INSIDERS' GUIDE® TO
THE TWIN CITIES

HELP US KEEP THIS GUIDE UP TO DATE

Every effort has been made by the authors and editors to make this guide as accurate and useful as possible. However, many things can change after a guide is published—phone numbers change, facilities come under new management, etc.

We would love to hear from you concerning your experiences with this guide and how you feel it could be improved and be kept up to date. While we may not be able to respond to all comments and suggestions, we'll take them to heart and we'll also make certain to share them with the authors. Please send your comments and suggestions to the following address:

> The Globe Pequot Press
> Reader Response/Editorial Department
> P. O. Box 480
> Guilford, CT 06437

Or you may e-mail us at:

> editorial@GlobePequot.com

Thanks for your input, and happy travels!

INSIDERS' GUIDE® SERIES

INSIDERS' GUIDE® TO
THE TWIN CITIES

FIFTH EDITION

TODD R. BERGER, HOLLY DAY, AND SHERMAN WICK

INSIDERS' GUIDE®

GUILFORD, CONNECTICUT
AN IMPRINT OF THE GLOBE PEQUOT PRESS

The prices and rates in this guidebook were confirmed at press time. We recommend, however, that you call establishments before traveling to obtain current information.

To buy books in quantity for corporate use or incentives, call **(800) 962–0973, ext. 4551,** or e-mail **premiums@GlobePequot.com.**

INSIDERS' GUIDE®

Text design by LeAnna Weller Smith
Maps created by XNR Productions Inc. © Morris Book Publishing LLC.

ISSN: 1525-7460
ISBN-13: 978-0-7627-3409-2
ISBN-10: 0-7627-3409-4

Manufactured in the United States of America
Fifth Edition/First Printing

CONTENTS

CONTENTS

Directory of Maps

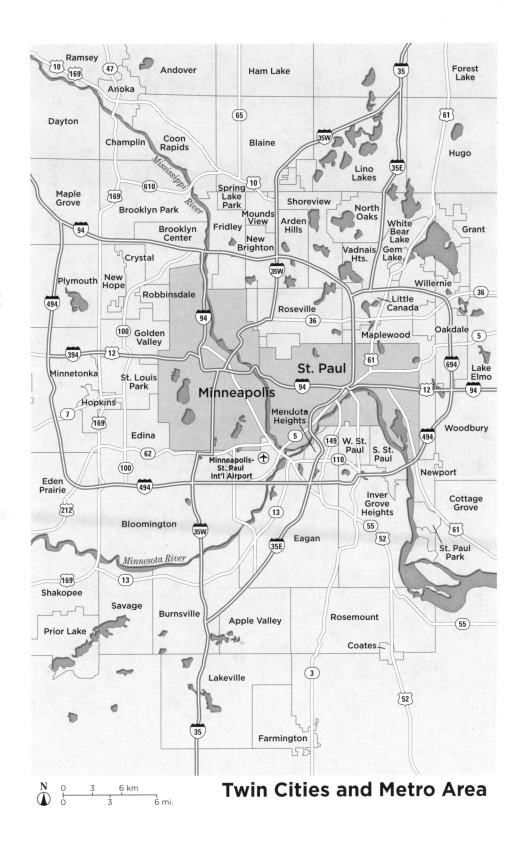

Twin Cities and Metro Area

Ramsey
Andover
Ham Lake
Forest Lake
10
169
47
35
Anoka
Dayton
61
65
Champlin
Coon Rapids
Blaine
35W
Hugo
Mississippi River
610
10
35E
Lino Lakes
Maple Grove
169
Spring Lake Park
Shoreview
North Oaks
Brooklyn Park
Mounds View
Arden Hills
White Bear Lake
Grant
94
Brooklyn Center
Fridley
New Brighton
Vadnais Hts.
Gem Lake
Crystal
35W
Willernie
Plymouth
New Hope
Robbinsdale
Little Canada
36
494
Roseville
Oakdale
Golden Valley
94
36
Maplewood
5
100
394
12
61
Lake Elmo
Minnetonka
St. Louis Park
Minneapolis
694
12
94
Hopkins
St. Paul
7
Mendota Heights
Woodbury
169
Edina
94
5
494
62
149
W. St. Paul
Newport
100
Minneapolis-St. Paul Int'l Airport
110
S. St. Paul
494
Eden Prairie
Inver Grove Heights
Cottage Grove
212
13
55
61
Bloomington
Eagan
52
St. Paul Park
169
35W
35E
Minnesota River
13
Shakopee
Rosemount
55
Savage
Burnsville
Apple Valley
Coates
Prior Lake
3
Lakeville
52
35
Farmington

N
0   3   6 km
0   3   6 mi.

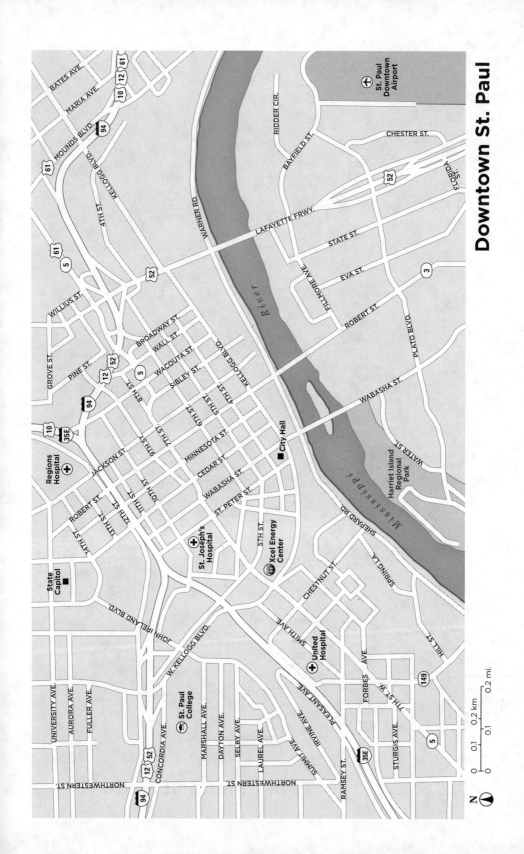

Downtown St. Paul

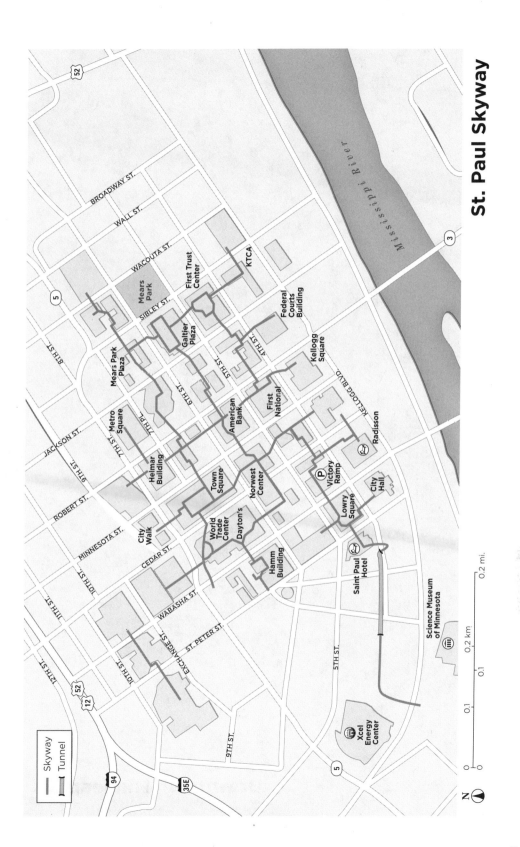

St. Paul Skyway

Legend:
— Skyway
▪ Tunnel

Streets and locations:
52, 5, 8TH ST., JACKSON ST., 9TH ST., ROBERT ST., MINNESOTA ST., CEDAR ST., 10TH ST., WABASHA ST., 11TH ST., ST. PETER ST., EXCHANGE ST., 10TH ST., 12TH ST., 52, 12, 94, 35E, 9TH ST., 5TH ST., 5, 3

BROADWAY ST., WALL ST., WACOUTA ST., SIBLEY ST., 6TH ST., 7TH ST., 7TH PL., 5TH ST., 4TH ST., KELLOGG BLVD.

Mississippi River

Locations:
- Mears Park
- First Trust Center
- KTCA
- Mears Park Plaza
- Galtier Plaza
- Metro Square
- Helmar Building
- American Bank
- First National
- Federal Courts Building
- Kellogg Square
- City Walk
- Town Square
- Norwest Center
- Victory Ramp (P)
- Radisson
- World Trade Center
- Dayton's
- Hamm Building
- Lowry Square
- City Hall
- Saint Paul Hotel
- Science Museum of Minnesota
- Xcel Energy Center

Scale: 0.1, 0.2 km / 0.1, 0.2 mi.

N

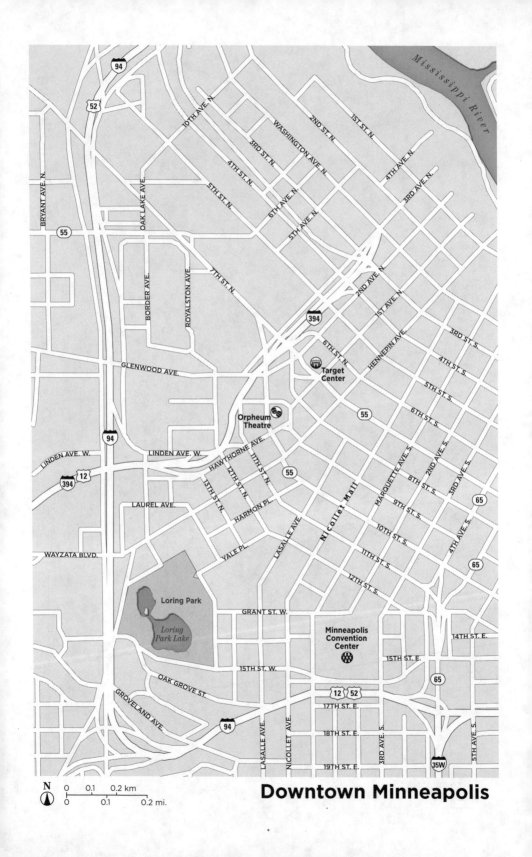

Downtown Minneapolis

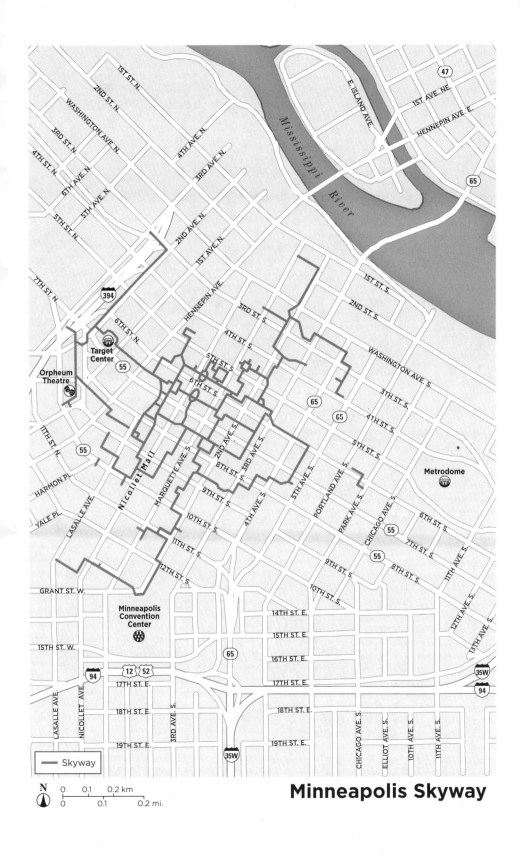

Minneapolis Skyway

Skyway

N
0   0.1   0.2 km
0   0.1   0.2 mi.

HOW TO USE THIS BOOK

For the most part, those of us who live in the Twin Cities don't consider ourselves Twin Cities residents—in the Metro we're either from Minneapolis or St. Paul. While both cities have much in common, differences in architecture, city layout, history, and industry set St. Paul and Minneapolis apart. Each has enough points of interest to fill a separate book by itself.

The *Insiders' Guide to the Twin Cities* is organized so that information can be accessed as quickly as possible. Besides the comprehensive table of contents and index, each separate chapter includes multiple subheadings. Chapters are divided by city where appropriate for easier navigation through the Cities and suburbs. Other chapters are organized alphabetically by subject or chronologically by event. You'll also find interesting tips scattered throughout the text, flagged with the 🛈 symbol. Look for the close-up features for an in-depth look at what makes the Cities special.

The book is structured with the reader in mind: It is written from the point of view of someone moving to or visiting the Twin Cities for the first time or visiting a given establishment for the first time. Accurate, useful information was the standard, and although perfection is never attainable, excellence is. You can feel confident that this book will steer you in the right direction 99 percent of the time as you use it to make choices based on your own preferences. Negative comments are few; if a certain restaurant, attraction, park, or hotel would rate negative words, it is not listed here. Why recommend rudeness, poor service, lousy food, bad atmosphere, or uninteresting "attractions"? That said, there are numerous worthy establishments in the Cities that do not appear in these pages because of time constraints and space constraints or because they are yet to be visited by the authors. Although we encourage you to use this guidebook and are confident that you will choose to visit places to your liking, we also encourage you to stop by that intriguing Ethiopian restaurant, visit that interesting shop selling bobblehead dolls or what have you, or buy a house in a neighborhood that "feels right," whether or not it is included in this book. This book is a diving board to get you into the pool; once there, you can swim wherever you like.

The modern skyscrapers of downtown Minneapolis. GREATER MINNEAPOLIS CONVENTION & VISITORS ASSOCIATION

AREA OVERVIEW

egend has it that the many lakes that cover the face of Minnesota are actually the filled-in footprints of Paul Bunyan and his mighty blue ox, Babe, created as they stomped around the countryside when Paul was just a boy. If this is true, then he must have been doing jumping jacks in the Twin Cities: St. Paul and Minneapolis alone have 22 lakes within their borders, with many more just outside their borders. There are much more logical explanations of why there are so many lakes in the area, but the Paul Bunyan theory is by far the most fun.

Even with all their beautiful historic buildings, bridges, and recent whimsical experiments in architecture, the most remarkable physical feature about the Twin Cities has always been their natural beauty. Where else can you find wildlife preservations, rich fossil beds, and fishing lakes, all a short walk from the two downtowns? We who live in either city are fully aware of how lucky we are, and any possibly detrimental change to the landscape—whether it be a proposed road widening in an area near a park or leveling of a historic building—is met with much more opposition than your average city planner is prepared for.

This, of course, was not always so. Minneapolis was partially built on the lumber industry, and thousands and thousands of old-growth trees were leveled and shipped out of state, almost completely destroying the Big Woods, a maple, oak, and basswood forest that once covered most of southern Minnesota. The Mississippi River valley Native American populations were decimated along with the forests that had been their home for thousands of years, and many of their spiritual centers, including the ill-fated Spirit Island that once rose out of the Mississippi River below St. Anthony Falls, were either gutted or dynamited in the name of progress.

With the founding of the two cities in the mid-1800s, however, a new level of civility and sophistication came to the residents. Multiple parks boards were established to protect wildlife areas, and even more groomed areas were set aside for outdoor activities. Today Twin Citians have the luxury of being able to walk past wetlands full of migratory waterfowl and turtles on their way to downtown Minneapolis, or through thickly forested areas housing species of rare native animals and birds just minutes outside downtown St. Paul. Kids who grow up in the Twin Cities get to share in pleasures usually reserved for children who grow up in the country, whether it be fishing in one of the many regularly stocked urban lakes, berry picking, or just enjoying being surrounded by trees, songbirds, and wildflowers in parks practically in their own backyards.

THE PERSONALITY OF THE CITIES

Minnesota has long suffered a reputation of being an American Siberia peopled with blond-haired, blue-eyed Scandinavian types who drive around in pickup trucks. And while it's true that some parts of the state do have six-month cold seasons, often complete with snow for the entire six months, the Twin Cities have been particularly blessed with relatively mild temperatures, partly due to our proximity to the swift-moving Mississippi River. Summers can top the scale at 100 degrees occasionally, and, conversely, winters can drop below zero. A good rule of thumb is to just be prepared for it to get cold in the winter and warm in the summer, and dress accordingly.

While most residents of the Twin Cities will go on and on about how much we love the changing of the seasons, to the point of ridiculing visitors who com-

Twin Cities Timeline

1680: Father Louis Hennepin, after being held captive in a village of the Mille Lacs Dakotas, is the first European to see the Falls of St. Anthony.

1819: The United States establishes Fort St. Anthony (renamed Fort Snelling in 1825) to protect the confluence of the Minnesota and Mississippi Rivers.

1837: Governor Henry Dodge of Wisconsin signs a treaty at Fort Snelling with the Ojibwes, who agree to cede all their pinelands on the St. Croix and its tributaries. A treaty is also signed at Washington, D.C., with representatives of the Dakotas for their lands east of the Mississippi. These treaties lead the way for extensive white settlements within the area of Minnesota.

1838: Franklin Steele establishes a claim at the Falls of St. Anthony in what is today Minneapolis; Pierre "Pig's Eye" Parrant builds a shanty and settles on the present site of the city of St. Paul, then called Pig's Eye.

1841: The Chapel of St. Paul is built and consecrated, giving the name to the future capital of the state.

1848: On August 26, after the admission of Wisconsin to the Union, the Stillwater Convention adopts measures calling for a separate territory to be named Minnesota. On October 30, Henry Hastings Sibley is elected delegate to Congress for the Minnesota Territory.

1855: On January 23 the first bridge to span the main channel of the Mississippi River anywhere along its length is opened between Minneapolis and St. Anthony.

1858: Minnesota becomes the 32nd state on May 11. At the time of its entry, Minnesota is the third-largest state in land area—only Texas and California are larger.

1861: On April 14 Governor Alexander Ramsey offers President Lincoln 1,000 men for the Civil War effort, making Minnesota the first state to offer troops to the Union. The first Minnesota regiment leaves Fort Snelling on June 22.

1862: The first railroad in Minnesota is opened between Minneapolis and St. Paul.

1881: Technological advances in flour milling made during the 1870s help turn Minneapolis into the flour milling capital of the world.

1883: The Northern Pacific Railroad completes its transcontinental route from Minnesota to the Pacific.

1884: The first iron ore is shipped from Minnesota, a product of the Soudan Mine on the Vermillion Range. Six years later iron is discovered on the Mesabi Range and shipped from there beginning in 1892.

1930: Minnesotan Frank B. Kellogg, serving as U.S. secretary of state, is awarded the Nobel Peace Prize for his work on the Kellogg-Briand Peace Pact, signed in Paris in 1928.

1944: The Democratic and Farmer-Labor Parties merge to form the Minnesota Democratic-Farmer-Labor Party (DFL).

1947: Engineering Research Associates, Inc., designs the ATLAS—the beginning of Minnesota's computer industry.

1948: The value of manufactured products exceeds cash farm receipts in the state for the first time.

1965: Hubert H. Humphrey becomes the first Minnesotan to win election to national executive office when he is sworn in as vice president on January 20.

1969: Warren Burger of St. Paul becomes chief justice of the United States Supreme Court.

1977: Walter Mondale becomes the second Minnesotan to win election to national executive office when he is sworn in as vice president on January 20.

1977: Rosalie Wahl becomes the first woman to serve on the state supreme court.

1987: The Minnesota Twins win the World Series.

1990: The Minnesota Supreme Court becomes the first state supreme court in the nation to have a majority of women seated as justices, following the appointment of Appeals Court Judge Sandra Gardebring.

1991: Casino gambling becomes legal in and around Minnesota's reservations.

1991: The Minnesota Twins win their second world championship in five years.

1992: The Mall of America, the nation's largest shopping and entertainment complex, opens in Bloomington.

1993: Minnesota loses professional hockey when the Minnesota North Stars move to Dallas.

1993: Sharon Sayles Belton is elected mayor of Minneapolis, the first African-American woman to preside over a major American city.

1999: On January 3 Reform Party candidate Jesse Ventura, whose only previous political experience was as the mayor of the Minneapolis suburb of Brooklyn Park, is sworn in as Minnesota's governor.

2000: NHL hockey returns to Minnesota on September 29 when the Minnesota Wild play their first game before a sold-out crowd at the brand-new Xcel Energy Center in downtown St. Paul.

2002: On October 25, 11 days before the election, U.S. Senator Paul Wellstone of Minnesota, his wife, daughter, three campaign workers, and two pilots die in a plane crash in northern Minnesota.

2004: The Twin Cities' first light-rail line, which runs between downtown Minneapolis and the Mall of America, opens on June 26.

plain about "a little snow," fact is, as soon as any of us have enough money to take a vacation somewhere warm during the winter, we're gone. Our snowbird migrations—RV-driving senior citizens who winter in the South and summer in Minnesota—are legendary. A brief jaunt to a tropical clime in the dead of winter is not an act of infidelity on any level—rather, we just want to protect the treasured memories we have of glorious old-growth trees covered with palm-sized green or flame-colored leaves, of hordes of Canada geese sunning themselves along the shores of the Mississippi, or of the way the brilliant white riverboats look heading down the St. Croix River in the middle of summer, mirror-reflected in the clear, tannin-tinted waters.

As soon as the weather is nice, however, anyone who can go outside, is outside. City parks get used here in the Twin Cities, from huge group picnics to locally organized volleyball and baseball games. Almost every neighborhood park has a splash pool for kids, and at any given time during the summer, families can be seen splashing around in the ridiculously shallow waters. At night the streets of downtown Minneapolis and St. Paul are full of people either out for a late-night walk in the balmy evening air or heading out on foot for a night on the town.

HOLLYWOOD AND THE TWIN CITIES

Minnesota has long been a favorite filming spot for moviemakers, especially those who need to shoot in snowy, cold areas with lots of open spaces. The Twin Cities are a logical spot to find actors and actresses to fill these scenes, as both Minneapolis and St. Paul have more than enough talent trained on the many professional and amateur theater stages in the area. Some of the films that have been shot in the Twin Cities metro area include *Airport, Beautiful Girls, Drop Dead Fred, Equinox, Fargo, Feeling Minnesota, Foolin'*

Around, Grumpy Old Men, Grumpier Old Men, Jingle All the Way, Mall Rats, The Mighty Ducks (I, II, and *III), The Personals, A Prairie Home Companion, Twenty Bucks,* and *Untamed Heart.* Brothers Joel and Ethan Coen, film directors and producers of such films as *Raising Arizona, Blood Simple, Barton Fink, Fargo,* and *O Brother Where Art Thou,* are from here, as is *Twin Peaks* producer Mark Frost and director of *The Sting,* George Roy Hill.

Television and big-picture actors and actresses who hail from the Twin Cities include Eddie Albert (*Roman Holiday, Green Acres*), Loni Anderson (*WKRP in Cincinnati*), Richard Dean Anderson (*General Hospital, MacGyver, Stargate SG-1*), James Arness (*Gunsmoke*), Julia Duffy (*Newhart, Designing Women*), Mike Farrell (*M*A*S*H, Providence*), Al Franken (*Saturday Night Live*), Peter Graves (*Mission: Impossible*), Tippi Hedren (*The Birds*), Josh Hartnett (*Pearl Harbor*), Charlie Korsmo (*Hook, Dick Tracy*), Dorothy Lyman (*All My Children, Mama's Family*), Kelly Lynch (*Drugstore Cowboy*), Mike Nelson (*Mystery Science Theater*), Kevin Sorbo (*Hercules, Andromeda*), Lea Thompson (*Back to the Future I, II, III; Howard the Duck, Caroline in the City*), and Robert Vaughn (*The Man from U.N.C.L.E.*).

LITERATURE AND MUSIC

There's nothing like a long, Minnesota winter to make you want to curl up with a good book—or sit down and write one. Some literary luminaries from the Twin Cities area have included *Prairie Home Companion*'s Garrison Keillor, Sinclair Lewis, F. Scott Fitzgerald, Meridel Le Sueur, Harvey Mackay, Robert Bly, Gordon Parks, cartoonist Charles Schultz, and journalist Eric Severeid. Folksinger Bob Dylan, blues legends Koerner, Ray and Glover, former Replacements' lead singer Paul Westerberg, Soul Asylum singer Dave Pirner, and Prince Rogers Nelson (a.k.a. Prince) also all made Minneapolis or St. Paul their home at one time or another.

GEOLOGY

The state of Minnesota is known throughout the world for its once-productive iron mines as well as its quarries of beautiful St. Peter sandstone and marble deposits. Of more scientific interest, some of the oldest exposed rock known in the world is also located in the Minnesota River valley, the Morton gneiss, which was formed approximately 3,600 million years ago. The Morton gneiss and "younger" (1,700- to 1,800-million-year-old) quarries of Minnesota granite and basalt have been prized as building materials throughout the world for years, as has St. Peter sandstone, marble, and fossil-rich kaolinite clay.

Millions of years ago the area now known as Minnesota lay submerged beneath shallow continental seas. During the Ordovician period (505 to 438 million years ago), Minnesota was located 10 to 40 degrees south of the equator, making the area about as tropical as Hawaii is today. The waters were rich with primitive animal life, much of which can be seen today as layers in the fossil record at paleontology digs throughout the state. Large amounts of corals, trilobites, snails, mussel and clam shells, and the ancestors of modern-day octopus and squid have been unearthed at sites such as Harriet Island/Lilydale Park and Shadow Falls in St. Paul and near Cannon Falls in Goodhue County.

Most of Minnesota is part of the Canadian Shield—a core of Precambrian rocks that contains the record of the history of the North American continent from about 3,600 million to 600 million years ago and is some of the oldest exposed rock in the world. Much of this ancient shield had been protected by the covering of the Ordovician seas, and later by layers of sediment and earth, but was again exposed by the eroding progress of glaciers over a mile thick that covered the area more than 12,000 years ago—the same glaciers that eventually carved out the 15,000-plus lakes and rivers that cross the face of the state today.

THE ORIGINAL SETTLERS

Before European settlement, Dakota (Sioux) and Ojibwe (Chippewa) tribes populated the Twin Cities area, and before that, an amalgam of people known as the Woodland Indians (or Hopewell Indians), who left behind thousands of burial mounds throughout the Midwest, six of which can still be seen at Mounds Park in St. Paul. The Mississippian cultures of the Dakotas and Ojibwes replaced these American Indians circa A.D. 800 to 1000.

While the Ojibwes' origins were to the east and north, the Dakotas were western Plains Indians who at the time of European exploration occupied the Twin Cities, western and southern Minnesota, and much of present day North and South Dakota. The French referred to the Dakotas as Sioux, a meaningless abridgement of the Ojibwe term, *Nadouissouix*, which meant "little viper" or "lesser enemy." The derogatory name stuck for centuries until recently, when the tribe began referring to itself by its original name. Both the Dakotas and Ojibwes were hunting societies, and their hunting techniques evolved by incorporating European tools, wares, and implements such as guns, hatchets, blankets, knives, and kettles. On a cultural level, the European introduction of glass beads and colored cloth and yarn to the Native peoples resulted in a revolution in American Indian artwork, producing the spectacular woven blankets and intricate beadwork that we associate with American Indian craftwork today.

The Twin Cities are home to the largest urban population of American Indians in the United States and are the birthplace of the American Indian Movement (AIM). AIM produces locally and nationally distributed literature that addresses Indian concerns on everything from legal issues

Twin Cities Vital Statistics

Founded: Minneapolis: 1848; St. Paul: 1819

Incorporated: Minneapolis: 1867; St. Paul: 1854

Size: Minneapolis: 54.9 square miles; St. Paul: 52.8 square miles

Elevation: 824 feet above sea level

Population: Minneapolis: 382,618; St. Paul: 287,151

Mayor: Minneapolis: R. T. Rybak; St. Paul: Chris Coleman

Governor: Tim Pawlenty

Airport: Minneapolis–St. Paul International Airport

Average temperatures: July: 73 degrees F
                              January: 13 degrees F

Average yearly precipitation: 28 inches

Colleges and universities: *Minneapolis:* Augsburg College, Capella University, Dunwoody, Minneapolis College of Art and Design, Minneapolis Community and Technical College, Northwestern Health Science University, the University of Minnesota–Twin Cities
St. Paul: Bethel College and Seminary, the College of St. Catherine, Concordia University–St. Paul, Hamline University, Luther Seminary, Macalester College, McNally Smith College of Music, Metropolitan State University, William Mitchell College of Law, Northwestern College, St. Paul College, University of St. Thomas

Daily newspapers: *Star Tribune, St. Paul Pioneer Press*

Radio stations: 38

Television stations: 8

Driving laws: Driver's license at age 16; maximum speed limit 65 mph (except in a few semirural stretches in the outer-ring suburbs where the speed limit is 70); seat belts mandatory for driver and all passengers; child seats mandatory for children under five or under 45 pounds; helmets mandatory for motorcycle riders.

to finding hospitals that practice Native American medicine.

St. Paul

Home to thousands of American Indians for centuries, the earliest known name for St. Paul is that given by the Indians: *Im-in-i-ja ska,* which translated into English means "White Rock," taken from the high limestone bluffs in the area. Fort Snelling (originally named Fort St. Anthony), the first European settlement in the area, was built in 1819, and soon after, seeking the nearby protection of the fort, the thriving community of Mendota was established.

Soon the more privileged military officers and the residents of Mendota became disturbed at the lifestyle of the residents of the squatter camp, most of whom were refugees from the ill-fated

Selkirk Colony in Manitoba. They were especially disturbed about the activities of a notorious and highly popular retired fur trapper whose talents had been turned to moonshining, Pierre "Pig's Eye" Parrant. The whiskey trade quickly infuriated the straitlaced Major Talliaferro, Fort Snelling's Indian agent, who issued a proclamation banishing the squatters from lands controlled by the fort. This forced them to move down the river to the northeast, just outside the fort's jurisdiction.

This site, then known as Fountain Cave, was located near what is now the southern part of St. Paul. A small monument today marks a spot on the riverbank near where the small group settled. Soon after they set up their new squatter camp, Major Talliaferro decided they were not quite far enough out of his sight and extended the jurisdiction of the fort to include the Fountain Cave site, sending his soldiers to burn the Fountain Cave encampment. The settlers were again forced to move farther down the river, this time settling on the north bank in what is now part of downtown St. Paul.

Institutions such as government and the Roman Catholic Church have been central to St. Paul's history since its earliest days. Since the beginnings of Minnesota Territory in 1849, St. Paul has served as the capital. At about the same time, it also became a Catholic diocese established by Father Lucian Galtier, who had come to save the souls in the crassly named settlement of "Pig's Eye."

Industry and technology were paramount in the historical development of St. Paul. Minnesota Mining and Manufacturing Company (3M) is one of the Cities' most important companies. 3M's history began in 1902 in Two Harbors, a small town north of Duluth, as a manufacturer of sandpaper. The company relocated to St. Paul in 1909, where sandpaper is one of important 3M products today. 3M has always placed a premium on producing and developing diverse new and innovative products, such as Scotch brand tape and

Post-it Notes. As time has passed 3M has grown into an international corporation and remains essentially a St. Paul company, even after relocating its headquarters to the adjoining suburb of Maplewood.

Minneapolis

The emergence of the other Twin City, Minneapolis, was far less colorful. In 1680 Father Louis Hennepin happened upon St. Anthony Falls, and 140 years later soldiers from nearby Fort Snelling constructed a sawmill and flour mill at the falls. Minneapolis and the across-the-river town of St. Anthony both began in the 1840s as milling and lumbering centers, when Franklin Steele settled in St. Anthony in 1838 and began his successful flour and sawmills. By the 1840s the village of St. Anthony had been established on the east bank of the Mississippi and the village of Minneapolis on the west bank. The two towns were soon linked by a suspension bridge, and in 1872 Minneapolis and St. Anthony were united to form one city.

Minneapolis was founded to process Minnesota grain with the tremendous power-generating capabilities of St. Anthony Falls, and by the late 19th century, Minneapolis became nationally known as the Mill City. Milling began on the Mississippi, in Minneapolis and St. Anthony, because of the falls. To businessmen in the area, the falls represented an unbridled source of energy for milling the vast wheat crops in the area, which rapidly expanded as Minnesota and the upper Midwest were settled. The milling industry became increasingly decentralized as the largest and most successful Twin Cities milling companies gradually diversified into related industries.

THE CITIES TOGETHER

Since the beginning of the 20th century, the Twin Cities economy has become increasingly diverse, depending less on a single industry—such as lumber, milling, or mining—and expanding into the technological, medical, retail, and agricultural fields.

Some companies' roots reach back to industry and manufacturing that began in the late 19th and early 20th century, as is the case with the 3M Corporation, while others quickly became important businesses because of technological innovation. Medtronic founder Earl Bakken began his company in a northeast Minneapolis garage in 1949, and it was the first of many medical supply companies that have made their home in the Twin Cities.

The Twin Cities is also home to one of the nation's largest retailers, the Target Corporation. For most of its long history in the Twin Cities, Target was known as Dayton Corporation, and later the Dayton Hudson Corporation. George Dayton opened the first Dayton's in downtown Minneapolis in 1902, and in 1962 Dayton Corporation's most nationally known retail store, Target, opened its door for the first time in nearby Roseville. Dayton Hudson officially changed its name to the Target Corporation in 2000.

Recent immigration is transforming the composition of the Twin Cities, much as it did in the late 19th and early 20th centuries. These new immigrant populations include Vietnamese, Laotians, Khmers (Cambodia), Hmong (Laos), east Africans, Russians, and Bosnians. With the exception of the Russians and Bosnians, Europeans are a relatively small component of the new immigration. The Twin Cities, in particular St. Paul, have the largest Hmong population in the nation.

The Hmong and other Southeast Asians have started more than 400 area businesses and have transformed St. Paul's Frogtown and Midway neighborhoods.

The new wave of immigration is just one parallel linking the Twin Cities past and present. Both Minneapolis and St. Paul are reviving important elements of their past on the Mississippi riverfront. Since the late 1980s Minneapolis has focused on regaining its greatest historical assets—the Mississippi River and the Mill District. Down the river in St. Paul, the renovated Harriet Island Regional Park celebrates its city's rich history.

THE SEVEN-COUNTY METRO AREA

Anoka County

Anoka County's history starts as far back as 1849, when the Minnesota territorial legislature organized the counties of Washington, Ramsey, and Benton. What is now Anoka County was originally parts of both Ramsey and Benton Counties, with the Rum River dividing the two. As more settlers came into the area, the plot of land bordering the Rum River's shores was given the name Anoka. The name originated from an American Indian word meaning "on both sides."

Anoka County was formed from Ramsey County on May 23, 1857. The original eight townships included Anoka, Watertown (Ramsey), Round Lake (Andover), Bethel, Columbus, St. Francis, Oak Grove, and Centerville. The original boundaries of Anoka County were the same as today except for a small portion of the southeastern tip of the county along the Mississippi River. This strip was a tiny county created from Ramsey County, possibly by a surveying miscalculation, the same day Anoka County was created. This tiny county was given the name of Manomin and occupied only about one-third of a congressional township; it functioned as an organized county until abolished and

Riverboats ply the waters of the Mississippi and St. Croix Rivers. GREATER MINNEAPOLIS CONVENTION & VISITORS ASSOCIATION

attached to Anoka County by constitu-
tional amendment on November 2, 1869.
As an organized township of Anoka
County, Manomin kept this name until it
was changed to Fridley in 1879.

Anoka County has grown from a
largely rural area in 1857 to the present-
day urban center. It is one of the largest
and fastest-growing counties in the state.
Anoka County, with its county seat in the
city of Anoka, encompasses a 430-
square-mile area, has a population of
approximately 299,000 and is the fourth-
largest county in Minnesota. Anoka
County is also the third most densely
populated county in the state, following
Ramsey and Hennepin Counties, and
includes the cities of Andover, Anoka,
Bethel, Blaine, Burns, Centerville, Circle
Pines, Columbia Heights, Columbus, Coon
Rapids, East Bethel, Fridley, Ham Lake,
Hilltop, Lexington, Lino Lakes, Linwood,
Oak Grove, Ramsey, St. Francis, and
Spring Lake Park within its borders.

Carver County

With the signing of the treaty of Traverse
de Sioux in March 1855, the formerly
Native American lands that soon became
Carver County were opened for settlement
by white pioneers. The county was named
in honor of explorer Jonathan Carver. The
original county seat was in San Francisco
Township, but in 1856 voters moved it to
Chaska, where it remains today.

Many of Carver County's initial settlers
were from the East Coast, but by the 1860s
many of the area's new settlers were immigrants from Germany or Sweden. The Germans founded towns like Hamburg, New
Germany, and Cologne, while the Swedes
settled in East Union and Watertown.

Calling in the Metro Area

The Twin Cities metropolitan area has four area codes (612, 651, 763, and 952), but callers do not have to dial "1" before calling other area codes. You can dial the seven-digit phone number for calls within your area code or the ten-digit number (area code plus phone number) for calls to areas outside your area code within the Metro. Your call will still go through if you dial "1" first, but you will be charged for a long-distance call.

Farming was the chief occupation of Carver County for 100 years. While many residents grew crops, others were dairy farmers, and creameries were so numerous that the county started calling itself the "Golden Buckle of the Dairy Belt." Oak Grove Dairy in Norwood–Young America and Bongards Creameries are still important forces in the dairy industry.

Carver County's most historically important farmer was Wendelin Grimm, a German immigrant who settled in Chanhassen. Grimm's claim to fame was in creating his own strain of hardy alfalfa, named Grimm alfalfa, which was at the time considered to be the most winter-hardy strain available. Grimm alfalfa was used throughout North America between 1910 and 1940 and is one of Minnesota's leading contributions to the history of agriculture.

Today Carver County has a population of approximately 68,000 people, divided among the cities of Carver, Chanhassen, Chaska, Cologne, Hamburg, Mayer, New Germany, Norwood, Norwood–Young America, Victoria, Waconia, and Watertown.

Dakota County

Located minutes south of the Twin Cities, Dakota County offers the amenities of the metropolitan area with the charm and serenity of a small town. Approximately 350,000 people live within the county's limits, making it the third most populous county in the state of Minnesota. Yet one-half of its land remains undeveloped or rural.

The quality of life in Dakota County is high due to its excellent schools, its proximity to renowned health care facilities, and pleasant neighborhoods. Parks, fishing lakes, trail systems, and recreation areas are in abundance, as well as the spacious grounds of the Minnesota Zoo, the second-largest zoo in the country. Businesses with roots and holdings in Dakota County include ConAgra, Hudson Manufacturing, Alexis Baily, Vineyard, Mead Paper, and Gumby Fancy, providing long-term employment for residents of the area.

Dakota County cities include Apple Valley, Burnsville, Eagan, Farmington, Hastings, Inver Grove Heights, Lakeville, Lilydale, Mendota, Mendota Heights, Miesville, New Trier, Randolph, Rosemount, Sunfish Lake, South St. Paul, and West St. Paul.

Hennepin County

Hennepin County, incorporated in 1852, forms part of one of the nation's major metropolitan areas, with Minneapolis as its largest city and county seat. The county has a broad-based economy with strong trade, service, and manufacturing sectors, and many major corporations are head-quartered in the county. The employment base is diverse, and employment remains relatively stable. The county's unemployment rate has consistently remained below the state and national averages.

More than 1,100,000 people live in the 611 square miles that make up Hennepin County, with the greatest percentage living in Minneapolis and the rest distributed among the cities of Bloomington, Brooklyn Center, Brooklyn Park, Champlin, Chanhassen, Corcoran, Crystal, Dayton, Deephaven, Eden Prairie, Edina, Excelsior, Golden Valley, Greenfield, Hamel, Hanover, Hopkins, Howard Lake, Independence, Long Lake, Loretto, Maple Grove, Maple Plain, Medicine Lake, Medina, Minnetonka, Minnetonka Beach, Minnetonka Mills, Minnetrista, Mound, Navarre, New Hope, Orono, Osseo, Plymouth, Richfield, Robbinsdale, Rockford, Rogers, Saint Anthony, Saint Bonifacius, Saint Louis Park, Spring Park, Tonka Bay, Wayzata, Woodland, and Young America.

The largest employers with holdings in Hennepin County include the state government, the University of Minnesota, General Mills, Cargill, Target Corporation, and the U.S. Postal Service.

Ramsey County

Ramsey County, established in 1849, is home to Minnesota's state capital, the city of St. Paul. More than 487,000 people live in the 156 square miles that make up the county, which includes the cities of Arden Hills, Blaine, Falcon Heights, Gem Lake, Lauderdale, Little Canada, Maplewood, Mounds View, New Brighton, North Oaks, North St. Paul, Roseville, St. Anthony, St. Paul, Shoreview, Spring Lake Park, Vadnais Heights, and White Bear Lake.

Ramsey County is the site of many popular attractions, both man-made and natural, including Como Park Zoo and Conservatory, Indian Mounds Park, Harriet

Island and Lilydale Parks, and the Alexander Ramsey House. St. Paul's suburbs are blessed with beautiful, historic neighborhoods built around lakes and parks for summer and winter recreation alike.

Scott County

Scott County, established in 1853 and named after Gen. Winfield Scott, is an area of 375 square miles located in the southwest corner of the Twin Cities metro area. The Minnesota River forms the northern border of the county, while the broad river valley cuts though glacial sediment into some of the oldest exposed rock beds in the state. The savanna that makes up most of Scott County once bordered the Big Woods, a hardwood forest that covered a majority of the state before it was logged in the mid-19th century.

Shakopee, the county seat, began in 1851 as a trading post nearby to the Dakota village of Chief Shakopee (or Shakpay). Town sites were established along transportation routes provided by the Minnesota River and the numerous oxcart trails that crisscrossed the region. Years later the railroad was the choice of transport in Minnesota, and highways developed along the oxcart trails and between communities.

Today urban sprawl and suburbanization are threatening this primarily rural county. Industry has taken hold, and transportation issues play a primary role in development decisions, just as they did in the past.

The county currently has a population of approximately 81,900 and is expected to increase to approximately 109,000 persons by the year 2010, according to Metropolitan Council estimates. Located within the county lines are the cities of Elko, Jordan, New Prague, Prior Lake, and Savage.

St. Paul honors its native son Charles Schulz with Peanuts *characters stationed throughout the city.* SAINT PAUL RCVA

Washington County

Washington County is located on the eastern edge of the Metro. Incorporated in 1849, its 423 square miles now house more than 205,000 people divided among the cities of Afton, Bayport, Birchwood, Cottage Grove, Dellwood, Forest Lake, Hastings, Hugo, Lake Elmo, Lake St. Croix Beach, Lakeland, Lakeland Shores, Landfall, Marine on St. Croix, Newport, Oak Park Heights, Oakdale, Pine Springs, St. Mary's Point, St. Paul Park, Scandia, Stillwater, Willernie, and Woodbury. The county seat is located in Stillwater, along the St. Croix River. Originally full of lumber towns, with an economy fueled by the lumber industry and made possible by the St. Croix River, industry in Washington County has grown to include major employers such as Anderson Windows, State Farm Insurance, 3M, and the Min-

nesota Correctional Facilities in Bayport and Oak Park Heights.

Washington County is full of historic sites that played key parts in the formation of the state. In 1849 the Minnesota territorial legislature met in Stillwater (at 102 South Main Street) and created nine counties in the new Minnesota Territory, including Washington County. Other historic places in the county include Gammelgården, Scandia, the site of the first Swedish settlement in Minnesota, and Cottage Grove, the birthplace of commercial agriculture in Minnesota.

Washington County has more than its share of beautiful natural areas. Located within county lines are Afton State Park, Lake Elmo Park Reserve, St. Croix Bluffs Regional Park, and Square Lake Park, as well as dozens of smaller protected wilderness areas. The county is bordered by the Lower St. Croix National Scenic Riverway.

GETTING HERE, GETTING AROUND

Transportation has long played a crucial role in shaping the Twin Cities. In the beginning the Mississippi, Minnesota, and St. Croix Rivers all made the lumber industry possible in Minnesota, turning communities like Stillwater, St. Anthony, and Minneapolis into important centers of commerce and trade. The rivers were also important in transporting iron, granite, sandstone, and marble from Minnesota to the rest of the world, and for bringing military supplies and luxury items from the rest of the world to Minnesota. Trains later replaced boats as the preferred means of transporting raw materials, and commuter trains became Twin Cities residents' favorite means of personal transportation. The Great Northern Depot in St. Paul, built in 1914, connected passengers to nearby resort destinations like Minnehaha Park and White Bear Lake as well as to the East and West Coasts.

Electric streetcars made their debut in the Twin Cities in 1889, and by the 1920s Minneapolis and St. Paul were home to one of the largest streetcar systems in the world. More than 1,000 cars on 500 miles of track took commuters to work and back home again each day, and the system was so extensive that it was possible to take a streetcar from downtown Minneapolis all the way to Stillwater or Excelsior. Unfortunately the streetcar system was abandoned in the 1950s. In 1954 street buses replaced the electric streetcars, and the electric tracks that crisscrossed the metro area were paved over to facilitate automobile use.

Today the Twin Cities are home to one large international airport and six smaller ones and a bus line that runs 24 hours a day in the busy downtown areas. Even if you're new to the area, fleets of friendly, reliable taxicabs and helpful bus drivers and information operators will make sure you get to your destination safely.

AIR TRAVEL

Minneapolis–St. Paul International Airport
Charles A. Lindbergh Terminal
4300 Glumack Drive, St. Paul
(612) 726-5555

Hubert H. Humphrey Terminal
7150 Humphrey Drive, Minneapolis
(612) 726-5800
www.mspairport.com

Minneapolis–St. Paul International Airport (MSP) is a sprawling complex of two terminals serving 22 passenger airlines, 17 cargo airlines, and 36 million people annually. The airport is located between Minneapolis and St. Paul on the southern side of the Metro, with relatively quick access to both downtowns and the rest of the Twin Cities region. MSP is a hub for Northwest Airlines (the company is based in Eagan, a St. Paul suburb) and, with a steady stream of takeoffs and landings, ranks as the eighth-busiest airport in the nation.

Getting to the Airport

MSP encompasses two terminals—the Lindbergh Terminal and the Humphrey Terminal. The Lindbergh Terminal is accessible from Minnesota Highway 5 via the Lindbergh Terminal exit. The Humphrey Terminal is accessible from Interstate 494 via the 34th Avenue South exit. Most commercial passenger airlines fly into Lindbergh, while Humphrey is the landing site for many charter airlines. Check your ticket carefully to determine your terminal before driving to the airport or instructing someone where to pick you up, although if you end up at the wrong terminal, you can hop on the light-rail to quickly get back on track—free of charge between terminals.

Design

If you havn't been through MSP for a few years, you probably won't recognize either of the terminals today. MSP and the six reliever airports operated by the Metropolitan Airports Commission (MAC) are wrapping up a $3.1 billion reconstruction project known as MSP 2010, and things have come a long way since work began in 1996.

Despite the changes, it is not difficult to find your way around either the Lindbergh or Humphrey Terminal. The top level of the Lindbergh Terminal is for ticketing and departures. You can be dropped off at this level via the elevated roadway just outside the doors. The gate concourses at Lindbergh are lettered sequentially, A through G. Generally, if your concourse letter is A through E, you will veer right after passing through the security checkpoints in between the check-in counters; if your concourse letter is F or G, you will veer left. You can easily find your gate by observing the concourse number and gate (for example, E8 would be Gate 8 on Concourse E). The lower the number of the gate, the shorter your walk down the concourse. Note that Concourses A and B, designated for smaller commuter airlines, are at the *end* of Concourse C, which passengers can access via the concourse tram.

People-mover walkways carry passengers down Concourses C and G, the two longest at MSP, and across the Skyway Connector between Concourses C and G. An aboveground shuttle tram also carries passengers the length of Concourse C, with several stops along the way, and an underground Hub Tram runs from Level T,

two floors below the ticketing and departures concourse, to escalators leading to the Skyway Connector. This tram also carries passengers to the outer Blue and Red parking ramps and to the Transit Center, where you will find the rental car counters, city bus stop, and the light-rail station.

At Lindbergh the baggage claim area is one floor below the ticketing and departures concourse. Electronic displays on this level indicate which of the 14 baggage carousels will deliver the luggage from your flight.

The much-smaller Humphrey Terminal, which reopened in a brand-new terminal building in 2001, will not make your feet as sore. Ticketing and departure counters, as well as the baggage claim area, are all located on the first floor of the terminal. The gates are one floor up and accessible via a short escalator ride. Taxis and shuttles to rental car centers can be found on the commercial roadway on the first level of the parking ramp.

Airlines

As noted, MSP is a hub for Northwest Airlines, and the carrier controls more than 60 percent of the local market. Some studies have concluded that Minneapolis–St. Paul's hub status leads to higher ticket fares. Then again, it also means that Twin Citians and visitors have a large selection of nonstop flights to destinations worldwide. If you are flexible about your departure time, plan far enough in advance, and look for sale fares online, you'll be less likely to experience sticker shock flying in or out of MSP.

Given the dominance of Northwest in Minneapolis–St. Paul, it is worth checking the airline's Web site (www.nwa.com) for cyberdeals if you are planning a trip to or from the Twin Cities. The airline offers specials, released every Wednesday, and if the special happens to be to or from your city, you can get a steep discount on your seat. On the Web site you can sign up for e-mail notices of these special offers.

Of course, Northwest isn't the only game in town. With the exception of Southwest Airlines, all major American carriers serve MSP, as do three international airlines and five charter airlines. Charter flights also often can get you a deal on your airline seat, although in Minneapolis–St. Paul most charter flights are from the Cities to warm-weather destinations, particularly in winter.

Domestic Airlines

AirTran Airways, (800) 247-8726; www.airtran.com
America West, (800) 235-9292; www.americawest.com
American Airlines, (800) 433-7300; www.aa.com
Comair Airlines (operated by Delta), (800) 354-9822; www.comair.com
Continental Airlines, (800) 525-0280; www.continental.com
Delta Airlines, (800) 221-1212; www.delta.com
Frontier Airlines, (800) 432-1359; www.frontierairlines.com
Mesaba Airlines (Northwest Airlink), (800) 225-2525; www.mesaba.com
Midwest Connect, (800) 452-2022; www.midwestairlines.com
Northwest Airlines, (800) 225-2525; www.nwa.com
SkyWest Airlines, (800) 221-1212 or (435) 624-3400; www.skywest.com
Sun Country Airlines, (800) 359-6786; www.suncountry.com
United Airlines, (800) 241-6522; www.ual.com
US Airways, (800) 428-4322; www.usairways.com

International Airlines

Air Canada, (888) 247-2262; www.aircanada.com
Icelandair, (800) 223-5500; www.icelandair.com
KLM Royal Dutch Airlines, (800) 374-7747; www.klm.com

Charter Airlines

Casino Express, (800) 258-8800; www.redlioncasino.com
Champion Air, (800) 922-2606; www.championair.com
Miami Air International, (305) 876-3600; www.miamiair.com
Omni Air International, (877) 718-8901; www.omniairintl.com
Ryan International, (888) 443-7926; www.flyryan.com

Ground Transportation

You can get to or from the airport via a variety of means. For the Lindbergh Terminal: For car rentals, city buses, hotel shuttles, or the light-rail station, take the Hub Tram on Level T to the Transit Center. For taxis follow the signs on Level T to the escalators to the taxi station.

Car rental agencies that have rental locations at the airport are **National Car Rental** (800-227-7368; www.national car.com); **Budget Car & Truck Rental** (800-527-0700; www.budget.com); **Avis Rent A Car** (800-831-2847; www.avis .com); **Alamo** (800-327-9633; www .alamo.com); **Dollar Rent A Car** (800-800-4000; www.dollar.com); **Enterprise Rent-A-Car** (800-325-8007; www .enterprise.com); and **Hertz** (800-654-3131; www.hertz.com).

At the airport it is easiest to catch a taxi at the taxi station, where you simply wait in line for the next available taxi. Let the attendant know if you have special needs, such as a cab that takes credit cards. For a list of taxi companies and their contact information, see the Taxis section later in this chapter.

City buses and the light-rail transit (LRT) are far and away the cheapest ways to get to and from the airport. If you're traveling light and in no big hurry, you can catch a city bus at the Transit Center. As a faster option, if your destination happens to be along its path, the LRT stops at the airport on its way between the Mall of

America and downtown Minneapolis. Contact **Metro Transit** at (612) 373-3333 or visit www.metrotransit.org for route and schedule information for buses or the light-rail. For more information on both, see the Public Transportation section later in this chapter.

Parking

Lindbergh Terminal offers short-term, long-term, and valet parking in the four ramps surrounded by the terminal concourses. Follow the signs as you enter the terminal area. Short-term parking is designed for stays of less than two hours; long-term parking is designed for stays longer than two hours. Receive $2.00 off short- or long-term parking with epark, a self-pay system used by inserting your credit card into a machine when you enter and exit. You can access the terminal from any of the ramps via enclosed skyways, the Hub Tram (accessible from the Transit Center), or Level T.

Humphrey Terminal offers short- and long-term parking in the ramp across the street from the terminal. Travelers can get to the terminal by walking across the street or using the enclosed skyway on the second level.

For off-airport parking, the following lots offer shuttle transportation to and from MSP every 5 to 10 minutes, 24 hours a day:

EZ Air Park (651-777-7275 and www.ezairpark.com); at 2804 Lexington Avenue, Eagan

Park 'N Fly (952-854-0606; www.pnf.com); 3700 American Boulevard East, Bloomington

Park 'N Go (952-854-3386; www.parkngo.net); 7901 International Drive, Bloomington

Team Parking, (651-690-1265); 1400 Davern Street and Shepard Road, St. Paul

For parking availability and information, call the **MSP Parking Information Line** at (952) 826-7000 or (888) 868-7001.

Amenities

With the last big series of expansions made to MSP in the 1990s, the Lindbergh Terminal's waiting area went from being a midsize airport to a minimall of shops and restaurant courts. The centerpiece of the terminal's lobby is Northstar Crossing, a collection of more than 75 retail shops and restaurants. The area features Minnesota-themed shops and nationally known retailers, including the first airport-based Lands' End. Throughout the terminal can be found McDonald's, Burger King, Cinnabon, Pizza Hut, Ben & Jerry's, Stage Deli, the first airport D.Q. Grill and Chill, and more. For libations (Lindbergh Terminal only) there are several City Martinis, a PS Air Pub, and the MSP Brewhouse. The Humphrey Terminal offers more limited services, with Lord Fletcher's restaurant, Dunn Bros. Coffee and Cafe, plus two shops selling magazines, newspapers, snacks, and gifts.

For passengers with disabilities, all airlines operating out of MSP provide wheelchairs for the flight. For carts, wheelchairs, or medical transportation, airline passengers should contact their travel agent, ticketing agents, flight attendants, or gate agents. Travelers Assistance (TA) can also help with wheelchair requests. TA volunteers may be reached by calling (612) 726-5500. Wheelchairs are also available for checkout at the information booth on Level T and at security checkpoints.

If you lose something at either of the terminals, call **Airport Lost and Found** at (612) 726-5141.

TRAIN TRAVEL

Amtrak
Twin Cities Passenger Station
730 Transfer Road, St. Paul
(651) 644-6012 or (800) 872-7245
www.amtrak.com

The Twin Cities share a train station in the industrial Midway District of St. Paul. To get to the station, take the Cretin Avenue/Vandalia Street exit from Interstate 94 and turn north at the stoplights. Turn east (right) at University Avenue, and then turn north (left) at the next stoplight (Cleveland/Transfer Road). The station is about a block up on the right. You can also get to the station from downtown Minneapolis or St. Paul on Metro Transit bus route 16 along University Avenue. The station and ticket counter are open 6:30 A.M. to 11:30 P.M. daily.

A single passenger train, the Empire Builder between Chicago and Seattle, stops at the station twice a day (once in each direction). If you're headed for points far afield, you can make connections in Chicago or Seattle to stations throughout the country.

Within Minnesota, the Empire Builder stops at Winona, Red Wing, St. Cloud, Staples, Detroit Lakes, and Fargo-Moorhead. While the train can be a fine option for travel to and from Red Wing and Winona, it's less convenient for the stations north of the Cities, where you arrive in the middle of the night, regardless of whether you are on the east- or westbound train.

BUS TRAVEL

Greyhound Lines
166 West University Avenue, St. Paul
(651) 222-0507

950 Hawthorne Avenue, Minneapolis
(612) 371-3325
www.greyhound.com
Greyhound is a Minnesota company, founded in Hibbing on northern Minnesota's Iron Range in 1914. St. Paul and Minneapolis each have a Greyhound station. St. Paul's station is just west of the State Capitol building on University Avenue and is open 6:45 A.M. to 7:30 P.M. daily. The downtown Minneapolis station is next to the Hawthorne Transportation

Some of the buses in downtown Minneapolis run 24 hours a day year-round. Call Metro Transit at (612) 373-3333 for specific bus information.

Center, a few blocks west of Target Center (First Avenue becomes Hawthorne Avenue as it heads west), and is open 6:00 A.M. to midnight daily.

Jefferson Lines serves both Greyhound terminals, the Lindbergh Terminal at Minneapolis–St. Paul International Airport, the University of Minnesota, Burnsville, and Anoka. Call (612) 332-3224 for more information.

CAR TRAVEL

Highways

Minneapolis–St. Paul has well-thought-out arterial and surrounding highways. However, politics and not-so-well-thought-out plans limit the number of lanes on many area highways, causing traffic jams and bottlenecks with predictable frequency. If you are driving to your destination in the Twin Cities, be aware that some major highways become parking lots during the morning and evening rush hours.

The Twin Cities are ringed by the Interstate 494/Interstate 694 loop. I-494 starts at the interchange with I-94 in the eastern suburb of Woodbury; arcs south around South St. Paul; heads due west through Eagan, Bloomington, and Eden Prairie; and then swings north through the western suburbs to reunite with I-94 in the suburb of Maple Grove northwest of Minneapolis. I-694 also starts at the intersection with I-94 in Woodbury but heads north through Oakdale, swings west to the intersection with Interstate 35E in Little Canada, and then meanders roughly northwest through the suburbs of New Brighton, Fridley, Brooklyn Center, Brooklyn Park, and Maple Grove, where it meets I-94 again.

Interstate 94 winds its way through downtown St. Paul and on to Minneapolis. TODD R. BERGER

The rough rectangle made by the I-494/I-694 loop is sliced by two branches of I-35 heading north-south through the Metro. I-35 splits into I-35W and I-35E in the southern suburb of Burnsville. I-35W heads due north through the western part of the Metro into downtown Minneapolis and then wiggles northeast of downtown through the northern suburbs to merge with I-35E in Columbus Township and become I-35 again. I-35E heads northeast from Burnsville into downtown St. Paul and then shoots north to briefly merge with I-694 before stretching north again for its eventual reunion with I-35W.

I-94 and I-394 split the I-494/I-694 rectangle east-west. I-94 rolls into the eastern Metro from Wisconsin, passing through downtown St. Paul and downtown Minneapolis before abruptly swinging north, where it merges for a few miles with I-694 in Brooklyn Center before going it alone again in its long march westward. Interstate 394 runs from the

western suburbs to downtown Minneapolis. The newest of the Twin Cities freeways, I-394 includes separate carpool lanes (open during times of heavy congestion), and its ramps take you right into the heart of Minneapolis's Warehouse District.

Several other federal and state highways crosshatch the I-494/I-694 loop. U.S. Highway 169 arrives in the Metro from southwestern Minnesota in the suburb of Eden Prairie, on the southwestern edge of the Cities, and then shoots due north through the western suburbs, crossing I-694 in Maple Grove just east of the intersection of I-694 and I-494. US 169 and the roughly parallel Minnesota Highway 100 are the principal north-south routes in the western suburbs.

Minnesota Highway 62 is the major east-west route through the southern Metro north of I-494. MN 62, referred to locally as the Crosstown, runs from its intersection with US 169 in Minnetonka in the southwestern Metro to its intersection with Minnesota Highway 55, just north of the Minneapolis–St. Paul International Airport. The Crosstown looks convenient on a map, but the highway briefly merges with I-35W in Richfield, and the resulting bottleneck is considered one of the worst in the nation.

Other useful highways in the south-central Metro include Minnesota Highway 77, which runs from the southern suburb of Apple Valley to its intersection with the Crosstown in the Lake Nokomis area of south Minneapolis. This highway passes, among other things, the Minnesota Zoo, the Mall of America, and MSP airport. MN 55 stretches all the way from the town of Hastings, 20 miles southeast of St. Paul, to downtown Minneapolis, passing over the Minnesota River via the 4,119-foot concrete-arch Fort Snelling–Mendota Bridge and skirting Fort Snelling State Park, MSP airport, and Minnehaha Park before gliding through the commercial districts of south Minneapolis. Known as Hiawatha Avenue along its path inside Minneapolis, this road is the route of the Hiawatha light-rail transit (LRT) leg from downtown Minneapolis to the airport. There are stoplights along parts of this route, but it can be a quick alternative to get downtown from the southeastern Metro.

The principal highways in the eastern Metro include Minnesota Highway 110, which starts at its intersection with I-494 just west of the intersection with U.S. Highway 52, then takes a short tour of the St. Paul suburbs of Inver Grove Heights, Sunfish Lake, West St. Paul, and Mendota Heights before intersecting with MN 55 just before the Fort Snelling–Mendota Bridge over the Minnesota River.

US 52 is perhaps more useful, arriving from southern Minnesota and intersecting I-494 in the southern St. Paul suburb of Inver Grove Heights. From there the highway conveniently heads through the suburbs of South St. Paul and West St. Paul right to downtown St. Paul, passing St. Paul Downtown Holman Field airport and crossing the Mississippi River in the process. The route into the city along US 52, particularly at night,

provides some of the most spectacular views of the St. Paul skyline.

U.S. Highways 10 and 61 unite in Hastings and follow the Mississippi River to I-94 just east of downtown St. Paul, passing through the suburbs of Cottage Grove, St. Paul Park, and Newport in the process. From there, US 61 veers north at Arcade Street, following city streets until hitting the suburb of Maplewood and then spiking north through the suburbs of Mahtomedi, Gem Lake, White Bear Lake, and Hugo before ending just north of Forest Lake about 25 miles north of downtown St. Paul. US 61 roughly parallels I-35E in the northern suburbs, and the interstate is almost always a better choice except during heavy rush-hour traffic.

US 10 takes the easy route after intersecting I-94 by merging with the interstate in the westbound direction, then turning north and merging with I-35E for a few miles, and then merging with I-694 and heading northwest to the northern suburb of Arden Hills. From there US 10 briefly follows its own route northwest, then merges with I-35W in Mounds View for a few miles, finally going it alone through the suburbs of Blaine, Coon Rapids, Anoka, Ramsey, and Elk River before skipping out of the Metro.

Minnesota Highway 36 is another useful eastern highway, running from its intersection with I-35W in the northern suburb of Roseville through Little Canada, Maplewood, North St. Paul, and Oakdale all the way to Stillwater on the St. Croix River. This highway has some stoplights, particularly in the stretch between I-35E and I-694 and on the approach into Stillwater, and is prone to gridlocked traffic during

---

Parking ramp availability signs are conveniently located on downtown St. Paul streets. The signs post the number of available parking spots and are helpful in guiding drivers to lots with spaces open.

rush hours; but it is the quickest outlet to the St. Croix Valley and a convenient artery leading to many shopping areas in the first-tier northern suburbs.

Minnesota Highway 280 provides an appreciated shortcut for motorists on I-94 on the western edges of St. Paul intent on reaching the northern suburbs. The highway runs from its intersection with I-94 just east of the Minneapolis city boundary due north through Lauderdale to intersect I-35W in Roseville after just a few miles. The highway provides access not only to the retail outlets of Roseville but also to the University of Minnesota–St. Paul Campus and Luther Seminary.

Twin Cities Streets

Minneapolis and St. Paul are two distinctly governed municipalities, separated along much of one boundary by the Mississippi River. For this reason, Minneapolis and St. Paul share a few important streets, which include University and Como Avenues. However, several streets change their names when crossing the county line. Most notably, Larpenteur Avenue in St. Paul becomes East Hennepin Avenue in Minneapolis, and Marshall Avenue in St. Paul turns into Lake Street after crossing the Mississippi into Minneapolis. More confusingly, both cities have streets that share names but are not connected to their counterparts across the river, including Minnehaha and Grand Avenues. These things happen when urban centers develop next to one another. Try to keep this in mind when navigating Twin Cities streets.

St. Paul Streets

It felt like all of St. Paul was mad at then Minnesota governor Jesse Ventura after he complained to David Letterman on national television that the downtown streets seemed to have been designed by drunken Irishmen. But people have been complaining about St. Paul's street plan for ages, and anyone thinking Ventura was in the habit of softening the blows should remember that the man was a pro wrestler.

The street plan really isn't *that* confounding, but it does get a little tricky where main thoroughfare Kellogg Boulevard takes a southeasterly bend to run along the Mississippi River. Kellogg connects the action at the southeastern end of the city (Xcel Energy Center, the Science Museum of Minnesota) with the artsy Lowertown district. The main streets unfolding away from the river, or northwest of Kellogg, are numbered beginning with 4th and reach 11th just before I-94 and I-35E rein in the city. These numbered streets are labeled "west" and "east" depending on which side of Wabasha Street they lie. Wabasha is a main northwest–southeast thoroughfare, and it, along with Robert and Smith Streets, crosses the Mississippi River to what's called St. Paul's West Side (it's actually on the city's south side), which is the premier Twin Cities Latino neighborhood. Seventh Street (again, labeled east or west in relation to Wabasha) is the main northeast–southwest route. It and all the other major arteries named here are prone to congestion during rush hour or major Xcel Center events, though St. Paul generally has less traffic than Minneapolis.

Another of St. Paul's main streets, Snelling Avenue (Minnesota Highway 51), starts on far western Seventh Street, northeast of MSP airport. It then runs north past the St. Paul neighborhood of Highland Park and through the university-riddled west side of the city, where it intersects major avenues such as Randolph, Grand, Summit, and University, as well as I-94, before continuing past the Minnesota State Fairgrounds into St. Paul's northern suburbs. Snelling is often busy, as is cross street University Avenue, which starts near the Minnesota State Capitol just north of downtown St. Paul, then parallels I-94 west on into Minneapolis.

Downtown St. Paul from Cathedral Hill in winter. TODD R. BERGER

East–west-running Grand and Summit Avenues are good to know, too. They're on a bluff on the northwest side of downtown, just 1 block from one another—Summit is the world's longest stretch of intact original Victorian housing, and Grand is St. Paul's main shopping and dining street.

Minneapolis Streets

Four key pieces of advice for drivers new to downtown Minneapolis. One: Get your numbered avenues and streets straight. Two: The myriad one-way streets generally alternate. Three: Keep your eyes peeled for the new light-rail on Fifth Street. Four: Never drive on Nicollet Mall, the city's pedestrian-friendly shopping artery.

We'll start with the numbers thing. The streets run northwest–southeast, beginning with First Street along the Mississippi River. They're named north or south depending on which side of the main thoroughfare Hennepin Avenue (a.k.a. Theater Row) they lie. Avenues, such as Hennepin, run northeast–southwest, and they have names more often than numbers. The city is bound by I-94, which runs east–west below Minneapolis before angling north–south along the city's west edge. Both Hennepin and Third Avenues have bridges across the Mississippi into St. Anthony and the hip Northeast neighborhood, with lots of locally owned shops, restaurants, and bars. The beautiful Stone Arch Bridge, like Nicollet Mall, is for peo-

ple and bikes only. All of downtown is congested during rush hours and when events are happening at the Metrodome (on the southeast side of downtown) or Target Center (on the northwest).

Things get easier both northeast and southwest of the city when the grid straightens out. At that point streets run plain-old north–south, and the avenues go, for the most part, east–west. Take Hennepin southwest out of downtown, for example, and you're headed to Loring Park, the Walker Art Center, and, once the street curves south, the Uptown shopping and dining district. Lake Street and Hennepin Avenue are at the heart of Uptown—follow Lake Street west a few blocks and you're at Lake Calhoun (one of this area's many lakes). Follow Lake Street east and you'll cross major north–south-running Lyndale Avenue and I-35W before eventually heading into St. Paul.

SNOW EMERGENCY INFORMATION

Although the words "snow emergency" may sound ominous to the uninitiated, such events are declared so that the city of Minneapolis or St. Paul can get people to park their cars in the proper places to allow plows through. Declaration of an "emergency" does not (necessarily) mean that you will need to stock up on batteries or canned chipped beef. Both Minneapolis and St. Paul have extensive and different snow emergency ordinances. In some situations, not complying with snow removal rules will result in the towing of a vehicle, a hefty fine, or both, so beware. Snow emergencies are announced through the local media. You can also check to see if restrictions are in effect in Minneapolis by calling (612) 348-SNOW or visiting www.ci.minneapolis.mn.us/snow. For St. Paul call (651) 266-PLOW, or check the Web at www.stpaul.gov/depts/publicworks/snowplow. It is your responsibility to know if a snow emergency has been declared; pleading ignorance will not

Numerous Twin Cities events offer park-and-ride opportunities. For example, the Minnesota State Fair has park-and-ride lots at the University of Minnesota, Har Mar Mall (in Roseville), and at other locations. Park and ride is an excellent way to avoid traffic and the hassle of commuting to popular Twin Cities events.

There is no overnight parking on this street during snow emergencies in St. Paul.

TODD R. BERGER

get you out of paying a fine or towing fees. The following is a list of guidelines and helpful hints for snow emergencies.

Minneapolis

Minneapolis does not set a minimum amount of snowfall to declare a snow emergency other than to describe it as "significant." Once a snow emergency is declared before 6:00 P.M., the entire city enters a three-day cycle that dictates where you can park your car. On the first day of a snow emergency, from 9:00 P.M. to 8:00 A.M., the city allows no parking on either side of Snow Emergency Routes, which are marked with red signs along the side of the street or blue street-name signs (non–snow emergency routes have green or brown street-name signs). You can park on either side of any non–snow emergency route and on parkways. On

the second day of the snow emergency, from 8:00 A.M. to 8:00 P.M., there is no parking on either side of parkways or on the even-numbered side of non–snow emergency routes; however, you can now park on plowed Snow Emergency Routes. From 8:00 P.M. to 8:00 A.M. on the second night of the snow emergency, you cannot park on the odd-numbered side of non–snow emergency routes. On the third day of the snow emergency, the parking ban continues on the odd-numbered side of non–snow emergency routes until the street is plowed to the curb.

Minneapolis offers free or reduced-fee parking on the first night of a snow emergency at five parking ramps near downtown and around the University of Minnesota. Call the Minneapolis snow emergency line or check out the Web site for more information.

St. Paul

St. Paul declares snow emergencies after 3 or more inches of snow accumulate at once, or accumulate over days. St. Paul divides its streets into "night plow" and "day plow" routes. The night plow routes are plowed between 9:00 P.M. and 6:00 A.M. on the night the snow emergency is declared. These routes are marked with permanent night plow zone signs. All downtown streets are plowed at night. Note that some north–south residential streets have signs reading NIGHT PLOW ROUTE THIS SIDE OF STREET. You *can* park on the nonsigned sides of these streets during the first night of a snow emergency. The snow is removed on day plow routes from 8:00 A.M. to 5:00 P.M. These routes, which are not marked with signs, include east–west residential streets and north–south residential streets without plowing signs.

PARKING

The rates at downtown Minneapolis and St. Paul parking ramps and lots range widely based on location, time of day, the owner of the facility, and whether a sporting event or other major happening is occurring in the area. Generally you can expect to pay $4.00 to $7.00 minimum for the first hour at downtown lots in either city, but there's usually a maximum amount you'll pay—likely somewhere between $8.00 and $20.00. To get the best price, look for surface lots near event sites or ramps/lots on the fringes of either city's downtown.

Both cities have many parking meters. Rates and enforcement times vary, so

Are you concerned about road conditions? Check out the Minnesota Department of Transportation Web site (www.dot.state.mn.us) or call (651) 296-3000 or (800) 657-3774.

check the signs carefully and carry plenty of quarters. It's illegal to replug in both cities. In downtown Minneapolis parking charges can be avoided by patronizing stores and restaurants that participate in the "Do the Town" parking program, where a $20 purchase after 4:00 P.M. and all day on weekends will get you a parking validation.

Keep in mind when parking downtown that you do not necessarily have to park right next to your destination when the winter winds blow and the temperatures plummet. In both downtown Minneapolis and downtown St. Paul, many buildings and parking ramps are connected through the Cities' respective skyway systems.

The skyway systems provide an added bonus in the summer, too—walking over the main pedestrian thoroughfares means you don't have to stop for traffic lights or crosswalks, or watch out for puddles or rogue automobiles.

Park-and-Ride Lots

More than 18,500 free parking spaces are available for city bus passengers at 113 Park-and-Ride lots throughout the Twin Cities metro area. For locations, call Metro Transit at (612) 373-3333, or visit their Web site at www.metrotransit.org.

PUBLIC TRANSPORTATION

City Buses

Metro Transit
(612) 373-3333
www.metrotransit.org
Metro Transit, the principal transportation provider in the Minneapolis and St. Paul area, is one of the country's largest transit systems, providing roughly 95 percent of the 72 million bus trips taken annually in the Twin Cities. Each weekday, customers board Metro Transit buses an average of 200,000 times. Buses run between the

Cities and the suburbs every day and evening—some downtown Minneapolis lines even run 24 hours a day. The system is made up of 125 routes served by a fleet of 830 buses, and Metro Transit has its own police department.

Adult rates for Metro Transit buses are $1.50 during non–rush-hour times and $2.00 for rush-hour times for local bus routes and $2.00 outside rush hour and $2.75 during rush hour for express routes. Rush hour is defined as 6:00 to 9:00 A.M. and 3:00 to 6:30 P.M., Monday through Friday (except holidays). Seniors over 65 and youths under 12 can ride at reduced fares during non–rush-hour times. Persons with disabilities can ride for 50 cents anytime.

Metro Transit buses are reliable and travel widely dispersed routes within the cities of Minneapolis and St. Paul, and it is very possible to live in either St. Paul or Minneapolis and not own a car. Service to the outer suburbs is less frequent, with only a few lines running out of town each day—usually one an hour at most. Downtown Minneapolis, downtown St. Paul, Uptown Minneapolis, and the Mall of America are Metro Transit's four main hubs, where most routes converge and transfers are easy to make. A quick phone call to Metro Transit will put you in touch with an operator who will plan your trip or mail you all the schedules you need to get around the area (please specify which ones you need, because there are hundreds of routes to choose from). Transit System maps are also available from Metro Transit.

On Metro Transit's Web site, you can determine routes, view route maps, print schedules, and plan itineraries by entering origination and destination addresses, landmarks, or nearest street intersections.

Light-Rail

The Twin Cities first light-rail line, the Hiawatha LRT, opened in 2004. The line stretches 12 miles from downtown Minneapolis, past the Metrodome and near the University of Minnesota West Bank Campus, and then follows Hiawatha Avenue through south Minneapolis past Lake Street, tunnels under Minnehaha Park, resurfaces to pause at the Veterans' Administration Medical Center, and then moves on to Fort Snelling State Park. The line dives underground again via tunnels to the Lindbergh Terminal and emerges to stop at the Humphrey Terminal at MSP airport, then travels to the Mall of America in Bloomington.

The line features 17 stations, all individually designed to fit in with the surrounding neighborhoods. Train fares are $2.00 during rush hours and $1.50 at other times—the same fares as local bus service. Rail riders must pay this fare before boarding trains and show proof of payment to transit police officers when asked. Ticket vending machines are available on rail platforms.

Light-rail transit, known as the LRT. GREATER MINNEAPOLIS CONVENTION & VISITORS ASSOCIATION

The Hiawatha LRT line was a source of great public debate for many years in the Twin Cities and in Minnesota state government—not surprising given the project's $715 million price tag. However, not long after the first south Minneapolis residents rode to the Mall of America, the first conventioneers boarded a train at the airport that dropped them off near their downtown Minneapolis hotels, and the first Metro commuters took advantage of the several park-and-ride lots for quick trips to their downtown jobs, the arguments were over. During the first 15 months of service, customers took 8.5 million rides—67 percent higher than projections.

Suburban Bus Systems

Several suburban areas have smaller bus systems serving outlying communities, with connections to the larger Metro Transit system in the Twin Cities. For more information on bus service in specific areas, contact the following organizations.

NORTHWESTERN SUBURBS

Maple Grove Transit
(763) 494-6005
www.ci.maple-grove.mn.us

Northstar Commuter Coach
(888) 528-8880
www.commutercoach.org
Northstar Commuter Coach serves the communities of Elk River and Coon Rapids.

Plymouth Metrolink
(763) 509-5535
www2.ci.plymouth.mn.us

SOUTHERN SUBURBS

Minnesota Valley Transit Authority
(952) 882-7500
www.mvta.com
The Minnesota Valley Transit Authority serves five southern suburbs just south of the Minnesota River: Apple Valley, Burnsville, Eagan, Rosemount, and Savage.

SOUTHWESTERN SUBURBS

SouthWest Metro Transit
(952) 949-2287
www.swtransit.org
SouthWest Metro Transit serves the communities of Eden Prairie, Chanhassen, and Chaska.

Taxis

While taxicabs are a common sight in both downtown Minneapolis and St. Paul, flagging one down on the street is nearly impossible. Your best bet is to call a cab company and have it send a ride over to you.

The one exception to this rule is at the airport. Parked cabs waiting for fares line up at the taxi station at Lindbergh Terminal and at the curb in front of Humphrey Terminal.

The following taxi company provides service in both the Twin Cities. Consult the Minneapolis or St. Paul yellow pages for further options, but understand that most companies don't have cabs in both cities.

Green & White/Suburban Taxi
Airport Service: (952) 884-8888
Minneapolis Service: (612) 522-2222
St. Paul Service: (651) 222-2222

HISTORY 🏛

Many Minnesota visitors are struck by a peculiarity of Twin Cities residents: their concern with the weather. As time has passed, the weather's impact on Twin Citians' lives has decreased considerably, and industry and technology have replaced the area's reliance on natural resources and agriculture. Still, in a state where temperatures have ranged from –60 degrees F to 114 degrees F, and where an Indian summer afternoon can transmogrify into a chilling winter blizzard in less than an hour, the interest in weather remains. After all, the Twin Cities were built on their abundant natural resources and fecund lands. Milling, mining, and lumbering were the cornerstones of the early Minnesota economy. These industries created links to numerous allied businesses that developed into the component parts of the area's diverse and dynamic 21st-century economy. So when you visit the Twin Cities, remember the area's concern with weather has an important historical antecedent. The number of farmers, millers, and lumberjacks may have dramatically decreased, but it is the basis of the area's early history. And at least indirectly, it continues to affect the personal and economic livelihood of Twin Citians.

THE ORIGINS OF THE TWIN CITIES

The history of the Twin Cities begins with two cities, Minneapolis and St. Paul, each with distinct yet similar developments. Minneapolis is nicknamed the "City of Lakes" and the "Mill City." In stark contrast, St. Paul is the "Saintly City" and the "Capital City." These differences have exacerbated competition between the cities, where frequently good-natured sparring has occurred. But there are more similarities than differences between the cities. One commonality is the first inhabitants of the area, the American Indians.

Before European settlement, the Dakotas and Ojibwe populated the Twin Cities area. However American Indian presence predates the Dakotas and Ojibwe. Archeologists and historians actually know more about the Woodland Indians because of the rich fossil record they left behind. Woodland Indian burial mounds were scattered throughout Minnesota when the state was settled. Mounds Park, overlooking downtown St. Paul, has one of the area's finest examples of Hopewell Indian mounds. The Mississippian cultures of the Dakotas and Ojibwe replaced these early peoples. Archeologists posit that this occurred between A.D. 800 and 1000. The mounds and their human remains, tools, and other artifacts are protected as the historical record of the first Twin Citians.

The Ojibwe, or Ojibwa, were in the past more often referred to as the Chippewas and had origins in the area near Sault Ste. Marie, Michigan. The skilled hunters' territories expanded to include parts of the northern metropolitan Twin Cities. While the Ojibwe's origins were to the east and north, the Dakotas were western Plains Indians, who at the time of European exploration occupied the Twin Cities, western and southern Minnesota, and much of present-day North Dakota and South Dakota. The French referred to the Dakotas as Sioux, a meaningless abridgment of the Ojibwe term, *Nadouissouix*. The word translates as "little viper" or "lesser enemy." The derogatory name stuck for centuries, until recently when the tribe was called the more respectful name Dakota. Both Indian tribes were hunting societies, and they evolved tremendously by incorporating European tools, wares, and implements such as guns, hatchets, blankets, knives, and kettles. The contact and cultural exchange transformed the local American Indians and the Europeans. The Europeans rapidly pushed the less densely populated American Indians from their lands through treaties and warfare. Frequently internecine warfare occurred between the Dakotas, usually supported and supplied by the British, and the Ojibwe, supported by the French. However, the French voyageurs were the first Europeans to leave a mark on the area, even if they did not establish a permanent settlement.

The names of French explorers and traders are found on the streets, avenues, counties, and institutions in the Twin Cities. Father Louis Hennepin, a Belgian, explored French territories that included the area that became the Twin Cities in 1680 and three years later wrote the then best-selling book *Description of Louisiana,* in which he exaggerated the splendor of the area's natural wonders. During his visit he named the Falls of St. Anthony after his patron saint. St. Anthony is located across the Mississippi River from the later birthplace of Minneapolis. In 1872 St. Anthony and Minneapolis merged. Hennepin's name is commemorated in Minneapolis's most famous thoroughfare, Hennepin Avenue, and the county of the same name. Fur trapping remained important in the area for well over a century, but a permanent settlement in the area did not occur until the United States won independence from England.

Fort Snelling was the first site permanently settled in Minnesota. The federal government established the fort to protect the most northwestern edge of the United States. Henry Leavenworth came to the present site of Fort Snelling in 1819, at the confluence of the Mississippi and Minnesota Rivers. The current location adjoins Minneapolis–St. Paul International Airport. Leavenworth failed miserably and was quickly replaced by Josiah Snelling. He performed his duties so well the federal government named it in his honor in 1825. The fort sits on a cliff overlooking the rivers, allowing for easy protection of

the area. It remains one of the Twin Cities' most scenic overlooks. When Fort Snelling was constructed, civilians began squatting in the area to serve the needs of soldiers and take advantage of the protection of the U.S. military.

The birth of St. Paul was a colorful page of Twin Cities history. Pierre "Pig's Eye" Parrant, a 60-year-old former voyageur, was the liquor bootlegger for the soldiers and citizens around Fort Snelling. Parrant's nickname, Pig's Eye, was the result of his disfigured and blind eye, and was the original name given to St. Paul. Not surprisingly, the thorny name for the city did not last. In 1840 a young Catholic priest, Lucian Galtier, arrived in Pig's Eye, where he christened the Chapel of St. Paul. Afterward the city was generally referred to as St. Paul's Landing. Following the arrival of the post office in 1846, the city's name was simply shortened to St. Paul.

Just up the Mississippi, the emergence of the other twin city, Minneapolis, was less colorful. Minneapolis and St. Anthony began in the 1840s as milling and lumbering centers; at first the two industries developed gradually. Franklin Steele settled St. Anthony in 1838, where he began successful flour and sawmills. On the other side of the Mississippi, Minneapolis was not founded until 1852, when Congress rescinded 26,000 acres from Fort Snelling's control. This allowed squatters such as Col. John H. Stevens to claim and develop the land that would become downtown Minneapolis.

Minneapolis's name has interesting origins. It is an amalgam of words from two languages, the Dakota word *minne*, meaning "sky-tinted water," and *polis*, the Greek word for "city." Minneapolis was founded on the west bank of the Mississippi River and St. Anthony on the east bank. In the 21st century it is difficult to believe that St. Anthony's importance early in its history eclipsed Minneapolis's, which had a relatively late start and was not chartered until 1867. But as time marched on, Minneapolis's growth significantly outpaced

St. Anthony's. In 1855 a suspension bridge was constructed to link the two communities. It was the first permanent bridge anywhere across the Mississippi, and it created extensive commercial and civic ties between the rapidly expanding urban centers. The two cities merged in 1872, which established a much larger Minneapolis. The Twin Cities' growth had a significant impact on Minnesota, which became a territory in 1849 and the 32nd state in 1858.

THE MILL CITY

In the late 19th and early 20th centuries, Minneapolis became nationally prominent as the "Mill City." The emergence of milling came as the lumbering industry began to decline because of competition from the west. The ascendancy of milling created numerous allied industries and was important to the development of the diverse

Minneapolis economy in the 20th century.

Milling began on the Mississippi, in Minneapolis and St. Anthony, because of the falls. Since the 19th century, industry and government programs have tamed much of the turbulence of St. Anthony Falls. To businessmen in the area, the falls represented a source of energy for milling the vast wheat crops in the area, which rapidly expanded as Minnesota and the upper Midwest were settled. As time progressed, each succeeding generation of mills became larger. This led to further consolidation, and industry leaders, internationally recognizable even today, emerged to dominate Minneapolis's market.

Innovations were instrumental in the development and dominance of General Mills. The corporation emerged gradually after a succession of mergers in Minneapolis's milling industry. Washburn-Crosby and Company is the major component of General Mills. The star of the company skyrocketed following an

St. Anthony Falls. GREATER MINNEAPOLIS CONVENTION & VISITORS ASSOCIATION

important innovation, "new process flour," which was brought to Washburn-Crosby and Company in 1871. The revolutionary new process flour involved milling spring wheat into white flour. No longer was winter wheat preferred. Quickly many Minneapolis mills acquired the revolutionary technology for producing new process flour. Many competitors acquired the information by dubious means. Washburn-Crosby and Company found tremendous success again in 1880, when they won the gold medal at the Millers' Exhibition in Cincinnati; thereafter the company marketed the Gold Medal brand of flour. The new technology catapulted General Mills and other Minneapolis mills to prominence as the nation's leading milling companies. By 1890 Minneapolis was the largest wheat market in the nation.

Minneapolis spawned many of the world's largest and most-important mills, and they have had a profound impact on the Cities' development. Pillsbury is another Minnesota-based company, and it began milling on the Mississippi in Minneapolis. The world's largest agribusiness company—Cargill—also has origins in Minneapolis, where it remains to this day, headquartered in Minnetonka, a Minneapolis suburb. Milling's influence still deeply pervades Minneapolis culture. Even the minor-league baseball team was named the Millers. Moreover, the call letters of one of Minneapolis's radio and television stations is WCCO. The station takes its name from Washburn-Crosby and Company, an early owner of the station. Diversification like this has spurred the increasingly dynamic Minnesota economy.

THE CAPITAL CITY

The nicknames of St. Paul are fundamental to its history. As the "Capital City" and the "Saintly City," its institutions play a pivotal role in the city's development. Unlike Minneapolis, St. Paul's economic history is not dominated by a single industry.

The institution of government has been central to St. Paul's history. Since the beginnings of the Minnesota Territory in 1849, St. Paul has served as the capital city. Early in its territorial history, it almost lost the capital to St. Peter in 1857. Joe Rolette, a territorial councilman, pocketed a bill passed by both houses of the legislature calling for relocating the territorial capital to St. Peter (south on the Minnesota River). Rolette hid with the bill for a week, but a copy of the bill was passed on to the governor, who signed it. Fortunately for St. Paul, the territorial governor was not reappointed. Later a federal district judge ruled that Minnesota Territory could not name another capital site. The capital remained in St. Paul. Political events continue to play an important role in St. Paul's history.

The Roman Catholic Church is another important institution in the city's history. Catholicism has always found more adherents in St. Paul. The city includes larger populations of Irish, German Catholics, and a small but significant number of Italian immigrants, while Minneapolis's immigration in the 19th century was dominated by Scandinavian and German Lutherans. Catholicism's influence began with the arrival of Father Lucian Galtier, who came to save the souls in "Pig's Eye." St. Paul was established as a diocese by 1850, and in 1888 it was expanded to become the archdiocese of St. Paul. The first archbishop of St. Paul, John Ireland, was involved in Irish immigration societies with St. Paul railroad magnate James J. Hill. The society populated the city and greater Minnesota with Catholics. In 1918 Ireland died, after initiating the erection of the spectacular Cathedral of Saint Paul, which continues today as one the city's most important landmarks. The archdiocese of St. Paul and Minneapolis remains headquartered in St. Paul.

Industry and technology were paramount in the historical development of St. Paul. Minnesota Mining and Manufacturing Company (3M) is one of the Cities' most important companies. 3M's history began in Two Harbors, a small town north of Duluth, in 1902 as a manufacturer of sandpaper. The company relocated to St. Paul in 1909. Over time 3M has grown into an international corporation and remains essentially a St. Paul company, even after relocating its headquarters to the adjoining suburb of Maplewood.

EUROPEANS SETTLE THE TWIN CITIES

Minnesota immigration in the 19th and early 20th centuries for the most part mirrored patterns throughout the United States. However, there were exceptions specific to the state of Minnesota and the Twin Cities. The national perception of Minnesota is of a state dominated by Scandinavians. This generalization is fairly accurate, if slightly exaggerated. German heritage is the most common ethnic background, followed closely by Norwegian, Swedish, and Irish ancestry.

Germans came to the state in greatest numbers from 1875 to 1900. Germans' contributions have been significant, especially in communities like New Ulm. In the south and west metropolitan area, there are numerous communities with German names and origins, such as New Germany, Hamburg, and Heidelberg. For the most part German heritage has been assimilated into the overall culture of the Twin Cities and Minnesota.

Minnesota's second most-numerous group of immigrants were the Norwegians, whose legacy is felt to this day. From 1875 until 1910 Norwegian immigrants came to Minnesota in the greatest numbers. O. E. Rolvaag was among this immigrant group. He wrote *Giants in the*

Earth (1927), a classic novel about Norwegian immigrant farmers. His son, Karl Rolvaag, served as governor of Minnesota.

The Swedish are the third-largest ancestral group in Minnesota. The Swedes followed similar immigration patterns as the Norwegians, and the two quickly became largely indistinguishable to outsiders. The legacy of Scandinavians is manifest in the cities they founded and settled, e.g., Scandia and Lindstrom. Moreover, public facilities bear the name of important past citizens of Scandinavian heritage. Olson Memorial Highway is named after governor Floyd B. Olson, who died suddenly in 1936 while running for the U.S. Senate.

Scandinavians dominated Minnesota politics during much of the state's history. Since Knute Nelson was elected governor in 1893, there have been 25 additional heads of state, and of this number only 6 were not of Scandinavian heritage. Even today Scandinavian heritage is an asset for Minnesota politicians. Congressman Martin Olav Sabo of Minneapolis makes his ancestry apparent by emphasizing his Scandinavian middle name.

The Irish are also an essential component of Minnesota's ethnic heritage. The Irish were influential in the development of St. Paul, especially in the formation of the Catholic Church under the leadership of Archbishop John Ireland. Heavy Irish immigration began in the 1860s and ended about 1890. The ethnic group quickly integrated into the community and ascended to government positions.

Additional immigrant groups came to Minnesota and the Twin Cities. From 1820 to 1890 small groups of Swiss, Belgians,

Several excellent Minnesota history books are available. The most recent, concise survey is A Popular History of Minnesota *by Norman K. Risjord, available from the Minnesota Historical Society Press.*

Larry Millett, Author

"I always tell people the most interesting place in the world is the place where you grew up," says Larry Millett, author of the award-winning books *Lost Twin Cities* and *Twin Cities Then and Now,* as well as several Sherlock Holmes mysteries that take place in Minnesota. "I've been a fan of local history for a long time because I find it intriguing. I grew up in the Cities and went to school in downtown Minneapolis and saw first-hand the demolition of the Gateway District. My father's family goes way back in Minneapolis—my grandfather owned a bar on Washington Avenue, and his wife was the granddaughter of one of the early founders of the city. So I have deep roots in this area."

Millett, who has worked as a reporter and editor at the *St. Paul Pioneer Press* for more than 30 years, has taken his love for architecture and history to write some of the most amazing and heartbreaking literary tours of the Twin Cities. Using

photos kept on record at the Minnesota History Center for more than 150 years, Millett's books show in great detail how much the cities have both changed and stayed the same over the past century. *Lost Twin Cities* is composed completely of photographs and the histories of the many architectural wonders that were destroyed over the years—including the beautiful Gateway Park, which became a hangout for homeless people during the Depression—while *Twin Cities Then and Now* provides side-by-side pictures of Twin Cities neighborhoods and business districts at various points in time.

"The cities are not hugely distinctive from each other architecturally, I think," says Millett about the Twin Cities today. "What happened historically is that there was a different set of architects for St. Paul and Minneapolis, so there were initial differences from the individual hands involved. But what's happened in St. Paul

and Dutch settled the area. Later, echoing national trends, southern, central, and eastern Europeans came to the Twin Cities. Compared with many other areas of the nation, they were smaller in number. However, they were a significant immigrant group from 1890 until 1920. Primarily Russians and various groups from the Austro-Hungarian Empire were included in this wave of immigrants. Unlike many other areas of the country, Italians and Greeks were a relatively insignificant immigrant group during this time in Minnesota.

Since the 1960s Twin Cities immigrants are predominately non-European.

THE DIVERSE TWIN CITIES 20TH-CENTURY ECONOMY

In the 20th century the Twin Cities diversified and developed an economy consistently among the strongest in the United States.

The milling industry became increasingly decentralized, as the largest and

since is that it's probably got a better stock of historic buildings than Minneapolis, while Minneapolis probably has a better stock of newer buildings. St. Paul has been more fortunate in preserving its historic housing stock than Minneapolis, and there are reasons for that that have more to do with relative lack of development and change than any great historic sentiment, I think. Minneapolis, since the turn of the century, has been a more dynamic city, and the more dynamic a city is, the more quickly its architecture tends to change."

Millett's favorite buildings today? "I love St. Paul's city hall," he says. "I think it's one of our country's great art deco buildings, as is the county courthouse. The public library in St. Paul, and the Hill Reference Library, which is next door and is part of the same building but a different institution. Of course Landmark Center, the State Capitol, St. Paul Cathedral, the basics. In Minneapolis, I'm very fond of the IDS building, I think that's a nation-ally and internationally significant sky-scraper, and the Norwest Tower (renamed the Wells Fargo Center) is very nice for its kind, too.

"It's amazing as a researcher to find out how many places aren't documented," finishes Millett. "There are places in both cities where basically there's no clue to how it looked 100 years ago because there are no pictures in the public collection. That's especially true of some of the residential neighborhoods. The downtowns of both cities are well documented, but once you get out to the residential districts, the documentation is much spottier. It all depends on how good a job the city's photographer did at the time. The Minnesota Historical Society has more than 140,000 images on their Web site (www.mnhs.org), so you can cruise through all those on their Web site now. It's really phenomenal what they have, all the images of the Twin Cities in particular."

most successful Twin Cities milling companies gradually diversified into related industries. The decline of Minneapolis milling occurred fairly rapidly, and in the 1920s flour production was halved from the production levels of the glory years before and immediately after the turn of the 20th century. Today Minneapolis is once again the largest producer of flour in the United States but holds considerably less domination over the industry, where it accounts for only 10 percent of the national total.

Washburn-Crosby and Company changed its name to General Mills in 1928. The corporation had developed Wheaties breakfast cereal in 1924 and Betty Crocker, a globally recognized cake mix, in 1921. The name change represented the growing national focus of the company. General Mills moved into other food-related businesses, including numerous breakfast foods, dough mixes, and frozen foods.

Pillsbury followed a similar path, diversifying its food lines and businesses throughout the 20th century. The home of

Rapid growth and new construction, particularly around the Xcel Energy Center, have fueled new businesses in downtown St. Paul. TODD R. BERGER

the Pillsbury Doughboy moved into prepared doughs as well as frozen and canned foods. The company entered the restaurant business in 1967, acquiring Burger King, and later became involved in additional restaurant ventures. Pillsbury underwent a significant change in 1989.

As the traditional industries of the Twin Cities diversified, new high-tech businesses asserted themselves as an important component of the local economy. Some companies' roots reach back to industry and manufacturing that began in the late 19th and early 20th centuries, as is the case with the 3M Corporation, while others quickly became important businesses in the area because of technological innovation.

One such Twin Cities company is Medtronic Inc. Earl Bakken, a University of Minnesota graduate student, began his company in a northeast Minneapolis garage in 1949. Medtronic's first big success came with the development of an implantable pacemaker in 1960. Medtronic diversified into numerous medical technol-

ogy fields and today is an internationally recognized corporation.

Honeywell is another important Twin Cities high-technology company. The origins of Honeywell date from a failed spring-powered thermostat company developed by A. M. Butz in 1885. Over time the fledgling company honed its technological devices. After success with its thermostat line, the company moved into heating, air-conditioning, and varied technological devices for industry and Cold War defense programs. Honeywell's military products became an important component of the company's revenues. As the Cold War came to an end, however, Honeywell ran into economic hard times.

The Twin Cities are also home to one of the nation's largest retailers, the Target Corporation. For most of its long history in the Twin Cities, Target was known as the Dayton Company, and later the Dayton Hudson Corporation. The Dayton Company opened for business in downtown Minneapolis in 1902. George Dayton started the business at a site in downtown

Minneapolis that, to this day, remains Dayton's. The Dayton Company started its most nationally recognized retail store, Target, in suburban Roseville, in 1962. Dayton Hudson officially changed its name to the Target Corporation in 2000.

As the 20th century came to a close, the Twin Cities saw significant corporate reorganization. Larger domestic and multinational corporations acquired several local firms. Several Twin Cities economists questioned the vitality of the area's economy, while many others felt the event was simply emblematic of global restructuring of the economy.

THE TWIN CITIES ENTER THE NEW MILLENNIUM

The Twin Cities underwent a substantial transformation during the late 1990s. The economy is still a topic of conversation because of acquisitions and mergers of several blue chip Twin Cities firms.

Corporations outside the Twin Cities acquired several area firms. Honeywell merged with a New Jersey company and then was bought by General Electric. Minneapolis-based ReliaStar, a financial products firm, was purchased by ING Group of the Netherlands in 2000. Norwest, a bank headquartered in the Twin Cities, was purchased by Wells Fargo of San Francisco.

Reflecting the strength of the local economy, there was a sharp increase in immigration over the past decade. The most recent Twin Cities immigrants are largely from Asia, Africa, and areas of the world that before the late '70s were absent from area demographics. The dynamic new immigrant population has significantly contributed to the complex of Twin Cities ethnicity.

The new wave of immigrants began to arrive in the late '70s. The new immigrant populations are largely émigrés who came to the United States to escape political tumult, repression, and warfare. The first group to arrive were displaced Viet-

namese, who were followed by numerous other Southeast Asian groups, which included Laotians, Khmers (Cambodia), and the Hmong (Laos). With the exception of Bosnians, Europeans are a relatively small component of the new immigration.

The Hmong are a significant immigrant group in the Twin Cities. Since the late '70s they have come from Laos, or relocated to the area from other American cities, to take advantage of the area's low unemployment and booming economy. Today there are more than 200,000 Hmong living in the United States. The Twin Cities, in particular St. Paul, have the largest Hmong population in the nation. The Hmong and other Southeast Asians have started more than 400 area businesses and have transformed St. Paul's Frogtown and Midway neighborhoods.

A more recent trend has seen East Africans settling in the Twin Cities. The first significant wave of African immigrants came from Ethiopia and Eritrea in the late '80s and early '90s. Today, Ethiopian and Eritrean restaurant businesses are scattered throughout the Twin Cities, and many of the former immigrants now hold government positions.

The Somalis are another East African immigrant group. An estimated 40,000 Somalis currently live in the United States, and approximately 20,000 reside in Minnesota. However, members of the Somali community feel the government numbers are low and believe there may be as many as 90,000 in Minnesota. The Somalis' presence is felt in the many small businesses owned and operated by the community.

The new wave of immigration is just one parallel linking the Twin Cities' past and present. Both Minneapolis and St. Paul are reviving important elements of their past on the Mississippi riverfront.

Since the late '80s, Minneapolis has focused on regaining its greatest historical assets—the Mississippi River and the Mill District. It began with the restoration of the James J. Hill Stone Arch Bridge—one of Minneapolis's most scenic vistas—and is

nearing its climax with the recently founded Mill City Museum. Opened in 2003, the museum is located in the historic Washburn-Crosby A Mill ruins. The museum celebrates the city's former status as the world's largest producer of flour. In addition, the Minneapolis Park and Recreation Board has completed the Mill Ruins Park.

Downriver in St. Paul the renovated Harriet Island Regional Park celebrates its city's rich history. During late summer 2000 more than 50,000 citizens attended the reopening of the park. The park represents the Cities' commitment to the riverfront.

ARCHITECTURE

The Twin Cities are composed of two cities with distinctly different histories and perspectives on architecture. Both cities draw architectural inspiration from different sources, and it is reflected in their respective architecture.

St. Paul has always looked to the East, and in particular Boston, as a source for civic inspiration. The design of the city reflects this perspective and was in large part developed by transplanted old-stock New Englanders. The streets, like Boston's, were platted much narrower than in Minneapolis. St. Paul views itself as a city of tradition and as the "Capital City." With a few exceptions, most notably the Minnesota World Trade Center, St. Paul's architecture has concerned itself with human-scale structures of elegance.

St. Paul's rival across the river has taken a considerably different approach to architecture. Minneapolis has always embraced progress and modernity. This distinction between the cities has only been exacerbated as Minneapolis architecture has increasingly grown vertically. Minneapolis streets are wider and for the most part straighter than those in St. Paul. Street addresses are much easier to follow because each block contains 100 potential addresses, thus addresses are clearly demarcated by intersections.

FUNCTION FIRST: THE BIRTH OF THE TWIN CITIES

Early Twin Cities architecture reflected national trends. When America was settled, functionality was of primary importance. Homes and civic structures were erected with safety and survival as main concerns. European settlers wanted protection from American Indians and from the severe Minnesota winters. Most early structures in the Twin Cities were log cabins, sod houses, and simple wooden structures.

Fort Snelling was the first permanent white settlement in the Twin Cities. Completed in 1820, it protected the north western-most edge of the United States. Thereafter, small wooden buildings were constructed in the two fledgling cities. Father Lucian Galtier dedicated a small log chapel in honor of St. Paul in November of 1841. Down the Mississippi almost a decade later, John Stevens created the first humble structure in the area that would soon be named Minneapolis. The little white house was soon surrounded by many similar structures.

Minneapolis and St. Paul rapidly developed into nationally prominent cities. During this epoch, buildings were constructed as quickly as possible to meet the needs of the expanding cities. As the cities developed, municipal institutions became necessary. Public buildings were the first opulent pieces of architecture in both cities, and they were public declarations of the importance of the Cities.

THE EMERGENCE OF THE TWIN CITIES

The Minneapolis City Hall (1906) represented the Cities' emergence as a nationally prominent municipality. In 1856 Minneapolis's population was 4,607, but by 1895 it had swelled to 192,823 and the city was the eighteenth largest in the nation.

St. Paul created structures to celebrate the Cities' ascendancy at the turn of the 20th century. The most significant architectural work was the Minnesota State Capitol, completed in 1904. Cass Gilbert designed the neoclassical structure. It is one of several outstanding pieces of government architecture in St. Paul.

Government and institutional structures marked St. Paul's entrance into the modern age. In contrast, Minneapolis was poised to begin its ascent skyward, which began with the Foshay Tower.

The Foshay Tower was the first skyscraper constructed in the Twin Cities. When it was completed in 1929, it was considered a feat of modern architecture. The 31-story obelisk was the largest building in the Twin Cities for more than 40 years. During the late 19th and early 20th centuries, both cities expanded upward with large concrete and metal structures, but none were as grand in scale as the Foshay.

In 1973 the IDS Center exceeded the Foshay by 26 stories, and the IDS was briefly lonesome atop the skyline. In the '80s and '90s new skyscrapers constructed of glass, concrete, and steel began to dominate downtown. The architecture is an eclectic modern mix of styles ranging from the interesting art deco–influenced Wells Fargo Center to less distinctive massive glass structures like the Piper Jaffray Tower. Unfortunately, the most recent additions to downtown, particularly on the south side of the Nicollet Mall, are less architecturally ambitious.

St. Paul also expanded upward in the late 20th century, but skyscrapers are not as prominent. The sixth-tallest building in Minneapolis, the Pillsbury Center, is taller than any building in St. Paul. The best architecture in downtown St. Paul is the city's government buildings. The St. Paul City Hall is a stunning structure, particularly its lobby, a fine example of art deco/moderne design. The Cathedral of Saint Paul is another architectural masterpiece; the baroque interior of the building suggests Europe rather than Minnesota. St. Paul architecture is not as vertical as Minneapolis; however, the Minnesota State Capitol and the Cathedral of Saint Paul make up for it in sheer size.

INTO THE 21ST CENTURY

As the Twin Cities enter the 21st century, both cities have recommitted themselves to the historic riverfront. Architecture and landscape design in the last decade have emphasized the Mississippi River.

In St. Paul the new Science Museum of Minnesota opened on the bluff above the river. The state-of-the-art museum makes fine use of its location with several scenic overviews of the river. In addition, the city reopened one of its most scenic parks, Harriet Island, across the river from downtown. Landscape architecture restored the park's links to the river through such features as the large concrete steps leading down to the river. Plans to redevelop the beautiful riverfront property to make better use of the river are in various stages of implementation. There is also a plan for residential development in the historic Irvine Park neighborhood on the Mississippi.

Minneapolis has shown a commitment to redeveloping the Mississippi riverfront with projects of its own. The first major project was the James J. Hill Stone Arch Bridge, which was renovated in 1994 by the Minnesota Department of Transportation. Then in 2003 the city opened the ambitious Mill City Museum (see the close-up later in this chapter for further details). The Minneapolis firm of Meyer, Scherer, and Rockcastle Ltd. created the design for the museum.

TWIN CITIES ARCHITECTURE IN DETAIL

The Downtown Minneapolis Skyline

Campbell Mithun Tower
222 South Ninth Street, Minneapolis
(612) 342–6000
Immense glass skyscrapers have transformed the look of downtown Minneapolis. Looking down Ninth Street, the chasm

between the past and present is highly visible. On the corner of Marquette Avenue and Ninth is the 31-story Foshay Tower. Continuing down Ninth Street to Third Avenue South is the Campbell Mithun Tower. By no means is it one of the most well-known pieces of architecture in Minneapolis, yet the structure easily eclipses the once-giant Foshay Tower in sheer size. Rising 42 stories, the Campbell Mithun Tower is the fifth-tallest building in the city. Constructed in 1985, it was an early addition to the skyward growth of downtown.

Dain Rauscher Plaza
60 South Sixth Street, Minneapolis
This is one of the many large glass skyscrapers erected in downtown Minneapolis in the '90s. Like all of the recent additions to the Minneapolis skyline, it has a system of skyways connecting it to the second and fourth levels of the Wells Fargo Center. At 539 feet and 40 stories, Dain Rauscher is the seventh-tallest building in Minneapolis.

The Foshay Tower
821 Marquette Avenue South, Minneapolis
(612) 359–3030
It is difficult to imagine that this obelisk once stood as the tallest skyscraper west of Chicago. It dominated the Minneapolis skyline and was the tallest building in the Twin Cities until the completion of the IDS Center in 1973. Today the Foshay Tower is surrounded by the modern glass-and-steel giants, which dwarf what is now the sixteenth-tallest building.

The Foshay Tower draws its name from the financier behind its construction, Wilbur H. Foshay. Foshay, a utilities magnate, became wealthy enough during the boom of the Roaring Twenties to construct a building modeled on the Washington Monument. The 32-story obelisk was topped with 10-foot-high letters that spelled out foshay. The Foshay's dedication in 1929 was one of the most lavish in the city's history. The festivities included

fireworks and a 75-piece brass band conducted by John Philip Sousa, which included his composition "Foshay Tower–Washington Memorial March." Unfortunately for Foshay, the good times were not to last. Shortly afterward the stock market crashed. Foshay's finances were decimated; in addition, he was convicted of fraud and sentenced to 15 years at Fort Leavenworth. President Franklin Delano Roosevelt pardoned Foshay after he had served three years.

Today the 447-foot Foshay is one of the Twin Cities' memorable sights, with its lights illuminating the Minneapolis sky. And it does this despite its relatively diminutive stature alongside the many larger skyscrapers built in the wake of the '80s and '90s. Features such as the open-air observatory are timeless and offer one of the most panoramic views of Minneapolis. Access is limited to late spring, summer, and early fall days because of the area's frequently inclement weather. For further information about the observation deck and prices, call (612) 359–3030. The Foshay Tower is a view not to be missed, especially during the splendor of a beautiful Minneapolis summer evening.

Hennepin County Government Center
300 South Sixth Street, Minneapolis
(612) 348–3000
The twin-tower exterior of the Hennepin County Government Center is unassuming enough. However, the 24-story atrium provides a truly spectacular view, which grows as you ascend the 25 stories of the building. There is another interesting feature to the building—Sixth Street passes directly under the structure.

The building was completed in 1977, and it serves Hennepin County (Minneapolis and suburbs) well. In addition to the wonderful atrium, the building includes an immense water fountain. The Hennepin Government Center has hosted public political rallies over the years. Prior to the 1992 election, former president Bill Clinton spoke at a huge rally on a lovely late summer evening.

IDS Center
80 South Eighth Street, Minneapolis
(612) 376-8000

The IDS Center supplanted the Foshay Tower as the tallest building in the Twin Cities when it opened in 1973—a position it has not relinquished. The IDS Center is arguably the most well-known building in the Twin Cities and is recognized as the centerpiece of the Minneapolis skyline. Seen from downtown Minneapolis and even the suburbs, the IDS Center looms large.

The IDS Center distinguishes itself in several other ways. The 57-story, 775-foot structure has more than 42,000 panes of glass as well as a 105-foot waterfall in Crystal Court, which was added during the 1998 renovation. Designed by world-renowned architects Philip Johnson and John Burgee, the skyscraper has frequently attracted national attention.

The grandeur of Crystal Court was featured in the *Mary Tyler Moore Show* and two motion pictures. The IDS observatory was a major Twin Cities attraction for years. Unfortunately, the observatory has since closed; however, Crystal Court is still one of the most beautiful shopping areas in the Twin Cities, and the IDS Center remains the centerpiece of the Minneapolis skyline.

225 South Sixth
225 South Sixth Street, Minneapolis

225 South Sixth is recognizable throughout Minneapolis by the crown that sits atop the large glass skyscraper. The building is the second tallest in Minneapolis. It was completed in 1992 as First Bank Place. The nationally respected firm of Pei, Cobb, Freed and Partners designed the 56-story 225 South Sixth, which, despite its size, receives far less attention than the Wells Fargo Center and the IDS Center.

US Bank Plaza
200 South Sixth Street, Minneapolis

Minneapolis was known throughout the nation as the Mill City during the 19th and early 20th centuries. As time has passed,

the importance of milling has been de-emphasized, and the "City of Lakes" nickname has moved to the forefront. However, milling and its many allied services and industries remain a vital part of the area's dynamic economy.

The building at 200 South Sixth Street was built as the Pillsbury headquarters. Pillsbury Center was completed in 1981. Then Pillsbury was acquired by General Mills, which relocated the company to its suburban Golden Valley campus. US Bank took up the empty space in Pillsbury Center, and soon after the building was renamed to reflect this change. US Bank Plaza is in the heart of downtown Minneapolis, where the 41-story building overlooks the city with its immense neighbors. It has two towers, and the beautiful atrium distinguishes it from other structures, with its eight stories of enclosed open space.

Wells Fargo Center
90 South Seventh Street, Minneapolis
(612) 344-1200

The Wells Fargo Center sits at the heart of downtown and perhaps is Minneapolis's most recognizable building at night, with its yellow-hued glow. The third-tallest building in the Twin Cities, like its neighbor the IDS Center it is 57 stories high. The building was completed in 1988 as the Norwest Center. The name changed when the Norwest and Wells Fargo banks merged.

The Norwest Center was constructed in the ashes of tragedy. A Thanksgiving 1982 fire destroyed the Northwestern National Bank Building. The structure itself was not as important a piece of architecture to the community as the "weatherball," which provided weather news 24/7 to Minneapolis. Norwest set out to construct a replacement.

The current building was completed in 1989. The heavily art deco–derived building was the work of Cesar Pelli and features a 100-foot-high domed ceiling rotunda as well as a more traditional lobby.

as the Digital Technology Center and the Science and Engineering Library. The recent renovation included restoring the staircase, lobby, and reading rooms to their original glory. The structure is built in the Roman Renaissance style, the dominant style of the campus's architectural epicenter, the Northrop Mall. It has the most decorative facade on the mall, making use of red brick and limestone trim.

Weisman Art Museum
333 East River Road, Minneapolis
(612) 625-9494

The Frederick R. Weisman Art Museum is one of the Twin Cities' most distinctive pieces of architecture. Opinions on the museum vary widely. Detractors have called the structure an ugly, discombobulated homage to the tin man in *The Wizard of Oz,* while enthusiasts glow incessantly about Frank Gehry's internationally acclaimed style. However, one fact is for certain: Gehry created a museum that is not, in the words of a former University of Minnesota president, Nils Hasselmo, "another brick lump."

Art critics from as far away as New York have lauded the Weisman. The museum features brushed stainless steel arranged in bold, undulating angles. Gehry links the museum to the more architecturally conservative buildings with terracotta bricks on the south and east sides. The interior of the museum includes extensive use of natural lighting sources, whether it is the skylights or large windows tastefully framing the view of downtown Minneapolis. The Weisman houses five galleries. Gehry has agreed to design an expansion, which is due to the art museum's success.

The Weisman has been home to the University of Minnesota's art collection since it opened in 1993. The museum emphasizes art of the recent vintage, just as the building is among the Twin Cities' most ambitious pieces of modern architecture. The Weisman is definitely worth a visit both for its fine galleries as well as its astounding architecture.

St. Paul's Architectural Treasures

Bandana Square
1021 East Bandana Boulevard, St. Paul
(651) 642-1509

During the past century the site of present-day Bandana Square has served several roles. The structure was constructed to serve as a train repair shop. As the railroad industry declined, the repair shop closed. After sitting vacant the huge building was renovated in the 1980s and reopened as a shopping mall. Unfortunately, the beautiful shopping center did not fare well. A few businesses have remained, but offices are the most common tenants at Bandana Square. Bandana Square hosts a link to its past—the Twin Cities Model Railroad Club—where fans of architecture can revisit the old train garage in miniature surrounded by facades of the historic Twin Cities.

Fort Snelling
Minnesota Highways 5 and 55, St. Paul
(651) 725-2413

Fort Snelling was the first permanent settlement in Minnesota and was once the most northwestern military post of the United States. The restored fort features examples of 19th-century architecture that emphasize practical, defense-oriented architecture over opulence. On the site are a hospital, forge, and a garrison for defending the confluence of the Mississippi and the Minnesota Rivers. Minnesota, like much of the Midwest, has a relatively brief history, and at Fort Snelling visitors can examine a restored version of the architecture of the first Minnesotans of European heritage.

Governor's Residence
1006 Summit Avenue, St. Paul
(651) 297-8177

The location of the governor's residence is ideal. Summit Avenue is the historical home of St. Paul's old wealth. The beautiful wide parkway is lined with trees and elegant Victorian homes and was the

St. Paul's tallest building, the Minnesota World Trade Center, towers over the Capital City.
TODD R. BERGER

childhood home of F. Scott Fitzgerald and railroad baron James J. Hill.

The governor's residence is a fairly recent tradition in Minnesota. Since the 1960s Minnesota's governor has called 240 Summit Avenue home. Before that date governors lived in their own homes and rented facilities for political events. William Channing Whitney, a prominent Twin Cities architect, designed the governor's residence in the English Tudor revival style. The interior has been renovated several times. Tours are available occasionally and by appointment.

James J. Hill House
240 Summit Avenue, St. Paul
(651) 296-6126

The James J. Hill House was once one of the largest mansions in the Midwest, appropriately built for one of St. Paul's wealthiest and most powerful men. In the

age of barons of industry, Hill was one of the area's most prominent citizens. Mansions like Hill's helped create the reputation Summit Avenue retains even today—as the street where St. Paul's old money resides.

James J. Hill ironically arrived via riverboat at age 17 from Ontario, Canada, in 1838. Hill was to play a central role in the development of another conveyance, the railroad, in the rapidly developing United States. Hill built a railroad empire, the Great Northern Railroad, from his adopted home of St. Paul.

Perhaps the most impressive aspect of the Hill House is its sheer size. The beautiful home was constructed with red sandstone and many examples of skilled craftsmanship. The carved woodwork and stained glass are of the finest quality. There are 32 rooms, 13 bathrooms, and 22 fireplaces, which were a necessity for

St. Paul's historic Landmark Center on Rice Park. SAINT PAUL RCVA

Minnesota's harsh winters when the house was constructed in 1891. Boasting 36,000 square feet of living space, it was a fitting residence for one of Minnesota's, and the nation's, greatest railroad tycoons.

Landmark Center
75 West Fifth Street, St. Paul
(651) 292-3228

Landmark Center is one of many architectural gems in downtown St. Paul's cultural quarter, which includes the Ordway Music Theatre, the Children's Museum, and the Science Museum. Landmark Center was erected in 1906 as the Federal Courthouse, where St. Paul's famous gangsters were once prosecuted. Today Landmark Center serves as the gallery for the Minnesota Museum of American Art, but the architecture continues to convey the structure's history. The building's tower overlooks Rice Park, which is surrounded by several of St. Paul's most attractive pieces of architecture.

Marjorie McNeely Conservatory at Como Park
Estabrook Drive and Aida Place, St. Paul
(651) 632-5111

The Marjorie McNeely Conservatory at Como Park is the architectural centerpiece of this lovely St. Paul public park. The park was designed by one of St. Paul's most important landscape architects, Horace W. S. Cleveland, and a German immigrant, Frederick Nussbaumer. Later Nussbaumer drew up the plans for the conservatory, which was inspired by London's Crystal Palace in Hyde Park.

The conservatory features a palm dome in the center of this glass structure, and the building is split into several wings displaying seasonally blooming flora. The conservatory is expertly integrated into the landscape of the rolling hills, ravine, and gardens that surround the structure. In 1993 a major face-lift restored the conservatory to a splendor far eclipsing its original beauty in 1915. The combination of architecture and flowers make the conservatory a treat for Twin Citians throughout the year.

Minnesota State Capitol
75 Constitution Avenue, St. Paul
(651) 297-3521

The Minnesota State Capitol is one of the area's architectural landmarks for several reasons. The 223-foot unsupported marble dome is the largest in the world. The architectural splendor also includes statues, columns, arches, and murals.

Cass Gilbert won a capitol design competition in 1898. Gilbert designed several Twin Cities buildings and the plan for the University of Minnesota's Northrop Mall (which was significantly modified) before moving on to national prominence with designs such as the Woolworth Building in New York City. The capitol was completed in 1904, and the cost of the new structure was the subject of great controversy. The third state capitol, most Minnesotans would agree today, was worth the hefty price tag.

St. Paul City Hall and Ramsey County Courthouse
15 West Kellogg Boulevard, St. Paul
(651) 266-8023

The St. Paul City Hall and Ramsey County Courthouse is an exemplary combination of neoclassical and art deco. The building's facade is an example of neoclassical style, while the art deco interior is where the building shines. It shares with New York's Rockefeller Center the then-modern art deco style that is paired with unmatched attention to materials and detail.

Constructed during the middle of the Great Depression, the St. Paul City Hall overflows with the finest craftsmanship. When the nation's economy hit rock bottom, many of the nation's most talented artists and artisans were unemployed. Not only did the cost of labor plummet but so did the price paid for materials. The results are breathtaking, particularly in the lobby, which glitters with black marble walls and features a 36-foot-high rotating statue named *Visions of Peace*. The original 1931 structure was renovated in 1993, restoring its luster.

Minnesota State Capitol. SAINT PAUL RCVA

St. Paul Public Library
80 West Fourth Street, St. Paul
(651) 227-9531

Twin Cities libraries are often distinguished by fine architecture. The St. Paul Public Library is an exceptional example, especially the James J. Hill Reference Library Reading Room. The reading room is an exemplar of Beaux-Arts classicism, and the two-story reading room is surrounded by the book stacks and Ionic columns, with abundant fine crafted woodwork and granite floors. Large comfy tables and chairs entice visitors to enjoy the resources available or quietly absorb the architecture. Recently renovated, the library is one of downtown St. Paul's many beautiful public buildings.

Union Depot
214 East Fourth Street, St. Paul

The Union Depot was constructed between 1917 and 1923. At the time the railroad was a prominent means of transportation, and a serpentine labyrinth of tracks circled the depot. Since then the importance of the railroad has dwindled, but the depot remains—although it serves a different purpose. Today the Union Depot is an awe-inspiring architectural work that takes advantage of a high ceiling, balconies, and plenty of stone. Restaurants occupy the immense lobby where passengers once arrived and departed, and visitors may dine in one of St. Paul's most historic and architecturally attractive settings.

Minnesota World Trade Center
30 East Seventh Street, St. Paul
(651) 297-1580

The Minnesota World Trade Center, completed in 1987, sits high atop the St. Paul skyline. It is the tallest building in St. Paul, and at 40 stories high, the building would

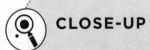

Mill City Museum

Minneapolis is most commonly known to visitors as the City of Lakes. The city's first nickname, and the name that elevated the city to national prominence, the Mill City, is rarely used today. Instead the city has focused on its chain of lakes, most notably Lake Calhoun, Lake Harriet, Lake Nokomis, and Lake of the Isles. Annually the city commemorates the lakes' importance during the Aquatennial, the only citywide annual event. The riverfront has undergone a renaissance in recent years as, piece by piece, elements of Minneapolis's past have been revived. The Mill City Museum, which opened in 2003, reclaimed the once-buried and nearly forgotten history of the city and restored it to the prominent position it deserves as the birthplace of a world-class city.

The Mill City Museum is located in the heart of Minneapolis's historic milling district. Shortly after the city was founded in 1852, small mills congregated on both the east bank (until 1872, St. Anthony) and the west bank of the Mississippi near St. Anthony Falls. At this only waterfall on the Mississippi, the river provided an exceptional source of power for milling the increasingly limitless wheat of the upper Midwest, and the number and size of the mills swelled. By 1890 Minneapolis had established itself as the nation's largest wheat market, and Washburn-Crosby and Company (the antecedent of General Mills) was among the Cities' leaders in the industry with its nationally recognized trademark, Gold Medal Flour.

To serve these needs, the company constructed the Washburn A Mill. Like its predecessor, the A Mill was plagued by fire, but none as deadly as the May 2, 1878, explosion, which killed 18. For many years the A Mill was left dormant, during which time the structure was seriously damaged. Parts of the old mill were destroyed and enormous gaping holes were left, exposing the structure to Minneapolis's harsh weather. This was the challenge for the Minneapolis architectural firm of Meyer, Scherer & Rockcastle Ltd., which designed the Mill City Museum. Surprisingly, the design uses the former dilapidation of the A Mill to the museum's advantage.

The Mill City Museum design retained many elements of the old mill: milling machinery, flour bins, rail corridor, engine house, and wheat house. While much of the mill has been restored, in some cases the architect has exploited scenic views created by fire damage, including a breathtaking view of St. Anthony Falls.

Architect Tom Meyer adapted this unique structure for the numerous attractions at the Mill City Museum. The museum emphasizes hands-on experiences, like those offered by the Minnesota Historical Society, and includes a water-power laboratory and a test kitchen. The eight-story "Flour Tower" ride features regional history. Another attraction is the open-air courtyard within the walls of the mill ruins.

The burned-out shell of Mill City gives way to a Mississippi River view. GREATER MINNEAPOLIS CONVENTION & VISITORS ASSOCIATION

The museum features several historical exhibits beyond milling, examining the influence of waterpower both in milling and in allied industries on the Mississippi River. The museum demonstrates the role of milling in the development of Minneapolis's dynamic economy and its impact on immigration patterns, railroad development, and agriculture.

The structure includes a bookstore, classrooms, and a restaurant. The mill also provides one of the most innovative and scenic living opportunities in the Twin Cities. The Brighton Development is located in the top five floors, with lofts available. The Brighton Development promises to become a part of an emerging neighborhood in downtown.

The Mill City Museum has a $24 million budget. Of these funds $20 million are from the state and federal government. The project has been the recipient of many endowments and private sector donations. The largest donations were received from the McKnight Foundation (3M) and Cargill Incorporated. Cargill, like General Mills, got its start in milling in Minneapolis.

fit in the much loftier Minneapolis skyline. The building is leased by different firms. The architectural design of the trade center is similar to many of the colossal Minneapolis structures. The exterior has plenty of dark glass, which reflects light on sunny summer days. Even in St. Paul, a city where tradition has always been emphasized, the Minnesota World Trade Center (a modern skyscraper) dominates the skyline.

HOUSES OF WORSHIP
St. Paul

Assumption Church
51 West Seventh Street, St. Paul
(651) 224-7536
The Assumption Church was constructed between 1869 and 1874. Located in an area of downtown St. Paul where architectural change has occurred at a rapid pace, the church remains a distinct and important piece of architecture.

As St. Paul developed, religious communities constructed churches to fulfill their spiritual needs. The ethnic heritage and denomination of the church often profoundly influenced the architecture of individual structures. This was certainly the case with the Assumption Church, which was formed to meet the needs of German Catholics. The Ludwigskirche in Munich heavily influenced the German Romanesque revival design of the church. For materials, the church makes use of Minnesota limestone. The twin towers are the most distinguishable features of the church. They rise 210 feet and are a perennial landmark in the ephemeral architecture of downtown St. Paul.

Cathedral of Saint Paul
239 Selby Avenue, St. Paul
(651) 228-1766
The Cathedral of Saint Paul is one of the Twin Cities' most recognizable landmarks. The sheer size of the structure is daunting, and it stands like a sentinel atop Cathedral Hill, where it overlooks downtown St. Paul, directly across the interstate from the massive Minnesota State Capitol.

The grand scale of the Cathedral of Saint Paul reflects its source of inspiration. The cathedral was modeled after Saint Peter's Cathedral in Rome, and designed by Emmanuel L. Masqueray. Also instrumental in the erection of the cathedral was Archbishop John Ireland, who envisioned and raised the money for the cathedral as a tribute to the faith of the archdiocese.

The features of the cathedral, completed in 1915, are breathtaking. The interior is baroque in design, makes use of Minnesota granite and travertine, and is decorated with stained glass and religion-inspired paintings, which include several beautiful frescoes. The dome extends 175 feet above the cathedral and can be seen from great distances. Guided tours are held Monday, Wednesday, and Friday at 1:00 P.M., where visitors may enjoy the Cathedral of Saint Paul's astounding beauty.

St. Clement's Episcopal Church
901 Portland Avenue, St. Paul
(651) 228-1164
Many are surprised to hear that this attractive and quaint church was designed by Cass Gilbert, who later served as architect for the colossal Minnesota State Capitol. The structure makes fine use of material but on a much smaller scale. Intimacy is stressed. The church is constructed of slate, stone, and wood; conveys a sense of solace; and is scaled to parishioner's size. St. Clement's Episcopal Church was completed in 1894, after which Gilbert went on to bigger, but not necessarily better, architectural projects.

Mount Zion Temple
1300 Summit Avenue, St. Paul
(651) 698-3881
www.mzion.org
The first Jewish house of worship in the Twin Cities was located at the first Mount Zion Temple. The present building is

Cathedral of Saint Paul. CATHEDRAL OF SAINT PAUL

located on Summit Avenue, where the old money in St. Paul resides. Eric Mendelsohn, an internationally renowned architect, designed the stylish, modern building.

Minneapolis

The Basilica of Saint Mary
88 North 17th Street, Minneapolis
(612) 333-1381

The Basilica of Saint Mary celebrated its first Mass on May 31, 1914, as a then-unique Catholic place for worship. It was the first basilica in America, an institution created to serve the needs of Minneapolis. While St. Paul completed its own breath-takingly beautiful cathedral in 1915 to serve its parishioners, the other Twin City was allowed by the Vatican to construct the basilica. As with the Cathedral of Saint

Paul, Emmanuel L. Masqueray (1861–1917) was the architect for the Basilica of Saint Mary.

Masqueray unveiled his design in 1906. The colossal basilica features a 200-foot dome and an impressive nave. At the time of its construction, the 140-foot by 82-foot nave was considered the widest in the world. The stained-glass windows, designed by Thomas Gaytee, are another extraordinary feature of the basilica.

The life of the namesake of the basilica, Mary, mother of Jesus, is artfully displayed on the stained-glass windows. The rose windows on both sides of the sanctuary portray the Immaculate Conception and the Crowning of Mary Queen of Heaven. Archangels in the windows of the entrance guard everyone who enters the basilica. Sculptures play a significant role in the architecture of the basilica and its grounds. The 12 apostles are depicted in the sanctuary, and there are half-scale replicas of the sculptures at Saint John Lateran in Rome. These are just a few of the sculptures, which include one of Father Louis Hennepin, who brought Catholicism to the area and looks out on the street that today bears his name (Hennepin Avenue).

Location is another superlative feature. Located on the edge of downtown Minneapolis, the building sits across the street from Loring Park and is within walking distance of the internationally acclaimed Walker Art Center and the numerous beautiful churches lining Hennepin Avenue (Hennepin Avenue United Methodist and Cathedral Church of St. Mark). All of these churches are examples of excellent Beaux-Arts architecture, but the Basilica of Saint Mary is certainly the largest in scale.

Cathedral Church of St. Mark
519 Oak Grove Street, Minneapolis
(612) 870-7800
The Cathedral Church of St. Mark was designed by one of the Twin Cities' most renowned architectural firms in the early 20th century, Brown and Hewitt. Between 1904 and 1930 the firm created several outstanding pieces of architecture, including this church, created in 1911. Edwin H. Hewitt was the primary designer of most of the firm's work, which was heavily influenced by the eclectic Beaux-Arts style. Emphasizing revivalism in architectural designs, Beaux-Arts works are symmetrical and balanced. The style was a popular foil for modernism.

As a member of the church, Hewitt set out to create a design appropriate to his faith. Denominationally, the church is Episcopalian; the design reflects this heritage. English Gothic revival dominates the church's architectural style. The tower is inspired by the example found at Magdalen College at Oxford, albeit significantly scaled down. Adding to the church's splendor is its location on the edge of Loring Park, which is one of Minneapolis's most beautiful parks.

Christ Church Lutheran
3244 34th Avenue South, Minneapolis
(612) 721-6611
Built in a humble working-class neighborhood in south Minneapolis, the Christ Lutheran Church is the last design of Eliel Saarinen. The world-famous Finnish architect created a design for the state of Minnesota, where Scandinavian Lutherans abound.

Saarinen constructed the church from 1949 to 1950 with the assistance of his architect son, Eero. Saarinen's great architectural pieces began with the railway station in Helsinki (1905-14). He went on to design a series of central European railway stations. Later, Saarinen immigrated to the United States, where his work culminated with the Cranbrook School (circa 1925). He was selected for the Christ Church Lutheran's design, which became his last architectural triumph.

Saarinen's forte was creating excellent institutional architecture, but the church's coffers did not overflow with money for a distinctive design. Hence, Saarinen created a work of great beauty out of a relatively limited budget. The church is small and intimate, and the exterior design is composed of minimalistic blocks. As parishioners or visitors approach the church, they walk under a large stone canopy. Inside the building are two wings, with a sanctuary on one end, and a fellowship hall, offices, and classrooms on the other. The interior is finely detailed and makes abundant use of yellow brick and complementary shaded wood. The exterior of the sanctuary has four sculptures representing faith, love, church, and hope. Saarinen died in 1950, the year Christ Church Lutheran was completed. The architect's legacy continues with one of the Twin Cities' most attractive small churches.

Hennepin Avenue
United Methodist Church
511 Groveland Avenue, Minneapolis
(612) 871-5303
www.themethodistchurch.org
The Hennepin Avenue United Methodist

Church is yet another impressive piece of architecture on Hennepin Avenue. Like the Cathedral Church of St. Mark, it was designed by Hewitt and Brown and is again an example of English Gothic Revival work. The octagonal base of the steeple and tall, slender spire set the church apart and position it among the Twin Cities' most spectacular architectural churches.

Our Lady of Lourdes Church
One Lourdes Place, Minneapolis
(612) 379-2259
www.ourladyoflourdes.com
Not only is Our Lady of Lourdes the oldest standing church in Minneapolis, but it also has a simultaneously tumultuous and intriguing history. During each successive turn in the history of the church, at least minimal architectural alterations were made. Surprisingly, despite the cobbled nature of the church's construction, it is an awe-inspiring work and a landmark in historic St. Anthony.

The church dates from 1854, when the First Universalist Church constructed the original structure. The front nave was built from native limestone. The original Greek temple–style church was significantly smaller than it is today. In 1877 the church was purchased by a group of Catholic French Canadian settlers in the area and rechristened Our Lady of Lourdes. The Canadians added the mansard roof, which remains on the eastern side of the church. In toto the structure was transformed into the French provincial style, which was one of the seven styles of church architecture then constructed in Quebec. Shortly thereafter, the church added a bell tower, sacristy, and a vestibule. Stained-glass windows were installed from the 1890s through the 1910s. However, the church was increasingly neglected over time.

In 1968 church leaders decided to demolish the church, but the Minneapolis city council intervened and the church was spared. Since then the church has undergone several renovations to restore it to its previous glory. In 1991 carillon bells

were mounted in the church tower. Today their sonorous chiming can be heard throughout historic St. Anthony.

West

Colonial Church of Edina
6200 Colonial Way, Edina
(952) 925-2711
The Colonial Church of Edina is a curiosity that stands in stark contrast to the architecture on Minnesota Highway 62. The church was modeled on a New England colonial village.

Architect Richard Hammel visited a church in Barnstable, Massachusetts, that was built by the Pilgrims in the 17th century. The Edina design, in keeping with the source architecture, is simple and subdued. The church makes use of gray with white trim and features a bell tower at the center. The colonial village design includes space for a sanctuary, lounges, and additional rooms for church activities.

East

St. Michael's Catholic Church
611 South Third Street, Stillwater
(651) 439-4400
www.stmichael.stillwater.mn.us
The Catholic missionaries arrived in Stillwater in 1849. The city, founded in 1843, rapidly developed as one of Minnesota's most important cities, which was due largely to the lumbering industry.

In 1873 the construction of St. Michael's Catholic Church began. The church sits atop a bluff overlooking the city of Stillwater and the St. Croix River Valley. The structure was built of native, blond Kasota stone. The church has impressive dimensions of 140 by 180 feet, with the gorgeous spire extending 190 feet above. In 1883 the church added the first chimes in the area, which to this day ring mellifluously above the valley, although today they chime via automa-

The Hennepin Avenue Suspension Bridge stands on the spot of the first bridge across the Mississippi River. GREATER MINNEAPOLIS CONVENTION & VISITORS ASSOCIATION

tion. Over the years St. Michael's has been renovated several times to maintain its striking beauty. In a city filled with architectural treasures, St. Michael's Church stands out as one of the city's most stunning pieces of architecture.

TWIN CITIES BRIDGES

Hennepin Avenue Suspension Bridge
Main Street SE and Hennepin Avenue, Minneapolis

The first Hennepin Avenue Bridge was completed in 1855; it was the first permanent span across the Mississippi and was necessary for the creation of Minneapolis in 1872. The cities of St. Anthony (east bank) and Minneapolis (west bank) could not have merged without the bridge.

The current bridge is the fourth struc-

ture on the site. It is a larger, architecturally scaled-down version of the bridge that stood here in the late 19th century. Three minimal, relatively short towers sit on both sides of the Mississippi. Despite its subdued architecture for a grand suspension bridge, it serves an important function and provides a panoramic view of the city's architecture.

High Bridge
Smith Avenue, St. Paul

The High Bridge is a landmark that provides one of the best scenic views of St. Paul. The original High Bridge was constructed in the late 19th century to link St. Paul's West Seventh Street and the upper West Side. The span of the bridge was an astounding 2,770 feet in length and constructed of over one million pieces of iron. It was no small accomplishment for its epoch; however, the bridge deteriorated over the course of almost a century. The bridge was razed in 1985.

St. Paul began the construction of a replica High Bridge. Once again, the bridge had a steep 4 percent grade. In addition, the bridge consisted of 11 spans. The largest span is an astounding 520 feet. Just as it did in the past, the bridge provides one of the best views of St. Paul and its numerous fine pieces of architecture.

Stillwater Lift Bridge
Wisconsin/Minnesota Highway 64 and Water Street, Stillwater
The Stillwater Bridge is one of the many pieces of architecture in the historic city, but its future is uncertain. The span linking Stillwater, Minnesota, to Wisconsin was constructed in 1931. It is a vertical-lift bridge, which must be raised for large vessels on the St. Croix River. Today there are only three extant vertical-lift bridges in Minnesota and Wisconsin. Despite the bridge's architectural significance, it has a questionable future because of the population growth in the St. Croix River Valley.

The Stone Arch Bridge is the best place in Minneapolis to view both Minneapolis's historic milling district architecture and the city's skyline.

Stone Arch Bridge
Main Street SE and Fifth Avenue, Minneapolis
The Stone Arch Bridge was constructed in 1883 for James J. Hill's Great Northern Railway. The bridge spanning the Mississippi took two years to complete. In 1982 the bridge was closed because of decreased train traffic. The bridge remained dormant until the state of Minnesota purchased it in 1992, and it was renovated to serve as a pedestrian walkway linking the old milling district and historic St. Anthony. Besides serving as an important piece of Minneapolis's architectural history, it provides one of the best panoramic views of downtown.

ACCOMMODATIONS

There are a few good rules to remember when trying to find hotel accommodations in the Twin Cities. First of all, winter rates for rooms are almost half that of spring and summer rates. Second, staying in St. Paul is cheaper than staying in Minneapolis, although this may change due to the new Xcel Energy Center in downtown St. Paul. Room rates can change drastically from month to month depending on what conventions are in town, sports events, high-profile local festivals, and rumors of a final break in winter or the first sign of fall. Most hotels in the Cities, however, have package plans that can knock up to a couple hundred dollars off the price of a room if you reserve the room a few months in advance and you plan to stay for two or more days. All major credit cards are accepted at the following establishments except where noted. Also, all the following hotels have both smoking and nonsmoking rooms unless otherwise noted; however, none of the bed-and-breakfasts listed here allow smoking inside the rooms. All hotels in the metro area are required to have wheelchair-accessible ramps outside and inside the hotels, although winter conditions may make some of these ramps hard to navigate if they're not properly maintained.

If you visit the Twin Cities during the chilly winter months, try to find a hotel connected to either the Minneapolis or the St. Paul skyway system. These wonderful second-floor walkways are climate controlled and link most of the downtown businesses, so you don't actually have to step outside unless you want to. You can enter the skyway system through the parking garages in both cities, and posted maps let you know where you are in the city at every junction.

Note: Accommodations are listed alphabetically under the headings Minneapolis, St. Paul, Neighboring Communities, and Bed-and-Breakfasts.

PRICE CODE

The following rate information is based on the cost of a standard, double-occupancy room in springtime (May–June), which is generally considered to be the peak tourist season in the Twin Cities.

$	Less than $100
$$	$101–$150
$$$	$151–$200
$$$$	$201–$250
$$$$$	$251 and higher

MINNEAPOLIS

Best Western Normandy Inn $
405 South Eighth Street, Minneapolis
(612) 370-1400
www.bestwesternnormandy.com
Conveniently located in the heart of downtown Minneapolis, this hotel is near the downtown skyway system and all the shopping, businesses, and entertainment of the area. The hotel offers guests a complimentary continental breakfast; indoor pool, Jacuzzi, and fitness room; and serves milk and chocolate chip cookies every night.

Crowne Plaza Northstar Hotel $$$
618 Second Avenue South, Minneapolis
(612) 338-2288
www.msp-northstar.crowneplaza.com
This hotel offers a comfortable stay for tourists and business travelers alike, with an eighth-floor Skygarden patio for relaxing outdoor seating May through October and a fitness center for the rest of the year. Each room includes an oversize desk with an ergonomic chair, individually controlled heating and air-conditioning, and high-speed Internet access. The hotel is in

Radisson Riverfront Hotel St. Paul $$
11 East Kellogg Boulevard, St. Paul
(651) 292-1900 or (800) 333-3333
www.radisson.com/stpaulmn
Right across the boulevard from the Mississippi River and in the heart of downtown St. Paul, this hotel sports the Twin Cities' only revolving restaurant, Carousel, located on the 22nd floor and offering a panoramic view of the Mississippi River. Hotel amenities include a heated indoor pool, a fitness center, high-speed Internet connections, and sleep-number beds.

Saint Paul Hotel $$$
350 Market Street, St. Paul
(651) 292-9292 or (800) 292-9292
www.stpaulhotel.com
Built in 1910 and located in the center of St. Paul on beautiful Rice Park, this premier luxury hotel is a member of the Historic Hotels of America. Fully restored to its original splendor (the most recent update was in 2005), the hotel offers guests a unique combination of turn-of-the-century charm and modern convenience. The hotel is within walking distance of St. Paul's RiverCentre, the Ordway Center for the Performing Arts, the Science Museum of Minnesota, and Xcel Energy Center, as well as the Mississippi River walk, plus more business and shops via the climate-controlled skyway. Amenities include a complimentary newspaper, 24-hour security, full-time concierge services, indoor parking and valet service, a rooftop fitness center, and turndown service at your request. The hotel has two restaurants, the elegant St. Paul Grill and the M Street Cafe. (For more information on eating at the St. Paul Grill, see the Restaurants chapter.) The Lobby Bar opened in 2005, and it's a cozy little place to stop for a nightcap. Shuttle service to and from destinations such as the Mall of America and Minneapolis is available at your request.

When you get into the Twin Cities, pick up a copy of the free weekly paper, City Pages, *for information on what's happening in the Twin Cities as well as for restaurant and event coupons.*

NEIGHBORING COMMUNITIES

Afton House Inn $$
3291 St. Croix Trail South, Afton
(651) 436-8883 or (877) 436-8883
www.aftonhouseinn.com
The Afton House Inn is located about 20 miles east of downtown St. Paul in the quaint town of Afton on the St. Croix River. Built in 1867, the 25-room hotel is on the National Register of Historic Places. The nicely furnished rooms include such amenities as gas fireplaces and Jacuzzis. The hotel also operates Afton Hudson Cruise Lines, with several boats that cruise the St. Croix. There are three on-site restaurants—two fine-dining rooms plus the casual Catfish Saloon and Café, which has outdoor seating.

Amerisuites $$
7800 International Drive, Bloomington
(952) 854-0700
This all-suite hotel is within a mile of the Mall of America and near Minneapolis–St. Paul (MSP) International Airport. The 128 rooms all have either king or queen beds, coffeemakers, minifridges, and other amenities. The hotel has an exercise room for its guests' use and operates a shuttle service to the airport. This is a good choice for business travelers wishing to be near the airport and to the mall.

Comfort Inn $
2715 Long Lake Road, Roseville
(651) 636-5800 or (800) 451-7258
www.choicehotels.com
Just outside of the metro area, the Comfort Inn provides easy access to the free-

The Afton House Inn is a short drive from the Twin Cities in the little town of Afton on the St. Croix. SAINT PAUL RCVA

ways leading to the Twin Cities, though Roseville is a pleasant, quiet suburb with several shopping centers. Rooms come with kitchenettes and wireless high-speed Internet as well as an upgraded continental breakfast.

Hampton Inn Airport/
Mall of America $$
7745 Lyndale Avenue South, Richfield
(612) 861-1000 or (800) 551-ROOM
www.hamptoninnrichfield.com

This comfortable hotel with few frills is set up especially with the business traveler in mind, with desks and modem hookups in many rooms. The hotel provides free shuttle transportation to the Mall of America and MSP airport, and there is an indoor swimming pool and whirlpool on the premises. There is no additional charge for making local phone calls.

The Lowell Inn $$$
102 North Second Street, Stillwater
(651) 439-1100
www.lowellinn.com

The elegant Lowell Inn in Stillwater (20 miles east of downtown St. Paul) harbors 21 individually decorated rooms featuring period antiques. Elmore Lowell established the Sawyer House on the land where the Lowell Inn now stands in 1848, the year Stillwater was incorporated as the Minnesota Territory's first city. The colonial inn standing today dates from 1930, and the interior brings to mind the regal atmosphere of southern plantation homes. The Lowell has three distinct dining rooms (see the Restaurants chapter for more information); guests can also relax during a Minnesota winter in front of the colonial fireplace in the Front Parlor. Room rates range widely depending on the room and its amenities, the day of the week (prices are higher on weekends), and whether guests prefer a package price including room, dinner for two, and breakfast.

Mystic Lake Casino Hotel $$
2400 Mystic Lake Boulevard, Prior Lake
(952) 445-9000 or (800) 262-7799
www.mysticlake.com
About 25 miles southwest of downtown Minneapolis, the 600-room Mystic Lake Casino Hotel rises next to the alcohol-free casino of the same name. The hotel features such amenities as an Olympic-sized pool with waterslide, 18-hole golf course, fitness center, and the largest casino in the Upper Midwest, with some 4,000 slot machines and 96 blackjack tables. Major celebrities regularly headline at the Celebrity Palace, and guests can partake in the massive buffet, routinely honored as the best buffet in the Twin Cities. The hotel is near Canterbury Park, which features betting on live horse racing during summer months and a card room year-round.

Radisson Hotel & Conference Center $$
3131 Campus Drive, Plymouth
(763) 559-6600 or (800) 333-3333
www.radisson.com/minneapolismn
_plymouth
The Radisson Plymouth is located near Interstate 494 and Minnesota Highway 55 in a parklike setting overlooking a 25-acre marshland preserve. All guest rooms include a minibar, two telephones, high-speed Internet, and a lighted work desk. Hotel facilities include a full-service fitness center and an indoor pool.

Sofitel Minneapolis $$$
5601 West 78th Street, Bloomington
(952) 835-1900
The French-style Sofitel is located at the intersection of I-494 and Minnesota Highway 100 on the Bloomington Strip. The hotel is about 10 minutes from the Mall of America and 15 minutes from MSP airport.

The 282-room hotel also hosts two French restaurants—La Fougasse, in particular, is worthy of destination dining.

BED-AND-BREAKFASTS

Covington Inn Bed and Breakfast $$$
100 Yacht Club, Pier One, Harriet Island, St. Paul
(651) 292-1411
www.covingtoninn.com
The only floating bed-and-breakfast in the Twin Cities, the Covington Inn is a renovated tugboat first launched in 1946 and now moored in the Mississippi River across from downtown St. Paul. Open year-round, the B&B has four comfortable rooms, all with fireplaces and private baths. The inn's common areas are trimmed in bronze, brass, and mahogany, and many salvaged fixtures suggest what it must have been like when the tug *Covington* pushed barges up and down the river. You can sit out on the deck and watch the mighty river flow by gleaming downtown St. Paul. The Covington's Harriet Island dock is a short walk from the Wabasha Street Bridge, which spans the Mississippi and leads to the museums, theaters, restaurants, and shops downtown.

Wales House $
1115 Southeast Fifth Street, Minneapolis
(612) 331-3931
www.waleshouse.com
Since opening to the public in 1994, this 10-bedroom bed-and-breakfast has been providing the charm of an old-world inn for faculty, staff, and other visitors to the University of Minnesota for extremely reasonable rates. Hundreds of visitors from more than 68 countries have stayed in this antiques-furnished turn-of-the-20th-century home, with stays ranging from one night to one year (room rates decrease significantly according to length of stay). The living rooms, which are open to guests, include a four-season

ACCOMMODATIONS

porch, large front parlor, fireplace room, lounge, dining room, and kitchen. Outside, guests can use the front patio. Amenities include free continental breakfast, private telephones in each room with free local calls, a furnished guest kitchen, on-site laundry, and a cleaning service.

William Sauntry Mansion   **$$$**
626 North Fourth Street, Stillwater
(651) 430-2653 or (800) 828-2653
www.sauntrymansion.com
Lumber baron William Sauntry had his 25-room Victorian mansion built in the booming sawmill town of Stillwater on the St. Croix River in 1881. Today this B&B, listed on the National Register of Historic Places, has six guest rooms, all with fireplaces, private baths, and double whirlpool tubs. The ornate house features wood floors, original chandeliers, stained-glass windows, and Victorian furnishings. The William Sauntry Mansion is close to downtown Stillwater, with its quaint antiques stores, lovely cafes, and antiquarian bookshops.

RESTAURANTS

With approximately 3,500 restaurants in the metropolitan area, the Twin Cities boast one of the best dining scenes in the country. Once considered the land of the smorgasbord or simple meat-and-potato fare, the Twin Cities today offer a vast array of culinary choices.

Traditional American and European fine-dining options are plentiful in the Twin Cities. Nicollet Mall, located in the heart of downtown Minneapolis, offers the highest concentration of fine-dining opportunities in the Twin Cities. St. Paul boasts fine restaurants in downtown and the thriving Cathedral Hill neighborhood.

The Twin Cities restaurant scene is diverse. Besides the more standard ethnic fare such as Chinese, Mexican, Thai, Middle Eastern, and Indian foods, the area boasts Kurdish, Cambodian, Afghani, Eastern European, and Ethiopian cuisine. Ethnic dining in the area starts on Nicollet Avenue, or Eat Street, which begins on the Nicollet Mall in downtown Minneapolis and leads into south Minneapolis. St. Paul offers ethnic food throughout town.

Dining options continue to expand in the suburban Twin Cities, especially the St. Croix River Valley east of Minneapolis and St. Paul. You'll find avant-garde cuisine, tropical flavors, and ethnic restaurants. In fact, there are many more Indian restaurants in the suburbs than in the Cities.

The chapter has been organized alphabetically by cuisine, followed by listings for sweets and treats and coffeehouses and teashops. In general each cuisine section is divided into regions: Minneapolis, St. Paul, and the suburbs north, south, east, and west. Also listed for most restaurants are business hours, reservation policies, and credit card policies. If the listing does not say otherwise, you can assume that the restaurant accepts all major credit cards. These policies frequently change, so call the restaurant if you have any questions. Both St. Paul and Minneapolis ban smoking in all restaurants and bars.

PRICE CODE

The following price code is based on one adult dinner entrée, without beverage, gratuity, and tax.

$	under $10
$$	$11–$20
$$$	$21–$30
$$$$	$31–$40

AFGHANI
St. Paul

Khyber Pass Café $$
1571 Grand Avenue, St. Paul
(651) 690-0505
Khyber Pass Café has served delicious Afghani cuisine since 1985. When entering the restaurant, the diner is immediately struck by its personality, charm, and aesthetic sense. The restaurant has a comfortable, clean, and cobbled-together feel, which integrates potted plants and Afghani crafts with numerous tasteful paintings.

The menu is composed of well-executed entrees. The possibilities include chicken, lamb, beef, and vegetarian dishes. The *korma-e-murgh,* boneless chicken in curry sauce with potatoes and peas, is one savory option. Another interesting choice is *kofta chalau,* which is made of meatballs, onions, and spices. The restaurant is open for lunch Monday through Friday and for dinner Monday through Saturday.

South

Da Afghan Restaurant $$
929 West 80th Street, Bloomington
(952) 888-5824
www.daafghan.com

Da Afghan serves Southwest Asian and Middle Eastern specialties, including spring lamb chops, *kabeli palow* with chicken or lamb, *mantou,* and many kinds of kabob. The beautiful restaurant is decorated with Afghani artifacts and Afghani rugs on the tabletops. Beer and wine are served. Da Afghan is open for dinner Tuesday through Sunday and for lunch on Thursday and Friday.

AMERICAN

Minneapolis

Al's Breakfast $
413 14th Avenue SE, Minneapolis
(612) 331-9991

This tiny hole-in-the wall near the University of Minnesota has been serving customers since the 1940s. College students and folks from the neighborhood have been known to line up around the block waiting for the place to open or to get a seat. Eggs, hash browns, and pancakes are served, as well as exotic omelets, many of which are named after Al's patrons or employees. Al's is open for breakfast and lunch (serving dishes off the breakfast menu) daily. Al's is a Twin Cities institution, and if you don't mind the wait or the grease, get your day started the wrong way at Al's. Al's accepts no credit cards.

The Uptown Bar and Café (3018 Hennepin Avenue South; 612-823-4719) is a rock club, but it serves food too. The breakfasts are especially good and large, and if you're a Bloody Mary fan, this is your place.

Annie's Parlour $
313 14th Avenue SE, Minneapolis
(612) 379-0744

Located just a couple of blocks from the U of M and the Bell Museum, Annie's Parlour is a great place to stop and get a bite to eat. This Dinkytown malt shop is as much a part of the university as Goldy Gopher himself, serving juicy burgers, chicken sandwiches, french fries, creamy malts, hot fudge sundaes, and banana splits. Since the restaurant is so appealing to college kids, this is the spot where many Twin Cities young ones are introduced to the U—they come to campus for a play or concert and Mom and Dad feed them here.

Aster Café $
125 Southeast Main Street, Minneapolis
(612) 379-3138

Located across the Mississippi River from downtown Minneapolis, this little cafe is the perfect place to stop by for lunch or grab a cup of coffee or a beer in the evening. The menu includes premade sandwiches and homemade soups, cookies, focaccia bread pizzas, and dessert bars. The dining area inside is large and opens up into the art gallery next door, and there's also a beautiful fenced-in outside patio that's nice for summer lounging. The cafe often books acoustic music but entertainment is also provided by people wandering in to play the piano set up in the corner of the shop. The cafe keeps about a dozen board and card games on hand for patrons who want to hang out past lunch—and there's a bowl full of dog biscuits under the counter for hounds accompanying patrons.

Birchwood Café $
3311 East 25th Street, Minneapolis
(612) 722-4474
www.birchwoodcafe.com

Birchwood, formerly a dairy and grocery store, has an old-fashioned stay-a-spell sense of welcome that makes it Seward's informal community center. The 1950s-era dining room has both indoor seating and an outdoor patio in summer and serves sandwiches on fresh country bread, rustic pizzas, daily changing entrees such as enchiladas and curries, soups, and half a dozen salads. Known for its fresh organic ingredients and extensive vegetarian and vegan dishes, the Birchwood menu also includes nonvegetarian items. Service is semicafeteria style; you get your salads, desserts, and beverages (no alcohol) at the counter, and hot or custom-made items are brought to your birchwood-topped table.

The Brothers Deli $
50 South Sixth Street, Minneapolis
(612) 341-8007
www.thebrothersdeli.com

The Brothers Deli offers authentic New York–style deli fare in downtown Minneapolis. This small deli, located on a busy second-floor skyway route in downtown, serves mouthwatering delicacies composed of only the best breads, meats, toppings, and condiments. The Broadway Danny Rose is a combination of corned beef and pastrami on fresh rye bread. Another top-notch sandwich is the Brother Sam, which melds the tastes of beef brisket and cheddar cheese on rye. The menu also features grilled sandwiches such as the tuna melt and Reuben, as well as matzo ball, chicken noodle, and tomato basil soups. Meals include potato salad, fresh pickles, and the best condiments available at a local deli.

Bryant-Lake Bowl $–$$
810 West Lake Street, Minneapolis
(612) 825-3737
www.bryantlakebowl.com

A bowling alley? Well, yes, but the Bryant-Lake Bowl in Uptown belies every stereotype of bowling alley eats, atmosphere, and culture. The atmosphere inside the restaurant is vintage 1940s, with beautiful woodwork and closely placed tables for intimate eating (with patrons at your neighboring table as well as your tablemates). Famous for its cheap-but-delicious breakfasts, including bison hash, several BLB Scrambles (eggs scrambled with a

choice of ingredients), and the ridiculously yummy Amy's Breakfast Burrito, the BLB serves lunch and dinner as well. Diners favor such specialties as the turkey, avocado, and bacon sandwich; grilled ahi tuna; and basmati rice and vegetables (with tofu or chicken optional). The BLB has a full bar, with many microbrews on tap. In addition to the 1950s-era bowling lanes, where you get to relearn the lost art of scoring your game by hand, the BLB is attached to a cabaret theater, where you can also order from the full menu. (See the Arts chapter for more information on the Bryant-Lake Bowl Theater.)

Café Brenda $$
300 First Avenue North, Minneapolis
(612) 342-9230
www.cafebrenda.com

Café Brenda is a chic little bistro where the emphasis is on ingredients obtained, as often as possible, from local farmers and prepared in ways that emphasize the current season. This is not a vegetarian restaurant, just a place where vegetarians and vegans feel totally at home; a place that knows being vegetarian doesn't mean you'd like a salad with fat-free ranch. Chef-owner Brenda Langton has been credited as one of the health-food movement's early pioneers, and this restaurant has been running in one form or another since 1978. While Langton makes magic with veggies, brown rice, and mock duck, she has her own flair—the diehard meat eaters in your group can get a sampling of what this means with an appetizer such as the sweet red pepper pomegranate dip or the wild mushroom and pistachio pâté. But there is plenty of healthy omnivorous fare, including free-range chicken and fresh fish (think sautéed fresh walleye with a blackberry teriyaki glaze). Café Brenda is open for lunch and dinner Monday through Friday and dinner only on Saturday. Reservations are accepted. In the evening, park in the pay lot at First Avenue North and Fourth Street, but get your ticket stamped at Brenda's for a full refund when you leave.

Chino Latino $$-$$$
2916 Hennepin Avenue South,
Minneapolis
(612) 824-7878
www.chinolatino.com

A popular spot for the hip dinner crowd, the foods of Thailand, Mexico, Jamaica, Polynesia, and Korea are represented on Chino Latino's true melting pot of a menu. Chino Latino's menu changes daily, and the foods here run the gamut of these countries' spiciest cuisines, including five-spice duck, taco plates, and peppery steamed mussels. The restaurant also serves a variety of sakes and tequilas to accompany your meal—and just about the biggest banana split in the state to finish it off. The global menu is perfectly matched with the wild, complicated decor, with its cushioned orange-vinyl wall, a satay bar, giant round booths, semi-unisex bathrooms (shared sinks), and an open kitchen.

French Meadow Bakery & Café $
2610 Lyndale Avenue South, Minneapolis
(612) 870-7855
www.frenchmeadow.com

There's no disputing the quality of the food at this trendy eatery in the Wedge neighborhood, which sells organic sourdough breads, coffees, elaborate cakes, and several kinds of quiches. French Meadow uses no oil, no preservatives, and no yeast in producing chewy and flavorful organic loaves in flavors ranging from multigrain to hemp to rye with sunflower seeds. Step to the counter to order up a French Meadow sandwich and you can request any of those breads with a tasty topping of hummus, roasted eggplant, rosemary chicken salad, whitefish, or smoked turkey. With a comfortable country decor that includes simple tables and chairs, dried grapevines winding up the walls, and enough antiques to keep you intrigued but not overwhelmed, French Meadow is the perfect place to get a cup of coffee and a sandwich for lunch.

Hamlin's Cafe $
512 Nicollet Avenue, Minneapolis
(612) 333-3876
www.hamlinscafe.com

Hamlin's serves golden, skin-on fries; hash browns made of real potatoes; giant onion rings; and pancakes, burgers, turkey melts, and grilled cheeses. It also makes homemade pies, which usually disappear with the morning crowd and won't be made again until the next day. One step into this little coffee shop off Nicollet Mall and you can pretend you're in the middle of small-town America and not in the bustling metropolis of Minneapolis.

Hell's Kitchen $-$$
89 South 10th Street, Minneapolis
(612) 332-4700
www.hellskitchen.com

This breakfast, brunch (on weekends), and lunch spot features wonderfully inventive dishes such as eggs Benedict with bison flank steak and tangerine jalapeño hollandaise sauce, wild-rice porridge, and walleye hash. Despite higher prices than most other breakfast places in the Twin Cities, Hell's Kitchen serves food that is a cut above the rest.

Jax Café $$$-$$$$
1928 University Avenue NE, Minneapolis
(612) 789-7297
www.jaxcafe.com

Jax has been a strange combination of kitsch and elegance since it opened in 1933 (right after Prohibition ended), with a long wooden bar accented by a stained-glass window depicting the seven dwarfs, and a trout stream in back. The menu includes shrimp cocktail, crab cakes, gigantic aged steaks, and salmon. In winter you'll want to be near the fireplace in the dark Round-table Room. During spring and summer request a place on the outside patio, where you can catch your own rainbow trout in the stream (and have the cook pan-fry it for you) or drink a cocktail and watch elegantly dressed patrons attempting to catch the wily fish themselves.

Joe's Garage $$
1610 Harmon Place, Minneapolis
(612) 904-1163
www.joes-garage.com

Loring Park is one of the most urbane areas in the Twin Cities. So it comes as no surprise that a restaurant like Joe's Garage exists at its location. Joe's integrates the culinary flavors of the world with traditional American fare. Burgers are among the menu items. An offering typical of the menu is the Greek lamb burger, a Middle Eastern take on a traditional burger, with feta, black olive pesto, tomato, and spinach. Other offerings include the spicy Asian pork burger and the classic beef burger. Pasta and risotto are also prominently featured on the menu.

The Malt Shop $
809 West 50th Street, Minneapolis
(612) 824-1352

Snelling Avenue at Interstate 94, St. Paul
(651) 645-4643

The Malt Shop serves gourmet burgers and sandwiches as well as shakes and malts. Besides the standard cheeseburgers and Reubens, there are items like the Malibu chicken, a sautéed chicken breast with Swiss cheese, bacon, and avocado. Most important are the malts and shakes, available in almost 40 flavors. They range from strawberry and chocolate to black cherry and cookies 'n' cream.

Manny's Steakhouse $$$$
1300 Nicollet Mall
(Hyatt Regency Hotel), Minneapolis
(612) 339-9900
www.mannyssteakhouse.com

With the bad rap cholesterol gets these days, it's hard not to feel a little bit naughty eating here. This bustling, Manhattan-style steakhouse serves obscenely huge and gloriously tender steaks, lobster, salmon, and chops—and that's about it besides the great wine list and a couple of desserts. Be prepared to either share dinner with a companion or get a doggy bag to go, because there's almost no way for one person to eat a whole dinner entree here.

Market Bar-B-Que $$
1414 Nicollet Avenue, Minneapolis
(612) 872-1111
www.marketbbq.com

Established in 1946 (although not always at this location), Market Bar-B-Que's been a Twin Cities family tradition for years. The menu includes fabulous, lean spareribs and beef tips, barbecue meat sandwiches, and an amazing "dessert trough" including Key lime pie and chocolate mud sundaes. The extensive wine list is printed on the side of giant empty wine bottles set on the tables. The decor is simple and comfortable, with large carved wooden booths and tables and black-and-white photographs of celebrities who have dined at Market, including Bobby McFerrin and Willie Mays. Each table is equipped with a small jukebox that carries popular music selections from the '50s to the present.

Matt's Bar $
3500 Cedar Avenue South, Minneapolis
(612) 722-7072

Matt's Bar is famous for one dish—the Jucy Lucy. And, yes, that is the correct spelling of the south Minneapolis super-cheeseburger. Matt's makes the best Jucy Lucy, although a couple of south Minneapolis bars disagree on where it was first created in the Twin Cities. The burger is composed of two beef patties sealed around a pool of American cheese. Jucy Lucy novices beware; the burger, when removed from the grill, is filled with steaming hot cheese. Diners are rewarded for their patience when the burger cools by the sumptuous taste of this south Minneapolis specialty. The menu also includes additional burger selections and sandwiches.

Modern Café $-$$
337 13th Avenue NE, Minneapolis
(612) 378-9882

The Modern is a magnet for university students and arty types who miss their mom's home cooking but don't want to eat at an actual diner. The restaurant serves pot roast with carrots, pork sandwiches on apple bread, omelets, and giant malts and milk shakes. To mix it up a bit, the cafe also makes walleye egg rolls, penne with goat cheese and crimini mushrooms, tomato risotto with capers and lemon zest, and heavenly chocolate crème brûlée.

Murray's $$–$$$$
26 South Sixth Street, Minneapolis
(612) 339-0909
www.murraysrestaurant.com

The double New York sirloin is a tradition for Twin Cities upscale dining. For three generations Murray's has satisfied its legion of dedicated customers with the Silver Butter Knife Steak, which is available for two or three diners. Other menu items are offered, but the many regulars come in droves for the steaks and the charming and elegant dining room. Reservations are a necessity. Even then, diners must compete with the regulars for a good table.

Rosen's Bar & Grill $–$$
430 First Avenue North, Minneapolis
(612) 338-1926

Rosen's is the popular restaurant and bar of longtime WCCO television sportscaster Mark Rosen. The location in downtown Minneapolis's Warehouse District is an especially busy spot on weekends, not only for the libations but also for the food. To accompany the suds there are appetizers such as fries, chicken fingers, and Rosen's Jumbo Buffalo Wings. For lighter appetites salads and stir-fries are included, and for hardier diners there is a certified Angus burger as well as entrees such as steaks, pork chops, and a Minnesota favorite, pan-fried walleye. Several pasta choices are available. Rosen's is open daily for lunch and dinner.

St. Martin's Table $
2001 Riverside Avenue, Minneapolis
(612) 339-3920
www.communityofstmartin.org

This small vegetarian restaurant run by the community of St. Martin will convert even the most agnostic palates with its menu (which changes daily) of fresh-baked breads, ingenious sandwiches, and savory soups. The restaurant uses organic produce, non–bovine growth hormone milk, and purified water in its dishes and is committed to serving simple, nutritious food that sustains our natural resources and supports growers. St. Martin's wait-staff are all volunteer and they donate their tips to local, national, and international charities. St. Martin's Table is open for lunch only Monday through Saturday. The restaurant does not serve alcohol. You dine well, and all for a higher purpose.

Sapor Café and Bar $$
428 Washington Avenue North, Minneapolis
(612) 375-1971
www.saporcafe.com

Diners in search of a sophisticated and difficult to classify fusion cuisine will love the Sapor Café. Entrees meld together high-quality, seemingly disparate ingredients to create piquant culinary delights. Dinners include a miso-baked salmon and a pork chop in jerk spices. The restaurant features a comfortable bar, which is frequented by a hip crowd.

Ted Cook's 19th Hole Bar-B-Que $–$$
2814 East 38th Street, Minneapolis
(612) 721-2023

Ted Cook's is a small takeout-only restaurant in south Minneapolis that serves some of the best barbecue in the Twin Cities. The restaurant is decorated minimally and functionally, and Ted Cook's elevates barbecue to an art. All aspects of the meats, sides, and desserts are carefully executed, and the end result is outstanding. The meats include pork ribs, beef ribs, and barbecue chicken and beef. The tender meat is accompanied by the rich and tasty barbecue sauce, which can be ordered mild or spicy. With each dinner, jo jo potatoes, coleslaw, and bread are served. Items from mom's kitchen—greens with corn muffins, black-eyed peas, and red beans and rice—are available as well as peach cobbler and sweet potato pie for dessert. Prices are very reasonable at Ted Cook's and even cheaper with lunch sandwich combinations. Ted Cook's is slightly off the beaten path but is well worth the trip south on Hiawatha Avenue (Minnesota Highway 55). In winter a picnic just down the avenue at Minnehaha Park sounds great. Unfortunately, the conditions outdoors won't allow it, but there is always Ted Cook's scrumptious takeout for an indoor picnic.

The Times Bar & Café $-$$$
201 East Hennepin Avenue, Minneapolis
(612) 617-8098
www.timesbarandcafe.com
The Times's big draw is its fondue—pots of cheese, oil, or chocolate are brought bubbling with a host of goodies for dipping. Beyond that, the menu features burgers, sandwiches, pizza, and pasta. On weekdays the menu offers blue plate special lunches that are exceptional deals, ranging from zingy tortilla wraps stuffed with chicken and cilantro to minipizzas and open-face roast turkey sandwiches. Most evenings the Times hosts live jazz or Latin bands (see the Web site for the restaurant's entertainment calendar).

Tuggs Tavern $
219 Southeast Main Street, Minneapolis
(612) 379-4404
The main thing this upscale burger joint and bar has going for it is the wonderful view from the dining porch. The food is good—Tuggs has several specialty stuffed burgers as well as a good fish-and-chips basket, and the tavern makes excellent fresh-squeezed lemonade—but it is literally the only restaurant on the St. Anthony's Wharf strip that has an unobstructed view of the Mississippi River and the downtown Minneapolis skyline. On hot summer nights, this is a beautiful spot to take a date to enjoy the cool breezes coming off the river and watch the full moon and the lights of downtown

reflected on the water. The bar makes great mixed drinks and uses wonderful fresh-squeezed lemonade in the house specialties.

Vera's Café $
2901 Lyndale Avenue South, Minneapolis
(612) 822-3871
www.verascafe.com
Open until midnight seven nights a week, Vera's is the premier late-night dining establishment in Uptown, serving homemade soups, huge sandwiches, six kinds of scrambled eggs, and European coffees. During the summer months the gated patio is a beautiful place to take in lunch or to hang out after a movie. Inside, Vera's is outfitted with antique-looking tables, ice-cream-parlor chairs, and velvet and mohair couches.

St. Paul

Andy's Garage $
1825 University Avenue West, St. Paul
(651) 917-2332
www.andysgaragecafe.com
Andy's Garage specializes in '50s-style American diner food. Several burgers, sandwiches, soups, and salads are on the menu, as well as daily specials and roasted turkey or beef sandwiches. The fries are especially good. The restaurant is popular for its excellent desserts, root beer floats, malts, and shakes. The thick, rich, silky malts are reminiscent of the glory days of the '50s that the restaurant's decor celebrates. The restaurant was originally a garage but was converted to the charming diner it is today. Andy's is located in the heart of University Avenue's summertime classic car cruising strip, where the retro '50s diner is greatly appreciated. Children love Andy's not only for its treats but also for the six "Little Mechanics" items offered. They include peanut butter and jelly sandwiches, corn dogs, and hamburgers. The restaurant goes out of its way to entertain children. One example is the toys provided to occupy kids. Andy's offers something

for all members of the family in a casual environment.

Café Minnesota $
345 West Kellogg Boulevard West (Minnesota History Center), St. Paul
(651) 297-4097
In most cases museums and attractions are not known for their food. However, Café Minnesota is a pleasant exception. The cafe is cafeteria style and serves lunch and dinner daily. Each week the restaurant offers a menu that includes an item from each of the following: the soup tureen, the Minnesota grill, the chef's carvery, the main course, and the feature sauté. Examples of dishes available on a given day include spicy sausage and shrimp soup, rosemary-roasted pork loin, and linguini and white clam sauce. The Café Minnesota is a great casual place for a bite to eat when enjoying the attractions at the Minnesota History Center.

Cecil's Restaurant, Delicatessen & Bakery $
651 South Cleveland Avenue, St. Paul
(651) 698-0334
www.cecilsdeli.com
Cecil's is St. Paul's best deli. The front of the building is a huge deli with fresh meats, cheeses, breads, and baked goods; in the back is a modest restaurant. But don't be confused by the decor, which looks much as it did decades ago. The food is as outstanding as it always has been and has not yielded to the prepared and health-food trends that now dominate the restaurant business. The menu contains almost every hot and cold sandwich imaginable. There are also several kosher selections. Cecil's house specialty sandwiches include the Nosher, which comprises roast beef, lettuce, and spicy dressing on a fresh kaiser roll, and five different Reubens, including a vegetarian version.

Day by Day Café $
477 West Seventh Street, St. Paul
(651) 227-0654
www.daybyday.com

Day by Day is a lovely spot just west of downtown St. Paul. The restaurant meanders through several rooms of multiple storefronts on busy West Seventh Street, and the plants, bookshelves, and tables at odd angles will make visitors feel right at home. Breakfast highlights include homemade buckwheat cakes, the Earth Breakfast (two eggs scrambled with hash browns and onions and covered with melted cheese), and the breakfast burrito. For lunch and dinner the restaurant features a guacamole burger, triple-decker clubhouse sandwich, and stir-fried sesame chicken or tofu. Each menu has unique handmade cover art.

Fabulous Fern's Bar & Grill $$
400 Selby Avenue, St. Paul
(651) 225-9414
www.fabulousferns.com
Located in St. Paul's historic Cathedral Hill neighborhood of brownstone townhomes, Fabulous Fern's is a casual spot with plenty of comfort food and an active bar. Restaurant specialties include wild rice and chicken salad with cranberry vinaigrette dressing, meat loaf sandwich, blackened ribeye steak with Louisiana cream sauce, and pecan-crusted walleye. Popular with sports fans who flock to Fabulous Fern's to watch the bar's 4 plasma TVs and 10 regular TVs, the place really gets hopping during Vikings games.

Forepaugh's $$-$$$
276 South Exchange Street, St. Paul
(651) 224-5606
www.forepaughs.com
Named for Joe Forepaugh, the dry-goods merchant who built the house in 1870, this Victorian beauty is neighbor to the equally impressive home of Alexander Ramsey, Minnesota's first territorial governor. Soft light in nine cozy dining rooms offers the warmth of Grandma's parlor, lace curtains and all. Forepaugh's main courses include duck, lamb, veal, steak, and the best beef Wellington in town. Forepaugh's offers a shuttle ride to and from the Ordway in downtown St. Paul,

very helpful if your evening includes a concert or show or if you plan to attend a Wild game at the Xcel Energy Center next to the Ordway. Ask about the shuttle when you make your reservations, which are recommended. The restaurant is open for lunch weekdays, for dinner Monday through Saturday, and for brunch and dinner on Sunday.

Hickory Hut $
647 University Avenue West, St. Paul
(651) 224-9464
The Hickory Hut serves up great barbecue in a fast-food and take-out environment. Wings, barbecue sandwiches, and ribs are the most popular items. Catfish, shrimp, and at least a dozen side dishes are available. All items come in large portions and are inexpensive. The barbecue sauce is superb and comes in both mild and spicy. If you are on the go and looking for barbecue or takeout, the Hickory Hut will certainly satiate your hunger.

Keys Restaurant $-$$
767 Raymond Avenue, St. Paul
(651) 646-5756
Six additional Twin Cities locations
Since 1973 Keys has been a favorite place for breakfast and traditional diner fare in the Twin Cities. Barbara Hunn established the first Keys on Raymond Avenue in St. Paul. Keys specializes in breakfast and lunch (though some locations are now open for dinner), which it serves in immense, heaping portions. The menu includes a vast array of omelets, pancakes, eggs, and combination breakfasts. The lunch menu is huge, with such American favorites as burgers, salads, and soups. Fresh fruit pies and cakes are featured for dessert. Hours vary significantly at Keys locations.

Mickey's Diner $
36 West Seventh Street, St. Paul
(651) 222-5633
Mickey's, on the National Register of Historic Places, serves up real ice-cream

Forepaugh's is a delicious upscale restaurant housed in a gorgeous Victorian mansion that's said to be haunted. Ask the waitstaff for details—if you dare.

malts, eggs any way you like 'em, burgers and fries, Mulligan stew, and pancakes 24 hours a day. Set in a '30s-era dining car with a chrome and Formica interior, the diner has been family owned and operated since 1939. Almost inevitably, movies shot in Minnesota, including *Jingle All the Way, The Mighty Ducks,* and *A Prairie Home Companion,* feature downtown St. Paul's most camera-friendly diner.

Muffuletta Café $$
2260 Como Avenue, St. Paul
(651) 644-9116
www.muffuletta.com
Located in the beautiful St. Anthony Park neighborhood near the University of Minnesota's St. Paul campus, Muffulletta serves an eclectic menu in a colorful, casual-yet-classy atmosphere. Specialties include tortellini with cream, peas, mushrooms, and prosciutto; pork tenderloin crusted with rosemary and pancetta; and the grilled chicken sandwich with grilled onions, avocado, and chipotle mayo. Muffuletta serves beer and wine, including a fabulous wine list courtesy of the sommelier on staff. The restaurant is open for lunch and dinner Monday through Friday, dinner only on Saturday, and brunch only on Sunday.

128 Café $$
128 Cleveland Avenue North, St. Paul
(651) 645-4128
www.128cafe.net
The 128 Café serves posh American cuisine from the basement of an apartment building in St. Paul. The restaurant features a seasonal menu developed by Brock and Natalie Obee, who serve as both chefs and owners. The 60-seat

St. Paul's historic Mickey's Diner is wildly popular among the downtown lunch crowd and curious tourists. TODD R. BERGER

restaurant serves penne, pork tenderloin, ribs, and much more. The penne is a combination of smoked chicken, sweet corn, bacon, leeks, cilantro, sun-dried tomatoes, and chipotle goat cheese. The baby back ribs are covered with barbecue sauce and accompanied by sautéed vegetables and garlic mashed potatoes. The restaurant also offers prix fixe dinners (a reasonably priced three-course meal). The 128 is open for dinner. In addition, the restaurant serves an excellent Sunday brunch (10:00 A.M. to 2:00 P.M.). Reservations are recommended.

Porky's $
1890 University Avenue West, St. Paul
(651) 644-1790

In the early 21st century, there are few drive-in restaurants. Porky's is one of them. And the pickup window is open regardless of Twin Cities weather. That's right, drive-in food is available 12 months a year at Porky's. The restaurant is a modified drive-in where you have the option of ordering at the drive-through pickup window or at a counter inside the restaurant. Diners may enjoy their food in their car under the large awning or, when weather permits, on the half-dozen picnic tables provided by the restaurant. Porky's menu is filled with drive-in favorites such as hamburgers, cheeseburgers, fried chicken, chicken wings, pork sandwiches, catfish, shakes, fries, and much more. Porky's opened in 1953, then closed briefly before reopening about a decade ago. Today Porky's serves as a meeting place for classic cars when the MSRA (Minnesota Streetrod Association) holds local events in the summertime. Porky's offers classic American drive-in food in a '50s environment.

St. Clair Broiler $-$$
1580 St. Clair Avenue West, St. Paul
(651) 698-7055
www.stclairbroiler.com

The St. Clair Broiler cooks up some of the best traditional American diner food in the Twin Cities. The highlights here are plentiful. First, the daily specials include roast turkey, Greek chicken, meat loaf sandwiches, and one of the best Friday all-you-can-eat fish fries in this area. The milk shakes and malts are as delicious as they were in the less health-conscious '50s and enormous enough to easily feed two. Kids' menus and seniors' specials are available. The Broiler is also a popular breakfast spot, with extra-large omelets, golden French toast, and choice steak and eggs.

St. Paul Grill $$-$$$$
350 Market Street, St. Paul
(651) 224-7455
www.stpaulgrill.com

If you enjoy traditional American dining in an elegant hotel, the St. Paul Grill is ideal. Located in the four-star Saint Paul Hotel, the restaurant overlooks Rice Park. Moreover, the restaurant is within walking distance of several cultural attractions including the Ordway Theater, the Xcel Energy Center, the Science Museum, and numerous downtown retail shops.

The St. Paul Grill serves upscale food and spirits. The menu includes beef and poultry as well as pasta, salads, and soups. The restaurant features an excellent wine list, which, like the cuisine, has received countless local and national awards. Reservations are highly recommended. The St. Paul Grill is open for lunch and dinner Monday through Sunday.

Tavern on Grand $-$$
656 Grand Avenue, St. Paul
(651) 228-9030
www.tavernongrand.com

Tavern on Grand is a Minnesota classic, serving up plates of walleye fillets to the masses. Sure, you can also come here for Black Angus top sirloin, baked chicken, and slow-roasted ribs, but you're unlikely to order walleye in Memphis, so get with the program and order up a plate of the exalted fish with all the trimmings. The restaurant has a north-woodsy feel like a lakefront lodge, complete with built-in fish tank, and the walleye is simply spectacular. Options abound, including a choice of a grilled or deep-fried (with "secret batter") one- or two-fillet dinner, the walleye basket,

Tavern on Grand restaurant. SAINT PAUL RCVA

the walleye sandwich, and the Lakeshore Special, which includes a fillet and an eight-ounce steak. You can also add a flaky fillet to any meal as a side order, if spaghetti, meatballs, and walleye is your thing. The waitstaff won't bat an eye.

W. A. Frost and Company $$$
374 Selby Avenue, St. Paul
(651) 224-5715
www.wafrost.com

W. A. Frost is located in the Cathedral Hill neighborhood of St. Paul in the elegant 19th-century Dacotah Building. The menu is brief but well executed and includes chicken breast, walleye, New York strip, and more. Since 1975 the beautiful old brownstone restaurant has been an integral part of the lovely neighborhood and has enticed diners to visit for food and spirits in one of the Twin Cities' most charming spots. During summer the restaurant serves meals on its expansive patio, one of the most beautiful and romantic locations for outdoor dining in the Twin Cities. W. A. Frost is open daily for lunch and dinner. Reservations are highly recommended.

South

Joe Senser's Sports Grill & Bar $-$$
4217 West 80th Street, Bloomington
(952) 835-1191

2350 Cleveland Avenue, Roseville
(651) 631-1781

3010 Eagandale Place, Eagan
(651) 687-9333
www.sensers.com

The three Joe Senser's Sports Grills are favorite places to watch sports and enjoy burgers, sandwiches, soups, or entrees. Unlike many sports bars, Joe Senser's offers plenty of choices. Featured are several burgers and sandwiches, such as the Flying Buffalo Chicken sandwich and the turkey bacon Parmesan sandwich. Also included are entrees such as barbecue ribs, pork chops, walleye, and pastas.

Besides the food, of course, there are the beers and the big-screen televisions.

East

The Bayport Cookery $$$$
328 Fifth Avenue North, Bayport
(651) 430-1066
www.bayportcookery.com

The Bayport Cookery is recognized locally and nationally for adventurous fine dining. The core of the restaurant's menu, which has monthly themes and varies weekly, is avant-garde cuisine. Unlike any other restaurant of its kind, it emphasizes the foods of Minnesota. The Cookery is a favorite among local foodies and tourists, who make the half-hour trek from downtown Minneapolis to the scenic St. Croix. The menu is based on availability of fresh items. For example, the month of January showcases truffles. Due to supply the savory menu often changes daily. The prix fixe menu varies greatly from month to month. Reservations are required.

Chickadee Cottage Restaurant $-$$
9900 Valley Creek Road, Woodbury
(651) 578-8118

The Chickadee Cottage Restaurant offers an extensive menu of American and European-influenced favorites. The cottage theme pervades the restaurant, with each room having a particular cottage motif (e.g., rustic lodge or rural getaway). Chickadee's breakfast menu is enormous and includes many fresh-baked goods as well as pancakes, waffles, eggs, omelets, and much more. The lunch and dinner menus also provide plenty to choose from, e.g., meat loaf sandwiches, grilled Caesar salad, scallops and shrimp, vegetable lasagna, and smoky apple pork chops. The restaurant is family friendly. Children are provided with crayons and a menu that includes pancakes and scrambled eggs for breakfast and grilled cheese or peanut butter and jelly sandwiches for dinner. Chickadee Cottage Restaurant is open Tuesday through Sunday for breakfast, lunch, and dinner.

The Lowell Inn $$-$$$
102 North Second Street, Stillwater
(651) 439-1100 or (888) 569-3554
www.lowellinn.com
The Lowell Inn is widely known for its Swiss fondue, served in the Stillwater inn's Matterhorn Room. But at the Lowell the Swiss cheese fondue is just the starter of a four-course meal (with optional wine accompaniment) featuring beef tenderloin, duck breast, or jumbo prawns with Minnesota wild rice pilaf. Desserts include grapes Devonshire and Swiss chocolate fondue. The whole shebang is delivered tableside for a set price. For those looking to choose individual dishes rather than a multicourse extravaganza, the Lowell's George Washington Room offers such entrees as duck breast, filet mignon, and lobster tail. (For more information on the Lowell Inn's guest rooms, see the Accommodations chapter.)

West

Park Tavern $-$$
3401 Louisiana Avenue, St. Louis Park
(952) 929-6810
www.parktavern.net
Bar and bowling alley food is generally not highly regarded for its taste. The Park Tavern is an exception. The appetizers are tasty and edible, with or without suds for lubrication, and include nachos, quesadillas, and chicken strips. Also featured are top-notch burgers and sandwiches such as the French dip au jus and the prime melt sandwich, which features prime rib topped with sautéed onions and cheese. Salads are another option for less ravenous diners.

Zaroff's Delicatessen Restaurant $-$$
11300 Wayzata Boulevard, Minnetonka
(952) 543-8687
When patrons open Zaroff's menu they first notice the glossary of terms. Despite the restaurant's Minneapolis suburban

Tavern on Grand is the place to get walleye—the restaurant serves more of the state fish that any other eatery in Minnesota. One new preparation method they're trying out: buffalo-sauce walleye nuggets.

location—Minnetonka—the menu proudly proclaims its Jewish deli roots. There are almost 20 Yiddish terms to aid patrons not yet experienced with Jewish-American culinary traditions. The extensive menu includes appetizers, numerous sandwich selections, entrees, burgers and franks, and eggs. Just a few highlights are the hot brisket of beef, the hot pastrami sandwich, and the Hebrew National frank on a bun. There are several specialty items, such as sautéed chicken livers, Hungarian goulash, and borscht. Zaroff's offers a wide selection of dessert items, including chocolate cake, apple pie, and ice cream. The cakes and cheesecake are flown in from the Carnegie Deli in New York. The full-service deli also has a wine and beer list. In Minnesota authentic New York–style delis are few and far between, and Zaroff's annually receives kudos for its fine foods.

CAJUN/SOUTHERN

Dixies on Grand $-$$$
695 Grand Avenue, St. Paul
(651) 222-7345
www.dixiesongrand.com
There are only a few Cajun and southern restaurants in the North Star State of Minnesota. Since Dixies opened in 1985, many other restaurants have incorporated Cajun items in their menu, but few have had the success of Dixies because they lack the dedication and specialization. Cajun- and southern-cooking purists may balk at the menu since it includes such foods as calamari and Cuban black bean soup and fusion foods like the Cajun burger. However, the vast majority of items are from the Cajun and southern food traditions. A

few specialty dishes are jambalaya, blackened catfish, shrimp and crawfish étouffée, and Carolina crab cakes. The ribs are another specialty at Dixies and are available in baby back and country-style pork ribs. Barbecue chicken is another popular menu item. Although dinner can be expensive, lunch offers much cheaper menu selections. Dixies has an extensive wine list as well as a large selection of domestic and imported beers. On Sunday the restaurant hosts a brunch, which includes red beans and rice, corn bread, country ham, barbecue chicken, and much more. The entire menu is available for take-out. Reservations for dinner are recommended, especially on weekend evenings.

CAMBODIAN

Cheng Heng $
448 University Avenue West, St. Paul
(651) 222-5577
Definitely a diamond in the rough, Cheng Heng is one of the most amazing deals (and best-kept secrets) in town. Located in one of the more dilapidated parts of St. Paul, Cheng Heng looks, to the casual observer, like just one more uninviting sign in a line of strip malls. But this is the only place in town where you can get a pile of beautifully steamed mussels in black bean sauce for under $10, and that's about the most expensive selection on the menu. The family-owned restaurant has won numerous critics' choice awards—just about annually—for everything from egg roll salad to shrimp-stuffed spring rolls. The couple who run the place take hospi-

tality to new levels, positioning fans to cool down your table when it's hot out and fussing over you as though you were their housé guest and not just another restaurant customer. They offer suggestions and menus with pictures to make even the pickiest of eaters comfortable with ordering Cambodian food for the first time and are more than willing to share their cooking secrets with curious customers. This has long been a favorite place to take relatives for special occasions or wow out-of-town friends when they come to visit. Cheng Heng is open daily for breakfast, lunch, and dinner.

CARIBBEAN

West Indies Soul Café $
625 University Avenue, Suite 102, St. Paul
(651) 665-0115
West Indies Soul began serving the Twin Cities at annual neighborhood festivals. The savory tastes of the Caribbean created a demand for catering and later a restaurant to serve jerk chicken, curry chicken and goat, fried plantains, and roti (Caribbean breads filled with meats). Though not a fast-food restaurant, the order-in and take-out counter-style dining facilitates quick service. Diners may select large or regular-size portions, and a sample platter is available for those interested in a culinary overview of the restaurant. Wraps and sandwiches, salads, and baskets are another option. They include a few non-Caribbean baskets such as rib tips and catfish strips. The restaurant serves homemade drinks of carrot punch, ginger beer, and lemonade but does not serve alcohol. West Indies Soul is open for lunch and dinner Tuesday through Saturday.

East

San Pedro Café $$
426 Second Street, Hudson, Wisconsin
(715) 386-4003
www.sanpedrocafe.com
San Pedro Café offers Mediterranean and

If you are an ethnic food novice but would like to sample the cuisine of another culture, look for ethnic restaurants with lunch buffets. The buffets provide an excellent overview of a culture's food at reasonable prices.

---

tropical cuisine and atmosphere in scenic Hudson, Wisconsin. Still considered a day trip to some Twin Citians, this community on the beautiful St. Croix River has seen a restaurant boom.

The menu overflows with flavor. There are sandwiches, wraps, pastas, salads, seafood, and Neapolitan pizzas. One fine example is an excellent Caribbean jerk chicken. The decor is pleasant and relies heavily on tropical blues and reds and exposed brick. The restaurant is located in a wonderful restored building in downtown Hudson and is packed with customers at all times of the day. A decade or so ago Twin Citians would have laughed if someone said Hudson and Stillwater would have some of the best restaurants in the area; today it is a well-established fact. The San Pedro Café is one of the best examples of the wealth of fine dining in the greater Twin Cities.

CHINESE

Minneapolis

China Express $-$$
409 14th Avenue SE, Minneapolis
(612) 379-6374
China Express's lunch express is an excellent fast-food alternative, where diners may select two items with white rice or pork fried rice for a low price. There are lunch specials such as kung pao shrimp, pepper steak, and *moo goo gai pan*. Chinese dinner specialties include Dragon and Phoenix (jumbo shrimp and chicken), and General Tso's chicken. China Express is open daily for lunch and dinner and offers delivery for orders over $15.

1st Wok $-$$
3236 West Lake Street, Minneapolis
(612) 922-8883
1st Wok features an extensive menu of Hunan and Szechuan-style Chinese food. Fine renditions of sesame chicken, kung

pao chicken, lo mein, and pepper steak are served, as well as numerous seafood items. The restaurant features specialties such as sesame shrimp, Double Wonder, and princess chicken and shrimp. Daily lunch specials are a steal and include an entree plus soup and fried rice. Vegetarian items include bean curd selections (kung pao bean curd and spicy bean curd Szechuan-style). 1st Wok is open daily for lunch and dinner.

Hong Kong Noodles Restaurant $-$$
901 Washington Avenue SE, Minneapolis
(612) 379-9472
Several excellent Chinese restaurants are in the vicinity of the University of Minnesota—this is arguably one of the best. The restaurant is rather small and seats no more than 50 people in an often-packed room. But it is the food that garners the restaurant accolades from its regular patrons and critics alike. With almost 300 menu items, Hong Kong Noodles offers plenty to choose from, but noodles are the restaurant's specialty. The menu is divided into extensive soup, chicken, beef, fried rice, hot pot, seafood, pork, and vegetable choices. In addition, the restaurant offers chef specialties and daily specials based on the available fresh produce and seafood. Finally, there is the restaurant's wide selection of noodles, which include rice noodles, pan-fried noodles, and lo mein. A few standouts are the Singapore-style rice noodles, seafood lo mein, and beef brisket fun. Hong Kong Noodles is open late daily, which is relatively uncommon in the Twin Cities. Hence, the restaurant does a booming business until midnight Sunday through Thursday. On Friday and Saturday evenings, the restaurant stays open until 2:00 A.M.

Peking Garden Chinese Restaurant $-$$
2324 University Avenue SE, Minneapolis
(612) 623-3989
The Peking Garden is one of the Twin Cities' favorite traditional Chinese restaurants. Located near the University of Minnesota, it draws large crowds of students,

Eat Street, also known as Nicollet Avenue and Nicollet Mall, hosts dozens of restaurants along its route through downtown and south Minneapolis. TODD R. BERGER

professors, and lovers of fine Chinese food. There are hundreds of choices on the extensive menu. Besides the typical beef, chicken, and pork entrees, there are seafood, duck, and soup choices.

Rainbow Chinese Restaurant & Bar $-$$
2739 Nicollet Avenue, Minneapolis
(612) 870-7084
www.rainbowrestaurant.com

Rainbow Chinese is one of the Twin Cities' favorite Chinese restaurants. The menu features exciting examples of Chinese cuisine prepared with fresh ingredients. Rainbow's signature dishes include Szechuan wontons, honey walnut shrimp and Singapore *chow mai fun,* and fried walleye pike with black bean sauce. There are many other options, including multiple vegetarian choices. Alcohol is available with meals and at the lovely bar, where diners can feel free to bask in the comely decor of the restaurant, which is superbly decorated in greens and yellows. Reservations are accepted only for groups of four or more. The restaurant serves lunch and dinner Monday through Friday but closes between 2:00 and 4:30 P.M. The restaurant is open all day on Saturday and Sunday.

Shuang Cheng Restaurant $-$$
1320 Fourth Street SE, Minneapolis
(612) 378-0208

Food critics and diners consistently recognize Shuang Cheng as one of the Twin Cities' best seafood restaurants. Shuang Cheng is modestly decorated with small, slightly uncomfortable chairs and a few booths along the wall. It is located in Dinkytown, just outside the U of M campus. On weekends it draws huge crowds, mainly for the delicious seafood prepared with a tantalizing Chinese flair. The menu includes shrimp, crab, scallops, oysters, clams, lobster, squid, and four walleye dishes. Chicken, beef, pork, and vegetarian options are available. Daily specials are posted on a whiteboard and erased when the item sells out. Here are just a few of the ever-changing daily specials: live lob-

ster, stir-fried bok choy, seafood and asparagus, and Black Sea bass. Shuang Cheng serves inexpensive lunch combinations aimed at thrifty university students.

Village Wok Restaurant $
610 Washington Avenue SE, Minneapolis
(612) 331-9041
www.villagewok.com

The Village Wok does some of the briskest business in the Twin Cities. Located on the edge of the U of M, it attracts a regular lunch, dinner, and late-night crowd of students, professors, and doctors. In addition, the restaurant draws throngs of Chinese diners with its traditional Chinese cuisine, especially the large seafood menu. Village Wok may have the largest menu in the Twin Cities, with sections dedicated to fried rice, chow mein, Cantonese specialties, Szechuan specialties, duck, hot pot, shrimp, scallops, squid, four types of noodles, plus the lengthy list of chef's selections and the late-night special menu. The menu features daily lunch combinations, such as shrimp Szechuan, cheese wonton and fried rice or sweet-and-sour chicken, egg roll, and fried rice. All lunch combinations are served for less than $5.00. The Cantonese-style dinners are another delicious bargain; they include beef with black bean sauce, roast duck, and shrimp with broccoli. Each of these enormous dinners is served with a choice of soup and a large bowl of rice and, at slightly more than $5.00, has fed countless financially strapped students.

Besides the Village Wok's Chinese dinner specials, the seafood menu is one of the largest in the area. Diners may choose from several preparations of trout, sole, salmon, and walleye. Each fish is prepared in a sauce such as black bean sauce, lemon sauce, or ginger sauce. A popular fish selection is the crispy whole walleye Hunan-style. Other seafood items include baked and fried lobster and oysters. The Village Wok is open for lunch and dinner daily. Unlike most area restaurants, it has late-night hours and does not close until 2:00 A.M. daily.

RESTAURANTS

85

St. Paul

Cleveland Wok Chinese Restaurant $
767 Cleveland Avenue South, St. Paul
(651) 699-3141

The Cleveland Wok offers an extensive menu of Chinese specialties. The restaurant follows the trend of many new Chinese restaurants in the Twin Cities—it provides an expanded menu of seafood and Chinese noodle dishes. Among the noodle selections are choices between pan-fried noodles (either egg noodles or rice noodles), lo mein, or chow fun. An excellent noodle item is the Singapore curry rice noodles, which marries roasted pork, shrimp, fried egg, carrots, green peppers, and lemongrass in a spicy complex combination that creates a savory sauce. There are also several chef's combo specials, where an entree such as curry chicken, kung pao chicken, or sesame chicken comes accompanied by fried rice and an egg roll or egg foo young. Numerous chicken, pork, and beef items are available. Cleveland Wok serves beer and wine. The restaurant is open Monday through Saturday for lunch and dinner.

My Le Hoa $-$$
2900 Rice Street (Market Place
Shopping Center), Little Canada
(651) 484-5353

Located in a suburban shopping center in St. Paul, My Le Hoa is routinely named one of the Twin Cities' favorite Chinese restaurants. Besides chow mein, fried rice, and egg foo young, the restaurant serves Cantonese noodle dishes, chicken, pork, beef, and numerous seafood items. Prawns, scallops, squid, and fish are all prepared in sauces ranging from curry and satay to black bean and oyster. The fish selection is impressive and includes salmon, sole, walleye, and cod. In addition, the restaurant offers four duck dishes. Duck is available half or whole. My Le Hoa is open for lunch and dinner Tuesday through Sunday.

North

Willow Gate II $
1885 West Perimeter Drive, Roseville
(651) 628-0990

Willow Gate's menu is extensive and features several hundred Chinese and Vietnamese items. At lunch there are combination meals for under $5.00, which include several seafood items. The curry shrimp and chicken fried rice are two favorites. Each is accompanied by a choice of two chicken wings or cheese wontons. Dinner offers larger combination plates as well as traditional Chinese fare, such as lo mein, egg foo young, fried rice, and seafood. Willow Gate serves beer and wine, and lunch and dinner are served daily.

East

Singapore!
Cuisine of China & Malaysia $-$$
1715 Beam Avenue Suite A, Maplewood
(651) 777-7999
www.singaporemenu.com

Singapore quickly became one of the Twin Cities' favorite Asian restaurants. Despite its unlikely location (suburban Maplewood), the restaurant features some of the area's most outstanding dishes. What sets the restaurant apart from the multitude of Asian restaurants? It's not the restaurant's superb versions of Chinese dishes, which are among the best in the area. Instead, the complex and savory Malaysian items distinguish Singapore from the crowd.

Singapore is the only Twin Cities restaurant to feature an extensive Malaysian menu, created by Chef Kin Lee. Included are *sambals*, a Malaysian specialty made of shrimp paste, ground chili peppers, and shallots. Sambal options range from mixed vegetables to prawns, scallops, shrimp, and other seafood choices. Complexly spiced curries and *rendangs* (dry curries) are also prominent menu items. The savory Captain's Curry boasts an astounding 27 spices. It is hard to go wrong at Singapore because all menu items are deft combinations of fresh vegetables, meats, and spices. And for vegetarians, there are several excellent choices. If diners have any questions, the friendly servers are more than happy to make suggestions or ask the chef to alter dishes to meet desired spice levels.

There are many excellent menu items for less adventurous diners. Despite the serious cuisine, Singapore is a relatively casual restaurant. But it is in the food where the restaurant truly shines. It comes as no surprise to local Asian food connoisseurs that the restaurant routinely wins awards from local weeklies and periodicals. Now there's a Minneapolis location as well, at 5554 34th Avenue South (612-722-0888).

West

Yangtze Chinese Restaurant $-$$
5625 Wayzata Boulevard, St. Louis Park
(952) 541-9469
The Yangtze Restaurant serves Szechuan, Cantonese, and Mandarin Chinese dishes. Menu favorites include sesame chicken, Mandarin shrimp, pan-fried noodles, pot stickers, and sizzling duck. Yangtze Restaurant is open daily for lunch and dinner and on weekends features one of the best dim sum in the Twin Cities.

CUBAN

Café Havana $-$$
119 Washington Avenue North,
Minneapolis
(612) 338-8484
In the 1950s cosmopolitan Havana spawned sizzling nightclubs, Latin rhythms, and a reckless, live-for-today attitude. Café Havana re-creates this paradise of privilege through telling details: the red carpet leading to the door, huge

sprays of flowers, sumptuous velveteen chairs and curtains, the whiff of good cigars, and the black dial telephone. Fans of true Cuban food—rice and pork dishes, plantains, and creamy three-milk cakes—will love Café Havana, which is also home to one of the posher bar scenes in the Cities. There's even a cigar room for post-dinner stogies. Owners Gladys and Peter Mendoza (mother and son) say that their family recipes are faithful to the Cuban dishes they left behind in 1969. Black beans and rice, the national dish, accompany many entrees, along with fried plantains. Items from cornmeal-crusted conch fritters to grilled chorizo with peppers and onions serve as appetizers. There's no goat on the menu, but the lamb shank and the traditional *ropa vieja* (shredded beef slow-cooked in sherry tomato sauce) are satisfying and delicious, and the seafood tastes as though it's just off the boat.

Victor's 1959 Café $
3756 Grand Avenue South, Minneapolis
(612) 827-8948
www.victors1959cafe.com
Serving Cuban and American breakfast and lunch cuisine, this tiny restaurant is packed with photographs and memorabilia of both Cuba and Castro. The yellow walls give a Caribbean feel to the restaurant, as does the Cuban music in the background. The menu includes eggs Havana, mango waffles, ranchero Cubano, the Bay of Pigs pork sandwich, fried yucca, both sweet plantains and fried green plantains, and Cuban coffee. The restaurant is a popular neighborhood stop, and with fewer than ten tables inside, the wait to get seated can be an hour or so.

EASTERN EUROPEAN

Kramarczuk Sausage Company $
215 Hennepin Avenue East, Minneapolis
(612) 379-3018

Specializing in the cuisine of Poland, Ukraine, and Russia, the casual Kramarczuk Sausage Company serves delicious, cheap eats in their cafeteria-style restaurant across the river from downtown Minneapolis. Specialties include *varenyky* (dumplings stuffed with meat, cheese and potato, or sauerkraut), *holubets* (cabbage rolls stuffed with rice and meat and topped with tomato sauce), *szegedin* goulash (meat, sauerkraut, and onions in a paprika sauce), and several selections of sausages. Soups include borscht and sausage vegetable, and Kramarczuk serves beer and wine. The restaurant also has an on-site deli and market. Live accordion music livens things up on Saturday night. Kramarczuk is open for lunch and dinner Monday through Saturday; the market and deli are open in the morning for sausages (and many other items) to take home and grill.

ETHIOPIAN
Minneapolis

Blue Nile $-$$
2027 Franklin Avenue East, Minneapolis
(612) 338-3000
www.bluenilempls.com
For more than a decade, Ethiopians and Eritreans have thrived in the Twin Cities. The immigrants have enriched the area with the wealth of their culture. One highly visible result is the many Ethiopian restaurants scattered throughout Minneapolis and St. Paul. Blue Nile was one of the first Ethiopian restaurants in the area. Its first location was in south Minneapolis, but it later relocated to the present location in Minneapolis's Seward neighborhood. Blue Nile moved into an expansive former supper club, where there is a huge dining room, bar, and space for dancing and live music.

Blue Nile features a menu filled with Ethiopian dishes as well as Middle Eastern specialties. Menu items include the *maraka hoolaa,* which is lamb flavored with ginger root and other exotic spices. The restaurant also features a shish kebab combo. Vegetarian menu selections are available. And for an excellent overview of the culinary treats offered at the Blue Nile, try the *gosa-gosa* C, which is a sampler of two of the menu's vegetarian entrees and maraka (Ethiopian stewed meat dishes). Blue Nile is open for dinner Monday through Sunday.

St. Paul

Queen of Sheba Café & Restaurant $-$$
2447 West Seventh Street, St. Paul
(651) 690-0068
Queen of Sheba serves primarily Ethiopian food—stewed beef, chicken, and vegetables spiced and served with *injera* (delicious, spongy pieces of flat bread made with ultrafine grain)—but the menu also has hot dogs, french fries, and hamburgers. It's a strange mixture of elegant and casual, as the restaurant is beautifully decorated with hand-embroidered tablecloths and framed needlepoints, but all the food is prepared to be eaten with your hands alone, although if you ask, they'll gladly bring you silverware. A counter at one side of the restaurant serves Ethiopian coffee.

FRENCH
Minneapolis

Restaurant Alma $$$
528 University Avenue SE, Minneapolis
(612) 379-4909
www.restaurantalma.com
Chef Alex Roberts, a veteran of such restaurant kitchens as New York City's Bouley and Union Square Café, serves up

incredible dishes following classic French techniques. Typical menu items include a Portuguese-style stew crowned with tender, in-the-shell clams, buttery squares of chicken, and spicy chorizo in a tomato broth; vegetarian corn *crespelle*; and prime, dry-aged ribeye steak. Reservations are highly recommended, especially on weekends.

Vincent $$$
1100 Nicollet Mall, Minneapolis
(612) 630-1189
www.vincentrestaurant.com
Vincent, named for head chef and owner Vincent Francoual, is a lovely spot for casual fine dining. Beautiful oak woodwork, high ceilings, and large windows overlooking Nicollet Mall and Orchestra Hall provide the upscale atmosphere for the restaurant's French-American specialties. The menu changes every two months, but some past dishes include pan-seared scallops with an orange sauce, seafood "cappuccino" with crab custard and a lobster froth, and fennel seed-crusted Atlantic salmon. Vincent is open for lunch Monday through Friday and dinner daily; reservations are recommended, particularly on weekends.

South

La Fougasse $$$
Sofitel Minneapolis Hotel, 5601 West 78th Street, Bloomington
(952) 835-0126
This hotel restaurant, formerly the site of two smaller French restaurants, serves a wide variety of elegant French dishes, including excellent onion soup, *fougasse*, and a huge collection of scrumptious desserts. Warm saffron, deep red, and azure blue monopolize every inch of this restaurant, giving it the ultimate Mediterranean look. Reservations are almost always required, as the place fills up quickly with hotel guests.

GERMAN
Minneapolis

Black Forest Inn $$
1 East 26th Street, Minneapolis
(612) 872-0812
The Black Forest Inn has been a favorite German restaurant for more than 30 years. It is located on the popular ethnic restaurant area of Eat Street (Nicollet Avenue). The restaurant has stood the test of time and remains a popular hangout for German food and, in summertime, outdoor dining. A canopy of trees with lots of green flora and a fountain shade the outdoor dining area. Another asset at the restaurant is the large bar stocked with imported German and domestic beers, which go great with the hearty German food, including such specialties as wiener schnitzel, sauerbraten, and *hasenpfeffer*, as well as sauerkraut and spaetzle (German dumplings somewhat similar to thick, doughy noodles). Dessert is outstanding, too, especially the decadent Black Forest cake.

St. Paul

Glockenspiel $-$$
605 West Seventh Street, St. Paul
(651) 292-9421
When Glockenspiel opened the Twin Cities was prepared for something special. After all, two of the restaurant's co-owners are the Wildmos, David and Mary, who own one of St. Paul's favorite restaurants, the Tavern on Grand. The location, a Czech and Slovak fraternal hall, is one of the restaurant's greatest assets. On entering the restaurant, you see a huge bar stocked with German beers. The dining area is a classy continuation of the bar and is decked out in plenty of blue against a large mural in the long, narrow, spacious dining area.

German specialties, especially pork, fill the large menu. The restaurant has daily specials, which include venison medallions on Saturday evening. Other specials during the week are salmon fillets and beef rouladen (beef rolled around a pickle). A few other entrees are *schweinhaxe* (pork hocks), Eisbach pfeffersteak (a German version of sirloin steak), and *schweinrippchen* (pork spare ribs). And for those with a smaller appetite, there are *kleine speise* (lighter fare) such as bratwurst, weisswurst, and a Reuben sandwich. Finally, for dessert the restaurant features tortes, cakes, and other German delights. Glockenspiel is open for lunch and dinner daily.

East

Gasthaus Bavarian Hunter $-$$
8390 Lofton Avenue North, Stillwater
(651) 439-7128
www.gasthausbavarianhunter.com
Gasthaus has specialized in the cuisine of south Germany since 1966, and the extensive menu offers something for everyone. The restaurant has the largest variety of schnitzels (cutlets) in the Twin Cities. Also featured are sausages, sauerbraten (a tangy beef), and, for large appetites, a couple of Bavarian combination platters. Surprisingly, the meaty restaurant has two *kein fleisch* (no meat) meals—vegetable rouladen and vegetable casserole. And don't forget to wash the meal down with a German beer, especially since the restaurant does not stock domestic brews. For diners' entertainment, polka music is performed on Friday and Sunday as well as for the many German events. The Gasthaus Bavarian Hunter is open daily for lunch and dinner.

The Gasthaus packs them in for its three annual festivals: Sommerfest in June, Waldfest on Labor Day, and Oktoberfest later in September. Sommerfest and Oktoberfest feature food, German beer in traditional one-liter mugs (and in smaller sizes), and polka music under the big tent in front of the restaurant. If you plan to partake in the festivities, make sure someone in your party is the designated driver, because the beer goes down fast and the location of the rural Stillwater-area restaurant makes for an expensive taxi ride back to the Cities.

Winzer Stube $$
516 Second Street, Hudson, Wisconsin
(715) 381-5092
One of the Twin Cities' best German restaurants is located in Hudson, Wisconsin, 25 miles east of downtown St. Paul. The restaurant has become a popular destination for Twin Citians who desire authentic German cuisine at reasonable prices. Located in the basement of the old opera house in downtown Hudson, the restaurant is decorated with lots of wood and German motifs.

The menu features several excellent dishes. One savory item is the roulade *mit speck und gurke*. The flavorful beef roll-ups are wrapped around a tasty pickle. Also outstanding is the *jägerschnitzel*. The fine pork cutlet is the restaurant's biggest seller and comes accompanied by spaetzle (homemade noodles) and *rotkraut* (red cabbage). The *schweinhaxe* (pork hocks) is a popular daily special that occasionally sells out during lunch. For smaller appetites there are soups and sausage platters (bratwurst, weisswurst, bauern mettwurst, and knackwurst) on the menu. The restaurant has a children's menu, and to end the meal there are outstanding dessert options such as Black Forest cake, apple strudel, and chocolate torte.

GREEK

Minneapolis

Gardens of Salonica
New Greek Café and Deli $-$$
19 Northeast Fifth Street, Minneapolis
(612) 378-0611
Anna and Lazaros Christoforide's sunny

restaurant serves fresh bread with delightful dips, like their zingy *skordalia* (potatoes, lemon juice, and garlic) and *tyro* (feta cheese blended with roasted peppers, garlic, and herbs); chicken souvlaki and lamb-and-beef gyro sandwiches; and fancier dishes like rice-stuffed squid baked in red wine sauce and the fresh artichoke-and-braised-lamb dish that's a spring special. The house specialty, popular for lunch or dessert, is *boughatsa:* phyllo pastries that come in sweet and savory varieties. Located in a turn-of-the-20th-century storefront on an obscure side street, this family-owned Greek cafe and deli draws patrons from all over the Metro.

It's Greek to Me $$
626 West Lake Street, Minneapolis
(612) 825-9922

This restaurant is casual and welcoming, with high pressed-tin ceilings, freshly painted wall murals, and new terra-cotta–like tiled floors. It's also inexpensive, considering that a dinner-size portion of anything costs around $10 and will usually leave you enough for tomorrow's lunch. The menu offers nearly two dozen appetizers to precede classic Greek specialties such as souvlaki and spanakopita, fried smelt, octopus, chicken gyros, and flaming cheese. It's Greek to Me maintains its status as one of the Lyn-Lake neighborhood's most popular eateries. Every night the place bustles with couples, small families, and intimate clusters of friends devouring spicy-hot feta cheese spread, roast leg of lamb, or vegetarian *dolmades*.

St. Paul

Acropol Inn Restaurant $
748 Grand Avenue, St. Paul
(651) 298-0151

The Acropol Inn is one of the Twin Cities' oldest Greek restaurants. The Apostolou family opened the restaurant in 1975 to serve gyros and other Greek specialties.

The restaurant serves all the traditional Greek standards—moussaka (meat and eggplant), *dolmades* (grape leaves stuffed with rice and meat), and *pasticcio* (a Greek version of lasagna). Wash the Greek cuisine down with a cold beer or glass of wine. The Acropol Inn Restaurant is open Monday through Saturday for lunch and dinner.

Christos Greek Restaurant $$
214 East Fourth Street, St. Paul
(651) 224-6000

2632 Nicollet Avenue, Minneapolis
(612) 871-2111
www.christos.com

Christos serves all your Greek favorites from two Twin Cities locations. The St. Paul restaurant is one the most beautiful and historical dining spots in the area, the Union Depot Place. Christos is situated in the middle of the immense former Union Depot, atop a riser, and is surrounded by columns and plenty of big windows and marble. It's hard for a restaurant to fail with such grandeur and beauty.

Both locations feature tasty versions of Greek cuisine. The menu includes gyros, *dolmades*, spanakopita, moussaka, and many other traditional Greek dishes. The prices are reasonable, especially for lunch, when the St. Paul location serves a buffet Monday through Friday. The buffet offers a relatively inexpensive introduction for Greek food novices as well as connoisseurs. The food selections are always delicious, and the unmatched ambience is free.

Spiro's Mediterranean Market $
2264 University Avenue West, St. Paul
(651) 645-4607

Besides a well-stocked Mediterranean market, Spiro's features a deli counter. There are two sandwiches offered—an Italian beef sandwich and, of course, a gyro. The gyro is big and tasty. The succulent gyro meat is surrounded by a fresh pita and topped with onions, tomatoes, and creamy Greek sauce. Also available are Greek salads and the deli's delicious homemade hummus. The hummus is among the best in the Twin Cities, with a tangy citrus taste in combination with the pureed chickpeas. Don't forget dessert. A couple of dessert treats are provided, and the baklava is a particularly good mix of phyllo dough, nuts, and honey. Spiro's is open for lunch Monday through Friday and early dinner (until 7:00 P.M. on weekdays and 5:00 P.M. on Saturday).

West

Santorini $-$$$
9920 Wayzata Boulevard, St. Louis Park
(952) 546-6722
Greek cuisine and American specialties dominate the menu at Santorini. For lunch and dinner there are numerous choices. Sandwiches ranging from a traditional burger to the Moroccan chicken, which features a unique pepper spread, onions, and cucumbers, are served along with pastas and more elaborate entrees. Shrimp, steaks, lamb chops, and much more are available as well as Greek combination platters.

INDIAN

Minneapolis

Passage to India $-$$
1401 West Lake Street, Minneapolis
(612) 827-7518
Passage to India is one of the many fine Indian restaurants in the Twin Cities. A few years ago this restaurant opened in the Uptown area of Minneapolis. With its opening came great expectations, since another branch is regarded as one of the best Indian restaurants in New York City. The Passage to India met most critics' expectations. The breads and tandoori choices are outstanding as are the special dinners. Each offers soup, appetizer, main course, and dessert for under $20. Pas-

sage to India is open until midnight most nights—a blessing in the Twin Cities, where so few restaurants have late-night hours.

North

India Palace $-$$
2570 Cleveland Avenue North, Roseville
(651) 631-1222
India Palace creates some of the area's best cuisine. Other than the facade of the building, the restaurant shows no signs of its previous tenants, a fast-food chain. Decorated with subtle Indian art, the restaurant is a favorite. Featured menu items include tandoori specialties, curries, and vindaloos. Also available is the lunch buffet, where seven days a week diners may enjoy the flavors of India. In addition, the restaurant offers take-out as well as an extensive beer and wine list. India Palace is open daily for lunch and dinner.

South

Tandoor Restaurant $-$$
8062 Morgan Circle South, Bloomington
(952) 885-9060
www.tandoormn.com
True to its name, the specialty of Tandoor Restaurant is the meats, seafood, and other foods cooked in the tandoor, a clay oven heated to high heat using charcoal. Favorites included tandoori chicken, tandoori naan bread, lamb *rogan nosh,* and chicken *makhani,* as well as various curry dishes. The restaurant features a lunch buffet. Tandoor Restaurant is open Monday through Saturday for lunch and dinner.

East

Taste of India $-$$
1745 Cope Avenue East, Maplewood
(651) 773-5477
www.tasteofindiamn.com

This Taste of India has different ownership than the St. Louis Park location and a slightly different menu. The restaurant features an extensive list of mainly north Indian dishes. Curries and tandoori specialties dominate the menu. The restaurant provides a daily lunch buffet, where diners can sample the flavors of India. Then wash it down with an exotic Indian drink, a beer, or wine. Taste of India serves lunch and dinner daily.

West

Taste of India $-$$
5617 Wayzata Boulevard, St. Louis Park
(952) 541-4865

The Taste of India offers an extensive menu of excellently prepared curries and tandoori (clay-oven) specialties. The Taste of India was one of the first restaurants of its kind in the area. Located in a comfortable strip mall in the suburbs, the restaurant specializes in north Indian cuisine, with treats from throughout the subcontinent thrown in to enthrall the taste buds. The tandoori items are especially tasty. The tandoori shrimp is an incredibly savory item. Large shrimp are covered in the tasty yogurt glaze and spices and then cooked to perfection; the shrimp is moist and packed with flavor. Indian specialty drinks (mango milk shakes, mango lassis, etc.) as well as wines and beers, both imported and domestic, are offered. The restaurant features a daily lunch buffet with one of the largest spreads in the Twin Cities. Taste of India is open daily for lunch and dinner.

IRISH

Kieran's Irish Pub $$
330 Second Avenue South
(Towle Building), Minneapolis
(612) 339-4499
www.kierans.com

Kieran's Irish Pub is a popular place to imbibe in the gaiety of the Emerald Isle. Owner Kieran Folliard satisfies the Twin Cities' love of Irish culture by providing beer, liquor, music, and food. The menu includes such Irish classics as lamb stew and corned beef and cabbage, as well as American favorites like the grilled New York strip. All menu items are influenced by Ireland; even the New York strip has an Irish flair (Irish whiskey sauce). And don't forget to order a Guinness to accompany the fare. Kieran's is especially busy during lunch and happy hour because of the immense downtown Minneapolis worker population. The restaurant is open Monday through Saturday for lunch and dinner.

The Local $-$$
931 Nicollet Mall, Minneapolis
(612) 904-1000
www.the-local.com

The Local is another successful restaurant created by Kieran Folliard. In 1997 Folliard developed an elegant Irish eatery where diners may select either inexpensive or haute cuisine food items. All food is served in a lovely dining room draped with velvet curtains and a charming bar, which is amply stocked with Irish, local, and domestic beers. The menu includes reasonably priced sandwiches and entrees. Among the sandwiches offered are the pot roast beef, chicken breast, and an Irish specialty, corned beef (topped with Swiss cheese). For lighter appetites, diners may choose from a half-dozen salads. Entrees include salmon, sirloin steak, fish-and-chips, and lamb steak. Reservations are recommended. The Local is open Monday through Friday for lunch and dinner. On the weekends, in addition to dinner the Local serves brunch until 2:00 P.M.

ITALIAN
Minneapolis

Auriga $$$
1930 Hennepin Avenue South, Minneapolis
(612) 871-0777
www.aurigarestaurant.com

Exotic cheeses, just-made breads, and European comfort food like sautéed polenta with organic scrambled eggs and baked Parmesan rind are the standbys here. Elegant foods include chestnut-and-duck-egg ravioli with watercress and truffle butter, special treats for special nights. The brief menu, which changes every two or three weeks, offers fish, chicken, beef or pork, game, and vegetarian dishes, including parsley root and porcini mushrooms generously dressing homemade pasta, brown rice and walnut croquettes, portobello mushrooms, and thin parsnip crisps. Deep jewel tones, metallic paints, and Prairie school light fixtures shine up the place, while stripped-to-concrete floors, industrial hardware, and candles lend a monastic simplicity.

Bobino Café and Wine Bar $$-$$$
222 East Hennepin Avenue, Minneapolis
(612) 623-3301
www.bobino.com

Named for the Monte Carlo theater where Josephine Baker last sang, Bobino's is a romantic little spot with citrus-colored walls, warm lighting, alcoves, arches, and artful windows that set the stage for romance. The five or six entrees offered each night might include grilled hanger steak, mussels, and a selection of fresh fish. (The menu changes monthly.) More than 50 wines and 20 tap beers are served here, as well as a half-dozen tapas plates and some really extraordinary desserts, such as champagne-infused vanilla custard poured over fresh fruit and rich chocolate tortes. The Bobino Starlite Lounge (212 East Hennepin Avenue; 612-623-3301), a martini bar, is nearby.

Broders' Cucina Italiana $
2308 West 50th Street, Minneapolis
(612) 925-3113
www.broders.com

Back in the early 1950s, Tom and Molly Broder founded this amazing neighborhood deli that served handmade pastas, imported olive oils, olives, cheese, meats, and other high-quality imported and homemade ingredients. Since then they've added spicy pizzas sold by the slice, sandwiches, take-out homemade pasta sauces, and deli treats from grilled asparagus to homemade cannolis to the menu. And they don't skimp on anything. Standbys include sandwiches such as the Tramezzino (roasted vegetables and feta on homemade focaccia), Genovese (tuna salad with red peppers, Dijon mayonnaise, tomatoes, and greens on French bread), and prosciutto cotto (roasted ham, baby Swiss cheese, and greens on focaccia). The deli serves a full range of desserts, including triple-chocolate cheesecake and tiramisu.

Broders' Southside Pasta Bar $$
5000 Penn Avenue South, Minneapolis
(612) 925-9202
www.broders.com

Made by hand by the excellent chefs at Broders', the different styles of pasta served here are all amazingly tender and rich, complemented by sauces and toppings that range from fresh Prince Edward Island mussels paired with beautiful, wine-soaked wild mushrooms to broiled fish and fresh herbs. It's about as far away from ordinary spaghetti as you can get, and for a price that's more than reasonable, especially for the quality of food Broders' serves. The one drawback is the no-reservation policy, and mere minutes after the doors open for dinner (generally 5:00 P.M.), the place is packed. In summer guests can sip drinks on the modest outdoor patio while waiting for a seat, but in winter latecomers will more than likely be left out in the cold.

Buca di Beppo $$
1204 Harmon Place, Minneapolis
(612) 288-0138

7711 Mitchell Road, Eden Prairie
(952) 934-9463

2728 Gannon Road, St. Paul
(651) 772-4388

14300 Burnhaven Drive, Burnsville
(952) 892-7272

12650 Elm Creek Boulevard,
Maple Grove
(763) 494-3466
www.bucadibeppo.com

Now a national chain, the first Buca di
Beppo opened in a charming basement in
Minneapolis—hence, the restaurant's
name, which means Joe's basement in
Italian. The southern Italian family-style
restaurant has become a popular place for
Twin Citians to celebrate. Diners order
immense portions of Italian favorites from
a chalkboard. The family-style meals are
best enjoyed with large groups so that
more items can be ordered and shared.
Menu items are ordered a la carte and
include numerous appetizers, salads, piz-
zas, pastas, and side dishes. All menu
items are enormous. A few standouts
include chicken marsala, chicken caccia-
tore, pizzas, and much more. The pasta
choices are extensive and include stan-
dards ranging from spaghetti marinara to
linguini *frutti di mare,* a combination of
mussels, clams, and calamari. In addition,
the restaurant serves a large selection of
wines. Reservations are accepted at all
area Buca di Beppos. The Minneapolis
Buca is open for dinner seven days a
week. On Saturday and Sunday the
restaurant opens at noon.

Campiello $$$
1320 West Lake Street, Minneapolis
(612) 825-2222

6411 City West Parkway, Eden Prairie
(952) 941-6868

Campiello is a great place to impress a

date. The smart lighting makes everyone
look fabulous, and the stunning presenta-
tions make everyone look like a big
spender without breaking the bank.
Campiello is high class without being
snobby, as is the waitstaff. Bond in his
tuxedo might feel a little overdressed, but
everyone else, from the blue jeaned to the
all in black, fits right in. On the menu the
crackly thin-crusted pizzas make for stunning appetizers, the salads are solid, and
the entrees (especially the pastas and the
rotisserie meats) are absolutely top
drawer.

D'Amico & Sons $
2210 Hennepin Avenue South,
Minneapolis
(612) 374-1858
www.damico.com
11 additional Twin Cities locations

D'Amico & Sons specializes in high-quality
deli fare for casual eating in or as take-
out. Where the D'Amico Cucina serves
upscale cuisine, this restaurant creates
delicious, reasonably priced items. The
restaurant features salads, pastas, pizza,
and sandwiches prepared with fresh
ingredients. Beers and wines are available.
D'Amico has the classiest and highest
quality casual dining in the Twin Cities.
D'Amico & Sons (Hennepin Avenue) is
open Monday through Sunday for lunch
and dinner.

D'Amico Cucina $$$
100 North Sixth Street, Minneapolis
(612) 338-2401
www.damico.com

The D'Amicos own restaurants through-
out the Twin Cities. The D'Amico Cucina
is their fine Italian dining restaurant. The
restaurant prepares some of the best
northern Italian cuisine in the area. For
wine lovers, the restaurant has a spec-
tacular wine list of vintages found
nowhere else in Minneapolis. D'Amico
Cucina is open Monday through Saturday
for dinner only. Reservations are highly
recommended.

Davanni's Pizza & Hot Hoagies $
2500 Riverside Avenue, Minneapolis
(612) 332-5551
www.davannis.com
17 additional Twin Cities locations

Since 1975 Davanni's has been one of the Twin Cities' favorite places for pizza and hot hoagies. The casual restaurant is a great place for students and families to enjoy one of the many delicious menu items. Diners have an option of three crust types: traditional, thin, and Chicago deep dish. The deep dish is especially tasty. The thick light crust is topped with a tangy tomato sauce, and the toppings and cheese are always fresh. Other popular menu items are the almost 20 hoagies, including salami, turkey, roast beef, meatball, pizza, and tuna. Delivery is also an important part of business—Davanni's is almost annually named the best take-out and pizza delivery in the Twin Cities.

Fat Lorenzo's $
5600 Cedar Avenue South, Minneapolis
(612) 822-2040
www.fatlorenzos.com

A southside neighborhood institution, Fat Lorenzo's tables are covered with white butcher paper for customers to doodle on with supplied crayons while they wait for their pizzas to show up. The menu features New York–style pizza and Italian specialties such as lasagna, baked rigatoni, spaghetti, and chicken cacciatore. Hot and cold hoagies (including meatball, turkey, and roast beef) round off the menu nicely.

Figlio Restaurant and Bar $$
3001 Hennepin Avenue, Minneapolis
(612) 822-1688
www.figlio.com

Located inside the Calhoun Square mall, this is where the wealthy, hip young crowd comes to drink and hold power lunches. Figlio's servings are generous, and the specialty dishes are absolutely decadent. Its seafood and pasta dishes are excellent, and its desserts have won numerous awards throughout the Twin Cities. The Death by Chocolate concoction is especially wonderful: layers of soft chocolate molded around a chocolate torte filled with chocolate mousse and drenched in warm chocolate sauce. You may want to call ahead for a reservation on weekend nights or holidays—this place fills up fast. Serving a full menu until 1:00 A.M. during the week and until 2:00 A.M. on Friday and Saturday nights, Figlio is a popular stop for patrons fresh from the bars and clubs of Uptown.

Golooney's East Coast Pizza $
2329 Hennepin Avenue, Minneapolis
(612) 377-8555

New York–style pizza shops are frequently imitated in the Twin Cities, but Golooney's East Coast Pizza is one of the best. The pizza is thick and cheesy with a fresh, piquant tomato sauce and a variety of delicious toppings. An important part of the restaurant's business is pizza by the slice, which serves the hungry, young, and hip Uptown neighborhood. For thrifty diners lunch specials are offered as well as take-out service. The menu also includes salads, sub sandwiches, and pitas. Golooney's is open daily for lunch and dinner.

Green Mill $-$$
2626 Hennepin Avenue, Minneapolis
(612) 374-2131
11 additional Twin Cities locations

Since 1976 the Green Mill has been one of the Twin Cities' favorite places for pizza. Since then the Green Mill has opened 30 franchises in four states and expanded the scope of its menu to include pasta, calzones, sandwiches, fish, fowl, and much more. The pizza remains the standout and the restaurant's best value. Green Mill offers flat, deep-dish, *pescara*, and numerous specialty pizzas.

Pane Vino Dolce $$-$$$
819 West 50th Street, Minneapolis
(612) 825-3201

Pane Vino Dolce offers fine Italian cuisine in a small, busy dining room. The menu includes small pizzas, risotto, ravioli, and seafood. All are prepared with fresh ingredients, and great attention is paid to presentation. Daily specials are offered. The restaurant is open daily for dinner. Pane Vino Dolce does not accept credit cards.

Pizza Lucé $-$$
119 North Fourth Street, Minneapolis
(612) 333-7359

3200 Lyndale Avenue South, Minneapolis
(612) 827-5978

2200 East Franklin Avenue, Minneapolis
(612) 332-2535
www.pizzaluce.com
Pizza Lucé specializes in, well, pizza, and many Twin Citians consider the restaurant's pies the best in town. Including the classic taste of the Lucé, which is made of Italian sausage, onions, garlic, and extra cheese, there are many gourmet pizza choices, such as the barbecue chicken and the luau (Canadian bacon, pineapple, green onions, and mozzarella). And if the large selection of gourmet pizzas doesn't meet your needs, then build your own pizza. The menu of more than 50 fresh ingredients includes meats, seafood, vegetables, and eight cheeses. In addition to pizza, the restaurant serves hoagies, spaghetti, lasagna, *mostaccioli,* and several vegetarian and vegan dishes. The Lyndale location serves beer and wine; the downtown and East Franklin locations have full bars.

All restaurants are open late, making Pizza Lucé a popular post-bartime nosh spot for the downtown club crowd.

Zelo $$$-$$$$
831 Nicollet Mall, Minneapolis
(612) 333-7000
This splashy restaurant is doing everything right to please couples in search of a memorable date, combining impeccable services with an accessible menu and a nicely focused wine list. Daily fish specials are the highlight, such as flaky walleye Milanese with a golden crown of Italian bread crumbs or a lusciously rare grilled ahi tuna moistened with Chinese mustard

Green Mill has expanded throughout the Twin Cities and to some others cities in the Midwest. The pizza parlor and brewpub serves up some of the tastiest pizza pie in the Metro. TODD R. BERGER

vinaigrette and served with green wasabi mashed potatoes. The next best thing to the fish is the *filettini*—delicate, pounded pork tenderloin slices in green peppercorn-cream-brandy sauce. Steaks, veal chops, and lemon-herb chicken round out the entrees, while commendable pizzas and pastas present more economical options. Their most popular dessert is their incredible tiramisu layered with mascarpone.

St. Paul

Carmelo's $$
238 South Snelling Avenue, St. Paul
(651) 699-2448
Carmelo's is a small, intimate Italian restaurant near the intersection of Snelling

and St. Clair Avenues in St. Paul's Mac-Groveland neighborhood. The busy, family-run restaurant is a nice choice for a romantic evening, with a hand-picked selection of wines and beers to complement such made-from-scratch dishes as chicken carmelo, seafood canneloni, and spinach and cheese ravioli. The restaurant is open for lunch Tuesday through Friday and dinner Monday through Saturday. If you can't find a parking place out front, park in the lot next to Sweeney Cleaners at the intersection of Snelling and St. Clair. Reservations are highly recommended for dinner, especially on the weekend.

Cossetta Italian Market & Pizzeria $
211 West Seventh Street, St. Paul
(651) 222-3476

Cossetta's is one of the busiest lunch spots in St. Paul. It draws throngs of patrons because of the fine pizzas and pastas prepared for eating in or take-out. The Chicago-style pizza is some of the best in the Twin Cities. The delicious chewy thick crust is topped with a piquant marinara sauce and tasty mozzarella and fresh ingredients. Huge pieces of pizza are ready to eat at the counter. Another counter offers lasagna, sausage and peppers, chicken marsala, sausage calabrase, chicken cacciatore, and more a la carte items. Ample seating is provided on two floors, where recordings by Italian-American singers such as Tony Bennett and Frank Sinatra are played over the sound system. A wine list is available for those who enjoy imbibing with their meals. Michael and Irene Cossetta opened the adjoining market in 1911, where the now-sprawling market and restaurant began. Today Cossetta's does booming business for lunch and dinner daily and looks to expand in the wake of the Xcel Energy Center just down the street.

Dari-ette Drive Inn $
1440 Minnehaha Avenue, St. Paul
(651) 776-3470

Not much to look at from the outside, this small drive-in Italian restaurant carries a huge selection of dishes you can eat right in your car. The menu includes wonderful, thick meatball, sausage, and pizza sandwiches (for a little extra, you can order peppers, onions, or mushrooms to go on the sandwich); hamburgers; Coney dogs; and fried shrimp baskets. The sandwiches come with either french fries or spaghetti on the side—we recommend getting the spaghetti because it is good, although a little messy to eat in the car. For dessert, there are ice-cream shakes, malts, sundaes, and excellent, cheap banana splits.

Luci Ancora $$-$$$
2060 Randolph Avenue, St. Paul
(651) 698-6889
www.ristoranteluci.com

Luci Ancora is another restaurant from the husband-and-wife team of Al and Lucille Smith and their large family. Luci Ancora has been influenced by the trend toward minimalist preparation and organic ingredients. The menu is brief, but all dishes are well executed. Each evening a four-course *prezzo fisso* meal is offered, which includes antipasto, soup or salad, pasta, and fish. In addition, wine and delicious desserts are offered. Call ahead for reservations. Luci Ancora is open for lunch and dinner Tuesday through Friday and for dinner only on Saturday, Sunday, and Monday.

Paisano's Pizza & Hot Hoagies $
619 Selby Avenue, St. Paul
(651) 224-3350

Paisano's deep-dish pizza is sold by the slice as well as in large, medium, and "solo" sizes. There are several specialty pizzas, which include the Classic, pepperoni, sausage, mushrooms, green peppers, and onions; the Tuscan, white sauce, Canadian bacon, red onion, fresh basil, and sun-dried tomatoes; and the Mediterranean, sun-dried tomatoes, artichoke hearts, feta cheese, Kalamata olives, and fresh spinach. There are a couple more specialty pies as well as 24 toppings to build a pizza to your liking. In addition, there are eight varieties of cold and hot hoagies. For the health conscious, house, classic Caesar, and Mediterranean salads are available. Paisano's is open seven days a week for lunch and dinner.

Pazzaluna Urban Trattoria and Bar $$$
360 St. Peter Street, St. Paul
(651) 223-7000
www.pazzaluna.com
Pazzaluna serves upscale regional Italian cuisine in downtown St. Paul. Specialties of the house include risotto alla Milanese, gnocchi alla Bolognese, *medalione di manzo,* and *carpaccio di manzo* alla Piemontese. A full bar features many Italian wines and several varieties of grappa, as well as single-malt scotches and numerous cordials. The elegant bar has a happy hour from 4:00 to 6:00 P.M. and 9:00 to 10:00 P.M. Monday through Friday. Reservations are recommended, and valet parking is available for bar and restaurant patrons.

Punch Neapolitan Pizza $$
704 Cleveland Avenue South, St. Paul
(651) 696-1066

8353 Crystal View Road, Eden Prairie
(952) 943-9557

3226 West Lake Street, Minneapolis
(612) 929-0006
Punch takes its plate-sized Neapolitan pizzas very seriously. Since the restaurant opened its first location, in St. Paul, in 1996, it has been a member of the Associazione Vera Pizza Napoletana, an Italian organization that regulates pizza purity. Since Punch's inception, owner John Soranno has adhered to the organization's guidelines requiring only the highest quality ingredients and methods. The result is an outstanding pizza. All pizzas are thin crusted and vary only in their high-quality toppings, such as the Puttanesca, which includes anchovies, capers, olives, onions, and oregano. With more than 20 pizzas, the choices are almost endless. Calzones and salads are other options on the menu. A wine list is also provided. Punch is open

Tuesday through Saturday for dinner.

Red's Savoy Pizza $
421 East Seventh Street, St. Paul
(651) 227-1437
Red's offers an excellent rendition of flat-crust pizza. The pizza has a zippy sauce and fresh cheese and ingredients. Diners may select from popular pizzas, such as pepperoni and sausage, or atypical pies, such as the tomato, bacon, and pickle. The pizzas are inexpensive, and they are available in regular or large. In addition, the restaurant serves burgers and several pastas. Another bonus at Red's is the dark and interesting ambience of the restaurant/bar, which feels like a movie gangster hangout.

Ristorante Luci $$-$$$
470 Cleveland Avenue South, St. Paul
(651) 699-8258
www.ristoranteluci.com
Ristorante Luci serves spectacular classical Italian cuisine in a modestly decorated location. The restaurant is owned by the Smith family, Al and Lucille, who own another nearby restaurant, Luci Ancora. The restaurant specializes in pastas and seafood, which are prepared to perfection. This is one of the reasons the neighborhood restaurant is a perennial favorite. Another is the wine list and the excellent desserts. Reservations are recommended. Ristorante Luci is open for dinner Tuesday, and Thursday through Sunday.

West

Daniel's Italian Restaurant $$
3220 West 70th Street (Galleria Mall), Edina
(952) 920-3338
Daniel's Italian Restaurant serves fine foods in the luxurious Galleria Mall in Edina. Of course, pasta is a featured menu choice as well as several seafood and veal dishes. Menu items include tortellini,

chicken parmigiana, and salmon lasagna. Plenty of free parking is available in the Galleria's parking lot. Daniel's is open for lunch and dinner.

Vescio's Italian Restaurant   **$-$$**
4001 Minnesota Highway 7,
St. Louis Park
(952) 920-0733

406 14th Avenue SE, Minneapolis
(612) 378-1747

Vescio's is a traditional place for Twin Citians to enjoy Italian food and more. The restaurant serves ravioli, rigatoni, tortellini, fettuccine, and spaghetti as well as sandwiches. The sandwiches are Italian-inspired creations that include the Big Boy Italiano (various meats and cheeses on French loaf) and sweet fried pepper sandwich. And don't forget Vescio's pizza. The pizzas are available in small and large and include one notable specialty: Sid's Special Pizza is topped with sausage, mushrooms, pepperoni, sweet fried peppers, extra cheese, and special seasoning and is named after longtime Minneapolis Star-Tribune sports columnist Sid Hartman, who often frequents the restaurant. The restaurant also goes out of its way to accommodate special diets. There are sections dedicated to diet dining, vegetarian selections, and a children's menu.

JAPANESE

Minneapolis

Fuji Ya Japanese Restaurant   **$$-$$$**
600 West Lake Street, Minneapolis
(612) 871-4055

465 Wabasha Street North, St. Paul
(651) 310-0111
www.sushicontrol.com

Fuji Ya is located in the Lyn-Lake neighborhood of south Minneapolis. It is the fourth location in the long history of the restaurant, which first opened its doors in downtown Minneapolis in 1959. A new St.

Paul location opened in 2005. Fuji Ya offers a wide array of Japanese food in all price ranges. For lunch, the restaurant's noodle soups as well as more expensive items are available, and there is also a sushi bar to satisfy lovers of the Japanese delicacy. Dinner specialties include shrimp tempura, sukiyaki and chicken teriyaki. Fuji Ya has an extensive list of beers and wines. In Minneapolis, lunch is served Tuesday through Friday; dinner is provided Tuesday through Sunday. Reservations are recommended.

Kikugawa   **$$-$$$**
43 Main Street SE, Minneapolis
(612) 378-3006

The best seats in the house are in the Kikugawa atrium, from which restaurant patrons can look out over the Mississippi and beyond to the Minneapolis downtown skyline. Inside, the lighting is romantically dim, reflecting off the large gold-leaf fans decorating the walls. The sukiyaki (a simmered beef dish) is the best in town, and the restaurant also offers a large selection of sushi and pickled vegetable appetizers. To drink, there are Japanese beers and flavored sakes to choose from. At night (if you're lucky) drinking businessmen and big-spending hipsters take turns at the karaoke machine, belting out hits from the '60s on up.

Koyi Sushi   **$-$$**
122 North Fourth Street, Minneapolis
(612) 375-9811

Koyi Sushi serves fresh sushi at some of the best prices in town, with some very tasty renditions. Some of the more popular choices include the Dynamite Roll (spicy salmon and yellowtail), the Dragon Roll (cooked tuna, *masago*, and spicy mayo topped with *unagi* and avocado), and the Marilyn Monroll (grilled chicken, asparagus, and avocado). Koyi offers sushi a la carte (two pieces per serving), as well as small and large rolls. Nonsushi offerings include *kalbee* (marinated and grilled beef ribs served with Korean vegetables) and seafood tempura. The restaurant is open daily for dinner.

St. Paul

Sakura Restaurant and Sushi Bar $-$$$$
350 St. Peter Street, St. Paul
(651) 224-0185

The price range speaks loudly about the possibilities at this fine downtown St. Paul restaurant. For novices to Japanese cuisine or those who are strapped for funds, lunch provides several options for under $10. The menu is divided into tempura, teriyaki, *donburi*, noodles, salads, and of course, sushi. Sushi is the most important menu item—although there are many other standouts from the rest of the large menu.

The sushi bar is prominently placed at the center of a large open room. With more than 30 types of the freshest sushi in town, connoisseurs have plenty of choices. The sushi bar offers California rolls, salmon egg, shrimp, crab, albacore tuna, scallop, and sea eel; all are beautifully presented. The restaurant has a relaxed atmosphere and lacks the snobbishness of some other Japanese restaurants. Servers are happy to help patrons navigate the menu. The excellent service resonates from owner Miyoko Omori, who frequently greets and seats customers. Reservations are recommended for dinner, which is offered late on Friday and Saturday. Sakura is open daily for both lunch and dinner.

Tanpopo Noodle Shop $
308 Prince Street, St. Paul
(651) 209-6527
www.tanpoporestaurant.com

There are numerous Vietnamese noodle shops in the area but few Japanese restaurants specializing in the fine delicacy. The act of making noodles is elevated to an art at Tanpopo. The menu changes seasonally, and the restaurant concentrates on a concise, inexpensive, well-executed menu for lunch and dinner composed of various *udon* (wheat flour noodles) and soba (buckwheat flour noodles) as well as *teishoku* (set meals). The Nabayaki Udon is one superb selection, which includes shrimp tempura, chicken, mushrooms, vegetables, and fish cake. There is also a vegetarian item, the *tanpopo tofu teishoku*. For dessert, try the tempura as well as green tea ice cream. The noodle shop is a beautiful renovated warehouse space in St. Paul's lower arts district. Tanpopo is open for lunch Tuesday through Saturday and dinner Monday through Saturday.

KOREAN
St. Paul

Mirror of Korea $-$$
761 Snelling Avenue North, St. Paul
(651) 647-9004

Snelling Avenue has several Korean restaurants. The Mirror of Korea was one of the first of its kind on the block. The restaurant moved into a building previously occupied by a pizza and sandwich shop. Its large menu belies the humbly decorated restaurant. Soups, stir-fries, and stews fill out the menu. One excellent dish is the *chop chae,* a traditional Korean dish of beef, vegetables, and rice noodles. There are also more exotic dishes, like the *yook hwae* (raw beef). The restaurant also offers Korean lunch specials. Mirror of Korea is open for lunch and dinner daily, except on Tuesday when the restaurant is closed.

Shilla Korean Restaurant $-$$
694 Snelling Avenue North, St. Paul
(651) 645-0006

Shilla Korean Restaurant is much larger than its neighbor, Mirror of Korea, just down the avenue, but both share many of the same menu items. The restaurant is a combination of '70s decor accented with Korean motifs and serves as the meeting place for many activities in the local

Korean community. The menu is extensive and includes all of your Korean favorites. A few standout dishes are *bi bim bop* (vegetable salad with a boiled egg) and *man do* (pork and vegetable dumplings). Bargain hunters will be happy to hear that the restaurant offers several lunch specials. Take-out is also available. Shilla is open Tuesday through Sunday for lunch and dinner and does not accept reservations.

Sole Café $–$$
684 Snelling Avenue North, St. Paul
(651) 644-2068

In an area with two additional Korean restaurants within walking distance, this restaurant is certainly the most authentic and arguably the best. The Sole Café is a friendly mom-and-pop operation, with usually one server for several tables. Despite this potential problem, the servers manage to be friendly and attentive to the needs of diners. The decor is a comfortable dining room with Korean motifs and a large bar at the front of the restaurant. Unlike its neighboring Korean restaurants, the menu is not extensive. It is, however, remarkably well executed. The menu includes traditional Korean favorites, such as *bulgogi* (the spicy Korean version of barbecue), *kim chi* soup, and *chop chae,* as well as less familiar items for American diners. The chop chae is an outstanding dish of tender beef and cellophane noodles, mushrooms, thinly sliced carrots, lemongrass, scallions, onions, and mild peppers. Soups and seafood are also prominent menu items, such as the *tae chee gae,* a swordfish soup with vegetables, and grilled salt adka fish. Sole Café is closed on Wednesday but open Thursday through Tuesday for lunch and dinner.

South

Hoban $
1989 Silver Bell Road, Eagan
(651) 688-3447

Hoban serves Korean dishes from its

southeast suburban location in an Eagan strip mall. The casual, small restaurant specializes in favorites such as dolsot *bi bim bop* (steamed vegetables over rice) and *kalbee* (thinly sliced marinated beef ribs that are grilled). The restaurant serves beer and wine and is open for lunch and dinner Tuesday through Sunday. The restaurant accepts Visa and MasterCard only.

KURDISH

Babani's Kurdish Restaurant $
544 St. Peter Street, St. Paul
(651) 602-9964

Babani's Kurdish is the first restaurant of its kind in the United States. The beautiful building on the outskirts of downtown St. Paul is decorated with Kurdish designs on rugs, pictures, and green curtains. The Kurds are a people without a national homeland, who live today in Iran, Iraq, Syria, and Turkey. A small population of Kurds resides in the Twin Cities. The restaurant provides an excellent opportunity to learn about Kurdish culture and cuisine. The servers are attentive and eager to answer questions regarding Kurdish food, which includes heavy influences of Middle Eastern, Indian, and Mediterranean cuisine. Chicken *tawa*, a sautéed chicken in lemon with vegetables over rice, is an excellent choice. The *biryani* (rice with almonds, raisins, vegetables, and spices) is also excellent and quite similar to the Indian dish of the same name. In total there are almost a dozen entrees for dinner on the menu, and each is served with a choice of soup or salad. Lunches are smaller and less expensive versions of dinner. Babani's serves lunch Monday through Friday and is open for dinner seven days a week.

LATIN AMERICAN

Conga Latin Bistro $$–$$$
501 East Hennepin Avenue, Minneapolis
(612) 331-3360

Latin American cuisine has experienced a tremendous boom in the Twin Cities. Several trendy Latin restaurants have opened, but few have the pedigree of Conga. The owners of Conga, the Thunstrom family, are also responsible for the perennially popular south Minneapolis Latin restaurant, El Meson. The nuevo Latino menu features a couple of paellas, the popular Spanish rice and seafood dish, as well as a wide selection of chicken, pork, beef, and seafood items. Other choices include the seafood casserole and Jamaican chicken. The beer and wine list is extensive, and there is also ample opportunity for dancing.

Machu Picchu   **$$-$$$**
2940 Lyndale Avenue South, Minneapolis
(612) 822-2125
Machu Picchu is a Peruvian restaurant that specializes in Latin seafood. Located in the heart of the Lyn-Lake neighborhood, an area overflowing with shopping, theaters, and coffee shops, the restaurant attracts a hip crowd looking for an exotic dining experience. *Arroz con mariscos* is a featured entree, and the Peruvian paella, which is composed of saffron rice studded with shrimp, clams, squid, mussels, and crab legs, is among the best seafood dishes in the Twin Cities. There are several additional seafood items, including specialty seafood soups. The *parihuela* includes shrimp, halibut, squid, clams, mussels, and crab legs in a spicy broth. Machu Picchu is open for dinner Tuesday through Saturday.

MEXICAN

Minneapolis

Chiapas Restaurant   **$**
2416 Central Avenue NE, Minneapolis
(612) 789-2971
Chiapas Restaurant serves authentic Mexican food in northeast Minneapolis. Silverio Perez, who also owns the Pancho Villa

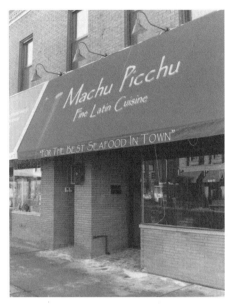

Machu Picchu in the Lyn-Lake neighborhood of south Minneapolis. TODD R. BERGER

restaurant in south Minneapolis, operates this 50-seat eatery. The restaurant specialties include chile relleno, enchiladas, and fajitas. Also featured are several vegetarian items. Chiapas is open daily for late breakfast, lunch, and dinner.

Chino Latino   **$$$**
2916 Hennepin Avenue South, Minneapolis
(612) 824-7878
www.chinolatino.com
Chino Latino is a chic hangout with a menu influenced by the food of Asia and Latin barrios. The food is often delicious and sometimes, well, interesting, such as one that caught the eyes of local animal lovers—guinea pig.

El Mariachi Restaurant   **$**
2750 Nicollet Avenue South, Minneapolis
(612) 871-5200
El Mariachi serves up a terrific *carne asada,* marinated with lots of lime and grilled to a chewy, charred perfection. They also make

a wonderful *puerco* en salsa verda with citrus-rich tomatillo sauce and delicious tacos filled with pork, chicken, or beef cooked in a variety of ways with homemade tortillas. Friday, Saturday, and Sunday nights you can listen to live mariachi music while you eat. On Friday night between 9:00 and 10:00, uninhibited customers can get up and sing with the musicians.

Me Gusta Mexican Cuisine $-$$
1507 East Lake Street, Minneapolis
(612) 724-6007

Me Gusta Mexican Cuisine is a Minneapolis favorite. For decades it has satisfied Twin Citians' needs for authentic Mexican cuisine. Today, there are numerous authentic Mexican restaurants in the area, but not that long ago Me Gusta was an oasis in a sea of bland, tasteless pseudo-Mexican eateries. The restaurant has introduced many Twin Citians to the savory tastes of Mexico.

Diners receive a complimentary bowl of homemade chips and salsa. Like the rest of the menu, the chips are fresh and the salsa is spicy. Then satisfy your thirst with Mexican beer, wine, or Jarritos, a sweet Mexican soda. The *comidas* (dinners) are large and are accompanied by refried beans, rice, and lettuce and tomatoes. The menu includes several burrito, fajita, and enchilada dinners and, for more adventurous diners, *nopales asados* (grilled cactus), the chile relleno, or the enchildas en mole. Several seafood items have recently been added to the menu. Me Gusta is open daily for lunch and dinner.

Pepito's Mexi-Go Deli $
4624 Nicollet Avenue South,
Minneapolis
(612) 825-6311

At a completely different, sister restaurant, Pepito's owner, Joe Senkyr, played actor Christian Slater's boss in the movie *Untamed Heart*. In reality Senkyr's small local chain of Mexican restaurants and delis carries an amazing selection of Mexican foods at reasonable prices, including vegetarian enchiladas and tacos, Azteca sandwiches served on *teleta*-style Mexican bread, huge nacho plates, and quesadillas made with homemade tortillas, all of which are excellent when topped with one of the six fresh-made salsas offered at the salad table. You can also take home buckets of prepared ground beef, grilled chicken, bags of homemade corn chips and tortillas, and lots of side dishes and sauces to use at your next get-together.

Taco Morelos $
1515 East Lake Street, Minneapolis
(612) 728-5437
Two additional Twin Cities locations

Taco Morelos serves authentic Mexican cuisine just around the corner from Eat Street. In an area of Minneapolis with numerous authentic Mexican restaurants, Taco Morelos was among the first. The restaurant features tacos, tamales, fajitas, enchiladas, burritos and all the Mexican standards. Wine and beer are offered at this comfortable and casual restaurant. The restaurant is open daily for lunch and dinner.

Tacqueria Don Blas $-$$
3764 Nicollet Avenue, Minneapolis
(612) 825-5410

Tacqueria Don Blas serves authentic Mexican food in a homey atmosphere. The service is often slow, and the ambience is nothing to write home about, but the food is inexpensive and wholesome. The menu features *tortas* (Mexican sandwiches), soups, combination platters, and a few seafood items. A lunch buffet is also served and provides an overview of some of the house specialties. Several types of meat are served with rice and beans. Delicious fresh tortillas are also included. The chicken mole is especially tasty. Quesadillas, tamales, and soup are available for a cheap and less filling lunch.

St. Paul

El Burrito Mercado $
175 Cesar Chavez Street, St. Paul
(651) 227-2192
www.elburritomercado.com

St. Paul's West Side is a historically diverse neighborhood and one of the first Chicano settlements in the Twin Cities. In this enclave there is a large Mexican grocery, bakery, and the cafeteria-style restaurant, El Burrito Mercado. Tucked in the back of the complex, it does astounding business by serving excellent Mexican food at reasonable prices. Get in line and make a selection from the menu, which features *tortas*, quesadillas, tamales, tacos, and burritos. After a shorter wait than at many fast-food restaurants, take a seat and enjoy a fine Mexican meal. El Burrito Mercado also serves breakfast, and don't forget to visit the bakery and grocery.

MIDDLE EASTERN
Minneapolis

Caspian Bistro & Marketplace $$
2418 University Avenue SE, Minneapolis
(612) 623-1113
The Caspian Bistro serves the best kabobs in the Twin Cities. The kabob options include beef, chicken, and lamb accompanied by basmati rice and salad. The menu also includes Middle Eastern treats such as gyro and lamb shank. Since 1986 the restaurant has served the nearby University of Minnesota with scrumptious Persian foods. The adjoining marketplace allows diners to purchase ethnic groceries for home. The 60-seat restaurant is open for lunch and dinner Tuesday through Saturday.

Falafel King $
701 West Lake Street, Minneapolis
(612) 824-7887
One additional Twin Cities location
The Falafel King provides Middle Eastern foods in a casual atmosphere. From the counter, diners may select from numerous appetizers, salads, sandwiches, combinations, and dinner entrees. Middle Eastern favorites such as kabobs, hummus, and falafel are served. Fettuccine Alfredo, chicken *shish tawk* (grilled chicken and

vegetables), and *foule muddammas* (Egyptian fava bean dip) are also featured. The restaurant serves omelets, and Greek and Middle Eastern–style breakfasts. The Falafel King is open daily and offers lunch and dinner buffets.

Holy Land Bakery, Grocery & Deli $
2513 Central Avenue NE, Minneapolis
(612) 781-2627
Holy Land is not only one of the best ethnic markets in the area, it also serves enormous portions of outstanding Middle Eastern cuisine on a disposable plate. The choices include kabobs, falafel, hummus, spinach pie, *shawarma* (gyro), and much more. The menu offers large pita sandwiches and much larger dinners, which generally include a salad and rice or hummus paired with one of several meats (shawarma, kabobs, combinations, etc.) and a basket of fresh pita. Select a self-service drink, and there will be plenty of leftovers for less than $10. The shawarma platter is colossal. Plus there are sampler plates of Middle Eastern cuisine as well as vegetarian meals. On request the deli offers halal meals to meet the dietary needs of Muslims. Holy Land does not serve alcohol. The busy restaurant provides seating beside the deli and grocery and has additional seating on the second floor. The Holy Land is open daily for lunch and dinner.

Jerusalem's $-$$
1518 Nicollet Avenue South, Minneapolis
(612) 871-8883
Jerusalem's, a perennial Best of the Twin Cities winner among readers of *City Pages,* dishes up the flavors and ambience of the Middle East in a surprisingly intimate atmosphere. The restaurant is

---

Are you looking for a unique ethnic meal? Try Babani's Kurdish Restaurant in St. Paul. It is the first restaurant to serve Kurdish food in the nation.

---

topped by a mosquelike onion dome, and stepping inside the otherwise unassuming building on Nicollet Avenue just before the bridge over Interstate 94 will transport you to another world filled with exotic spices, sights, and sounds.

Jerusalem's serves a pan–Middle Eastern menu. Lovers of hummus, kibbe (bulgur, beef, onion, and pine nuts), and stuffed grape leaves will find plenty of choices to satisfy their taste buds. Entrees include *shawarma* (thin slices of spiced beef and lamb), spinach pie, chicken shish kebab, and the lamb curry dinner. Many of the dinner dishes are available in smaller plate or sandwich form for lunchtime diners and take-out.

Desserts are simple but tasty, including baklava and *krima*. Do not leave the table without a demitasse of Turkish coffee; the restaurant serves a just-sweet-enough version with a floating cardamom seed that is perhaps the best this side of Ankara.

If your schedule allows, come to Jerusalem's on a Friday or Saturday night, when belly dancing wiggles on stage and through the dining room, although be sure to call ahead for reservations; the small restaurant is often packed on those nights. The sword dance is a crowd pleaser, and don't be shy about sticking a few bucks in the elastic bands on the dancer's costume when she shimmies by your table. You'll get a big smile and a few extra wiggles in return.

The Signature Café $-$$
130 Warwick Street SE, Minneapolis
(612) 378-0237
If you are looking for Egyptian cuisine, you'll find it in an unexpected area in Minneapolis. The Signature Café is located in the ritzy Prospect Park neighborhood, where it sits in the middle of a residential block. The cafe's exterior suggests the successions of diners that once occupied this lovely spot. Egyptian music and decorations greet patrons upon entering, and the aromas of the kitchen fill the air. The

menu is divided into several sections ranging from lighter fare—salads, soups, and sandwiches—to Egyptian main courses. Also featured are a couple of pasta selections. The options include *kofta,* falafel, and *shawarma*. Vegetarians are in luck at the cafe, where almost half the menu satisfies their dietary needs. *Koshary,* an Egyptian comfort food, is included and is made of garbanzo beans, fried onions, lentils, and tomato sauce served over rice. In addition, there are a few children's menu items. And don't forget the selection of desserts and Egyptian drinks. The Signature Café is open Monday through Saturday for lunch and dinner.

Sinbad Café & Market $-$$
2528 Nicollet Avenue, Minneapolis
(612) 871-6505
Sinbad Café & Market is a Middle Eastern grocery store and restaurant. Food may be ordered for take-out or eaten in the comfortable sit-down restaurant. The menu includes falafel, spinach pie, gyro, and most Middle Eastern favorites, as well as Moroccan couscous. The restaurant also features Turkish coffee, mango drink, hibiscus drink, baklava, and several more dessert and beverage options.

Trieste Café $
10 South Fifth Street, Minneapolis
(612) 333-4658
Trieste Café is an international eatery with flair. The beverage list is extensive, with several types of coffee, lemonade, mineral waters, malts, and shakes. The menu also has hot hoagies, subs, international favorites, and salads. The international favorites are where the Trieste Café shines. The gyro is of particular note and recognized by many as one of the best in the Twin Cities. Other international items include hummus, falafel, spanakopita, and tabbouleh salad. The Trieste Café occupies a small, cramped space on the ground floor of the historic Lumber Exchange building and is open from breakfast until 6:00 P.M. on weekdays. Hurry over before the end of

rush hour, when the Trieste's doors close, and enjoy one of the best gyros in town.

North

El Bustan $-$$
4757 Central Avenue NE, Columbia Heights
(763) 502-8888
As the Twin Cities Middle Eastern population has grown, restaurants like El Bustan have appeared to meet the needs of this burgeoning community. The Columbia Heights restaurant features halal foods (in accordance with Islamic dietary laws), no alcohol, and a *shisha*, a traditional water pipe. The menu is an extensive survey of Middle Eastern standards and includes delicious hummus, kabobs, and shrimp *sayyadiya*. The latter dish is a spicy combination of shrimp in tomato sauce served over a bed of rice. El Bustan is open daily and accepts Visa and MasterCard.

The Olive Tree Restaurant and Market $
3700 Central Avenue NE, Columbia Heights
(763) 782-9900
The Olive Tree offers Middle Eastern fare at rock-bottom prices. Two people can easily eat a filling lunch for less than $10. The menu is composed of salads, appetizers, sandwiches, and entrees. It ranges from Middle Eastern favorites like *shawarma*, kabobs, and falafel to lamb chops and chicken *musahab*, a Cornish hen marinated and charbroiled in a special sauce. The deli is cramped next to the market, but the lunch bargains more than make up for this slight inconvenience.

NEPALI AND TIBETAN

Everest on Grand
1278 Grand Avenue, St. Paul
(651) 696-1666
www.hotmomo.com
Everest on Grand fills a much-needed spot in Twin Cities cuisine, serving Nepali and Tibetan dishes to tuna casserole–leaning Midwesterners. The restaurant specializes in Tibetan *momos*, tasty steamed dumplings mixed with vegetables, pork and turkey, or yak. Nepali specialties include a variety of vegetarian and meat or fish (chicken, goat, lamb, cod, or shrimp) curries and *daal-bhatt,* traditional Nepali combination meals. During the week the restaurant features a lunch buffet, allowing patrons to sample many of the kitchen's Himalayan dishes at a set price.

PUERTO RICAN

Puerta Azul $-$$
1811 Selby Avenue, St. Paul
(651) 646-7003
This friendly, beautifully lit and decorated restaurant is considered by many a St. Paul treasure, serving a small but enticing menu of Puerto Rican food that leaves customers waffling between exactly what to get and coming back to try whatever it was they didn't get the last time. Chef Sonia Gonzales Sadr grew up in Puerto Rico, and the wonderful dishes served at Puerta Azul are either from traditional recipes or her own variations. The base of many is *sofrito,* a blend of garlic, onions, green pepper, cilantro and tomato, which stands out in the arroz con pollo and the beans and rice. Sofrito-flavored beans or fried plantain are served with most entrees, such as their excellent pork kabobs or roast marinated in garlic and ginger, marinated sliced beef fried with onions, and fish in Spanish sauce. Using a sweeter base is the mango chicken and the guava chicken dishes, which are also as close to perfect as you can get. For dessert, the coconut mango ice cream is sweet and refreshing, while the cream cheese flan with homemade caramel sauce is indescribably delicious. The restaurant serves beer and wine. Puerta Azul is open daily for lunch and dinner.

SEAFOOD

Minneapolis

McCormick & Schmick's
Seafood Restaurant $$$
800 Nicollet Mall, Minneapolis
(612) 338-3300

The best downtown happy-hour food is to be found in the bar here from 4:00 to 6:00 P.M. and again from 10:00 to 11:00 P.M., as that's when a couple of bucks will get you a luscious pan of mussels, a cheeseburger with fries, or a fish taco plate. The restaurant's dark rich wood, shiny brass, and sparkling beveled-glass decor sets off the Tiffany-style stained-glass ceiling beautifully, making this the place to take people you want to impress. Fresh seafood is flown in twice daily: scallops from Florida, swordfish from Hawaii, and oysters from British Columbia, and the menu includes big and beautiful Dungeness crab and bay shrimp cakes with red pepper aioli, fresh oysters, and excellent clam chowder.

Oceanaire Seafood Room $$$$
1300 Nicollet Mall (in the Hyatt Regency Hotel), Minneapolis
(612) 333-2277

A sidecar, clams casino, and lobster thermidor are just a few factors that make up the Oceanaire's decor. The fish here is all fresh, flown in daily from both coasts, and, depending on the catch of the day, the restaurant serves meals like black bass in black butter; a zesty cioppino boasting an immense catch of mussels, clams, shrimp, and fish; yellowfin tuna with wild mushrooms and rich red-wine sauce; Chilean sea bass; and a fantastic oyster bar. The menu changes daily, according to what's available, and the fish fresh on any given day are identified at the top of the menu with a check mark.

Seafood Palace Chinese
Restaurant $-$$
2523 Nicollet Avenue, Minneapolis
(612) 874-7721

As Chinese restaurants have diversified over the past decade, several specialty restaurants have opened. The Seafood Palace Chinese Restaurant has met the need for fresh seafood. The restaurant's menu begins with extremely reasonable lunch specials, then moves on to the dinner specialties, which include shrimp, scallops, mussels, lobster, and crab as well as traditional Chinese favorites like fried crispy duck, sweet-and-sour pork, and vegetarian dishes such as bean curd with brown sauce and mushrooms with Chinese cabbage. Dinner prices are inexpensive for seafood, especially for lobster and Vancouver Dungeness crab, and both are served in black bean sauce. Shrimp choices are numerous and include *chow fun,* honey walnut, fried rice, lo mein, black bean sauce, and many more.

St. Paul

Mac's Fish & Chips $
1330 Larpenteur Avenue West, St. Paul
(651) 489-5299

Mac's is tiny, none too fancy, and take-out oriented, but for fish-and-chips that would make a Londoner proud, it is a must-visit restaurant in the Twin Cities. Mac's specializes in halibut fillets, and the lightly breaded, deep-fried fish pieces seem as light as clouds and taste otherworldly. You can get the best deal if you buy a basket, which includes halibut fillets, shrimp, chicken strips, or a combination thereof, along with fries, coleslaw, bread, and a beverage. You can also buy the halibut fillets and shrimp by the piece, chicken strips in six-strip servings, half and full orders of fries, and plenty of slaw, allowing you to customize the size of your meal. Mac's harbors a few tables in its dining room, but it is best to call ahead and pick up your order, heading back to your hotel or home with a basket or two of fish-and-chips for a low-key, inexpensive, filling feast.

SOUTHWESTERN
Minneapolis

Bar Abilene   **$-$$**
1300 Lagoon Avenue, Minneapolis
(612) 825-2525
www.barabilene.com
The flavors of the Southwest are available in the Twin Cities at Bar Abilene. Located in the Uptown neighborhood of Minneapolis, the restaurant does brisk business and draws a hip clientele. For starters the menu features Texas tapas that include potato chipotle gouda flautas, Maryland blue crab-corn quesadillas, and tortilla soup. Dinner is divided into burgers and southwestern specialties. The burgers include several restaurant specialties such as the Hill Country Burger, which combines mild green chili and Monterey jack cheese on an onion bun. The restaurant's other specialties range from the savory jalapeño skewered shrimp to the wild mushroom quesadillas.

West

Tejas   **$$**
3910 West 50th Street, Edina
(952) 926-0800
www.tejasrestaurant.com
Tejas is a casual, rustic, eclectic restaurant serving southwestern-influenced dishes. House specialties include the chicken burrito with mango/habañero sauce, braised lamb shank with horseradish whipped potatoes, and wood-roasted beef tenderloin with barbecue béarnaise sauce and cayenne onion rings. Closed Sunday, Tejas is open for lunch and dinner every other day of the week.

SPANISH
Minneapolis

El Meson   **$-$$**
3450 Lyndale Avenue South, Minneapolis
(612) 822-8062
El Meson features Spanish and Caribbean cuisine in a relaxed, comfortable atmosphere. A few popular dishes include the *arroz con mariscos* (rice with seafood) and the paellas (a Spanish rice and seafood dish). In addition, the restaurant serves various chicken and pork dishes with savory rice and beans. For lunch the restaurant offers an ever-popular buffet of home-style Latin favorites. The restaurant has repeatedly received kudos for its delicious, nutritious cuisine. El Meson serves beer and wine.

La Bodega Tapas Bar   **$$-$$$**
3005 Lyndale Avenue South, Minneapolis
(612) 823-2661
Tapas, small servings of Spanish food, have become a trendy cuisine nationally. The Twin Cities' first tapas bar, La Bodega is a popular restaurant in the Lyn-Lake neighborhood of south Minneapolis. The tapas are small portions, and the majority of diners purchase at least two or three. Seafood is featured prominently among the tapas choices, which include fried calamari and garlic shrimp. The restaurant offers extensive wine selections to accompany the tapas as well as Spanish flamenco music and dancing on weekends. La Bodega is open daily for lunch and dinner.

SRI LANKAN

Sri Lanka Restaurant   **$$-$$$**
3226 West Lake Street, Minneapolis
(612) 926-0110
This lovely restaurant specializes in the bounty of tastes from Sri Lanka, where

fresh fruits, vegetables, meats, and spices are combined to make exciting dishes. A warning to those who are inexperienced with Sri Lankan cuisine: Spice is very important. However, the cooks will spice the dishes to meet diners' tastes. Seafood and vegetarian items are prominent on the menu. The malu curry is a complex combination of halibut or salmon with Asian mustard and vegetables. The Harak Mas Mallum is one of several dishes served exclusively at the restaurant. The dish is composed of sliced beef and veg-etables flavored with an imported fish from the Maldive Islands. Several roti (breads) and noodle entrees are also offered. The restaurant serves a brunch on Friday, Saturday, and Sunday. The brunch is one of the best in the area and features salads, meats, vegetables, and desserts. The range of flavors and combinations of tastes are astounding. Sri Lanka Restau-rant is open daily for dinner; reservations are recommended.

THAI

St. Paul

Pad Thai Grand Café $–$$
1659 Grand Avenue, St. Paul
(651) 690-1393
www.padthaigrandcafe.com
Pad Thai Grand Café specializes in authentic Thai food in a beautifully deco-rated restaurant. The decor is loaded with Thai elephant motifs, murals, and plants. Red is abundant and complements the exposed brick. Besides the lovely indoor dining space, outdoor seating is available.

The food at the Pad Thai Grand Café includes excellent items. The spring rolls are delicious and unique and come with a tangy spicy fish sauce. The pad Thai, the specialty, is also superb. A wonderful mix-ture of contrasting flavors are melded together including rice noodles, bean

sprouts, onions, ground peanuts, and lemon. The menu includes seafood and vegetarian options as well as a wine list. The service is friendly, and the chef will spice dishes according to patrons' desired heat level. Pad Thai is open Monday through Saturday for lunch and dinner and Sunday for dinner only.

Ruam Mit Thai Café $–$$
475 St. Peter Street, St. Paul
(651) 290-0067
www.ruammitthai.com
Ruam Mit Thai Café is tucked into a quiet stretch of St. Peter Street in downtown St. Paul, near the Fitzgerald Theater and the Minnesota Children's Museum. The restau-rant is considered by many the finest Thai restaurant in the Twin Cities. The menu includes Thai favorites such as spring rolls, pad Thai, roast duck curry, and bamboo shoot salad. The restaurant serves beer and wine and is open for lunch and dinner Monday through Saturday. During week-days the restaurant serves a popular lunch buffet.

Taste of Thailand $
1671 Selby Avenue, St. Paul
(651) 644-3997

1753 Old Hudson Road, St. Paul
(651) 774-6905

7890 University Avenue NE, Fridley
(763) 571-1188
The main location of Taste of Thailand, in a residential area on Selby Avenue west of Snelling Avenue in St. Paul, won't wow you with its intimate atmosphere. But it more than makes up for lack of ambience with its extensive menu of wonderful Thai dishes. The restaurant has all the classics, including oh-so-light spring rolls, fiery *miang kham,* the house specialty *tom yum* soup, and the ever-popular pad Thai. Other notable dishes include *pad goong, pad med mamnang himaphane,* and *gaeng ped pla.* If it's summertime, wash it all down with a glass of Thai lemonade.

North

Royal Orchid   **$-$$**
2401 Fairview Avenue, Roseville
(651) 639-9999
www.thebestthaifood.com
Royal Orchid serves authentic Thai cuisine
in a restaurant decorated in subdued pastel purple and lilac with a few murals featuring elephants and other Thai motifs.
Beyond the pleasant ambience, Royal
Orchid creates unique Thai cuisine. Instead
of cooking with cliché tastes and using
shortcuts, the Royal Orchid marries complex spices, vegetables, and meats. The
masmon curry is like no other because of
this. Besides the pad Thai and curries, the
menu includes several interesting salads,
such as the Moslem salad, which includes
lettuce, cucumber, scallion, tofu, peanut
dressing, and sweet potato chips. The
entree selection is also extensive. Pineapple rice and Thai-flavor fish are two standouts. Also available are beef, chicken, pork,
tofu, scallops, and shrimp, which all can be
prepared with eight different sauce
choices, from garlic to saffron curry, satay,
and mock ginger chili with green beans.
Royal Orchid accepts Visa and MasterCard
only and is open for lunch and dinner Monday through Saturday.

VIETNAMESE

Minneapolis

Camdi Chinese-Vietnamese
Restaurant   **$**
1325 Fourth Street SE, Minneapolis
(612) 331-4194
Camdi Chinese-Vietnamese Restaurant's
daily lunch special is one of the best bar-
gains in the Twin Cities. For under $4.00
diners may select one of the specials,
which include curry chicken, Vietnamese
chow mein, hot-and-spicy chicken, sweet-
and-sour chicken, Buddha's Delight (a
vegetarian dish), and several more
choices. The lunch specials are big and
tasty. The menu includes a number of

larger dinners and wonderful egg rolls
with fish sauce. The small, humble restaurant has served the Dinkytown neighborhood (next to the University of Minnesota)
for years with its inexpensive Vietnamese
cuisine.

The Lotus Restaurant   **$**
313 Southeast Oak Street, Minneapolis
(612) 331-1781
Three additional Twin Cities locations
Each Lotus location has its own unique
character, and this location reflects its
proximity to the University of Minnesota.
For starters the Lotus has many fine
options, especially the egg rolls and
spring rolls. The menu includes favorites
such as Vietnamese beef salad and cur-
ried chicken Vietnamese-style. Lunch specials are also offered; the Mustard Chicken
is particularly good and includes chicken
and onions in a spicy mustard sauce. The
Lotus Restaurant is closed Monday but
provides a casual environment for lunch
and dinner the rest of the week.

Lucky Dragon Riverside
Restaurant   **$-$$**
1827 Riverside Avenue, Minneapolis
(612) 375-1690
Lucky Dragon specializes in reasonably
priced Vietnamese and Chinese fare.
Lucky Dragon's menu includes soups,
combination meals, noodles, stir-fried
entrees, and numerous Vietnamese specialties. Vegetarian items are available, and
the entire menu contains no MSG. There is
a large lunch and dinner buffet Monday
through Friday—one of the best Vietnamese buffets in the Twin Cities. The egg
rolls, hot-and-spicy chicken, and beef in
black bean sauce are exceptional and usually available with the buffet.

Quang Restaurant   **$-$$**
2719 Nicollet Avenue South, Minneapolis
(612) 870-4739
Quang Restaurant has received local and
national attention for innovative versions
of traditional Vietnamese cuisine. The *New
York Times* praised the restaurant as one

of the best restaurants for business travelers, which came as no surprise to many Twin Citians. The hip restaurant serves fine renditions of Vietnamese favorites. Popular items include caramelized lemongrass chicken, grilled pork chops, and the seafood noodle soups. In addition to fine versions of egg rolls and spring rolls, the menu features such dishes as grilled sugarcane shrimp (*banh hoi choi*). The restaurant does not serve alcohol. Quang Restaurant is closed Tuesday and open for lunch and dinner the rest of the week.

St. Paul

Saigon Restaurant & Bakery $
601 University Avenue West, St. Paul
(651) 225-8751
Saigon Restaurant is the best and most affordable authentic Vietnamese restaurant in the Twin Cities. The specialties are *pho* and *banh mi*. Pho, the national dish of Vietnam, is a huge bowl of soup. It includes vegetables, noodles, and a choice of meats from roast pork to several delicious seafood combinations. Another signature dish at the Saigon Restaurant is the banh mi, a savory Vietnamese sandwich composed of pâté, cilantro, cucumber, Vietnamese mayo, and any of a number of meats combined on a fresh baguette. There is a deli counter where banh mi and baked goods are available for take-out, all at incredibly low prices.

Vina Highland Vietnamese Restaurant $
756 Cleveland Avenue South, St. Paul
(651) 698-8408
Two additional Twin Cities locations
The casual Vina serves delicious, inexpensive dishes. The menu is filled with Vietnamese favorites such as curry shrimp, egg roll salad, and hot-and-spicy chicken. The hot-and-spicy chicken is an excellent rendition of the Vietnamese favorite and is composed of chicken with onions, lemongrass, and red peppers. All items are

spiced to order and contain no MSG. For lunch, Vina features more inexpensive combination meals, where Chinese menu items are an important part. Vina is open seven days a week for lunch and dinner. There are two additional locations in the Twin Cities with slightly different hours and menu items. They are Vina Vietnamese Restaurant (6401 Nicollet Avenue, Richfield; 612-866-5034) and Vina Plus (1821 University Avenue, St. Paul; 651-644-1384).

South

Kimson Vietnamese Cuisine $
8654 Lyndale Avenue South, Bloomington
(952) 885-0230
Kimson is another one of the excellent Vietnamese restaurants in the Twin Cities. With more than 200 items, the menu provides plenty of pork, chicken, beef, tofu, seafood, and vegetarian selections. Vietnamese favorites including hot-and-spicy chicken, sautéed beef over fried potatoes, curry chicken, and egg rolls are offered. The menu serves extensive vegetarian items and six types of eggplant, e.g., curry eggplant and eggplant with bean curd, broccoli, and celery. There are nearly a dozen tofu entrees, which range from chow mein and sweet and sour to ginger bean curd. Kimson is open daily for lunch and dinner.

Kinhdo Restaurant $
2755 Hennepin Avenue, Minneapolis
(612) 870-1295

2709 Winnetka Avenue North, New Hope
(763) 544-8440
Kinhdo Restaurant has two unique Twin Cities locations, but both serve excellent renditions of Vietnamese cuisine as well as a few favorite Chinese food items. The menu features exceptional values on Vietnamese favorites like hot-and-spicy chicken, beef and potatoes, and egg rolls

with fish sauce. The menu also features such Chinese items as chow mein, egg foo young, and a great version of sweet-and-sour chicken.

SWEETS AND TREATS

Minneapolis

Award Baking International $
1101 Northeast Stinson Boulevard,
Suite 3, Minneapolis
(612) 331-3523 or (800) 333-3523
www.oblaten.com
Award Baking International is the place to go to get *oblaten*—those thin, crisp, delicately flavored cookies that upscale ice-cream parlors serve with sundaes—as well as biscotti, both of which are made by Award Baking. The little store—hidden behind a nondescript door in the side of a warehouse—also carries a good selection of teas and imported English fruit candies and licorice.

Caruso's Gelato Cafe $
3001 Hennepin Avenue South, Calhoun
Square, Minneapolis
(612) 822-2629
The gelato fad has reached the Midwest, and Caruso's promises to be only the first of many such cafes to spring up throughout the Twin Cities. Caruso's carries more than 30 flavors of the creamy, sticky Italian dessert, including chocolate chip, cappuccino, mango, coconut, strawberry cheesecake, lemon, banana, and tiramisu, which can be carried out either in a waffle cone or in a cup.

Dairy Sales Room Store $
Andrew Boss Meat Science Building
University of Minnesota
1354 Eckles Avenue, St. Paul
If your timing is right, you can find some of the best ice cream and cheeses in the Twin Cities in this little-known and rarely open outlet on the University of Minnesota's St. Paul Campus. Open only 3:00

to 5:00 P.M. Wednesdays, customers line up early to get their hands on dairy products produced by university students and researchers. Don't worry, no failed experiments make it to the sales floor, and if you're willing to make the effort to find the store, you will be treated to rich (12 percent fat!) and creamy ice cream in a variety of flavors and a range of cheeses, the weekly selection depending on what is available from the university's work and the time of year. The store may (or may not) have on hand such favorites as Gopher Gold ice cream (French vanilla and raspberry), aged cheddar, and Nuworld, a spreadable variety of blue cheese that is all white. Quantities available for sale are always limited: Arrive early for the best selection.

Sebastian Joe's $
1007 Franklin Avenue West, Minneapolis
(612) 870-0065
When Italian immigrant Sebastiano Pellizer arrived in the Twin Cities in the 1930s, he was almost immediately rechristened Joe by his employer, a construction-crew chief. The moniker stuck, and in 1984 when his grandchildren Mike and Todd founded this ice-cream shop, Sebastiano gave them permission to use his name. Sebastian Joe's has become nearly synonymous with handmade ice cream in the Twin Cities. The ice-cream list tops 80 flavors (15 daily) and includes both new spins and old favorites, such as basil strawberry, chocolate, fresh strawberry, vanilla made from ground vanilla beans, ginger cream, and cayenne pepper–laced Chocolate Coyote.

Wuollet Bakery $
2447 Hennepin Avenue, Minneapolis
(612) 381-9400

1080 Grand Avenue, St. Paul
(651) 292-9035
Four additional Twin Cities locations
www.wuollet.com
What began more than 70 years ago as a neighborhood bread-baking concern grew

to include cakes, pastries, and a following. Yet Wuollet is still a family-run bakery, watched over by two brothers, their uncle, and a cousin. In the hands of Wuollet's cake artists, traditional white-on-white wedding cakes can ascend to seven tiers covered in white chocolate ropes, orchids, and other amazements, while soufflé cakes featuring genoise (egg-rich sponge cake) disappear under drifts of Bavarian cream. A sweets table covered in prof- iteroles, fancy French pastries, cheese- cake, and trifle is a reception addition that uses Wuollet's skills to their tastiest advantage. Wuollet also offers chocolate long johns smothered in rich chocolate frosting, brownies, and blondies so but- tery they melt on the tongue like the rich- est fudge or caramel. The shop also sells delicious doughnuts and princess tortes layered in Bavarian cream and raspberry preserves.

St. Paul

Café Latte $
850 Grand Avenue, St. Paul
(651) 224-5687
Look no further than Café Latte to find the ultimate in cheesecakes in a myriad of flavors, including the tin roof cheesecake with layers of nuts and chocolate. Latte is renowned for its decadent turtle cake— dark chocolate cake layers separated by and topped with buttery caramel and pecans—as well as the tart key lime pies, raspberry marzipan, thick scones served with crème frâiche, jams, and fresh fruit and fudge tarts.

Grand Ole Creamery $
750 Grand Avenue, St. Paul
(651) 293-1655
The Grand Ole Creamery has been creat- ing some of the most imaginative and delicious ice-cream flavors in its parlor since 1984. And the flavors, including Irish coffee eggnog and chocolate malt banana, aren't just interesting experiments in flavor, they're also very, very good.

The store serves up to 32 flavors from a master list of more than 100, and customers can satisfy their chocolate, strawberry, or vanilla cravings or try the black walnut, cinnamon, or sweet cream. At the bottom of each ice-cream cone is a malted milk ball carefully placed so that the ice cream doesn't leak out onto your shirt. The prices (around $4.00 for a single-scoop waffle cone) are a little high but well worth the extra expense to true ice-cream connoisseurs. The store also makes thick, rich malts and shakes, banana splits, and sundaes. During the dog days of summer, folks line up out the door to indulge in this stuff.

Izzy's Ice Cream Cafe $
2034 Marshall Avenue, St. Paul
(651) 603-1458
www.izzysicecream.com
This 16-seat ice creamery, open since 2000, is sparse and clean, with outdoor seating and tables for kids. The store serves an amazing variety of homemade ice cream, including lemon raisin bar, blue- berry cheesecake yogurt, granola, choco- late cherry, ginger, hazelnut, pistachio, crème de menthe, pineapple, Oreo cookie, and coffee ice cream that's flecked with coffee grounds. The beauty of it all is that if there's another flavor that you weren't really sure on but would like to try, you can ask the server to make that flavor your izzy—a small scoop added to the top of your first choice. If you're not in the mood for a homemade waffle cone, you can order a malt, shake, float, sundae, or an egg cream.

Just Truffles $
1326 Grand Avenue, St. Paul
(651) 690-0075
www.justtruffles.com
Like its name says, this store carries just truffles: thick, rich, gigantic homemade chocolate truffles kept in a refrigerated glass case until purchase. Originally located in the famous Saint Paul Hotel, this store sells its chocolates to locals and celebrities passing through (their auto-

graphed pictures line the walls of the con-
fectionery) in dozens of flavors, including
champagne, peanut butter, Kahlua, and
raspberry. The edible chocolate boxes are
a special and delicious way to send the
truffles as a gift.

Regina's Candy Kitchen & Store $
2073 St. Clair Avenue, St. Paul
(651) 698-8603

1905 South Robert Street,
Southview Square,
West St. Paul
(651) 455-8864
Founded in 1926 by a young Greek crafts-
man and his bride, Regina, and passed on
to their children and grandchildren,
Regina's uses old-world craftsmanship in
making its amazing (and amazingly inexpensive) caramels, chocolates, toffees, and
more than 20 flavors of dark chocolate
truffles. You can't tell from the nondescript painted-brick building and the
block-letter sign on the bright blue
awning that Regina's Candies is much
more than a hole-in-the-wall, but inside
you'll find a timeless candy-filled shop
with enough kinds of chocolates to make
your head spin.

Taste of Scandinavia
Catering and Bakery $
2900 Rice Street, Little Canada
(651) 482-8876

845 Village Center Drive, North Oaks
(651) 482-8285
www.tasteofscandinavia.com
This charming European bakery has luscious desserts spinning inside a glass
case—the strawberry torte layers yellow
sponge cake with chocolate mousse, fresh
banana slices, and raspberry preserves
and is covered in strawberries and peaks
of cream. Sweets from elegantly decorated layer cakes to muffins and cookies
to Finnish cinnamon *pulla* can also be
found. On late afternoons the bakery
offers many half-price deals, so stop in
late and indulge yourself.

Grand Ole Creamery on Grand Avenue in St. Paul. TODD R. BERGER

COFFEEHOUSES AND TEASHOPS

Minneapolis

Acadia Café $
1931 Nicollet Avenue, Minneapolis
(612) 874-8702
www.acadiacafe.com
If you weren't hungry when you first
walked in, a few seconds of standing by
the counter and inhaling all the wonderful
scents of fresh chocolate croissants and
cookies baking is sure to start your stom-
ach rumbling. Aside from all the coffee
and espresso drinks you could ever want,

Acadia makes fresh soups, sandwiches, store-made bread, yogurt parfaits, and homemade Belgian waffles with fruit and whipped cream that are worth waking up early for. There's lots of comfortable seating and large tables for eating, too, making this more than just a place to drop by to grab a cup of coffee and a quick bite to eat.

Recorded light jazz and blues fill the open, airy coffeehouse, where owner and commercial photographer Tom Berthiaume displays his black-and-white portraits against exposed-brick walls. If you'd like to see more artwork, a full-fledged gallery with changing shows is connected.

Blue Moon Coffee Café $
3822 East Lake Street, Minneapolis
(612) 721-9230

Everything about the Blue Moon breathes comfort and relaxation. The soothing purple and blue color scheme and sparkling strings of white and colored Christmas lights make the cafe the perfect place for a calming evening of quiet revitalization. There are many coffee drinks on the menu and a choice of eight different kinds of coffee, 20 types of tea, homemade biscotti, pastries, sandwiches, and a big ice-cream cooler that carries Häagen-Dazs bars and other treats. Outside seating is available, but the large selection of comfy couches is hard to resist even on the nicest summer evenings.

Bob's Java Hut $
2651 Lyndale Avenue South, Minneapolis
(612) 871-4485

This funky little coffeeshop stays open past midnight in the summer months and closes earlier depending on how many customers linger in the winter. Don't be intimidated by the odd-looking crowd that hangs out here—they're mostly art students with time on their hands and a budget that includes copious amounts of hair dye. The menu is predominately coffee drinks and juice, with a few baked goods for the morning and lunch crowds.

The house specialty is Kool-Aid. No one else in town bothers putting it on the menu, and lots of people who come here order it. On warm days and nights, the large storefront window rolls back to let fresh air and conversation from the outside patio in.

Dunn Bros. Coffee $
201 Third Avenue South, Minneapolis
(612) 692-8530
www.dunnbros.com

This old brick warehouse is the home of one of the nicer Dunn Bros. coffeehouses in town (there are about over three dozen throughout the Twin Cities), with live music most summer weekend nights and a beautiful, comfortable interior, furnished with large potted plants that make it feel like it's springtime year-round. The best thing about the coffee shop, however, is the location—attached to the Milwaukee Road building, an indoor ice-skating rink/farmers' market (depending on season) that was once a train depot and was only recently renovated and opened to the public. The shop serves all the coffee and espresso drinks you could want as well as cookies, muffins, and a changing menu of other treats, depending on the mood of the staff.

La Société du Thé $
2708 Lyndale Avenue South, Minneapolis
(612) 871-5148
www.la-societe-du-the.com

This well-stocked, comfortable teahouse offers 130 varieties of specialty and whole-leaf teas, ranging from $20 to $200 per pound. The helpful staff gives careful instructions about heating water, steeping time, and the story behind each particular type of tea, all of which are preserved in air-tight canisters. Come in for a soothing cup of boiled leaves—come away understanding at least part of the spiritual art of making and drinking tea.

May Day Café $
3440 Bloomington Avenue South,
Minneapolis
(612) 729-5627
Situated in the old Powderhorn Co-Op
grocery spot just off the edge of Powderhorn Park, this small, cozy place is remarkable for its quality coffee and wonderful
sweet breads (sweet potato pound cake,
cranberry, and zucchini bread in season).

Muddy Waters $
2401 Lyndale Avenue South, Minneapolis
(612) 872-2232
This long-established coffeehouse, furnished like a college student's first apartment, caters specifically to the quirky
hipster crowd, with menu items like Pop
Tarts and Spaghetti-Os. There's lots of
indoor seating, and in the summertime the
crowds of caffeine addicts spill out to fill
the tables spread out in front of the building. Saturday-morning cartoons are often
featured on the TV screens.

Pandora's Cup $
2516 Hennepin Avenue South,
Minneapolis
(612) 381-0700
This old two-story house-turned-cafe in
Uptown offers two roomy front porches
(one downstairs, one upstairs) that look
out onto the bustle of Hennepin Avenue.
The cozy rooms inside are crowded with
mismatched kitchen and living-room furniture, video games, bookshelves, local artwork, and teens and twenty-somethings.
Pandora's Cup has a full coffee/espresso
menu, lots of loose teas, a wide selection
of lesser-known soda pops (including Rat
Bastard Root Beer), sandwiches (tomato,
basil pesto, and cheese; peanut butter and
jelly), vegetarian soups, and a pile of
cookies and muffins. With tons of great
music on the 100-CD changer, Pandora's
has become a home away from home for
urban and suburban teenagers, who
crowd the modest space at night.

Purple Onion $
326 14th Avenue SE, Minneapolis
(612) 378-7763
This low-frills coffeehouse revels somewhat
in its hipness, with loud alternative music
playing at all times on the stereo and purposefully blank walls offsetting the large,
comfortable, and insular wooden booths
and tables (perfect for reading or studying) that may or may not have been left
over from the diner that was once here.
This is almost strictly a coffee/espresso-
serving establishment, with just a few
other items on the menu.

Sister Sludge Coffee Café $
4557 Bloomington Avenue South,
Minneapolis
(612) 722-3933

330 2nd Avenue South, Minneapolis
(612) 371-4395
This funky little neighborhood coffeehouse serves coffee, espresso, and chai
drinks to patrons either crowded into the
small shop or spread out comfortably
among the tables set outside. The menu is
small and consists mostly of Rice Krispie
bars, muffins, and cookies, but it's a comfortable place to spend an afternoon or
catch a cup of coffee before officially
starting your day.

St. Paul

Brewberry's—The Coffee Place $
475 Fairview Avenue South, St. Paul
(651) 699-1117
Located across the street from the College of St. Catherine, this coffeehouse has
a huge and loyal clientele of professors,
students, and people from the neighborhood who come here in the morning to
loudly discuss everything from modern
politics to classical literature. While it is a
nice neighborhood coffeehouse, the feel is
somewhat cafeteria-like, probably because
it is so busy, with three to four counter-
persons running around at all times trying
to keep up with customer orders. There

are two rooms to sit in, though, and the smaller front room is quieter and more relaxed than the back room, so if you don't want to get dragged into the heady conversations of the day, you can hide out here to read your newspaper—this is also the room with the free newspaper and magazine rack. The menu includes made-to-order sandwiches and soups, fruit smoothies, many flavors of biscotti, and a wide variety of baked desserts, as well as all the coffee and espresso drinks you could ever need.

Ginkgo Coffeehouse $
721 Snelling Avenue North, St. Paul
(651) 645-2647
www.gingkocoffee.com
Three additional Twin Cities locations
By day, Ginkgo is a friendly java joint with mismatched furniture, potted plants, and a few outdoor tables in summer. A couple of nights a week, however, the atmosphere changes, and this coffeehouse on the edge of St. Paul's Hamline University campus becomes a dimly lit, cozy, acoustic-music venue. In addition to local singer-songwriters trying out their material on an invariably friendly audience, acoustic acts from throughout North America stop by to perform and sell CDs and demo tapes here. If the artist is particularly popular, arrive early.

Lori's Coffee House $
1441 Cleveland Avenue North, St. Paul
(651) 647-9007
Lori's is a nice little corner coffeehouse that makes wonderful, homemade soups on-site and throws a couple of huge slices of also-homemade bread in for free. There's coffee and espresso, cookies, muffins, a good selection of bottled juices to pick from, and fresh-squeezed orange juice. Lots of college kids hang out here, and there's definitely room for them—while the inside is spacious and airy, most people opt to sit around one of the many tables spread out on the lawn.

Sarah Jo's Coffee Café $
327 West Seventh Street, St. Paul
(651) 224-3890
This establishment caters specifically to the breakfast and lunch crowd, opening earlier than most places in the neighborhood and closing around 5:00 P.M. The menu is wonderfully diverse, with a large selection of hot and cold fresh sandwiches to choose from—including beef French dip and barbecue meatball—as well as homemade soup, smoothies, muffins, and all the usual selections of coffee and espresso drinks. There's lots of seating space, and the tables are actually big enough for two or three to set down their food and drinks. The coffee shop is also walking distance from the Xcel arena and downtown St. Paul, making it a great place to park and stop before seeing the sights of the area.

Tea Source $
752 Cleveland Avenue South, St. Paul
(651) 690-9822
www.teasource.com
Owner Bill Waddington personally selects the fine teas he sells to customers of all tastes. Although Tea Source is a retail store selling loose teas, you can also stop in the Highland Park store just north of Ford Parkway and enjoy a cup or pot of your favorite tea in the store—a perfect spot for an afternoon read, a break from shopping, or conversation. With dozens of options among black, green, oolong, tisanes (herbal teas), and blends, you can pick out a few ounces of your favorite or an adventurous alternative to take home. A detailed guide available in the store helps make sense of the inventory (which can be overwhelming to those used to gas station coffee), and Tea Source offers similar information in its catalog and online.

North

The Corner Coffee House $
87 West County Road C, Little Canada
(651) 482–1114

One of the few true coffeehouses in the suburbs, the Corner Coffee House is a big, friendly-looking, yellow two-story house with a large back patio, several cozy rooms inside for neighborhood get-togethers, and lots of lot parking. The menu includes a couple dozen coffee and espresso drinks, huge fresh-fruit smoothies topped with whipped cream, breakfast pastries, and Italian desserts. Art and knickknacks are for sale, most of which are made by local artists, and live musicians stop by to play weekend afternoons and evenings. If you don't feel like stopping in but still want the coffee, there's even a drive-through window in back for a quick pickup.

The Dakota Bar and Grill. GREATER MINNEAPOLIS CONVENTION & VISITORS ASSOCIATION

NIGHTLIFE ⓨ

A casual drive through the Twin Cities might lead you to think that Minnesotans have a serious drinking problem. There are literally hundreds of little drinking holes throughout the region, sometimes spaced less than a city block apart from another. The truth is that Minnesotans just like to be together, especially in the winter. Around December the local bar provides a place for people to gather to play Trivial Pursuit, watch TV, and buy tickets to win the traditional bar "meat raffle," which usually consists of some lucky customers winning 10 pounds of bologna or olive loaf. There's no better fun in January than getting bundled up tight as the sun goes down and heading out to the neighborhood bar to meet with friends and neighbors.

If your idea of a night on the town is catching a good live band, you're in luck— nearly all the bars and coffee shops in the Twin Cities metro area offer at least one night of local or acoustic live music a week. There are clubs that cater to just about every musical taste you can imagine. Downtown Minneapolis, particularly the Warehouse District, has the largest concentration of dance clubs. The Uptown area of Minneapolis has many hip bars, some with live music, and the area around the University of Minnesota has numerous, somewhat grittier bars filled with younger, drunker patrons. Downtown St. Paul is much tamer in terms of live music, though new brewpubs and bars that have sprung up near Rice Park and around the Xcel Energy Center are certainly livening things up, and the Artists' Quarter jazz club has long made patrons feel as though they'd stumbled upon a subterranean gem. Several elegant drinking establishments inhabit the Selby-Dale area just west of the cathedral, and St. Paul has two excellent spots for live Irish music, Half Time

Rec near Como Park and the Dubliner Pub in the Midway. The numerous pubs in neighborhoods across the Saintly City offer plenty of local color.

ALTERNATIVE MUSIC AND ROCK CLUBS

Minneapolis

The Cabooze
917 Cedar Avenue, Minneapolis
(612) 338–6425
www.cabooze.com
Since 1974 the Cabooze has opened its doors to nationally-recognized touring rock, folk, and instrumental acts as well as many local bands that never get outside the Twin Cities. The club often pairs lesser-known local acts with major touring bands, too, giving good smaller bands the greater exposure they need to hit the tour circuit themselves. The Cabooze features musical acts Wednesday through Saturday. It has a large dance floor for those who don't feel like just standing around, as well as the largest bar in the Twin Cities.

Club 3 Degrees
113 North Fifth Street, Minneapolis
(612) 781–8488
www.club3degrees.com
Kind of a rarity in the Twin Cities, especially with the demise of everyone's favorite all-ages club, the Foxfire, Club 3 Degrees is an alcohol-free, smoke-free nightclub for audiences of all ages (until 11:00 P.M., when the club allows only those 18 and over). The club mostly books politically correct punk bands and Christian rock, but the occasional acoustic act makes its way in now and again.

Fine Line Music Café
318 First Avenue North, Minneapolis
(612) 338-8100
www.finelinemusic.com

Offering a decent blend of folk music, adult contemporary rock, and up-and-comers not quite ready for the bigger venues, the Fine Line is a fairly small, intimate, and comfortable club on good nights and extremely packed and uncomfortable on bad nights. The stage is poorly placed way in the back of the club, and when an act has a good draw, it's nearly impossible to see the stage from anywhere but directly in front of the stage. A small menu with American basics such as salads, steak, and pasta is available on nights featuring national touring acts.

First Avenue/Seventh Street Entry
701 First Avenue North
(612) 338-8388
www.firstavenue.com

Yes, this is that place from *Purple Rain*. Not only did Twin Citian Prince film parts of his movie at First Avenue, he also spent his fair share of time here when the cameras weren't rolling, onstage and in the crowd. The world-famous First Avenue has been a popular hangout for bands, musicians, and club goers since Joe Cocker took the stage on opening night in 1970. Since then the club has featured top-40, alternative, and classic rock acts and has opened its floors to crowds dancing to techno, house music, salsa, hip-hop, reggae, and likely any other type of music you can think of. First Avenue sometimes holds all-ages shows, but the upstairs is always for ages 21-plus. With its own fully stocked bar and a wall-length window providing a view of

the action below, upstairs is a great place to retreat from the downstairs crowds. The real beauty of First Avenue is the layout. No matter where you stand in the club, whether it be on the massive dance floor or upstairs at the bar, you always get a decent view of the stage.

Set in a side room, with its own separate entrance on Seventh Street, the Entry is the more intimate venue. The stage setting is great here, too, and though the room gets packed quickly, on good nights this is about as close to having a major-label act play in your living room as you can get. The dress code is informal, and the bar offers some of the cheapest tap beer you'll find at a live-music venue. Expect to pay less than $10 for a cover charge, and feel free to check out what's going on next door after you receive a hand stamp. Main room ticket prices average $15, with shows a minimum of three nights a week. During spring and fall the club's booked almost every night. For show and ticket information, pick up a club schedule (found at any record store in the Twin Cities, both venues are listed on the same schedule), check out the Web site, or just give First Avenue a call.

400 Bar
400 Cedar Avenue South, Minneapolis
(612) 332-2903
www.400bar.com

The bartender's surly, the beer's expensive, and the doorman thinks everybody who comes in is up to no good; but the sound man knows what he's doing, and a lot of touring acts stop here specifically because they sound so incredibly good in this club. The owners' former association with Soul Asylum helped bring people into the club when the band was big, but it's the club's reputation as a good venue to play that brings the bands in now. Everything from alternative rock to folk to blues acts (and everything in between) from all over the world make this club a regular stop on their tours. If you don't get here when the doors open, you probably won't be able to get in because of the huge crowds.

First Avenue/Seventh Street Entry gives out free passes to upcoming shows and events with each ticket purchased. Usually if you buy one ticket, you get enough free tickets to get you into three or four other shows or dance club nights.

First Avenue music club. CLINT BUCKNER

Ground Zero/The Front
15 Northeast Fourth Street, Minneapolis
(612) 378-5115

Ground Zero offers diverse theme nights three times a week. One of the club's most popular dance nights is "Bondage a go-go," where every Thursday and Saturday dancers perform relatively tame S&M; some patrons dress in corresponding attire.

Besides the large dance floor, Ground Zero has a smaller, cozier lounge room, the Front. Theme nights include Funky Friday, with old-school soul, disco, and R&B; and Astro Lounge, with disco, hip-hop, house, and whatever the DJ feels like playing.

Lee's Liquor Lounge
101 Glenwood Avenue, Minneapolis
(612) 338-9491
www.leesliquorlounge.com

Located in a former industrial area just south of downtown's Warehouse District, Lee's is a little off the beaten path, and the one-way streets in the area sometimes make it tricky to find. It's worth finding. Lee's hosts live music almost every night, and covers generally run $5.00 or less for the local and touring acts. (Musicians from Austin, Texas, seem to love this place.) The sight lines are good, and the bar is clean and comfortable, despite its slightly rough-around-the-edges roadhouse feel. This is the type of place where you're equally comfortable tossing back a few beers while bobbing your head or doing your thing on the dance floor. And who doesn't benefit from the mix of music, wood paneling, and taxidermy every once in a while?

Mayslacks Polka Lounge
1428 Northeast Fourth Street, Minneapolis
(612) 789-9862
www.mayslacks.com

This place can be the best bang for your buck so far as seeing live music. The cover is rarely more than $3.00, and bands usually play for a good two or three hours—and for the low cover, you can see anything from a brand-new band made up of neighborhood kids to a major label act. The downside is that there are rarely opening bands for acts, so by the time the headliners are finished playing, they're sometimes panting, out of breath, and usually very drunk. The sound system is better than you might expect from a neighborhood bar, and a lot of groups play here just because they like the way they sound onstage. The beer's moderately priced, too, and on football/soccer/hockey/bartender's-in-a-good-mood nights, the lounge has some really great specials.

The Quest Club
110 North Fifth Street, Minneapolis
(612) 338-3383
www.thequestclub.com
The Quest is a beautiful nightclub that brings in major national acts, with several conveniently located bars on both floors so that you don't have to fight too much to get a bartender's attention. The brightly lit stage is set so that you can see the performers pretty much anywhere you stand in the club, and the second floor has comfortable booths and tables you can wrestle other patrons to secure. The club is tucked away in an unassuming stately old office building, and the main floor's ceiling stretches up to the top of the building, giving it an open, airy feeling even when the floor is packed. The VIP room is amazing, with fake palm trees, fiberoptic twinkling stars, and an active

fountain that completes the illusion of being outside. One drawback of the club is that it does push the house dress code occasionally, but staff can be pretty lenient about it depending on the band you're coming to see.

Terminal Bar
409 Hennepin Avenue East, Minneapolis
(612) 623-4545
Most of the patrons of this bar are people from the neighborhood who like to stop by after work for a beer and kids coming to see local bands perform on the small stage in the back. The draft beer is a little high priced, but there's a popcorn machine always full of popcorn, and if you ask nicely, you can always sample the bar favorite, a hard-boiled egg on a Ritz cracker with a little mustard. The cover charge, if there is one, is usually around $3.00, a relative bargain in Minneapolis.

The Uptown Bar and Café
3018 Hennepin Avenue South, Minneapolis
(612) 823-4719
www.uptownbarandcafe.com
Once known for attracting the loudest national and local acts, the Uptown Bar and Café briefly stopped booking bands in the mid-1990s; despite good attendance, the bar was losing money and decided to concentrate only on food and drink. When the bar returned to booking bands, it featured a scaled-back all-local schedule, mostly composed of roots rock and acoustic music. Once again, the bar drew well in Minneapolis's hip Uptown neighborhood and has expanded to music on Tuesday through Saturday.

Lyn-Lake is a neighborhood at the intersection of Lyndale Avenue and Lake Street and abuts the Uptown neighborhood of Minneapolis. In recent years there has been significant renewal at the intersection of two of the city's major thoroughfares. Many shops and restaurants call Lyn-Lake home.

Whiskey Junction
901 Cedar Avenue, Minneapolis
(612) 338-9550
www.whiskeyjunction.com
With lots of local music and beer and food specials, Whiskey Junction, just down the street from the Cabooze, attracts a slightly grungy crowd, including plenty of students from the nearby U of M and Augsburg Col-

lege. Two bars keep thirsty patrons busy, and the bar has several pool tables and TVs, often flickering with various sporting events (the bar is the base for the unofficial Cleveland Browns Fan Club, making a brave statement in Vikings country). Whiskey Junction has an excellent selection of tap beers, including the local favorite, Summit, as well as rarer finds on tap, such as Beamish Stout, Boddington Cream Ale, Fullers India Pale Ale, and Paulaner Hefe Weizen.

The Whole Music Café
Coffman Memorial Union
300 Washington Avenue SE,
Minneapolis
(612) 625-2272
www.coffman.umn.edu/whole
The Whole, originally called the Gopher Hole, occupies the basement of Coffman Union on the University of Minnesota–Minneapolis campus. The 40-year-old venue has a venerable history, including early days as a coffeehouse featuring folky songsters and poets and later as a haven for new wave, punk, and indie-rock bands and their devoted student (mostly) fans. When Coffman Union underwent a $71 million renovation, improvements to the Whole included such coveted features as bathrooms and a rocking sound system. But the architects wisely left the gritty, down-in-the-cellar atmosphere much as it always has been, a nod to the tradition of this little underground club in the heart of the university.

St. Paul

Christiansen's Big V's Saloon
1567 University Avenue West, St. Paul
(651) 645-8472
Another relic of the old days of St. Paul, Christiansen's Big V's Saloon features live music from local and national indie bands every weekend and most weekdays. The decor of the bar is fabulous—the walls are covered with an old menu from the 1940s (don't try ordering the 15-cent pancake

breakfast, because it doesn't actually exist), while the bar itself is a classy antique curved wooden affair with a mirrored backdrop. The placing of the stage is a little inconvenient, tucked back where only patrons in the back room can actually see the stage, but considering that the saloon doesn't usually charge more than $5.00 cover, not many people complain.

Station 4
201 East Fourth Street, St. Paul
(651) 298-0173
www.station-4.com
Station 4's music is aimed at a younger demographic. Local rock and some national touring bands are standard. The club is divided into two parts, one with a long bar with lots of dartboards and the other for the music. There is a large stage and lots of seating for the young bar crowd, who on weekends fill the club. Station 4 always runs shuttles to Wild hockey games and other big events at Xcel Energy Center.

Turf Club
1601 University Avenue, St. Paul
(651) 647-0486
www.turfclub.net
Billing itself as the "Best Remnant of the '40s," St. Paul's Turf Club combines upscale sophistication with the feel of an old-fashioned cowboy bar. Local, domestic, and imported beers are on tap, and the club features an elegant, curved wooden bar for customers to perch at, as well as booths and tables throughout the establishment. Long having a reputation for giving local original bands a much-needed performance outlet, the Turf Club is one of the hippest hangouts in the Twin Cities, with music almost every night for ridiculously low cover charges. The Turf Club clientele is refreshingly free of the "beautiful people" crowd found at many downtown Minneapolis dance clubs, and the music here ranges from foot-stomping country to ska. Downstairs is a second bar formerly known as the Clown Lounge. At press time, this interesting space was in

flux, as Turf changed ownership in 2005. The clowns are now gone, but the place retains an intimate, basement-rec-room feel, with wood paneling and taxidermied fish. It's definitely worth checking out if you're around on an evening this downstairs bar is open. It provides a good aural break if the music upstairs doesn't turn out to be your thing.

The Suburbs

Medina Entertainment Center
500 Highway 55, Medina
(763) 478-6661
www.medinaentertainment.com
About 5 miles west of Interstate 494 in the western suburb of Medina, the Medina Entertainment Center hosts local bands like the disco kings Boogie Wonderland and the White Sidewalls, a '50s and '60s cover band. On Wednesday and Thursday in Rascals Bar within the complex, you can consult with psychic Ruth Lordan for insight into your present and future. In addition to live music, the Medina often has poker events.

COFFEEHOUSES

Lori's Coffeehouse
1441 Cleveland Avenue North, St. Paul
(651) 647-9007
Located near the University of St. Thomas campus, Lori's sometimes hosts live music for the entertainment of the clientele—swing by and take your chances on who's performing. There's never a cover charge, and this is really a pretty pleasant place to hang out to get the feel of the neighborhood.

White Rock Coffee Roasters
769 Cleveland Avenue South, St. Paul
(651) 699-5448
This great neighborhood coffeehouse has live local music on Saturday night; usually something acoustic, often a singer-songwriter. The crowd will probably consist of students from the many

area colleges as well as nonstudent folk from the neighborhood, who enjoy the coffee shop's caffeinated beverages and wireless Internet service by day.

COMEDY CLUBS

Minneapolis

Acme Comedy Company
708 North First Street, Minneapolis
(612) 338-6393
www.acmecomedycompany.com
Acme hosts local and national comedians in its Warehouse District space inside the Itasca Building. The club has shows nightly except Sunday, with free open mike on Monday. The on-site restaurant serves pasta, steaks, and ribs, and you have the choice of buying a ticket for the comedy show alone, for $15, or a dinner and show special for $27.

ComedySportz
Calhoun Square, 3001 Hennepin Avenue South, Minneapolis
(612) 870-1230
www.comedysportztc.com
Part of the national ComedySportz chain, this club sets up refereed comedy teams that compete for the biggest laughs and the most points for their unscripted, improvisational performances. Audience members are encouraged to heckle the teams as well as throw out suggestions for comedy themes. But make sure your suggestions are clean, or the referee could call the "Brown Bag Foul" on you and you'll end up wearing a paper bag over your head. Shows are every Thursday at 8:00 P.M. and every Friday and Saturday at 8:00 and 10:30 P.M.

DANCE CLUBS

BarFly
711 Hennepin Avenue, Minneapolis
(612) 333-6100
www.barflyminneapolis.com

BarFly (tagline: "More quaint than a club. More liberal than a lounge.") sits in the old Skyway Theater on busy Hennepin Avenue. DJs spin for the beautiful people dancing and bellying up to moodily lit bars. This club is open Wednesday through Sunday and offers specials every night such as free cocktails for the ladies from 9:00 P.M. to midnight on Thursday and two-for-one martinis (from 8:00 to 10:00 P.M.) and $2 shots (from 10:00 to 11:00 P.M.) on Friday.

Escape Ultra Lounge
600 Hennepin Avenue South, Minneapolis
(612) 333-8855
www.escapeultralounge.com
This 12,000-square-foot 18-plus club is right above the Hard Rock Café in the heart of Minneapolis's entertainment district on Hennepin Avenue. A "fashionable" dress code is enforced here, where plasma screens, leather couches, and serious uplighting make for a hip, high-tech mood. Two VIP rooms up the swank factor. Escape is open from 5:00 P.M. to 2:30 A.M. seven days a week and features drink specials and a range of music including hip-hop, latin, R&B, rock, and dance hall.

Spin
10 South Fifth Street, Minneapolis
(612) 333-5055
www.spinmn.com
In Minneapolis's hip Warehouse District, this place is designed for people to see and be seen—and to dance. The sound and the lighting are state-of-the-art amazing, and the ambience can't be beat. There are 40-foot ceilings, a 20-foot water wall, blasts of fog, and the bathrooms—you must visit the bathrooms, where plasma screens perch above the urinals and the stall doors are clear glass that turn opaque when they are closed. Spin's annual November Studio 54 party is totally hot and totally '70s. The club is open Thursday through Sunday from 9:00 P.M. to 2:00 A.M. Watch for nightly specials, and be aware that the dress code is enforced.

FOLK, IRISH, AND ACOUSTIC MUSIC
Minneapolis

Cedar Cultural Center
416 Cedar Avenue South, Minneapolis
(612) 338-2674
www.thecedar.org
The Cedar Cultural Center is an absolutely amazing place to see musicians perform. The auditorium is designed specifically for listening to music, with beautiful hardwood floors, a large raised stage in the front, excellent acoustics, and a soundman who actually pays attention to musicians' cues. Exciting acts perform at this venue, from traditional Irish bands to folk duos to world-famous acoustic soloists such as Pierre Bensusan and Didier Malherbe. The Cedar is also the home of the annual Nordic Roots festival, a three-day-long event that features elemental, contemporary, and experimental groups from the Nordic countries. The refreshment bar is worth noting, too—this establishment includes cheap, good beer on tap, wine, homemade cookies, and Indian samosas on the menu.

Jitters at the Times
205 Hennepin Avenue East, Minneapolis
(612) 617-1111
Originally a downtown Minneapolis coffee shop, restaurant, and bar famous for introducing new bands and local spoken word performers to the Cities, Jitters recently moved to northeast Minneapolis to become almost exclusively a bar with a limited menu and an even more limited repertoire of live shows. The decor is interesting, almost as though someone went piano bar–hopping in Vegas and picked out a selection of disparate elements from those clubs to make one big one. The walls are made of metal siding and silver paint; the couches are covered in red velvet fabric; the tables are small, art deco affairs set with roses in mismatched vases; and the lighting is provided by metal lamps that look as though they were stolen from the

Care for a Drink?

"Bar time" in Minnesota is 2:00 A.M. although many bars close earlier. Some bars and restaurants, such as First Avenue and Figlio, stay open later but do not continue to serve alcohol. Liquor stores in the Twin Cities can be open from 8:00 A.M. to 8:00 P.M. Monday through Thursday and until 10:00 P.M. Friday and Saturday, as well as on July 3 and New Year's Eve. Liquor stores are closed on Sunday, though some convenience stores sell 3.2 beer on Sunday.

Renaissance Faire. However, there's no admission charge, the beer is cheap, and the music is free.

Kieran's Irish Pub & Restaurant
330 Second Avenue South, Minneapolis
(612) 339-4499
www.kierans.com

One of the few truly Irish bars in Minneapolis, Kieran's has a full bar and an excellent menu that includes traditional U.K. foods like fish-and-chips and bangers-and-mash. The bar usually has live Irish and folk music playing on two different stages Friday and Saturday nights and infrequently during the week, with the occasional open-mike night and scheduled poetry readings on the smaller stage. During the summer, Kieran's sets up an outside bar and lots of tables for clients, with the occasional live band set up outside to serenade both patrons and random passersby.

St. Paul

The Dubliner Pub
2162 University Avenue West, St. Paul
(651) 646-5551

The Dubliner Pub is an old-style Irish theme bar for its working-class industrial location. The cozy, box-shaped pub is painted green and has a beautiful long bar, where Irish, English, and domestic beers are on tap. There is also a small stage for Irish music on the weekends as well as darts and free popcorn.

Half Time Rec
1013 Front Avenue, St. Paul
(651) 488-8245

The Half Time Rec is the most authentic neighborhood Irish bar in the Twin Cities. It began as a bar catering to the Irish immigrants arriving in St. Paul during the '70s, but it now serves a much larger cross section of the Twin Cities population. Weekend business is extremely busy and attracts young and old as well as people from the Como Park neighborhood where it is located.

The Half Time Rec features a long, comfortable, U-shaped bar and an adjoining room with a stage for music Tuesday through Saturday. The rooms are comfortably furnished, and the stage is draped with both the Irish and the American flags. At the Half Time Rec, patrons vociferously have fun. They frequently sing along with the music or get up and dance to the authentic Irish music, which sometimes includes a few American via Ireland–inspired covers. The beers are reasonably priced and the Guinness is prepared with the correct amount of head. For patrons' enjoyment, there is a boccie court in the basement. The Half Time Rec is a few miles from the major thoroughfares, but it is well worth the effort if you enjoy authentic Irish music and fun.

GAY BARS

Gay Nineties Theatre Cafe & Bar
408 Hennepin Avenue, Minneapolis
(612) 333-7755
www.gay90s.com

The state's largest gay club, the Gay Nineties pretty much offers something for everyone, from live music to a weekly (and very popular) drag show at the La Femme Show Lounge on the second floor. The club has a dedicated straight following as well, who come for the strong mixed drinks and the excellent dance music with no cover charged—Friday and Saturday nights are packed, and there's nearly always a line to get inside. The club has nine different bars on the premises, two discos, a supper club, male strippers, and a game room.

The Saloon
830 Hennepin Avenue, Minneapolis
(612) 332-0835

The Saloon is one of the most popular bars and dance floors for Twin Cities gay men, featuring a large, dark dance floor with plenty of loud music and a large bar in the back for socializing and imbibing. The Saloon is conveniently located on busy Hennepin Avenue in downtown Minneapolis.

JAZZ, BLUES, AND R&B

Minneapolis

Bunker's Music Bar & Grill
716 Washington Avenue North, Minneapolis
(612) 338-8188

A popular lunch spot serving soups and sandwiches during the day, this neighborhood bar turns into a blues and rock club at night. The acts booked range from pop and alternative rock bands to blues, R&B, and jazz acts. The cover charge is pretty low—usually under $5.00—and there are also pool tables and video games for entertainment.

The Dakota Bar & Grill
1010 Nicollet Avenue, Minneapolis
(612) 332-1010
www.dakotacooks.com

At least once a week, a national headlining jazz act comes through town to play at this club, and while the ticket prices are high (usually around $30) for the area, jazz fans will definitely get their money's worth. The cuisine served is elegant and as improvisational as the music: trout in maple sauce, walleye cheeks with pepper-garlic sauce, and the signature brie and apple soup. There's an extensive wine list, a full bar, and a happy hour Monday through Friday from 4:00 to 6:00 P.M.

Famous Dave's BBQ & Blues
3001 Hennepin Avenue South, Calhoun Square, Minneapolis
(612) 822-9900

Not only does Famous Dave's have some of the best barbecue ribs and fried catfish in the Twin Cities (especially for a chain restaurant), the Uptown branch also books some of the rawest blues in the area. Bands perform after 9:00 most nights of the week, giving parents time to feed their kids and drop them off at the sitters' before coming back to sit in on blues sessions. The music is free, and the drinks are reasonably priced.

Sophia
65 Southeast Main Street, Minneapolis
(612) 379-1111

Located right next to the Mississippi River in St. Anthony Main, Sophia serves a wide selection of fairly expensive dishes and has a full bar. Starting around 8:00 almost every night, local soft jazz acts take the small stage set near the bar and play until closing. There's no cover charge for the music, although there is a two-drink minimum after 9:00 P.M. Nominated by local papers time and again for the best romantic restaurant and best jazz club in Minneapolis for its classy music and dancing, this is an excellent place to take a date you want to impress.

The Viking Bar
1829 Riverside Avenue South,
Minneapolis
(612) 332-4259

The Viking Bar does not live up to the image its name projects. It is not a Minnesota Vikings sports bar, nor is it involved in the preservation of Scandinavian culture. Instead the Viking is one of the Twin Cities' grittiest venues for American roots music. Local R&B, jazz, and blues musicians play the small stage and even smaller stage. The Viking Bar is as close as the Twin Cities get to the seedy clubs of New Orleans and Chicago, with all their inherent charm and oddness.

St. Paul

Artists' Quarter
408 St. Peter Street, St. Paul
(651) 292-1359
www.mnjazz.com

This basement jazz club has great potential that has yet to be realized. The acoustics are great in the small basement space, the stage is big enough to hold a full piano and an accompanying band, and the bar serves clean, cheap tap beer as well as liquor, but so few nationally recognized jazz acts pass through the Twin Cities that most nights are booked by local artists that have a lot more heart than talent. Still, the club is a great place to stop by late at night to unwind—the bartenders are friendly, the cover charge is usually under $5.00 (rare for jazz clubs here), and if you're not a jazz purist, the bands that do play here are usually a lot of fun.

LOUNGES, PUBS, AND BREWPUBS
Minneapolis

Brit's Pub & Eating Establishment
1110 Nicollet Mall, Minneapolis
(612) 332-3908

This upscale downtown bar is almost always packed on weekends, usually with drinking-age kids from college or graduate school. The main room is lavishly furnished with mock-Georgian lounges and armchairs as well as beautiful wooden bar stools set next to tables and wall outcroppings to set your beer on throughout the room. The far walls are hung with large mirrors, giving the illusion that the main room is a lot larger than it actually is. There's a large back room to Brit's, but it's usually reserved for private parties at night. During summer Brit's opens its rooftop patio for outdoor libations surrounded by Minneapolis's skyscrapers. You can also watch lawn bowlers practicing their avocation on the rooftop grassy field, the only elevated lawn bowling field in the country. For a fee you can attempt to roll your "bowl" as close as possible to the "jack."

Chatterbox Pub
2229 East 35th Street, Minneapolis
(612) 728-9871

This bar's big claim to fame is the huge collection of Atari video games available for customers. In short, this bar's perfect for those who like tipping back a few while bathing in the warm green and blue glow of Frogger and Space Invaders.

Gluek's Restaurant & Bar
16 North Sixth Street, Minneapolis
(612) 338-6621
www.glueks.com

Gluek's is Minneapolis's original brewpub. Since 1902 Gluek's has served Minneapolis with its delicious and uniquely tasty beer. Located in the historic Warehouse District, Gluek's draws huge crowds with its brew, other domestic and foreign beers, and liquors. Gluek's is across the street from the Target Center, home of the Minnesota Timberwolves, and within walking distance of downtown Minneapolis. With all these advantages, it is no surprise Gluek's remains one of Minneapolis's great brewpubs.

The Herkimer Pub & Brewery on Lyndale Avenue in south Minneapolis. TODD R. BERGER

The Herkimer Pub & Brewery
2922 Lyndale Avenue South, Minneapolis
(612) 821-0101

The Herkimer Pub & Brewery offers a large selection of fresh beers at reasonable prices. Despite its location in the Lyn-Lake neighborhood, the beers made in-house cost less than a bottle of domestic. The Herkimer specializes in its in-house-brewed beer. Each day there are different "Today's Brews" written on a chalkboard, including light lagers and heavier dunkels (German for dark). The restaurant and bar are clean and comfortable, with plenty of booths and tables. The Herkimer serves food and appetizers until midnight, all reasonably priced, as is the beer.

Lyle's Bar and Restaurant
2021 Hennepin Avenue South, Minneapolis
(612) 870-8183

On the edge of Uptown, one would think that Liquor Lyle's, as most area residents call this establishment, would tend toward a hipster crowd. But this neighborhood watering hole attracts everyone from construction workers to artists to its somewhat smudgy, dated-yet-colorful ambience. The booths have vinyl seats, the men's restrooms have trough urinals, and the bouncer is big and hairy; but if you want to share a pitcher of beer and a basket of deep-fried cheese curds with a friend on a day when you haven't taken a shower, Lyle's is hard to beat.

MacKenzie
918 Hennepin Avenue, Minneapolis
(612) 333-7268

MacKenzie specializes in Scottish beers and liquors but also has a large selection of American libations, all at reasonable prices. The inside of the bar is decorated with Scottish decor and theater posters on lots of beautiful exposed brick. Located next to the historic Orpheum Theatre and within walking distance of several others, MacKenzie is a great stop before or after Hennepin Avenue theater events.

Mario's Keller Bar
2300 University Avenue NE, Minneapolis
(612) 781-3860
www.gasthofzg.com
Mario's Keller Bar occupies the large and comfortable basement of the Gasthof zur Gemuetlichkeit Restaurant. The Keller Bar features polka on Friday and Saturday nights and rock music Tuesday through Thursday. A festive atmosphere overtakes the club, especially on weekends, when fraternity members pack the dance floor and consume massive quantities of beer, which comes as no surprise considering the excellent selection of imported German beers on tap and available by the glass, pint, or enormous glass boot. Connoisseurs of German beers will enjoy the bar's selection, which runs a bit pricey, while many others will revel in the joyous German beer-hall atmosphere.

The Summit Brewing Company of St. Paul brews some of the finest micro-brews around, and most Cities bars and restaurants have at least one Summit beer on tap. The brewery makes Extra Pale Ale, Grand Pilsner, India Pale Ale, and Porter year-round and such seasonal varieties as Maibock and Winter Ale.

O'Donovan's Irish Pub
700 First Avenue North, Minneapolis
(612) 317-8896
O'Donovan's is a nice addition to the small Twin Cities Irish pub scene. Unlike the Dubliner Pub or Kieran's Irish Pub, O'Donovan's authenticity to all that is Irish is mostly left to the beautiful decor. The walls are covered with Irish murals and the rooms are furnished with comfortable booths. O'Donovan's draws a young, collegiate-type crowd, who enjoy the pub's live

music selection, which is not Irish reels but often includes top-40 hits performed on a keyboard. Location is a prime asset for O'Donovan's—the Target Center and First Avenue/Seventh Street Entry are directly across the street.

Triple Rock Social Club
629 Cedar Avenue South, Minneapolis
(612) 333-7499
www.triplerocksocialclub.com
The Triple Rock Social Club is *the* punk rock bar and restaurant of the Twin Cities. Owned by Erik Funk, a member of local punk legend Dillinger 4, it provides beer and food in a comfortable and relaxed atmosphere. The jukebox is particularly interesting—filled with a surprisingly eclectic range of music, from punk to R&B to metal—patrons' selections never cease to amaze and create an interesting atmosphere. Also of note is the wide selection of beers on tap, a dozen at last count, served at reasonable prices. The Triple Rock's menu contains sandwiches, salads, burgers, and one of the Twin Cities' largest and best selections of vegetarian and vegan items.

Urban Wildlife Bar & Grill
327 Second Avenue North, Minneapolis
(612) 339-4665
www.urbanwildlifebar.com
Urban Wildlife is one of the most popular Twin Cities hangouts for hip 20-somethings. During the summer the bar and outside seating are packed, particularly during the weekends. This is not surprising considering its location in the heart of the cool and busy Warehouse District of Minneapolis. Urban Wildlife takes advantage of the view by having windows along the perimeter of the two exposed walls. A small menu of bar food is available.

Whitey's World Famous Saloon
400 Hennepin Avenue East, Minneapolis
(612) 623-9478
Geared somewhat to the college crowd, Whitey's is your standard, comfortable neighborhood bar that has weekend spe-

cials on Jägermeister shots and about half a dozen domestic and locally brewed beers on tap. The interior is beautiful—the bar is an elegant, curved length of carved wood surrounded by high-backed stools, and in summertime customers can sit inside the bar or at the tables set outside on the fenced-in patio.

St. Paul

Great Waters Brewing Company
426 St. Peter Street, St. Paul
(651) 224-2739
www.greatwatersbc.com
Great Waters Brewing Company serves flavorful microbrews from its location inside the Hamm Building. The brewpub's beers include cask-conditioned ales, served at cellar temperature of 52 degrees F and "hand pulled" from casks in the basement, and pushed beers, which are served at 38 degrees F, similar to other tap beers in the United States. Beers include the Saint Peter Pale Ale, Martin's Bitter, Brown Trout Brown Ale, and Pot Hole Porter. Great Waters also brews its own root beer and has an outdoor patio and full menu, featuring several pastas, grilled duck breast, and a top-notch London broil.

O'Gara's Bar & Grill
164 Snelling Avenue North, St. Paul
(651) 644-3333
www.ogaras.com
O'Gara's is a popular St. Paul bar for several reasons. First, the beer prices are reasonable, with some taps as cheap as a couple bucks. Second, it has plenty of comfortable space, nicely decorated with beautiful exposed brick, for enjoying the libations. Third, it has an entire wall dedicated to the late *Peanuts* cartoon creator, Charles Schulz. Schulz grew up in one of the apartments above O'Gara's, and his father also worked at a barbershop that today is part of O'Gara's Bar. A barber pole, Snoopy cartoons, and prints commemorate the bar's place in history.

O'Gara's also features a brewpub with several of its own beers, some of which are seasonal; a few specialty brews include Sligo Red, Oktoberfest, Light Amber Ale, and, for more adventurous beer connoisseurs, selections such as Dublin Apricot Wheat, which includes a subtle hint of apricot.

Sweeney's Saloon
96 North Dale Street, St. Paul
(651) 221-9157
Sweeney's is a local pub with beautiful woodwork and a secluded (though usually packed) patio bar open during the summer. With many excellent beers on tap, lots of booths, and a pub-food menu, Sweeney's is a neighborhood institution attracting young, cute singles and attached (or not) 30-somethings looking for a pint or a pitcher in a busy, friendly setting.

MOVIE THEATERS
Minneapolis

Asian Media Access
3028 Oregon Avenue South, Minneapolis
(612) 376-7715
www.amamedia.org
Asian Media Access specializes in the best of Asian cinema from the present and the past. Lacking a theater of its own, the organization rents two local theaters (Riverview and Oak Street) on a regular basis for screenings. Asian Media Access provides action-packed Hong Kong cinema, contemporary Japanese film, Chinese comedies, and more. Be sure to call or check the Web site. for details about upcoming events.

Bell Auditorium
U of M Campus
10 Church Street, Minneapolis
(612) 331-3134
www.mnfilmarts.org
Formerly home to the University Film Society, the Bell Auditorium has been a

pioneer in film locally and nationally for 43 years. Since its inception, the Bell Auditorium has hosted directors and film scholars of the likes of Robert Altman, Jean-Luc Godard, and Roberto Rosellini. It is the nation's first and only dedicated nonfiction film screen.

Block E 15
Block E, 600 Hennepin Avenue, Minneapolis
(612) 338-5900

Minneapolis's newest theater complex and the only cinema downtown, the Block E 15 inside the new Block E shopping and entertainment complex shows first-run movies in full digital sound with stadium seating. Students with an ID get a discount, and parking in the complex's underground ramp is only $2.00 for up to three hours.

Landmark's Lagoon Cinema
1320 Lagoon Avenue, Minneapolis
(612) 825-6006

Lagoon Cinema is part of the Landmark's national art theater chain. Arty, indie, and a few foreign hits are often held over at the Lagoon after playing its sister theater, the Uptown. The Lagoon screens smaller-budget films for a longer duration and others that would not otherwise have been shown. The five theaters in this multiplex are roomy and comfortable, with excellent sound and large movie screens, but they lack the charm of the Uptown Theatre.

Oak Street Cinema
309 Southeast Oak Street, Minneapolis
(612) 331-3134
www.mnfilmarts.org

Oak Street Cinema is the only Twin Cities theater dedicated to classic film revivals. Occasionally new films from famous directors or student films are shown, but beyond that Oak Street Cinema sticks to reviving cinema's illustrious as well as forgotten past.

The nonprofit organization is the place where Twin Cities cineastes catch their fix of film's rich history. Schedules have

included great films of the '70s, the French New Wave, and the films of directors such as Tarkovsky, Bergman, Mel Brooks, Bunuel, and a host of others. Thematic scheduling such as the best of vampire films or silent films is common. Oak Street Cinema is one of the Twin Cities great artistic treasures.

Parkway Theater
4814 Chicago Avenue South, Minneapolis
(612) 822-3030

This south Minneapolis theater has a knack for consistently showing the best of second-run indie and mainstream films. Despite the Parkway's less than spectacular ambience, this old mom-and-pop theater more than makes up for it in value. Ticket prices are low, and concession prices are a steal. If you are curious about what is playing at the Parkway, give the theater a call; the message on the answering machine is always homey and interesting.

Riverview Theatre
3800 42nd Avenue South, Minneapolis
(612) 729-7369
www.riverviewtheatre.com

The Riverview Theatre presents second-run movies in one of the Cities' most beautiful facilities. The theater is a fine example of art deco architecture and furnishings. The lobby is of particular distinction—appearing today as it probably did 50 years ago—decorated with art deco lamps and sofas.

Films screened at the Riverview are usually popular second-run films. There are occasional deviations. *The Wizard of Oz* and other cinema classics have been shown at this Minneapolis gem. Prices for tickets are a bargain ($3.00 for most shows), and concessions are much cheaper than at the suburban multiplexes, especially if you purchase a combo. The seats are comfortable, with stadium seating available in the back of the theater. The Riverview is a treasure, providing its south Minneapolis neighborhood with inexpensive entertainment in a wonderful theater.

St. Anthony Main Theatre
115 Southeast Main Street, Minneapolis
(612) 331-4723
This theater is in Minneapolis's beautiful St. Anthony area. It is also within walking distance of Nicollet Island and the Stone Arch Bridge and close to downtown.

St. Anthony Main Theatre has much more charm than your average suburban multiplex. The individual theaters and seating are comfortable and the concessions comparable to other theaters in town, but once again, the theater's real selling point is its location, right next to the picturesque St. Anthony area. Go for a walk and enjoy the grandeur and the sights of downtown and St. Anthony, then stop by the theater for a movie.

Suburban World Theater
3022 Hennepin Avenue South, Minneapolis
(612) 825-0717
The historic Suburban World Theater was renovated into a one-screen cinema and restaurant. The theater reflects the Uptown neighborhood, so the food and beverages are different from the usual grub. The menu includes the usual burgers and pizza as well as wraps, salads, tapas, and sandwiches, plus wine and beer—all served during shows. Also included is the exceptional beauty of the theater.

The Suburban World first opened in 1928 as the Granada Theatre. It was and is an example of Spanish-Moorish architecture, adorned with stucco facades of balconies, plants, and statues. The combination of the food and the architecture makes this an interesting place to see a revival or second-run film. The theater hosts special television sports events, concerts, and live performances.

Uptown Theatre
2906 Hennepin Avenue South, Minneapolis
(612) 825-6006
The Uptown Theatre is where most art and indie cinema debuts in the Twin Cities. Films frequently are screened at the Uptown exclusively before moving to Landmark's Lagoon Cinema and suburban Twin Cities theaters.

In the heart of Minneapolis's hip Uptown neighborhood, the Uptown Theatre is a stunning piece of architecture. Since the 1930s it has been the best single-screen theater in the area, in part because of its size—as large as most of the suburban multiplexes. The balcony is huge and the seating is comfortable. Unfortunately, despite its breathtaking architecture, details such as the restrooms and paint on the walls have not been as well maintained. Nevertheless, the Uptown Theatre remains one of the most enjoyable movie venues in the Twin Cities.

St. Paul

Grandview Theater
1830 Grand Avenue, St. Paul
(651) 698-3344
Two neighborhood theaters showing first-run movies survive in St. Paul, and the Grandview, opened in 1933, lives on at its Grand Avenue location near Macalester College and the University of St. Thomas. The theater has two screens, a large theater downstairs and a smaller room upstairs (originally the theater's balcony). Designed in the art moderne style, the classic theater is a neighborhood treasure.

Highland Theater
760 Cleveland Avenue South, St. Paul
(651) 698-3085
This 1938 art deco theater in St. Paul's Highland Park neighborhood shows first-run movies. Competition from suburban megacomplexes has hit many one- and two-screen cinemas in the Cities hard over the years, and the Highland, along with its sister theater, the Grandview, is a holdover from another era.

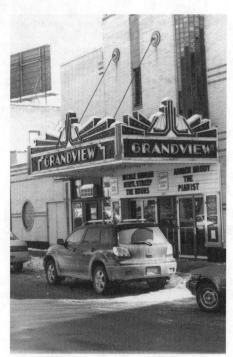

St. Paul's historic Grandview Theater on Grand Avenue in St. Paul. TODD R. BERGER

The Suburbs

Har Mar 11
2100 North Snelling Avenue, Roseville
(651) 636-2664
www.generalcinema.com
If you want to see the most recent Hollywood blockbusters with a few indie and art house film leftovers, this is the spot. Har Mar and the retail complexes in Roseville are some of the largest in the Twin Cities, with the exception of the Mall of America, so go ahead and catch a film and do some shopping all in one visit. There are three large theaters where the most recent box office smashes are shown daily on big screens and eight smaller theaters with a smaller multiplex feel.

Heights Theatre
3951 Central Avenue NE,
Columbia Heights
(763) 788-9079
www.heightstheater.com
Once a dilapidated second-run theater, the Heights was transformed into one of the most beautiful theaters in the Twin Cities when the inside and outside were painted, comfortable new seats installed, and a vintage theater organ put in place. The organ allows silent film classics to be scored for the audience's pleasure.

Besides occasional silent film revivals, the Heights books second-run and classic films as well as special events such as Tromafest, a festival dedicated to the kitschy horror of Troma Studios (see "The Heights" close-up). For adventurous film lovers the Heights is one of the most interesting movie theaters in the Twin Cities.

Pavilion at Crossroads
County Road B2 and Snelling Avenue,
Roseville
(651) 777-FILM
These theaters are part of the United Artists theater chain and show the Hollywood hits with a few art and indie films. Pavilion at Crossroads has excellent sound and seating and has the advantage of proximity to Minneapolis and St. Paul and easy accessibility via Minnesota Highway 36.

Regal Brooklyn Center 20
6420 Camden Avenue North
(763) 560-6300
www.regalcinemas.com
Regal Brooklyn Center 20 has the most screens and the most modern theaters in the Twin Cities. Carmike Oakdale Stadium 20 is the only other theater in the area with 20 screens. The Regal, like the other megaplexes, has stadium seating, high-back adjustable chairs, and digital sound in all of its theaters. Despite its size, Regal feels more comfortable due to its design, which includes larger individual theaters decorated with minimalistic murals. This immense yet comfortable megaplex

The Heights

Once considered an eyesore in an already rundown part of town, the Heights Theatre has been reborn as the centerpiece of a cultural revolution in the Columbia Heights suburb of Minneapolis. Under the guidance of proprietors Tom Letness and Dave Holmgren, who bought the theater in 1998 and funded the renovation with profits from the Dairy Queen franchise they own right next door, the tacky turquoise aluminum siding facade was stripped to reveal the beautiful brickwork underneath. Inside, the garish green walls were replaced with red velvet drapes and a deep purple coat of paint. The sound system and projectors were replaced with up-to-date equipment as well as an antiquated 70mm projector. With this new hardware it's now possible for the Heights to screen silent Frank Capra classics, the original 70mm prints of *Lawrence of Arabia,* and an amazing selection of Bollywood Hindi-language action films that have packed the 410-seat theater to capacity on a regular basis. They put in a restored Wurlitzer theater organ, and classic silent films now have the live organ accompaniment they did when they were first screened.

Aside from the wide selection of art house, classic, and foreign films it shows, the Heights holds special, irregularly scheduled events where independent filmmakers passing through town come into the theater to speak about their work and sign autographs. In 2000 Lloyd Kaufman of Troma Films stopped in on his way to the Sundance Film Festival to lecture, sign copies of his book about the history of his company, and give out free T-shirts and video copies of his movies to audience members. The event was accompanied by a weeklong film retrospective of Troma classics. The Heights also hosts the Minnesota Film Festival in conjunction with the area's annual spring Art-A-Whirl gallery tours as well as the annual late summer Minneapolis/St. Paul International Film Festival. All during the holiday season (starting with Halloween), holiday-specific classics and new films are shown.

The neighborhood the Heights is nestled in has undergone a similar reawakening. With the influx of immigrants coming into the Twin Cities metro areas, everything from Balkan coffee shops serving Bosnian foods to Middle Eastern restaurants and grocery stores have taken root and blossomed in northeast Minneapolis. Gone are the days when the main sources of entertainment were tiny diners and bowling alleys huddled in the shadows of the giant cereal factories and industrial warehouses—northeast Minneapolis today is a true, working melting pot of customs and cultures.

Despite being an art house theater on par with those in uptown Minneapolis, the Heights retains its everyman's appeal. With its more-than-reasonable door prices (usually $5.00 per adult), cheap concessions, and free street parking, the Heights has managed to keep itself accessible to the working-class Columbia Heights neighborhood, which only recently started having coffee shops that were more than greasy spoons. The Heights doesn't pretend to be a highbrow establishment, either. It mixes black-and-white horror and science fiction classics with popular second-run films and true art films. The theater has a loyal core crowd of locals who show up to see everything it runs, and, depending on what's on for the night, the rest of the audience comes from every imaginable walk of life to the suburban theater.

includes a cafe stocked with coffees and ice creams and a video game room for kids of all ages.

Roseville 4 Theatres
1211 Larpenteur Avenue West, Roseville
(651) 488-4242
Roseville 4 shows all the Hollywood block-buster hits—and does it for cheap. Tuesday night tickets are only $1.00 and concessions are reasonably priced. These bargains make Roseville 4 a perennially favorite hangout for teens in the Twin Cities. The theater is located conveniently near the busy Roseville shopping area.

Showplace 16 Theatres
Minnesota Highway 52 at Upper 55th Street, Inver Grove Heights
(651) 453-1916
www.kerasotes.com
One of the first mammoth megaplexes in the Twin Cities, Showplace 16 Theatres is also one of the best. With some of the largest movie screens, comfortable stadium seating, and a great view of the screen anywhere, Showplace 16 is one of the many new colossal multiplexes in the Twin Cities suburban area.

Mall of America

AMC Mall of America 14
401 South Avenue, Mall of America,
60 East Broadway, Bloomington
(952) 777-3456
This is one of the better theaters for watching movies in the Twin Cities. The theaters are large and comfortable, with huge screens and clear sound. AMC Mall of America occasionally is the site for local and even national premieres as well as quirky bookings. The "Terror at the Mall" Halloween series is one great example, when recent and classic horror films were shown at midnight during the month of October. But there are disadvantages at the Mall of America. The theaters are almost always busy; however, the complex is well designed for handling large crowds.

The concessions are as extensive as any theater in the Twin Cities. Pizza and coffee are available as well as the traditional popcorn and soda.

SPORTS BARS
Minneapolis

Big Ten Restaurant & Bar
606 Washington Avenue SE, Minneapolis
(612) 378-0467
The Big Ten Restaurant & Bar is a University of Minnesota institution, known both for good subs and for covering Minnesota Golden Gophers athletics. The restaurant and bar is filled with memorabilia from Gophers sports; included are numerous autographed photos of triumphs in football, basketball, and hockey. For atmosphere alone, this is the place to catch a Gophers game, not to mention the beer and the excellent bar food. The televisions may not be as large and fancy as at the suburban bars, but they make up for it in spirit and tradition—and isn't that what college athletics are about after all?

City Billiards Bar & Café
25 North Fourth Street, Minneapolis
(612) 338-BALL
City Billiards is the pool hall for downtown Minneapolis. Though smaller than its suburban counterparts, it has the advantage of being situated in the shadows of Minneapolis's skyline. Available at City Billiards are beer, sandwiches, and pizza. The prices are reasonable for the pricey Warehouse District, and specials are available for pool, food, and drinks.

Dub's Pub & Grill
412 14th Avenue SE, Minneapolis
(612) 331-4111
Over the years this has been the site of numerous restaurants, bars, and grills. All have served a similar purpose as the local watering hole for the student population of the University of Minnesota. Dub's is a

popular place to go for Minnesota Golden Gophers basketball, football, and hockey. The big-screen television and the reasonably priced burgers and subs are also big draws. So if you visit the state and are curious about Minnesotans' obsession with hockey—or would like a tall glass of tap beer—stop by Dub's.

William's Uptown Pub & Peanut Bar
2911 Hennepin Avenue South, Minneapolis
(612) 823-6271

If you are looking for variety in domestic and imported beers, William's is the place. This Uptown establishment boasts 217 different bottled beers from around the world, including Russia, Thailand, Africa, Finland, and Greece. In addition, William's offers plenty of daily specials on domestic beers and appetizers. The appetizers are enormous and go great with their wide selection of tap beers. William's is divided into a pub on the first floor and a more casual peanut bar in the basement where, not surprisingly, peanuts and popcorn are complimentary. Despite the sophisticated beer selection, the clientele at William's is mostly the young Uptown set, who enjoy the billiards and darts available on both floors.

St. Paul

Billy's on Grand
857 Grand Avenue, St. Paul
(651) 292-9140
www.billysongrand.com

Billy's on Grand offers something for all who are looking for a drink and a good time. The rooms at Billy's provide unlimited possibilities, from sports bar to lodge to patio seating in the summer. The beer prices are reasonable, too. Also available is a full menu, which includes burgers and prime rib. The variety of options at Billy's is one of the reasons it is extremely busy on weekends and is such a popular nightlife spot among young St. Paulites.

Tom Reid's Hockey City Pub
258 West Seventh Street, St. Paul
(651) 292-9916
www.tomreids.com

The name of this pub says it all. Hockey returned to Minnesota in 2000 at the Xcel Energy Center in St. Paul; in its wake, many new bars and restaurants have sprung up. And who better to open a pub than Tom Reid, a former National Hockey League player with the Minnesota North Stars (now the Dallas Stars) and current Minnesota Wild broadcaster? Not only does the pub broadcast the game on television screens but it also hosts a radio pregame on KFAN, the local sports radio station.

The Suburbs

Biff's Sports Bar & Grill
7777 NE Minnesota Highway 65, Spring Lake Park
(763) 784-9446

Biff's provides inexpensive pool, darts, food, and sports viewing for the northern suburbs of the Twin Cities. Televisions range in size from big to bigger screens at Biff's, where you can watch all your Vikings game-day action. Besides the sports bar there are more than 25 pool tables, where the local working-class clientele play in organized pool leagues and enjoy Biff's many beer specials.

Billiard Street Café
7178 University Avenue NE, Fridley
(763) 574-1399
www.billiardstreet.com

Since 1988 Billiard Street Café has served as a pool hall with a cafe and a proshop, and in 2005 it added a bar. It is inconspicuously located in a strip mall; despite this, it is one of Minnesota's largest billiard clubs, with more than 50 pool tables. In-house eight ball leagues make the Billiard Street Café busy, and it is sometimes difficult to reserve a table on weekday evenings, although they are usually available after a wait. The late night/morning hours also provide ample opportunity for billiards. If you are looking to play pool in the Twin Cities, Billiard Street Café might be the place for you.

Joe Senser's Sports Grill & Bar
2350 Cleveland Avenue, Roseville
(651) 631-1781

4217 West 80th Street, Bloomington
(952) 835-1191

3010 Eagandale Place, St. Paul
(651) 687-9333
www.sensers.com

Joe Senser's Sports Grill & Bar is a popular spot for Minnesota Vikings fans. With three locations, it easily serves much of the area and provides excellent coverage on several big-screen televisions as well as numerous smaller monitors. Joe Senser, a former Minnesota Viking, is the local legend/owner and also participates in a Vikings postgame show, *Vikings Unsensored* (on Twin Cities sports radio station KFAN), after each game. In addition, Senser's features college football and basketball, as well as professional basketball, baseball, and hockey. Offering a wide selection of beers, Senser's has plenty of food to accompany the suds.

Park Tavern
3401 Louisiana Avenue, St. Louis Park
(952) 929-6810

5221 Viking Drive, Bloomington
(952) 844-0335
www.parktavern.com

The Park Tavern is one of the Twin Cities' premier sports bars. Twin Citians come in hordes to watch sports on the big-screen televisions and enjoy the kitchen's excellent food. This is where Park Tavern has the competition beat. Many other sports bars treat the food as secondary, but the Park Tavern excels, with delicious burgers and sandwiches, not the everyday bar fare. Plus it has some of the best beer specials in town for Vikings games, and the St. Louis Park location boasts the best bowling alley in the Twin Cities.

UNIQUE TO THE TWIN CITIES

Grumpy's Downtown
1111 Washington Avenue South, Minneapolis
(612) 340-9738
www.grumpysbar.com/downtown.html

Although we're told this looks kind of divey from the outside, especially since the interior lights are kept low at all times, this is actually a really interesting bar to check out. Intermittently, tables are moved around to make way for performance artists, poets, and acoustic and electric bands to set up in one corner, or a movie screen and projector are brought in and art house films, black-and-white classics, and new films from local filmmakers are showcased, including those from the ex-Minnesotan Coen brothers. There are several pool tables and an ATM on the premises. About a dozen beers are on tap and a decent selection of food on the menu—especially for a bar—and the waitstaff is attentive and friendly.

Nye's Polonaise Room
112 Hennepin Avenue East, Minneapolis
(612) 379-2021
www.nyespolonaise.com

Now this is a fun place to drink. Nye's, a northeast Minneapolis tradition since 1949, features live polka music in one half of the bar and a piano bar in the other most nights of the week, and everyone comes here to dance. The crowd is about as mixed as you can get, with senior citizens manning the accordions in Ruth Adams' Polka Band and barely 21-year-old hipsters hanging out on the dance floor. The bar looks much the same as it did when it first opened, with scarlet walls and carpets and dark, polished wood accents everywhere. The bar serves Polish and American food that's good enough to come in for even if you don't want to polka.

SHOPPING

"Shopping trip" means so many different things when in the Twin Cities. It could mean a sunny, summer walk down picturesque Grand Avenue in St. Paul, where beautiful two-story Victorian houses have been converted into antiques shops, custom clothiers, or flower shops with multihued wares spilling out onto the sidewalk. It could mean window-shopping in busy downtown Minneapolis, where importers, clothiers, and jewelers have set up shop in the ornate storefronts of 100-plus-year-old buildings. It could mean braving the immense Mall of America, the largest indoor mall in the country.

But whatever "shopping trip" means to you, you're sure to find satisfaction shopping in the Twin Cities. There are tiny neighborhood shops, heady metropolitan areas, and suburban malls that carry everything from sports to celebrity memorabilia; specialty grocery complexes that sell novelty items and foods from around the world; and stores that carry everything you'd ever need to have a successful and beautiful wedding, professional social event, or child's theme birthday party.

ANTIQUES SHOPS
Minneapolis

City Salvage and Antiques
505 First Avenue NE, Minneapolis
(612) 627-9107
Mantels, archways, buffets, stained glass, and other high-end items salvaged from pre-1950s buildings fill this store. The changing inventory has at times included Charlie the Tuna lamps, a full bar complete with booths, and church pews. Owner John Eckley has more than two decades' experience in architectural salvage.

St. Paul

Wescott Station Antiques
226 West Seventh Street, St. Paul
(651) 227-2469
Wescott Station Antiques is a family-run antiques business offering seven rooms full of antique furniture, glassware, lamps, and more. Literally thousands of antiques and collectibles line the walls of this tightly packed store, making a visit here as much a treasure hunt as it is a shopping spree.

West

Battlefield Military Antiques
3915 Minnesota Highway 7,
St. Louis Park
(952) 920-3820
www.battlefieldstore.com
Battlefield Military Antiques is absolutely packed with war memorabilia, including rows and rows of books, magazines, and unopened boxes of model soldiers, frontiersmen, warplanes, and boats. The books, new and used, cover every era of combat from Hadrian's Wall to Vietnam, in incredible levels of both technical and strategic detail. What catches the eye first, though, are the neatly racked and displayed antiques: a clothing store's worth of old uniforms, helmets worn by both good guys and bad guys, blue and green caps topping the shelves in perfect rows, ribbons, and medals. Collectors will also appreciate the boxes of limited-edition G.I. Joes.

Blake Antiques
1115 Excelsior Avenue East, Hopkins
(952) 930-0477
www.carlsonantiques.com
Blake Antiques carries refinished antique

furniture ready to bring home and display without even needing to be dusted. The store also carries fine sterling jewelry and flatware, original oil paintings, Oriental rugs, fine porcelain (including unusual arts and crafts–movement designs), pottery, and an eclectic collection of costume and fine jewelry.

BOOKSTORES
Minneapolis

Amazon Bookstore Cooperative
755 Chicago Avenue South, Minneapolis
(612) 821-9630
www.amazonfembks.com
Amazon opened in the late 1960s, making it the oldest independent feminist bookstore in the country. The bookstore in south Minneapolis stocks some 10,000 fiction and nonfiction titles as well as gifts, music, and art all by, for, and about women. The bookstore, which specializes in titles from small feminist presses, is a worker cooperative, and the friendly staff will steer you to titles of interest.

Big Brain Comics
1027 Washington Avenue South, Minneapolis
(612) 338-4390
This small, well-stocked comic book store focuses more on unusual and underground comic books and magazines than the superhero type that Marvel and DC put out. There are lots of imported comics in the stacks, as well as American independent and collectible comic books.

The Bokhandel
2600 Park Avenue, Minneapolis
(612) 871-4907
www.americanswedishinst.org
Located inside the beautiful American Swedish Institute building, the Bokhandel sells books, prints, cards, gift items, compact discs, and cassette tapes relating to Sweden and Scandinavia. Titles are available in both English and Swedish.

Book House in Dinkytown
429 14th Avenue SE, Minneapolis
(612) 331-1430
The Book House has been a mainstay of the U of M's Dinkytown area for more than 30 years, carrying hardcover and softcover books. With more than 150,000 volumes in stock, this store has bookshelves that run from floor to ceiling and has excellent fiction, drama, and poetry sections, not to mention rows and rows of foreign language material and an entire basement level dedicated to scholarly works. Book House buys tons of used books, so it's worth checking back regularly to see what's new in stock.

B H Biermaier's Books
809 Fourth Street SE, Minneapolis
(612) 378-0129
Bill Biermaier has been selling books from his Minneapolis location for a quarter century and is proud of his success in locating hard-to-find copies of out-of-print or obscure books. Arts, literature, and children's books dominate the store's collection in sheer number, but Biermaier's is a good source for just about any genre of book, including rare and collectors' editions. With ceiling-high stacks and books spilling out into the aisles, this place practically begs you to browse for hours. Finding a specific book can become a daylong challenge, but if you need to get out in a hurry, Bill can find it for you awfully quick.

BookSmart
2919 Hennepin Avenue South, Minneapolis
(612) 823-5612
BookSmart is the place to go to buy cheap used books, with a huge selection of mysteries and a great biography section. Turnover is quick, so if you see something you want in stock, you'd better buy it or someone else will.

Cummings Books
417 14th Avenue SE, Minneapolis
(612) 331–1424
www.cummingsbooks.com
This is a bookstore for book *and* pet lovers—expect to see cats, dogs, and a couple of birds as you browse the stacks. The variety of books include literary criticism, special interest, and Canadian history. If you can't find what you're looking for, Cummings Books's friendly staff is more than willing to help you look.

DreamHaven Books & Comics
912 West Lake Street, Minneapolis
(612) 823–6161
www.dreamhavenbooks.com
In addition to Jupiter-size selections of new and used books, DreamHaven is a dream destination for fans of comic books, Japanese anime, kung fu movies, and everything pop-cultural, from Dr. Who to Asterix. An online catalog and a mail-order service mean that even out-of-state patrons can enjoy DreamHaven. DreamHaven is also responsible for putting on some of the larger science fiction and fantasy fan conventions in the Twin Cities and holds many in-store book signings when science fiction and fantasy authors pass through town.

Lien's Bookstore
507 Hennepin Avenue East, Minneapolis
(612) 362–0763
Not your ordinary used book store, Lien's is a treasury of the printed word. First editions and rare, out-of-print, and gorgeous art and history volumes live in this picturesque corner-store collection. The store holds 4,000 square feet of books and specializes in European and American history, with a particular emphasis on military books as well as classic literature. The knowledgeable staff will help track down those hard-to-find old books the store may not have on hand.

Magus Books & Herbs
1309^{1}/$_{2}$ Fourth Street SE, Minneapolis
(612) 379–7669
www.magusbooks.com

Magus Books sells new books on tai chi, Wicca, magic, tarot, astrology, and the like, as well as herbs, candles, incense, scented oils, jewelry, and meditation and New Age tapes and CDs. The staff is informative and can direct you to exactly whatever it is you're looking for, as well as provide helpful historical background information on products you purchase.

Paperback Exchange
2227 West 50th Street, Minneapolis
(612) 929–8801
www.paperbackexchange.com
Paperback Exchange carries more than 300,000 used paperback books covering pretty much all subjects, from pulp mystery to criticism, depending on what's in their current, quick-turnover stock. The store rents hardcover books for nominal charges, many of which are brand-new and not yet available at local libraries.

Present Moment Books & Herbs
3546 Grand Avenue South, Minneapolis
(612) 824–3157
www.presentmoment.com
One of the nation's largest purveyors of herbs and homeopathic remedies, Present Moment offers more than 36,000 new and used book titles. Whether your New Age and wellness needs run to *Cooking with Herbs* or *The Spirit of Place: A Workbook for Sacred Alignment,* it's present at Present Moment. Their specialties include books on alternative health, world religions, New Age, Wicca, and yoga, as well as women's studies and environmental publications.

St. Martin's Table Bookstore
2001 Riverside Avenue, Minneapolis
(612) 339–3920
www.communityofstmartin.org
St. Martin's Table Bookstore shares a space with St. Martin's Table (see the Restaurants chapter), with racks of books devoted to peace, religion, and social-justice issues. The bookstore holds Friday-night readings and performances September through May.

 CLOSE-UP

Nicollet Mall

Nicollet Mall is Minneapolis's main artery. It's the center of the action, a 12-block stretch of stores, restaurants, and hotels between Washington Avenue and Grant Street that hums year-round. This is a pedestrian mall—no cars allowed. It's all about people here.

In spring people, after being cooped up all winter, descend from their offices in the Minneapolis skyscrapers and exit the skyways to savor the season on Nicollet Mall. In summer they stroll along the mall, pick up dinner ingredients or flower bouquets at the bustling farmers' market, and eat on streetside patios. In winter it's true that a lot of the action stays indoors, but you can count on the Holidazzle Parades to draw people back out. On cold, snowy days, well-insulated folks line Nicollet Mall up to an hour before the nightly twinkle-lit parades begin, which are held from just after Thanksgiving until Christmas. After each parade, the spectators turn into holiday shoppers flitting in and out of businesses along the parade's mall route.

Visitors and new Twin Cities residents, remember the "no cars allowed" rule. It's easy to get caught up in finding your way around downtown and make a wrong turn onto the mall. Cars were banned from Nicollet Mall in the 1960s as part of a broader plan to keep people shopping in the city. By eliminating cars and adding wide sidewalks, trees, and places to sit, Minneapolis encouraged people to shop, dine, and socialize downtown.

The fact that the mall exists today shows that the plan worked, though this stretch of downtown has had its ups and downs. Not everyone wants to stay downtown after work or make the trip into the city when the largest mall in America beckons only a few miles away. But there's business downtown, and where there's business there're people, and this is who the mall was built for.

There's a two-story Target here (the discount store's headquarters are on the mall, too) and name-brand stores await in the stretch's shopping centers: Neiman Marcus, Marshall Field's, a Sak's outlet, and lots of smaller stores you'd find in any major shopping center. There are a few independent stores here, too—though if that's what you're seeking, you're better off walking a few blocks to the Warehouse District, where storefront rents are cheaper.

In the last few years, city promoters gave the mall a nickname: Restaurant

Shinders
733 Hennepin Avenue, Minneapolis
(612) 333-3628
www.shinders.com
With 13 locations throughout the Twin Cities metro area, locally owned Shinders is a great place to pick up major newspapers from around the country, comic books, games, sports collectibles and trading cards, hard-to-find independent magazines, and books from both major and independent publishing houses.

Outdoor dining on Nicollet Mall. GREATER MINNEAPOLIS CONVENTION & VISITORS ASSOCIATION

Row, It's easy to see why. One of the coolest things about this side of the mall is that the dining options run the gamut from fancy fusion to basic deli to Irish pub food. As soon as Nicollet crosses Grant Street, on its southwestern end, it changes from Restaurant Row to Eat Street, well established and known for its range of ethnic restaurants.

Activities, too, draw people to Nicollet Mall, and those go beyond the street performers and the biweekly farmers' market. Peavey Plaza, next to Orchestra Hall, has lots of free concerts throughout the summer and a Rockefeller Centeresque ice-skating rink in the winter. Marshall Field's continued the traditions of its predecessor, Dayton's, Minnesota's old school department store born on Nicollet Mall. These include a spectacular garden show every spring and a storybook holiday show each winter, both free, and both Twin Cities family traditions. Branch out just a block or two from the mall and you've got the clubs of the Warehouse District, the theaters of Hennepin Avenue, the events of Target Center, and more. It's a good thing, this desire to coax people downtown. And it's a good thing, for the people and for the city, that it worked.

Uncle Edgar's Mystery Bookstore/Uncle Hugo's Science Fiction Bookstore
2864 Chicago Avenue South, Minneapolis
(612) 824-6347 or (612) 824-9984
www.uncleedgar.com or
www.unclehugo.com

Specialization is the name of the game for many independent booksellers in these days of giant chain bookstores, but Uncle Edgar's/Uncle Hugo's was at it long before the trend began in the late '80s. Uncle Hugo's opened in 1974, and Uncle Edgar's opened in 1980. The two shops merged into one location in south Minneapolis in 1984. With a huge selection of their respective genres, both new and used, they sponsor many author readings every month. Check their shared Web site for information about upcoming events.

St. Paul

Midway Used & Rare Books
1579 University Avenue West, St. Paul
(651) 644-8786
www.midwaybook.com
With three stories of used and rare books that include huge pulp fiction and small-press poetry sections, this store seems almost too good to be true. The prices are incredibly reasonable, and if whatever it was you originally came to find isn't available, you're sure to find one or two things that are easily good enough to take home.

The Red Balloon Bookshop
891 Grand Avenue, St. Paul
(651) 224-8320
www.redballoonbookshop.com
This spacious bookstore, specializing in educational and fun books for kids, is located in a beautiful converted Victorian house on St. Paul's Grand Avenue. The store carries books, audio- and videotapes, and selected toys for young people from birth to junior high age. The bookstore offers nonprofit discounts; takes mail and phone orders; and hosts a storyline as well as in-store events. Several times a year visiting authors and educators speak at the Red Balloon. You can call the storyline 24/7 for a story at (952) 352-1350. Or visit www.storylineonline.net.

 Most downtown Minneapolis restaurants and stores participate in the "Do the Town" parking program, where a $20 purchase after 4:00 P.M. and all day on weekends will get you a parking validation.

Sixth Chamber Used Books
1332 Grand Avenue, St. Paul
(651) 690-9463
www.sixthchamber.com
Sixth Chamber Used Books is a clean, well-organized, and spacious used book store featuring hardcover and paperback editions in most major categories. Especially notable is the used science fiction and fantasy section, which takes up several ceiling-to-floor shelves in the back of the store. The prices are extremely reasonable, and staff is both quick and efficient. Sixth Chamber holds irregular in-store book signings and author readings.

CLOTHING STORES

Minneapolis

Hubert White
747 Nicollet Mall,
IDS Crystal Court, Minneapolis
(612) 339-9200
Hubert White has been the quality standard for men's apparel since it opened its first store in Minneapolis in 1916. Today the men's clothier carries brand-name men's contemporary, casual, and formal wear, including Gran Sasso, Bobby Jones, Scott Barber, Canali, Oxxford, Tallia, and Burberry. The professional staff is helpful in both assisting with selecting purchases and arranging alterations at the last minute.

Lava Lounge
3037 Lyndale Avenue South,
Minneapolis
(612) 824-5631
www.lavalounge.com
Lava Lounge's inventory makes it a one-stop shop for club clothes. Beyond the staples—shiny, leathered, glittery, synthetic clothes—it also carries an impressive array of cuffs, handbags, and eyewear, with brand names like Miss Sixty, Betty Blush, and Merc stocked for all seasons. Lava Lounge's annual patio sale occurs during

the Lyn-Lake Festival in August, when prices on cool clothes are significantly dropped.

Nate's Clothing Company
27 North Fourth Street, Minneapolis
(612) 333-1401
A fixture in the Minneapolis Warehouse District since 1916, Nate's carries a staggering collection of worsted wool, nubby tweed, and linen suits and shirts. The store carries suits and sportcoats from designers like Bill Blass and Ralph Lauren, and Nate's expert staff can find something sharp and classy for even hard-to-size guys. The store's sales are legendary, so sign up for Nate's mailings for the inside scoop on sale dates.

Saint Sabrina's Parlor in Purgatory
2751 Hennepin Avenue South, Minneapolis
(612) 874-7360
www.saintsabrinas.com
Decorated in deep black and red tones, Saint Sabrina's is a decadent shopping experience. The store has club clothes, sunglasses, shoes, bondage clothes, leather jackets, and even an in-store piercing booth. The clearance rack is a good place to pick up marked-down stuff that was cool yesterday and will probably be cool and expensive again tomorrow.

Top Shelf Clothiers & Consultants
3040 Lyndale Avenue South, Minneapolis
(612) 824-2800
www.topshelfinc.com
Located inside a turn-of-the-20th-century former home, Top Shelf is divided into many small, friendly rooms that are perfect for the personalized business of creating custom clothing. A formal dining room now acts as the library for a collection of the finest offerings of suit, sportcoat, pant, and topcoat materials from the woolen mills of England, Italy, Spain, and the United States. Well-known fabric lines such as Zegna, Loro Piana, Roger La Viale, Scabal, Reda, Barberis, Cerruti, Holland,

Sherry, and many others are available for custom designs, including shirts. From the selection of fabric to measurement and styling, the customer is encouraged to follow the process and participate in laying the groundwork for satisfying future orders.

St. Paul

Artgarbs Gallery
796 Grand Avenue, St. Paul
(651) 229-0204
www.artgarbs.com
Most pieces of clothing in Artgarbs Gallery are an original concept and design, hand painted by owner and resident artist Lisa J. Omodt. The clothing is 100 percent cotton or linen and is machine washable.

C'est Fou Showroom
1128 Grand Avenue, St. Paul
(651) 602-9133
This French boutique–style retail store carries one-of-a-kind and custom-made clothes as well as elegant shoes and eclectic and glamorous jewelry and accessories. The store offers free alterations on all clothes purchased here, with an emphasis on creating a flattering fit for customers. The store displays and sells a rotating stock of artwork and jewelry created by local artists.

There is no sales tax on clothing in Minnesota.

Coat of Many Colors
1666 Grand Avenue, St. Paul
(651) 690-5255
This Grand Avenue store specializes in natural fabric women's clothing in all sizes, as well as jewelry and gifts from around the world. Most of the jewelry is handmade, focusing on sterling silver set with

semiprecious stones, bone, seeds, and metals. Coat of Many Colors is a socially and environmentally conscious store that returns 20 percent of its profits to Third World development projects.

Grand Jeté
975 Grand Avenue, St. Paul
(651) 227-0331
www.grandjete.com
Grand Jeté is a retail store carrying dancewear for children and adults, including dance tights, leotards, and skirts and ballet, pointe, tap, and jazz shoes in a full range of sizes. The store staff is especially helpful in assisting customers in the selection and proper fit of pointe shoes.

West

Oh Baby!
3515 Galleria, Edina
(952) 928-9119

743 East Lake Street, Wayzata
(952) 404-0170
Oh Baby! offers some of the Twin Cities' most precious selection of clothing for infants, toddlers, and growing boys and girls, along with bedding, furnishings, accessories, and gifts. Much of the inventory is imported from Europe, while in-house designers can be hired to fully customize children's rooms with hand-painted walls, furniture, and custom bedding.

Whymsy
3360 Galleria, Edina
(952) 924-4176
www.whymsy.com
Whymsy is a retailer of creative attire and accessories for women, including distinctive one-of-a-kind and limited-edition items. The store is full of brand-name lines of upscale, coordinated women's clothing and accessories, with a focus on elegant casual and special occasion attire for the nontraditional woman.

FARMERS' MARKETS

Aldrich Arena Farmers' Market
1850 White Bear Avenue, Maplewood
(651) 227-6856
www.stpaulfarmersmarket.com
8:00 A.M. to 12:00 P.M. Wednesday.

At the Farm
8880 East Minnesota Highway 5, Waconia
(952) 442-4816
www.atthefarmwaconia.com
10:00 A.M. to 5:00 P.M. daily.

Axdahl's Garden Farm
7452 Manning Avenue, Stillwater
(651) 439-2460
www.axdahlfarms.com
Call for hours.

Burnsville Farmers' Market
Diamondhead Senior Campus,
200 West Burnsville Parkway, Burnsville
(952) 227-6856
www.stpaulfarmersmarket.com
8:00 A.M. to 1:00 P.M. Saturday, noon to 5:00 P.M. Thursday

Cal's Market and Greenhouse
6403 Eagan Drive, Savage
(952) 447-5215
8:00 A.M. to 8:00 P.M. Monday through Saturday, 10:00 A.M. to 6:00 P.M. Sunday.

Excelsior Farmers' Market
Lyman Park on Water Street, Excelsior
(952) 474-5330
www.excelsioronline.com
2:00 to 6:00 P.M. Thursday.

Gerten's Farm Market
2900 East 65th Street,
Inver Grove Heights
(651) 450-0001
9:00 A.M. to 6:00 P.M. daily.

Minneapolis' Farmers' Market on Nicollet Mall. GREATER MINNEAPOLIS CONVENTION & VISITORS ASSOCIATION

Herb Man
24149 Chippendale Avenue West,
Farmington
(651) 463-2504
www.herb-man.com
9:00 A.M. to 6:00 P.M. Monday through Friday, weekends at St. Paul Downtown Farmers' Market (see listing).

Hopkins Farmers' Market
16 Ninth Avenue South, Hopkins
(952) 922-7703
www.mfma.com
7:30 A.M. to noon Saturday.

Jordan Ranch
6400 Upper Afton Road, Woodbury
(651) 738-3422
9:00 A.M. to 6:00 P.M. Tuesday through Sunday.

Marketfest
3rd Street and Washington,
White Bear Lake
(651) 426-2271
6:00 to 9:00 P.M. Thursday.

Minneapolis Farmers' Market
312 Lyndale Avenue North, Minneapolis
(612) 333-1737
www.mplsfarmersmarket.com
6:00 A.M. to 1:00 P.M. weekdays, 6:00 A.M. to 2:00 P.M. weekends.

Minneapolis Farmers' Market
on Nicollet Mall
Nicollet Mall between 4th and 10th
Street, Minneapolis
(612) 333-1737
www.mplsfarmersmarket.com
6:00 A.M. to 6:00 P.M. Thursday, 8:00 A.M. to 3:00 P.M. Saturday. The Saturday market may be closed during Nicollet Mall events.

Morrie's Market
7170 Minnesota Highway 7, Excelsior
(952) 472-1135
Open daily from July to October; hours vary.

Northfield Area Farmers' Market
Riverside Park on Seventh Street,
Northfield
(651) 463-3577
Call for hours and dates.

Pahl's Market
6885 160th Street, Apple Valley
(952) 431-4345
9:00 A.M. to 8:00 P.M. Saturday, 10:00 A.M. to 5:00 P.M. Sunday.

Peterson Produce
8910 Minnesota Highway 12, Delano
(763) 972-2052
8:00 A.M. to 6:00 P.M. daily.

Richfield Farmers' Market
6335 Portland Avenue, Richfield
(612) 861-9385
www.ci.richfield.mn.us
7:00 A.M. to noon Saturday.

Riverside Farm Market
Minnesota Highway 10, Elk River
(763) 427-6023
8:00 A.M. to 7:00 P.M. daily.

Seventh Place Mall Farmers' Market
7th Street and Wabasha Street, St. Paul
(651) 227-6856
www.stpaulfarmersmarket.com
10:00 A.M. to 2:00 P.M. Tuesday and Thursday.

St. Luke's Church Farmers' Market
1079 Summit Avenue, St. Paul
(651) 227-6856
www.stpaulfarmersmarket.com
1:15 to 5:00 P.M. Friday.

St. Paul Downtown Farmers' Market
5th Street and Wall Street, St. Paul
(651) 227-6856
www.stpaulfarmersmarket.com
6:00 A.M. to 1:00 P.M. Saturday, 8:00 A.M. to 1:00 P.M. Sunday, noon to 5:00 P.M. Friday.

West St. Paul Farmers' Market
Signal Hills Shopping Center, Butler and
Robert Street, West St. Paul
(651) 227-6856
8:00 A.M. to noon Friday.

White Bear Lake Farmers' Market
Corner of Third Street and Washington
Square, White Bear Lake
(651) 429-8566
8:00 A.M. to 1:00 P.M. Friday.

Woodbury Farmers' Market
Central Park lot on Radio Drive,
Woodbury
(651) 227-6856
www.stpaulfarmersmarket.com
8:00 A.M. to 1:00 P.M. Sunday.

FLOWER AND GARDEN SHOPS
Minneapolis

Brown & Greene
4400 Beard Avenue South,
Minneapolis
(612) 928-3778
www.bgfloral.net
Brown & Greene floral designer Lyn
Williams has been creating beautiful, nontraditional arrangements from her historic
neighborhood store since 1989. Her
designs are centered around customers'
color choices and feature unusual flower
combinations, like gerberas and black
calla lilies with roses and more conventional flowers. Bouquet prices range from
$30 to more than $200, depending on the
arrangements, and reservations for weddings must be made at least six months in
advance.

Indulge & Bloom
651 Nicollet Mall, Minneapolis
(612) 343-0000
Indulge & Bloom, which also has a
Wayzata location, carries beautiful,
strange, and unusual flowers and plants
from all over the world, including Ecuado-

Farmers' markets and roadside produce spring up just about everywhere during summer and early fall. Check for official summer opening dates and business hours, as they're subject to change and are dependent on growing seasons.

rian roses, orchids, and topiaries. Staff
members pride themselves on their pro-
fessionalism; wedding arrangements are
their specialty. Wedding flowers can range
from $1,000 to $30,000 and up, and
reservations should be made 9 to 12
months in advance. The store also features home-decor items, Waterford crystal, bath-and-body products,
garden-related items, ornaments, books,
cards, truffles, and children's gifts.

St. Paul

Laurel Street Flowers
1129 Grand Avenue, St. Paul
(651) 221-9700
www.laurelstreetflowers.com
Located in a cottage house on historic
and picturesque Grand Avenue, this
store's arrangements fit perfectly into its
surroundings. The shop's guiding style
leans to English and French provincial,
and typical arrangements include fresh
blooms such as tulips and lilies of the valley in spring and summer to boutonnieres
shaped as miniature Christmas wreaths
for winter weddings. Owner and designer
Paula Flom uses a European hand-tie
method in her bouquets instead of plastic
holders, and her creations often include
such unusual choices as mixed fruits in
dark colors dripping from centerpieces
and viney garlands hanging from chandeliers. Prices run the gamut of boutonnieres
starting at $11 to wedding bouquets cost-
ing around $125. Flom starts wedding
couples with a free consultation and esti-
mate and suggests that couples make

arrangements a year before the wedding date.

Stems & Vines
17 Grand Avenue, St. Paul
(651) 228-1450
Six additional Twin Cities locations
This store's location in historic St. Paul adds to its ambience and charm. Stems & Vines designs flower bouquets and events around personalities instead of colors and styles. Stems & Vines designers are booked well in advance; it's recommended that reservations be made no later than nine months prior to your event date. Stems & Vines is a sponsor of the Twin Cities Bridal Association and holds exhibitions at every bridal and floral event in town.

MUSIC STORES

Cheapo Discs
5151 Central Avenue NE, Fridley
(763) 574-2308

80 North Snelling Avenue, St. Paul
(651) 644-8981

1300 West Lake Street, Minneapolis
(612) 827-8238
www.cheapodiscs.com
Cheapo is the Twin Cities' largest independent seller of new and used CDs. The store opened decades ago as Cheapo Records but moved into the more popular CD format for recorded music—although not completely (Cheapo Records is located next to Cheapo Discs in St. Paul). Today Cheapo has three Twin Cities locations, where new and used rock, country, R&B, and much more are bought and sold 365 days a year until midnight. Applause, Cheapo's new and used classical and jazz CD store, is located across the street from the St. Paul store, at 71 North Snelling Avenue (651-644-5115). Cheapo is a big carrier of local music and *the* place for hard-core fans to pick up new releases on Monday at midnight.

Electric Fetus
2000 Fourth Avenue South, Minneapolis
(612) 870-9300
www.efetus.com
The Electric Fetus is one of the Twin Cities' favorite stores to purchase CDs because of its wide selection of releases in all genres. The store features plenty of sales and reduced-price items. It stocks a superb selection of rock and pop as well as jazz, blues, country, reggae, and ska. Also available are used CDs, clothing, gifts, and tobacco-related accessories.

Extreme Noise Records
407 West Lake Street, Minneapolis
(612) 824-0100
www.extremenoise.com
Extreme Noise Records is a co-op specializing in punk rock records and CDs. The store sells its merchandise at lower prices because of the largely volunteer staff. Whether you are looking for classic Buzzcocks, the Ramones, the Germs, or GG Allin, or more recent punk stars such as local boys Dillinger 4, Extreme Noise usually will have it. Punk records and CDs are available from throughout the world. The store also features "zines," books, and videos regarding the punk rock lifestyle. The store sells records unavailable at other Twin Cities music sellers and serves as an important part of the local community by supporting punk rock in the area.

Roadrunner Records
4304 Nicollet Avenue South,
Minneapolis
(612) 822-0613
www.landspeedrecords.com
Roadrunner Records specializes in CDs and vinyl in all genres of music. The largest selection can be found in the rock area; however, the store also features jazz, punk, and world music. Roadrunner's world music selection is one of the best in the Twin Cities.

ODDS 'N' ENDS
Minneapolis

Beezwax Home Decor
3001 Hennepin Avenue South, Calhoun Square, Minneapolis
(612) 822-6169
www.beezwaxhomedecor.com
Beezwax Home Decor carries both scented and unscented candles in all shapes and sizes. Made from a natural, renewable resource, these pure beeswax candles are clean burning and long lasting. Also in stock are beautifully scented natural aromatherapy candles, perfume oils, aromatherapy oils, bath products, and scent diffusers. The shop's unique selection of home decor, includes chandeliers, wall sconces, and candle holders of all sizes.

Colección y Elegancia
1515 East Lake Street, #118, Mercado Central, Minneapolis
(612) 728-5416
Colección y Elegancia, a small store tucked into Mercado Central, carries beautiful music boxes, snow globes, porcelain figurines, and other objets d'art. The prices are reasonable for the quality of work, and inventory moves quickly because of that.

Golden Leaf, Ltd.
3032 Hennepin Avenue South, Calhoun Square, Minneapolis
(612) 824-1867
Golden Leaf carries premium cigars from the leading companies in the industry. The walk-in humidor contains more than 250 brands of the freshest and best-priced cigars in Minnesota. Other products for sale include accessories, humidors, pipes, tobacco, newspapers, lighters, and other smoking accessories.

Ingebretsen Scandinavian Gifts & Foods
1601 East Lake Street, Minneapolis
(612) 729-9333
www.ingebretsens.com
Ingebretsen carries Norwegian pewter,
Scandinavian crystal (Hadeland, iittala, Nybro), dinnerware from Porsgrund, candles and holders, housewares, linens, wood carvings, and rosemaling and other folk art. The clothing includes Norwegian sweaters, jackets, skirts, T-shirts, and sweatshirts. The jewelry case holds beautiful pieces wrought in silver, pewter, bronze, leather, porcelain, enamel, and wood. At the needlework shop next door, you can find fabrics, kits, books, and supplies for Danish counted cross-stitch, Hardanger embroidery, Norwegian Klostersøm needlepoint, lace making, and Norwegian knitting. The select food section includes such Scandinavian delights as lutefisk and lefse, Swedish meatballs and sausage, herring, cheeses, lingonberries, chocolate, and flat bread. You'll also find cookware for making specialty items like *lefse, krumkake, aebleskiver, kransekake,* rosettes, and other treats in your own kitchen. The library in back contains folk tales, children's books, language materials, cookbooks, fiction, culture and tradition, travel, history, art, music, and picture books for sale, as well as CDs and cassettes of Scandinavian folk music, classical, jazz, and popular music and Nordic humor.

Kitchen Window
3001 Hennepin Avenue South, Calhoun Square, Minneapolis
(612) 824-4417
www.kitchenwindow.com
Kitchen Window is considered a key destination for quality kitchen products in the Twin Cities metro area.

The store is filled with such brands as All Clad, Calphalon, and Le Creuset cookware; Wusthof Trident, Chef's Choice, and Lamson cutlery; Rosle kitchen tools; and Cuisinart, Kitchen Aid, Krups, and Panasonic small appliances. Kitchen Window features espresso machines and coffeemakers, teamakers, mugs, carafes, and press pots. It also carries items for ethnic cooking that range from *lefse* griddles and *krumkake* irons to pasta makers, tortilla presses, sushi mats, and gadgets of all kinds. Kitchen Window holds cooking

classes. Check the Web site or call for more information.

Paper Source
3048 Hennepin Avenue South,
Minneapolis
(612) 377-0700
www.paper-source.com
This aptly named shop carries a stagger-ing range of paper-related products—from stationery sets to bookbinding glue, greeting cards, rubber stamps, blank books, and lots and lots of paper. The paper stock runs from affordable typing and computer paper to beautiful imported sheets of handmade paper worthy of being framed and displayed.

Party City
1630 New Brighton Boulevard,
Minneapolis
(612) 781-9025
www.partycity.com
Four additional Twin Cities locations
Whether you're looking to buy small rub-ber dinosaurs, warming trays, balloons, or paper plates in bulk, Party City is the greatest place to stop for kids' and adults' party supplies. The extensive wedding section includes paper samples for invita-tions, a huge selection of cake toppers, and cake decorating kits. The all-season aisles hold every color of plastic flatware (with matching plates and napkins) you can imagine. The shop also sells warming trays, racks, and canned heat at extremely reasonable prices as well as plastic punch bowls and ladles.

Patina
2057 Ford Parkway, St. Paul
(651) 695-9955

1009 Franklin Avenue West, Minneapolis
(612) 872-0880

5001 Bryant Avenue South, Minneapolis
(612) 821-9315

2305 18th Avenue NE, Minneapolis
(612) 788-8933
www.patinastores.com
Patina offers stylish and relatively inex-

pensive gift options—many under $25. This is the type of place where you can find a present in nearly any price range for nearly anyone—and lose track of time doing so. There's lots to look at: contem-porary photo frames, bed-tent tops for kids, trendy jewelry, designer stationary, leather passport cases, and Band-Aids that look like bacon. Patina now has online shopping, with free shipping on orders over $75.

Sister Fun
1604 West Lake Street, Minneapolis
(612) 672-0263
The name says it all—this store is just amazingly fun to poke around in. File cab-inet drawers reveal everything from tiny plastic airplanes to tin trains with wind-up cranks, baby doll parts, and cheap novelty key chains. On the shelves can be found 3D renditions of *The Last Supper,* coin purses with pictures of the Pope on them, Elvis paraphernalia, snow globes contain-ing tiny nuns, Brady Bunch lunchboxes, reissues of Godzilla movies, mood rings, miniature tin carousels, etc., etc., etc. You can get lost in this place, but don't worry—everything is priced much, much lower than you'd expect, despite being such a chic, campy, and popular shopping stop for college kids, artists, and adults going through their second childhood.

St. Paul

Ax Man Surplus
1639 University Avenue West, St. Paul
(651) 646-8653

1021 East Moore Lake Drive, Fridley
(763) 572-3730

8008 Minnetonka Boulevard,
St. Louis Park
(952) 935-2210
www.ax-man.com
Ax Man has everything you want that you never thought you wanted at more than reasonable prices, including iron lungs, ancient airplane models, antiquated TI-80

computer keyboards, beads, buttons, Pogs, snail shells, seashells, remote control wiring, police tape, public address horns, maps, huge bags of shredded money, rock videos, test tubes, copper cable, bar magnets, refrigerator magnets, transformers, all sizes of electrical motors, music box innards, marbles, bicycle tires, and doll heads. The stock is constantly changing, and some truly strange things wind up for sale, including school bus fenders and fake cheese.

The Bead Monkey
867 Grand Avenue, Victoria Crossing Mall, St. Paul
(651) 222-7729

With several other locations spread throughout the Twin Cities, the Bead Monkey is the place to go to buy pipes of inexpensive glass beads, charms, jewelry-making supplies, beading needles and wire, and semiprecious stones. If you like beading but aren't sure how to go about a project, the knowledgeable staff can either help you on the spot or refer you to one of the many beading classes for persons of all ages.

Bockstruck Jewelers
400 St. Peter Street, St. Paul
(651) 222-1858
www.bockstruck.com

Family owned and operated since 1883, Bockstruck Jewelers has an eclectic collection of brand-name watches and jewelry by Ebel, Tag Heuer, Mikimoto, Bertolucci, and Chopard. Bockstruck Jewelers guides you through the diamond-selection process and has financing available.

The Crossroads Shoppe of Crocus Hill
619 Grand Avenue, St. Paul
(651) 225-4467

The Crossroads Shoppe presents Red Wing Stoneware and heirloom-quality Amish handcrafted quilts and furniture. Some of the Amish-crafted items sold here include gorgeously embroidered wall hangings, table runners, thick quilts,

braided and woven rugs, straw baskets, and cloth dolls.

Garden of Eden
867 Grand Avenue, St. Paul
(651) 293-1300
www.gardenofedenstores.com

This luxury bath shop carries soaps, oils, perfumes, bath candles, and aromatherapy items. Soaps include handmade bars of glycerin with ribbons of flowers and herbs in them to novelty bars with "Satan Be Gone" emblazoned across the package. While most of the items here are aimed at women, the shop also carries aftershave and other men's products.

Bibelot means "small decorative object," and you'll discover a lot of these at eclectic Bibelot stores found all around the Twin Cities. This is a good place to purchase a last-minute gift for just about anyone. Check the phone book for the Bibelot closest to you.

Irish on Grand
1124 Grand Avenue, St. Paul
(651) 222-5151
www.irishongrand.com

Irish on Grand, the premier Irish shop in Minnesota, offers Irish products, including music, books, food, teas, crystal, china, artwork, and more. Aside from the usual T-shirts with shamrock themes, Irish on Grand carries beautiful woolen capes and throws, sweaters, mittens, scarves, and hats, as well as fine silver and gold jewelry.

Legacy Art & Gifts
1209 Grand Avenue, St. Paul
(651) 221-9094

Legacy Art & Gifts carries items created by mostly local artists showcased in a fabulous converted Victorian house. The shop features pottery, etchings, handblown glass, watercolors, textiles, wood boxes, one-of-a-kind jewelry, and more.

St. Patrick's Guild
1554 Randolph Avenue, St. Paul
(651) 652-9767

St. Patrick's Guild, established in 1949, is a huge Catholic-themed store that carries religious books, drawers full of rosaries, medallions dedicated to different saints, holy water bottles, religious figurines, children's Bibles, and concrete garden statues.

Stogies on Grand
961 Grand Avenue, St. Paul
(651) 222-8700
www.stogiesongrand.com

Stogies on Grand is a premier tobacconist that also offers a comfortable smoking lounge, complete with big-screen TV, newspapers, and board games, for those who want to immediately try out the cigars and tobacco they just purchased. Stogies carries more than 300 premium cigars in their large walk-in humidor and a wide selection of pipes, tobacco, humidors, lighters, cutters, and other tobacco-related accessories.

Ten Thousand Villages
867 Grand Avenue, St. Paul
(651) 225-1043
www.tenthousandvillages.com

Ten Thousand Villages, located in Victoria Crossing West shopping mall, is a nonprofit shop featuring handcrafted jewelry, gifts, clothing, and home furnishings from around the world, with many pieces contributed by artists in developing nations. The profits from purchases made at Ten Thousand Villages go directly back to the artists of these nations in an effort to provide them with a fair living income for their work.

Twin Cities Magic & Costume
241 West Seventh Street, St. Paul
(651) 227-7888
www.twincitiesmagic.com

There is really no place like Twin Cities Magic & Costume. The store has just about everything you need to embark on your career as a magician or for those days you need to be disguised as a gorilla, Little Bo Peep, or Dracula. Costumes, the-atrical supplies, and special effects equip-ment are for sale and rent, including fog machines, strobe lights, explosive paper and powders, wigs, hats, boas, fake mus-taches and teeth, tiaras, and more.

South

BareBones
2210 Eden Prairie Center, Eden Prairie
(952) 484-8719

BareBones, with a second location at the Mall of America, is a wonderful "toy" store for kids and adults alike, a place where the doctor's office meets the novelty store. BareBones carries toys and books dealing with human anatomy, including 3D puz-zles, sex-ed books, human anatomy posters, and coffeetable books.

West

Ampersand
3448 Galleria, Edina
(952) 920-2118

Ampersand, which also has a Wayzata location, is a home store that carries everything you might possibly need for a party, whether it be a very formal affair or a casual lawn party. Ampersand has boxed invitations for every event under the sun, including birthdays, weddings, showers, anniversaries, barbecues, and cocktail parties, as well as silver olive forks, Italian pottery, designer cork tops, hand-painted dishware, flatware, elegant crystal punchbowls, and a huge selection of candles.

Gabberts Furniture & Design Studio
3501 Galleria, Edina
(952) 927-1500
www.gabberts.com

Named the No. 1 home furnishings retailer in America by *House Beautiful* magazine, Gabberts has earned acclaim for its fine home furnishings that suit every lifestyle and span the spectrum of design from traditional to casual to contemporary. The stock changes with the seasons and times and is always amazing—hand-painted desks, tables, and chairs with farm motifs or ocean scenes, or primary-color furniture that looks like adult versions of a kid's playset. Gabberts also carries lush, soft leather couches, beautiful lamps, chandeliers, and pretty much anything else you need to make your home truly yours.

Que Sera
3580 Galleria, Edina
(952) 924-6390

This eclectic store, identified in front by a detailed chipped-tile mosaic, carries vintage-inspired home furnishings, lighting, beautiful costume jewelry, and knick-knacks of all sorts. Que Sera offers custom upholstery and slipcovered sofas and chairs incorporating vintage fabrics, hand-painted furniture, custom iron and wood beds, custom bedding, hand-blown glass chandeliers, table lamps, candles, mirrors, frames, and more.

SPECIALTY GROCERS

Minneapolis

Holy Land Bakery, Grocery and Deli
2513 Central Avenue NE, Minneapolis
(612) 781-2627

This Mediterranean deli and grocery store sells everything you need to make your own lamb kabobs, hummus, spinach pie, and falafel, although chances are you probably won't be able to make them quite as well as the Holy Land deli counter does. The store stocks items such as pita (made fresh in the bakery every day), meats, gigantic bags of basmati rice, roasted and dried chickpeas, at least six types of feta cheese, black and green olives, specialty coffees, and a wide selection of Middle Eastern cookies, candies, and specialty chocolates.

Shuang Hur Oriental Market
2710 Nicollet Avenue, Minneapolis
(612) 872-8606

Shuang Hur is the largest Asian supermarket on Eat Street, carrying thousands of products from China, Taiwan, and Thailand. The full-service grocery store has a large fresh-produce section with melons, bean sprouts, and crates of aged duck eggs; freezers full of egg roll and spring roll wraps and desserts; and a Chinese BBQ deli that carries whole roasted pigs and BBQ duck and chicken meat. In the dry goods sections are rows and rows of dried mushrooms, noodles, soups, spices, rice, and shrimp crackers. A couple of rows over are about a hundred different types of festively colored packaged candy and cookies.

Surdyk's
303 East Hennepin Avenue, Minneapolis
(612) 379-3232
www.surdyks.com

This Minneapolis shop is a wine connoisseur's dream come true. Surdyk's carries a great selection of wines and other spirits, plus a gourmet cheese shop that makes this the place to consider when planning cocktail or dinner parties. Cigar smokers will appreciate the large humidor, which was a part of the store long before puffing cigars became trendy.

St. Paul

El Burrito Mercado
175 Concord Street, St. Paul
(651) 227-2192

El Burrito Mercado is an all-purpose Mexican and Latin grocery store located in St. Paul's West Side. The immense store features a bakery where you can purchase fresh pastries, fruit turnovers, breads, and cookies; a meat counter that carries fresh seafood, shredded pork, chicken, and beef, as well as gigantic fried pork rinds; a restaurant that whips up tacos, quesadillas, and burritos as quick as most fast-food restaurants, except the ingredients here are fresh, spicy, and good for you; and a full-service grocery carrying everything from Mexican coffees and candies to fresh, homemade corn chips and statues of tiny, sombrero-wearing skeletons playing guitars.

Spiros Mediterranean Market
2264 University Avenue West, St. Paul
(651) 645-4607

This wonderful Greek deli and grocery carries items for making Greek foods, like frozen beef and lamb for gyros, cucumber sauce, and a good selection of cheeses. The grocery section has Mediterranean candies, coffees, beans, pastas, fruit preserves, nuts, flour, jars of olives, pickled squid, and anchovy paste. The deli counter has some of the best baklava in town, as well as hummus and Greek salad, and makes gyros and other sandwiches fresh to order. In the freezer section are trays of moussaka and frozen spinach pies made fresh in the store.

SPORTS AND RECREATION OUTFITTERS

Minneapolis

Alternative Bike & Board Shop
2408 Hennepin Avenue, Minneapolis
(612) 374-3635
www.altbikeboard.com

Alternative Bike & Board Shop has been an Uptown institution since 1974, carrying all the respected bicycle, skateboard, and snowboard brands like Burton, Clicker, Nitro, and K2. It also carries clothing, accessories, and gear and has a knowledgeable staff that can help set you up

Thrifty Outfitters, located upstairs inside the Midwest Mountaineering store in Minneapolis, sells new and used outdoors equipment, clothing, and boots at steep discounts.

with anything you need to get out on the road or on the slopes. A trustworthy repair department offers a quick turnaround time on repairs for a reasonable price.

Erik's Bike Shop
1312 Fourth Street SE, Minneapolis
(612) 617-8002
www.eriksbikeshop.com
Eight additional Twin Cities locations

This chain of local shops offers an excellent selection of equipment and is operated by a knowledgeable staff who can help you out with everything from information about bike and ski trails to what kind of equipment would suit you best. Cyclists will find an extensive assortment of mountain, road, touring, and BMX bikes from Cannondale, Specialized, and Haro, as well as cycling accessories, including car racks, helmets, parts, and apparel. Winter enthusiasts will be pleased by Erik's selection of snowboards, clothing, and boots. Erik's also has a full-service bike shop for quickie to major repairs and offers lots of extras, such as a low-price guarantee and free services when you purchase new bikes and boards.

Freewheel Bike
1812 South Sixth Street, Minneapolis
(612) 339-2219
www.freewheelbike.com

Freewheel Bike carries mountain, road, and tandem bikes from Trek, Fisher, LeMond, Schwinn, Univega, Bontrager, Klein, and Santana, but its best feature is arguably the Public Shop, where, for under $10 an hour you can use the store's racks and tools to fix your bike—if you get in over your head, the staff is on hand to offer assistance. Freewheel also hosts maintenance classes jointly with Open U, rents bikes, and sponsors riding groups and teams.

Midwest Mountaineering
309 Cedar Avenue South, Minneapolis
(612) 339-3433
www.midwestmtn.com

Midwest Mountaineering takes up nearly an entire block of Cedar Avenue on the

University of Minnesota's West Bank and is one of the most complete retail stores for brand-name outdoor adventure gear (including a giant outdoors-related book section) and one of the few outfitters to rent kayaks and other gear for whitewater paddling. The store's "cave" offers bouldering opportunities for climbers looking to try out equipment or just wanting a quick overhang workout. Once you sign a waiver, you're free to hit the walls. The store's staff is extremely helpful and can direct you to some of the better climbing, rafting, or hiking opportunities in the region.

St. Paul

Finn-Sisu
1841 University Avenue West, St. Paul
(651) 645-2443
www.finnsisu.com
This tiny Midway shop stocks cross-country and racing skis as well as equipment and supplies by all the top makers. The prices are a little high, but it's all top-quality merchandise, and the staff is very good at matching people with just the right gear. The store is also conveniently located near Como Park, giving you a chance to try out your new toys mere minutes after leaving the store.

Joe's Sporting Goods
33 Country Road B, St. Paul
(651) 488-5511
www.joesportingoods.com
Joe's carries a solid selection of top-of-the-line fishing equipment, from rods, reels, and flies to clothes, boots, and hats, as well as a complete array of hunting, camping, and snow-sport gear. The knowledgeable sales staff at the big, new store is quick to answer any questions you might have or direct you to someone who can help.

Stillwater's P. J. Asch Otterfitters, about a block from the Lower St. Croix National Scenic Riverway, has a climbing wall inside its converted-grain-bin retail space.
TODD R. BERGER

East

P. J. Asch Otterfitters
413 East Nelson Street, Stillwater
(651) 430-2286
www.pjaschotterfitters.com
The owners of P. J. Asch Otterfitters converted four old grain bins in downtown Stillwater into four cozy climbing rooms, then added an outdoor store to augment the climbing facilities. With 6,000 square feet of climbing surface—and walls that reach 42 feet—the place attracts climbers of all skill levels. Much of the business comes from first-time climbers, so plenty of beginner routes and lessons are provided, with instructors on hand to teach

you the ropes. For experienced climbers, P. J. Asch has four advanced climbing routes (with corner smears and a lieback crack). You also can rent sea kayaks here, mostly for use on the nearby St. Croix River.

VINTAGE CLOTHES AND THRIFT STORES

Minneapolis

Corner Store
900 West Lake Street, Minneapolis
(612) 823–1270
Corner Store specializes in brand-name jeans and western apparel such as cowboy boots, brass belt buckles, and fringed suede jackets, as well as motorcycle jackets, costume jewelry, and sequined cloth-

For the stylish in a vintage sort of way, Lula is likely to stock duds that will attract attention (the good kind). TODD R. BERGER

ing. For more elegant occasions, Corner Store has vintage tuxedos for rent.

Everyday People Clothing Exchange
323 14th Avenue SE, Minneapolis
(612) 623–9095
www.everydaypeopleclothing.com
This vintage and resale store, with an Uptown location as well, carries an eclectic (and sometimes hilarious) collection of disco clothes, old band T-shirts, go-go boots, comfortably broken-in Levis, and studded leather and plastic belts. The owners of this locally owned business are meticulous about everything they sell, and it shows. Anything with holes has them for a good and fashionable reason.

Tatters
2928 Lyndale Avenue South, Minneapolis
(612) 823–5285
Originally called Tatters and Platters, a retailer selling apparel and vinyl, Tatters has been a Twin Cities retro-alternative clothing establishment for many years. Tatters offers freshly laundered used and vintage clothing that spans decades, carrying seasoned motorcycle and letter jackets, Hawaiian and bowling shirts, party dresses from the 1940s onward, and lots and lots of Levis. It also stocks new apparel ranging from partywear to T-shirts and underwear.

St. Paul

J. T.'s Wooden Truck Mercantile
644 Smith Avenue North, St. Paul
(651) 230–4346
Longtime thrifters remember J. T.'s Como location, a cavernous space packed with vintage clothes. This shop, just across the High Bridge from downtown St. Paul, is less cavernous but similarly packed with men's and women's vintage clothing, including, of course, J. T.'s amazing amassment of vintage ties. Browse the superspecific tie categories, such as "fun animals, 1930s."

Lula
1587 Selby Avenue, St. Paul
(651) 644-4110

Lula boasts beautiful vintage clothes and accessories, including especially large and eclectic collections of women's dresses, men's shirts, and coats and jackets. The reasonably priced clothing moves quickly, and it's largely from the 1970s and earlier, though the owner is appropriately aware of the 1980s' fresh vintage classification. She's been known to load up dressing rooms with all sorts of possibilities you may have overlooked. Trust this woman. She's totally into selling you vintage clothes that make you look and feel incredible.

Jerabek's New Bohemian
63 West Winfield Street, St. Paul
(651) 228-1245

If you're looking for vintage clothes or housewares, try Jerabek's New Bohemian, a coffee shop tucked into St. Paul's West Side that's been around for 100 years. Not only is Jerabek's famous for its home-made pastries, it doubles as a vintage shop.

Unique Thrift Store
1657 Rice Street, St. Paul
(651) 489-5083

2201 37th Avenue NE, Columbia Heights
(763) 788-5250

4471 Winnetka Avenue West, New Hope
(763) 535-0200

Once a year, *City Pages* puts out its "Best of the Twin Cities" list of stores in the metro area, and when it does, the Unique Thrift Store almost always gets the best thrift store award. Unfortunately, for about two weeks after receiving the award, prices in the store go up, the selection of great shoes and clothes gets cleaned out by a mad new-customer rush, and it's suddenly just another thrift store stocked with dusty junk at outrageous prices. Before and after this annual tradition, however, all three Unique Thrift Store locations are the place to go to get beautiful, barely worn summer dresses, business suits, boots and shoes, ice skates, in-line skates, leather jackets, winter coats, and kids' stuff at unbelievable prices. You can pretty much buy a fashionable, brand-name wardrobe for your son or daughter for a whole growing season, including shoes and a coat, for under $50; prices on adult clothes and shoes are just as reasonable.

ATTRACTIONS

There is never a reason to be bored in the Twin Cities. On top of all the educational opportunities and artistic venues the area is famous for, the metro area is host to amusement parks, a bevy of hands-on historical exhibits, one of the largest zoos and one of the best free zoos in the country, and lots of interesting spots to just hang out for the day. In winter flocks of teenagers and adults head to the Mall of America to spend the day walking among the still-green trees and surreal landscape that make up the always-summery Camp at MOA, or to the tropical canopies of wild orchid displays that fill Como Park's spectacular Marjorie McNeely Conservatory. In summer there's no excuse for staying inside on the weekend—several water parks are nothing but cool, watery roller coasters, wave machines, and swimming pools.

PRICE CODE

The following price code is based on the cost for general admission for one adult. Most sites offer considerably discounted tickets for children and seniors, and some allow discounts or even free entry for employees, members of the military, and certain organizations.

$	$5 and under
$$	$6–$15
$$$	$16–$30
$$$$	$31 and up

AMUSEMENT AND WATER PARKS

The Park at MOA $$$
Mall of America, 5000 Center Court, Bloomington
(952) 883–8600
www.theparkatmoa.com
Located at the center of Mall of America,

this seven-acre indoor theme park offers more than 30 rides and attractions. The largest indoor theme park in the nation, the Park at MOA sits right on top of the old Met Stadium site—in place of a baseball diamond are 400 live trees, artificial cliffs meant to evoke the St. Croix River, all of those rides. Unlike outdoor amusement parks such as Valleyfair!, a stroll through the Park at MOA costs you nothing (in fact, cutting through the park is often the fastest route between stores at the mall). Rides require tickets, which you can buy at booths or at automated machines. Tickets for rides and attractions are based on a point system. A point is worth 80 cents, with rides and attractions costing three to six points each. You can also purchase Ticket Point Packages and all-day wristbands, two money-saving options if the little ones (or you) plan to get on a lot of rides.

For small children, there's the Americana Carousel, a hand-painted contemporary version of the classic carousel, and Lil' Shaver, a smaller, slower version of the roller coaster that circles the park (the Ripsaw Roller Coaster). For everyone else, there's the Skyscraper Ferris Wheel that takes visitors 74 feet high, Paul Bunyan's Log Chute—a watery ride that includes a drop over a 40-foot waterfall—and more than enough other rides and features to take your mind off shopping, including the Mighty Axe, the Screaming Yellow Eagle, and the Treetop Tumbler. There's also a full-service child care facility, Kids Quest, which charges by the hour and entertains kids with toys, nonviolent video games, karaoke, and more.

Valleyfair! Amusement Park $$$$
1 Valleyfair Drive, Shakopee
(952) 445–7600 or (800) 386–7433
www.valleyfair.com
With more than 75 rides, the Midwest's

largest theme park has something to offer the littlest kid and the bravest adult alike. You can take an inner tube down a gently sloping canal for a relaxing, meditative ride; bumper cars and electric car tracks; exciting water rides like the Flume, which sends passenger boats off a 50-foot drop at the end of the ride; and the Excalibur, a high-speed wooden roller coaster with a 105-foot drop and lots of quick twists and turns. The Steel Venom impulse coaster plummets at speeds up to 68 mph, corkscrewing you straight toward the ground before veering to a horizontal ride just before impact. For those with no fear of heights, the 275-foot Power Tower will take you high in the air and then, well, drop you. There are lots of rides for the really little guys, too, from bumble bee–shaped electric cars to a multilevel foam-ball factory to an antique carousel. An IMAX theater is an added attraction to the park and a great place to hide out during sudden late-summer showers. The park is open mid-May through September.

ANIMALS AND PLANTS

Como Zoo/Marjorie McNeely Conservatory at Como Park   Free
1225 Estabrook Drive, St. Paul
(651) 487-8200
www.comozooconservatory.org
This zoo offers intimate exhibits housing great apes, giraffes, zebras, wolves, and more. One of only four free metropolitan-area zoos in the country (although a small donation is requested), Como Zoo has been an institution in St. Paul for more than 100 years. The first Siberian tigers successfully bred in captivity were born here in 1958, and the big cat display is still one of the best features of the zoo, including a single breeding pair of lions that has had several healthy pairs of cubs over the past decade. There is also a great primate exhibit, with about a dozen ring-tailed and brown lemurs, spider monkeys, a couple of breeding pairs of tamarins that have successfully given birth every

spring, and orangutans and gorillas that have been with the zoo for more than 10 years.

Located right next door to the zoo is the Marjorie McNeely Conservatory at Como Park, the region's largest botanical garden. The Victorian-style, glass-domed conservatory features hundreds of plants from throughout the world and is divided into eight sections featuring palms, ferns, tropical food plants, bonsai trees, seasonal flowers, orchids, Japanese landscapes, and butterfly-friendly plants. In summer a side door opens into the Como Ordway Memorial Japanese Garden, a sansui (mountain and water) design created by St. Paul's sister city, Nagasaki, Japan, for the park.

The antique wooden Cafesjian's Carousel is beautifully restored, and the brightly painted and mirrored wooden animals are available to ride throughout the summer for a nominal charge. Como Town, the park's newest addition, is an amusement park for little ones.

Both the Como Zoo and the Marjorie McNeely Conservatory at Como Park are open year-round.

Minnesota Landscape Arboretum $$
3675 Arboretum Drive, Chaska
(952) 443-1400
www.arboretum.umn.edu
The Minnesota Landscape Arboretum, Minnesota's largest public garden, is part of the Department of Horticultural Science at the University of Minnesota. Its mission is to provide a community and national resource for horticultural and environmental information, research, and public education; to develop and evaluate plants and horticultural practices for cold climates; and to inspire all visitors with beautiful, healthy plants in well-designed and maintained displays, collections, model landscapes, and conservation areas.

The arboretum features 1,000 acres of public gardens, including spectacular annual and perennial display gardens, collections of plants developed for northern climates, natural and native areas, and

Como Park's conservatory is a visual treat. MARJORIE MCNEELY CONSERVATORY

demonstration gardens. The arboretum grounds include miles of summer hiking trails and winter cross-country ski trails that take you through northern woodlands, native prairie, and natural marshes. In spring, summer, and fall, trams can be boarded for a guided tour around the beautiful 3-mile drive, and volunteer-guided walking tours can be taken through the many display gardens for free.

The arboretum is open daily from 8:00 A.M. until 8:00 P.M. or sunset, whichever comes first. Volunteer-guided walking tours that focus on the plant collections near the building (dwarf conifers, roses, perennials, herbs, annuals, host glade, Japanese gardens, and home demonstration gardens) last 60 minutes. Visitors can take their own personal 30-minute audio walking tour of the demonstration gardens (equipment is available in the lobby of the Snyder Building for no extra charge).

Minnesota Zoo   **$$**
13000 Zoo Boulevard, Apple Valley
(952) 431-9500 or (800) 366-7811
www.mnzoo.org

Located in the southern suburb of Apple Valley, a few minutes south of the Mall of America, and housing more than 2,000 species of animals from five different continents, the Minnesota Zoo and its IMAX theater see a million visitors per year. The zoo's 500 acres include an indoor tropical rain forest populated by an amazing variety of birds and animals, a family of gibbons, and a large and smelly South American tapir. At Discovery Bay, there are dolphins that officially perform for audiences every afternoon and unofficially any time enough people gather around their huge, glass-walled tank; a walk-through aquarium with sharks, fish, and deep-sea plants; an education center where kids can pet different kinds of sharks; and the Minnesota animal exhibit with beavers, foxes, fruit bats, and porcupines. Outside the main exhibit building, you can find ducks and swans, a prairie dog town, wild horses, camels, tigers, and many, many other animals, some of which are on the endangered species lists and are almost an exclusive at the zoo, such as the red panda. Domesticated animals like pigs and chickens get their day in the sun at the Wells Fargo Family Farm exhibit. It's home to two cloned cows.

Also at the zoo is the 600-seat 3D IMAX theater. In the Weesner Family Amphitheater, the zoo often features big-name human stars, like Los Lobos and the Brian Setzer Orchestra.

Underwater Adventures Aquarium $$
Mall of America, 120 East Broadway, Bloomington
(952) 883-0202 or (888) DIVE-TIME
www.underwateradventures.net
Underwater Adventures is a huge (1.2 million gallons) walk-through aquarium located under the Mall of America. The facility features more than 4,500 different sea creatures from around the world in eight different displays. For a one-time admission charge, visitors can walk through a 300-foot glass-walled tunnel that leads them through the middle of the three freshwater exhibits: Turtley Awesome Woods, Fisherman's Hollow, and the Mighty Mississippi, and five ocean exhibits: Shark Cove, Rainbow Reef, Seacrits of Hollywood, Circle of Life, and Starfish Beach, where children can touch harmless sharks and stingrays.

CASINOS AND RACETRACKS

Canterbury Park Racetrack and Card Club
1100 Canterbury Road, Shakopee
(952) 445-7223 or (800) 340-6361
www.canterburypark.com

Canterbury Park, located about 25 miles south of both downtown St. Paul and Minneapolis, hosts live horse racing with on-site paramutual betting mid-May through the beginning of September and on-site teleracing betting on simulcast horse races around the country throughout the year. Canterbury also has a card room, including the Poker Room, featuring such games as Texas hold 'em, seven-card stud, and Omaha, and the Casino Games Room, with games like blackjack, Caribbean stud, and Super 9. Canterbury is about 3 miles from Mystic Lake Casino.

For a reasonable charge, kids can buy Dixie cups of fish to throw to the seals at Como Zoo.

Mystic Lake Casino
2400 Mystic Lake Boulevard, Prior Lake
(800) 262-7799
www.mysticlake.com
Besides its trademark high-stakes bingo, Mystic Lake Casino has nearly 4,000 slots and 96 blackjack tables as well as restaurants, including a huge buffet. The gaming facility offers concerts, celebrity shows (think Wayne Newton, George Carlin, and the Oak Ridge Boys), a hotel, and free daily shuttles across the Twin Cities. It is operated by the Shakopee Mdewakanton Sioux Community.

Treasure Island Resort and Casino
off Minnesota Highway 61
Red Wing
(800) 222-7077
www.treasureislandcasino.com
Located 45 minutes southeast of St. Paul near the Mississippi river town of Red Wing, Treasure Island features 2,500 slots, 44 game tables, bingo, and smoking and nonsmoking gambling areas. Guests can take a cruise down the scenic Mississippi River aboard the *Spirit of the Water,* the casino's 150-passenger yacht. There's also

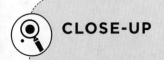

Rice Park

Rice Park is arguably the most lovely urban green space in the Twin Cities. It is one preserved block carved out of St. Paul's core, surrounded by cobblestone streets and towering buildings and replete with benches and trees. One of St. Paul's oldest parks, the square was donated to the city in 1849, the same year St. Paul was incorporated as a town and nine years before Minnesota became a state. The man who donated the park, Henry Mower Rice, was first a fur trader, and then a businessman and one of the town's first cheerleaders. If only Henry knew what his gift would become.

Benches around the huge circular fountain at Rice Park's center make nice spots to eat lunch or listen to a concert in the square. There's a statue of F. Scott Fitzgerald, who wrote and published *This Side of Paradise* while living on Summit Avenue, the swanky St. Paul street full of Victorian mansions just up the bluff. (Incidentally, Henry Rice built one of the first homes on this prime stretch of real estate.) There are bronze statues of Charlie Brown and Snoopy, too, part of a larger collection of *Peanuts* statues spread throughout St. Paul, tributes to *Peanuts* comic strip creator and another St. Paul homeboy, Charles Schulz. During the Winter Carnival each year, the park holds the festival's ice-sculpting contest. Massive frosty sculptures glow amid trees dressed in twinkling white lights for as long as the weather allows.

But the park is defined as much by what's around it as what's in it. On the north side, along Fifth Street, sits the Landmark Center, built in 1902. It has

huge stone towers, the tallest of which holds a clock. Landmark Towers was originally the federal courthouse and post office for the upper Midwest, during which time it saw the trials of many big-name gangsters. Take a peek inside. Now a National Historic Landmark, the building holds lots of offices of nonprofit organizations and is open for tours. The atrium is amazing, and some of the courtrooms and judges' chambers have been restored to their original grandeur.

Along the park's south side, the stately marble Italian Renaissance revival rectangle that is the St. Paul Central Library inspires awe from its spot on Fourth Street. It cost $1.5 million dollars (and that's in 1917 dollars) to construct. It's still a library today, and thankfully, it recently benefited from a $15.9 million restoration. Central Library is on the National Register of Historic Places. Inside, it's all handsome stone and wood, and there's even a nice little coffee shop and store to visit.

On the park's west side, along Market Street, is one of the premier accommodations in all of the state, the Saint Paul Hotel. It was the luxurious brainchild of St. Paul businessman Lucius Pond Ordway, designed to wow back in 1910 with a grand ballroom, a fine dining room, and guestrooms with scenic views. This is the kind of hotel with a doorman in a top hat, afternoon teas by the fire, and huge arrangements of fresh flowers everywhere. The hotel regularly attracts stars, politicians, and royalty—Calvin Coolidge, Bill Clinton, Bing Crosby, and Bill Murray are among recorded visitors. The hotel's

Landmark Center on Rice Park. GREATER MINNEAPOLIS CONVENTION & VISITORS ASSOCIATION

St. Paul Grill is still known around the Cities as a premier dining spot, the ballroom still hosts events, and the view is still—well, try to get a room overlooking Rice Park.

Directly across from the Saint Paul Hotel, on Washington Street, is the Ordway Center for the Performing Arts, which opened in 1985. Sally Ordway Irving, Lucius's granddaughter, is behind this theatrical gem. By far Rice Park's newest structure, its creators met the architectural challenge of fitting in with the neighbors. The Ordway doesn't pretend to be old, and it holds up yet defers to its surrounding—the low-lying building's soaring glass-walled lobby gives audiences a reason to linger over a spectacular view.

Despite all this history and elegance, Rice Park is a wonderfully and comfortably low-key spot. It gets nice and quiet here, especially at night after the Ordway show has let out and the fancy St. Paul Grill diners have finished and the carriage that waits outside the hotel has gone home. You can practically feel the city's breath in this park, its heart. Depending on the angle, Rice Park could be now or 65 years ago, but it's unquestionably St. Paul, with its best foot forward.

a venue for live, nationally known celebrity entertainment and accommodations in the casino's 250-room tropical-themed resort.

Should you get hungry, there are plenty of great places to eat at Treasure Island, including the Tradewinds all-you-can-eat buffet and Java's Restaurant for meals ranging from steak to seafood.

GUIDED EXCURSIONS

RiverCity Trolley $$$
(612) 378-7833
www.minneapolis.org/gmcva/trolley

Sit back and enjoy the ride on the RiverCity Trolley as friendly conductors tell the history of Minneapolis, the City of Lakes, during this 60-minute tour of turn-of-the-20th-century city buildings, sky-scrapers, and other points of interest. The trolley travels along the Mississippi River past St. Anthony Falls to Main Street in the heart of the historic milling district. Sights include the Walker Art Center, the State and Orpheum Theatres, and the Minneapolis Sculpture Garden.

Kids will love riding on the brightly painted, Mr. Rogers–style trolley cars. The trolleys are climate controlled and comfortable, and the seats are high enough that it's easy for smaller children to look out the windows. Your best bet is to get an all-day pass so that you can hop on and off the trolley while you take in the sights of the milling district and St. Anthony Falls (Downtown Minneapolis Tour) or the shores of the many beautiful lakes (Chain of Lakes Tour). Look for trolley signs around downtown, where you

Down in History motorcoach tours (651–224–1191), led by costumed actors, are a fun way to get oriented to the Twin Cities and learn a little in the process. The Gangster, Twin Town Tacky, and Uff Duh Tours are among your choices.

can hop on or off at your leisure. The season runs from May to October.

Padelford Packet Boat Company, Inc. $$-$$$$
Harriet Island Regional Park, St. Paul
(651) 227-1100 or (800) 543-3908
www.riverrides.com

Hop on one of six riverboats leaving from Harriet Island in St. Paul for a Mississippi River excursion. These paddleboat river tours offer an excellent way to experience the river up close.

One of the riverboats, the *Harriet Bishop,* named for St. Paul's first school-teacher, is the fleet's newest and largest Mississippi riverboat. The riverboat offers two enclosed decks that seat 300 for dinner plus the open third deck. Bars and rest rooms can be found on all three decks, and the top deck features a dance/band area as well as a 48-tone Tangley calliope.

Another of the riverboats is one of the few truly authentic sternwheelers on the Mississippi River. The all-steel *Jonathan Padelford* is named for the tenth great maternal grandfather of Capt. William D. Bowell Sr., founder of the Padelford Packet Boat Company, Inc. The engines are identical to the old steam engines but run hydraulically.

Padelford Packet Boat Company offers two narrated daily public excursions seven days a week in June, July, and August and at 2:00 P.M. every Saturday and Sunday, May and September. Elegant evening dinner cruises depart Fridays, June through September, as does the Sunday brunch cruise. A lunch cruise, a showboat cruise, a birding cruise, private charters, and more are also available.

HISTORICAL ATTRACTIONS

Alexander Ramsey House $$
265 South Exchange Street, St. Paul
(651) 296-8760
www.mnhs.org/ramseyhouse

Completed in 1872, this is one of the country's best-preserved Victorian homes. The

Ramsey House is one of the most detailed and intimate historical sites in the Twin Cities. The only owners were the Ramsey family, and so the history stayed in the house. More than 90 percent of the furnishings are original, which is rare for historical sites.

Costumed guides lead visitors on a tour of the impressive home of Alexander and Anna Ramsey. Ramsey was the first territorial governor and the second state governor, and he held many other prominent positions in public life.

The Ramsey House features original furniture, crystal chandeliers, carved walnut woodwork, and marble fireplaces. The costumed interpreters offer more than just a dry recitation of facts, playing out vignettes showing the life of the times. Free fresh-baked cookies are handed out by the "servants." There are special events and tours throughout the year, particularly during holidays. Tours run year-round on Friday and Saturday between 10:00 A.M. and 3:00 P.M., with expanded hours during summer and the holiday season.

American Swedish Institute $
2600 Park Avenue, Minneapolis
(612) 871-4907
www.americanswedishinst.org
Set in a spectacular, 33-room turn-of-the-20th-century mansion that looks more like a castle than a former residence, the American Swedish Institute is the largest and oldest museum of Swedish culture, arts, and history in the country. Completed in 1908, the châteauesque structure is all ornately carved Indiana limestone on the outside. The inside is a marvel of hand-carved wood, with intricate designs lining the walls, and each sculpted plaster ceiling is a work of art. There's also a *kakelugnar* in each of eleven rooms, which is basically a colorful, porcelain-wrapped Swedish fireplace. Once the home of Swan J. Turnblad, publisher of North America's foremost Swedish-language newspaper, the house was donated to the American Swedish Institute (which Turnblad founded) in 1929. Also exhibited at

the museum are Scandinavian artifacts from the Turnblad family.

While taking in the decor, expect also to be taken with tales of immigrants who left Scandinavia to settle in Minnesota, which bears similar scenery, albeit sans mountains and fjords. The museum is a rich resource for local history as well as a showcase for artwork by Swedish and Swedish-American artists and artisans. There are concerts and theater performances in the upper rooms and lectures and other events in the modernized lower level. (It's a special treat to visit when the mansion is decked out at Christmastime.) There are also fiddling and dancing groups that come through to entertain visitors, special festivals with music and food, and Swedish language classes for kids and adults.

The Ard Godfrey House   Free
50 University Avenue NE, Minneapolis
(612) 379-9707
Built in 1849, the Ard Godfrey House was the family residence for the Maine millwright who helped build the first dam and sawmills to put the waterpower of the Falls of St. Anthony to use. The oldest wood frame house in the Twin Cities, this Greek revival structure was restored and refurbished by the Woman's Club of Minneapolis as a gift to city residents.

The Godfrey House was reopened to the public in 1979. Today the house is available for guided tours weekends May through August and for private tours by appointment year-round.

Fort Snelling $$
Minnesota Highways 5 and 55, St. Paul
(612) 726-1171
www.mnhs.org/fortsnelling
Built on a bluff overlooking the Mississippi and Minnesota Rivers in 1820, Fort Snelling was once the westernmost U.S. outpost in the mostly unexplored wilds of the north and was the center of frontier commerce and government on the upper Mississippi. At the time, an outpost on the confluence of the Minnesota and Missis-

sippi Rivers meant control of river traffic throughout the Minnesota Territory; British fur traders, American outlaws, and warring American Indian nations could be held in check. Today themed tours provide insight into what life was like at the fort, with costumed guides reenacting scenes from military, civilian, and Native American life of the 1800s. Not only are these some of the oldest surviving buildings in the state, but both Twin Cities trace their pedigrees to the fort. Soldiers from the fort built the first sawmill at St. Anthony Falls, and the first residents of St. Paul were moved there after being sheltered as immigrants.

This reconstruction of the first permanent settlement in Minnesota is open May through October and is staffed by costumed guides portraying fort life in 1827. Events at the fort include demonstrations, historical skits, practice military drills, watching or joining in with residents of the 1820s military post as they prepare the harvest for storage and winter use, and book readings and lectures from Minnesota authors and historians. Contact the fort directly to hear about special events year-round.

Gibbs Museum of Pioneer and Dakota Life   **$$**
2097 Larpenteur Avenue, Falcon Heights
(651) 646-8629
www.rchs.com/gbbsfm2.htm
Near the farm fields that make up the northern border of the University of Minnesota's agriculturally focused St. Paul campus, you'll find this quaint little barn and farmhouse, which date from the 19th century. They're preserved in their original state as an educational opportunity for those who would like to step back in time. On summer weekends expect to see people in period dress doing farm chores like churning butter on the porch. Interpreters share the process and results of their extensive archeology of this site, displaying excavated artifacts and explaining their historic significance to the public. The Gibbs Museum's medicine and veg-

etable gardens are especially interesting, with many native plants that no longer exist naturally in the area but were especially important to Native Americans and pioneer settlers.

A point of interest is that the history most spoken about at this archeological site is that of Jane Gibbs, a young woman raised by missionaries and used as an interpreter between the Dakota Indians and settlers for many years, and not that of her husband, Heman Gibbs, who helped build the two houses on the property as well as the barn in back. The Gibbses, who first moved to the Minnesota property in the 1840s from Illinois, lived for five years in a tiny sod house—replicated in astounding detail and now a part of the tour—before building the main house. Guided tours cover everything that's left of the original Gibbs property. Gibbs Museum is open mid-April through mid-November.

Henry Sibley House Historic Site   **$**
1357 Sibley Memorial Highway, Mendota
(651) 452-1596
www.mnhs.org/sibleyhouse
Henry Sibley, an American For Company regional manager and Minnesota's first governor, lived in a limestone home amid a trading post in the riverside hamlet of Mendota. Today visitors can walk through three of the structures in one of Minnesota's oldest European-American settlements, including the home of Sibley and his neighbor, Jean Baptiste Faribault. Sibley's restored house is full of fur trade stuff and the trappings of frontier gentility—pelts, muskets, and loads of blue china. The guides' stories of Sibley and company are vivid snapshots of the difficulties faced by these tough frontiersmen living in a wild world.

The Sibley House offers many theme tours and events, including Children's Day—where kids can learn about Dakota techniques used since the 1680s for turning natural materials into tepees, bowstrings, and fishing lines—and the 1850 Holiday Theme Tours, where visitors of all ages can tour the Sibley and Faribault Houses decorated as they were for the winter holidays in 1849–50. During the Holiday Tours, guides discuss the different celebrations by Yankees and French-Canadians, upper and lower classes, Presbyterians and Catholics, and the Dakota peoples. The site is open weekends May through October, with expanded summer hours.

Minneapolis Riverfront
Minneapolis
(888) 676–MPLS
www.minneapolis-riverfront.com
St. Anthony Falls defined Minneapolis as the world leader in flour milling for more than 50 years. With the completion of the restored Stone Arch Bridge and various revitalization projects, the area is a redis-covered historical treasure.

Originally called "curling waters" by the Dakota Indians, St. Anthony Falls were renamed by Father Louis Hennepin after his patron saint, Saint Anthony of Padua. Known as the birthplace of Minneapolis, this landmark is the only waterfall on the Mississippi River. Great viewing of the falls is available from the Stone Arch Bridge. The falls originally traversed a limestone ledge and, in their natural state, fell 16 feet to rapids below. In the 1960s, when the Upper Lock and Dam were constructed, the degrading ledge was covered with a concrete apron to protect it from further erosion. Today the falls stand between 12 and 15 feet above water level, dependent on the level of the Mississippi River.

A year-round walking trail provides a self-guided tour of the St. Anthony Falls Historic District with its nationally signifi-cant homes, buildings, and archeological ruins of former flour mills. Visitors can fol-low the Heritage Trail around St. Anthony Falls and learn about historic structures and archeological sites from exhibits. The trail offers a spectacular view of the river from the historic Stone Arch Bridge and is a great way to get away from the bustle of the city without actually leaving Min-neapolis.

Head across the bridge and back in time on Nicollet Island. Nicollet Island was

the stepping-stone to the settlement of Minneapolis, and many of the 19th-century homes and row houses are still on the island. For an extra treat, a horse-and-carriage ride around the island can some-times be picked up at Nicollet Island Inn.

Minnesota State Capitol   **Free**
75 Rev. Dr. Martin Luther King Jr.
Boulevard, St. Paul
(651) 296–2881
www.mnhs.org/statecapitol
Soaring domes, monumental arches, columns, statues, and symbolic murals dominate the scene for visitors today as they did when the Minnesota State Capitol was completed in 1905. The first two capi-tols, one destroyed by fire and one out-grown, were in downtown St. Paul. The current structure is the stark, white capitol topped by a magnificent marble dome and the four golden horses—the Quadriga—that are usually what people remember after their visit to this master-piece of Italian Renaissance architecture.

Today the State Senate, House of Rep-resentatives, and Supreme Court have been restored to their original appear-ances, as has the Rathskeller Cafe, now open to the public during the legislative session. Guided tours of the capitol leave every hour; self-guided tour brochures are available at the front entrance. (Groups of ten or more, please call ahead for reserva-tions.) The State House and Senate are easily accessible to visitors, and if your timing's right, you can hear important issues being decided. The tours showcase amply captioned oil portraits of Minnesota governors around the rotunda, and go on to give insight to the history of the build-ing, including information on the Civil War, and on architect Cass Gilbert's role in selecting art and furnishings for this, his magnum opus. The capitol is open daily year-round.

Murphy's Landing   **$$**
2187 East Highway 101, Shakopee
(763) 694–7784
www.murphyslanding.org

Murphy's Landing is a living-history site that preserves and interprets 19th-century life in the Minnesota River Valley. More than 40 period buildings were moved here from 1969 to 1972 with the intent of re-creating a 19th-century village; today the village includes a fur trading post, a homestead, and a storefront, all of which are arranged in chronological order by date of construction. Costumed inter-preters demonstrate the rigors of the daily life of Minnesota's settlers, from metal-smiths to weavers and merchants. Special seasonal events are planned around the holidays for history buffs of all ages. Mur-phy's Landing is open daily year-round.

Stevens House   **$**
4801 Minnehaha Avenue South,
Minneapolis
(612) 722-2220

The Stevens House, built in 1849 and origi-nally located in the present-day riverfront spot of the Minneapolis Post Office, is the first permanent settler's home in Min-neapolis. The home of Col. John H. Stevens and his family served as the social and civic hub of the new city. People met here to discuss a name for the city and to organize local schools and government. It was here that John Stevens drew up the original territorial boundaries for Hennepin County. The first county elections were held here in 1852.

The house was reopened to the public in 1985 after being closed since the turn of the last century. It was pulled to Min-nehaha Park in 1896 by more than 10,000 schoolchildren in the first act of historic preservation in the state of Minnesota, but lack of funding prevented it from being anything but a curious landmark in the park for decades. Now an interpretive museum, exhibits, and tour guides inside the house tell the story of the city, found-ing father Stevens, and the importance of this little white house. The Stevens House is open May through September on Satur-day, Sunday, and holidays.

Wabasha Street Caves   **$-$$$**
215 South Wabasha Street, St. Paul
(651) 292-1220
www.wabashastreetcaves.com

Burrowed into the sandstone bluffs that line the Mississippi River on St. Paul's West Side, this is the site of the late Castle Royal nightclub, which was a speakeasy during the days of Prohibition and, before that, a mushroom farm. There's a lot of St. Paul history here, especially for those interested in the city's incarnation as a gangster mecca. Considering that the city of St. Paul was built around a cave (Pig's Eye Parrant's cavern and tavern), a cave is an appropriate dwelling for a night out. Dancers come to the caves on Swing Night, held every Thursday as well as select Fridays and featuring live big bands. The Historic Cave Tour covers the history of the Wabasha Street Caves, while the St. Paul Gangster Tour stops at several sites outside the caves where infa-mous crimes took place. Each October motorcoach tours depart from the caves to deliver St. Paul's haunted history. The caves are open year-round (call for tour times and reservations).

INDOOR RECREATION

Hubert H. Humphrey Metrodome
900 South Fifth Street, Minneapolis
(612) 332-0386
www.msfc.com

This multipurpose facility, home of the Minnesota Vikings, Twins, and the U of M Gophers football team, features events year-round. First-time visitors to the Metrodome are awed by its interior vol-ume; regular fans sometimes feel they're watching theater, not sports. The Metrodome is big enough to host motocross events and monster-truck ral-lies as well as football games, occasional rock concerts, and in-line skaters.

During evenings November through March, when there's no previously sched-uled event, the Metrodome turns into the Rollerdome—hordes of skaters take over

The Hubert H. Humphrey Metrodome forms the most horizontal part of the downtown Minneapolis skyline. GREATER MINNEAPOLIS CONVENTION & VISITORS ASSOCIATION

its half-mile concourses, taking advantage of the tremendous workout the field provides. Skaters addicted to speed zoom around the upper concourse, while less-rabid skaters enjoy the Dome's smooth skating surface on the lower concourse. It's a great cure for cabin fever.

No one gets turned away wearing traditional skates, but Rollerdome is In-line Central. Rollerblade sponsors these skating sessions, where free protective gear is dispensed on a first-come, first-served basis and safety teams patrol to keep in-liners in line.

Parking for Rollerdome and the Metrodome is free in the Metrodome lot, which you can enter at the intersection of South Fifth Street and 11th Avenue. Enter the Dome at Gate D. No cameras, recording devices, or outside cans, bottles, coolers, or containers are allowed at the Metrodome or Rollerdome, but concessions are available inside on weekends in case you get peckish.

Mall of America
60 East Broadway, Bloomington
(952) 883–8800
www.mallofamerica.com
This gigantic mall says only one thing about the state of American shopping: Fantasy moves product. And at this cement-and-plastic Bloomington behemoth, there's a lot of product to move. The largest shopping and entertainment complex in the United States, the megamall—at 4.2 million square feet—is the size of seven Yankee Stadiums and home to more than 520 stores, 50 restaurants, a 14-screen movie theater, an indoor amusement park, and an aquarium. To make your shopping experience more pleasurable, the mall rents strollers, wheelchairs, shopping carts, and lockers. In case you change your mind about shopping and decide to get married instead, there's a wedding chapel conveniently located inside the mall.

MUSEUMS

The Bakken: A Library and Museum of Electricity in Life $$
3537 Zenith Avenue South, Minneapolis
(612) 926-3878
www.thebakken.org

Established in 1976 by Earl E. Bakken, inventor of the first transistorized cardiac pacemaker and cofounder of Medtronic, a Twin Cities company on the cutting edge of electrocardio technology, this Tudor-style mansion houses an incredible collection of rare books, manuscripts, and scientific thingamajigs that are all related to the role electricity plays in life. Bakken's fascination with the life-saving capabilities of electricity led to the establishment of this museum, and his similar interest in homeopathic medicine led to creating the herbal gardens outside the museum, full of Old and New World medicinal plants.

A $6 million renovation, completed in 1999, doubled the original size of the museum. The expansion created more space for exhibits and classrooms, added a workshop geared toward student experiments, and expanded the library. One of the most popular exhibits is "Frankenstein: Mary Shelley's Dream," in which visitors step back to the early 1800s for a dramatic multimedia immersion into Victor Frankenstein's laboratory and Mary Shelley's study. In "Electricity in the 18th Century," visitors learn about Benjamin Franklin and other electricity pioneers and then play with electricity as those scientists did.

The Bakken Museum is open Tuesday through Saturday; the museum's research library is open Monday through Friday.

Bell Museum of Natural History $
University of Minnesota,
10 Church Street SE, Minneapolis
(612) 626-9660
www.bellmuseum.org

The Bell preserves an impressive collection of stuffed creatures that would interest 19th-century taxidermists as well as current students of the natural sciences. The animals are displayed in simulated natural environments, with background murals painted by landscape artist Francis L. Jaques. These scenes are curious testaments to the exotic hobbies of scientists of the past, especially in regard to the exhibits displaying passenger pigeons and other now-extinct creatures.

The exhibits of stuffed birds, mammals, and fish are extremely clean and tastefully exhibited, with beautiful painted backdrops of seascapes and woodlands for the animals on display. The exhibits are primarily Northland animals and confined to North America, with emphasis on Minnesota wildlife including porcupines, bears, moose, and ground squirrels. There is also a temporary exhibit hall that features artwork, animal remains, and fossils from around the world, changing approximately every two months.

The Touch and See Room, located on the second floor of the museum, is a veritable paradise for children interested in the natural sciences. Living snakes, turtles, and lizards are on display in tanks around the room, and with assistance from one of the friendly attendants, children can even hold some of these creatures. The room is full of horns, antlers, bones, fossils, and rocks, all for the handling—there's even a big, leathery elephant ear for kids to pick up and examine. There's also a rain-forest plant exhibit and a hall for traveling exhibits and artwork.

The Bell Museum is closed Monday and major holidays. Admission is free every Sunday.

Hennepin History Museum $
2303 Third Avenue South, Minneapolis
(612) 870-1329
www.hhmuseum.org

Founded by the Hennepin County Territorial Pioneers Association in 1858, the Hennepin History Museum has long been dedicated to preserving the history of Hennepin County. Today the Hennepin History Museum serves as the gateway to historical resources. Housed in the George H. Christian mansion, designed by Hewitt and Brown, the museum offers a series of rotating exhibits focusing on everything from toys to technology. Past exhibits have highlighted Ojibwe and Dakota cultures, period clothing design, toys, quilt making, technology, innovations, local artists, and decorative arts. City Kids' Gallery is one place where touching the artifacts is not only allowed but encouraged.

The museum contains a vast number of items relating to Hennepin's history, including household items, government documents, restaurant menus, business advertisements, and more. Of special interest are the *Diaries of Gideon Pond,* the musings of an early missionary; early 20th-century real estate photos; and a collection of first editions on local history.

The Hennepin History Museum is open varying hours Tuesday through Sunday.

Minnesota Air Guard Museum $
Off Minnesota Highways 62 and 55
Minneapolis–St. Paul International Airport
(612) 713-2523
www.mnangmuseum.org
This small but historically important museum displays vintage aircraft and memorabilia of the Minnesota Air Guard. The memorabilia—airplane pictures, portraits, helmets, patches—is crowded into a couple of cramped rooms in a hangar. The museum's focus is on local flyboys, and the only globally relevant information pertains to when these local boys left town. Twenty-two cool old planes are on display on the tarmac outside, including fighter jets, transports, and the terrifying black A-12, the CIA's favorite superfast spy plane.

Because the museum is located on an active military base, visitors must arrive by vehicle (rather than light-rail transit) and must show a photo ID. It's open weekends May through August.

Minnesota Children's Museum $$
10 West Seventh Street (Seventh and Wabasha), St. Paul
(651) 225-6000
www.mcm.org

Einstein said that "play was the highest form of research," and if you have children, you will appreciate the diversion this museum can offer your kids. Traveling exhibits have included items on Peter Rabbit and Mister Rogers, while permanent exhibits are interactive and give children a chance to crawl through simulated ant colonies, operate a giant crane to transport foam blocks, or take the stage in a TV studio. Look into the membership rate here, as it will give you and your family unlimited admission throughout the year and discounts on programs and museum birthday parties. This is an especially popular place for graduate students to take their kids, as it keeps the youngsters entertained while letting education-minded parents comfortably take a study break. Recommended for children six months to 10 years of age and for parents looking to entertain their brood during the winter. Museum hours vary. Call ahead.

An admittance stamp at the Minnesota Children's Museum lets you come and go from the building all day, so you can sneak out and get a decent lunch and still come back and play for no extra charge.

The Minnesota History Center $$
345 West Kellogg Boulevard, St. Paul
(651) 296-6126 or (800) 657-3773
www.mnhs.org/places/historycenter
The History Center is an architectural masterpiece constructed from Minnesota's own Rockville granite and Winona limestone. The view of the city from several vantage points inside the museum is breathtaking. There are exhibits and events all year focusing on Minnesota's past. Encounter early settlers in "Tales of the Territory" or learn the facts about our storied weather in "Weather Permitting." The History Center has a gigantic library of books and photographs about Minnesota

events, regions, family genealogy, and other artifacts; visitors are allowed to pore through the collection for free.

The center is a wonderful resource of artifacts, historical texts, and changing and permanent exhibits that chronicle much of the history of Minnesota. A few of the permanent exhibits are particularly kid friendly. Grainland includes an authentic 24-ton boxcar and a model grain elevator that children can climb through as they learn how grain gets to the marketplace. Juke boxes, interactive kiosks, and recording equipment keep kids busy in "Sounds Good to Me: Music in Minnesota."

The museum also presents lecture series and book readings from local historians and authors. Justice Rosalie Wahl, the first woman on the Minnesota Supreme Court, has spoken here on her experiences with task forces on gender bias and racial fairness, as has "Super V-man" John Velek, a Vikings football fan, who brought rare Vikings memorabilia from his collection to display temporarily at the History Center. The museum has hosted musical exhibits from members of the St. Paul Chamber Orchestra and the Minnesota Youth Symphonies Solo Competition, in which 10 to 12 youth finalists perform in a two-hour solo competition. An extensive research library rounds out this amazing historical resource, housing maps, books, photographs, newspapers, and census records. Anyone can use these resources, and classes are available for those who want help. The History Center museum is closed Monday; the research library is open Tuesday through Saturday.

Minnesota Transportation Museum $-$$$
various locations
(651) 288-0263
www.mtmuseum.org

Discover the history of transportation at the museum's exhibit sites. Among other things, visitors may ride diesel-powered trains in Osceola, Wisconsin; or view locomotive restoration up close at Jackson Street Roundhouse in St. Paul.

Minnesota Transportation Museum's Osceola and St. Croix Valley Railway's trains start at the Osceola, Wisconsin, depot (715-755-3570) about an hour northeast of the Twin Cities. There are two trips. One trip heads west 10 miles along the lovely St. Croix River to the adorable town of Marine on St. Croix, Minnesota. A highlight of this 90-minute ride is crossing the river from Wisconsin to Minnesota on the large Cedar Bend swing bridge. Your second choice from Osceola is to head 5 miles east to Dresser, Wisconsin, a former Soo Line junction town. Check out the original 1886 wooden Soo Line depot on this 50-minute trip. Trains run weekends and holidays, April through October. In addition, the railway operates special events all season long.

The Jackson Street Roundhouse, located at 193 East Pennsylvania Avenue in St. Paul (651-228-0263), is the first railroad maintenance shop in Minnesota and the oldest known railroad in St. Paul—not bad for a city whose history has been dominated by railroading. Here, train lovers can climb aboard train cars of varying eras and styles and learn the state's railroad history through vintage posters and railroad maps. There's a gift shop, a working turntable (used to turn the locomotives), a kids' play area, and a working shop, too, where the Minnesota Transportation Museum restores all types of railroad equipment and cars. They'll even take you behind the scenes for a glimpse of the latest work in progress.

The Science Museum of Minnesota $$
120 West Kellogg Boulevard, St. Paul
(651) 221-9444
www.smm.org

With eight indoor acres of both permanent and temporary exhibits that include an extensive collection of dinosaur, mammal, insect, and fish fossils, plus a set of T. rex jaws you can operate, there's lots of interaction at this museum. In the Cell Lab, kids don lab coats and check out what their cheek cells look like under the microscope. They can bring rocks and seashells and such into the Collector's Corner, where they help identify their treasure and can then swap it for something else in the trading collection. In the Mississippi River Gallery, kids pretend to drive a real tugboat as they look out over the river. There are river views everywhere, both from the museum's patios and soaring glass windows and from the new exhibits on the museum's 10 outdoor acres. The nine-hole mini-golf course is actually a lesson in river science, and the prairie maze is made from native Minnesota plants and grasses.

The Museum of Questionable Medical Devices, formerly located in Minneapolis, is now housed in the Science Museum. Located in the Collections Gallery, level four, about a dozen items from the original 300-piece collection give visitors a peek at machines from the past 100 years that were designed to "cure" what ails the average human. In some cases these failed remedies were honest mistakes, but many others were deliberate frauds. A few examples include the phrenology machine, which looks like an old-fashioned, hood-style hair dryer and supposedly "reads" the bumps on your head to tell you about your personality; a fluoroscope, a shoe-fitting X-ray machine; the Kellogg Vibratory Chair, an electric-powered chair that shook violently and was reputed to cure constipation and improve respiration; and an aerobic exercise kit.

The museum's education center offers classes to kids on subjects as diverse as animation and film making and archeology. For a less hands-on experience, but just as thrilling, check out the nation's first convertible dome Omnitheater and the 3D Cinema, both located inside the museum.

The Science Museum of Minnesota offers really cool one-shot classes for kids and families and also hosts birthday parties.

**Twin City Model Railroad Museum $
Bandana Square, 1021 Bandana
Boulevard East, St. Paul
(651) 647–9628
www.tcmrm.org**
Since 1939 this museum has been dedicated to the promotion and understanding of the role played by railroads in the history and development of Minnesota. An extensive collection of railroad artifacts and art is available, including a changing photo exhibit in the museum focusing on a different historic train or train line each month.

The centerpiece of the museum is the scale-model railroad of the re-creation of the Twin Cities pre-1950. Up to six trains at once glide through the depots and tunnels of the incredibly detailed model, while miniature streetcars seen running back and forth over the Third Avenue Bridge model are sometimes brought out to run on the tracks as well. Re-creations of historic steam engines like the Twin Cities *Hiawatha* can be seen pulling passenger cars in and out of the 1914 Great Northern passenger depot, peopled with tiny engineers and waiting passengers. The museum is closed Monday.

KIDSTUFF 👫

We Minnesotans have a great love for our children, and it's no more evident than in the way our major metropolitan areas are laid out. In both Minneapolis and St. Paul, neighborhoods are centered around parks with community centers, swimming pools, and, in winter, ice-skating rinks. Public schools have initiated many after-school programs to help parents who can't be at home when the school day officially ends, and during summer these same schools offer fun classes for kids that include swimming lessons and summer sports.

There are more than enough activities for your children in the Twin Cities, from science and nature-oriented attractions to water parks and bumper cars. And we like to drag our kids to museums and art events here an awful lot. Luckily, most places are fully prepared to receive and entertain children, even those without specific arts programs geared toward kids.

As for dining options, you're welcome to bring your kids into plenty of Twin Cities establishments—bars that double as restaurants in the daytime welcome underage patrons (accompanied by adults) until just before happy hour. The restaurants in this chapter try to make children feel comfortable, from the menu to service to decor. We've tried to pick places that are easy on the wallet.

PRICE CODE

The following price code is based on the cost for general admission for one adult. Most sites offer discounted tickets for children and seniors, and some allow discounts or even free entry for members of their respective organizations.

$	$5 and under
$$	$6–$15
$$$	$16–$30
$$$$	$31 and up

AMUSEMENT AND WATER PARKS

The Park at MOA $$$
Mall of America, 5000 Center Court, Bloomington
(952) 883–8600
www.theparkatmoa.com
Located right in the center of the Mall of America, the Park at MOA, the largest indoor amusement park in America, has more than 30 rides and attractions for kids and adults alike. For the little guys, there's the Americana Carousel, a hand-painted contemporary version of the classic carousel, and Lil' Shaver, a smaller, slower version of the roller coaster that circles the park (the Ripsaw Roller Coaster). For everyone else, there's the Skyscraper Ferris Wheel that takes visitors 74 feet high in the air, the Log Chute—a watery ride that includes a drop over a 40-foot waterfall—and plenty of other rides and activities to take your mind off of shopping. Admission to the park is free; you purchase points or a wristband for rides. If you like to sneak some kid-free shopping in, drop the little ones off at Kids Quest in the Park at MOA. It charges by the hour, and there's plenty for kids to do here, including read books, sing karaoke, and play nonviolent video games.

Cascade Bay $$
1360 Civic Center Drive, Eagan
(651) 675-5577
www.cascadebay.com
Seven-acre Cascade Bay in the St. Paul suburb of Eagan is the largest outdoor municipal water park in the Midwest. Its lazy river, multiple slides, sand beach, and more are extremely popular with people of all ages. Cascade Bay is pretty inexpensive, too.

Como Town $$$
1301 Midway Parkway, St. Paul
(651) 487-2121

The Como campus, already a kid magnet for its free zoo, conservatory, and lovely sprawling grounds, sweetened the pot in 2005 with the opening of Como Town. It's the new version of what regular park visitors remember as a few low-scale rides tucked into a corner of the zoo. What a welcome change. The park's small, with about 12 attractions geared toward kids ages 2 to 12, who can fight pretend fires with a personal truck and water cannon, navigate ministreets by kiddie car, and climb, swing, and bounce their way through a mega-jungle gym called Hodge Podge Park. A couple of rides have some height and speed, too. Admission to the park is free, then you buy rides with one to four 75-cent tickets.

Grand Rios $$-$$$
6900 Lakeland Avenue North,
Brooklyn Park
(763) 566-8855
www.grandrios.com

Grand Rios is located inside the Grand Rios hotel in the Minneapolis suburb of Brooklyn Park. At 45,000 square feet, it's Minnesota's largest indoor water park. Grand Rios is a Caribbean-themed affair with water basketball, spas, a lazy river, a 500-gallon dumping bucket, and multiple tube slide, one of which dumps into Hurricane Plunge.

Valleyfair! $$$$
1 Valleyfair Drive, Shakopee
(952) 445-7600 or (800) 386-7433
www.valleyfair.com

With more than 75 rides, Valleyfair! is the upper Midwest's largest theme park, with something to offer the littlest kid or the bravest adult. Take an inner tube down a gently sloping canal for a relaxing, meditative ride on Ripple Rapids, or take a boat off a 50-foot drop on the Flume. The park is packed with twists, turns, flips, and freefalls, from the classic wooden High Roller to the Xtreme Swing, like your typical playground version on steroids, new in 2006. There are many rides for the really little ones, too, from bumble bee–shaped electric cars to a multilevel foam-ball factory to an antique carousel.

Water Park at the Depot $$$
225 Third Avenue South, Minneapolis
(612) 375-1700
www.thedepotminneapolis.com

With 15,000 square feet, this locomotive-themed water park includes a three-story waterslide, multiple pools, and a slide/train that sprays water. It's pretty pricey for its size (or lack thereof), but it's connected to hotels that offer package deals and it's downtown, near many other attractions.

Twin Cities parents love Toddler Tuesday at the Mall of America for its great deals, including free meals and activities.

ANIMAL ADVENTURES

Como Zoo   Free
1225 Estabrook Drive, St. Paul
(651) 487-8229
www.comozooconservatory.org

One of only four free (donation requested) metropolitan-area zoos in the country, Como Zoo has been an institution in St. Paul for more than a century. The first Siberian tigers successfully bred in captivity were born here in 1958, and the big cat display is still one of the best features of the zoo. It includes a single breeding pair of lions that has had several healthy pairs of cubs over the past decade, providing valuable insight to professionals and the public alike on how well lions do in captivity when allowed to stay together as a family instead of being separated immediately after mating and birth, as is customary at many other zoos. There is a great primate display, with about a

Children love Cafesjian's Carousel at Como Zoo in St. Paul. SAINT PAUL RCVA

dozen ring-tailed and brown lemurs, spider monkeys, a couple of breeding pairs of tamarins that have successfully given birth every spring, and orangutans and gorillas that have been with the zoo more than 10 years. There are bears, giraffes, zebras, buffalo, and the ever-popular Sparky the Sea Lion show, held Memorial Day through Labor Day. There's also a pair of wolves in a large, specially designed exhibit area that is designed to make the wolves feel comfortable having people watch them, with thick tree cover in the back of the enclosure for them to hide in when they don't feel like company.

But it doesn't stop at the animals. There's also an antique wooden carousel, Cafesjian's Carousel, for kids and adults to ride in a building near the entrance of the zoo, and in summer check out amusement park Como Town. In late October the zoo opens in the evening for its annual "Zoo Boo," where kids come in their Halloween

costumes and are given candy and gifts by more than 300 volunteers.

Minnesota Zoo $$
13000 Zoo Boulevard, Apple Valley
(952) 431–9500 or (800) 366–7811
www.mnzoo.org
Located in the southern suburb of Apple Valley (a few minutes south of the Mall of America) and housing more than 2,000 animals from five different continents, the Minnesota Zoo and its IMAX theater see a million visitors per year. The expansive grounds include an indoor tropical rain forest populated by an amazing variety of birds and animals, ranging from colorful African hornbills to a family of gibbons and a large and smelly South American tapir. There are also dolphins that officially perform for audiences every afternoon and unofficially any time enough people gather around their huge, glass-walled tank; a walk-through aquarium with

sharks, fish, and deep sea plants; Discovery Bay, where kids can touch different kinds of sharks; and the Minnesota Trail, with beavers, foxes, fruit bats, and porcupines. Outside the main exhibit building, you can find ducks and swans, a prairie dog town, wild horses, camels, tigers, and many, many other animals, some of which are on the endangered species lists and are almost an exclusive at the zoo.

One of the most popular exhibits at the zoo is the seasonal and extremely hands-on Wells Fargo Family Farm. This reproduction of a working farm is surrounded by fields of crops—you can either walk up the hill to the farm itself or wait at the stationhouse for a tractor or horse cart to give you a ride. The farm has a huge selection of domestic animals, from beautiful show chickens and roosters to plow horses to many varieties of cows, including two that were cloned. The chicken coop has an incubator with hatching eggs, and an assistant

is on hand most hours to show children how to pet and hold the baby chicks properly. There's a petting pen full of goats, and you can even enter the pen to feed and play with the friendly animals.

Underwater Adventures Aquarium $$
Mall of America, 120 East Broadway, Bloomington
(952) 883-0202 or (888) DIVE-TIME
www.underwateradventures.net

Underwater Adventures is a huge (1.2 million gallons) walk-through aquarium featuring more than 4,500 different sea creatures from around the world in eight exhibits. For a one-time admission charge, visitors can walk through a glass tunnel that leads them underneath the three freshwater exhibits: Turtley Awesome Woods, Fisherman's Hollow, and the Mighty Mississippi, and five ocean exhibits: Shark Cove, Rainbow Reef, Seacrits of Hollywood (with famous fish like Nemo),

Underwater Adventures Aquarium offers a chance to walk underneath sharks and other sea creatures. GREATER MINNEAPOLIS CONVENTION & VISITORS ASSOCIATION

Starfish Beach, and Circle of Life, where children can touch harmless sharks and stingrays.

BERRY PICKIN'

Driving out to the country to pick fresh strawberries, blueberries, or apples is a Minnesota-childhood staple. For a small per-bucket fee, the following farms let visitors pick as much fruit as they can carry home, and there are often bonus attractions such as petting zoos, wagon rides, and gift shops. For apples, we suggest you stop by **Aamodt's Apple Farm,** 6428 Manning Avenue North, Stillwater (651-439-3127; www.aamodtsapplefarm .com); the **Afton Apple Orchards,** 14421 South 90th Street, Hastings (651-436-8385; www.aftonapple.com); or **Sponsel's Minnesota Harvest Apple Orchard,** 8251 Old Highway 169 Boulevard, Jordon (952-492-2785; www.minnesotaharvest .net). For strawberries and blueberries, try either the **Bauer Berry Farm,** 10830 French Lake Road, Champlin (763-421-4384; www.bauerberry.com); or **Covered Bridge Farm,** 18655 Forest Boulevard North, Forest Lake (651-464-0735). For a comprehensive list of basically anything grown in the state that you can buy directly from farms, contact **Minnesota Grown** (651-201-6539 or 800-657-3878; www.minnesotagrown.com).

ARTS AND CULTURE

The Children's Theatre Company $$$
2400 Third Avenue South, Minneapolis
(612) 874-0400
www.childrenstheatre.org

Berry-picking conditions and the availability of apple varieties can change overnight. Call farms and orchards ahead to avoid disappointment.

Since 1965 the Tony Award-winning Children's Theatre Company and its cast of incredibly talented children and professional adult actors have been putting on performances at its 746-seat facility—recently remodeled to include a second stage. Most of the performances are based on children's stories and fairy tales, such as *A Year with Frog and Toad,* but there's a healthy dose of impressive original works as well, such as *Korczak's Children,* a story about the Holocaust through children's eyes, and *The Monkey King,* based on a 500-year-old Chinese story about a trickster on a quest with pious monks to recover sacred scrolls.

In the Heart of the Beast Puppet
and Mask Theatre $$
1500 East Lake Street, Minneapolis
(612) 721-2535
www.hobt.org

Unusual masks and large, fantastical puppets teach themes of natural and cultural understanding here. Outside of regular original performances and the much-lauded May Day parade, Heart of the Beast offers kids' performances every Saturday morning for $3.00, with a $2.00 discount if you're from the neighborhood.

Minneapolis Sculpture Garden   Free
725 Vineland Place, Minneapolis
(612) 375-7600
www.walkerart.org

Located right next to the Walker Art Center, this beautiful collection of large sculptures made by local and internationally known artists is a great place to take kids because it's outside, it's interesting, and it's free. Kids can run around and enjoy the 11-acre grounds without worrying about keeping silent while the grown-ups enjoy art—and who knows? They might learn something about art appreciation themselves. Right across the street is Loring Park, with restrooms, a wading pool, a playground, and lots of sunny spots for a relaxing summer picnic.

Minnesota Center for Book Arts $
1011 Washington Avenue South, Suite 100,
Minneapolis
(612) 215-2520
www.mnbookarts.org

The Minnesota Center for Book Arts, the largest independent book arts facility in the nation, offers classes to children, teens, families, and adults on making paper, binding books, and working in a printing-press studio. Kids can take their literary creations to the next level by making a beautiful cover out of found objects and binding their books using traditional methods, or they can create their own newspapers in the letterpress studio using both modern and antiquated letterpress equipment.

MUSEUMS AND HISTORICAL ATTRACTIONS

American Swedish Institute $
2600 Park Avenue, Minneapolis
(612) 871-4907
www.americanswedishinst.org

If your kids have an interest in mythical castles, bring them here, since it's the closest they'll get to walking through a real one in this country. Set in a spectacular 33-room turn-of-the-20th-century mansion that looks more like a castle than a former residence, the American Swedish Institute is the largest and oldest museum of Swedish culture, arts, and history in the country. Gargoyles and turrets adorn the outside. If all the Scandinavian artifacts inside don't keep the kids' attention, turn them on to the carved wood throughout the house—they can count the cherubs or fish or winged lions. Fiddling and dancing groups entertain visitors on a regular basis, and the institute also hosts special festivals with music and food. Kids can cozy up in the third-floor storytelling space for story hour on the first Wednesday of each month, which also happens to be free-admission day.

The Bakken: A Library and Museum of Electricity in Life $$
3537 Zenith Avenue South, Minneapolis
(612) 926-3878
www.thebakken.org

It starts in the lobby, where kids dive into the shocker machine, thought a cure-all in the 1920s, while parents read about the museum's founder, Earl E. Bakken, inventor of the first portable pacemaker. The rest of the electricity-related thingamajigs throughout this Tudor-style mansion are often hands-on—adults tend to hog the theremin, that instrument that makes B-movie UFO sounds, and kids really like the crack and spark that comes from cranking out 60,000 volts. Nine informational exhibits include the popular "Frankenstein: Mary Shelley's Dream." Recommended for ages six and above. Make-and-take projects are held weekly on Family Science Saturday from 10:00 A.M. to 4:00 P.M.

Bell Museum of Natural History $
University of Minnesota, 10 Church Street SE, Minneapolis
(612) 626-9660
www.bellmuseum.org

While most museums of taxidermied animals have fallen out of favor, this is one of the more pleasant traditional natural history museums in the country. The Bell Museum is designed to preserve the past, protect the future, and bring people closer to nature. How else is your kid going to get the chance to pet a Kodiak bear? The Touch and See Room lets children handle history, such as a 10,000-year-old wooly mammoth tusk; various fossils, bones, and rocks; and live animals including lizards and turtles. The museum has two floors of clean and tasteful diorama-style exhibits featuring North American mammals and birds, with an emphasis on Minnesota wildlife, including a bald eagle, moose, and squirrels. There's also a rain-forest plant exhibit and a hall for traveling exhibits and artwork. Plan ahead for the crafty, hands-on family program held 1:00 to 3:00 P.M. on the second Saturday of each month.

Fort Snelling $$
Junction of Minnesota Highways 5
and 55, St. Paul
(612) 726-1171
www.mnhs.org/fortsnelling

Built on a bluff overlooking the Mississippi
and Minnesota Rivers in 1820, Fort
Snelling was once the last American out-
post in the mostly unexplored wilds of the
north and was the center of frontier commerce and government on the upper Mississippi. Themed tours provide insight into
what life was like at the fort, with costumed guides reenacting scenes from military, civilian, and American Indian life of
the 1800s. Kids can join in the fun by taking up a musket and pretending to be a
soldier, scraping hides with fur traders, or
"working" in the laundry or kitchen of the
fort. New programming includes day
camps and kids' activities.

Gibbs Museum of Pioneer
and Dakota Life $$
2097 Larpentur Avenue, Falcon Heights
(651) 646-8629
www.rchs.com/gbbsfm2.htm

The history most spoken about at this
archeological site is that of Jane Gibbs, a
young woman kidnapped by missionaries
and used as an interpreter between the
settlers and Dakota Indians. Jane arrived
here with her husband, Heman, in 1849,
the year Minnesota became a territory.
They lived in a tiny sod house for five
years until the main house was built. Both
homes are included in the tour (the sod
house has been replicated in astounding
detail) as are the schoolhouse; gardens
full of indigenous plants; reconstructed
Dakota lodges and tepees; and a barn
with sheep, chickens, ducks, and other
animals. The main home is furnished with
the Gibbs family artwork, furniture, photographs, and essentials as well as period
pieces donated by members of the Ramsey County Historical Society, including a
full kitchen with a wood-burning stove
and a crank-operated washing machine.
The hourlong tour is comprehensive but
big on talking, not really suitable for fidg-

ety children under age nine. However, the
farm does put on seasonal events geared
toward youngsters, including metal forg-
ing, crop gathering, and milking demonstrations, plus summertime craft-making
days and ghost-story readings held
around Halloween.

The Jackson Street Roundhouse $
193 Pennsylvania Avenue East, St. Paul
(651) 228-0263
www.mtmuseum.org

It's all about trains here at the first railroad
maintenance shop in Minnesota. Climb
aboard train cars of varying eras and
styles. Learn the state's railroad history
through vintage posters and railroad
maps. There's a gift shop, a kids' play area,
and a working shop, too, where the Minnesota Transportation Museum restores
locomotives. Staffers will even take you
behind the scenes for a glimpse of the latest work in progress.

Mill City Museum $$
704 South Second Street, Minneapolis
(612) 341-7555
www.millcitymuseum.org

Here's a perfect example of a museum
done right. Tell your kids you're taking
them to a flour-milling museum in a former working mill and you might not hear
cheers of excitement. But then tell them
about the ride. The Flour Tower takes you
on an eight-story-high journey that relates
the history of this mill in employees'
words. And mention the explosion. Mill
explosions were common at the turn of
the 19th century, when Minneapolis produced more flour than any city in the
world, and here you can watch a small
explosion and find out why it happened.
From the top of the building, look down
at St. Anthony Falls, the only natural falls
along the Mississippi, which provided the
power that drew the mills in the first
place. And that's not all. Lots of hands-on,
kid-friendly exhibits here make Minneapolis's flour-milling saga intriguing for both
child and adult. Seeing the building itself
is worth the trip. A fire nearly destroyed

the mill, and the museum was built around the ruins. Mill City Museum is a must-do attraction in the heart of Minneapolis's ongoing riverfront renovation.

Minnesota Children's Museum $$
10 West Seventh Street, St. Paul
(651) 225-6000
www.mcm.org

While kids up to age 9 or 10 might still appreciate this wonderful resource, this museum is geared to younger children, from infants to eight-year-olds. The great thing about this museum is that all the exhibits are hands-on. We had no idea how much our own son would enjoy pretending to be a bus driver or a shopkeeper or a restaurant owner until he politely refused to leave the One World Gallery exhibit hall until all the possibilities the exhibit had to offer had been exhausted. While in the World Works Gallery, kids can operate a crane to pick up blocks, build a house foundation out of rubber masonry, or learn how to make art out of recycled newspaper. The Earth World Gallery has a giant anthill (populated by giant ant statues and nests) that kids can crawl through, pulley-operated clouds that can be moved across the ceiling by remote control, and a beaver dam and a giant hollow log that kids can climb in and out of.

For toddlers ages six months to four years, there's a wonderful playroom, the Habitot, that's set up like a nature preserve, with a giant "pond" playpen filled with plush lily pads and frog, turtle, and fish puppets at one end and a padded crawl-through cave filled with more stuffed animals and puppets at the other end. Changing rooms are connected to the exhibit, too, so parents don't have to rush to the other end of the building to take care of emergencies. Performances and activities take place in the second-floor atrium at scheduled intervals throughout the day.

Another nice feature is that as long as you leave your museum admission sticker on, you can come and go all day, which is great because the dining facilities consist of vending machines and there are a lot of great restaurants in the immediate vicinity to take the family instead. You're also welcome to bring a picnic.

The Minnesota History Center $$
345 West Kellogg Boulevard, St. Paul
(651) 296-6126 or (800) 657-3773
www.mnhs.org/places/historycenter

The Minnesota History Center is a wonderful resource of artifacts, historical texts, and changing and permanent exhibits that chronicle much of the history of Minnesota. A few of the permanent exhibits are particularly kid friendly. Grainland includes an authentic 24-ton boxcar and a model grain elevator that children can climb through as they learn how grain gets to the marketplace. Juke boxes, interactive kiosks, and recording equipment keep kids busy in "Sounds Good to Me: Music in Minnesota."

Murphy's Landing $$
2187 East Highway 101, Shakopee
(763) 694-7784
www.murphyslanding.org

This living-history site that preserves and interprets 19th-century life in the Minnesota River Valley. More than 40 period buildings were moved here from 1969 to 1972 with the intent of re-creating a 19th-century village. The village includes a fur trading post, a homestead, and a storefront, all of which are arranged according to date of construction. The site is peopled by "villagers" who are clothed in period costumes and perform such duties as weaving, metalsmithing, and farming—visitors are encouraged to ask questions about what villagers are doing. Kids can play house 1880s-style in the Pioneer Kids' Play Area. Educational seminars and lec-

In both Minneapolis and St. Paul, there's a park in every neighborhood for you to stop and let the kids get out and stretch their legs.

The Science Museum of Minnesota in downtown St. Paul offers hours of fun exhibits and experiments for curious kids. SCIENCE MUSEUM OF MINNESOTA

tures are ongoing, and special seasonal events are planned around the holidays.

Science Museum of Minnesota $$
120 West Kellogg Boulevard, St. Paul
(651) 221-9444
www.smm.org

When the Science Museum moved to this Mississippi riverfront location, it improved upon what it already did well: thoroughly engage kids in science. Cool fossils and dinosaur skeletons, including a set of T. rex jaws you can operate, are at the heart of the museum. But there's lots more interaction among the eight indoor acres of permanent and temporary exhibits. In the Cell Lab, kids don lab coats and check out what their cheek cells look like under the microscope. They can bring rocks and seashells and such into the Collector's Corner, where they help identify their treasures and then can swap for something else in the trading collection. In the Mississippi River Gallery, kids pretend to drive a real tugboat as they look out over the river. There are river views everywhere, from the museum's patios and soaring glass windows and from the new outdoor exhibits—the nine-hole mini-golf course is actually a lesson in river science, and the prairie maze is made from native Minnesota plants and grasses. There's an IMAX theater, too, as well as one-shot kids' and family classes with activities such as fossil hunting, robot building, and experimenting with dry ice.

Twin City Model Railroad Museum $
Bandana Square, 1021 Bandana Boulevard East, St. Paul
(651) 647-9628
www.tcmrm.org

A great treat for children and adults alike, this exhibit will particularly impress anyone even slightly interested in history, railroads, or miniatures. In existence in one form or another since 1939, the Model Railroad Club has been educating and entertaining the public with model locomotives, building its incredible panoramic sets to scale to complete the illusion. The museum is set inside a former passenger-train repair shop that houses a wonderful scale model of the Twin Cities and the surrounding communities, including parts of the Mississippi River and the old Mill District in Minneapolis prior to 1950, when trains were still the main means of transporting goods throughout the country. Up to six different trains run at once through the model, disappearing into tunnels and climbing through the tree-filled landscapes with their tiny headlights blazing. The exhibit changes monthly—miniature streetcars run back and forth over the Third Avenue Bridge model, or steam engines like the Milwaukee *Hiawatha* pull passenger cars in and out of the 1914 Great Northern passenger depot. There's a changing photo exhibit in the museum, too, focusing on a different historic train or train line each month. In the winter, the museum stays open a little later on Saturday to show off the special "Night Trains" exhibit, where all the lights are turned off in the museum and the lights on the trains and miniature buildings become the only source of illumination in the room. Thomas the Tank fans can check him out on the tracks on the first and third Sunday of each month, and there are always Thomas play stations and merchandise in the gift shop.

PARKS (FAVORITES OF LITTLE INSIDERS)

Edinborough Park $
7700 York Avenue South, Edina
(952) 832-6790
www.edinboroughpark.com

This densely landscaped one-acre park has a huge playground, pathways, an amphitheater, a junior Olympic–sized pool, and more than 6,000 plants, trees, and flowers. It's also indoors—this *is* Minnesota, land of the six-month winter. Edinborough generated a buzz among Twin Cities parents when it added Adventure Peak, one of the largest indoor play structures in the country, in 2003. It's hard to drag kids out of Edinborough, what with the 30-foot climbing tree, the slide tunnels, the nets, the telescopes, the giant inflatable air bounce, and more. The park has scheduled activities and concerts, too, that are never rained out.

Harriet Island Regional Park   Free
West of Wabasha and Water Streets, St. Paul
(651) 632-5111
www.stpaul.gov/depts/parks/special services/Harriet_Island/index.html

In the shadow of St. Paul sits the largest urban river park in North America. Seems there's always an event going on at Harriet Island, such as the summer children's concert series and the Taste of Minnesota, the state's popular annual Independence Day celebration (both of which are free, by the way). The Padelford Packet Boat Company launches riverboat tours from here. And you'll find, among other things, a riverboat-themed playground, the floating River Boat Grill, and big, wide steps that head right down into the Mississippi.

Lake Calhoun   Free
3000 Calhoun Parkway, Minneapolis
(612) 230-6400
www.minneapolisparks.org

Lake Calhoun is part of Minneapolis's inner-city chain of lakes, which are immensely popular during summer, espe-

cially with families. This particular lake has a little bit of everything, including sandy beaches, a fishing dock, picnic areas, walking and biking paths, and a tot lot. You can rent canoes, kayaks, and paddleboats at the Lake Calhoun Pavilion on the east side of the lake. The waterside pavilion houses a restaurant called Tin Fish, with all kinds of seafood, snacks, and kid-friendly items such as hot dogs, grilled cheese, fish-and-chips, and root-beer floats.

RESTAURANTS THAT LIKE KIDS (AND VICE VERSA)

Andy's Garage Cafe
1825 University Avenue West, St. Paul
(651) 917-2332
www.andysgaragecafe.com
This 1950s-style diner (and former gas station) is *the* place to take kids in the Twin Cities, as local publications have proclaimed for years. After you walk in, select from the bowling-bag game packs, cars, and throwback toys and games available for use at your table. Once there, send

junior off to stick a quarter in the jukebox or in the mechanical horse. Or let the youngsters hunt for Mr. Potato Head—his location changes daily, and if you find him, you get a Tootsie Pop. On Saturday night, family-friendly throwback bands play, and on nice days, the garage doors roll open. Birthday boys and girls of all ages get a plastic blow-up flamingo and a free malt or sundae. Speaking of food, it's good, and exactly the type you'd expect from a '50s diner: golden fries, juicy burgers, and overflowing tuna melts. Servers can get swamped and therefore be slow, but there's lots to entertain you and the kids while you wait.

Convention Grill & Fountain
3912 Sunnyside Road, Edina
(952) 920-6881
Here's a clean, authentic diner that's thankfully light on kitsch as well as on the pocketbook. Choose a booth seat or one at the stainless-steel counter overlooking the double-wide grill. The jukebox plays as servers zip around with vanilla Cokes, hamburgers, skin-on fries, and malts served as they should be—with a long

Andy's Garage Cafe in St. Paul's Midway neighborhood is the place to take kids. SAINT PAUL RCVA

spoon and the overflow in the metal cup each malt was made in.

cupcake
3338 University Avenue SE, Minneapolis
(612) 378-4818
www.cup-cake.com

This is the kind of place you wave in front of your kids as a reward for good behavior, never letting on that you want to go as badly as they do. *Cupcakes,* people. The cafe/coffeehouse rotates randomly through about 50 tried-and-true cupcake recipes, and you'll find up to 12 varieties offered on any given day. One kid favorite is the Betty Crocker, if solely for its swirly pink frosting and pretty pastel sprinkles, but look for Boston Crème, Red Velvet, Lemon Sunshine, S'More, and Coco Loco as well. The menu holds soups, sandwiches, and pizzas, too—kids can order cheese pizza, PB&J, or egg salad or try the more adventurous adult fare.

Galactic Pizza
2917 Lyndale Avenue South, Minneapolis
(612) 824-9100
www.galacticpizza.com

Superheroes deliver the pizza from Galactic. Generic superheroes, not Spidey or Superman, but spandex and capes are involved. Delivery service, by electric vehicle, is limited to an area southwest of the city, though it does extend to downtown Minneapolis during lunch. Travelers can order pizza delivered to their hotels. Or they can opt to eat on-site. The clean, multicolored storefront has brightly colored, child-height tables outdoors, retro Formica kitchen tables inside, and some toys older kids might like, including pick-up sticks, dominoes, and chess. Galactic is more kid friendly than kid oriented, though, and the nighttime crowd is primarily adult. The restaurant theme is social responsibility—you'll see a lot of words like *hormone-free, recycled,* and *organic* on the menu. The pizza can be plain or exotic, meaty or vegan, whatever you want. (The Paul Bunyan, with bison sausage, morel mushrooms, and wild rice

is surprisingly delicious.) Give the kids a heads-up: Your server will *not* be wearing a superhero outfit, alas, but you'll catch glimpses of the caped ones as they head off on their pizza-delivery missions.

Pop! A Neighborhood Restaurant
2859 Johnson Avenue Northeast,
Minneapolis
(612) 788-0455
www.poprestaurant.com

Pop! possesses hard-to-find qualities in a restaurant: a casually upscale atmosphere that still welcomes children, gourmet food at reasonable prices, and a drink menu that holds both a solid wine list and an even bigger selection of pop, the preferred word for sweet, carbonated beverages here in Minnesota. There's more than a hint of Latin America in the menu, where tamale and empanada exist alongside pasta and burger, and where smoked jalapeño mayo and avocado find their way onto the chicken sandwich. Trust the chef. He knows what he's doing. And try to save room for dessert.

WE ALL SCREAM FOR . . .

Grand Ole Creamery
750 Grand Avenue, St. Paul
(651) 293-1655
www.grandolecreamery.com

Do not be deterred by the line snaking out the door, spilling out onto the sidewalks of boutique-street Grand Avenue. This ice cream is worth the wait, as evidenced by the aforementioned line you're sure to find on warm summer days. The waffle cones are made fresh daily and plugged with a malted milk ball to prevent

The Greater Minneapolis Convention and Visitor's Association has a new Web site for visitors with children. See www .minneapolis-kids.com for information about discounts, family-friendly hotels, and kid-approved sights.

sticky hands and ice-cream-smeared shirts. There are 175 flavors, and the 31 available on any given day tend toward the seasonal—strawberry kiwi sorbet in the summer, German chocolate and pumpkin apple strudel in the fall, and choices like egg nog and Winter Wonderland (loaded with peppermint candy) in the winter.

Izzy's Ice Cream Café
2034 Marshall Avenue, St. Paul
(651) 603-1458
www.izzysicecream.com
Izzy's opened in part because its owners wanted to create a place where parents would feel totally comfortable bringing the kids. The ice-cream shop has since become a local favorite not only for its kid friendliness but also for its namesake feature: An "izzy" is the extra one-ounce scoop of ice cream that tops your single- or double-scoop cone here. With 32 of Izzy's 100-plus artisan options spread out before you, it's hard enough to choose a flavor, let alone decide which izzy would be the best complement. Even your basic vanilla is delicious, but then you'll find temptations such as the Norwegian Chai, with chai tea and Norwegian cardamom toasts, both from local shops; and the Dark Chocolate Zin, made with red zinfandel and balsamic vinegar. Kids go gaga over the Bubble Gum and the blue Cotton Candy. The one-ounce izzy cone is a nice size for young children, and it costs just over a dollar.

SHOPPING KID-STYLE

Creative Kidstuff
4313 Upton Avenue South, Minneapolis
(612) 927-0653
Five additional Twin Cities locations
www.creativekidstuff.com
This neat little local toyshop chain offers educational and creative toys for both kids and parents to salivate over. Hands-

on is the motto here. Lots of toys have been removed from their packaging and scattered about the store for kids to try out. There are three big sales a year—a storewide event in June and clearance sales in July and after Christmas. Creative Kidstuff holds in-store kids' events throughout the year, too.

The Red Balloon Bookshop
891 Grand Avenue, St. Paul
(651) 224-8320
www.redballoonbookshop.com
Located in a house on St. Paul's cozy Grand Avenue, the Red Balloon has been turning kids on to books since 1984. The selection is comprehensive, with classics past and future, and the staff obviously loves what they do—they're ready with suggestions if you need ideas. There's nearly always an event scheduled, whether it be a story hour or an author reading or lecture. The latter two are good examples of how the Red Balloon caters to children's book lovers, regardless of age.

Wild Rumpus Books for Young Readers
2720 West 43rd Street, Minneapolis
(612) 920-5005
www.wildrumpusbooks.com
The front door of this 2,000-square-foot destination bookstore hints at what's to come. It actually holds a door within a door, giving kids an entrance that's their own size rather than the same old adult-height doorway. This place is definitely designed for kids. The name, plucked from Maurice Sendak's *Where the Wild Things Are,* fits. Animals are everywhere—chickens, cats, birds, ferrets, tarantulas, geckos, fish, and even a rat, whose cage is appropriately placed in the floor of the scary books reading shack. You'll find old and new favorites as well as lots of books from smaller presses that you simply can't find at your local chain bookstore—one of many refreshing ways this bookshop differentiates itself from the big guys.

ANNUAL EVENTS AND FESTIVALS

Festivals are an important part of Minnesota life. In the winter, elaborate festivities like the Holidazzle Parade and the St. Paul Winter Carnival stave off cabin fever. With the coming of spring, just about anything can kick off a festival, from an abundance of wildflowers blooming to charitable functions and building restoration projects. Entire city blocks are roped off for block parties in the summer, and the streets are filled with cars decorated with seashells, ribbons, sculptures, and big painted flowers. Just about every tiny town in the state holds at least one spring and summer festival, complete with parades, concession and merchandise kiosks, and live music.

The following calendar lists only events that have been around for a while and that we expect will continue to be around.

JANUARY

St. Paul Winter Carnival
Various locations around St. Paul
Last week of January through first week of February
(651) 223-4700
www.winter-carnival.com
The St. Paul Winter Carnival is by far the coolest celebration in the Midwest and one of the oldest winter festivals in the country. More than 50 events—including amazing snow and ice-sculpture exhibits, live music, and sporting events such as a 5K run and half marathon, and softball on ice—are a part of this annual festival, with the crowning events being the King Boreas Grande Day Parade and the more decadent evening Vulcan Victory Torchlight Parade.

FEBRUARY

Kidfest
RiverCentre/Touchstone Energy Place,
175 Kellogg Boulevard, St. Paul
(651) 265-4800
Kidfest, in January or February is Minnesota's longest-running children's event, with multiple stages of live entertainment, dozens of free activities and games for kids of all ages, and Minnesota's largest inflatable playground (featuring a super-slide, Velcro wall, maze, sports challenges, and much more), all guaranteed to keep your kids busy for at least a day, maybe two. The Saturday and Sunday festival features celebrity visits from national childrens' artists (usually of Nickelodeon fame). In addition, there's the perennial favorite, the petting zoo, a rain-forest stage filled with exotic creatures and pony rides.

Twin Cities Food & Wine Experience
Minneapolis Convention Center,
1301 Second Avenue South, Minneapolis
A mid-February weekend
(866) 895-7658
www.foodwineshow.com
Although tickets for this annual event get into the pricey range, around $55, you are likely to get your money's worth even if you come hungry. About 300 Twin Cities restaurants; local, national, and international wineries; and other exhibitors serve

The Twin Cities Infoline (612-379-CALL) provides an automated list of events, arts and entertainment, restaurants, sports scores, and other happenings throughout the Twin Cities metro area.

up their gourmet specialties to the masses. Additional events (at an additional charge) include wine seminars and wine lunches at restaurants throughout the Metro.

MARCH

St. Patrick's Day Parade
Downtown St. Paul
(651) 292-3225

St. Paul's annual St. Patrick's Day Parade picks up at Fourth and Wacouta Streets and heads west all the way down Fourth Street, ending at Rice Park. The parade features Irish music and performers, and food, drink, and merchandise kiosks are set up along the parade route for the remainder of the day.

The parade is all part of St. Paul's annual Irish Celebration, paying homage to the many Irish immigrants who settled in the city. Entertainment, crafts, Irish foods, and beer (Irish and otherwise) are all part of the festivities, centered around Landmark Center in downtown St. Paul.

APRIL

Minneapolis/St. Paul International Film Festival
Various locations,
sponsored by U Film Society
Three weeks in April
(612) 331-3134
www.mnfilmarts.org

In 20-plus years, the Film Society's International Film Festival has gone from a weekend-long event to the present high-water mark where about 150 flicks from more than 60 different nations are screened during three full weeks in April. The festival's participating theaters include the Oak Street Cinema, Bell Auditorium, State Theatre, and other Twin Cities film houses.

Ironman Bike Ride
Lakeville High School, Lakeville
Last Sunday of April
(651) 251-1495
www.ironmanbikeride.org

An annual event for more than 40 years, the Ironman Bike Ride takes 5,000 participating bicyclists through 33-mile, 66-mile, or 100-mile scenic tours through the Minnesota countryside. The $25 entrance fee goes to benefit Hosteling International.

MAY

Festival of Nations
RiverCentre, St. Paul
(651) 647-0191
www.festivalofnations.com

Founded in 1932 and held generally in late April or early May, the Festival of Nations has been an event of the people who helped create it for their pleasure and the ethnic values they treasured. Its underlying philosophy has been that as Americans of all backgrounds—native citizens and naturalized citizens alike—share experiences, their differences become less significant and barriers to understanding are removed. Today Minnesota's largest multicultural event showcases more than 100 ethnic groups through food, dance performances, cultural exhibits, folk art demonstrations, an international bazaar, and more.

Cinco de Mayo Fiesta
District del Sol, St. Paul
First week in May
(651) 222-6347
www.districtdelsol.com

The Cinco de Mayo Fiesta lights up the District del Sol on the west side of St. Paul, across the Robert Street Bridge from downtown (for visitors, the "west" side of St. Paul is actually south of downtown). More than 100,000 people teem the streets of the Hispanic neighborhood to take in Mexican entertainment and food and to watch the Cinco de Mayo Parade. It's one of the 10-largest Cinco de Mayo celebrations in the country.

The Cinco de Mayo Fiesta in the District del Sol across the Mississippi from downtown St. Paul brings many smiles. SAINT PAUL RCVA

In the Heart of the Beast
May Day Parade
Powderhorn Park, 3400 15th Avenue
South, Minneapolis
First Sunday of May
(612) 721-2535
www.heartofthebeasttheatre.org
For more than 30 years, In the Heart of the Beast Puppet and Mask Theatre's annual May Day parade has been as true a sign of spring returning to the Twin Cities as robins choosing their mates. The brilliantly colored ensemble of friendly and scary creatures on stilts, children dressed as flowers, and other magical images travels along Minneapolis's downtown Bloomington Avenue and ends in a colorful pageant in Powderhorn Park, where puppets sail across the pond in boats. This is probably the largest, funkiest celebration of spring in the entire Midwest, paired with an entire day of dance, music, fun, and food all along the parade route.

JUNE

Improv in the Parks
Lake Harriet Rose Gardens, Roseway
Road and Lake Harriet Parkway,
Minneapolis
Sunday, June through August
(612) 825-1832
www.stevierays.org
Stevie Ray's Improv Troupe performs in the great outdoors, creating comedy sketches on the spot based on audience suggestions. Sometimes the troupe incorporates unsuspecting audience members in the act. Bring something to sit on (blanket, lawnchair, etc.). The troupe performs twice each summer Sunday, at 5:00 and 7:00 P.M., although shows are canceled if it rains or the grass is wet. The shows are free.

Alive After Five Concert Series
Peavy Plaza, 11th Street and Nicollet
Mall, Minneapolis
(612) 338-3807
www.d-a-n.org

Unwind after the workday with good food and music on the mall throughout June. Local and touring bands can be seen at the plaza for free, and drink and food kiosks are set up close to the stage.

Grand Old Day
Grand Avenue, St. Paul
First Sunday of June
(651) 699-0029
www.grandave.com
More than 220,000 people show up for this granddaddy of Twin Cities celebrations—the largest one-day street festival in the Midwest—with everything from a strongman contest to local bands performing on one of the fourteen entertainment stages. Lots of food vendors and merchant kiosks, and various family attractions are featured during the event, as well as the 10:00 A.M. kiddie parade followed at 10:30 by the Grand Old Day parade.

The festival engulfs 30 city blocks and is packed with more than 150 outdoor vendors offering every delicacy imaginable, from Cokes, pizza, and corn dogs to gyros, egg rolls, and Jamaican beef.

Edina Art Fair
50th and France, Edina
First weekend of June
(952) 922-1524
www.50thandfrance.com
Nearly 300 local, regional, and national artists whose works include clothing, dolls, woodcarving, and more are featured at this annual festival.

Red Hot Art Festival
Stevens Square Park, Second Avenue and 18th Street, Minneapolis
First weekend in June
(612) 874-2840
Works by local emerging artists are showcased at this event, along with food, music, and other entertainment.

St. Anthony Main Summer Music Series
219 Southeast Main Street, Minneapolis
(612) 378-1226
www.saintanthonymain.com
Throughout the summer, weekends and July 4, you can catch live music for free on the stage outside Tuggs Tavern, located right across the street from the Mississippi River.

St. Anthony Park Arts Festival
St. Anthony Park neighborhood, St. Paul
First Saturday of June
(651) 642-0411
www.stanthonyparkartsfestival.org
More than 100 Midwestern artists showcase their goods annually in one of St. Paul's prettiest neighborhoods, with food and music available all along Como Avenue from Carter to Luther Seminary. You can find spectacular deals on truly unusual items at this juried art show.

Tater Daze
Downtown Brooklyn Park
A weekend in June
(763) 493-8122
Tater Daze began in 1965 and celebrates Brooklyn Park's potato-growing heritage. The weekend festival kicks off with a parade on the first night and is followed by a host of community events, including live music and lots of family activities.

Art on the Lake
Downtown Excelsior
A weekend in June
(952) 474-6461
For more than 20 years, Excelsior's juried Art on the Lake has showcased the work of local and national artists through art competitions, demonstrations, and other related activities aimed to get the public interested in art. Food, live music, and entertainment are almost as important a part of this festival as the art itself.

Father Hennepin Festival
Downtown Champlin
Second weekend in June
(763) 421-2820

This is a family-oriented festival, featuring fireworks, powerboats, personal watercraft races, and amusement park rides.

South St. Paul Kaposia Days
Various locations, South St. Paul
(651) 451-2266
www.kaposiadays.com
This family festival includes a street dance, a treasure hunt, a grand parade, children's activities, a flea market and craft sale, royalty pageants, bingo, water war games, fireworks, and athletic tournaments.

St. Louis Parktacular
Various locations, St. Louis Park
(952) 924-2550
www.parktacular.org
St. Louis Park's annual community celebration features a carnival, live music, a parade, food vendors, a silent auction, and an art fair.

Stone Arch Festival of the Arts
Mississippi Riverfront, Old St. Anthony
Main, Minneapolis
Father's Day weekend
(612) 378-1226
www.stonearchfestival.org
More than 200 vendors, artists, bands, and street performers congregate along the riverfront, making this a fun festival to either take Dad for the afternoon or shop for a present for him. The festival also features free dance, theater, and music performances; kids' art projects; free cooking demonstrations; and an "Art of Classic Cars" car show, featuring more than 150 vintage vehicles.

Midsommar Celebration
American Swedish Institute,
2600 Park Avenue South, Minneapolis
Mid-June
(612) 871-4907
www.americanswedishinst.org
Celebrate Midsommar in the Swedish tradition with music, folk dance, and food. Join the museum's costumed guides and performers in this traditional festival that celebrates everything good about summer.

Midsommar Dag
20880 Olinda Trail, Scandia
Third Saturday in June
(651) 433-5053
Midsommar Dag kicks off the festival season in the picturesque town of Scandia, located at the edge of the metro area near Marine on St. Croix. Sponsored by the Gammelgarden Museum, the festival is a bright affair of parades, traditional Scandinavian dancing and costumes, and lots of food.

Buckhorn Days
Long Lake
A weekend at the end of June
(952) 476-1408
This weekend-long festival in the western suburb of Long Lake features live music, dancing, carnival games, fishing contests, "mad scientist" exhibits and concession stands.

Earle Brown Days Festival
Downtown Brooklyn Center
Last week of June
(763) 569-3400
www.cityofbrooklyncenter.org
This annual festival, honoring civic leader and activist Earle Brown, features a parade, fireworks, arts and craft fair, ice-cream social, live music and entertainment, and special events aimed specifically at kids and teens, including a kids' fishing contest and lots of games.

Minnetonka Summer Festival
Various locations, Minnetonka
Last Saturday in June
(952) 939-8206
www.eminnetonka.com
This citywide festival includes family-oriented activities for all ages: live entertainment, rides, games, food vendors, and fireworks.

MSRA's Back to the '50s
Minnesota State Fairgrounds, St. Paul
End of June
(651) 641-1992
www.msra.com

Every year, the Minnesota Street Rod Association (MSRA) heads to the state fairgrounds to show off its members' street rods, classic cars, and custom cars. More than 10,000 show cars can be seen at the event, which also features food and merchandise kiosks, commercial exhibits, and live music.

Twin Cities GLBT Pride Festival
Various locations, Minneapolis
Two weeks at the end of June
(952) 852-6100
www.tcpride.org
The largest and probably the oldest annual gay/lesbian/bi/transsexual pride festival in the upper Midwest includes a parade, music, food, and more. An estimated 400,000 people show up for the festival over the course of two weeks.

JULY

Basilica Block Party
Corner of Hennepin Avenue and 17th Street, Basilica of Saint Mary, Minneapolis
Beginning of July
(612) 317-3511
www.basilicablockparty.org
Proceeds from this annual outdoor festival go to restore the historic Basilica of Saint Mary, which in turn offers outreach and charitable programs to poor and impoverished people throughout the state. More than 20,000 people of all ages and denominations come to this event, which features big-name bands, food, and drink.

Taste of Minnesota
Harriet Island Regional Park, St. Paul
Five days ending July 4
(651) 772-9980
www.tasteofmn.org

The Taste of Minnesota festival is a good way to sample many local restaurants in one place.

This huge event offers food prepared by more than 50 of the Twin Cities' best restaurants, and dozens of national and regional performers. Each night concludes with fireworks.

Eden Prairie's Fourth of July "Home Town" Celebration
Round Lake, 7550 Constitution Avenue
Fourth of July
(952) 949-8450
www.edenprairie.org
This celebration finishes with spectacular fireworks at the Eden Prairie Center at 10:00 P.M. Daytime activities at Round Lake Park include a kiddie parade, youth baseball tournament, live music, games, and concession stands.

Minneapolis Riverfront Fourth of July Celebration
Old St. Anthony Main, Minneapolis Riverfront
Fourth of July
(612) 378-1226
www.mpls4thofjuly.com
One of the best Fourth of July fireworks displays in the Twin Cities, with music and self-guided tours of the area's Mississippi River bridges. The best seat in the house is anywhere on Nicollet Island, where the fireworks seem to explode directly overhead.

Pan-o-Prog
Downtown Lakeville
First week of July
(952) 985-9558
www.panoprog.org
Since 1967 Lakeville has celebrated its Panorama of Progress festival, now called Pan-o-Prog, which features family entertainment including races, picnics, pet shows, dances, a scholarship pageant, Fourth of July fireworks, and a parade.

Anoka Riverfest & Craft Fair
Historic Downtown Anoka
Second Saturday of July
(763) 421-7130
www.anokariverfest.com
This all-day riverfront festival includes a

Fireworks over the State Capitol during the Taste of Minnesota. GREATER MINNEAPOLIS CONVENTION & VISITORS ASSOCIATION

craft/artisan fair, historical society events, live music, youth activities, and, of course, lots of food.

Summer Music and Movies
Loring Park, 1382 Willow Street, Minneapolis
(612) 375-7622
www.walkerart.org
Every Monday night from mid-July through August, free live music is followed by a movie. This is a collaboration between the Walker Art Center and Minneapolis Parks and Rec.

Hennepin Avenue Block Party
Hennepin Avenue from 4th Street to 10th Street, Minneapolis
Third weekend in July
(612) 376-7669
www.d-a-n.org
Part of the Minneapolis Aquatennial Celebration, this free outdoor concert always features big-name bands and even bigger crowds.

Minneapolis Aquatennial
Various locations around Minneapolis
Third full week of July
(612) 376-7669
www.aquatennial.com
Royalty pageants, parades, boat races, and other events are featured in this citywide celebration of the 10 Best Days of Summer. The Aquatennial has one of Minnesota's largest parades, the nation's fourth-largest fireworks show, milk carton boat races, sand castle competitions, a triathlon, programs for juniors and seniors, and tons of family-oriented activities. One of the highlights of the celebration, the milk carton boat races, invites participants of all ages to create full-size boats out of hundreds of sealed milk cartons and race—the largest creation was Tetra Pak's 1993 25,000-milk-carton boat that held 150 passengers.

In 1978 millionaire and philanthropist Percy Ross rode in the Minneapolis Aquatennial's Torchlight Parade and threw $16,500 worth of silver into the crowd. This would get Percy in big trouble today—throwing objects from parade floats is now illegal in Minneapolis.

Country Market Rockin' Ribfest
Harriet Island Regional Park, St. Paul
A weekend in July
www.ribamerica.com
This four-day food and music festival features award-winning barbecue teams from throughout the country, as well as national and regional entertainment daily.

Lumberjack Days
Lowell Park, Stillwater
Second to last weekend of July
(651) 430-2306
www.lumberjackdays.com
This huge, weekend-long event features live concerts from major-label recording stars, tons of concession stands, Minnesota's fastest 10-mile and 5K runs, kids' events, a huge parade, and Minnesota's biggest fireworks display—all located in historic downtown Stillwater. Wine tasting, ice-cream socials, lumberjack exhibits, logrolling and pie-baking contests are just a few of the events that you can expect to be torn between, not to mention the annual Treasure Hunt.

Blooming Day on Grand
Grand Avenue, St. Paul
Last Saturday of July
(651) 699-0029
www.grandave.com
Celebrate summer on St. Paul's Grand Avenue. This one-day event is made for strolling, shopping, and having fun. From 10:00 A.M. to 2:00 P.M., the businesses of Grand Avenue give out free flowers and desserts. Strolling along Grand Avenue will become even sweeter than normal, a visual spectacle of gardens and floral displays and exhibits of local artisans' work.

AUGUST

Uptown Art Fair
Uptown Minneapolis,
Lake Street and
Hennepin Avenue
First full weekend of August
(612) 823-4581
www.uptownminneapolis.com
The Uptown Art Fair is the largest art fair in Minneapolis, featuring work from hundreds of local and national artists as well as food and live music. Painting, photography, sculpture, jewelry, ceramics, and fiber are on display and for sale at the event.

Powderhorn Art Fair
Powderhorn Park, 3400 15th Avenue
South, Minneapolis
First weekend of August
(612) 729-0111
www.powderhornartfair.org
The popular Powderhorn Art Fair, which usually runs concurrent with the Uptown Art Fair, is a winning attraction for crafts-fair fans. The weekend-long festival—originally billed as an alternative to the "big one down the street"—has developed a flavor of its own, exposing an eclectic variety of both artwork and artists to the public. Free bus service connects it with the Uptown and Loring Park Art Fairs.

Minnesota Fringe Festival
Various venues in Minneapolis
First two weeks of August
(612) 872-1212
www.fringefestival.org
This annual celebration of theater has hundreds of performances in multiple venues throughout Minneapolis. Musicals, puppetry, dance, and performance art are just some of the events during the festival.

Old Time Harvest Festival
Fairview Lane, across from the
Scott County Fairgrounds, Jordan
First weekend of August
(952) 492-2062
www.scottcarverthreshers.org
This family-oriented festival has antique

farm equipment displays, a flea market, an antiques auction, and an antique car show, as well as demonstrations of threshing, sawing, spinning, and quilting. There's even an antique farm equipment parade each afternoon.

Minnesota Irish Fair
Harriet Island, St. Paul
Second weekend of August
(952) 474-7411
www.irishfair.com
From bagpipes to bodhrans, corned beef to ceilis, this free three-day celebration of Irish culture features Irish music, dance, theater, exhibits, sports, a marketplace, genealogy information, and a special children's area.

Minnesota State Fair
State Fairgrounds, 1265 Snelling Avenue North, St. Paul
Twelve days ending on Labor Day
(651) 642-2200
www.mnstatefair.org
One of the largest fairs in North America—usually drawing crowds of over a hundred thousand a day—this fair has big-name entertainment, exhibits, competitions, food, demonstrations, horse shows, auto races, a huge midway carnival, and lots of food on a stick. There's also a bust of the festival's princess sculpted in butter, farm animal shows and competitions, a huge garden show, and juried arts and crafts from state elementary, high school, and college students.

Woodbury Days
Ojibway Park, Woodbury
Last weekend of August
(651) 714-3500
www.woodburydays.com
Woodbury Days is a community event with lots of activities for the whole family, including Midway Carnival Rides, games and food, the Woodbury Days Annual Bike Ride, inflatable slides, water fights, a petting zoo, the Rod & Custom Car Club

Car Show, fireworks displays, a daily parade, and live music.

Stiftungsfest
Downtown Norwood Young America
Last full weekend of August
(952) 467-3365
www.stiftungsfest.org
There's something for everyone at this celebration of German heritage and culture: German choirs, dancers, polka bands, arts, crafts, ethnic foods, and beverages. Stiftungsfest, founded in 1861, is the oldest festival in Minnesota.

Minnesota Renaissance Festival
3 miles south of Shakopee on Minnesota Highway 169
Mid-August through the end of September
(952) 445-7361 or (800) 966-8215
www.renaissancefest.com
Jump back in time to experience life in the 16th century, or at least the fun parts of it. For more than 30 years, Minnesota has been host to the largest themed event in the United States. Food, fun, sword fights, games, comedy, dancers, singers, music, 12 stages of continuous entertainment, and royalty are regular staples of this annual event, which is open weekends in mid-August, Labor Day, and through the end of September. The site of the Minnesota Renaissance Festival is a bustling 16th-century village filled with hundreds of costumed villagers, period buildings, and a huge marketplace.

SEPTEMBER

Excelsior Apple Day
Downtown Excelsior
First Saturday after Labor Day
(952) 474-6461
Excelsior Apple Day is a main street festival with antiques, crafts, apples, produce, entertainment, food, and the children's Red Wagon and Doll Buggy Parade.

Sunbonnet Day
Riley-Jacques Barn, 9096 Riley Lake
Road, Eden Prairie
Second Sunday in September
(952) 949-8450
Each September, Eden Prairie steps back in time on Sunbonnet Day, with old-fashioned wagon rides, pony rides, a farmers' market, and games of Pennies in the Hay.

Johnny Appleseed Bash
Utley Park, 50th Street West & Woodale
Avenue, Edina
Third weekend of September
(952) 920-0595
This annual benefit for St. Stephen's Episcopal Church takes place in Utley Park. Food, live entertainment, a silent auction, a petting zoo, and pony rides are just a few of the things you can expect at this community-oriented festival.

Lone Oak Days
Historic Holz Farm, 4665 Manor Drive,
Eagan
End of September
(651) 675-5500
www.eaganmn.com
Hayrides, farming demos, games, and self-guided tours of 1940s-era farm life at Holz Farm highlight Eagan's heritage festival.

Harvest Festival
Gibbs Museum of Pioneer and Dakota
Life, 2097 West Larpenteur at
Cleveland, Falcon Heights
Late September or early October
(651) 646-8629
An annual event with food, music, and square dancing. Guests can participate in crop gathering, kitchen duty, and other farm activities.

OCTOBER

Twin Cities Marathon
Minneapolis and St. Paul
First weekend of October
(763) 287-3888
www.twincitiesmarathon.org

The Twin Cities Marathon's unique scenery and aesthetics have earned it the distinction as the most beautiful urban marathon in America. It's also ranked as one of the nation's top marathons. The 26.2-mile course begins near the Metrodome in Minneapolis and finishes at the State Capitol on John Ireland Boulevard in St. Paul. The course is easy to navigate, mostly asphalt, and very scenic with mile after mile of parkways, lakes, rivers, and tree-lined boulevards. Prospective runners should register early for the race, as this race attracts contestants from around the country. Good viewing spots include the Lake Harriet Rose Garden, Minnehaha Falls, and along Summit Avenue.

Anoka Halloween
Downtown Anoka
Mid-October through Halloween
(763) 427-1861
www.anokahalloween.com
Anoka celebrates more than 80 years as the Halloween Capital of the World with three parades and many other activities for young and old alike. The celebration begins with a football game dubbed "the Pumpkin Bowl." Other events include cemetery tours, a house-decoration contest, ghost stories, costume contests, a haunted house, and a 5K Grey Ghost Run.

NOVEMBER/DECEMBER

Samhain Celtic New Year
Newell Park, Fairview Avenue and Pierce
Butler Route, St. Paul
November First
(651) 641-0485
This celebration consists of traditional Irish music, food, storytelling, dancing, and games.

LGBT Film Festival
Oak Street Cinema, 309 Oak Street SE,
Minneapolis
Mid-November
(612) 331-3134
www.mnfilmarts.org

This popular and longstanding festival shows a variety of queer-themed documentaries and features from around the world.

Autumn Festival/Arts and Crafts Affair
Canterbury Park, 1100 Canterbury Road, Shakopee
November
(952) 445-1660 or (800) 574-2150
The largest crafts show in the upper Midwest, the Autumn Festival draws more than 500 vendors from all over the country.

Victorian Christmas at the Historic Courthouse
101 West Pine Street, Stillwater
Weekend before Thanksgiving
(651) 430-6233
Fine handmade crafts by local artists are displayed at the elegantly decorated Stillwater courthouse. The building, beautifully decorated in Victorian style, resounds with laughter and music, while vendors in costume offer their wares to the public. Volunteers in period clothing offer jail tours, an exhibit, an old-fashioned tearoom, and music of the season. This event is considered the gateway to the holiday season in Stillwater.

TCF Holidazzle
Nicollet Mall, Minneapolis
Friday after Thanksgiving through December 23
(612) 376-SNOW
www.holidazzle.com

If you call ahead of time (612-616-7669), you can volunteer to march in the TCF Holidazzle. The Holidazzle organizers offer a variety of costumes to volunteers, from elfin outfits to Old Saint Nick himself. Call early for the best costumes and your preferred date. And don't forget the long underwear.

Costumed children, adults, and festooned floats covered with one million colored lights make up the TCF Holidazzle. These free, 30-minute night parades head down Nicollet Mall from 12th to Fifth Streets, beginning at 6:30 P.M. Wednesday through Sunday. Fairy tale–themed floats, marching bands, celebrity grand marshals, and, of course, Santa in his sleigh can be seen in the parade.

Old-Fashioned Holiday Bazaar
Landmark Center, 75 West Fifth Street, St. Paul
A weekend in November or December
(651) 292-3225
www.landmarkcenter.org
Stroll through a marketplace of more than 80 exhibits featuring beautiful and unique gift items, all handcrafted by the area's finest artisans. Participating in this annual event is considered an important tradition by many, who get their holiday shopping done here.

The Weisman Art Museum is one of the most striking buildings in the Twin Cities. GREATER MINNEAPOLIS CONVENTION & VISITORS ASSOCIATION

THE ARTS

The Greater Twin Cities have been dubbed a "cultural Eden on the prairie," where people widely support more than a hundred theater companies and classical music ensembles. Sir Tyrone Guthrie pumped up the theatrical boom back in 1963, enrolling large-scale local assistance to establish the classical repertory company named after him. The Cities now have more theater seats per capita than any Metropolitan area in the United States apart from New York City.

Minneapolis and St. Paul are also serious museum towns, with a number of important collections housed in several world-famous buildings. Many, many more little galleries spread throughout the metro area take up any slack the major museums might have missed, displaying everything from concrete anatomy molds to metal mechanical sculptures.

More than 100 performing arts groups and organizations flourish in the Twin Cities area, ranging from tiny neighborhood-based production companies to full-fledged touring troupes. The **Metropolitan Regional Arts Council** (2324 University Avenue West, Suite 114, St. Paul; 651-645-0402; www.mrac.org) keeps pretty good track of who's who and where in town.

ALL ABOUT BOOKS

Open Book
1011 Washington Avenue South,
Minneapolis
(612) 215-2520
www.openbookmn.org
The first literary arts complex of its kind in the nation, this renovated historic building opened in 2000. Visitors can watch the book printing and binding process from beginning to end, explore the exhibitions gallery, or simply stretch out on the sofa

in the literary commons with a good book from the center's library. Other amenities include occasional live performances, literary readings, writing workshops, family reading space, and a cafe. Located in the building is the Minnesota Center for Book Arts, the largest independent book arts facility in the nation; the Loft, which offers classes on writing and publishing; and an excellent performance space for visiting authors and lecturers. Open Book is fun to just walk around in, as so much of the original structure and facades were saved in the restoration process, including pieces of the original wallpaper, staircases that go nowhere, and ancient bakery and factory signs painted on the brickwork itself.

ART GALLERIES

AZ Gallery
Northern Warehouse Building, 308
Prince Street, St. Paul
(651) 255-6624
www.theazgallery.org
This prominent Lowertown St. Paul gallery holds opening receptions on the first Friday of each month, hosting artwork premieres of two featured artists plus a group exhibit. The 2,000-square-foot gallery also puts on performing arts events throughout the year.

CIRCA Gallery
1637 Hennepin Avenue South,
Minneapolis
(612) 332-2386
www.circagallery.org
CIRCA Gallery displays art in exhibits that show how a gallery with coherent vision can unite widely different artists. Everything from encaustic prairie landscapes with mottled-wax finishes to intensely colored abstractions fit into this vision, as do bronze sculptures inspired by primitive

> *Almost every arts venue in town offers a discount to students with a valid student ID.*

altars and acrylic paintings that look like aerial shots of bombed-out civilizations.

CIRCA Gallery's mission is to provide awareness and appreciation of contemporary styles, media, and expressions. The gallery represents 40 regional and national artists, with an exhibition rotation approximately every five weeks.

Dolly Fiterman Fine Arts Gallery
100 University Avenue Southeast, Minneapolis
(612) 623-3300

Dolly Fiterman Fine Arts represents American and European contemporary artists in a turn-of-the-20th-century landmark marble building. The gallery's collection emphasizes sculptures, painting, drawings, and graphics, and the gallery is known globally for its advanced and avant-garde international scope.

Works from artists like Lichtenstein and Moore encircle the main room, and special exhibits are in the affordable range ($500 to $50,000). The clean, white walls and the well-lit spaces make the modern artworks, even the sketches, seem to pop off the walls. The layout allows for casual contemplation, and if you're lucky, the energetic Dolly Fiterman herself might come and show you around the gallery personally.

Groveland Gallery
25 Groveland Terrace, Minneapolis
(612) 377-7800
www.grovelandgallery.com

Groveland Gallery represents the work of 30 regional artists and specializes in contemporary representational painting and drawing. Established in 1973, this elegant gallery is located in a restored 1890s mansion and carriage house on the edge of downtown Minneapolis. On the premises is a second gallery, the Annex, which features work by emerging local artists. Exhibitions in both galleries change every six weeks.

Inside Out Gallery
Interact Center for the Visual and Performing Arts, 212 Third Avenue North, Suite 140, Minneapolis
(612) 339-5145
www.interactcenter.com

Interact is a studio for actors and artists with disabilities. The organization's Inside Out gallery has four exhibitions each year that are open to the public. Interact's theater company, supported by professional actors as teachers and peers produces two major shows per year.

Intermedia Arts
2822 Lyndale Avenue South, Minneapolis
(612) 871-4444
www.intermediaarts.org

The graffiti on Intermedia's facade isn't just a nice concession to local taggers—giving them the space is part of the gallery's mission. More than perhaps any other gallery in town, Intermedia is dedicated to being a neighborhood space, with shows often focusing on the work of artists from the semibohemian streets of Lyn-Lake. (An annual show called 55408 accepts only artists from this local zip code.) As a result, Intermedia's exhibits lack the gloss and commercial appeal of other galleries' shows, but they do offer a compelling artistic window into the soul of a community.

Intermedia Arts presents more than 50 visual, media, and performing arts events each year. Recent events include B-Girl Be, a celebration of women in hip-hop, and the Wheels ArtCar Parade, in which community members work with artists to decorate their bikes, wheelchairs, and in-line skates to lead a parade of similarly decorated motorized vehicles.

Katherine E. Nash Gallery
University of Minnesota Department of Art, Regis Center for Art, 405 21st Avenue South, Minneapolis
(612) 624-7530

The mission of the Katherine E. Nash Gallery is to create an accessible environment for University of Minnesota faculty and students to exhibit their work and to show art in various media by artists from regional, national, and international sources. The gallery got a beautiful, brand-new 4,900-square-foot space in 2003. While outside artists are its focus, there are the occasional grad-student shows.

Kellie Rae Theiss Red House Gallery
3413 West 44th Street, Minneapolis
(612) 339-1094
www.theissgallery.com
The Kelly Rae Theiss Red House Gallery features original classical, surrealistic, and impressionistic paintings and sculpture. This intimate gallery exclusively represents local and regional artists, both in solo and group exhibitions, on an seven-week rotation.

Minnesota Center for Photography
163 13th Avenue NE, Minneapolis
(612) 824-5500
www.mncp.org
The Minnesota Center for Photography offers works from local and national artists. Ranging through the cute, creepy, conventional, commercial, and creative, there's something here for everyone with an interest in the photographic arts. The gallery encourages strong community involvement and is a good place for budding photographers to begin exploring the professional side of their craft.

Northern Clay Center
2424 East Franklin Avenue, Minneapolis
(612) 339-8007
www.northernclaycenter.org
Northern Clay Center's mission is the advancement of the ceramic arts. Ongoing programs include classes and workshops for children and adults at all levels of proficiency, more than 10 exhibitions a year of functional and sculptural work by regional and national clay artists, studio facilities and grants for artists, and a sales gallery representing many of the top ceramic artists across the region and country.

The Soap Factory
518 Second Street SE/loading dock, Minneapolis
(612) 623-9176
www.soapfactory.org
The Soap Factory is an exciting, and expanding, nonprofit arts organization dedicated to supporting emerging artists, enhancing the public's understanding and appreciation of their artistic expressions, and fostering strength and vitality within the arts, cultural, and education communities of the Twin Cities. With its hardwood floors and old prefab office walls, the Soap Factory building could easily double as a phenomenal nightclub or revolutionary headquarters. The Soap Factory has put the space to good use, however, filling it with shows that are always balanced between avant-garde sensibilities and good old-fashioned representationalism. It maintains an open-door submission policy, and artists and potential curators are invited to submit their work and proposals at the end of each year.

Each year, the Soap Factory presents several large-scale visual exhibitions featuring a wide range of media from local, national, and international emerging artists as well as performance art, film, video, and spoken-word events. New exhibitions open with special events and artists' talks that provide artists and their audiences with the opportunity to interact. The gallery also puts on an annual Fourth of July independent film festival.

Vern Carver & Beard Art Galleries
LaSalle Plaza, 800 Lasalle Avenue, Minneapolis
(612) 339-3449
www.verncarverbeard.com
Vern Carver & Beard is the oldest gallery in the Twin Cities. Founded in 1886, the gallery features fine original art by regional artists of past and present, antique prints, and art glass (stained glass,

blown glass, etc). The gallery also provides custom framing for prints and paintings.

ART MUSEUMS

Frederick R. Weisman Art Museum
333 East River Road, Minneapolis
(612) 625-9494
www.weisman.umn.edu

The Weisman is impossible to miss—it's the huge metal structure on the east side of the Washington Avenue bridge that either looks stunningly beautiful or stunningly pretentious, depending on your mood and the time of year. On the outside the museum faces the Mississippi River with an undulating, dramatic facade covered in polished aluminum, especially beautiful at sunset. In comparison the interior is surprisingly conservative, and the modestly scaled and wonderfully lit galleries inside

Minneapolis Institute of Arts. GREATER
MINNEAPOLIS CONVENTION & VISITORS ASSOCIATION

are so attractive that the *New York Times* called them "possibly the five best rooms for viewing art in the world."

The mostly 20th-century permanent collection contains the world's largest assemblage of works by Marsden Hartley and Alfred Maurer as well as paintings and prints by Georgia O'Keeffe, Arthur Dove, and Robert Motherwell, among others. The entrance is dominated by Roy Lichtenstein's *World's Fair Mural.* Be sure to take in the river view from the tiny balcony, located one floor above the galleries.

A teaching museum for the university and the community, this sculptural stainless-steel and brick landmark building designed by architect Frank Gehry provides a multidisciplinary approach to the arts through programs and a changing schedule of exhibitions. Admission is always free.

The Minneapolis Institute of Arts
2400 Third Avenue South, Minneapolis
(612) 870-3131
www.artsmia.org

The Minneapolis Institute of Arts, one of the outstanding art museums in the country, features art and artifacts from around the world, from ancient sculptures to photography and film. Housed in a 1915 Beaux-Arts marble building designed by McKim, Mead, and White near downtown Minneapolis, the museum contains a world-class collection of nearly 100,000 objects representing artistic traditions and treasures spanning 5,000 years. Unlike many big-city art museums, which have the tendency to overwhelm casual visitors, the MIA can be easily explored in a few hours—and, unlike many big-city museums, no admission fee is charged.

Highlights of the museum include a small but exceptional collection of French impressionist and postimpressionist paintings, including works by Monet and van Gogh; an extensive collection of carved Oriental jades; *Lucretia,* considered by art historians to be the best Rembrandt in the country; and works by old masters Titian, El Greco, and Poussin as well as 19th- and

Walker Art Center. GREATER MINNEAPOLIS CONVENTION & VISITORS ASSOCIATION

20th-century American and European artists. There's an amazing collection of tapestries, photography, and prints as well.

The Minnesota Museum of American Art
**Corner of Kellogg Boulevard
and Market Street, St. Paul
(651) 266-1030
www.mmaa.org**
The Minnesota Museum of American Art— St. Paul's art museum—recently moved from its home at Landmark Center to a new 6,000-square-foot riverfront space just a few blocks away. (Look for the big ART HERE sign on Kellogg.) The museum features American art by national and regional artists from the 19th century to contemporary times. Special exhibitions highlight significant American artists and movements. This is a place for the traditional and the unconventional. The diversity of art and artists past, present, and emerging is revealed through music, performance, dance, fashion, painting, film, and sculpture.

Schubert Club
**Museum of Musical Instruments
Landmark Center, 75 West Fifth Street,
St. Paul
(651) 292-3267
www.schubert.org**
Considering how small this museum is, its collection of keyboards, phonographs, and musical instruments is amazingly complete. Owned and operated by the Schubert Club, this museum is a popular stomping ground for music aficionados of all types, local and otherwise.

Walker Art Center/Minneapolis
**Sculpture Garden/Cowles Conservatory
1750 Hennepin Avenue, Minneapolis
(612) 375-7600
www.walkerart.org**
For years the Walker's been the foremost modern art museum in the state. The museum is the only place in town to consistently bring in artists who tweak, poke, or outright stab at comfortable midwestern sensibilities, organizing concept-centered

 Admittance to the Walker Art Center is free every Thursday and the first Saturday of every month.

shows with a sociopolitical awareness. The displays include a permanent collection of 20th-century American and international art, including works from Willem de Kooning, Andy Warhol, Sol LeWitt, and Dan Flavin; the Walker also sponsors vanguard music, dance, theater, film, and video events throughout the year, as well as innovative education programs and visionary new media initiatives. Artists and filmmakers from around the globe have lectured and performed at the Walker, including filmmaker John Waters and composer Philip Glass. The popular monthly After Hours parties offer previews of new shows, live music, and cocktails.

Located right next to the Walker Art Center is the Minneapolis Sculpture Garden's beautiful collection of large sculptures made by local and internationally known artists. The 11-acre garden holds more than 40 sculptures, including work by George Segal, Jenny Holzer, and David Nash, set among tree-lined courtyards. The garden is one of the most-visited sites in Minneapolis, for good reason—the works of art combined with the ever-changing landscape make it a year-round delight.

The garden's entrance is framed by a pair of monumental granite columns titled *Ampersand* by the sculpture's creator, Martin Puryear. The garden's most famous statue, however, is the whimsical *Spoonbridge and Cherry* fountain, a 52-foot spoon topped by a 1,200-pound red Bing cherry, designed by Claes Oldenburg and Coosje van Bruggen. The glass-walled Cowles Conservatory, located in the garden, is a perfect place to hide from gloomy weather, with a changing display of blooming plants and a palm court dominated by Frank Gehry's *Standing Glass Fish*.

CINEMA—ART HOUSE AND SPECIALTY THEATERS

Bell Auditorium
University of Minnesota Campus, 10 Church Street SE, Minneapolis
(612) 331-3134
www.mnfilmarts.org
Formerly home to the University Film Society, the Bell Auditorium has been a pioneer in film exhibition both locally and nationally for 43 years. Since its inception the Bell Auditorium has hosted many directors and film scholars, including Robert Altman, Jean-Luc Godard, Roberto Rosellini, and countless others. It is the nation's first and only dedicated nonfiction film screen.

The Heights Theatre
3951 Central Avenue NE, Columbia Heights
(763) 788-9079
www.heightstheater.com
The Heights is one of the last of the great one-screen theaters. Renowned for showing first-run films that are actually interesting, the Heights is a classic place to catch a film without being assaulted by the Surround Sound/THX onslaught coming through the paper-thin walls of the movie cell next to you. In fact, the Heights introduces movies with Wurlitzer organ music on Friday and Saturday night. As an added bonus, refills on soda and popcorn are always free.

Landmark's Lagoon Cinema
1320 Lagoon Avenue, Minneapolis
(612) 825-6006
If you're into art house, indie, or critically acclaimed film fare, chances are you'll end up here. Lagoon Cinema is part of the Landmark franchise, which consistently snatches up the best new films and markets them aggressively to a niche of self-described art housers. The facilities are relatively distinctive for a cineplex, with swirled carpet and abstract light trees. Even more impressive, the theater is designed for optimum viewer friendli-

ness—cushy yet supportive seats, no center aisles, and sharp floor inclines.

Oak Street Cinema
309 Southeast Oak Street, Minneapolis
(612) 331-3134
www.mnfilmarts.org
What more could you want from a repertory house? Never mind that Oak Street offers films ranging from mainstream classics to obscure art house fare, with room to include work from all over the globe, too. And forget for a second that its occasional highlighting of rave-ups lets you be cheap and almost up-to-date about your moviegoing. Oak Street makes film obsession as entertaining as it could ever be. Oak Street's not too stuffy to include edgy crowd-pleasers but still serious enough to give a fair share of time to Antonioni and Hitchcock films. With this kind of film resource in the city, it's a wonder people still rent DVDs.

Riverview Theatre
3800 42nd Avenue South, Minneapolis
(612) 729-7369
www.riverviewtheatre.com
The first impressive thing about this king of all budget movie theaters is the cool '50s lobby straight out of *The Jetsons*. And then there's the popcorn—it's one of the few places where you buy the popcorn because it tastes good—there's even a discount on takeouts. The theater itself is enormous, and the elevated-back seats allow you to sit back and put your feet up. In addition to their regular second-run fare, they play the *Rocky Horror Picture Show* the first and third Saturday of each month at midnight for $5.00.

Uptown Theatre
2906 Hennepin Avenue South, Minneapolis
(612) 825-6006
Uptown is the granddaddy of all local single-screen theaters, boasting the biggest screen around and some of the roomiest seats. This place not only stands out as a great space to see films but also ranks as one of Minneapolis's landmarks.

DANCE

James Sewell Ballet
528 Hennepin Avenue, Suite 205,
Minneapolis
(612) 672-0480
www.jsballet.org
Founded in New York City in 1990 by James Sewell, the James Sewell Ballet relocated to Minnesota in 1993. The ballet specializes in original contemporary ballet, and the beautiful performances run the gamut from classical choreography to improvisation of entire movements. During the Minnesota Twins playoff run in 2002, the troupe even improvised a movement to the live play-by-play broadcast of the American League Divisional Series. The James Sewell Ballet performs at the State Theatre and at O'Shaunessy Auditorium on the College of St. Catherine's campus in St. Paul, but the troupe ventures to other venues across the state and has performed across the country and internationally.

Ragamala Music and Dance Theater
711 West Lake Street, Suite 309,
Minneapolis
(612) 824-1968
www.ragamala.net
Ragamala presents original works of dance, music, and poetry based on the ancient classical dance of southern India, Bharatanatyam. The cross-cultural performances of the company have developed a strong reputation for innovation, and the company's school offers classes from introductory to advanced levels. Ragamala performs across the country as well as at O'Shaunessy Auditorium on the College of St. Catherine's Campus in St. Paul and at the Southern Theater in Minneapolis.

Zenon Dance Company
528 Hennepin Avenue, #400,
Minneapolis
(612) 338-1101
www.zenondance.org
Zenon commissions original works of modern and jazz dance from emerging

choreographers in Minnesota as well as established masters. The high-energy performances of the company appeal to communities not regularly reached by dance troupes, and its outreach program takes it to children in communities in Minnesota and around the nation. Zenon performs regularly in the Twin Cities as well as around the state and nation and operates a school teaching not only modern and jazz dance but also yoga, hip-hop, tap, and break dancing.

MUSIC ENSEMBLES AND COMPANIES

Greater Twin Cities
Youth Symphonies (GTCYS)
528 Hennepin Avenue, Suite 404,
Minneapolis
(612) 870-7611
www.gtcys.org
Heralded as one of the nation's top youth music organizations, GTCYS boasts six orchestras and a student body with 600-plus members. It presents fall, winter, and spring concerts and the Young Soloists' Concerto Showcase. GTCYS sponsors a summer orchestra program as well.

Minnesota Chorale
528 Hennepin Avenue, Suite 211,
Minneapolis
(612) 333-4866
www.mnchorale.org
Under the direction of Kathy Saltzman Romey, the Minnesota Chorale has become the state's preeminent symphonic chorus and ranks among the best in the nation. At around 150 voices, the chorale is the principal chorus for the Minnesota Orchestra and the St. Paul Chamber Orchestra. Its nationally recognized Bridges series seeks to build musical and social bridges through artistic collaboration.

The Minnesota Opera
620 North First Street, Minneapolis
(612) 333-2700
www.mnopera.org

Since 1963 the internationally renowned Minnesota Opera has produced more American and world premieres than any other company in the United States. From November through May, more than 40,000 operagoers enjoy performances at the Ordway Center for the Performing Arts in St. Paul. An anchor tenant at the acoustically perfect Ordway, the Minnesota Opera also offers classes at its Minnesota Opera Center in the Minneapolis Warehouse District ($15 to $20). Walk-ins are welcome.

The Minnesota Orchestra
1111 Nicollet Mall, Minneapolis
(612) 371-5656 or (800) 292-4141
www.minnesotaorchestra.org
The Minnesota Orchestra performs nearly 200 concerts each year ranging from classical to pops. Performances are scheduled in Orchestra Hall. The orchestra's award-winning concert broadcasts, produced by Minnesota Public Radio and distributed by American Public Media to more than 120 radio stations nationwide, reach approximately 200,000 people each week.

The Minnesota Youth Symphonies
790 Cleveland Avenue South, Suite 203,
St. Paul
(651) 699-5811
www.mnyouthsymphonies.org
The Minnesota Youth Symphonies are open to students of all income levels from elementary school through high school. Co-music directors Claudette and Manny Laureano oversee four advanced orchestras. The MYS presents major concerts at Orchestra Hall in Minneapolis. Auditions are held at the end of August of each year.

The St. Paul Chamber Orchestra
408 St. Peter Street, Third Floor,
St. Paul
(651) 292-3248
www.stpaulchamberorchestra.org
With 35 members, the St. Paul Chamber Orchestra is about one-third the size of the average symphony orchestra. But that

definitely doesn't mean it doesn't sound as "big" as any other orchestral ensemble. As the only full-time professional chamber orchestra in the United States, the SPCO has an extensive discography, with 64 recordings. This ensemble presents more than 150 concerts annually and reaches millions more through radio broadcasts and regional, national, and international touring.

The Schubert Club
Landmark Center, 75 West Fifth Street,
#302, St. Paul
(651) 292-3267
www.schubert.org
The Schubert Club is Minnesota's oldest arts organization, presenting world-renowned artists and local and regional musicians to Twin Cities audiences through various grants and private funding. The Schubert Club Instrument Museum is located in Landmark Center as well.

VocalEssence
1900 Nicollet Avenue, Minneapolis
(612) 547-1451
www.vocalessence.org
VocalEssence is recognized internationally as one of America's premier choral arts organizations. The chorus offers innovative programming under the direction of founder Philip Brunelle.

THEATERS AND PERFORMANCE SPACES

Acadia Cafe Cabaret Theater
1931 Nicollet Avenue South, Minneapolis
(612) 874-8702
www.acadiacafe.com
This space wasn't necessarily designed to hold theater performances—it's a second room for the Acadia Cafe, equipped with riser seating and a permanent stage. But any eccentricities fade away when the shows start. Seven nights a week, Acadia hosts a performance—music, improv, comedy, poetry, or performance art—anything

The Minnesota Orchestra in Minneapolis's spectacular Orchestra Hall. GREATER MINNEAPOLIS CONVENTION & VISITORS ASSOCIATION

at all, so long as it's original. The space has the perk of being within a cafe, which offers food and a 24-rail tap. And while it may not be the best theater space in town, it holds some of the most intense productions to be found.

Brave New Workshop Theatre
2605 Hennepin Avenue South,
Minneapolis
(612) 332-6620
www.bravenewworkshop.org
The country's longest-running satirical comedy theater, founded by Dudley Riggs in 1958, features original shows and late-night improvisation on Friday and Saturday for just a dollar. The Brave New Workshop is known for its satirical takes on pop-culture icons of the moment, from Prozac to *Who Wants to be a Millionaire* to the Christian Right, bringing cutting-edge

shows like *Beanie Baby Barbecue* and *I Think, Therefore IBM* to the stage. The theater offers classes on improvisation, acting, and writing.

Bryant-Lake Bowl Theater
810 West Lake Street, Minneapolis
(612) 825-3737
www.bryantlakebowl.com
The Bryant-Lake Bowl Theater space has become a mainstay of local performance acts, bringing live music (including opera), dance, comedy, and theater to an intimate stage tucked behind the bowling alley. On any given night you may wander in and find the tiny performance area packed in support of local talent. No matter where you decide to sit, make sure to take advantage of the extensive beer and wine lists.

Cedar Cultural Center
416 Cedar Avenue South, Minneapolis
(612) 338-2674
www.thecedar.org
The Cedar offers an eclectic selection of world music. It perfectly fills the niche that the majority of Twin Cities venues have missed, booking acts that include the very best—and very often underappreciated— of global and ethnic musicians, including folk, Irish, African, blues, and bluegrass. Some past performers include French guitar virtuoso Pierre Bensusan and American performer Ani DiFranco. The Cedar is also host to the annual Nordic Roots Festival, which brings Nordic and Nordic-style performers from around the world to play the weekend event.

Chanhassen Dinner Theatres
501 West 78th Street, Chanhassen
(952) 934-1525
www.chanhassentheatres.com
The Chanhassen Dinner Theatres complex is the nation's largest professional dinner theater, featuring four stages under one roof including its 600-seat main stage, and producing one lavishly costumed Broadway musical comedy after another year-round. This facility is also the largest restaurant in the state.

Children's Theatre Company
2400 Third Avenue South, Minneapolis
(612) 874-0500
www.childrenstheatre.org
Since 1965 the Children's Theatre Company (CTC) and its cast of incredibly talented actors and actresses, young and old, have been performing at the 746-seat facility—recently remodeled to include a second stage. Most of the performances are based on children's stories and fairy tales, such as *A Year With Frog and Toad*. There's a healthy dose of impressive original works as well, such as *Korczak's Children,* a story about the Holocaust through children's eyes, and *The Monkey King,* based on a 500-year-old Chinese story about a trickster on a quest with pious monks to recover sacred scrolls. One of the country's leading theater groups for youths, the Tony Award-winning CTC produces an annual season featuring more than 390 mainstage performances and a touring production that performs in 50 Midwest communities. Its public performances, school matinees, and Theatre Arts Training Program serve more than 350,000 people each year.

The Fitzgerald Theater
10 East Exchange Street, St. Paul
(651) 290-1221
www.fitzgeraldtheater.publicradio.org
Opened in 1910 as the Schubert Theater and long known as the World Theater, this comfortable classic structure was renamed in 1994 after St. Paul's famous literary figure and social gadfly, F. Scott Fitzgerald. The man behind the restoration and renaming of the theater is its well-known tenant, Garrison Keillor, host of *A Prairie Home Companion* radio show. As St. Paul's oldest surviving theater space, now restored to its former elegance, the Fitzgerald Theater presents its shows in a two-balcony, 1,000-seat hall with excellent acoustics and sightlines. The theater's many pleasant features make it popular with touring acts that could probably sell out much larger venues. The theater schedules classical, jazz, folk, country, and

The Fitzgerald Theater in Saint Paul is the home of A Prairie Home Companion, *the wildly popular radio show of Garrison Keillor.* SAINT PAUL RCVA

pop music events as well as film screenings and theater productions.

Guthrie Theater
725 Vineland Place, Minneapolis
(612) 377-2224
www.guthrietheater.org

Anyone who knows American theater knows the Guthrie, the Minneapolis theater founded in the early '60s by legendary director Sir Tyrone Guthrie. The company's métier has always been intriguing interpretations of classic drama. The largest nonprofit theater between New York and San Francisco, the Guthrie is renowned for its productions of classic, comedic, and contemporary plays. The mainstay of Twin Cities professional theater, the Guthrie has a shared entry with the Walker Art Center. The Guthrie's season (six shows a year, including an annual *Christmas Carol* production) is more tradi-

tional than the smaller venues in town, choosing to stick to mostly classic and Broadway productions and not veering much into experimental territory.

The theater's larger-budget productions and prominent location translate into ticket prices ranging from $15 to $45 on average, but the theater offers discount rush tickets 10 minutes before showtime.

Guthrie Lab
700 First Street North, Minneapolis
(612) 377-2224
www.guthrietheater.org

Essentially, the Guthrie Lab is the experimental wing of the Guthrie Theater. While the Guthrie Theater is known for its big-name, high-budget performances, productions at the Guthrie Lab are known for taking chances with much bolder productions. Their performances revolve around ingenious staging, costuming, and even lighting, and although the Lab is hidden deep within Minneapolis's Warehouse District, when you find it you'll be blown away with what it can do with theater. The Guthrie's much-anticipated new $125 million home on the Minneapolis riverfront is scheduled to open in 2006.

In the Heart of the Beast Puppet and Mask Theatre
1500 East Lake Street, Minneapolis
(612) 721-2535
www.heartofthebeasttheatre.org
In the Heart of the Beast's unique theater production is marked by elaborate costuming; stories are told through puppets or actors hidden behind gigantic masks, giving performances a mystical and magical quality. For more than 25 years, this unique theater company has used the ancient tradition of puppet and mask theater to explore issues, events, and values of contemporary society. Though some performances are adaptations of children's stories, all shows are a wonder for eyes of any age.

Puppets are hand-hewn by those involved with the show, and the traveling company stages shows both regionally and nationally. Residencies, educational programs, and special events are offered in the permanent facilities.

Jungle Theater
2951 Lyndale Avenue South, Minneapolis
(612) 822-7063
www.jungletheater.com
The Jungle Theater has a reputation for straightforward performances scripted by lesser-known or more poetic playwrights, offering a year-round season of plays from classic and contemporary sources in an intimate, off-Broadway setting. The red-velvet-seated theater has put on plays by Dylan Thomas and Tennessee Williams and was the site of the world premiere of playwright Karl Gajdusek's *Silver Lake*.

Mixed Blood Theatre
1501 South Fourth Street, Minneapolis
(612) 338-6131
www.mixedblood.com

Walking around Minneapolis's West Bank, it's hard not to notice Mixed Blood's sign and wonder what lurks beneath. Far from anything runaway imaginations may concoct, Mixed Blood is a professional theater company whose mission is to expose and promote the Twin Cities cultural melting pot. Founded in 1976 by Jack Reuler to provide voice and venue for actors of color, Mixed Blood has branched out into the working world to tackle hot topics like race, culture, gender, sexual orientation, and disability. The main stage is housed in a turn-of-the-20th-century brick firehouse, while the touring company itself performs in schools and organizations throughout the region.

Northrop Auditorium
84 Southeast Church Street, Minneapolis
(612) 624-2345
Located on the University of Minnesota campus in Minneapolis, this is the primary venue for big-name dance company tours and classical, jazz, and alternative music acts. The old, ornate theater has the grandiose feel of a palace, with high ceilings, velvet curtains, ornate gold and marble trimming, and beautiful acoustics. The annual Northrop Dance Season is an exceptional mix of traditional and cutting-edge dance performances from around the world, while the annual Jazz Series brings acts such as the Buena Vista Social Club and Sonny Rollins.

Old Log Theater
5175 Meadeville Street, Excelsior
(952) 474-5951
www.oldlog.com
You could call the Old Log one of the Twin Cities' legendary theaters. When it was founded in 1940, however, the forested shoreline around meandering Lake Minnetonka was not considered part of the Twin Cities but a distant retreat from the urban core, a summer playground for the wealthy. Now, of course, it's the leviathan of the western suburbs, but this large log cabin of a dinner theater—one of America's oldest professional

theaters—still stands among the trees near the banks of Lake Minnetonka.

At the Old Log, you'll find American and British comedies with all of the slamming doors, mistaken identities, and double-entendres inherent in the genre. Typically running for months at a time, the productions are crowd-pleasers for conservative audiences but are usually not adventurous enough for those who enjoy theater with an edge.

Orchestra Hall
1111 Nicollet Mall, Minneapolis
(952) 371-5656

The Minneapolis counterpart to St. Paul's Ordway, Orchestra Hall is the place to go to hear the Minnesota Orchestra. The modern exterior can put you off a little, but once inside, visual distractions are kept to a minimum. The minimalist auditorium, which seats 2,400, has a large main floor with three balconies symmetrically girding it. Behind the natural wooden stage and on the ceiling loom what look like enormous sugar cubes hurled by some mythical giant. These blocks provide hundreds of surfaces that deflect sound, making Orchestra Hall among the most acoustically perfect theaters in the nation. The hall lobby opens to Peavy Plaza, which holds the orchestra's popular outdoor summer music festival.

Ordway Center for the Performing Arts
345 Washington Street, St. Paul
(651) 224-4222
www.ordway.org

While Minneapolis's Orchestra Hall is modern and glassy like the downtown around it, St. Paul's Ordway is elegant and old world, conforming admirably to the high and somewhat stuffy standards set forth by its older neighbors, Landmark Center, the Saint Paul Hotel, and the St. Paul Public Library. Both the hall and the lobby are tastefully designed, with the wooden walls of the auditorium making for outstanding acoustics, especially for a relatively small ensemble like the St. Paul Chamber Orchestra, as well as for touring Broadway

Ordway Center for the Performing Arts.
ORDWAY CENTER FOR THE PERFORMING ARTS

productions like *Peter Pan*. Rich in contemporary details, the handsome 1,900-seat theater is laid out in the manner of a European opera house, with spacious lobbies overlooking Rice Park from a continuous, three-story bank of windows.

Orpheum Theatre
910 Hennepin Avenue South, Minneapolis
(612) 339-7007
www.hennepintheatredistrict.org

When it opened in 1921, the Orpheum was one of the nation's premier vaudeville houses. For a time in the mid-1980s, it was owned by singer Bob Dylan and had seen better days. In 1988 the city bought the Orpheum and spent over $10 million on its restoration, which was completed in 1993. Today the Orpheum's most stunning element is the auditorium's glittering dome, lined with 30,000 leaves of silver and lit by a 2,000-pound brass and Italian crystal chandelier.

Like the State Theatre, the Orpheum hosts both musical concerts and many of

THE ARTS

the Broadway musicals that come to town. The old-style marquee blinking over downtown can't be missed. The renovated theater has showcased the world premieres of *Victor/Victoria,* starring Julie Andrews, and Disney's *The Lion King.*

Park Square Theatre
20 West Seventh Place, St. Paul
(651) 291-7005
Located in the heart of downtown St. Paul in the center of Park Square—a block-long brick street that's for pedestrians only—Park Square Theatre offers great professional theater in a reasonably large setting. The sets and costumes are beautiful, and there are no bad seats in the house. The shows range from contemporary plays to classical works.

Penumbra Theatre
270 North Kent Street, St. Paul
(651) 224-3180
www.penumbratheatre.org
As the only professional African-American theater company in Minnesota, the Penumbra has a large following and a great reputation. Founded by artistic director Lou Bellamy with the mission of creating artistically exceptional productions that address the African-American experience, the troupe has a rich history of excellence that has included Pulitzer Prize–winning playwright August Wilson as a member.

The Playwrights' Center
2301 East Franklin Avenue, Minneapolis
(612) 332-7481
www.pwcenter.org
This former church converted into theater space stands in the middle of the Seward neighborhood on Franklin Avenue. If people know about it, it's because they read the name in another theater's playbill—usually because the Playwrights' Center gave a donation to the performing company. Behind the scenes the center helps actors and writers workshop their new ideas. It also houses the occasional performance.

Plymouth Playhouse
2705 Annapolis Lane, Plymouth
(763) 553-1600
www.plymouthplayhouse.com
The Plymouth is the flagship space of Troupe America, which specializes in dinner-theater productions long on laughs and music. *Nunsense, Pump Boys and Dinettes,* and revues featuring the Twin Cities' own Lovely Liebowitz Sisters have had extended runs here. Their popular long-running production, *How to Talk Minnesotan,* was adapted for the stage by the book's author, Howard Mohr. More recently, *Church Basement Ladies* poked similar fun at the stereotypical Minnesotan.

Rarig Center
Univeristy of Minnesota Campus,
330 21st Avenue South,
Minneapolis
(612) 625-4001
The Rarig Center, located on the West Bank, hosts University Theatre and Xperimental Theater productions throughout the year in four theaters: a proscenium, a thrust, an arena, and a black box. The Mainstage shows are usually the more popular ones, such as *As You Like It,* and the smaller theater spaces offer experimental shows. The X Theater productions are directed and performed exclusively by undergraduate U of M students. At University Theatre, student and professional actors, designers, and directors write and direct musicals, comedies, and dramas. The *Minnesota Centennial Showboat* offers performances each summer aboard a sternwheeler riverboat anchored at Harriet Island in St, Paul.

Red Eye Theater
15 West 14th Street, Minneapolis
(612) 870-0309
www.theredeye.org
One of the smaller theater venues in the Twin Cities, the Red Eye Theater is by far the most experimental, a place were work is developed and presented. Just off Nicollet Avenue, the Red Eye's theater space hosts film and video productions

and dance events, both local and imported, but its main thrust is theater. The venue itself has hosted fringe performances over the last few years, an example of how Red Eye is committed to energizing and establishing artists' work. The Red Eye's performing space is a long, rectangular black box that's also used by other companies who enjoy its versatility and intimacy.

Roy Wilkins Auditorium
RiverCentre, 175 West Kellogg Boulevard, St. Paul
(651) 265-4800
www.theroy.com
Roy Wilkins Auditorium (named for the longtime NAACP head, a St. Paul native) is all that's left of the old St. Paul Auditorium. Half the auditorium and its adjoining theater were razed to build the Ordway Center. This cavernous hall, part of the sprawling RiverCentre complex, has seen a revival thanks to big-ticket touring dance DJs (Chemical Brothers, Moby) and cutting-edge rock acts (Marilyn Manson, Deftones). What Roy Wilkins loses in acoustics, it makes up for in breathing room. If a show has festival seating, you can quench your fanaticism and get quite close to the stage or take a break and find respite near the exit doors.

Southern Theater
1420 Washington Avenue South, Minneapolis
(612) 340-1725
www.southerntheater.org
The Southern has increasingly become a venue for dance due to its rebuilt stage floor. Many local dance companies perform here, and everything from flamenco to classical Indian dance to modern dance can be seen in this venue. Exposed-brick walls enclose the auditorium, lending a comfortable warehouselike feel to the performance experience. Every January the Southern hosts Out There, a notably high-quality series of theatrical performances.

Stages Theatre Company
1111 Main Street, Hopkins
(952) 979-1111
www.stagestheatre.org
Stages, formerly Child's Play Theatre Company, produces a full season of plays for young audiences. Housed in the Hopkins Center for the Arts, it offers acting, singing, and directing classes for youth ages 5 through 18.

State Theatre
805 Hennepin Avenue South, Minneapolis
(612) 339-7007
www.hennepintheatredistrict.org
Downtown Minneapolis has become a theatrical center due in large part to the renovation of this gem of a theater. Painstakingly restored between 1989 and 1991 to its former 1920s glory, which includes a golden proscenium arch, glittering chandeliers, and intricate murals, the 2,200-seat State Theatre now showcases a steady stream of touring plays and musicals, concerts, and lectures. Smaller than its neighbor the Orpheum Theatre (which is owned and managed by the same group), the historic State Theatre is similar in its beautifully restored interior, complete with a grand sloping balcony that hangs over the rear half of the main floor. Broadway touring productions sometimes set up shop here for months at a stretch. Rock concerts, comedians, and dance performances fill in the rest of the schedule.

Theatre de la Jeune Lune
105 North First Street, Minneapolis
(612) 333-6200
www.jeunelune.org
The Jeune Lune is located in the Warehouse District of downtown Minneapolis and is known for its elaborate and poignant commedia-style productions. The space itself is justification for buying the first ticket, after that most theatergoers are hooked. The facade of the building was designed by renowned architect Cass Gilbert, and the theater is listed on the

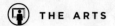
National Register of Historic Places. The interior is a large bricked space, which lends itself to authentic-looking street and/or exterior house scenes in a variety of plays.

This theater ensemble is known for its highly physical, visually spectacular productions. Jeune Lune's acclaimed *The 3 Musketeers* was the hit of the 1997 Spoleto USA Festival. The Jeune Lune received the Regional Theatre Tony Award in 2005.

Theatre in the Round Players, Inc.
245 Cedar Avenue South, Minneapolis
(612) 333–3010
www.theatreintheround.org
Theatre in the Round, the oldest community theater in the Twin Cities, performs drama and comedy on a unique arena stage. Because the audience surrounds the stage entirely, sets are minimal, making the action between the actors more intense. Props are also very important because of the lack of stage settings. Most of the plays presented are classics, but the players perform a few well-done area premieres each year.

PARKS 🌳

T he Three Rivers Park District, formerly Hennepin Parks, is an independent park district established by
the state legislature in 1957 and is responsible for maintaining most of the parks
around the Twin Cities metro area. As a
special park district, Three Rivers is
charged with acquiring, developing, and
maintaining large park reserves, regional
parks, and regional trails for the benefit
and use of the citizens of suburban Hennepin County, Scott County, the metropolitan area, and the state of Minnesota.
Three Rivers' policy for planning and management of natural resources distin
guishes it from other park and recreation
agencies in Minnesota. The policy speci-
fies that no more than 20 percent of a
park reserve may be developed for active
use and that at least 80 percent of a park
reserve shall be restored to and retained
in a natural state. As a result, once-rare
osprey, bald eagles, sandhill cranes, and
trumpeter swans are now nesting in the
park reserves. Woodland and prairie
restorations have been accomplished
using native wildflowers, shrubs, and trees
produced from seeds collected in the park
reserves.

Twin Citians have the luxury of being
able to walk past wetlands full of migratory waterfowl and turtles on their way to
downtown Minneapolis, or through thickly
forested areas housing species of rare
native animals and birds just minutes outside St. Paul. Kids who grow up in the
Twin Cities share in pleasures usually
reserved for children in the country,
whether it be fishing in one of the many
regularly stocked urban lakes, berry picking, or just being surrounded by trees,
songbirds, and wildflowers. Even in the
dead of winter, you'll find people outside
cross-country skiing, snowshoeing, or ice
fishing in the many city and suburban
parks around the Cities. Take a trip to any

of the following, and you'll soon see why
we Minnesotans are rabidly protective of
our wilderness areas.

MINNEAPOLIS

Boom Island
Plymouth Avenue and Northeast
Eighth Street, Minneapolis
(612) 230-6400
www.minneapolisparks.org
Boom Island Park is a jewel in the crown
of the nationally acclaimed Minneapolis
parks system. Situated above historic Main
Street, Nicollet Island, and the St. Anthony
Lock and Dam, Boom Island is a veritable
playground for families and tourists wishing to experience the majesty and beauty
of the Mississippi River. The park is well
used and threadbare in spots, but not
enough to lose its luster as a popular destination for picnicking, tossing a Frisbee,
sightseeing on a riverboat, launching one's
own boat, or simply relaxing by the river
on the plaza overlooks.

Attention to details, with few notable
exceptions, makes this park highly accessible to persons with disabilities. Low-
grade rampways have been integrated
into the overlooks and boarding docks.
Water fountains and the public telephone
all incorporate current accessible features,
and level asphalt pathways connect all the
critical areas of the park. The park can
serve as a nice starting or ending point on
a journey on foot or by bike to the nearby
Heritage Trail around historic Main Street
and St. Anthony Falls or going north up
the river to connect with the Mississippi
River Regional Corridor Trail that takes
you to Anoka Riverfront Regional Park,
Islands of Peace Park, and, eventually, East
and West Coon Rapids Regional Parks.

The boat launch is located on the
north side of the main parking area in a

small, protected channel about 300 feet away from the water's edge and the dock area to the boat slips. Several sets of stairs and a wheelchair-access ramp go to the boat slip dock area, and a lovely promenade/plaza area is just downriver of the riverboat landing. This area provides a nice overlook to the river as well as a stunning view of downtown Minneapolis. Another small plaza area with wood decking adjacent to the boat landing affords visitors an opportunity to view the comings and goings of both the riverboats and the private boats being launched nearby.

Boom Island is home to St. Anthony Falls' miniature "lighthouse," which sits on a prominent point overlooking the riverboat dock and river. The lighthouse is not functional but makes a nice destination for visitors, especially kids. The view is great from this area—almost like being out on the water.

Cleary Lake Regional Park
18106 Texas Avenue, Minneapolis
(763) 694-7777
www.threeriversparkdistrict.org
The 1,045-acre Cleary Lake Regional Park, southwest of Burnsville, is one of the most popular year-round recreation spots in the southern metro area. A distinctive three-season pavilion, available by reservation, is a favorite Cities site for large group gatherings, while golfers find challenge in the par 3, nine-hole golf course and driving range. Water sports available include swimming, boating, and fishing in Cleary Lake. Winter activities include cross-country skiing on groomed trails and snowshoeing anywhere in the park except the ski trails. Boats, bicycles, in-line skates, and cross-country skis are available for rent at the visitor center; reservation picnic areas and group campsites are also available.

Loring Park
1382 Willow Street, Minneapolis
(612) 370-4929
www.minneapolisparks.org
Modeled after New York's Central Park, although about 800 acres smaller than the real thing, Loring Park is a hip city park with just about everything. There's a large, beautiful lake (Loring Lake) full of mallards, wood ducks, and Canada geese that come up on the shore regularly, demanding handouts; friendly squirrels; lush, green rolling hills; and, in summer, free live music and movies in the outdoor amphitheater several nights of the week. There's also a concession cart parked conveniently near the amphitheater most nights, which sells snack foods and ice cream. The park is well maintained, with lots of paved trails that take you around Loring Lake and the stunning fountain and bronze sculpture of Norway's esteemed violinist Ole Bull.

A short walk across the street takes you to either the Basilica of Saint Mary or the internationally acclaimed Walker Art Center and its sculpture garden, depending on which way you point your feet.

Mill Ruins Park
On the Mississippi River at St. Anthony Falls, Minneapolis
(612) 341-7555
www.millcitymuseum.org
Mill Ruins Park is next to the Mill City Museum, the historic Crosby A Mill now preserved to celebrate the history of the flour mills that built the city of Minneapolis. The park overlooks the locks and St. Anthony Falls, and visitors can watch the barge traffic making its way through the locks and on down the Mississippi. The park connects to the Stone Arch Bridge, a pedestrian and bicycle pathway across the river, and to the bike trail system winding up and down the Mississippi and throughout the Twin Cities.

Minneapolis Chain of Lakes/
Rice Creek Regional Parks
Cedar Lake, 25th Street West
and Cedar Lake Parkway
Lake Calhoun, Calhoun Parkway
and Lake Street
Lake Harriet, 4135 Lake Harriet
Parkway East

Lake Nokomis, Minnehaha Parkway East and Cedar Avenue
Lake of the Isles, 25th Street West and Lake of the Isles Parkway East
(612) 661–4800

About 2,500 acres of parkland surrounds Minneapolis's Chain of Lakes, which includes Lake Harriet, Lake Calhoun, Lake of the Isles, Cedar Lake, and Lake Nokomis. The lakes are all connected by Rice and Minnehaha Creeks, which makes canoeing through much of the parkland a fun trip that involves little or no docking to get from lake to lake. Both boat and shore fishing are popular in the Chain of Lakes, and many fishing piers and easily accessed shore fishing sites can be found throughout the parks.

The lakes are surrounded by paved bike and walking trails, and the bike trails connect to the larger system surrounding and cutting across the city of Minneapolis, including the Cedar Lake Trail, the Minnehaha Creek Trail to the Mississippi (which will also get you to the St. Paul bike trail system), and the Midtown Greenway, which follows the railroad tracks along 29th Avenue through south Minneapolis and Uptown.

Thomas Sadler Roberts Bird Sanctuary, located on the north shore of Lake Harriet, consists of 13 acres of unapologetically wild land that attracts more than 200 bird species each year. The sanctuary is named for Thomas Roberts, the late Minneapolis physician and University of Minnesota ornithology professor who in 1932 wrote what remains the definitive work on local avian culture, *Birds of Minnesota*. Created by the Minneapolis Park Board in 1936 as Lyndale Park Bird Sanctuary, its name was changed after Roberts's death to honor the man who led so many field trips here.

Minnehaha Falls and Park
Hiawatha Avenue and Minnehaha Parkway, Minneapolis
(612) 230–6400
www.minneapolisparks.org

This historic, well-used, and recently refurbished 193-acre regional park gives visitors little wonder where Henry Wadsworth Longfellow got the inspiration to write his epic poem *Song of Hiawatha,* which was inspired by accounts the poet had read about Minnehaha Falls, though he never actually visited them. The impressive falls are the primary destination point for most park visitors, with several wonderful overlooks and steps that take you to the bottom of the falls. From the bottom, you can pick up the Minnehaha Trail and follow it and the river to the Lower Glen area of Minnehaha Regional Park. There you'll find a wide, open field, old stone bridges that cross the water at regular intervals, limestone cliffs, and areas of restored prairie and undeveloped wetlands. Throughout the park are statues, plaques dedicated to historic events, and historic buildings, including the historic Minnehaha Depot, built in 1875 to serve as a recreational gateway for visitors to the falls and as a departure point for soldiers from nearby Fort Snelling, and the Col. John H. Stevens House, which is open to visitors most weekends mid-May through mid-September.

The main area of the park, around the picnic areas and the falls, can be busy during summer months. There are lots of walkers, bikers, and skaters, so keep one eye out as you go from overlook to overlook. You can easily walk south of the falls, however, and find quieter, more reflective surroundings in which to relax and enjoy the natural beauty of the park. Benches are strategically placed in and among statuary, gardens, and a unique pergola (covered walk). About 1 mile south of the main park entrance is a paved hike/bike trail that goes from Minnehaha Falls to

While Minnehaha Park is beautiful in summer, it's a real treat to go there in winter and see the powerful waterfall frozen solid. Most of the park trails are closed then, but you can still walk down to see the falls.

Fort Snelling State Park. The trail is mostly paved, with a few sections in disrepair, but it's quiet, little used, and takes bicyclists and hikers all along the upper river bluffs and past a magnificent river overlook at a pedestrian bridge that crosses to the Old Soldier's Home.

The park is also connected to the Minnehaha Creek Bike Trail, which follows the creekbed all the way to Lake Harriet; the Mississippi River Trail leading north to the University of Minnesota; and downtown Minneapolis, and the St. Paul bike trail system via the Ford Parkway bridge.

Nicollet Island Park
Off Historic Main Street at East Hennepin Avenue, Minneapolis
(612) 230-6400
In summertime this little island located in the middle of the Mississippi River is a haven for native wildlife of all sorts, including the occasional deer. In winter the park is converted into a giant ice-skating rink. Year-round the park is a beautiful place for an afternoon or evening stroll—at night the lights of downtown Minneapolis reflect off the Mississippi River, giving one the feeling of being downtown yet still walking through a quaint, small town. Horse-and-carriage rides are available from the nearby Nicollet Inn, and fireworks displays can be seen from the park's rolling green hills on New Year's Eve, Fourth of July, and during the Aquatennial celebration.

St. Anthony Falls Heritage Trail
Main Street, Minneapolis
(888) 676-6757
www.minneapolisriverfront.com
This amazing stretch of land is often overlooked because the entrance is tucked behind the giant Pillsbury flour mill, next to Minneapolis's historic Main Street retail area directly across the Mississippi River from downtown. This park and trail celebrate the founding of Minneapolis.

The Heritage Trail is a highly accessible asphalt multiuse trail (bike, hike, jog, and skate) that takes visitors on a 1.8-mile loop, connecting them to most of the historic and natural features of early Minneapolis, including natural vistas of the tree-lined banks of the Mississippi River as well as many ruined brick arches from the days of the bustling milling industry. The trail is widely interpreted along the way, making this an excellent self-guided trail.

The centerpiece of the park, the Stone Arch Bridge, was built by railway baron James J. Hill in 1883 to speed his trains across the Mississippi. Now beautifully restored, the bridge provides serene transit for walkers, joggers, and anybody who wants the best possible view of St. Anthony Falls, whose churning power first made Minneapolis a milling capital. Trail users can cross the river over the historic bridge, which offers a spectacular vista of the river, the downtown Minneapolis skyline, and the highly accessible St. Anthony Falls Lock and Dam at the other end. A beautiful promenade parallels the river on its west bank and is a favorite destination of noontime walkers and others who wish to sit, read, or watch the river flow by. There are plenty of overlooks and bench areas on the trail, and water and toilets are located at developed areas on both sides of the river.

ST. PAUL

Como Park
1360 North Lexington Parkway, St. Paul
(651) 632-5111
www.stpaul.gov/depts/parks
This 450-acre urban park, more than 100 years old, is one of the most visited sites in the Twin Cities, offering large group picnicking areas and a conservatory, zoo, Japanese garden, a small amusement park with pony rides, and summer concerts and plays. There's also an 18-hole golf course that turns into a cross-country ski area in the winter; seasonal equipment rentals and refreshments are available at Como Lakeside Pavilion.

In the middle of a tough Minnesota winter, there's no palliative like a visit to the lush, green-filled Marjorie McNeely Conservatory at Como Park, which houses such exotic plants as 125-year-old palm trees (botanical souvenirs from world tours by the city's elite) and papaya trees (grown in Como greenhouses from the seeds of grocery store papayas). Outside, the teahouse in the Como Ordway Memorial Japanese Garden offers a traditional *chanoyu* tea ceremony several times throughout the summer. Look for the beautiful goldfish pond stocked with giant, colorful, friendly fish. (See the Attractions chapter for information on Como's zoo and conservatory.)

The historic Cafesjian's Carousel, which operated for three-quarters of a century at the Minnesota State Fairgrounds, found a new home in 2000 at the park, just south of the conservatory. The carousel and its beautiful antique horses are available to the public during the summer, and a ride on the carousel is a great way to end a day at the park.

Crosby Regional Park and Hidden Falls Park
**East Mississippi River Boulevard, St. Paul
(651) 632-5111
www.stpaul.gov/depts/parks**
Hidden Falls Park dates from 1887, when the area was identified as one of four major park sites for the city of St. Paul. The park got its name from both the small, spring-fed waterfall hidden deep inside the park and the historic Crosby Farm, formerly owned by English immigrant Thomas Crosby, who once farmed 160 acres of this land. Today hiking and biking trails run along shady, wooded bottomlands next to the river and along the marshes of the two lakes before connecting to Mississippi River Boulevard. (If it's rained recently, bike slowly through the lower, shadier spots or a slippery patch of mud may wreck your outing.) The primary park features include a well-developed picnic area with pavilion and modern toilet facilities, a boat launch ramp, picnic sites, and access to a 7-mile hiking/biking path that follows the Mississippi River.

Panfish can be caught from the banks of the Mississippi River or from over the side of a boat.

The hiking/biking trail, which converts to a cross-country ski trail in the winter, takes users along the Mississippi River, where the flora and fauna of river life can be observed up close. Songbirds migrate and nest nearby, and deer and rabbits can be seen in the thick wooded areas around the park. At points along the trail, historic Fort Snelling can be seen on the high bluffs across the river. The Crosby Regional Park section has an open floodplain meadow, two lakes, and wooded areas.

Fort Snelling State Park
**101 Snelling Lake Road, St. Paul
(612) 725-2724
www.dnr.state.mn.us/state_parks**
For hundreds of years before Europeans arrived, generations of Dakotas lived in villages along the Mississippi and Minnesota Rivers that meet in what's now Fort Snelling State Park. The river confluence was believed to be the place of origin and center of the earth by the bands of Mdewa-kan-ton-wan Dakotas, the "Dwellers by Mystic Lake." By the late 1600s Europeans had visited the area. In the 1820s Fort Snelling was built on the bluff above the two rivers to control the exploration, trade, and settlement on these waterways.

Established as a state park in 1962, the 3,400-acre park is located in the Mississippi River Sandplains Landscape Region at the confluence of the two great rivers. During the last Ice Age, retreating glaciers left thick moraine deposits over the bedrock in the area. As the glaciers melted, torrential meltwaters carved through the deposits to form the valleys of what are now the Minnesota, Mississippi, and St. Croix Rivers. Most of the park is on the Minnesota River floodplain and is thickly wooded with large cottonwood, silver maple, ash, and willow trees along the braided channels of the Minnesota River. Picnic sites, a beach, and river and lake fishing invite visitors to enjoy the recreational opportunities

Fort Snelling State Park, along the Minnesota and Mississippi Rivers, offers miles of hiking and skiing trails less than 15 minutes from both downtowns. TODD R. BERGER

offered by this historic and beautiful park nestled in the shadow of city freeways and airport flyways. The swimming beach, added in 1970, remains a popular recreation attraction in the park. In 1997 a new visitor center opened to the public.

Conveniently located in the heart of the Twin Cities, this park offers extensive hiking, bike, and ski trails that link to Minnehaha Park and the Minnesota Valley National Wildlife Refuge. Canoe on Gun Club Lake, play golf, swim in Snelling Lake, or hike or ski to Pike Island, at the confluence of the Mississippi and Minnesota Rivers. Interpretive exhibits and films on display in the Thomas C. Savage Visitor Center give visitors a good background on the history and resources of the park and area. Trails also allow visitors to hike up to historic Fort Snelling for a view of military life in the 1820s. The Pike Island Interpretive Center hosts exhibits concerning historic Fort Snelling and the region in

general. Throughout the park, the forest bottoms and marshes have an abundance of wildlife consisting of white-tailed deer, foxes, woodchucks, badgers, and skunks. Visitors might also come across the native, nonvenomous fox snake, which is almost identical in appearance to a rattlesnake. Snapping, soft-shell, and painted turtles can be seen basking in the sun along the river or in one of the lakes.

During winter, the park maintains 10 miles of groomed cross-country ski trails and 6 miles of groomed skate-ski trails—snowshoeing is permitted anywhere in the park except on groomed ski trails. The park also has 7 miles of hiking trails available for use in the winter, with even more available during summer. Golf equipment and canoes are available for rent in the park, and naturalist programs ranging from bird-watching tours to nature and snowshoe hikes are offered year-round.

Indian Mounds Park
Earl Street and Mounds Boulevard, St. Paul
(651) 632–5111
www.stpaul.gov/depts/parks

Built to enshrine six 2,000-year-old Hopewell Indian burial mounds, Mounds Park occupies what was the choicest residential land in St. Paul in the 1860s. Today the bluffs of the park give visitors one of the best "aerial" views of the Twin Cities, with the Minneapolis skyline on the left, the St. Paul skyline on the right, and the Mississippi River below. The mounds are surrounded by metal rail fences but are easily seen and approached—the remains of the chiefs have long since been removed, but the mounds are still standing as a sacred memorial. Visitors are not permitted to climb on the mounds. A brass plaque describing the site stands near the brick pavilion. The park is also the site of the first visit by Europeans to the Twin Cities area; Father Louis Hennepin and two other Frenchmen were brought here in 1680.

Two more historic features nearby are the reconstructed aerial beacon used for many years by aircraft approaching the Holman Field airport directly across the river and the Carver's Cave outlook. Information about this beacon is posted on signage adjacent to the beacon tower located a short distance from the mounds. It's best to park at the Mounds parking lot, approaching this site via the asphalt path. The Carver's Cave overlook commemorates Jonathan Carver, a forward scout for Maj. Robert Rogers's expedition to find a Northwest Passage, whose travels brought him up the Mississippi River. In 1766 he discovered an ancient cave with artifacts and hieroglyphics along the bluff at about this point. A plaque at the overlook describes the history.

The park is actively used by families, groups, skateboarders, cyclists, hikers, and others. It is a well-worn park with old restrooms and access routes developed before accessibility regulations were in place, but there are plenty of picnic and play space for people of all ages and accessible parking spaces at many points in the park.

Lilydale/Harriet Island Park/ Cherokee Park
South side of Mississippi River at Wabasha, St. Paul
(651) 632–5111
www.stpaul.gov/depts/parks

The river-oriented Lilydale/Harriet Island Park includes the natural area of the Lilydale portion below the river bluffs and Harriet Island itself. Harriet Island, situated on the Mississippi River across from downtown St. Paul, was one of the first recreational sites in the city. Named for pioneer schoolteacher Harriet Bishop, the park was a true island separated from the mainland by a channel of water until 1950, when the channel was filled. At the top of the bluffs is Cherokee Park, which has picnic grounds and good spots for viewing the entire park.

Harriet Island has long been a playground for St. Paul citizens who come alone or with friends and family to fish, launch their boats, cruise on a historic riverboat, picnic, take walks, and simply enjoy nature. The park has landscaped river edges, beautiful flower gardens that attract native and migratory songbirds, and a marina from which park visitors can board several large paddleboats to tour the waterways.

Lilydale, formerly a residential community, extends to the west of Harriet Island and is now an undeveloped floodplain. It used to be the site of former Twin City Brick Co.'s mining operations, until the company exposed extensive fossil beds, making the area well known among professional and amateur paleontologists, who are sometimes allowed to accom-

---

As of 2005, parking is free in all parks in the Three Rivers Park District (formerly known as Hennepin Parks).

---

pany professionals on guided digs at the park. A connected pond and about 200 acres of marsh and woodlands provide habitat for varied flora and fauna.

Mears Park
366 Sibley Street, St. Paul

Located near Galtier Plaza in the distinctive, anachronistic Lowertown neighborhood of St. Paul, Mears Park serves as the neighborhood's village commons. The park is a popular lunchtime and evening gathering spot and is filled with trees, flowers, benches, sculpture, and even a rippling creek. Summertime brings outdoor concerts, performances, events, and festivals. In winter the park's many trees are covered with hundreds of thousands of twinkling lights. Restored bridges across Interstate 94 serve as beautiful gateways to the neighborhood.

Phalen Regional Park
Off Wheelock Parkway and East Larpenteur Avenue, St. Paul
(651) 632–5111
www.stpaul.gov/depts/parks

Founded in 1899, Phalen Regional Park surrounds the quiet residential area around Phalen and Round Lakes in northeast St. Paul, with 3.2 miles of paved trails, an amphitheater, a beach, an 18-hole golf course, and a picnic shelter and pavilion. The park is named for Edward Phelan (whose name was spelled various ways), the earliest settler of the land around Phalen Creek. The park's trails connect to the Gateway State Trail, a paved biking and walking trail stretching from downtown St. Paul to Pioneer Park, north of Stillwater.

Rice Park
140 Washington Street, St. Paul

In the shadow of Landmark Center, the Ordway Center for the Performing Arts, the St. Paul Public Library, and the Saint Paul Hotel, St. Paul's Rice Park is a restful yet active square of greenery and monuments. Young trees provide a little shade during the day, but the park is at its best for summer concerts and as the ice sculpture hub of the annual St. Paul Winter Carnival.

GREATER METRO AREA

Afton State Park
6959 Peller Avenue South, Hastings
(651) 436–5391
www.dnr.state.mn.us/state_parks

Five miles south of the town of Afton, Afton State Park is a 1,702-acre wilderness area set along the St. Croix National Scenic Riverway. Opened in 1969 specifically to both preserve the native landscape and to give visitors the opportunity to see Minnesota wilderness up close, the park is located in a landscape of rolling glacial moraines and rocky bluffs, surrounded by thick hardwood woodlands and pine trees, with protected remnants of original prairie being aggressively restored by park management. In spring the grassy fields are sprinkled with prairie pasqueflowers and woodland ephemerals. In summer and early fall, the landscape gives way to thick bunches of butterfly weed, puccoons, sunflowers, and blazing star. Throughout the park visitors get picture-perfect glimpses of the slow-moving St. Croix River.

Among the activities visitors enjoy at Afton, bird-watching is one of the most popular. Red-tailed hawks hunt for rabbits, and eagles soar high above the bluffs. Native and migratory waterfowl can be seen along the riverbanks, while bluebirds, meadowlarks, and migratory birds make their homes in the prairie grasses each year. The park is home to an amazing diversity of wild animals native to Minnesota, including deer, fox badgers, squirrels, and wild turkeys. This is a great spot for fishing in summer and winter; walleye, sauger, and smallmouth bass can be caught either along the riverbank or over the side of your canoe.

Afton State Park has more than 20 miles of paved and groomed trails for horseback riding and hiking in spring and

Elegant Rice Park is one of the many small parks in St. Paul. SAINT PAUL RCVA

summer. In winter many of these trails are left open for cross-country skiers and snowshoers to explore. The park office has maps of the park available for visitors, and, while the park does not have a naturalist on staff, many activities are offered throughout the year by volunteers who lead snowshoe hikes, demonstrate bird-banding practices, and teach visitors how to identify many of the birds that visit the park. There are also several primitive camping sites with nearby access to hiking trails—reservations are needed from April to November but not from November to April.

For kids Afton is a great place to play year-round. In summer Afton has a large, clean swimming beach near a picnic area and public restrooms. In winter Afton has a great sliding hill for sleds, toboggans, and tubes, as well as a warming house to huddle in before and after playing in the snow. The visitor center offers one-day classes for kids on flower and bird identification, hiking, snowshoeing, and cross-country skiing.

Anoka County Riverfront Regional Park/Islands of Peace
5100 East River Road, Fridley
(763) 757-3920
www.anokacountyparks.com
This Anoka County park's biking, hiking, and ungroomed cross-country skiing trails are right in the Twin Cities metropolitan area, offering nice views of the Mississippi River all along the trails. Canoes can be rented from the park, and fishing is permitted from the shore and the river. If you're lucky enough to hook some lunch, grills and picnic shelters are also available.

The Islands of Peace segment of the park, located north of Interstate 694, has been developed by the Foundation for Islands of Peace. Chase's Island and the adjacent riverfront land are used as a recreational facility for the general public and for adults and children with disabilities. A reception center has a fireplace, restrooms, a library, a lounge, and meeting rooms for use by the public. A walk bridge and paved trail link the center to Chase's Island facilities, which include paved trails, shelter, river viewing, and picnic facilities—all with wheelchair access. The 57-acre Durnam Island segment, located in the river west of Chase's Island, has only recently been developed into nature trails to accommodate the disabled and the general public, with a boat shuttle service back and forth from the island.

The Anoka County Riverfront Regional Park also acts as a trailhead for the trail segment to the south along East River Road, connecting the Minneapolis trail system and the trail segment to the north to Islands of Peace in Fridley. An additional trail link to Brooklyn Center exists as well, with a trail crossing over the I-694 bridge.

Rice Park and Mears Park in downtown St. Paul are picturesque stroll-worthy urban pockets, especially in winter, when they're decorated with myriad white lights.

Baker Park Reserve
County Road 19, between Minnesota
Highways 12 and 55
(763) 479-2473
www.threeriversparkdistrict.org
Located on Lake Independence in central Hennepin County, just a 20-minute drive from much of the metro area, Baker Park Reserve's 2,700 acres offer diverse outdoor activities in natural surroundings. Baker Park offers a 213-site campground, golf at the Baker National Golf Course, swimming and boating in Lake Independence, and a playground for kids. The kids' playground area is truly spectacular, almost fortresslike, and is one of the reasons that this is such a popular family

park and a great place to take kids of all ages. Kids scramble over ramps, platforms, and paths made of recycled rubber mats that protect against minor falls and bumps and bruises.

In winter a sliding hill, a cozy warming chalet, and groomed cross-country ski trails are opened. In summer paved hiking and biking trails wind through one of the remnants of a Big Woods forest. Boats, bikes, and skis are available for rent through the park's visitor center.

Bald Eagle–Otter Lakes Regional Park
5800 Hugo Road, White Bear Township
(651) 748-2500
www.co.ramsey.mn.us/parks
Bald Eagle–Otter Lakes Regional Park, comprising 884 acres, is located in White Bear Lake in the northeast corner of Ramsey County. The park is a large natural area in a developing suburban neighborhood, with extensive woods, wetlands, and grasslands. The park is home to many species of wildlife, including red foxes, deer, woodcocks, herons, turtles, minks, beavers, and muskrats. Two relatively rare species of wildlife, osprey and otters, have also been sighted in this park. More than 3 miles of paved and woodchip-covered hiking trails offer visitors the opportunity to experience nature up close. The two lakes at the park, Fish Lake and Tamarack Lake, are open to shore and lake fishing, and Fish Lake is a popular spot for ice fishers in winter.

The Tamarack Nature Center offers a variety of programs, including bird-watching tours, syrup making, guided summer hikes, and winter snowshoe walks. Inside the nature center itself are mounted displays of many animals native to the area, several of which were made by famous taxidermist Walter Breckenridge, former director of the Bell Museum of Natural History.

Battle Creek Regional Park
2300 Upper Afton Road East, St. Paul
(651) 748-2500
www.co.ramsey.mn.us/parks

Battle Creek Regional Park, consisting of 1,840 acres in the southeast corner of St. Paul and southern Maplewood, provides a large natural area in a highly developed urban environment. The park's extensive areas of woods, wetlands, and grasslands provide habitat for many species of wildlife, including deer, foxes, herons, egrets, and hawks. Biking and hiking trails offer visitors the opportunity to view the birds and animals as well as the beauty of the vegetation. Winter visitors can tour the park on groomed cross-country trails. A large picnic pavilion accommodates groups of up to 500 people, and smaller picnic shelters are also available. In summer the park has a weekly concert series that showcases everything from local alternative acts to acoustic jazz combos.

Baylor Regional Park
County Road 33, Norwood
(952) 466-5250
www.co.carver.mn.us/parks

Baylor Regional Park is located in the extreme southwest corner of the Twin Cities, so far removed from the bright lights of the downtowns that it's a favorite observation point for junior astronomy clubs and amateur stargazers of all ages. Perched on the shoulder of Eagle Lake and surrounded by farmers' fields, Baylor preserves a rich mix of native habitats, from the large grove of mature maple trees that are tapped in early spring each year for maple syrup, to the floating boardwalk that carries visitors over wetland marshes to get a glimpse of turtles, waterfowl, and wildflowers.

The park offers a 50-site tent and RV campground with 30 utility sites, two shower facilities, a swimming beach and bathhouse on Eagle Lake, two large picnic shelters, tennis courts, and 5 miles of hiking trails. A community room in the park barn is available with advance reservations for group usage. In winter the 5 miles of hiking trails turn into a neatly groomed cross-country ski trail, and a warming house is available for outdoor enthusiasts from 8:00 A.M. to sunset daily.

Three Rivers Park District's 25-foot climbing wall regularly moves to different parks in the park system—contact Three Rivers (763-694-7718; www.threeriversparkdistrict.com) to find out its current location. You can rent the wall on- or off-site, too.

Bryant Lake Regional Park
6800 Rowland Road, Eden Prairie
(763) 694-7764
www.threeriversparkdistrict.org

Bryant Lake Regional Park is located south of Minnesota Highway 62 and west of Shady Oak Road on Rowland Road and has a three-season concession plaza, three-season pavilion, a paved boat launch, a fishing pier, a swimming beach, a boat rental building, and 3 miles of turf and paved hiking/biking trails. The 170-acre park also provides habitat for deer, waterfowl, and songbirds; fishing, boating, swimming, and ice fishing are just some of the ways visitors can get close to the natural beauty of this metro-area park. Located in the suburb of Eden Prairie, the park is set in a vista of rolling hills that block out the surrounding city lights and sounds, making it a perfect spot for an urban escape.

Carver Park Reserve
7025 Victoria Drive, Victoria
(763) 694-7650
www.threeriversparkdistrict.org

Visiting a park as large as Carver Park Reserve in the suburbs may seem natural today, but it was quite controversial when first proposed. Carver Park was authorized for purchase in 1964, and a lawsuit requesting the purchase be found illegal was soon filed by developers who wanted the land for housing. The claim was rejected in 1966, and Hennepin Parks (now Three Rivers Park District) went on to purchase parkland in Anoka, Scott, and Wright Counties. Today folks throughout the metro area are the beneficiaries of the park district's early imperialist urges, and the trailblazer, Carver Park Reserve, is one of the crown jewels of the system, with 3,500 acres with lakeshore frontage on six major lakes.

At the head of the reserve is Lowry Nature Center, designed for adults, schoolchildren, and families alike. Lowry Nature Center offers programs that focus on Carver's abundant natural resources, ranging from fall bird migration and waterfowl watches to the springtime activity of maple-syrup making and stargazing in the summer, as well as tracking mink, voles, and foxes and building snowcaves. The park itself is home to deer, foxes, owls, hawks, and many other animals that can be seen from roads and trails. Wetland animals can be seen from more than 1,700 feet of boardwalk that takes you through marsh and tamarack swamps. For small children, Habitats, a creative education play area, features larger-than-life flowers to climb on, dragonfly eyes to peer through, and a beaver lodge to sit in.

Park facilities include a boat launch, 54 campsites at Lake Auburn, and four different lakes for canoeing, fishing, and ice fishing as well as trails for hiking, horseback riding, cross-country skiing, snowmobiling, and snowshoeing. On winter weekends the park turns a wood-heated barn into a warming house for outdoor enthusiasts, with snack counters and restroom facilities conveniently located nearby. Cross-country skis, Norwegian kick sleds, and bicycles can be seasonally rented from the park.

Coon Rapids Dam Regional Park
103 West River Road, Brooklyn Park
(763) 694-7790
www.threeriversparkdistrict.org
Situated on the banks of the Mississippi River, the 610-acre Coon Rapids Dam Regional Park offers visitors the chance to see our nation's greatest river up close. The centerpiece of this large regional park

is the refurbished Coon Rapids Dam, which spans the Mississippi River. A wide dam walkway, usable by pedestrians, bicyclists, and in-line skaters, allows visitors a unique opportunity to walk across a working dam, with a scenic view of the riverway above and below the dam.

Interpretive signs describing the history of the dam and natural features related to the river line the bridge on the river side of the railing; the visitor center provides outstanding exhibits about the history and construction of the dam, especially focusing on the economic, cultural, and environmental impact the Mississippi River has on the lives of people who live and depend on having a clean and well-managed riverway that extends all the way south to New Orleans. Boating is allowed north of the visitor center, with a boat launch for accessing the north Mississippi River waterway through a naturally sheltered backwater.

Trout fishing is also allowed in Cenaiko Trout Lake, a beautiful lake stocked with rainbow and brook trout (Minnesota fishing license with State Trout Stamp affixed required), located at the east side of the park. Fishing piers are also located on the southern shore of Cenaiko Trout Lake, and bank fishing is reasonably clear with some brush and weeds. Bait and tackle supplies can be purchased at the visitor center for reasonable prices. Bicycles and in-line skate rentals are available at the visitor center for use on many of the paths.

The stunning Native Prairie Restoration Area is on the nearby banks of the river, just past the visitor center entrance and extending to the picnic plaza. The park has two well-developed and conveniently linked and accessible asphalt bike/hike trails—all part of the extensive Mississippi River Trail Corridor that leads users south into Anoka Regional Park and eventually connects users with the Minneapolis Parkway Trail System at Boom Island and the Heritage Trail at historic Main Street in Minneapolis.

Cottage Grove Ravine Regional Park
Half a mile east of Washington County
Road 19 and Minneapolis Highway 61,
Cottage Grove
(651) 430–8240
www.co.washington.mn.us
This handsome 506-acre park stays pretty quiet except when the high school teams are practicing. The park name refers to the nearby town (organized in May 1858) and the wooded ravine that was formed in glacial times and may once have been a channel of the St. Croix River. The park is home to native Minnesota wildlife, including the pileated woodpecker. These spectacular birds have a flaming red crest and can reach 16 inches in height. If a loud jackhammering sound breaks the silence, you'll know they are close by.

In winter this is a great park for the experienced skier, with almost 150 feet in elevation change and some great downhill runs through heavily wooded, dramatic ravines. It is also a popular spot for ski skaters.

Crow-Hassan Park Reserve
West of Rogers on Sylvan Lake Road,
Rogers
(763) 694–7860
www.threeriversparkdistrict.com
A visit to the 2,600-acre Crow-Hassan Park Reserve invokes images of the early pioneers as they crossed the wilderness in covered wagons. On the prairies of Crow-Hassan, those days are replicated with wagon rides during the annual Prairie Fest, not to mention in the wide, open spaces of the restored prairies themselves. No matter what time of year one visits, the prairie is colorful: Spring brings delicate blue and violet wildflowers, summer produces stands of tall grasses that dance in the breeze, fall offers a spectacular, fluorescent-hued display of reds and oranges, and winter leaves white snow, drifting like ocean waves. It's hard to imagine an endless sea of grass flowing from Minnesota to the Rocky Mountains now that trees, crops, houses, and billboards muddy the view. But one of the

best places in the Twin Cities to catch a glimpse of that sweeping landscape is this park, where 600 acres of old farm fields have been transformed back into prairie.

The reintroduction of native grasses and forbs began here in 1969, using seeds from a two-acre remnant of virgin prairie located in the park near Prairie Lake. Other sources were also tapped to complete the collection of nearly 100 species that have been planted since, and with the reintroduction of native grasses and plants, native animals have slowly made their way back to the land as well. Deer, foxes, coyotes, trumpeter swans, hawks, and bald eagles may be seen from the many miles of trails that wind through the park as well as on the nearby Crow River.

For pet owners, more than 30 acres of open space allows dogs to run off leash; a special permit is required and is available from Three Rivers Park District Headquarters for about $25 per year. This is also a popular park for horseback riders, with more than 15 miles of trail dedicated for just this purpose. In winter cross-country skiing and snowmobiling bring crowds of enthusiasts. The beauty of Crow-Hassan, though, is that in between the rolling hills, the deep prairie grass, and the thick tree cover, you can come out here and be as completely alone as you want to be, even if the park is at peak season.

Elm Creek Park Reserve
County Road 81 and Territorial Road,
Osseo
(763) 694–7894
www.threeriversparkdistrict.org
The Elm Creek Park Reserve, located northwest of Osseo, is a beautiful and varied park and nature reserve that makes a concerted effort to provide access to people of all abilities and ages. A swimming beach, creative play area, and a concession stand with volleyball, horseshoe, and bike rentals are located on the premises, and horse trails, cross-country ski trails, hiking trails, and bicycle paths interlace the entire park.

At 4,900 acres, Elm Creek Park

Reserve is the largest in the Three Rivers system. Wildlife is abundant in Elm Creek because of the numerous streams and marshes: Herons, ducks, and beavers can be viewed from miles of trails. Coyotes are also known to roam the wilds of Elm Creek, though your chances of seeing one are slim. Five lakes, three streams and wetlands, hardwood forest, and reclaimed farmland provide plenty of elbow room for wildlife and parkgoers alike.

The Eastman Nature Center provides stimulation for curious minds of all ages, with displays giving a concise overview of the reserve's habitat. From here hikers can go on self-guided tours ranging from wild-flower walks to a trip through turtle country. If the displays don't move you into the woods, the enthusiastic naturalists and creative courses (on tagging monarch butterflies, for example) offered will. On late afternoon weekend days in January and February, Eastman packs them in to view the white-tailed deer that come to feed.

Elm Creek also has a good-size creative play area and is another recipient of the Playground Appreciation Association Award, voted on by kids of the Minneapolis Public School System.

French Regional Park
12605 County Road 9, Plymouth
(763) 694-7750
www.threeriversparkdistrict.org
French Regional Park, usually shortened to "French Park" by locals, was named for the first superintendent of the Hennepin County park system, Clifton E. French. Under French's direction, the park system underwent an unprecedented period of development through the 1960s until his retirement in 1984. Under his guidance, Hennepin Parks (now Three Rivers Park District) became the largest landowner in the county and acquired parcels in four adjacent counties.

Located on 310 acres on Medicine Lake—which was originally called / (mouth) *ca-pa go!* (beaver) *ca-ga-sta-ka* (free from ice, broken) *mde* (lake) by the Dakota Indi-

ans—French Regional Park features water-based activities. A self-guided canoe trail through the backwaters of beautiful Medicine Lake provides intimate views of wetland wildlife. Monthly outdoor education programs for the public feature such activities as maple syruping, bird-watching, and guided hikes to beaver lodges. The open landscape of rolling glacial hills is broken along the lake and lagoons with second-growth forest. Windy days can be chilly, but the fine vista of the downtown Minneapolis skyline in the late afternoon sun is well worth it. This is not a place to come for solitude. The park's central location attracts more than 20,000 skiers—half at night—during a good season.

The visitor center has a concession area with rental equipment, from cross-country skis to volleyballs. A creative play area is available for people of all ages and abilities, and a shuttle tram runs throughout the summer season between the visitor center and the swimming beach. French Park's playground has won recognition from the Playground Appreciation Association, sponsored by the Minneapolis Public School System and voted on by kids of the schools themselves, for having the best "training ground" for tag players for its "many opportunities for climbing, rolling, running, falling, and navigating through cargo nets."

Hyland Lake Park Reserve
10145 Bush Lake Road, Bloomington
(763) 694-7687
www.threeriversparkdistrict.org
When visiting the 1,000-acre Hyland Lake Park Reserve, one can hardly believe it's located in the middle of the bustling metropolis of Bloomington. The parklands, which include prairie lands, deciduous woods, and Normandale, Hyland, and Bush Lakes, have more than 9 miles of trails for hiking, an additional 5 paved miles for bicycling, and, in winter, 8 miles of groomed trail set aside for cross-country skiing. The first cross-country ski trail in the Twin Cities was cut here, near the old Bush Lake ski jump in the winter of

1965–66. Hyland Lake Park Reserve is now one of the finest and most popular cross-country facilities in the area.

On the lakes there's a boat landing with a newly built rental/storage facility for canoes, rowboats, and paddleboats, as well as a large fishing pier for shore fishing. Bush Lake has a clean swimming beach with picnic shelters nearby. Skis, bicycles, paddleboats, and seasonal recreation equipment can be rented at the visitor center for reasonable rates.

The Richardson Nature Center, located inside the park, is home to deer, pheasants, and wild songbirds. Richardson's spacious center focuses especially on raptors and raptor recovery, with programs on eagles, owls, hawks, and falcons. You can see ospreys banded and meet live owls, hawks, and kestrels. Other classes taught by naturalists include how to build bluebird houses, identify birds and waterfowl, use natural plant materials to dye things—Easter eggs, yarn, paper—or create nature-friendly lawns.

Interstate State Park/ Glacial-Pothole Trail
On Minnesota Highway 8 in Taylors Falls
(651) 465–5711
www.dnr.state.mn.us/state_parks
Carved by glacial meltwater, Interstate State Park follows the cliffs and bluffs bordering the beautiful St. Croix River. Established in 1895 when Minnesota and Wisconsin created separate parks across from each other on the St. Croix River, this was the first example of an interstate collaboration in the country. During the late 1930s Interstate State Park received the highest number of visitors of any park in the state—327,496 in 1937 alone.

The main attraction of the park, besides the St. Croix, are the unusual basalt formations and potholes and greenstone cliffs that were formed before there was any complex life on Earth. The Pre-cambrian basalt boulders make up the Glacial-Pothole Trail, which is amazing to explore. The Glacial-Pothole Trail is a rough-hewn pathway through the maze of

"potholes"—deep, perfectly circular holes carved into the hard basalt by glaciers—some of which are hundreds of feet deep and the deepest known glacial potholes in the world. Interstate State Park also holds annual wildflower exhibits, and some of the flowers that bloom here no longer naturally grow anywhere else in the state.

There is much to do at Interstate State Park. Visitors can climb the cliffs of the St. Croix River Dalles, canoe the flatwater, watch kayakers rush through the rapids, or relax on an excursion boat. Spring brings wildflowers, and in fall the St. Croix River Valley forest is ablaze in the autumn colors of red, gold, and orange. The geology that formed this park intrigues visitors and brings geologists from all over the world. At least 10 different lava flows are exposed in the park, along with two distinct glacial deposits and traces of old streams' valleys and faults. The park's visitor center is carved out of the dense, black basalt that makes up most of the Glacial-Pothole Trail and the Glacial Gardens. During the summer a park naturalist provides tours of the glacial potholes, a landmark of the park, and programs detailing the natural history of the area.

The park has a 22-acre summer campground with 22 electric sites located near the Glacial-Pothole Trail and Glacial Gardens that fills up quickly in the summer months—reservations are highly encouraged. Canoes can be rented at the nearby boat dock and can be reserved by calling the park.

Lake Elmo Park Reserve
1515 Keats Avenue North, Lake Elmo
(1 mile north of I-94 on Washington County Road 19)
(651) 430–8370
www.co.washington.mn.us
The Lake Elmo Park Reserve is 2,165 acres of forest, wetlands, and prairie restoration lands. Eighty percent of the parkland is set aside for preservation and protection, and because of this, Lake Elmo is home to a huge variety of native animals, birds, reptiles, and fish. People come to Lake

The Big Deal about the Big Woods

The Big Woods was a forest that once occupied 3,030 square miles in south-central Minnesota. The forest was composed of maple, basswood, white and red elm, red oak, tamarack, and red cedar on the banks of numerous lakes. The trees were so thick that sunlight couldn't penetrate to the forest floor in some places. French explorers who came to the area called the forest "Bois Grand," or "Bois Fort," which was later amended by English settlers to the "Big Woods." Today farms, towns, suburbs, and industry have replaced much of the Big Woods. Fortunately, the 1,590 acres located at the northern edge of what was once the Big Woods retain a remnant of the grandness of these original forests as Lake Maria State Park.

Elmo year-round for both shore and boat fishing, canoeing, hiking, swimming, and cross-country skiing. There are also four campgrounds with a total of 108 campsites, restroom facilities, lighted picnic shelters with electricity, hand pumps for water, and a two-acre swim pond that's regularly maintained by the park.

Lake Maria State Park
11411 Clementa Avenue NW, Monticello
(763) 878-2325
www.dnr.state.mn.us/state_parks
Visitors who come to Lake Maria State Park will enjoy one of the few remaining stands of the Big Woods, a maple, oak, and basswood forest that once covered part of southern Minnesota. The park is perfect for hikers, backpackers, horseback riders, and cross-country skiers who enjoy the challenge of the rolling terrain. Take a stroll on the boardwalk that winds through a marsh. Backpack sites, located on remote lakes and ponds throughout the park, are just 2 miles from the trail-head parking lot. New log camper cabins, located near lakes and ponds, provide bunk beds for six people and a table and benches for campers who want more of the creature comforts.

The park maintains more than 20 miles of summer hiking trails, 16 miles of groomed cross-country ski trails, and 3 miles of winter hiking trails. Snowshoeing is permitted anywhere in the park except on groomed ski trails, and snowshoes can be rented at the visitor center for about $6.00 a day. Boat and canoe rentals are available through the visitor center in summer, and three camper cabins and numerous secluded primitive campsites are available for rent year-round.

Although there is no full-time naturalist on staff, interpretive programs are available year-round. The marshes, potholes, and lakes here provide excellent habitat for wildlife, and approximately 205 different species of birds have been reported living in, or passing through the park on seasonal migrations. Visitors have seen bald eagles, Cooper's hawks, Franklin's gulls, osprey, egrets, loons, trumpeter swans, great blue herons, marsh hawks, and goldfinches, as well as screech, great-horned, snowy, and short-eared owls. Shrews, bats, moles, rabbits, woodchucks, red and gray squirrels, pocket gophers, beaver, mice, fishers, muskrats, mink, striped skunks, red foxes, and white-tailed deer also make Lake Maria State Park their home. Lake Maria is one of the last remaining natural habitats of the endangered Blanding's turtle, easily identified by bright yellow spots on its shell.

Lake Minnetonka Regional Park
4610 County Road 44, Minnestrista
(763) 694-7754
www.threeriversparkdistrict.org
This 292-acre park features picnic areas, a visitor center, a fishing pier, a boat launch with 48 car or trailer parking spaces, a unique 1.75-acre upland swimming pond with chlorinated water, and a wheelchair-accessible swimming ramp that extends into the pond. The visitor center, which was formerly a private residence, contains meeting rooms, a reception area, exhibits concerning the area around Lake Minnetonka and the people and activities associated with it, and an exterior garden containing a huge variety of native medicinal and herbal plants.

The park has a nice fishing pier, with two seated angler stations, that allows people of all abilities the opportunity to not only enjoy fishing but also to sit on the water and enjoy the beautiful view of the lake. There's a concession stand next to the changing rooms/bathrooms by the picnic area with accessible tables where folks can purchase goodies while enjoying the water. The beach is well maintained, with large umbrellas located around the water for families to use to keep themselves cool on the hottest summer days.

Lake Minnewashta Regional Park
Off Minnesota Highway 41 between Minnesota Highways 5 and 7, Chanhassen
(952) 466-5250
www.co.carver.mn.us/parks
Lake Minnewashta Park is a large, suburban park that contains remnants of the Big Woods that once covered this area. Some of the oak trees here are so old that they're more than 12 feet in circumference. An ambitious reforestation project that included the planting of 25,000 new hardwoods was completed a few years ago but will realistically take many years to re-create the leafy canopy that once covered the park.

This park is really tucked away and is visited mostly by locals, and at times you probably have a better chance of seeing deer than people while visiting. Lake Minnewashta is a popular fishing lake, allowing powerboats, canoes, and sailboats in summer and ice fishing in winter.

Lake Rebecca Park Reserve
9831 County Road 50, Rockford
(763) 694-7860
www.threeriversparkdistrict.org
From canoeing on the Crow River to boat and ice fishing on Lake Rebecca, this 2,200-acre park reserve offers outdoor activities in settings that suggest you are much farther away from the metropolitan area than you actually are. Lake Rebecca Park Reserve's gently rolling landscape, with numerous wetland areas, provides a haven for wildlife, including deer, beavers, and waterfowl. This park reserve is also one of the sites for the trumpeter swan restoration program, and several overlooks along hiking trails provide glimpses of these swans, which are the world's largest waterfowl. Boats are available for rent from the park's visitor center, and nonmotorized boat launching is permitted. Reservation picnic areas and group campsites are available.

Lebanon Hills Regional Park
Pilot Knob Road South of Cliff Road, Eagan
(651) 554-6530
www.co.dakota.mn.us/parks
Less than 30 minutes from both downtown Minneapolis and St. Paul, this Dakota County park covers more than 2,000 acres of lakes, marshes, beaches, and trails. Open year-round, the park is divided into east and west sections connected by an immense network of trails. Nearly every outdoor activity is available—swimming in Schultz Lake (one of the few local beaches with lifeguards present), RV and tent camping, hiking, picnicking, horseback riding, mountain biking, and cross-country skiing. Fishing and all nonmotorized boats are allowed on Jensen Lake, and in winter ice fishing is allowed on the lake as well.

Lebanon Hills is a popular destination for winter sports enthusiasts. The park has two great ski areas: the 4K skate-ski lanes just off of Johnny Cake Road offer long, tough uphills and fast, winding downhills and is definitely not a place for beginners (this area doubles as a mountain bike area in summer, and the rock-and-dirt trails don't hold snow all that well), and the 19.8K classic-track area, just east of Pilot Knob Road. The trail system was originally laid out for hiking and horse paths, so some downhill corners can be awkward for skiers. Cross-country ski and snowmobile trails snake through the park's wooded, hilly terrain, and hot cocoa and snacks are available at the warming house at Schultz Lake.

Long Lake Regional Park
1500 Old MN 8, New Brighton
(651) 748–2500
www.co.ramsey.mn.us/parks

Long Lake Regional Park is located in the city of New Brighton in the northwestern part of Ramsey County. The 218 acres of parkland include 1.5 miles of shoreline on Long Lake and a natural area around Rush Lake, a nonrecreational lake. Rush Lake is surrounded by cattail marshes, oak woods, and a nine-acre restored prairie, seeded in 1987, which is now reaching maturity and offers a beautiful display of prairie flowers throughout the summer.

The park features an extensive trail system, a beautiful swimming beach, and a large picnic area near the swimming beach. Visitors can watch mallards paddle through the cattail marshes, take a stroll through the oak woods, or bike around the nine-acre restored prairie. After a dip in Long Lake, make tracks to the beach house for snacks, restrooms, changing rooms, and showers. A large picnic pavilion is complete with kitchen and public restrooms, and the group picnic area features a game field, a volleyball court, hiking/biking trails, and a wheelchair-accessible play area. On the south end of Long Lake, you can launch your boat and park your trailer—or just fish off the pier. Although the grounds are spread out quite a bit (the fishing

pier is a couple of miles away on the south end of Long Lake, while most of the park is on the north end of the lake), the layout of the park's facilities is actually very convenient. The pier has its own parking area with restrooms and a clean water source, and access from there to the pier is a paved walkway that's level and free of obstacles. Seated angler stations are situated on the pier for additional comfort and convenience.

Minnesota Valley National Wildlife Refuge and Recreation Area
3815 American Boulevard, Bloomington
(952) 854–5900

Only minutes from the Twin Cities and the airport, Minnesota Valley National Wildlife Refuge and Recreation Area is dedicated to preserving the wildlife of Minnesota River habitats. This archipelago of river-valley land parcels functions as a federally managed nature preserve, particularly for waterfowl and migrating birds using the Minnesota River flyway. All told, 10,514 acres are at your disposal, including the Minnesota Valley Trail, which links Fort Snelling State Park and units of the Minnesota Valley National Wildlife Refuge to waysides and other public lands. The area is ideal for hiking, biking, cross-country skiing, mountain biking, and snowmobiling. The landscapes are just as diverse as the trail system and include wetlands, floodplain forest, remnants of farmlands settled in the late 1800s, and blufftop oak savanna. Wildlife observation and bird-watching are popular activities year-round, while seasonally canoeing, cross-country skiing, bicycling, snowshoeing, and camping give visitors additional views of the park.

In the Minnesota Valley Recreation Area you can see the only remaining building from the town of St. Lawrence, visit the Jabs Farm Homestead, or ride your bike across a 1900s railroad bridge.

Today a brightly lit, modern interpretive center in the park contains engaging displays of Minnesota River Valley history, ranging from its pollution perils—and comebacks—to a primer on the glacial forces that created the valley. The refuge's real strength is in its programs led by talented naturalists, who offer field trips to the woodcock dancing grounds in spring and to the heron rookery in winter via cross-country skis. The wildlife refuge occupies only a fraction of the Minnesota Valley Recreation Area, which is classified as a Minnesota State Park and stretches about 75 miles from historic Fort Snelling to Le Sueur.

Murphy-Hanrehan Park Reserve
15501 Murphy Lake Road, Savage
(952) 447–6913
www.threeriversparkdistrict.org
The glacial ridges and hilly terrain of northwest Scott County make Murphy-Hanrehan one of the most challenging cross-country ski areas found in the Twin Cities. With the exception of the trails, this 2,400-acre park remains undeveloped. The park's hilly terrain attracts mountain bikers, horseback riders, and endurance hikers in summer and cross-country skiers, snowmobilers, and especially brave downhill skiers in winter.

Noerenberg Memorial Gardens
2840 North Shore Drive, Wayzata
(763) 559–6700
www.threeriversparkdistrict.org
In 1972 the last surviving child of Frederick and Johanna Noerenberg—heirs to the Grain Belt brewery fortune—bequeathed the family lakeside estate to Hennepin County. The bequest stipulated that the 73 acres of flower beds, shade trees, and ornamental grasses be opened to the public, and that the enormous Queen Anne house, built in 1890 and one of the first constructed on Lake Minnetonka's shores, be torn down to prevent a roving public from wandering through the intimate remains of the past. The bequest also called for a memorial to be constructed from the housing materials, which became the white-pillared colonnade that now stands on the grounds. The family grape arbor and gazebo/boathouse

were also left standing; they are the sole man-made structures on the premises.

Today the park features beautifully sculpted flower gardens that include unusual annuals and perennials, an assortment of grasses, and a large daylily collection. The park is a beautiful spot to stroll through and enjoy the flowers—however, part of the bequest of the Noerenberg family states that no picnics or boating activities are to be permitted on the premises, so mild hiking and sightseeing covers the range of what park visitors can do here.

St. Croix Bluffs Regional Park
10191 St. Croix Trail South, Hastings
(651) 430–8240
www.co.washington.mn.us
Five miles south of Afton, this 579-acre regional park is made up of rolling hills, blufftop hardwood forests, and nearly a mile of scenic St. Croix River shoreline. Woodlands and ravines cut through tight bluffs to the riverbanks, making great bird-watching areas for everything from eagles to wild turkeys. The park is located on the west bank of the St. Croix River and has 0.75 mile of river frontage. Swimming is not allowed in the St. Croix, but boating, fishing, and ice fishing are.

St. Croix National Scenic Riverway
401 Hamilton Street,
St. Croix Falls, WI
(715) 483–3284
www.nps.gov/sacn
The St. Croix River stretches more than 150 miles and partially forms the boundary between Minnesota and Wisconsin. It is the only river in the world that's protected along its entire length. Beginning near Gordon, Wisconsin, it flows southerly to St. Croix Falls. The Lower St. Croix flows from St. Croix Falls dam to Prescott, Wisconsin, where it joins the Mississippi River. The Lower St. Croix is deeper, wider, and slower moving than the Upper St. Croix, making it a great place to fish, canoe, water-ski, and swim. Hot air balloon rides are available year-round and

provide an excellent view of the river and its lush banks from on high. Winter activities include ice fishing, downhill and cross-country skiing, tubing, snowmobiling, and sledding. Nearby Lake St. Croix is formed by a dam on the Mississippi River and is popular for water recreation.

Spring Lake Park Reserve
Off County Road 42, Hastings
(651) 438-4660
www.co.dakota.mn.us/parks
Enjoy the feel of northern Minnesota while hiking or skiing the scenic trails that wind through the woods and along the bluffs high above the Mississippi River. Spring Lake Park Reserve provides a scenic and peaceful setting for nature lovers to appreciate, as well as a model airplane flying field that will delight adults and children alike and a challenging, state-of-the-art archery trail. A youth campground with a heated lodge and an outdoor classroom is also available to youth groups interested in outdoor educational/ recreational activities.

Square Lake County Park
15450 Square Lake Trail North, Stillwater
(651) 430-8370
www.co.washington.mn.us
The 27-acre Square Lake County Park is known for having one of the clearest lakes in Minnesota, making it a popular spot for scuba divers, swimmers, and anglers alike. The lake is regularly stocked with trout and has a 950-foot clean sand beach, a concession stand where food and fishing supplies can be purchased, and restrooms with showers.

Theodore Wirth Park
1339 Theodore Wirth Parkway, Minneapolis
(612) 230-6400
www.minneapolisparks.org
Theodore Wirth first toured the parkland he would oversee in January 1906 using two horses and a sleigh, crossing what was then open country as he traveled from park to park. Wirth spent the next four decades developing these natural resources into one of the finest municipal park systems in the country. After he retired his favorite park of the bunch was named in his honor.

Theodore Wirth Park, or just Wirth Park, as it's usually called, is a huge chunk of land extending from Minneapolis at Glenwood Avenue to Lowry Avenue and from Vincent Avenue into Golden Valley. This beautiful 500-acre park surrounds Wirth Lake, which has a swimming beach as well as a boat launch. There's also an archery range, a playground, tennis courts, the Theodore Wirth Golf Course, and the Eloise Butler Wildflower Garden.

This is a popular park for locals in winter. Behind Theodore Wirth Park's great sledding hill (on the golf course's 10th fairway) is the lighted snow-tubing hill, which isn't too steep and has a tow rope. Cold, hungry snow tubers will appreciate the nearby Swiss Chalet, which has a fireplace and serves fast-food fare such as burgers and fries. Completed in 1923, the Swiss Chalet is the perfect headquarters for a winter recreational retreat and is based on a miniature chalet that Theodore Wirth had brought back from his honeymoon in Switzerland years before. Both a skate-skiing course and an intermediate traditional trail start from the chalet. From the top of the skiing hill, the Minneapolis skyscrapers glittering in the afternoon sun may startle you with their closeness. This is known as one of the prettiest places in the Cities for nighttime skiing.

Named for schoolteacher Eloise Butler, who is buried in the bird sanctuary, the Eloise Butler Wildflower Garden and Bird Sanctuary is a favorite spot for urbanites to escape the realities of city life and walk among the brilliant wildflower plots that are tended as carefully as they were when Butler was still alive. Eloise Butler feared that the wild beauty of Minnesota would be destroyed the way the old-growth hardwood forests near her childhood home in Maine had been, and she set about turn the three acres of land she owned into an immense wild garden full of native plants and grasses. After her death the Minneapolis Park Board created a preserve for native flora in her honor, which included her own original garden and has grown over the years to include an additional 12 acres. The park draws crowds of native and migratory songbirds, including meadowlarks, redwing blackbirds, and finches.

Wild River State Park
10 miles north of Center City
(651) 583-2125
www.dnr.state.mn.us/state_parks

Wild River State Park was established to protect the area's natural and cultural resources and to provide recreational opportunities along the St. Croix River. The park's name, Wild River, is derived from the fact that the St. Croix River was one of the original eight rivers protected by the U.S. Congress through the Wild and Scenic Rivers Act of 1968. Nearly 5,000 of the park's total 6,803 acres were donated by Northern States Power Company (now Xcel Energy).

Wild River State Park attracts people who enjoy camping, hiking, horseback riding, canoeing, interpretive programs, self-guided trails, and cross-country skiing. Day visitors can enjoy a leisurely paddle down the St. Croix River from the Sunrise River access to the southern park river access. The park provides opportunities for semimodern camping, group camping, backpack camping, canoe camping, and walk-in camping. Visitors who want modern amenities can reserve the guesthouse, which provides a living room, dining room, kitchen, and fireplace. The park also has two camping cabins, with bunk beds, a table, and benches. An all-season trail center is a great spot to relax after hiking or cross-country skiing on the 35-mile trail system. A visitor center with exhibits and environmental education programs is open year-round.

Naturalist programs at the park are available year-round to individuals as well as schools and other groups upon request. The park maintains 35 miles of groomed cross-country ski trails, 1.5 miles of packed hiking trails, and 1.5 miles of snowshoe trails—snowshoeing is permitted anywhere in the park except on groomed ski trails. Guided snowshoe tours include a visit to a beaver pond, identifying and following animal tracks, or a challenging trip down a short, steep slope to a hidden prairie (basic instructions on how to snowshoe are covered before the hikes, and snowshoes are provided at no charge for participants). The park also offers one-day classes on tapping maple trees for sap and making maple syrup.

Wild River provides habitat for a variety of wildlife. Hawks, owls, eagles, and a diversity of songbirds are common. The tracks of beaver, raccoons, foxes, coyotes, otters, mink, and deer are often seen in the soft earth or snow. Northern pike, walleye, and smallmouth bass are found in the St. Croix River. Squirrels and other small mammals thrive in oak forests and savannas; the prairie restoration sites are home to flocks of meadowlarks and sparrows.

Dogs are permitted on Regional Trail corridors and on designated turf trails in all parks. Pets must be on a leash no more than 6 feet long, and owners must clean up after pets and dispose of pet feces in a sanitary manner.

William O'Brien State Park
16821 O'Brien Trail North,
Marine on St. Croix
(651) 433-0500
www.dnr.state.mn.us/state_parks

A great "getaway" park only 45 minutes from the Twin Cities, the 1,520 acres of William O'Brien State Park provide a beautiful setting for quality recreation along the banks of the St. Croix River. The park is named for William O'Brien, a pioneer lumberman in the St. Croix River Valley, its man-made lake is named for O'Brien's daughter, Alice, who donated an additional 180 acres to the park in 1945.

O'Brien is an extremely popular camping spot, and in the summer the first-come, first-served campsites fill up quickly, especially on weekends; campsite reservations are strongly encouraged. The lower campground offers great river views, while the upper has both sunny, open spots and deeply wooded ones. The park has 125 drive-in campsites, 61 electric with a 60-foot RV limit, 2 walk-in sites, 7 wheelchair-accessible sites with wheelchair-accessible flush toilets and showers, 4 group camps, and a select number of camping cabins available to the public. Conveniently, the park's open picnic shelter sells firewood and ice to campers, and public phones are also available for campers' use.

Hiking trails offer quiet exploration of the park's rolling, wooded hills. For anglers, the channels of the St. Croix have northerns, walleye, bass, and trout. Ideal for canoeing, the river is also a migratory pathway that offers visitors an exciting diversity of sights and sounds. Canoes can be rented from the park for an outing on the St. Croix or on Lake Alice. Swimming in the river isn't allowed, but Lake Alice has a sandy beach and shallow water close to shore. On clear days you can see Taylors Falls from one overlook, and, although the park is heavily used, the 12 miles of hiking trails are rarely crowded. Many of these hiking trails (11.5 miles' worth) become cross-country trails for intermediate and expert skiers during winter. The park maintains 12 miles of groomed cross-country ski trails and 11 miles of skate-ski trails—snowshoeing is permitted anywhere in the park except on groomed ski trails. The park also has a warming house for huddling in after playing in the snow.

SPECTATOR SPORTS

People in the Twin Cities love sports. It is, however, a love tempered by regional priorities and perspectives on life. There are sports fanatics in this town, men and women whose hearts bleed the purple of the Minnesota Vikings football team or have not missed a Twins game in decades, but most Twin Citians practice a little more restraint. They love the local teams but also value a summer trip "up north" to the cabin at the lake or a night at the other entertainment options the Cities offer.

Twin Cities sports fans love winners. Win or lose, the teams receive support, but when they win, the area erupts. The Twins' two world championships in '87 and '91, as well as their improbable trip to the American League Championship Series in 2002 in a year Major League Baseball tried to contract the team, created a colossal public outpouring of local pride. St. Paul and Minneapolis streets were flooded with happy citizens waving their "homer hankies" and celebrating their team.

When in the Twin Cities, be sure to watch our sports teams. There is definitely something for everyone. Unlike in many other cities, parking is relatively easy to attend games at Cities sports facilities, which are surrounded by parking ramps and pay lots. Ticket prices are more reasonable than many larger markets; always check ahead, since ticket prices frequently change. The only exception is Minnesota Vikings games, which in recent years have routinely sold out before the start of the season; ticket prices start at around $50 per seat. If you want to see the Vikings, plan early to secure tickets.

AUTO RACING

Elko Speedway
26350 France Avenue, Elko
(952) 461-7223 or (800) 479-3630
www.goelkospeedway.com
For more than 20 years, Elko Speedway has been affiliated with NASCAR. Over the past decade Elko Speedway has witnessed spectator counts double and competitor counts more than double.

Elko Speedway is one of only 60 short racetracks in the nation sanctioned by NASCAR and a member of the Winston Racing Series. Late-model NASCARs race at Elko Speedway. The $^3/_8$-mile track has an asphalt and granite aggregate surface and high banking.

Elko Speedway usually has races from April through September, with races beginning in the early evening on Friday and Saturday.

Raceway Park
1 Checkered Flag Boulevard, Shakopee
(952) 445-5500
www.goracewaypark.com
Raceway Park offers NASCAR racing. This track has had racing for more than 49 years and emphasizes racing in a safe, family-oriented atmosphere. Raceway Park is in Shakopee, a beautiful town in the Twin Cities area, which is also home to Valleyfair! Amusement Park.

The most talented local drivers race at Raceway Park. There are racing events at the track geared toward children, such as novelty events.

Parking problems can be avoided by taking hotel shuttle buses to Twin Cities sporting events. Check with your hotel to see if this stress-saving option is available.

Xcel Energy Center, home of the NHL's Minnesota Wild. XCEL ENERGY CENTER

BASEBALL

Minnesota Twins
Metrodome, 34 Kirby Puckett Place,
Minneapolis
(612) 33–TWINS or (800) 33–TWINS
www.twins.mlb.com

In 2002 the Minnesota Twins shocked most of Major League Baseball by advancing to the American League Championship Series, where they finally fell to the eventual World Champion Anaheim Angels. For years under longtime manager Tom Kelly and the tight wallet of owner Carl Pohlad, the Twins organization cut salaries by signing young, unproven players. However, under new manager Rod Gardenhire in 2002, the Twins proved they were quite talented at spotting raw talent and developing young players into champions. Much of the championship team remains in Twins uniforms, and their future seems bright.

The Twins play at the Hubert H. Humphrey Metrodome ("the Dome" in local parlance), a large concrete structure capped with an expansive Teflon bubble located in downtown Minneapolis and surrounded by parking lots. Fans of the Dome enjoy its steady temperature, in the low 70s. Detractors find the Dome's environment sterile and dull and at times incredibly loud. The stadium has been renovated several times since opening in 1982 and is clean and comfortable, especially during a spring blizzard. However, there are some significant disadvantages for baseball fans. Seating down both the third base and first base lines requires patrons to crane their necks because of the sight lines, which were developed for football. Visiting outfielders and infielders fielding pop-ups complain about the roof, which is almost exactly the color of a baseball. Despite its shortcomings, the Dome is an adequate professional baseball facility.

Minnesota Twins baseball. MINNESOTA TWINS

Hopefully, in the near future the Twins and local politicians can amicably resolve "stadium issues."

Twins tickets can be purchased several ways and are readily available. For the 2005 season, ticket prices ranged from $6.00 for upper deck general admission to $41.00 for the "lower club" area behind home plate. These prices are subject to change.

The Twins have special offers and promotional events. One is Twins Culvers Kids Days games. Kids Days allow a paying adult to bring children to games for free. The free seats are always upper level general admission, and the sponsor and number of children who get in for free frequently changes. This has been a popular promotion since the '70s.

Twins tickets are available on the team's Web site, by phone, and in person. The Twins ticket office is located on the west side of the Dome facing the Minneapolis downtown skyline. Twins tickets can also be purchased at Twins Pro Shops in Apple Valley and Roseville and by mail by writing to Minnesota Twins Ticket Office SDS 12-1466, P.O. Box 86, Minneapolis, MN 55486-1466; be sure to include $4.00 for shipping and handling, and provide the game dates, seating preferences, and a legible return address.

St. Paul Saints
Midway Stadium, 1771 Energy Park
Drive, St. Paul
(651) 644–6659
www.saintsbaseball.com
On September 6, 1995, the independent minor-league St. Paul Saints had 4,637 fans attend their playoff game, while only 2,700 showed up for the Twins game.

The Saints create an ambience reminiscent of the glory days of baseball. All seats at Midway Stadium have a great view of the game. There are also good concessions and the omnipresent tailgating. Because of long and harsh winters, Twin Citians love outdoor baseball— a beer, a hot dog, summer sun, and baseball.

St. Paul Saints baseball stadium. ST. PAUL SAINTS

The St. Paul Saints are a hot ticket in the Twin Cities. The methods of purchasing Saints tickets are limited. The Saints can be reached by phone at (651) 644-6659 for phone orders, and tickets may be purchased at the stadium ticket office. Keep in mind that games can and frequently do sell out. As of this writing, it is not possible to purchase Saints tickets on their Web site or by e-mail.

Ticket prices are reasonable, considering there is not a bad seat at Midway Stadium, and in the past have ranged from $4.00 to $10.00, with special discounts for seniors and children ages 14 and younger. The Saints accept Visa, MasterCard, and Discover cards.

Parking is readily available for a small fee in the large parking lot abutting Midway Stadium. Feel free to bring some food for tailgating.

BASKETBALL

Minnesota Golden Gophers
Men's Basketball
Williams Arena, 1925 University Avenue SE, Minneapolis
(612) 624-8080 or (800) U-GOPHER
www.gophersports.com

The Twin Cities are great places if you're a basketball fan. The area boasts both men's and women's professional teams as well as the collegiate Big Ten men's team, the University of Minnesota Golden Gophers.

Since the 1895-96 season the Minnesota Golden Gophers basketball team has played in one of the most august and competitive conferences in collegiate sports, the Big Ten. Former NBA stars Mychal Thompson and Kevin McHale wore the Gophers' maroon and gold, as have a number of other NBA players currently playing and retired. Today coach Dan Monson is rebuilding the program that was hurt by an academic-fraud scandal in the 1990s.

Gophers boosters abound in the Twin Cities. The Gophers play at Williams Arena, a great place to watch basketball. It is a beautifully renovated brick building

The St. Paul Saints offer outdoor baseball at its best, but there's a lot besides baseball going on at the ballpark—get a massage by a nun, watch the between-game antics, or rent the hot tub seating in left field.

that feels comfortable yet electric because of the U of M students and alumni who attend games at "the barn."

You may purchase Gophers tickets by phone, online, or in person at Williams Arena. The University of Minnesota accepts Visa, MasterCard, Novus, and American Express. There is plenty of parking for Gophers basketball in lots on Oak Street.

Minnesota Golden Gophers
Women's Basketball
Williams Arena, 1925 University Avenue SE, Minneapolis
(612) 624-8080 or (800) U-GOPHER
www.gophersports.com

In 2002 the Minnesota Golden Gophers women's basketball team finished with its best record in more than 20 years, finishing 22-8 just one year after finishing a more typical 8-20. The Gophers finished second in the Big Ten (the best finish in the Big Ten standings in school history), advanced to the NCAA tournament, and finished the season ranked 19th in the country. Under coach Pam Borton, who took over the team in 2002, the future of Golden Gophers women's basketball looks bright.

Golden Gophers women's basketball has been in action since 1973 and competed as part of the Big Ten for the first time during the 1982-83 season. Tickets are available by phone, online, or in person at Williams Arena.

Minnesota Lynx
Target Center, 600 First Avenue North, Minneapolis
(612) 673-8400
www.wnba.com/lynx

After beginning play in 1999, the Minnesota Lynx are building a growing fan

Historic Williams Arena, home of the University of Minnesota Golden Gophers basketball teams. TODD R. BERGER

base with the WNBA's brand of basketball. The WNBA may not be as flashy as the NBA, but it shines on many other levels. Women's basketball is more team oriented, with plenty of well-executed passes, plays, and teamwork. Both on and off the court, the WNBA puts a premium on community involvement. The Lynx have several community initiatives. Events occur frequently, such as the Great Basketball Dribble. Annually fans, coaches, and players dribble basketballs to raise funds for early detection of breast cancer and breast cancer research. Other events are aimed at young children, including tickets for underprivileged kids and youth-beat reporter tryouts.

The Lynx share the Target Center with the Timberwolves; the season begins in late May and ends in early August. There are many seating options. Tickets are available in person at the Target Center and by phone. There is ample parking in

the several municipal ramps behind the arena. Prices ranged from $10 to $108 in 2005.

Minnesota Timberwolves
**Target Center, 600 First Avenue North, Minneapolis
(612) 763-1600
www.nba.com/timberwolves**
Professional basketball has a long history in Minnesota, going back long before the Timberwolves' recent successes. The Wolves debuted during the 1989-90 season, but did not reach the playoffs until the 1996-97 season. The Wolves 2003-04 season was the most successful in the team's history, when the team advanced to the Western Conference finals.

The Target Center was constructed for the Wolves in 1990 as a single-sport arena. This allowed the Wolves always to have the home-field advantage. The Target Center was the first Twin Cities facility

for one major-league franchise. Since then, Minnesota's NHL expansion team, the Wild, has opened the Xcel Energy Center exclusively for the Wild, and the Wolves now share the Target Center with the WNBA's Minnesota Lynx. Nevertheless, the Target Center feels like, and is, the home of the Wolves.

The Target Center is ideally located at the intersection downtown of the Warehouse District and the theater district. The structure fits tightly on its lot and almost spills out onto the street. It is comfortable on the inside, despite its size. Target Center has a capacity of 19,006.

Wolves tickets for the 2005–06 season ranged from $10 to $500 for a single game. There are several ticket plans, including full-season, half-season, 14-, and 7-game plans. Tickets are available in person at the Target Center and by phone. There is ample parking in the municipal ramps behind the arena.

FOOTBALL

**Minnesota Golden Gophers Football
Metrodome, 34 Kirby Puckett Place,
Minneapolis
(612) 624–8080 or (800) U–GOPHER
www.gophersports.com**
Long before the Minnesota Vikings arrived as an NFL expansion team, the Gophers were the Twin Cities' principal football team. They play in one of the premier NCAA conferences, the Big Ten, which has presented a significant hurdle for the team. The football team, like their basketball counterparts, lacks the recruiting base of many other Big Ten schools. Nevertheless, in recent years the Gophers football squad has risen to the upper tier of the Big Ten.

The Gophers play at the Hubert H. Humphrey Metrodome. Tickets for Gophers football games are available by phone, online, or in person at the Mariucci Arena ticket office on campus at 4 Oak Street SE, Minneapolis. You cannot buy Gophers football tickets at Metrodome

When Minnesota was awarded an NBA franchise in 1987, the name-the-team contest turned up possibilities such as the Flakes, the Purple Cows, and the Fighting Norsemen. "Timberwolves" was chosen because Minnesota has more of the animal than any state in the Lower 48.

ticket outlets. Single game tickets for the 2005 season ranged from $20 to $47. Gophers football tickets are often a matter of supply and demand.

**Minnesota Vikings
Metrodome, 34 Kirby Puckett Place,
Minneapolis
(612) 338–4537
www.vikings.com**
Are the Vikings among the NFL's elite or aren't they? And what's in store now that former owner Red McCombs sold the team to Zygi Wilf in 2005? It's anybody's guess. Despite the uncertainty, and despite sometimes less than stellar performances, the Vikings are wildly popular with Minnesota sports fans.

The Vikings play at the Hubert H. Humphrey Metrodome. The Dome is a multipurpose stadium that the Twins and the Vikings call home; however, the seats have better sight lines for football than baseball. When modified for football, the Dome seats 64,121 fans. The Vikings have a tremendous home-field advantage at the Dome. Dome Vikings fans cheer loud enough to create a near-deafening din. The Vikings' "Dome field advantage" acts as the twelfth man on the field at Vikings home games.

The Vikings have several community-based programs. The Vikings Children's Fund is the team's major fund-raising project. The team is given only one day off during the regular season, known as "community Tuesday." On Tuesday the Vikings perform a host of charitable activ-

Dome Souvenir Plus & The Original Baseball Hall of Fame Museum of Minnesota

When you walk down Third Street en route to the Hubert Humphrey Metrodome, it's just about impossible to miss the building. A loudspeaker mounted on the outside of Ray Crump's deceptively small establishment invites passersby in, warning them that they'll be paying twice as much for the same souvenirs inside the Metrodome.

Few people passing by the brick storefront would confuse the building for the National Baseball Hall of Fame in Cooperstown, New York, but on entering the store, they'll be amazed by the wealth of local and national baseball history. The museum houses an impressive Wall of Celebrities, featuring a rotating display of the store's 10,260 signed photos, baseballs, and bats. The museum is free, and the adjoining Dome Souvenir Plus stocks extensive sports souvenirs and team-related merchandise for all the Twin Cities sports teams at reasonable prices.

Ray Crump arrived in Minnesota after the Twins relocated from Washington, D.C., for the 1961 season. Crump's career in Major League Baseball began as a batboy for the Washington Senators, where he would later assume the position of equipment manager. His career spanned 36 years with the Senators and then the Twins, where he was able to acquire the unique sports memorabilia found at the museum. An affable and insightful man, Ray Crump has written and published a book detailing his professional baseball experiences, *Beneath the Grandstands.*

Vintage Minnesota Twins collectibles are prominently displayed at the Original Baseball Museum, including the complete uniforms of retired Twins stars Harmon Killebrew, Tony Oliva, and Rod Carew. There is a special section dedicated to former Twins great Kirby Puckett, as well as plenty of Twins '65, '87, and '91 World Series memorabilia. Included is a prominent display focusing on the Washington Senators relocation to Minnesota. Unique displays include baseballs autographed not only by baseball stars but also by a wide array of nonsports stars; e.g., Jerry Lewis, Hubert Humphrey, and Louis Armstrong. The Elvis Corner displays personal items from the King of Rock 'n' Roll.

Crump's Wall of Celebrities includes autographed photos of such stars as

ities in the area, including visiting area hospitals, the Ronald McDonald House, and area schools or helping with Special Olympics activities. The Vikings provide exciting football action on the field and also make many contributions to the community off the field.

Minnesota Vikings tickets are available through Ticketmaster (651–989–5151; www.ticketmaster.com) or in person at

Muhammad Ali, Hulk Hogan, Liberace, and Bill Cosby shown posing with a younger Ray Crump. Many of the photos were autographed long before the personalities became stars. "When I got the photo taken with Bill Cosby, no one knew who he was," says Crump. "He was some guy who had done a Jell-O commercial. I also have a baseball signed by Frank Sinatra, except he signed it 'Francis Sinatra.' Years later this woman who worked for him told me he never signed anything except business papers 'Francis,' and that he never signed autographs with anything but 'Frank.'"

When Ray Crump opened the museum and store, there was no Wall of Celebrities. These autographed photos of the stars were considered personal and cherished by the Crump family. Crump decided to display the autographs after making an observation: Many women seemed bored at the museum while their husbands refused to leave. He quickly realized displaying the celebrity photos made the museum more fun for the entire family.

And the focus of the museum is on family fun. "This is a family business," explains Crump. "My wife's right back there behind the counter most days, and my two sons frequently help me up front or in the snack bar. I like working at the snack counter better than the front of the store because it gives me a chance to talk to people more. I really enjoy talking to customers about the museum and all the souvenirs we've got here." At least one Crump family member will be available when the museum/store is open to serve the needs of Minnesota sports fans.

The amiable Crump gushes with interesting stories and minutiae about memorabilia and Major League Baseball. How many people can give you a detailed explanation of the differences between the National and American Leagues' method for taking attendance, or know that the Vikings lease at the Dome does not expire until 2011? If you have any questions about sports at all, Crump probably knows the answer or can tell you who does. As far as souvenir shopping goes, Dome Souvenir Plus has a huge selection of items at reasonable prices. Whether you are looking for a Twins hat, Vikings barbecue sauce, or a collectible bobblehead doll, Dome Souvenir Plus has it.

Dome Souvenir Plus & The Original Baseball Hall of Fame Museum of Minnesota is conveniently located 1 block directly north of the Dome, across from gate A (910 South Third Street, Minneapolis). For further information call (612) 376-9707 or, to order merchandise, (888) 375-9707. They also can be visited at www.domeplus.com.

the Metrodome ticket office. A limited number of single-game tickets go on sale in mid-July, but they sell out quickly.

There is plenty of parking, with tremendous variation in prices. The lots next to the Dome are expensive, but north of Washington Avenue there is ample reasonably priced parking.

HORSE RACING

**Canterbury Park Racetrack
and Card Club
1100 Canterbury Road, Shakopee
(952) 445-7223 or (800) 340-6361
www.canterburypark.com**

Canterbury Park has been the state's only horse track since 1985. Canterbury Park's horse racing is also the only sport in the Metro where gambling is legal. Live racing begins in mid-May and runs through the beginning of September. The track is open year-round for simulcast racing.

Admission is reasonable, anywhere from free to $3.00. Anyone under age 18 must be accompanied by an adult and is admitted free of charge. Besides horse racing, the track also has a card club (see the Attractions chapter for more information). Parking at the track is free.

Canterbury Park is approximately 25 minutes from downtown Minneapolis and 15 minutes from the Mall of America.

HOCKEY

**Minnesota Golden Gophers
Men's Hockey
Mariucci Arena, 1901 Fourth Street SE,
Minneapolis
(612) 624-8080 or (800) U-GOPHER
www.gophersports.com**

The Golden Gophers men's hockey team has a rich tradition at the University of Minnesota. It is the only Western Collegiate Hockey Association (WCHA) team in the Twin Cities and the largest university team in the area. In a state with so many sports entertainment options, Gophers fans are diehards. They have been rewarded with a team that has consistently played high-caliber hockey in one

i *Minnesota is arguably the hockey capital of the United States. In fact, our love of hockey mirrors our neighbor to the north, Canada.*

of college hockey's toughest conferences, the WCHA.

The year 2002 brought glory back to Golden Gophers hockey, when for the first time since 1979, the Golden Gophers reigned as WCHA National Champions.

The Gophers play at beautiful Mariucci Arena, a facility built specifically for the team. Here they have a significant home advantage behind the enormous enthusiasm of students and alumni.

Regular-season ticket prices were $30 in 2005-06. Tickets can be purchased by phone, online, or in person at Mariucci Arena.

Plenty of parking for Gophers hockey is available in the lots across from Mariucci Arena on Oak Street.

**Minnesota Golden Gophers
Women's Hockey
Ridder Arena, 1815 Fourth Street SE,
Minneapolis
(612) 624-8080 or (800) U-GOPHER
www.gophersports.com**

The Golden Gophers men's hockey team is not the only hockey team on the U of M campus, nor is it the only team with a recent national championship. Women's hockey is blossoming in Minnesota, from young kids all the way to Division I athletics. In 1999-2000 the Gophers won the AWCHA National Championship. Not bad for your third season of existence.

Since taking the title, the Gophers continued their winning ways, winning the WCHA-Women's League regular season title in 2000-01 and 2001-02.

The Golden Gophers women's hockey team is the only women's hockey team in the country with an arena built specifically for it. Ridder Arena, a gorgeous 3,400-seat arena next door to Mariucci Arena, opened for the 2002-03 season and is considered by many to be the finest women's collegiate hockey arena in the country.

Tickets are available by phone, online, or in person at the Mariucci Arena ticket office. Tickets are a relative bargain, ranging from $4.00 to $10.00 for the 2005-06 season. Parking is widely available at lots and ramps near Ridder Arena.

Minnesota Wild
Xcel Energy Center, 175 West Kellogg Boulevard, St. Paul
(651) 602-6000
www.wild.com

The Minnesota Wild were an expansion team for the 2000–2001 NHL season. However, a lot of work went into luring professional hockey back to Minnesota after losing the North Stars. In fact, the NHL decision to come to St. Paul was incumbent on a new hockey-only facility. Efforts by city officials and fans led to the new, state-of-the-art Xcel Energy Center.

The Xcel Energy Center is located in downtown St. Paul. It is equipped with four 9-foot by 16-foot, high-definition scoreboards as well as two 16-foot by 24-foot, high-definition marquees outside the arena. A truly spectacular ribbon board circles the entire arena at the suite level, showing statistics and ads in 16.7 million shades of color. When the Wild score a goal, the lighthouse in the northeast corner of the arena sounds its foghorn, and the Wild fans go nuts.

Seating in the facility is comfortable and all seats have an excellent view of the action. There are 18,600 seats in the arena, with ticket prices ranging from $10 to $70. Tickets can be purchased for individual games through Ticketmaster at (651) 989-5151 or www.ticketmaster.com. They may also be bought at the box office at the Xcel Energy Center. Wild tickets are a hot commodity in the Twin Cities, and you may have difficulty finding tickets at any price level after the season begins. When tickets become available for an upcoming game, the Wild typically run ads in the sports sections of the *StarTribune* and *St. Paul Pioneer Press.* However, the availability of tickets, especially for some seating, is not guaranteed. There are many readily available parking options in downtown St. Paul.

Before the first puck was dropped in the Wild's NHL inaugural season, the team established an important charitable initia-

Minnesota Wild hockey team. MINNESOTA WILD

tive: the 10,000 Rinks Program. The program takes its name from the state's motto, the Land of 10,000 Lakes. The program is ambitious and sets out to accomplish several initiatives: youth hockey clinics, funding inner-city youth hockey, and a program for creating diversity in hockey. The Wild will also offer "life skills messages" for youth on their radio network.

The Minnesota Wild value children and seem to realize that the kids they are helping will in the future be the team's fan base and players. The first few years are difficult for expansion teams, but the Wild will prosper with the support of its fans. Principal owner Bob Naegele Jr., retired the number one symbolically in the Wild's first game to commemorate the importance of the fans to the team.

SOCCER

Minnesota Thunder
James Griffin Stadium, 275 North
Lexington Parkway, St. Paul
(651) 917–TEAM
www.mnthunder.com
Professional soccer has appeared in the Twin Cities in various franchises. All the franchises have had modest success, but not enough to remain in business. However, after several seasons the Thunder continue to increase their Twin Cities fan base.

The Thunder arrived for the 1994 season in the USISL. They have been successful both on the field and in attracting fans. The Thunder have appeared in the A-League Championship three times in the past few years, losing the 2000 A-League Championship game to Rochester. The Thunder appear poised to continue their success.

The Thunder's slogan is "the world's game . . . Minnesota's team." As the area becomes increasingly more diverse, soccer has developed a larger fan base. Soccer is the world's most beloved team sport, and in the Twin Cities soccer is especially popular among children and teens. The Thunder's season ticket sales have steadily increased. These factors, and the team's success, bode well for the future of the Thunder.

Tickets for individual Thunder games may be purchased for VIP or general admission seating; they ran from $12 to $20 for the 2005 season, reasonable for professional sports tickets. The Thunder also offer discount tickets for youth ages 19 and younger. Tickets are available by phone or in person at the James Griffin Stadium.

SUMMER RECREATION

Minnesotans know how to appreciate the warm weather. It seems like every day free of winter's cold is spent in the great outdoors. Casual visitors to the Twin Cities are often amazed by how much space inside the metro area is left unpaved and untouched, that near downtown Minneapolis the banks of the Mississippi are covered with greenery and lined with thick forests. The only human concessions are the paved hiking trails and handrails that weave in and out of the cliffs along the river. In St. Paul the bird sanctuary of Harriet Island can be found just across the Mississippi from the bustling downtown area, set in a beautiful flower garden that just doesn't feel like it's in the middle of a city.

In short, the best way to describe what to do in the Twin Cities during the summer is Go Outside. In this chapter we list not only where to go to play but also the local associations responsible for organizing many of the outdoor recreational events. We also list some of the more reasonable places to rent gear, from bicycles to canoes to scuba equipment. Whether you're looking for something for the whole family to do or seeking a quiet, beautiful spot to escape from city traffic and shopping malls, you're sure to find it in the Twin Cities.

BIKING

Minnesota has more miles of paved trails than anywhere else in the country. Mountain biking trails wind their way through forests and along cross-country ski trails in the off-season, and easy-to-navigate paved trails follow the shores of nearly every metro area state park lake. Lakes, creeks, waterfalls, bluffs, rivers—you can bike near them all without ever having to leave the metro area.

Inside the Cities proper, there are four especially nice paved bike trails to choose from. In Minneapolis the **Grand Rounds Parkway** follows the perimeter of the Chain of Lakes and encircles the city. Considered the crown jewel of metropolitan biking, this 38-mile scenic trail traces the shorelines of Lake Nokomis, Lake Hiawatha, Shingle Creek, Bassett Creek, Minnehaha Creek, and part of the Mississippi River.

The other three trails are located in St. Paul. **Como Park**'s 1.7-mile bike trail circles Como Lake and heads toward the Como Park Zoo and Conservatory area. **Hidden Falls/Crosby Farm**'s 6.7-mile bike path follows the shady, wooded bottomlands along the banks of the Mississippi and is an especially pleasant ride to take during the dog days of summer. **Phalen Park**'s 3.2-mile bike trail circles Lake Phalen and its beautiful swimming beach, a layout that makes it oh-so-convenient to stop riding and go in for a dip.

Other parks in the metro area with paved biking trails include Anoka County Riverfront, Baker Park Preserve, Bryant Lake, Bunker Hills, Burlington-Northern Regional Trail, Carver Park Preserve, Central Mississippi Riverfront, Cleary Lake, Coon Rapids Dam, Elm Creek Park Reserve, Fish Lake, French, Hyland-Bush-Anderson Lakes, Lake Elmo Park Reserve, Lake Minnetonka Regional Park, Lake Rebecca Park Reserve, Lebanon Hills, Lilydale/Harriet Island, Long Lake Regional Park, Minnehaha Parkway, Mississippi Gorge, Murphy-Hanrehan Park Reserve, North Hennepin Trail Corridor, Rice Creek–West Regional Trail, Rum River Central, Snail Lake, Southwest Regional LRT Trail, Theodore Wirth, and the Wirth-Memorial Parkway (see the Parks chapter for details about many of these parks). For more information about biking in the Twin Cities, call the **Minnesota Community**

Bike lanes along St. Paul's historic Summit Avenue serve both crosstown pedaling commuters and recreational cyclists. SAINT PAUL RCVA

Bicycle Safety Project at (612) 625–9719, the **Minnesota Safety Council** at (651) 291–9150, or the **Minnesota Office of Tourism** at (888–TOURISM), or visit the latter's Web page at www.explore minnesota.com.

There are several good places in the metro area to rent bicycles and get geared up. In Minneapolis you can rent bicycles at reasonable prices from **Calhoun Rental** (612-827-8231) at 1622 West Lake Street, **Campus Bikes** (612-331-3442) at 213 Southeast Oak Street, or from **Kenwood Cyclery** (612-374-4042) at 2123 West 21st Street.

Several in-town organizations hold annual bike-riding marathons worth checking out. One example: the **Minnesota Chapter of the Multiple Sclerosis Society** (612-335-7900; www.mssociety.com) holds three separate MS Bike Tours in the Cities each summer to raise funds for multiple sclerosis research and treatment.

The **Minnesota Cycling Federation** (www.mcf.net) comprises bicycle racing clubs in the upper Midwest, whose purpose is the education and promotion of bicycle racing skills and safety and the promotion of races for bicycle racers. The federation provides cycling enthusiasts with the most current information about area race calendars, race results, MCF member clubs, the NCS Velodrome, and the Youth Cycling League.

CAMPING

Although plenty of people, mostly ice fishers and hunters, go camping in wintertime, camping is really something to enjoy in the warmer months. Camping sites in the metro area are scarce and quickly snatched up, so it's a good idea to reserve a site at least two weeks in advance. To make camping reservations, call the campground directly and indicate where you want to camp (by the water, near hiking trails, etc., or the name of the specific campsite) and when you want to do it. For a free copy of the *Minnesota Alliance of Campground Operators' Minnesota Campgrounds and RV Parks,* call the **Minnesota Department of Tourism** (888–TOURISM; www.exploreminnesota.com).

Three Rivers Park District manages several family campsites around the Twin Cities in Baker Park Reserve, Carver Park Reserve, and Cleary Lake Regional Park, all listed below. Sites are available from May through mid-October. Call the reservations office at (763) 559-6700 at least one week in advance of your desired reservation date, or call the campground directly for reservations with less than two days' notice. A $7.50 nonrefundable service fee per site is charged for all campground reservations and for any changes made to your reservation. Check-in time is 4:00 P.M. and check-out time is 3:00 P.M. Beer and wine are permitted. Kegs, other bulk containers, and hard liquor are not allowed. The maximum length of stay is 14 days within a 30-day period. Weekend reservations must include both Friday and Saturday nights; three nights will be required for all holiday weekends.

Baker Park Reserve (763–694-7662; www.threeriversparkdistrict.org) Campground is on Lake Independence, 20 miles west of Minneapolis on County Road 19, between U.S. Highway 12 and Minnesota Highway 55. There are 210 sites, including 98 with electricity. Each has a picnic table and fire ring and can accommodate two tents or one tent and one RV, with a maximum of six people per campsite. There are showers and flush toilets (wheelchair accessible) and an RV dump station. Daily fee: $17 per site, $22 per site with electricity.

Lake Auburn Campground is in **Carver Park Reserve** (952–443-2911; www.threeriversparkdistrict.org), near Victoria on County Road 11 between Minnesota Highway 5 and Minnesota Highway 7. Each site at Lake Auburn has a picnic table and fire

Three Rivers Park District sells gift cards that can be used to purchase services, programs, or merchandise (rounds of golf, ski lessons, and books, for example) at park district facilities that accept credit cards.

ring and can accommodate two tents or one tent and one RV, with a maximum of six people per campsite. There are 54 sites plus 2 hike-in sites. This is rustic camping—there are pit latrines (wheelchair accessible), a hand pump, no showers, and no electricity. There is an RV dump station (for a fee). Daily fee: $11 per site.

The Red Pine Hike-In Family Camping Area is in **Cleary Lake Regional Park** (763–694-7777; www.threeriversparkdistrict.org), near Prior Lake on County Road 27 (Texas Avenue) just south of County Road 21. Red Pine has five sites with fire rings and picnic tables and can accommodate tent camping only. There are pit latrines (wheelchair accessible), a water pump nearby, no showers, and no electricity. Daily fee: $11 per site.

There are beautiful state parks with campsites within an hour's drive or so of the Twin Cities. Among the most popular are **William O'Brien** (651–433-0500), northwest near Marine-on-St. Croix; **Interstate** (651–465-5711), northwest near Taylors Falls; and **Afton** (651–436-5391), southwest near Hastings. Check out the parks online at www.dnr.state.mn.us/state_parks or contact the DNR reservations center (866-85PARKS, www.stayatmnparks.com). You'll need a day permit ($7.00) or an annual permit ($25.00), available at the parks, for your vehicle. Fees are $11 per night for a rustic site (no showers) and $15 for semimodern (showers).

CANOEING AND ROWING

The benefits of canoeing are immeasurable. Not only is it a great way to stay in shape, but it's also a pleasant way to get close to nature without noisy motors or worrying about getting hung up on waters too shallow for outboard motors. In the Cities several parks are perfect for canoes and kayaks. **Lake Calhoun** in Minneapolis is a popular canoeing lake surrounded by swimming beaches and fishing piers. The lake has a great view of the downtown Minneapolis skyline and is absolutely spectacular at sunset. Connected to Lake Calhoun is **Lake of the Isles,** an especially beautiful place to take a canoe, with narrow waterways overhung with old stone bridges, wide areas full of friendly ducks and geese, and a small forested island in the middle of the lake. A city-run building on the Lake Calhoun grounds rents canoes and sailboats to park visitors.

Also in Minneapolis, and adjacent to Lake Calhoun, is **Lake Harriet,** a wide-open lake heavily used by canoes, sailboats, and motorboats alike. The lake has several public swimming beaches and a refreshment stand on its northwestern shores—the perfect place to stop after a heavy workout on the water.

Other metro area parks that have waterways suitable for canoeing include Anoka County Riverfront, Baker Park Preserve, Bald Eagle–Otter Lakes, Bryant Lake, Carver Park Preserve, Cleary Lake, Como, Coon Rapids Dam, Crow-Hassan, Fish Lake, French, Hidden Falls-Crosby Farm, Hyland-Bush-Anderson Lakes, Lake Byllesby, Lake Elmo Park Reserve, Lake George, Lake Minnewashta, Lake Rebecca Park Reserve, Lebanon Hills, Lilydale/Harriet Island, Long Lake Regional Park, Martin-Island-Linwood Lakes, Minneapolis Chain of Lakes, Nokomis Hiawatha, Phalen-Keller, Rice Creek/Chain of Lakes, Rice Creek–West Regional Trail, Rum River Central, Snail Lake, and Theodore Wirth (see the Parks chapter for more parks information).

The **Minneapolis Rowing Club** (612-729-1541; www.mplsrowing.org) has participated in regattas around the country almost every year since its founding in 1877. The club sponsors classes on rowing for youths of all ages as well as beginning adult rowers.

To rent canoes in the Cities, try **Aarcee Rental** (612-827-5746; www.aarceerental .com) at 2910 Lyndale Avenue South in Minneapolis, or rent canoes through specific parks in the **Three Rivers Park District** (763-559-6700; www.threerivers parkdistrict.org).

CAR SHOWS

For more than 30 years, the **Minnesota Street Rod Association** (www.msra.com) has been sponsoring car shows in and around the Twin Cities area with the purpose of promoting interest in the hobby and sport of street rodding. More than 13,000 enthusiasts belong to the MSRA, a fact that's never more apparent than when the association's annual Back to the '50s show comes to town in June and the streets of St. Paul are filled with beautifully restored vintage hot rods.

DISC GOLF

Sort of a combination of Frisbee and golf, disc golf now has an official home in the Twin Cities. Located in the relaxing **Bryant Lake Regional Park** in Eden Prairie, Three Rivers Park District's first disc golf course is 12 holes in length and features a short course and a long course. The course is open for play from sunrise until sunset, and there is no fee to play. Reservations are required for groups, leagues, or tournaments; call (763) 559-6700. Discs are available for rental from 9:00 A.M. to 7:00 P.M. weekdays and from 9:00 A.M. to 8:00 P.M. weekends at the concession area for $2.00 per hour, The popularity of the sport prompted another Three Rivers park to open a course. **Hyland Ski & Snowboard Area** in Bloomington is a premier disc golf course with 18 tournament-level holes offering challenging elevations and spectacular views of the Twin Cities. Brace yourself for hole 18—it's 700 feet long. The course is open from 8:00 A.M. to sunset daily, weather permitting. No advance tee times are sold. Cost is $3.00 for one round and $5.00 for all-day play. Children 10 and under play free with a paying adult. Disc rental is free with greens fee. There's also a clubhouse with pro shop, disc sales, food, and beverages (alcoholic and otherwise).

FISHING

Many of the 1,000-plus lakes in the Twin Cities metro area have either been stocked with fish by the DNR or are naturally just great fishing holes. For more information about licensing requirements and where to drop your line, see the Fishing and Hunting chapter.

FOOTBALL

Cities Sports Connection (612-929-9009; www.cscsports.com) offers coed and men's outdoor and indoor touch football leagues for all levels of player. Rec B teams consist of players of low to moderate skill level. Rec A teams consist of a mix of players with average to good skill proficiency and game knowledge. Intermediate teams consist of players with good skill proficiency and game knowledge. CSC touch football leagues are offered year-round. CSC is open to all adults 18 or older—no membership or nonmember fees are charged to participate in CSC leagues.

GOLF

With hundreds of acres of flat, open plains and gently rolling hills, Minnesota is naturally home to some of the most incredible golf courses in the country.

Some of these courses belong to the Three Rivers Park system and are located in the parks themselves (see the Parks chapter for information about individual

parks). **Baker National Golf Course,** located in the Baker Park Preserve at 2935 Parkview Drive, Medina (763-494-7640), has both an 18-hole course and a 9-hole course with a driving range/practice area, clubhouse, pro shop, and snack bar on the premises. Rates for the Championship Course and the Evergreen Course are $36 and $14, respectively, with discounts available to seniors and juniors (17 and under). Golf carts are available for rental. Telephone reservations for the courses are highly recommended.

Glen Lake Golf & Practice Center (763-694-7824), located in Glen Lake Park at 14350 County Road 62 in Minnetonka, is a nine-hole golf course with a driving range/practice area, clubhouse, snack bar, and golf store on the premises. Carts and clubs can be rented at the store, and groups from two to four are permitted on the course. General rates are $15.50 per person on weekends, with discounts available for seniors, juniors, and weekday play. Tee times may be reserved up to five days in advance.

Cleary Lake Golf Course (763-694-7777) in Cleary Lake Regional Park, located at 18106 Texas Avenue in Prior Lake, is a nine-hole course with a visitor center, snack bar, and golf store on the premises. Clubs and carts can be rented at the course. General rates are $13 per person with discounts available for juniors (under 15) and senior citizens on weekdays.

St. Paul has four golf courses located within the city's park system: Phalen, Como, and two in Highland Park. **Phalen Golf Course** (651-778-0413) at 1615 Phalen Drive in Phalen Park, is an 18-hole course with a clubhouse and a banquet room that seats 200. The course plays to a par 70, measures approximately 6,100 yards, and has a rating of 67.5 and a slope of 116. The course includes a driving range, a full-service pro shop, and a snack bar.

Como Golf Course (651-488-9673), located at 1431 North Lexington Parkway in Como Park, is an 18-hole golf course

The Minnesota Department of Natural Resources has publications dealing with camping, fishing, hunting, and boating in Minnesota. Call (800) 285–2000 to have information mailed to you about any of these activities.

with a clubhouse, a full-service pro shop, and a snack bar on the premises. Como is a short, hilly course that plays to a par 70, measures approximately 5,800 yards, and has a rating of 68.5 and a slope of 115.

Highland 18-Hole Golf Course (651–695–3774), 1403 Montreal Avenue, opened to the public as an 18-hole facility in 1927 and is the longest of the parks courses, measuring about 6,600 yards. It plays to a par 72 with a rating of 71.2 and has a full-service pro shop, a driving range, and food service operation. **Highland 9-Hole Golf Course** (651–695–3708), 1797 Edgcumbe Road, opened in 1972 and is a favorite of beginning golfers. The course plays to a par 35 and measures 3,000 yards. The course includes a snack bar that also sells a limited line of golf supplies (balls, gloves, tees, etc.).

All the St. Paul parks courses charge the same rate scale of $25 per game, with discounts available to students (21 and under), seniors, and for weekday and evening play; reservations for courses may be made via phone or online.

River Oaks Golf Course (651–438–2121; www.riveroaksmunigolf.com), located in Cottage Grove at 11099 South Minnesota Highway 61, has an 18-hole golf course with a grass practice facility. The course plays to a par 71 and measures approximately 6,483 yards. General rates for the 18-hole course are $28 for weekdays and $30 on weekends. Discounts are available to residents, juniors under 17, and senior citizens. There is a restaurant on the premises and a pro shop where golfers can rent carts and clubs.

The **Falcon Ridge Golf Course** (651–462–5797; www.falconridgegolf.net) is a favorite spot for corporate outings and charity tournaments. Located at 33942 Falcon Avenue in Stacy, the grounds include an 18-hole regulation course and a 9-hole short course, as well as a resident PGA golf professional available for individual or group lessons. General rates for the 18-hole course are $20 on weekdays and $25 on weekends; rates for the 9-hole course are $13 on weekdays and $15 on weekends. A pro shop where carts and clubs can be rented is located on the premises.

HIKING

Just about every park in the Twin Cities metro area has a hiking trail that wanders in and out of forests, follows rivers and streams, passes close by natural waterfalls, or follows along the shores of the Mississippi River. Area parks with easy to moderate paved and turf hiking trails include Anoka County Riverfront, Baker Park Preserve, Bald Eagle–Otter Lakes, Battle Creek, Baylor, Bryant Lake, Bunker Hills, Burlington-Northern Regional Trail, Carver Park Preserve, Central Mississippi Riverfront, Cleary Lake, Como, Coon Rapids Dam, Cottage Grove Ravine, Crow-Hassan, Elm Creek Park Reserve, Fish Lake, French, Hidden Falls–Crosby Farm, Hyland-Bush-Anderson Lakes, Lake Byllesby, Lake Elmo Park Reserve, Lake George, Lake Minnewashta, Lake Rebecca Park Reserve, Lebanon Hills, Lilydale/Harriet Island, Long Lake Regional Park, Martin-Island-Linwood Lakes, Minneapolis Chain of Lakes, Minnehaha, Minnehaha Parkway, Mississippi Gorge, Murphy-Hanrehan Park Reserve, Nokomis Hiawatha, North Hennepin Trail Corridor, Rice Creek/Chain of Lakes, Rice Creek–West Regional Trail, Rum River Central, St. Croix Bluffs, Snail Lake, Southwest Regional LRT Trail, Spring Lake, Springbrook Nature Center, Theodore Wirth, Wirth-Memorial Parkway, and Wood Lake Nature Center (see Parks chapter for the parks listings).

For more experienced hikers, **Fort Snelling State Park** in St. Paul (612–725–

2389), at 101 Snelling Lake Road, has 18 miles of turf hiking trails that wind through the park's nature preserve, and **Minnesota Valley State Recreational Area** in Jordan (952–492–6400), at 19825 Park Boulevard, has 47 miles of turf and paved hiking trails to explore. The **Gateway Trail** runs more than 18 miles from St. Paul to Pine County Park north of Stillwater. You can pick up the Gateway Trail in Phalen Park (see the Phalen listing in the Parks chapter for more information).

If you're interested in meeting other hikers, **Friends of the Mississippi River** (651–222–2193; www.fmr.org), located at 240 Summit Avenue in St. Paul, organizes bird-watching tours and wildflower hikes at different spots along the Mississippi River. For women who don't like hiking in the backwoods of Minnesota alone, the Department of Natural Resources' **Becoming an Outdoors Woman in Minnesota** (651–296–6157) organizes group hikes for women as well as other solo and group gender-specific outdoors experiences ranging from canoeing to big-game hunting.

HORSEBACK RIDING

Many of the parks in the metro area allow horses to share paved and dirt paths with cyclists and pedestrians. The trick is finding a place to rent horses. Tourists and residents alike can rent horses or arrange for guided rides at many locations throughout the metro area suburbs for an average of $15 an hour.

North of the Twin Cities, horses can be rented at **Brass Ring Stables,** 9105 Northwest Norris Lake Road, Elk River (763–441–7987); **Valley View Horse Ranch,** 5168 County Road 33, Buffalo (651–682–2928); **Bunker Park Stables,** 550 Bunker Lake Boulevard, Coon Rapids (763–757–9445; www.bunkerparkstable.com); **Rockin' R Ranch**, 8540 Kimbro Avenue North, Grant City (651–439–8800); and **Roselawn Stables,** 24069 Rum River Boulevard NW, St. Francis (763–753–5517).

In the eastern suburbs, horses can be rented at the **Diamond T Riding Stable,** 4889 Pilot Knob Road, Eagan (651–454–1464); the **Windy Ridge Ranch,** 2700 Manning Avenue South, Woodbury (651–436–6557); and **Woodloch Stable & Tack,** 5676 North 170th Street, Hugo (651–429–1303).

South of the Twin Cities and just outside Carver, horses can be rented at **River Valley Ranch,** 16480 County Road 45 (952–361–3361).

Parks in the metro area with specified horse paths are Baker Park Preserve, Carver Park Preserve, Crow-Hassan, Elm Creek Park Reserve, Lake Rebecca Park Reserve, and Murphy-Hanrehan Park Reserve (see the Parks chapter for more information).

HORSESHOE PITCHING

In Coon Rapids, Minnesota's oldest nudist resort, the **Oakwood Club Inc.** (763–408–9004; www.oakwoodclub.com) holds extremely informal horseshoe-throwing competitions at its beautiful, secluded facilities adjacent to a state nature preserve.

HOT AIR BALLOONING

There's nothing quite as inspiring as riding a hot air balloon over the St. Croix River Valley in the middle of summer, when the rolling fields below are bright green and the water is at its bluest. **Balloon Adventures** (952–474–1662) in Chanhassen and **Aamodts Balloons** (651–351–0101; www.aamodtsballoons.com) in Stillwater offer balloon adventures from champagne rides to daylong trips. Call companies for specific takeoff times and sites. To learn how to pilot one of these big colorful beasts by yourself, **Wiederkehr Balloon Academy** in Lakeland (651–436–8172), located at 130 North St. Croix Trail, offers classes in balloon navigation.

To find other people to enjoy the outdoors with, Twin Cities Transplants (not a singles' club), www.imnotfromhere .com, has been matching newcomers with residents for more than 10 years to help new residents get acclimated to the Twin Cities.

IN-LINE SKATING

Both cities have plenty of paved paths open to in-line skates. Some of the parks that allow in-line skates to share paved walking paths are Lilydale/Harriet Island, Minneapolis Chain of Lakes, Nokomis Hiawatha, and Theodore Wirth (see the Parks chapter for listings). Two other particularly nice places to skate are along Lake Calhoun and Lake of the Isles; both the trails follow the lakeshore all the way and are wide enough that you don't have to worry about knocking pedestrians over or being hung up behind them for too long.

Skate parks have their place here, too, and the most impressive one is in the western suburb of Golden Valley. **Third Lair Skatepark** (763-79-SKATE; www.3rdlair.com), 850 Florida Avenue South, has indoor and outdoor parks plus a really good skate shop. The **Tri-City Skate Park** at the Southdale YMCA (952-835-2567; www.ymcatwincities.org/ skatepark/skatepark.htm), at 7355 York Avenue South in Edina, has a skate park, too—the first all-concrete, in-ground, continuous-bowl skate park in the upper Midwest. You can sign up for summer skateboarding classes, too.

For more information about in-line skating events around town, contact the **Minnesota In-line Skate Club** (612-827-3205; www.skate.minnesota.com). This club has trail information and organizes weekly skates.

KICKBALL

Cities Sports Connection (612-929-9009; www.cscsports.com) organizes and coed kickball leagues for players ages 18 and over. Teams consist of players with lower to average and decent skill proficiency and game knowledge, with a focus on sportsmanship, having fun, and getting a good workout. No membership or non-member fees are charged to participate in CSC leagues, and teams play events all over the metro area and are not tied to one specific area. CSC provides paid officials for all league action and free T-shirts for participants.

MINIATURE GOLF

Definitely a kid's sport or a fun place to take a date, a round of miniature golf makes for a relaxing, mildly competitive evening out. Although there aren't any miniature golf parks in the Twin Cities proper, there are several in the suburbs. **Adventures Garden Miniature Golf** (612-861-9169), located at 64th Street and Portland Avenue South in Bloomington, is the largest of the bunch, with more than enough windmills and castles for any minigolf enthusiast. In Eagan, **Grand Slam Sports and Entertainment Center** (651-452-6569), at 3984 Sibley Memorial Highway, has a midsize golf park that makes for a good quick night out.

NATURE INTERPRETATION AND BIRD-WATCHING

Many of the metro area parks have ongoing wildlife conservation projects open to the public, which are a great way to get an up close look at Minnesota's wildlife. Bald eagles, hawks, egrets, deer, porcupines, and the occasional skunk are just a few of the animals you might see while walking in the Minnesota woods. In the Cities, raccoons and Canada geese are plentiful along the banks of the Mississippi River. Some of the metro area parks that have specific areas set aside for nature interpretation include Bald Eagle-Otter Lakes, Baylor, Bunker Hills, Carver Park Preserve, Como, Coon Rapids Dam, Elm Creek Park Reserve, French, Harriet Island, Hidden Falls-Crosby Farm, Lake Minnetonka Regional Park, Lebanon Hills, Minneapolis Chain of Lakes, Noerenberg, Memorial Park, Rice Creek/Chain of Lakes, Springbrook Nature Center, Theodore Wirth, and Wood Lake Nature Center (see the Parks chapter).

Part of the **Minnesota River Valley Birding Trail** (651-739-9332; www.birding trail.org) lies in the southern Twin Cities, and many parks have bird-watching hikes. Check with Three Rivers Park District (763-694-7750; www.threeriverspark district.org), St. Paul Parks and Recreation (651-266-6400; www.stpaul.gov/depts/ parks), and the Minneapolis Park and Recreation Board (612-230-6400, www.minneapolisparks.org) seasonally for more information.

PAINTBALL

This could be considered either a winter sport or a summer sport, but isn't it more fun running around outside in cutoffs and T-shirts, chasing down your opponents with mock artillery in the hot summer sun than dealing with the limited cover and even more limited area of an indoor range? You have your choice of outdoor or indoor paintball arenas at **Adventure Zone** in Burnsville (952-890-7961; www.theadventurezone.net) at 13700 Nicollet Avenue, and at **Splatball Inc.** (612-378-0385; www.splatball.com), at 2412 University Avenue SE in Minneapolis. The biggest outdoor paintball center is **St. Paul's Paintball Park** (651-488-7700), at 1870 Rice Street. The park is open to groups of six or more (up to 24 participants per group), and reservations are required.

SAILING AND SAILBOARDING

There's really nothing quite as pretty as the white triangles of sailboats bobbing in the placid waters of Minnesota's wide blue lakes. There's also nothing quite as pleasant as actually being on one of the boats, enjoying the hot summer sun as you dangle your fingers and toes in the cool, clear water. Many lakes in the metro area are perfect for sailing and sailboarding alike, including Lake Harriet in Minneapolis, White Bear Lake in White Bear Lake, Keller Lake in St. Paul, Lake Minnetonka in Minnetonka, Medicine Lake in Plymouth, and Lake Nokomis in Minneapolis.

State parks in the metro area that allow sailboats and sailboards in the park lakes (and provide convenient boat launches for the same) include Baker Park Preserve, Bald Eagle-Otter Lakes, Bryant Lake, Carver Park Preserve, Cleary Lake, Fish Lake, French, Hyland-Bush-Anderson Lakes, Lake Byllesby, Lake Elmo Park Reserve, Lake George, Lake Minnewashta, Long Lake, Martin-Island-Linwood Lakes, Minneapolis Chain of Lakes, Nokomis Hiawatha, Phalen-Keller, Rice Creek/Chain of Lakes, and Snail Lake (see the Parks chapter).

The **American Red Cross** in St. Paul (651-291-6789; www.stpaulredcross.org) offers sailing classes and events throughout the summer, as does **Blue Water Sailing School** at 2337 West Medicine Lake Drive in Plymouth (763-559-5649); **Lake Calhoun Yacht Club and Sailing School** in Minneapolis (612-927-8552; www.lake

---

One popular 5K race for runners (and walkers) of all levels is named after a beer. September's James Page Blubber Run has a halfway stop at a bar and ends at a party on Peavey Plaza in downtown Minneapolis.

Sailboarders on Lake Calhoun in Minneapolis. GREATER MINNEAPOLIS CONVENTION & VISITORS ASSOCIATION

calhoun.org), at 3010 East Calhoun Parkway; and **Scuba Center** (612-925-4818; www.scubacenter.com), at 5015 Penn Avenue South in Minneapolis and 1571 Century Point in Eagan (651-681-8434).

SCUBA DIVING

Yes, there is scuba diving in Minnesota. Divers from around the world come to Minnesota to dry-suit dive in the frigid waters of Lake Superior, where hundreds of shipwrecks, including the famous *Edmund Fitzgerald,* can be found miles off the coast and underwater life found only in this region can be studied up close. If you feel like exploring the bottom of a less cold and much less deep lake, pretty much any spot that has a swimming beach is fine for diving and snorkeling. Classes on scuba diving, scuba certification, and gear rental are provided by **Scuba Center** (612-925-4818; www.scuba

center.com), at 5015 Penn Avenue South, Minneapolis and at 1571 Century Point, Eagan (651-681-8434); and **Scuba Dive and Travel** (612-823-7210; www.scuba diveandtravel.com), at 4741 Chicago Avenue South in Minneapolis. **FantaSea Scuba & Travel** (952-890-3483; www .fantaseadivers.com), at 3429 East Minnesota Highway 13 in Burnsville, offers both classes and certification and arranges Minnesota scuba adventure packages for amateur and novice divers alike.

SKYDIVING

The **Minnesota Skydivers Club** offers static line and tandem airplane jumps as well as free-fall jumps to those who have satisfactorily completed five static line jumps. Ground training is provided for beginning jumpers, with instruction given by jumpmasters and instructors who have been certified by the United States Parachute Association. For jump times and site information, contact the Minnesota Skydivers Club at (507) 351-7001; www.mnsky dive.com.

SOCCER

Cities Sports Connection (612-929-9009; www.cscsports.com) offers coed outdoor and indoor soccer leagues at the following skill levels: Rec teams consist of players of low to moderate skill level, Inter-A teams consist of players with average to good skill proficiency and game knowledge, and Competitive teams consist of competitive, higher-skilled players with good skill proficiency and game knowledge. CSC soccer leagues are offered outdoors in spring (May–July), summer (June–August), and early fall (October). CSC also runs two indoor leagues, winter1 (January) and winter2 (April). CSC is open to all adults 18 or older—no membership or nonmember fees are charged to participate in CSC leagues.

SOFTBALL

Cities Sports Connection (612-929-9009; www.cscsports.com) organizes coed softball leagues at all skill levels. CSC softball leagues are offered in the spring (April–June) and summer (June–August). Teams consist of 10 players (coed means 6 men/4 women) on the field at all times, with rosters of 15-plus people per team. CSC is open to all adults 18 or older—no membership or nonmember fees are charged to participate in CSC leagues.

If you're looking to form a softball team in the Twin Cities proper, the **Amateur Softball Association** can help. Contact this group through **Minnesota Sports Federation** (763-241-1789; www.msf1.org).

United States Slowpitch Softball Association (763-571-1305; www .mnusssa.com) can help you put together a slow-pitch softball team. The association will send you the information you need or at least get you in touch with your local park and recreation department. The USSSA oversees suburban leagues, sets up tournaments, and helps teams find places to play.

SPRINTS, 10KS, AND MARATHONS

The **Twin Cities Marathon, Inc.** (763-287-3888; www.twincitiesmarathon.com) is a nonprofit corporation that organizes and directs the annual Twin Cities Marathon, TC 10 Mile, and Saturday events as a community service for the Minneapolis–St. Paul area. The Twin Cities Marathon is often referred to as the most beautiful urban marathon in America and runs alongside the Mississippi River and through many metro area parks.

The **Minnesota Distance Running Association** (952-927-0983; www.run mdra.org) promotes running and serves as a resource for runners in Minnesota. For a $20 membership fee, members of MDRA receive a subscription to the organization's magazine, *RunMinnesota,* the *Running Minnesota Annual* with details about running events throughout Minnesota, and the chance to participate (for free) in the many training runs the association sponsors year-round to help runners get in shape for distance runs. To contact the MDRA, write to 5701 Normandale Boulevard, Edina, MN 55424. For information about MDRA-sponsored races in the metro area, call the MDRA raceline at (952) 925-4749.

SWIMMING

Summertime is beach weather, and all together there are more miles of swimming beaches in Minnesota than in California and Florida combined. There are more than 1,000 lakes throughout the seven counties in the Twin Cities metro area, and almost all of them are used for one form of recreation or another. In Min-

Lake Calhoun beach. GREATER MINNEAPOLIS CONVENTION & VISITORS ASSOCIATION

neapolis swimmers are welcome at Lake Calhoun and Cedar Lake—the former does not have lifeguards, but Cedar Lake does. At the northern edge of St. Paul, swimmers share Keller Lake with the occasional boater, while at the northwestern corner of St. Paul is beautiful Lake Josephine, a family outing tradition for residents and visitors of the area for generations. White Bear Lake in White Bear has five public areas set aside for swimming, and in Minnetonka the 1,500-acre Lake Minnetonka is surrounded by swimming beaches and boat launches. Outside Minneapolis, Plymouth's Medicine Lake has two public beaches with lifeguards and has an on-site outfitter that rents small boats and canoes. State parks in the metro area with swimming beaches are Baker Park Preserve, Bald Eagle–Otter Lakes, Baylor, Bryant Lake, Bunker Hills, Cleary Lake, Como, Elm Creek Park Reserve, French, Hyland-Bush-Anderson Lakes, Lake Byllesby, Lake Elmo Park Reserve, Lake George, Lake Minnetonka Regional Park, Lake Minnewashta, Lake Rebecca Park Reserve, Lebanon Hills, Long Lake Regional Park, Martin-Island-Linwood Lakes, Minneapolis Chain of Lakes, Nokomis Hiawatha, Phalen, Rice Creek/Chain of Lakes, Snail Lake, Square Lake Park, and Theodore Wirth (see the Parks chapter for more information).

If you want to take a quick dip in a pool, nearly every neighborhood park in the Twin Cities has a free wading pool for kids and adults to splash around in, while several parks have full-size pools for public use. In Minneapolis full-size public swimming pools can be found at **North Commons Water Park** (612-370-4945), at 1701 Golden Valley Road; **Rosacker Pool** (612-370-4937), at 1520 Johnson Street NE; and **Webber Pool** (612-370-4915), at 4300 Webber Parkway. In St. Paul full-size public swimming pools can be found at

Como Pool (651-489-2811), in Como Park at Como Avenue and Lexington Parkway; **Highland Swimming Pool** (651-695-3773), at 1840 Edgcumbe Road; and **Oxford Pool** (651-647-9925), at North Lexington Parkway and Iglehart Avenue.

VOLLEYBALL

Cities Sports Connection (612-929-9009; www.cscsports.com) offers indoor and outdoor (sand and grass) coed volleyball leagues at all skill levels, from the very beginning volleyball player to the advanced, highly competitive player. CSC volleyball leagues are offered indoors in the fall (September–December), winter (January–March), and spring (March–May). CSC leagues move outdoors for early summer (May–July, sand), summer (June–August, grass), and late summer (July–September, sand). CSC is open to all adults 18 or older—no membership or nonmember fees are charged to participate in CSC leagues.

WINTER RECREATION

Minnesota is transformed during winter. Familiar landmarks are completely obliterated by giant piles of soft, white snow, and the horizon stretches out seemingly forever, no longer blocked by the lush green foliage of the spring and summer landscape.

With the change in scenery comes a change in the mood and activities of the people. Summer streets are always packed with pedestrians, and the parks are full of picnicking families and nature lovers. However, when the temperature drops below 20 degrees F—and in January and February, below 0 degrees F— many of these same people couldn't be pried out of their houses for anything but the absolutely necessary drive to work or trip to the grocery store. Those who do venture outside engage in ice-skating, sledding, snowmobiling, sledding, ice hockey, and skiing.

Following are examples of some traditional Minnesota winter activities (and the places to do them at), as well as a few nontraditional indoor activities that take you outside the home without leaving you out in the cold.

BOWLING

A great winter sport, bowling gets you out of the house and in someplace warm and friendly. Leagues and tournaments take place in bowling centers throughout the metro area. Stop in at your local lanes to inquire.

If you just want to bowl a couple of games with friends, there are dozens of bowling alleys to choose from. The **Brunswick Eden Prairie Lanes** (952–941–0445), located at 12200 Singletree Lane in Eden Prairie, has 40 lanes and is open until midnight Sunday through Wednesday and 2:00 A.M. Thursday through Satur-

day. This is the original Twin Cities home of Cosmic Bowling, during which the lights fade to black, pins glow, fog machines blow, and laser lights keep time to '50s through '90s dance music. There are also pool tables, video games, and dartboards, as well as the largest bar in Eden Prairie. Another option: the 36-lane **Earle Brown Bowl** (763–566–6250), located in Brooklyn Center at 6440 James Circle North. **Memory Lanes** (612–721–6211), at 2520 26th Avenue South in Minneapolis, is where cosmic hipsters come to toss glow-in-the-dark bowling balls and drink reasonably priced fancy mixed drinks. Lights-out Thunder Alley runs weekday evenings and some weekends. Memory Lanes also has a full-service kitchen and 14 TVs in the bar—a hot spot on Sunday during football season thanks to its NFL package in high-definition format. **Park Tavern** in St. Louis Park (952–929–6810; www.parktavern.net), located at 3401 Louisiana Avenue, is another hot bowling spot. Every Friday and Saturday night, the Park Tavern holds Rock and Bowl (for ages 21 and over) with a spacey light show and music added to the bowling experience. Be sure to show up early to reserve a lane on these nights, because the 20 in-house lanes are booked fast. **Bryant-Lake Bowl** (612–825–3737), 810 West Lake Street in Minneapolis, is a throwback to bowling alleys of the past. The 1950s-era lanes in this small bowling alley provide loads of atmosphere, and the BLB does not have electronic scoring, so you get to practice scoring by hand, something many of us haven't done since childhood. Bowling is cheap here, but the lanes are first-come, first-served, and no reservations are accepted. Expect to wait on busy weekend nights, although the numerous microbrews on tap will make the wait enjoyable.

BOXING

Boxing is no longer a sport confined to men alone, and boxing rings have sprung up at health clubs all over the metro area, while those that have been long established have found new participants and audiences of both genders. In St. Paul, **Brunette Boxing Gym** (651–779–6248, www.brunetteboxing.com), at 1135 Arcade Street, is the oldest boxing gym in the metro. It hosts boxing competitions and offers personal training for men and women of all ages, from beginners to professionals. **Uppercut Boxing Gym** (612–822–1964; www.uppercutgym.com), at 1324 Quincy Street NE in Minneapolis, provides boxing training for all fitness levels, amateur to professional.

BROOMBALL

Similar to hockey, except using brooms instead of sticks and an actual ball instead of a puck, broomball is becoming a popular sport throughout the world and here in the Midwest. The **Minneapolis Parks and Recreation Board** (612–230–6475) organizes broomball teams for competitions and informal meets. The **Twin Cities Sport Connection** (612–929–9009) organizes coed and men's broomball leagues for informal and intermediate competitions.

    Cities Sports Connection (612–929–9009; www.cscsports.com), also offers coed and men's broomball leagues of all skill levels each winter (December–February) and can easily incorporate individuals and small groups. CSC broomball teams consist of men's 5 and coed 6 (3 men, 2 women, and a goalie). League fees include paid officials for all league games, official broomball game balls, a six-game league schedule and play-off tournament, stylish CSC T-shirts, and prizes for winners. Teams and individuals need to supply their own brooms and additional equipment as desired.

CROSS-COUNTRY SKIING

There's nothing quite as exhilarating as exploring the Minnesota backwoods on a pair of cross-country skis. Nearly every park in the metro area has well-groomed ski trails for enthusiasts and beginners alike, taking skiers through everything from heavily wooded marked forest paths to gently sloping open spaces with incredible views of frozen waterfalls, lakes, and streams. On top of that, nearly every golf course in the metro area doubles as a cross-country ski park as soon as there's sufficient snow to do so. In the Cities, St. Paul's **Como Park,** at 1431 North Lexington Parkway, has a 5K trail that loops around the park. Cross-country ski lessons are offered at the park's pavilion on an irregular basis—call (651) 488–9673 for details. Also in St. Paul are **Fort Snelling State Park** (612–725–2389), which is located at 101 Snelling Lake Road and offers 12 miles of groomed trails for cross-country and skate-ski use; **Hidden Falls/Crosby Regional Park** (612–632–5111), at Crosby Farm Road and Shepard Road, which has 13.9K of trails for ski use; **Highland Nine Hole Golf Course** at 1797 Edgcumbe Road, which has a 5K groomed track for experienced skiers and a 3K loop across the street for beginners; and **Phalen Golf Course** at 1615 Phalen Drive, which has 10K of groomed track for cross-country skiers. For more information on these and other St. Paul trails, call St. Paul Parks and Recreation at (651) 266–6400.

    Metro area parks with groomed trails for cross-country skiers include Baker Park Preserve, Carver Park Preserve, Cleary Lake, Coon Rapids Dam, Cottage Grove Ravine, Elm Creek Park Reserve, French, Hyland-Bush-Anderson Lakes, Lake Minnewashta, Lebanon Hills, Murphy-Hanrehan Park Reserve, and Theodore Wirth, Wirth-Memorial Parkway. (See the Parks chapter for more park information.)

    Cross-country ski gear can be rented or purchased in Minneapolis at **AARCEE** at 2910 Lyndale Avenue South (612–827–5746) and at **Midwest Mountaineer-**

When the snow falls, cross-country skiers shush around Minneapolis's Chain of Lakes. GREATER
MINNEAPOLIS CONVENTION & VISITORS ASSOCIATION

ing at 309 Cedar Avenue South
(612–339–3433). In St. Paul ski gear can
be rented or purchased at either **Finn-Sisu**
at 1841 University Avenue West (651–645–
2443) or **Joe's Sporting Goods** at 33 East
County Road B in Little Canada (651–
488–5511).

CURLING

Resembling a combination of ice hockey
and shuffleboard, curling has gone from a
popular sport confined mostly to Canada
and the United Kingdom to an Olympic
event and a well-loved, albeit still relatively
obscure, winter sport in the Midwest USA.
The **St. Paul Curling Club,** the largest
member-owned curling club in the country, organizes curling matches and practices at its home on Selby Avenue in St.
Paul (651-224-7408; www.stpaulcurling
club.org).

DOGSLEDDING AND SKIJORING TRAILS

Dogsledding and skijoring—in which a
skier is pulled along by a horse or a vehicle—are permitted on designated trails in
some metro area parks. With the exception of the multiuse trail at **Baker Park**
Reserve, a special-use permit is required
for both activities; call the Three Rivers
Park District reservations office at (763)
559–6700 for further information, permits,
and maps.

Sections of snowmobile trails at **Crow-**
Hassan Park Reserve and **Elm Creek Park**
Reserve are open for skijoring and
dogsledding on weekdays during the day
and weekends and holidays from 5:00 A.M.
to 10:00 A.M. **Crow-Hassan Park Reserve,**
located west of Rogers on Sylvan Lake
Road, has 5.5 miles of trail designated for
dogsledding/skijoring use; **Elm Creek Park**

Reserve, located northwest of Osseo on County Road 81, has 11 miles of trail designated for dogsledding/skijoring use; the **North Hennepin Trail Corridor,** connecting the Coon Rapids Dam Regional Park in Brooklyn Park to Elm Creek Park Reserve in Maple Grove, has 6 miles of trail designated for dogsledding/ skijoring use. These trails are usually packed, so be prepared for lots of company. A special-use permit and annual Park Patron permit are required to use the trails.

Murphy-Hanrehan Park Reserve, located near Prior Lake on County Road 75, has 3 miles of trail designated for dogsledding and horseriding—no snowmobiles are allowed. The trail is open all week during daylight hours and is not usually packed. A special-use permit is required to use the trails.

Baker Park Reserve, located 20 miles west of downtown Minneapolis on County Road 19, has 4 miles of trails set aside for dogsledding, skijoring, mountain biking, and snowshoeing. No special-use permit is required.

DOWNHILL SKIING AND SNOWBOARDING

In the immediate Twin Cities metro area, there aren't a lot of options for downhill skiing or extreme snowboarding. But let's face it—this is farm and lumber country, and mountains don't really figure into our natural geography. For real downhill skiing, you have to make the three- to four-hour trek up to Duluth and the North Shore, where you'll find the **Giants Ridge Golf & Ski Resort** (218-865-3000; www.giantsridge.com), in the town of Biwabik off County Road 138; **Spirit Mountain** (218-628-2891; www.spiritmt.com), at 9500 Spirit Mountain Place in Duluth; and **Lutsen Mountains** (218-663-7281; www.lutsen.com) found between Duluth and the Canadian border on Ski Road Hill near Lutsen. All three ski areas are also resorts, and discounts are offered seasonally on rooms and lift tickets for those

who purchase a combination of both—advance reservations are highly recommended.

Closer to home—but again, not as tall or as steep as the North Shore slopes—is **Buck Hill** in Burnsville (952-435-7174; www.buckhill.com) located at 15400 Buck Hill Road; **Hyland Ski Area & Snowboard Area** in Bloomington (763-694-7800; www.hylandski.com), at 8800 Chalet Road; **Afton Alps** (651-436-5245; www.aftonalps.com), located near Afton off County Road 20; **Welch Village Ski and Snowboard Area** (651-465-6315; www.welchvillage.com), located in Welch on Minnesota Highway 61 and County Road 7; and **Wild Mountain Ski** (651-257-3550 or 800-447-4958; www.wildmountain.com), located off Minnesota Highway 8 near Taylors Falls at 37200 Wild Mountain Road.

FENCING

The **Twin Cities Fencing Club** (651-225-1900; www.twincitiesfencing.com) is one of the top fencing clubs in the country. Fencers from TCFC have represented the United States at international competitions, won national championships (both senior and junior), and earned medals at local, regional, and national competitions. Head coach Roberto Sobalvarro has coached U.S. National Teams at the World Championships, World Cup competitions, and the U.S. Olympic Festival. The club serves fencers of all ages and all levels of experience, from beginner to national champion.

FORMAL DANCING

What better way to chase away the winter blues and meet new people than dancing? Several clubs in the Twin Cities area bring like-minded dance partners together, including the **Twin Cities Rebels Swing Dance Club** in Bloomington (952-941-0906; www.tcrebels.com), which has regular swingin' get-togethers all over the metro area, and the **Twin Town Twirlers Square Dancing Club** (763- 503-5976, www.tripletdance.com), which meets on Monday and holds monthly dances. To find out about a variety of dance classes and events, contact the **Minnesota Chapter of the U.S. Amateur Ballroom Dancers Association** (www .usabda-mn.org).

HEALTH CLUBS

What better way to stay in shape through the winter than a health club membership? The Twin Cities proper have several gyms and health clubs to choose from, many of which offer free child care and youth programs such as swimming lessons and martial arts. **Lifetime Fitness** has two locations in St. Paul—at 2145 Ford Parkway in the Highland Park neighborhood (651-698-5000) and at 340 Cedar Street (651-227-7777), downtown. There is also a downtown Minneapolis branch at 615 Second Avenue South (612-752-7000) in the Grand Hotel Minneapolis (branch is for executive members), and several locations in the suburbs, including the women-only location at 2480 Fairview Avenue North in Roseville (651-633-4444). The facilities include Cybex, Nautilus, Gravitron, and ski machines as well as stair-climbers. Aerobics, dance, and karate classes are offered, as are massage, tanning beds, personal training, nutrition seminars, and free child care. Reciprocity is included in regular membership fees, and this is the only health club chain in town that is open 24 hours a day.

Los Campeones Fitness & Body, 2721 Franklin Avenue East in Minneapolis (612-333-8181), features free weights and cable machines, treadmills and other cardio machines, a juice bar, and an on-site pro shop offering items including vitamin supplements. Special student and couple rates are available. The **Sweatshop Health Club** in St. Paul (651-646-8418; www .sweatshopfitness.com), located at 167 Snelling Avenue North, offers personal weight-training programs, kickboxing, spinning, and Pilates mat classes and has a child care facility on the premises. **The Firm** (612-377-3003; www.thefirm workoutstudio.com), located at 245 Aldrich Avenue North in Minneapolis, is known for its trendsetting, urban approach to fitness—classes like striptease and funk aerobics add spice to the core necessities you'd expect from any top-notch gym.

A national standard in women's gyms, the **YWCA** has three branches in Minneapolis—downtown at 1130 Nicollet Mall (612-332-0501), in Midtown at 2121 East Lake Street (612-215-4333), and in Uptown at 2808 Hennepin Avenue South (612-874-7131). The YWCA also has one location in St. Paul at 375 Selby Avenue (651-225-9922). All facilities have indoor swimming pools, weight machines, fitness programs, and day care.

The **YMCA** has multiple locations throughout the Twin Cities metro area, including one in downtown Minneapolis at 30 South Ninth Street (612-371-8700), and one in downtown St. Paul at 194 East Sixth Street (651-292-4143). All locations offer weight rooms, aerobic workout equipment, lap pools, gyms, and day care.

Minnesota winters are usually coldest (with many days consistently below 0 degrees F, depending on the year) between mid-January and mid-February, so if you are going to go out and play in the snow, your best bet is to do it before or after those weeks.

HOCKEY

Kids in Minnesota start playing hockey about as soon as they can walk, and both boys and girls participate in the sport with equal fervor. Every winter, parks in the Twin Cities metro area are flooded to make ice-skating rinks for skaters and

Winter Car Safety

The American Red Cross and other organizations sometimes sell winter car safety kits that include a flashlight and batteries, a snack food item, flagging tape, a candle, matches, a pencil and notepad for messages, a guide for safe winter travel, and other roadside necessities. But you don't have to wait for these occasional special offers—you can compile your own emergency car kit. For tips on how to make one, contact Minnesota's Division of Homeland Security and Emergency Management (651-296-2233; www.hsem.state.mn.us) or the Minnesota Safety Council (651-291-9150; www .mnsafetycouncil.org).

hockey players, and formal and informal hockey teams are formed among children and adults alike. During hockey season, large amounts of television time are blocked off on more than one station to bring live coverage of local high school and college hockey playoffs.

Traditionally St. Paul has been a much more dedicated hockey town than Minneapolis, and it shows. St. Paul has the Minnesota Wild's Xcel Energy Center arena and is home to groomed ice hockey rinks, including **Conway Ice Skating Park** at 2090 Conway Avenue (651-501-6343), **Desnoyer Ice Skating Rink** at 525 Pelham Boulevard (651-298-5753), **Edgcumbe Ice Skating Rink** at 320 South Griggs, (651) 695-3711, **Griggs Ice Skating Rink** at 1188 Hubbard Avenue (651-298-5755), **Langford Ice Skating Park** at 30 Langford Park (651-298-5765), **Linwood Ice Skating Rink** at 860 St. Clair Avenue (651-298-5660), **Merriam Park Ice Skating Rink** at 2000 St. Anthony Avenue (651-298-5766).

For more locations and information, contact St. Paul Parks and Recreation at (651) 266-6400 or www.stpaul.gov/depts/parks/specialservices.

ICE FISHING

Ice fishing entails setting up camp on top of a frozen lake, cutting a hole in the ice, and waiting for some sluggish fish to come along and snap up your bait. There are lots of fancy variations on this, including bringing portable houses, space heaters, camping refrigerators, and televisions out onto the ice with you, but this is basically the blueprint to every ice fishing trip. For more information, see the chapter on Fishing and Hunting.

ICE-SKATING

Just about every park in the Twin Cities metro area, if not every park in Minnesota, has a picturesque area that gets flooded every winter and turned into a free neighborhood ice-skating rink. One great example is the **Wells Fargo WinterSkate** (651-291-5608) on Landmark Plaza at St. Peter and Fifth Streets in downtown St. Paul. It's a new addition to Twin Cities rinks, but a beautiful one. Rice Park's white lights twinkle nearby as you skate in the shadow of the massive old courthouse that is now Landmark Center. Skate rental is $2.00 (or free if you produce your Wells Fargo credit or check card), and there's a warming tent with hot chocolate and snacks.

In St. Paul, you can find well-groomed skate rinks at **Conway Recreation Center Rink** at 2090 Conway Avenue, (651) 501–6343; **Desnoyer Ice Skating Rink** at 525 Pelham Boulevard, (651) 298–5753; **Eastview Recreation Center Rink** at 1675 East Fifth Street, (651) 772–7845; **Edgcumbe Ice Skating Rink** at 320 South Griggs, (651) 695–3711; **Griggs Recreation Center Rink** at 1188 Hubbard Avenue, (651) 298–5755; **Hazel Park Recreation Center Rink** at 945 North Hazel Avenue, (651) 501–6350; **Langford Recreation Center Rink** at 30 Langford Park, (651) 298–5765; **Linwood Recreation Center Rink** at 860 St. Clair Avenue, (651) 298–5660; **Merriam Park Recreation Center Rink** at 2000 St. Anthony Avenue, (651) 298–5766; **North Dale Recreation Center Rink** at 1414 North St. Albans, (651) 298–5812; and **Northwest Como Recreation Center Rink** at 1550 North Hamline, (651) 298–5813. There are many more options. Contact St. Paul Parks and Recreation for information at (651) 266–6400 or www.stpaul.gov/depts/parks/specialservices.

Minneapolis skating rinks, including those at **Lake Harriet** 1300 42nd Street East, (612) 230–6475; **Bryn Mawr Park** 1905 Mt. View Avenue, (612) 230–6400; **Longfellow Park** 3435 36th Avenue South, (612) 370–4957; and **Loring Park** 1382 Willow Street (612) 370–4929. Downtown Minneapolis converted the Old Milwaukee Road Train Depot at Fifth and Washington Avenues into a seasonal indoor skating rink. The **Depot Rink** (612–375–1700; www.thedepotminneapolis.com) is a gorgeous ice sheet inside the historic, glass-walled depot. Skate rentals are available.

For more information on Minneapolis

rinks, contact the Minneapolis Park and Recreation Board at (612) 230–6400 or www.minneapolisparks.com.

ROCK CLIMBING

While there aren't any mountains or even many steep hills in the Twin Cities metro area, there are several organizations that can put together mountaineering excursions for solo or group climbers, as well as a few gyms with indoor climbing walls for varying skill levels.

REI (952-884-4315; www.rei.com), located at 750 West American Boulevard in Bloomington, has information on REI's annual trips to such destinations as the Summit Challenge in Nepal and the Kilimanjaro Climb. Staff can also direct you to local climbing spots. REI is a complete gear shop and can hook you up with anything you need to prep yourself for any level of climb. The Bloomington store has an indoor climbing wall available free to members (for a one-time fee of $15) and for $10 to nonmembers.

Midwest Mountaineering (612–339–3433, www.midwestmtn.com), located at 309 Cedar Avenue South in Minneapolis, is another great gear shop with clinics and information about local climbing spots for all levels of climbers. The store has erected an on-site climbing cave that's free and open to the public during store hours. Shoe rental is available for $3.00.

For indoor climbing, **Vertical Endeavors Indoor Rock Facility** (651–776–1430), at 844 Arcade Street in St. Paul, has practice climbing options for all skill levels as well as on-site climbing instructors. It also holds clinics and organizes trips.

SLEDDING/TOBOGGANING

There aren't really rules regarding or areas set aside for sledding or tobogganing—most Twin Cities metro parks have great sledding hills either built or already existing for kids and adults to use. Use your

A nice winter date is indoor ice-skating at the Depot, a historic glass-walled rink in downtown Minneapolis. There are bars and restaurants nearby to complete the night.

common sense and don't pick a hill that terminates in a busy street, and don't try to take your sled on a ski or snowboard slope. **Como Park** in particular has great areas built up especially for sledding/tobogganing—call (651) 488-9673 for more information.

SNOWMOBILING

An incredible sense of freedom comes with riding a snowmobile, and Minnesota has 18,000 miles of public and private snowmobile trails that cross wide-open frozen lakes and follow paths cut through thick Minnesota forests. With just a few commonsense rules to "limit" the snow-mobiler, this is a great way to see the out-doors in Minnesota. You can download a copy of the Snowmobiler's Safety Laws, Rules & Regulations from the **Department of Natural Resources** Web page at www.dnr.state.mn.us/snowmobiling, or call the DNR at (651) 296-6157 for a copy by mail. You are required to have a Snowmo-bile State Trail Sticker ($16 per sticker) on your vehicle before you can take to the trails, so you'll probably want to give the DNR a call anyway. Maximum speed in Minnesota for snowmobiles is 50 mph. All resident snowmobiles must be registered with the DNR.

You are allowed to ride snowmobiles anywhere within the seven-county metro area on your own land (although you'd better be on good terms with your neigh-bors if you try it in the Cities), on land that has signs posted saying SNOWMOBILES ALLOWED, and on land where you have express written or spoken consent from the owner or lessee. Parks within the metro area that have trails specifically groomed for snowmobiles include Baker Park Preserve, Carver Park Preserve, Cleary Lake, Crow-Hassan, Elm Creek Park Reserve, Lake Rebecca Park Reserve, Lake Theodore, Lebanon Hills, Minnetonka Regional Park, Lebanon Hills, and Murphy-Hanrehan Park Reserve (see the Parks chapter for com-plete park listings). Additional information

on trails, trail maps, and snowmobiling events can be obtained by calling the **Min-nesota United Snowmobilers Association** at (763) 577-0185 or www.mnsnow mobiler.org.

SNOWSHOEING

Snowshoeing is an ideal means of trans-portation after a fresh snowfall. The wide, flat paddles make it possible to walk safely over the top of snowdrifts. Once you've mastered walking in snowshoes, you will practically glide over the soft snow.

The following parks have areas set aside for snowshoers: Baker Park Pre-serve, Carver Park Preserve, Coon Rapids Dam, Crow-Hassan, Elm Creek Park Reserve, French, and Murphy-Hanrehan. Individual parks hold events like full-moon and naturalist-led hikes. Call ahead or check out the activities listed with Three Rivers Park District (763-694-7750;

A young snowshoer high-steps through the powder. GREATER MINNEAPOLIS CONVENTION & VISITORS ASSOCIATION

i *If venturing onto frozen lakes, watch for warning signs, brightly colored buoys, or anything else that seems out of place. Minnesotans are intensely aware of the dangers of thin ice, and if nobody else is playing on a frozen public lake, it's a good idea to steer clear of it yourself.*

www.threeriversparkdistrict.org), St. Paul Parks and Recreation (651-266-6400; www.stpaul.gov/depts/parks/special services), or Minneapolis Park and Recreation Board (612-230-6400; www .minneapolisparks.com).

SNOW TUBING

Unlike sledding or tobogganing, you need to have a decent hill to get real speed on an inner tube. Some of the places that have designed and built special hills for snow tubing are **Eko Backen** (651-433-2422; www.ekobacken.com), at 22570 Manning Trail in Scandia; **Green Acres** (651-770-6060; www.greenacresrec.com),

at 8989 55th Street North in Lake Elmo; **Trapp Farm Park** (651-675-5511), at 841 Wilderness Run Road in Eagan; **Valley-wood Golf Course and Park** (952-953-2323), at 4851 125th Street West in Apple Valley; and **Theodore Wirth Park** (612-230-6400), at 1301 Theodore Wirth Parkway in Minneapolis. Inner tubes can be rented at all of the aforementioned facilities for a nominal fee.

YOGA

Depending on how you approach it and what you want to get out of it, yoga is a religion, an exercise routine, or a great way to forget about being trapped in a subzero climate. There are many different types—Hatha, Vinyasa, Ashtanga, and more. Find your style in Minneapolis at **Grasshopper Yoga Studio** (612-824-0278; www.grasshopperyogastudio.com), 810 West 31st Street, or **One Yoga Studio** (612-872-6347; www.one-yoga.com), 2100 B Lyndale Avenue South. Or in St. Paul at **Yoga Center** (651-644-7141; www.stpaul yogacenter.com) 1162 Selby Avenue, or **Sol Yoga & Massage** (651-224-8800; www .sol-yoga.com), 758 Grand Avenue.

HUNTING
AND FISHING

Hunting and fishing have been an important part of Minnesotans' lives and the state's economy since nomadic indigenous peoples and, later, European explorers discovered the dense, rich hardwood forests that harbored deer, bear, moose, and elk, or the lakes and streams that teemed with fish and furbearing animals like otter and beaver. Much, much later, wealthy socialites from Chicago made annual treks to Minnesota to swim and fish in the clear waters, giving rise to vacation and health resort towns all along the banks of Lake Superior, Lake Minnetonka, and many other Minnesota lakes.

These traditions stand today. There are hundreds of hunting and fishing resorts all over the state, many of which can sell you your fishing licenses right on the premises, as well as bait, ammunition, and rod and boat rentals. **Hospitality Minnesota** (651-778-2400; www.hospitalitymn.com) and the **Minnesota Office of Tourism** (888-TOURISM; www.exploreminnesota .com) issue an annual booklet that lists resorts in detail and will mail you a free copy if you call or contact them through either Web site.

Hunters and anglers are encouraged to be ethical, safe, and responsible. Minnesota's Department of Conservation, now the Department of Natural Resources (DNR), has been working since 1931 to make sure that there will always be game and fish for future generations, and strict fines and imprisonment are some of the penalties imposed on poachers and careless hunters who disregard the laws. The DNR offers many valuable resources to hunters and anglers, including information booklets on the best places to go hunting and fishing, a regularly updated Web site

(www.dnr.state.mn.us) with specific information about breeding and stocking programs for game animals and fish, and the convenience of applying for hunting and fishing licenses over the telephone for a nominal extra charge.

HUNTING

Hunting is a heavily regulated sport in Minnesota, requiring specific licensing dependent on game targeted, whether you're hunting with firearms or bow and arrow, the area you plan to hunt in, and the age of the hunter. If you purchase a small-game license but do not specify that you plan to hunt migratory birds (waterfowl, woodcock, snipe, rails, etc.), you are not allowed to hunt those birds; you must reapply for the same license and specify that you do plan to hunt migratory birds. Deer and big game licenses are awarded on a lottery basis depending on how many animals the Minnesota DNR considers an expendable excess.

Trespassing laws are rigidly enforced, and if you're caught hunting on private property or on land that is not zoned for hunting, you'll be fined. (Fines vary by county.) Exceptions to the trespassing laws include entering private land on foot and without a weapon to retrieve a wounded animal that was lawfully shot or to retrieve a hunting dog. If a landowner

The Minnesota Deer License and Registration Tag now come as a two-part form—the upper half is the actual license; the bottom half is the site tag to be cut off and attached to the deer itself.

does not allow you onto his land to retrieve a wounded animal, you must leave the private property immediately without the game animal.

Hunting dogs are not allowed to chase down, wound, or kill big-game animals. A dog that is observed doing so may be legally killed by a person other than a DNR conservation officer between January 1 and July 14. Hunting dogs may not be killed by anyone other than a DNR conservation officer any other time, as many hunters legally use dogs to track upland game, waterfowl, rabbits, raccoons, foxes, and coyotes.

For current licensing rates for game hunting, call the **Minnesota DNR** at (651) 296–6157 or (888) 646–6367, or check out the Web site at www.dnr.state.mn.us. Most licenses, both hunting and fishing, can be picked up at almost any bait shop or convenience store near the popular hunting areas (more than 1,800 licensing facilities are spread throughout Minnesota), but the DNR can immediately issue small-game licenses electronically if you call (651) 296–4506 or (888) MINN–DNR, or if you apply through the DNR's Web site. Hunters are encouraged to apply for all licenses early, as the number of licenses issued is dependent on game availability.

Animal poaching is a serious crime in Minnesota. **Turn In Poachers (TIP), Inc.,** is a nonprofit organization founded by hunters and concerned citizens to stop poaching in Minnesota. TIP offers cash awards for information leading to a poacher's arrest; all tipsters remain anonymous. For more information call the toll-free TIP hotline at (800) 652–9093.

The following listings are only general rules that apply to hunting and trapping game in Minnesota. Most parks and wildlife preserves have specific rules and restrictions regarding hunting and trapping, and it's important to check with both the DNR and with the specific park/preserve in question before going out.

Big Game

When hunting big game (deer, moose, bear, etc., as dictated by law) in Minnesota, the minimum caliber of rifle, shotgun, muzzleloader, or handgun that can be used is .23, and only single-projectile ammunition can be used. It's illegal to harvest big game with a bow and arrow while in possession of a firearm, with the exception of hunting bear, where possession of a firearm while in possession of archery equipment is allowed. Bows must have a minimum pull of 40 pounds at or before full draw in order to effectively kill big game. Arrowheads used must have a minimum of two sharp metal cutting edges and be barbless. Crossbows are not allowed for either big- or small-game hunting, except by special permit given only to disabled hunters. Big game may only be hunted from one-half hour before sunrise to one-half hour after sunset.

BEAR

Bear hunting is legal in much of northern and central northern Minnesota. Residents and nonresidents can obtain bear hunting licenses, which are usually made available by mid-March, from the DNR. More than 16,000 bear hunting permits were issued during the 2004 hunting season, but the number of permits issued is dependent on actual animal population.

DEER

Open season for deer hunting generally begins in early November and lasts

Some parts of Beltrami, Lake of the Woods, Koochiching, Roseau, and St. Louis Counties are Chippewa territories and are closed to nonband hunters and anglers except by special permission from the tribal council. Consult the DNR regarding specific contact information and how to acquire permission.

through early December. Archery season for deer traditionally begins in mid-September. Call the DNR for specific dates, as they vary from year to year. Any deer harvested by a hunter must be tagged according to DNR specifications. Brochures on proper tagging procedures are available at any of the 1,800 licensing stations across Minnesota or from the DNR Information and License Center at 500 Lafayette Road, St. Paul, MN 55155-4040, www.dnr.state.mn.us, (888) 646-6367.

A limited number of Special Area Permits are issued each year to hunters in places where the number of hunters must be limited to control the harvest or for public safety. Permits are awarded by a lottery system dependent on a head count and estimation of expendable deer available. Hunters who receive Special Area Permits may also hunt deer outside that Special Area if they apply to do so and have it specifically punched on their hunting license. Laws can change significantly from year to year. For the most current hunting regulations, contact the Minnesota DNR at (888) 646–6367 or look online at www.dnr.state.mn.us.

ELK

During years when elk hunting is permitted, the season is open only to residents of Minnesota, and hunters must apply in parties of two. Elk hunting permits are not issued every year; contact the DNR to find out more about whether there will be a hunt and for more information about applying for permits. Permits are issued by random drawing, and the hunt is a once-in-a-lifetime event.

MOOSE

Minnesota's annual moose hunt is open only to Minnesota residents and is a once-in-a-lifetime event—each hunter is allowed to take down only one moose in his or her lifetime. Moose licenses are awarded annually on a lottery basis determined by actual animal populations. Some years no

moose permits are issued. Generally the moose hunting season runs from late September to mid-October. Contact the DNR for more specifics.

Small Game, Waterfowl, and Migratory Birds

It's no accident that Minnesota has an abundance of wildlife in its parklands, wildlife preserves, and even in the cities. Careful monitoring of habitats and hunter/game interaction by Minnesota conservation officers has been an important facet of state government for more than a century, with the goal of creating safe hunting opportunities for residents and visitors while preserving as much of the native Minnesota wildlife as possible. Limits on migratory birds and many species of small game are strictly enforced.

BEAVER, MINK, MUSKRAT, AND OTTER

It is unlawful to trap any furbearing animals within any state-owned game refuge without first obtaining a permit from the appropriate wildlife manager. Most of the state parks and state wildlife refuges allow trapping of furbearing small game as long as you get prior permission and have a small-game hunting license.

FOXES, RACCOONS, SQUIRRELS, RABBITS

A small-game hunting license is required, unless you are hunting on your own land.

MIGRATORY WATERFOWL

A State Migratory Waterfowl Stamp (State Duck Stamp), purchased from the DNR for a nominal fee, is required for hunting geese, ducks, and mergansers. All hunters—resident and nonresident—between the ages of 18 and 65 are required to have a valid State Duck Stamp in their possession while hunting migratory waterfowl, with the exception of those taking down waterfowl on their own property or who are in the U.S. Armed Forces and are stationed outside Minnesota with official military leave papers on their person.

Waterfowl hunting seasons and bag limits are set in late summer, and season dates are announced in early September. Contact the DNR for more information.

A special permit is also required for hunting Canada geese in season. During early September and late December, the entire state is open to hunting geese. Daily bag limits range from two to five geese per hunter, depending on the DNR-specified hunting zone, and shooting hours last from one-half hour before sunrise to sunset every day. Possession limits are double the daily bag limits. Migratory waterfowl must be transported in an undressed condition (with head and wings attached) at all times until delivery to either the hunter's home or to a commercial processing facility.

It is unlawful to take geese, ducks, mergansers, coots, or moorhens with lead shot or while having any lead shot in possession. Only nontoxic shot approved by the U.S. Fish and Wildlife Service may be used. These nontoxic shot restrictions are responsible for preventing lead poisoning of more than 400,000 wild ducks nationwide each year.

WILD TURKEY

Spring and fall (check with the DNR for specific dates) are open for hunting wild turkey in Minnesota. Generally application deadlines for Wild Turkey Stamps are five or six months before the season begins. Smaller, quicker, and smarter than domestic turkeys, these native Minnesota birds can also fly up into trees to hide, making them a competitive target for traditional firearm and bow hunters alike. Although a small-game license is not necessary for taking wild turkey, you must purchase a

Wild Turkey Stamp from the DNR to legally hunt the birds. Bag limit is one bird of either sex in the fall season per hunter and one male bird per hunter in spring.

Only fine shot size number 4 and smaller may be used to hunt turkey, and nothing smaller than a 20 gauge shotgun can be carried on turkey hunts. Bows must have a pull of no less than 40 pounds, and arrows must be sharp, have at least two metal cutting edges, and be at least $7/8$ inch in diameter. Poison- or explosive-tipped arrows may not be used to hunt any game animal or bird in Minnesota. Hunting dogs are not allowed on turkey hunts, and neither are electronic tracking devices. Every hunter who takes a wild turkey must personally present the bird for registration at one of the 1,800 registration stations throughout Minnesota; the feathers, head, and feet must remain on the bird until it is officially registered.

Protected Animals

There is no open season for hunting bobwhite quail, prairie chickens, cranes, swans, hawks, owls, eagles, herons, bitterns, cormorants, loons, grebes, or any other species of birds except specified game or unprotected birds. Crows may be taken without a license in season (September 1 through February 28) or at any time when they are doing or are about to do damage. There is also no open season for hunting caribou, antelope, gray wolf, wolverine, cougar, or spotted skunk ("civet cat").

Unprotected Species

Minnesota residents are not required to have a license to hunt unprotected species. Weasels, coyotes, gophers, porcupines, striped skunks, and all other mammals for which there are no closed seasons or are not under protected status may be hunted year-round. They may be taken in any manner, except with the aid of artificial lights or by using a motor vehicle to chase, run over, or kill the animal. Poisons may not be used except in accordance with restrictions stated by the Minnesota Department of Agriculture.

House sparrows, starlings, common pigeons, chukar partridge, quail other than bobwhite quail, mute swans, and monk parakeets are all unprotected and may be hunted year-round.

No person may take a wild animal with a firearm or by archery from a motorized vehicle except a disabled person with an appropriate permit on a stationary vehicle. Also, it's against the law to transport an uncased firearm or shoot from any motorized vehicle in Minnesota.

FISHING

In the Land of 10,000 Lakes, it's no surprise that fishing is one of the most popular summer recreational activities. To meet the demand of thousands of dedicated anglers, the Minnesota DNR runs fisheries all over the state that are in charge of keeping some of the most popular lakes and fishing holes well stocked with walleye, pike, muskellunge, trout, bass, catfish, crappie, bluegill, and, in Lake Superior, salmon. Fishing licenses are available at any of the 1,800 licensing agents located at convenience stores, bait shops, and sports outfitters across the state. Since March 2000 the DNR has also been issuing fishing licenses electronically over the telephone (call 888–MNLicense for more information) and through its Web site at www.dnr.state.mn.us.

Regulations for fishing areas change per year according to species populations, so it's a good idea to call the DNR to request a current fishing guide or to ask about a specific fishing spot before heading out. The DNR's Web site regularly posts updated fishing information and regulation changes, if any.

Common Catches

NORTHERN PIKE

Although walleye is the most popular fish in Minnesota, the most widely spread game fish in the state is the northern pike. With its abundance of marshes and shallow streams, Minnesota has as much or more northern pike habitat than any other state. Given relatively clean water, an adequate food supply, and enough shoreline marshes and wetlands to spawn in, northern pike will propagate in abundance all on its own.

Northern pike does so well on its own, in fact, that stocking lakes with the fish is usually unnecessary. The feisty carnivorous fish, which can grow to weigh 20 pounds, will eat just about any other fish, and lakes with an abundance of northern pike tend to have low populations of all other fish. Eventually the food supply runs out, and pike populations start dropping off as well.

This practice of allowing pike populations to grow on their own has problems. It's every sport angler's dream to catch a giant trophy northern pike, but it usually takes at least 15 years for a northern pike to grow to weigh 20 pounds and another 10 to reach 30 pounds. You can usually count on a few 20-plus pounders to be caught each year, but most northern pike caught are only two or three pounds on average. The DNR encourages anglers to view the northern pike as a trophy fish only, and that all small fish carefully caught and released can be caught again year after year for sport until they are big enough to be mounted.

Pike are a fun sport fish for all levels of angler, as they are fearless, toothy creatures and will snap at just about any bait you use. This makes catch-and-release tactics especially practical, as northern pike can be lured with harmless artificials as easily as live bait and tend to release their grip on artificials a lot easier than they do tasty organic bait.

Year-round Twin Citians take to the Metro's lakes. GREATER MINNEAPOLIS CONVENTION & VISITORS ASSOCIATION

Northern pike season generally runs mid-May through mid-February of the following year. Contact the DNR for specific season dates. A possession limit of three is in effect, and only one pike longer than 30 inches can be taken each day.

Northern pike are best caught in cool waters, so winter, early spring, and late fall are the best times to pursue these fish. Some of the state-managed lakes and streams known for their strong northern pike populations are Baudette River, Rainy River, and Winter Road River in Lake of the Woods County; Warroad River in Roseau County; Andrew Lake, Burgen Lake, and Rachel Lake in Douglas County; Big Birch Lake, Big Swan Lake, and Little Sauk Lake in Todd County; Coon-Sandwick Lake in Itasca County; Dudley Lake and Kelly Lake in Rice County; East Battle Lake, Twenty One Lake, and Norway Lake in Otter Tail County; Medicine Lake and North Twin

Lake in Beltrami County; Sallie Lake and Melissa Lake in Becker County; Platte Lake in Crow Wing County; Reeds Lake and St. Olaf Lake in Waseca County; Sissabagamah Lake and Wilkins Lake in Aitkin County; and Stieger Lake in Carver County, Sturgeon Lake in Paine County, Ten Mile Lake in Cass County, and Sullivan Lake in Morrison County.

BASS

Bass are some of the scrappiest, most wildly gymnastic fish in Minnesota's waters and can fight an angler after being hooked for several hours before either wearing out or breaking free. Because of their aggressive reaction to being hooked, catch-and-release fishing is often not a viable option; these fish literally throw themselves into the air and against boats and rocks trying to escape, sometimes ripping hooks completely out of their bodies while doing so. Both smallmouth and largemouth bass are very strong for their size, and anglers should expect a good fight no matter what size the catch.

Largemouth bass are especially adaptable and prolific fish. They live and successfully spawn in a variety of conditions, and only very few stocked bass are required to populate a large body of water. Male largemouth bass viciously guard largemouth fingerlings until they're old enough to leave the nest, which almost guarantees that many of the tens of thousands of largemouth eggs laid each year will someday become full-grown fish. Consequently, stocking plays a very small role in largemouth bass management and is usually only done in newly filled basins, winterkill lakes, or chemically rehabilitated waters.

What largemouth bass do need to flourish is spawning areas with a firm bottom of sand, mud, or gravel; heavy cover such as beds of rooted aquatic weeds or logs large enough for fingerlings to hide in or under; and adequate dissolved oxygen levels in the water, especially in the winter, when the fish hibernate under ice. Largemouth bass are a warmwater fish and do best in waters that are as warm as 80 and 90 degrees. In winter, largemouth bass go into a state of near-hibernation, settling lethargically near the bottom of lakes until temperatures rise to a comfortable 60-degrees-plus again.

Smallmouth bass don't usually get much larger than two or three pounds, although those who catch them swear they're at least twice that big in the water because of their incredible strength. A native Mississippi watershed fish, smallmouth are abundant throughout the Mississippi River and its tributaries. The smallmouth is also naturally found in many Minnesotan lakes, though it is far less common in this environment than are largemouth bass. Unlike largemouth bass, smallmouth bass prefer to live in cool water and need to be in 60-degree water in order to spawn. Like the largemouth bass, though, smallmouth males guard their nests until the fingerlings are at least two weeks old, guaranteeing a successful population in any area they find comfortable enough to settle.

Stream-based smallmouth bass are migratory fish, and in late fall these migrations take them 50 miles or more from their spawning grounds to their "hibernacula"—places where large groups of smallmouth bass crowd together under the ice, eating and moving little while they wait out the winter.

Largemouth and smallmouth bass season generally runs mid-May through mid-February of the following year; the dates change year to year and depend on what part of the state you intend to fish. In 2006 it is illegal to catch and keep any smallmouth bass after September 8 (catch and release is okay). Contact the DNR for specific season dates. A six-fish possession limit of combined smallmouth and largemouth bass is in effect.

Some of the state-managed lakes and streams that are excellent for catching largemouth and smallmouth bass are Otter Tail River, Clitherall Lake, Fladmark Lake, and Annie Battle Lake in Otter Tail County; Bavaria Lake, Minnewashta Lake, Stieger Lake, and Waconia Lake in Carver County; Chisago Lake and South Lindstrom Lake in Chisago County; DeMontreville Lake, Jane Lake, and Olson Lake in Washington County; Flour Lake, Hungry Jack Lake, Pike Lake, and Two Island Lake in Cook County; Green Lake and Long Lake in Kandiyohi County; Little Sauk Lake and Moose Lake in Todd County; Mink Lake and Somers Lake in Wright County; Moccasin Lake and Portage Lake in Cass County; and Pelican Lake in St. Louis County, Pierz (Fish) Lake in Morrison County, Turtle Lake in Ramsey County, Bear Creek Reservoir in Olmsted County, Clear Lake in Waseca County, Crooked Lake in Anoka County, and Little Mantrap Lake in Hubbard County.

All along the Mississippi River Valley and the Mississippi River itself are also very good places for catching smallmouth bass. Largemouth bass can be found in the warmer runoff pools and tributaries of the Mississippi River.

CATFISH AND BULLHEADS

Catfish and their close cousin, the bullhead, are incredibly hardy fish that can live on just about anything. Both fish, especially bullheads, are often stocked in urban ponds and lakes that have low oxygen levels due to high concentrations of algae or detritus, where they can be fished for fun by kids and those with limited mobility. Minnesota has two native catfish species, channel and flathead, and three species of bullheads—black, brown, and yellow. Found throughout the state, the fish prefer fertile waters but respond well to stocking programs that put them in waters other than where their populations would naturally occur. During winter catfish and bullheads seek deep waters where boulders or logs provide refuge

Minnesota actually has 11,842 lakes to angle in, significantly more than the 10,000 the state's motto proclaims.

from currents, and they sink into a torpor so deep that silt often collects on their bodies.

An old myth concerning catching catfish claims that they're armed with poisonous spikes and that they should be handled as little as possible. Truth is, while they do have sharp spines along the leading edges of the dorsal (top) fin and the two pectoral (side) fins that stand erect when the fish is alarmed, the spines are not poisonous, and any pain experienced comes from being poked by them and not from any toxin. As long as you avoid grasping the dorsal and pectoral fins, catfish and bullheads can be handled as safely as any other fish.

Flathead catfish, also called "mud cat" or "yellow cat," are most commonly found in Minnesota's large, slow-moving rivers, such as the Minnesota River, the St. Croix at Taylors Falls, and the Mississippi River below the Coon Rapids Dam. Distinguished by the broad, flat head from which it got its name, it is the largest catfish in Minnesota and has been reported to grow up to 100 pounds. Flatheads occupy deep pools with dense cover, such as logjams, and feed primarily on other fish—because they eat such great numbers of other fish, fish managers sometimes introduce them to lakes with large numbers of undesirable fish, such as carp, to try to control those populations. They have an acute sense of smell and therefore don't generally go for artificial lures, dead bait, or "stink bait," preferring live bait instead.

Channel catfish are steel gray and peppered with dark spots that disappear with age. Similar in appearance to the flathead, their distinguishing characteristic is their deeply forked tail. Much smaller than flatheads, rarely growing to exceed 20 pounds and usually averaging one to four pounds, channel cats can navigate much better in the faster waters of the Mississippi, St. Croix, Red, and St. Louis Rivers than flatheads do. While channel cats prefer deep, still, clean waters, they often move to murky waters to spawn, as the limited visibility protects their fry from predators.

Bullheads are the toughest of the catfish, requiring nothing but a puddle of warm water and some wet grass to survive. Ideally, though, these omnivorous fish prefer weedy, deep lakes and ponds with bottom cover (logs, thick weeds, etc.) for them to lay their eggs. All bullheads are relatively small members of the catfish family—yellow bullheads, found in southern Minnesota, weigh about a pound on average, while black bullheads and brown bullheads, naturally found in the Mississippi, Minnesota, St. Croix, and Red Rivers, usually don't grow to be longer than 10 inches.

Catfish are plentiful throughout the state and are not usually stocked in lakes or streams unless they're there to control other fish populations, or are stocked in inner-city ponds to give kids and those with limited mobility a chance to enjoy the sport of fishing.

As of 2006, the season for both bullhead and catfish is year-round. A possession limit of 100 fish is set for bullhead and 5 fish for catfish. Contact the DNR for more information.

CRAYFISH

Licensed anglers and children under age 16 may take home up to 25 pounds of crayfish for personal use during crayfish season, as determined by the DNR. Crayfish cannot be sold as bait or for aquarium use.

MUSKIE AND TIGER MUSKIE

The muskellunge is one of the largest and most elusive fish in Minnesota and is also one of the most prized trophy fish sought by sports anglers. Closely related to the northern pike, muskies can grow to surpass 40 inches long and weigh 30 pounds and up. Light-colored with dark bars running up and down their bodies, muskies can be silver, green, or brown, with large, strong, tooth-lined jaws for dragging down prey.

As with northern pike, stocking lakes and waterways with muskies is unnecessary. For one thing, they prefer larger fish as prey, so introducing them to a fishing lake only guarantees the eventual annihilation of the already-existing bass and trout populations. Muskie are also very particular about their environment, requiring well-oxygenated, cool water (60 degrees and cooler) that's clear enough for these sight-feeding fish.

Because muskies are perceived as trophy fish only, and because large muskies are scarce and usually very old, Minnesota imposes a possession limit of one muskie per licensed angler, with a minimum length of 40 inches (30 inches in Shoepac Lake within Voyageurs National Park). The muskie season generally runs early June through mid-February of the following year. Contact the DNR for specific season dates.

Tiger muskie, a sterile hybrid of the northern pike and the muskellunge, has characteristics of both parents. Tiger muskies have distinct bars that run along their light-colored bodies similar to the bars on a full muskie, fins and tail lobes rounded like a northern pike's, and cheekscale patterns that fall somewhere between those of both fish. The hybrid grows slightly faster than either pure-strain parent and can exceed 30 pounds in less than 10 years. Because of their quick maturation rate and because they are sterile, tiger muskie are often stocked in lakes and streams in heavily fished lakes and streams throughout Minnesota, including some Twin Cities metro area lakes.

Some of the state-managed lakes open to fishing these amazing trophy fish are Bald Eagle Lake in Anoka County, Eagle Lake and Rebecca Lake in Hennepin County, Elk Lake in Clearwater County, Little Wolf Lake in Cass County, Owasso Lake in Ramsey County, and Plantanganette Lake in Hubbard County.

PANFISH

Panfish are not actually any particular species of fish but a blanket term referring to any number of small food fishes, especially those caught with hook and line,

generally not available on the market. Minnesota has quite a few good-tasting "panfish," and it's common practice to take home a few of them to eat to make up for all the undersized trophy fish you caught and had to let go.

Crappies and bluegills are probably caught for eating more often than any other fish in Minnesota. Crappies are easy to catch and produce sweet-tasting fillets, and they travel in schools, which make them even easier to find and catch. Bluegills are Minnesota's biggest and most popular panfish, found in about 65 percent of Minnesota's lakes and slow streams, including the backwaters of the Mississippi. Though they occasionally exceed a pound, an 8-inch bluegill is considered a big fish.

Closely related to the bluegill are the pumpkinseed, the green sunfish, and the orange-spotted sunfish. Like the bluegill, the pumpkinseed lives in many of Minnesota's lakes and streams. Almost as large as the bluegill, the pumpkinseed can be distinguished from its dark olive cousin by the bright orange spot at the tip of its ear flap. Green sunfish are a drab, gray color and are much smaller than pumpkinseed and bluegill—usually about 5 inches long. The brightest, smallest, and most colorful member of the sunfish family is by far the orange-spotted sunfish, which rarely reaches 4 inches long. Although their bodies are the same olive tones of the other sunfish species, orange-spotted sunfish are often streaked with orange-red lines on their cheeks and gill covers, while their stomachs and lower fins are tinged red. Because they're so small, orange-spotted sunfish aren't usually taken home by anglers, but they're very pretty to see in the water while you're fishing,

Black and white crappies are among Minnesota's most popular panfish. Black crappies are much more widely distributed than white crappies and can be found in most of the state's lakes. The two fish are very similar in appearance—in fact, the only real difference in appearance is that the black crappies are a slightly darker gray color than white crappies. Both fish rarely grow to weigh more than two pounds, and both species travel in large schools that are easy to spot.

Rock bass are stout and heavy compared with sunfish and crappies, measuring 10 inches on average and weighing around a pound. With its red eyes and brassy-colored, black-spotted flanks, it's an easy fish to identify when caught. Rock bass live in many streams and lakes in Minnesota, generally preferring well-oxygenated, hard-water walleye lakes with boulder and sand bottoms. White panfish and yellow bass, despite their names, are not related to largemouth and smallmouth bass. They're actually a cousin of the much larger Atlantic striped bass. Yellow bass populations are limited to the backwaters of the Mississippi below Lake Pepin, while the white bass can be found in the Minnesota River, the St. Croix, and the Mississippi and many of its tributaries and reservoirs. Both fish are thick bodied, occasionally exceeding two pounds.

The season for most of Minnesota's panfish runs year-round, with varying bag limits. Contact the DNR for more details.

WALLEYE, SAUGER, AND PERCH

Walleye is the most sought-after fish in Minnesota, and Minnesota anglers and restaurant patrons alike go crazy over the thick-filleted perch. Each year anglers in Minnesota catch and keep almost four million pounds of walleye, keeping the DNR's hands full stocking Minnesota lakes and rivers with the elusive fish.

The average walleye weighs one to two pounds, although some specimens caught have weighed in at as much as 10 pounds. The fish is torpedo shaped, with opaque, pearly eyes (for which the fish is named), and its color ranges from dark olive-brown to yellowish gold. Unlike its near cousin, the sauger, the walleye lacks spots on its dorsal fin, except for a dark patch on the rear base of the fin, which the sauger does not have. Also, the lower tip of the walleye's tail is white, while the lower lobe of the sauger's tail is all dark.

Both the walleye and the sauger are native fish, although walleye is much more commonly found in Minnesota's waterways than the sauger. The walleye prefers large, shallow lakes with gravel shoals, such as Mille Lacs, Leech Lake, Winnibigoshish, Upper and Lower Red Lakes, Lake of the Woods, and Lake Vermilion. Because of its popularity as a game and food fish, the walleye has been introduced to waterways all over the state and now occupies more than 1,600 lakes and 100 warmwater streams throughout the Midwest. The walleye's low-level vision and sensitivity to light keep it hidden in the deep parts of lakes until dawn and dusk, at which point walleyes come to the shallows to feed. Their diet consists almost solely of fish, and their biggest prey is yellow perch, which can't see well in the dark and are easily caught by the night-feeding walleye. Because of their sensitivity to light, walleyes are best caught at dawn or dusk, or when the skies are overcast.

Sauger are similar to walleye in appearance and habits, although their distribution throughout Minnesota is more limited. They can usually be found in Lake St. Croix, the Minnesota River, the Mississippi River, Lake of the Woods, Rainy Lake, and Lake Kabetogama. Saugers seldom exceed three pounds and are generally much slimmer than walleye.

Yellow perch, cousin to both walleye and sauger as well as a shared common prey, are also found throughout Minnesota's lakes and streams. They're often infected with parasites, and even the healthy ones are usually too small to reasonably consider eating. Walleye and yellow perch populations often coincide with each other, and lakes where the yellow population is strong are also home to big, healthy walleye—who may not be hungry

Kids under age 16 do not need a license to fish in Minnesota when accompanied by an adult with a fishing license.

enough to be interested in bait.

Some of the state-managed lakes and streams that are good for walleye are Ann Lake and Knife Lake in Kanabec County; Big Sand Lake in Hubbard County; Big Stone Lake in Big Stone County; Borden Lake in Crow Wing County; Crane Lake, Kabetogama Lake, Sand Point Lake, Little Vermilion Lake, Loon River, Namakan Lake, and Rainy Lake in St. Louis County; Crawford Lake, Wright Lake, and Somers Lake in Wright County; Farm Island Lake, North Big Pine, and South Big Pine in Aitkin County; Goose Lake and Green Lake in Chisago County; Lake of the Woods in Roseau County; Little Elk in Sherburne County; Little McDonald Lake and Norway Lake in Otter Tail County; Little Sauk Lake and Osakis Lake in Todd County; Red Lake in Beltrami County; and Stieger Lake and Waconia Lake in Carver County.

The season for walleye and sauger generally runs mid-May through mid-February of the following year, with a limit of six fish. The opening of walleye season is an annual event in Minnesota, opened with much fanfare by the governor casting a line in a chosen outstate lake with cameras clicking and TV cameras rolling. Perch season is year-round, with a limit of 10 fish per day. Contact the DNR for more details.

SALMON

Three species of Pacific salmon have been introduced to Lake Superior in the past few decades: the chinook (or king) salmon, the pink (or humpy) salmon, and the coho (or silver) salmon. All three species feed in Lake Superior until they reach sexual maturity and then swim up rivers to spawn and die. The chinook salmon has been the most successful of the three species, growing to weigh more than 30 pounds and being the most resistant to disease.

There is no closed season for salmon fishing—however, you must get a Trout and Salmon Stamp on your fishing license

in order to legally catch them. Bag limits for catching all species of salmon change with each year as newly hatched young come back to Lake Superior to mature. Contact the DNR for more information.

TROUT

Minnesota has four species of trout inhabiting its streams and lakes, two of which are native species (brook trout and lake trout) and two of which were introduced to Minnesota waters in the late 1800s—the rainbow trout, originally from western North America, and the brown trout, which was brought over from Germany. Brown trout have done exceptionally well here and are the hardiest of the trout species, able to tolerate warmer and murkier waters than any other species in the state. You must buy a Trout and Salmon Stamp for your fishing license to fish in Minnesota's trout streams and lakes, including Lake Superior. Funds from stamp sales pay for habitat improvement and raising and stocking trout and salmon.

Most trout streams are located in southeastern Minnesota and along the North Shore. The southern streams are populated with mostly brown trout, some rainbow trout, and, where the water runs cold and clear, a few brook trout. Northern streams have mostly "brookies," while the deep, cold lakes up north and Lake Superior itself make a comfortable home for lake trout as well as a lake and brook trout hybrid called a splake. Also up north is a specific type of rainbow trout, called a steelhead, that lives only in Lake Superior and grows exceptionally large.

Out of all the trout species represented in the state, the pink-striped rainbow trout and the silvery steelhead are the most prized as gamefish among anglers; they put up a good, dramatic fight when hooked, sometimes leaping several feet into the air to free themselves from a line, as opposed to the brown trout, which is too suspicious to be easily lured by bait, and the brook trout, which is gullible and will bite at just about anything floating in the water.

Hundreds of streams course through Minnesota's woods and farmlands. Some are naturally fertile and have always been excellent fishing holes; others are poor in nutrients and soil quality and have to be regularly stocked by the DNR. A good trout stream has rich siltbeds, a profuse insect population, and adequate groundwater, creating a suitable streambed ecology for healthy trout to flourish in. Though brown, rainbow, and brook trout have evolved over time to live and breed in cool, fast-moving streams, they actually grow much bigger when they're removed from streams and put in lakes. Because of this, the Minnesota DNR regularly removes young trout from streambeds and stocks about 160 deep, clean, coldwater lakes throughout the state to give anglers a chance to catch some real trophy trout. The DNR also stocks these same lakes with plenty of splake—a cross between a male brookie and a female lake trout. As with most other hybrids, splakes grow much faster and bigger than either of their parent species and are popular fish because they're big, they taste good, and they're very easy to catch.

Some of the state-managed stocked lakes open to trout fishing are Beaver Creek, Cold Spring Brook, West Indian Creek, and Zumbro River in Wabasha County; Bunker Hill Creek and Little Rock Creek in Benton County; Camp Creek, Canfield Creek, Duschee Creek, North Branch Creek, Root River, and Trout Run Creek in Fillmore County; Whitewater River and Trout Valley Creek in Winona County; Boys Lake, Thrush Lake, and Turnip Lake in Cook County; and Foster Arend Lake in Olmsted County, Square

Lake in Washington County, Eagle Creek in Scott County, East Beaver Creek in Houston County, Hay Creek in Goodhue County, and Ann Lake in Carver County. Trout seasons and bag limits range widely, depending on the species and where you are fishing. Stream trout (rainbow, brook, and brown) can be fished only in summer, although lake trout have both summer and winter seasons. Contact the DNR for more details.

Harmful Aquatic Species

Several plant and animal species introduced to Minnesota waters over the past century, have caused severe damage to native species populations. Among these are zebra mussels, Eurasian watermilfoil, ruffe, and round goby.

Eurasian watermilfoil is a water plant similar in appearance to duckweed that reproduces quickly in shallow water and can interfere with water recreation as well as harm oxygen levels in lakes and ponds. Even the tiniest of fragments clinging to boats and trailers can spread the prolific plant from one body of water to another. Zebra mussels, originally from Asia, can quickly displace native mussels, disrupt lake ecosystems, and clog industrial equipment. Their microscopic larvae can accidentally be transported in bait buckets or by moving a boat from one confined body of water to another. The best way to prevent the spread of Eurasian watermilfoil and Zebra mussels is to make sure you wipe dry any excess water from your boat before moving it from one body of water to another, and dump bait buckets on land and dry them thoroughly before putting them back in water.

Ruffe is a small, perchlike fish from Europe that has taken over parts of Duluth harbor, displacing many native fish. Also from Europe is the bottom-dwelling round goby, which has displaced many fish in Minnesota lakes and is a serious

ℹ️ *Don't know what you've caught? The DNR can send you free information describing in detail how to tell which fish is which, describing species' markings to the minutest detail to avoid confusion.*

threat to the fisheries in the Great Lakes, which it has already entered. The spread of both fish can be attributed to being transported from one body of water to another in bait buckets and livewells.

Ice Fishing

This sport is a longtime tradition of both Minnesotan and Alaskan anglers, inspired by Alaskan indigenous anglers who had no choice but to catch fish this way. The basic principle of ice fishing is to walk out on a deep lake with enough ice cover to safely support your weight (ice should be a minimum of 6 inches thick for walking, a foot or more for vehicles), cut a hole in the ice, and sink a hook through it with hopes of luring the few fish that aren't in a state of torpor to take your bait. Over the years this simple idea has expanded to include portable ice fishing houses for anglers to sit in comfort while waiting for fish to bite, equipped with televisions, suspended heating elements, radios, furniture, and the requisite cooler stuffed with beer.

Your best bet in ice fishing is to stake out lakes and rivers known for having good trout or muskie populations, as these fish actually get more energetic as the weather grows cooler.

Some metro area parks with lakes deep enough (and enough lively coldwater fish) for ice fishing include Baker Park Preserve, Bald Eagle–Otter Lakes, Bryant Lake, Carver Park Preserve, Como, Coon Rapids Dam, Fish Lake, French, Hidden Falls–Crosby Farm, Lake Byllesby, Lake George, Lake Minnewashta, Lake Rebecca Park Reserve, Lebanon Hills, Long Lake Regional Park, Martin-Island-Linwood Lakes, Minneapolis Chain of Lakes, Nokomis Hiawatha, Phalen, Rice Creek/Chain of Lakes, Snail Lake, and Theodore Wirth (see the Parks chapter for parks listings).

Metro Fishing

Both Minneapolis and St. Paul have a surprising number of good fishing lakes within city limits, as do their nearby suburbs. At least 23 city lakes and rivers in the metro area are regularly stocked and monitored by the Minnesota DNR, with the purpose of providing safe, fun fishing lakes for urbanites, children, and those with limited mobility.

Some of the best fishing lakes in Minneapolis are Lake Calhoun, Lake of the Isles, Cedar Lake, Lake Harriet, and Lake Nokomis. Lake Calhoun, located about 3 blocks west of Lake Street and Hennepin Avenue, is a deep (82 feet deep in spots) fishing and boating lake with largemouth bass, northern pike, crappie, sunfish, tiger muskie, walleye, perch, catfish, and carp swimming in its waters. Rental canoes are available at the concession stand, which also sells fast food but no bait. Calhoun has a couple of great fishing piers and three swimming beaches.

Connected to Lake Calhoun by a canoe-navigable channel is Lake of the Isles, located by land just south of Franklin Avenue and 1 mile west of Hennepin Avenue. Many of the same types of fish as in Lake Calhoun are in these waters, with a huge population of sunfish and crappies, much to the delight of the many species of waterfowl that also frequent these waters.

Cedar Lake, located just south of Interstate 394 and east of Minnesota Highway 100, is stocked with healthy populations of largemouth bass, northern pike, crappie, sunfish, tiger muskies, perch, carp, and catfish and is a great shore fishing spot due to the deep water right next to shore. Anyone willing to bushwhack along the brushy banks can usually find some good-size largemouth bass hanging out along the lake's north shore.

Lake Harriet, another great Minneapolis fishing and boating lake with waters as deep as 87 feet in places, is located 1 mile west of Lyndale Avenue just north of 50th Street. Shore fishing at Lake Harriet is surprisingly good, considering that most of the really deep water is near the middle of the lake. Muskies, bass, sunfish, perch, catfish, and walleye can be caught here. The lake has a fishing pier and a boat rental facility nearby as well as a swimming beach and playground.

Lake Nokomis, located south of Minnehaha Parkway between Cedar and Hiawatha Avenues, is one of the best crappie lakes in the Twin Cities. Because it gets more sun and warms up quickly, the north shore fishing pier is the best spot to stake out in the spring. Also found in Lake Nokomis are northern pike, sunfish, tiger muskie, carp, bullhead, perch, and walleye.

St. Paul has a couple of excellent fishing spots for more serious anglers—meaning no picnic area, no playground, and little or no paved paths leading down to the water. Hidden Falls Regional Park, located just south of Ford Parkway, is an excellent summer fishing spot for walleye, catfish, crappie, sunfish, white bass, smallmouth and largemouth bass, northern pike, and carp. If the water level is high, anglers can fish from the grassy picnic area, but if it's low you must descend a steep bank to reach the water.

Pike Island and Snelling Lake, both located in St. Paul's Fort Snelling State Park, are two rustic yet excellent fishing holes. Pike Island is good for early-season walleye fishing, as the fish pass here while moving upstream to spawn below Ford Dam. The best fishing is where the channel north of Pike Island meets the Mississippi River, where you can catch carp, catfish, smallmouth bass, walleye, white bass, and crappie. Snelling Lake has some nice paved paths leading to the shoreline, although to get to the best fishing areas, you have to stand in the marsh. There's also a good fishing pier here, from which you can catch largemouth bass, crappie, sunfish, northern pike, carp, and bullhead.

Other metro area parks that have areas set aside for fishing include Anoka County Riverfront, Baker Park Preserve, Bald Eagle–Otter Lakes, Baylor, Bryant Lake, Carver Park Preserve, Central Mississippi Riverfront, Cleary Lake, Como, Coon Rapids Dam, Fish Lake, French, Lake Byllesby, Lake Elmo Park Reserve, Lake George, Lake Minnetonka Regional Park, Lake Minnewashta, Lake Rebecca Park Reserve, Lebanon Hills, Lilydale–Harriet Island, Long Lake Regional Park, Rice Creek/Chain of Lakes, Rice Creek–West Regional Trail, Rum River Central, Snail Lake, and Theodore Wirth.

Becoming an Outdoors Woman in Minnesota (888-646-6367), at 500 Lafayette Road in St. Paul, and **Women Anglers of Minnesota** offer angling, ice fishing, and shore fishing classes for women interested in either taking up the sport or finding other women to fish with. Contact them at P.O. Box 580653, Minneapolis, MN 55458 or through www.up-north.com/womenanglers.

DAY TRIPS AND ⊖ WEEKEND GETAWAYS

Any way you point your vehicle, you're sure to end up somewhere extraordinary. Minnesota is dotted with hundreds of little towns settled in the early days of the state, and just about all of them are worth exploring. Although there are more than enough attractions and sights in the Twin Cities to fill up your time, there's nothing like a good, long road trip through the countryside to clear one's mind of the hustle and bustle of the Metro life.

The best time (we think) to hit the road is early spring, the last two weeks of April and the first two weeks of May, or when autumn is in full swing, the last two weeks of September and the first two weeks of October. There is nowhere better to see the changing of the seasons than out in the country, amid the old hardwood forests that line the state highways and the charming old farmhouses—many of which are still in use—that dot the gently rolling fields and coulees outside the Cities. Here is a sampling of the road trips well worth taking from the Twin Cities.

DULUTH

Located on the shore of Lake Superior and a major shipping port, Duluth was once the fastest-growing city in the country and was expected to surpass Chicago in size by 1870. When Jay Cooke, the wealthy Philadelphia land speculator, picked Duluth as the terminus of the Northern Pacific, Lake Superior, and Mississippi Railroads, Duluth's future appeared prosperous. Unfortunately, Jay Cooke's empire crumbled when the stock market crashed in 1873, and Duluth almost

disappeared from the map. By the late 1800s, with the continued boom in lumber and iron mining and with the railroads completed, this shipping port again bloomed. By the turn of the 20th century, there were almost 100,000 inhabitants, and it was again a thriving community. At its economic height, more millionaires lived in Duluth than anywhere else in the world.

Much of this history is reflected in present-day Duluth, both in the fantastic architecture and in the huge boats that serve as floating museums. The signs that Duluth is once again experiencing an economic revival have never been more obvious. Most of the old warehouses by the Maritime Center and along the harbor have been converted into picturesque shopping centers and family-owned restaurants, many with the original facades left intact to give a historical perspective of what the region once looked like. Uphill from busy Canal Park Drive, the streets are lined with row houses and red-brick churches, many of which have been closed up but left intact. While driving up the steep roads in Duluth is a little nerve-racking (especially in winter), the harbor looks absolutely stunning from the heights. An incredible stretch of blue water dotted with white sailboats and gigantic ore boats greets you, while the far, far shore of Lake Superior is barely visible even on the clearest days.

For more information on the sights and attractions of Duluth, call the **Duluth Convention & Visitor Bureau** at (218) 722-4011 or (800) 4-DULUTH, or check out its extensive Web page at www.visit duluth.com.

Getting There

Getting to Duluth from the Twin Cities is easy. Just take Interstate 35E north or I-35W north (depending on where you are in the Twin Cities). The highways merge into I-35 north of the Metro, and the interstate shoots straight north to Duluth.

Attractions

Most of Duluth's attractions are located around the Duluth Harbor, so it's easy to walk from one to the next to make a full day of sightseeing. The newest of Duluth's offerings is the **Great Lakes Aquarium** at 353 Harbor Drive (218-740-FISH; www .glaquarium.org), which houses the largest freshwater aquarium in America. While the main focus of the GLA is the gigantic aquarium that houses every known species of fish from Lake Superior (including several giant sturgeons), there are also many hands-on exhibits geared toward children. One of the favorites is a joystick-operated microscope hooked up to a video monitor that's focused on a tank full of fish. Kids also love the very friendly otter on the first floor that shows off for visitors. Ticket prices are $6.95 for children up ages 3 to 11 and $12.95 for adults.

Right next door to the aquarium at 301 Harbor Drive is the **S.S. *William A. Irvin*** (218-722-7876; www.williamairvin .com), a giant ore ship turned museum. The ship is open for tours Memorial Day through mid-October, with a special "Ship of Ghouls" exhibit around Halloween. For serious maritime buffs there's also the **Lake Superior Maritime Visitor Center,** 600 Lake Avenue South (218-720-5200; www.lsmma.com), owned and operated by the U.S. Army Corps of Engineers. Movies, model ships, and rotating exhibits are housed both inside and outside the museum year-round. The museum also hosts a boat watchers' hotline (218-722-6489) and has a Web cam trained on the harbor. Admission to the museum is free.

At 506 West Michigan Street inside the depot is the **Lake Superior Railroad Museum** (218-733-7519; www.lsrm.org), which houses a rotating exhibit of historic railway cars, locomotives, and engines, most of which can be boarded for a close-up view of turn-of-the-20th-century machinery. On permanent display is a dining car china exhibit, the William Crooks (Minnesota's oldest engine), and the oldest known rotary snowplow in existence. The depot is also home to the **Duluth Children's Museum** (218-733-7543; www.duluthchildrensmuseum.org). The depot is full of hands-on exhibits for kids as well as education programs and tours, the Duluth Art Institute, the St. Louis Historical Society, and a performing arts wing where community and touring ballet companies, plays, and concerts take place throughout the year.

At 72nd Avenue West and Grand Avenue is the **Lake Superior Zoo** (218-730-4900), home to more than two dozen endangered and threatened species from around the world. Admittedly on the small side, the zoo is a preservation project and educational tool as well as a tourist attraction.

For a little highbrow entertainment, check out the **Karpeles Manuscript Library Museum** at 902 East First Street (218-728-0630; www.rain.org/-karpeles). This museum displays a rotating selection of original manuscripts from all over the world, including the original draft of the Bill of Rights and Einstein's description of his general theory of relativity. The **Tweed Museum of Art,** located on the University of Minnesota–Duluth campus at 1201 Ordean Court (218-726-8222; www.d umn.edu/tma), features nine separate galleries and exhibits dating from the 15th century. For a glimpse of what life was like for the well-to-do during the Iron Range boom, the historic **Glensheen Estate** at 3300 London Road (888-454-GLEN; www.glensheen.org), holds tours of its seven-acre grounds throughout the year (call for times and reservations).

For wintertime fun head to **Spirit Mountain** (800-642-6377; www.spirit

Duluth's historic lift bridge allows freighters from all over the world to reach the city's inner harbor. TODD R. BERGER

mtn.com), just outside Duluth, for cross-country and downhill skiing and, of course, snowboarding. Spirit Mountain has five chairlifts (including a covered one for skiers wanting to take a little break from the cold), and the 175-acre site has 23 separate downhill runs geared for all levels of skiers and two huge freestyle parks, one for skiers and one for snowboarders. New in 2005—a magic carpet, great for beginners. Spirit Mountain has all sorts of package plans for extended stays in the area, including discounts on lodging, meals, and lift tickets. Call area hotels and motels directly for package information.

Accommodations and Camping

Right on the waterfront and steps away from Canal Park Drive, the following hotels are relatively new buildings designed with easy access to the hot spots of Duluth in mind. The **Canal Park Inn,** at 250 Canal Park Drive (800-777-8560; www.canal parkinnduluth.com), features an indoor heated pool and hot tub, and all guests receive a complimentary breakfast each morning. The **Hampton Inn** at 310 Canal Park Drive (218-720-3000 or www .hamptoninn.com) offers the same amenities with a full hot breakfast, while the **Inn on Lake Superior** at 350 Canal Park Drive (218-726-1111 or 888-ON-THE-LAKE; www.innonlakesuperior.com) offers a lakefront view with its balcony suites. Downtown lodging is, to be expected, more affordable than the lakefront hotels. At 131 West Second Street is the **Best Western Downtown** (218-727-6851 or 800-570-9802), located close to the skyway system that connects downtown Duluth. Two blocks away at 200 West First Street is the **Holiday Inn** (218-722-1202 or 800-477-7089; www.hiduluth.com), which has two pools and a sauna on the premises.

Also downtown is the **Radisson Hotel** at 505 West Superior Street (218-727-8981 or www.radisson.com/duluthmn), **Fitger's Inn** at 600 East Superior Street (218-722-8826 or 888-FITGERS; www.fitgers.com), and the **Voyageur Lakewalk Inn** at 333 East Superior Street (218-722-3911 or 800-258-3911; www.visitduluth.com/voyageur).

Duluth has many beautiful bed-and-breakfasts designed to make guests feel right at home. In town is the **Mathew S. Burrows Inn** at 1632 East First Street (218-724-4991 or 800-789-1890; www.1890inn.com), the **Ellery House** at 28 South 21st Avenue East (218-724-7639 or 800-355-3794; www.elleryhouse.com), and the **Firelight Inn on Oregon Creek** at 2211 East Third Street (218-724-0272 or 888-724-0273; www.firelightinn.com). All of these establishments are historic landmarks furnished with period antiques, built around the turn of the 20th century with only a few modern conveniences added to the original designs.

While there aren't any campsites in Duluth proper, there are several notable ones right outside the city limits. Ten miles south of Duluth is **Buffalo Valley Camping,** located at 2590 Guss Road, Proctor (218-624-9901; www.buffalohouseduluth.com), which has a full bar and restaurant at the campsite as well as showers and electrical, sewer, and water hookups for RVs. Take exit 239 off I-35 and you'll find the **Knife Island** campsite at 234 Minnesota Highway 61, Esko (218-879-6063), located right in the middle of the ghost town of Slateville and the adjacent abandoned logging camp. Water and electrical

hookups are available at almost all the 30 available sites, and firewood is provided by the camp.

Shopping

Unless you're just out for groceries, most of your Duluth shopping is going to take place around the museums and walkways in the Canal Park Drive and Lake Avenue area. Here original warehouse structures from Duluth's manufacturing past have been converted into shopping malls and restaurants, while new structures have been built to integrate perfectly with the brickwork of the older buildings.

If you're into antiquing, the **Canal Park Antique Mall** at 310 Lake Avenue South (218-720-3940) is your best bet. The largest antiques and collectibles mall in Duluth is where you're sure to find that perfect knickknack for yourself or souvenir to take home to family and friends. If you prefer collecting old literature, **Old Town Antiques & Books** at 102 East Superior Street (218-722-5426) is a good place to stop.

And while you're on Superior Street, try out **Torke Weihnachten Christmas & Chocolates** at 637 East Superior Street (218-723-1225 or 800-729-1223) for both specialty candies and European Christmas ornaments. Check out the wonderful **Electric Fetus,** 12 East Superior Street (218-722-9970), for the best selection of records, CDs, and tapes in this part of the state (visit its sister store in Minneapolis when you come back).

Along the Canal Park area is the **DeWitt-Seitz Marketplace** at 394 Lake Avenue South, home to both **Hepzibah's Sweet Shoppe** (218-722-5049), with its wonderful homemade and imported candies, and toy and gift store **J. Skylark Company** (218-722-3794). Outside the mall and along Lake Avenue are even more gift shops—this is a great place to catch up on your window-shopping in the summer.

The University of Minnesota–Duluth offers reasonably priced accommodations for senior citizens during the summer months. Call the campus at (218) 726-8222 for more information and rates.

Restaurants

Traditional American fare dominates the restaurant scene in Duluth, with steakhouses on the high end of the scale and hamburger and french-fry joints at the low end. In the Fitger's Brewhouse complex at 600 East Superior Street is **Bennett's on the Lake** (218-722-2829; www.bennetts onthelake.com) and **Fitger's Brewhouse Brewery and Grill** (218-279-BREW; www.brewhouse.net). The first is very fancy and almost requires you call ahead for reservations on weekends. The second more casual, offering live music entertainment most nights, homebrewed beer, and gourmet sandwiches. There are also four separate Grandma's restaurants along the Lakeway, as well as Perkins Family Restaurants just about everywhere. For Asian food, we recommend **Taste of Saigon** in the Dewitt-Seitz Marketplace at 394 Lake Avenue South (218-727-1598)—its food and selection are as good as the portions are large and generous. For late-night dining and carousing, the **Top of the Harbor** at the Radisson Hotel on 505 West Superior Street (218-727-8981) is a rotating restaurant that gives you a full view of the city every 72 minutes. The Radisson also has the **Fifth Avenue Lounge** on street level.

An invaluable resource to pick up when in Duluth is the local free paper, *Ripsaw*—each issue has dining information and a calendar of events that is informative to even the most experienced of Duluth visitors. Well written and fun to read even if you don't need help picking out something to do for the day, *Ripsaw* is available at most retail centers and newsstands around town.

HINCKLEY

Established in 1885, the little town of Hinckley—population 1,291—is rich with fishing holes, hiking trails, natural beauty, and history. The site of the Great Hinckley Fire in 1894 that killed more than 400 people, Hinckley is a monument to a community's triumph over tragedy. For more information, contact the Hinckley Convention and Visitors Bureau at (320) 384-0126 or (800) 952-4282; www .hinckleymn.com.

Getting There

From the Twin Cities, take either I-35E or I-35W north until it merges into I-35 north, then follow I-35 all the way to the Hinckley exit. From there you can go west into downtown Hinckley, or east on Minnesota Highway 48 to the Hinckley Grand Casino.

Attractions

Hinckley's history stretches back to the early 1800s, to the days when it was mostly fur trading posts and Ojibwe lands. The Great Hinckley Fire destroyed most of the original settlements, but what could be saved is on display or documented at the **Hinckley Fire Museum** at 106 Old Highway 61 South (320-384-7338), open May through mid-October. A large obelisk memorial has also been set up in the town cemetery to commemorate the disaster. The route of the railroad used by settlers fleeing the Great Hinckley Fire is now part of the **Willard Munger State Trail,** the longest paved hiking trail in the country, stretching from Hinckley all the way to Duluth. In winter the trail is open to snowmobilers and cross-country skiers and in summer to hikers, bicyclists, in-line skaters, and horseback riders.

The other major attraction in the area is the Mille Lacs Band of Ojibwe's **Grand Casino Hinckley,** 777 Lady Luck Drive (800-472-6321; www.grandcasinohinckley .com), located 1 mile east of I-35 on MN 48 just outside Hinckley. The casino features more than 2,000 slot machines, blackjack tables, poker tables, pull tabs, and live bingo competitions. There are five restaurants on-site, from snack bar to buffet to lounge with live music.

For nature lovers there's **St. Croix State Park** (320–384–6591), located 15 miles east of Hinckley on MN 48; then 5 miles south on County Road 22. St. Croix State Park is Minnesota's largest state park, with over 33,000 acres of campsites and hiking, horse, snowmobile, bike, and ski trails. A swimming beach and six canoe landings are along the St. Croix River. Twelve miles north of Hinckley on I-35 is **Banning State Park** (320–245–2668), which is the home of the beautiful Kettle River. This is a great place to catch a glimpse of the native wildlife (deer, raccoons, etc.) while traveling down the river. There is limited camping available, so it's a good idea to call and check with the park before making long-term plans.

Annual events in Hinckley include the Corn and Clover Festival, Octoberfest in October, and Grand Celebration & Pow Wow in July; the Arts & Crafts Festivals in August and November; and Santa Days in December. The Grand Casino's outdoor amphitheater also hosts a summer concert series May through August.

Accommodations

There are quite a few places to spend the night at Hinckley, both at the Grand Casino or in town. The **Grand Northern Inn,** I-35 at exit 183 (320–384–4702 or 800–558–0612), offers a complimentary continental breakfast, an indoor swimming pool, and a 24-hour casino shuttle service, while the **Days Inn** at 104 Grindstone Court (320–384–7751; 800–559–8951), has an indoor pool, a free deluxe continental breakfast, and a 24-hour casino shuttle. The **Travelodge** (320–384–6112), at the Minnesota Highway 48 exit off I-35, has snowmobile trails that lead right off the parking lot, a free 24-hour shuttle service to take you to the casino, and a coin laundry on the premises. The **Grand Hinckley Inn** (800–737–8675) is located across the

parking lot from Grand Casino Hinckley and has rooms with private hot tubs, and an indoor pool. The two bed-and-breakfasts in the area are the **Dakota Lodge,** located 10 miles east of Hinckley on MN 48 (320–384–6052; www.dakota lodge.com), which has rooms with whirlpools and fireplaces, and the newly built **Woodland Trails** (320–655–3901; www.wood landtrails.net), on 500 acres with trails, a stocked catch-and-release pond, and an entertainment room with a big-screen TV and an English pool table.

Shopping

Many shops in Hinckley are located in the downtown area on Main Street. **Just Like New,** 114 East Main Street (320–384–7741), has brand-name consignment clothes for the whole family—tags are color coded for different discounts monthly—as well as handcrafted knickknacks and collectibles. **Antiques America Mall,** located at the junction of I-35 and MN 48 (320–384–7272), houses 50 dealers of antiques and collectibles.

Your options at the neighboring Grand Casino Hinckley are much more limited. It's only fair to note here that cigarettes sold on Indian reservations are much, much cheaper than those sold off the reservations, and that you can buy cartons of them at extremely reduced prices at the Grand Casino, which is run by the Mille Lacs Band of Ojibwe. Other than that, though, the casino isn't the greatest place to purchase gifts for friends and family, unless they like cigarettes, previously used casino playing cards, or Vikings paraphernalia.

Restaurants

Most of the dining establishments in Hinckley are fast-food restaurants, with just a few exceptions. **Tobies** (320–384–6174) is more of a campus than a plain-old restaurant. There's family dining, a bar, a gas station, a gift shop, and a bakery that serves gigantic caramel rolls.

Dining options at the **Grand Casino Hinckley** are good—however, we must warn you that the casino is a serious smoking establishment and even the non-smoking sections of the restaurants get a little congested. **Cherry's Snack Bar** located at the junction of I-35 and MN 48 is a good place to stop for lunch, while **Grand Buffet** is a good place to stop for dinner, if you can get in. There's usually a long line to get into the buffet, so you may want to try **Grand Grill Americana** or the **Winds Steakhouse** instead, which aren't as good a deal as the buffet but are less crowded and farther away from the noise of the casino.

Nightlife

Like most other small towns, the doors close pretty early here, so all the nightlife (after 6:00 P.M.) is at or near the **Grand Casino Hinckley. The Silver Sevens Lounge** is mostly cover bands; **Tobies Lounge** usually has live bands Friday and Saturday and karaoke on Sunday. The **Grand Casino Events and Convention Center** brings in well-known golden oldies singers as well as the occasional comedian, and the **Grand Casino Amphitheater** is a 5,756-seat outdoor affair that books top country stars and the occasional pop star.

NEW ULM

Founded in 1857 by two German immigration societies, New Ulm reflects the town's German heritage. The shadow of the Hermann Monument, set high on a hill just outside the business district, rises in the distance and is visible from just about anywhere in town. Often referred to as the "City of Charm and Tradition," New Ulm's colorful history is reflected in its attractions and many seasonal festivals.

Getting There

New Ulm is easily accessible by taking U.S. Highway 169 south from the Twin Cities to Minnesota Highway 99 west. From there, go west on U.S. Highway 14 (the Laura Ingalls Wilder Highway), which will take you into downtown New Ulm.

For further information, brochures, or directions, be sure to visit the **New Ulm Area Chamber of Commerce/Visitors Information Center** at 1 North Minnesota Street (507-233-4300 or 888-463-9856), located a short walking distance from most of the area attractions, shopping, and restaurants.

Attractions

At the forefront of New Ulm's attractions is the **Hermann Monument.** Representing the Teutonic hero, Hermann Arminius of Cherusci, the monument overlooks the city from the bluff on Center and Monument Streets. Dedicated in 1897, the monument stands 102 feet tall in Hermann Heights Park—a beautiful park with a panoramic view of the city below. The Hermann Monument is open Memorial Day through Labor Day and costs a nominal fee of $1.00, but you may visit the adjoining Hermann Heights Park year-round for free.

Another attraction is the **Glockenspiel/Schonlau Park** at Fourth and Minnesota Streets. The glockenspiel is one of the few freestanding carillon clock towers in the world. The glockenspiel chimes at noon, 3:00, and 5:00 P.M. daily and features a revolving stage of 3-foot-high characters that depict the city's history.

Brown County Historical Society and Museum at Center and Broadway Streets (507-233-2616; www.browncounty historymnusa.org) provides an excellent overview of the history of the New Ulm area. The building was once the New Ulm Post Office, and it was placed on the National Register of Historic Places in

1976. The Brown County Historical Society houses three floors of regional history: a Dakota Indians exhibit, a Brown County settlers area called "Made in Brown County," seasonal displays, and much more. All of the information is insightfully presented with great detail, and the admission charge is a meager $3.00.

New Ulm is filled with beautiful historical homes, but the **John Lind Home,** at the intersection of Center and State Streets (507-354-8802), is especially aesthetically pleasing and historically significant. This lovely structure is an excellent example of Queen Anne–style architecture and was the home of the 14th governor of Minnesota and the first Swedish member of the United States Congress, Minnesota representative John Lind. Admission is $2.00 for adults, children age 12 and under are free. Afternoon tours are held daily in summer, Friday through Sunday in spring and fall, and by appointment in winter.

Beer brewing was New Ulm's first industry. The **August Schell Brewing Company,** 1860 Schell Road (507-354-5528 or 800-770-5020; www.schells brewery.com), was founded in 1860, and since its inception Schell's has produced premium-quality crafted and specialty beers at reasonable prices. Before the popularity of microbrews, Schell's was the area leader in providing libations. Tours of the brewery, gardens, and park are available daily Memorial Day through Labor Day. The brewery tour and tasting cost $2.00. Schell's now owns the Grain Belt brand of beer, a well-known Minnesota brew of American lager formerly made in the Twin Cities. If you can't make it to Schell's Brewery, be sure to visit one of New Ulm's restaurants and bars for a bottle or draught of Schell's Bock, Dark, or Original, or of the 1919 Root Beer it also produces.

New Ulm has a wealth of additional attractions. For lovers of the classic children's book *Millions of Cats,* author Wanda Gag's childhood home, the **Wanda Gag Home,** 226 North Washington Street

(507-359-2632), is open on weekends in June, July, August, and December and during the rest of the year by appointment.

Yet another attraction of historical significance is the **Turner Hall,** at the intersection of First Street South and State Street (507-354-4916). The New Turnverein opened in 1856 and was dedicated to improving the health of New Ulmers through gymnastics and exercise. Parts of the Turner Hall building date from 1865, including 70 feet of murals in the Ratskeller, a bar and restaurant. The Turner Hall is free and open daily to the public 10:00 A.M. to 10:00 P.M.

New Ulm has a full slate of annual festivals and events. New Ulm celebrates Christmas with traditional German hoopla. Included are the Christmas **Parade of Lights,** which celebrates the arrival of Santa Claus on the Friday evening after Thanksgiving and the traditional German **St. Nicholas Day,** December 6; **Fasching,** a German version of Mardi Gras, occurs annually in late February or early March concurrent with **Schell's Bock Beer Fest.** Summer has an active festival schedule with both **Bavarian Blast** and **Polka Days** at the end of July, plus **River Blast** in Riverside Park over Labor Day weekend, which features a floating parade. **Oktoberfest** in October features traditional German food, music, and, of course, beer.

Accommodations

New Ulm has ample accommodations, including bed-and-breakfasts as well as hotels. As with all other aspects of New Ulm, most of the accommodations have a German flavor.

The **Holiday Inn,** at 2101 South Broadway Street (507-359-2941 or 877-359-2941), is the largest hotel in New Ulm. It hosts Oktoberfest for two weekends each fall and has a swimming pool, restaurant, and cocktail lounge for your convenience. The **Budget Holiday,** 1316 North Broadway

Street (507-354-4145), was renovated in 2002. Another New Ulm hotel is the **Colonial Inn** at 1315 North Broadway Street (507-354-3128 or 888-215-2143), a relatively small, 24-unit hotel that offers free HBO during your stay.

The New Ulm area has many bed-and-breakfasts. The **W. W. Smith Inn** at 101 Linden Street SW in nearby Sleepy Eye (507-794-5661 or 800-799-5661), for example, is located 14 miles from New Ulm. The W. W. Smith Inn has much to offer lovers of bed-and-breakfasts. Listed on the National Register of Historic Places, this elegant Queen Anne structure was constructed in 1901 for a wealthy area banker. In New Ulm, **Deutsche Strasse B&B** at 404 South German Street (507-354-2005 or 866-226-9856; www .deutschestrasse.com), offers five rooms, two with queen-size beds and three with full-size beds, and all with private baths. Also included is a full breakfast.

Shopping

If you're looking for specialty shops with a German flair, you'll find them in New Ulm. New Ulm boasts businesses devoted to antiques, crafts, sweets, dolls, and sausages. The vast majority of shops are conveniently located on Minnesota and Broadway Streets, in the heart of beautiful old downtown. **Edelweiss Flower Haus,** 304 North Minnesota Street (507-354-2222; www.edelweissflowerhaus.com), specializes in flowers, and shoppers can watch floral artists create arrangements before their eyes. In addition, there's **NadelKunst, Ltd.,** 212 North Minnesota Street (507-354-8708), specializing in knitting, crocheting, beading, and cross-stitch.

Of course, New Ulm has stores that specialize in German merchandise: the **Guten Tag Haus,** 127 North Minnesota Street (507-233-HAUS; www.gutentag haus.com), and **Domeier's New Ulm German Store,** 1020 South Minnesota Street

(507-354-4231). Unlike the aforementioned businesses, Domeier's is located 10 blocks south of the downtown business district.

The **Christmas Haus,** 203 North Minnesota Street, and **Lambrecht's,** 119 North Minnesota Street, share an owner, a phone, and a Web site (507-233-4350; www.lambrechtsgifts.net). The former specializes in German and seasonal goodies, and the latter has two entire floors of flowers and gift items, from greeting cards and framed prints to lace, lamps, and shirts. At **August Schell's Brewing Company,** 1860 Schell Road (507-354-5528), there is something for every shopper. Naturally, there are many Schell and Grain Belt clothing and collectibles, plus gourmet food and novelty items.

Restaurants

Surprisingly, German food does not dominate New Ulm's restaurant options. German food is often included with traditional American fare. Certainly the place to start when discussing New Ulm's restaurants is the **Veigel's Kaiserhoff,** 221 North Minnesota Street (507-359-2071). The Kaiserhoff's most popular dish is the barbecue ribs; diners have enjoyed the restaurant since 1938. The menu also includes many German favorites such as bratwursts, schnitzels, landjaeger, and German chocolate cake. Don't forget to wash down the Kaiserhoff's cuisine with a delicious Schell's beer, brewed in New Ulm. Another restaurant with heavy German influences is the **Otto's Feierhaus and Bier Stube** at 2101 South Broadway Avenue (507-359-5300). Otto's is conveniently located for travelers in the New Ulm Holiday Inn and serves American food and German specialties.

Traditional American food is popular in New Ulm. **Hy-Vee's Kitchen** in a grocery store at 2015 South Broadway Avenue (507-354-8255), is a local cafe-style restaurant. The **Ulmer Café,** 115 North Minnesota Street (507-354-8122), is right in the middle of New Ulm's shopping area and features breakfast and lunch in a hometown cafe.

For families, **Happy Joe's,** 1700 North Broadway Street (507-359-9811), specializes in food kids and adults love, such as pizza and chicken. There is also a smorgasbord at Happy Joe's, which outside Minnesota is called an all-you-can-eat buffet. **DJ's,** 1200 North Broadway Street (507-354-3843), is another family diner featuring lunch and dinner specials daily.

Main Jiang House is an authentic Chinese restaurant at 400 North Minnesota Street (507-354-1218). New Ulm also has several sandwich, burger, pizza, and taco chain restaurants.

NORTH SHORE DRIVE

The North Shore Drive, officially U.S. Highway 61, is lined with rental cottages, bed-and-breakfasts, RV parks, and motels, while the shore is dotted with rent-by-the-day boat docks and marinas. The first real town outside Duluth is Two Harbors, a virtual mecca of restaurants and gift shops, while the residences themselves are relatively new and tucked away some distance from the downtown area. Two Harbors is a good place to sit down and get a bite to eat or rest for the night

---

 Keep an old plastic credit card–type hotel key in your wallet in case you find yourself with an ice-covered windshield and no scraper.

---

before heading on to the beautiful parks that make up the attractions in this area, or to pick up a bag of regionally grown wild rice, fresh honey, fruit preserves, or a lighthouse-shaped refrigerator magnet.

Attractions

Thirteen miles northeast of Two Harbors on US 61 is **Gooseberry Falls State Park** (218-834-3855), which holds an amazing series of relatively untouched waterfalls that are open to the public to walk out on—literally. This is not recommended for those struggling with a fear of heights, as it's possible to climb to the very top of the waterfalls via hiking trails and walkways and walk right to the edge of the rocky face to peer over the edge—without the presence of handrails or safety mesh. A visitor center features exhibits on Lake Superior and the history of the park itself.

Split Rock Lighthouse State Park (218-226-6377), also on US 61 about 20 miles northeast of Two Harbors, surrounds the lighthouse that has been a landmark on the Lake Superior shore since 1910. Now a state-run historic site, it and the neighboring lighthouse keeper's houses and fog signal building have been restored to 1920s appearance and opened to visitors and tour groups. Call the lighthouse directly for tours: (218) 226-6372. The attached History Center shows films and exhibits on the lighthouse, commercial fishing, and shipwrecks through most of the summer.

For more energetic travelers, the **Superior Hiking Trail** winds through the forested ridgeline of the coast for 200 miles. There are many small and midsize fishing lakes and tiny craft shops to be found all along the drive that parallels the trail—call the Superior Hiking Trail Association in Two Harbors: (218) 834-2700; www.shta.org.

Accommodations and Camping

The **Lighthouse Bed & Breakfast,** at the harbor in Two Harbors (218–834–4814 or 888–832–5606; www.lighthousebb.org), is one of the few B&Bs on the Great Lakes housed inside a working lighthouse, built in 1892. The B&B has four rooms decorated with period antiques, and all have a view of Lake Superior. For more pedestrian comforts, **AmericInn Lodge and Suites,** 1088 US 61 West, Two Harbors (218–834–3000), offers guests an indoor pool, hot tub, and sauna, while just outside Two Harbors on the shoreline is the **Grand Superior Lodge,** 2826 US 61 (218–834–3796 or 800–627–9565), a beautiful resort with individual log homes, an on-site restaurant and cocktail lounge, and an indoor pool and spa. A more rustic resort is the **Beachway Motel & Cabins,** 5119 North Shore Drive, Duluth (218–525–5191; www.lake-superior-explorer.com/beach), with full kitchenettes, evening campfires, and playgrounds for the kids. The motel and cabins are open May through October.

Shopping

It's a tradition of ours to make the trek up to the North Shore every summer for one reason—wild rice. The tiny one-quarter pound bags of wild rice you get at the supermarket in the Cities usually cost you a couple of dollars, while just about every store in Two Harbors on up sells four-pound bags for around $8.00. Wild rice is much richer than your typical white variety rice and adds a wonderful, hearty dimension to soups, poultry stuffing, and anything else that calls for rice.

All along the North Shore Drive can be found tiny houses converted into shops where you can buy anything from jars of wild clover honey to homemade preserves to lighthouse-shaped refrigerator magnets

and, of course, fish bait. One is **Beaver Bay Agate Shop and Museum,** 1003 Main Street in Beaver Bay (218–226–4847), which is exactly what it sounds like, with jewelry and key chains made from agates found along the Lake Superior shoreline as well as permanent displays of man-made artifacts and geological marvels found in the area.

Listing the shops along the North Shore Drive is a tricky business, because the area is so tourist related. Not many people are willing to brave the winding roads that follow Lake Superior during winter, or the little stores that line the roadside, and winter sometimes lasts three-quarters of the year here.

But the remote shops in the sticks and in the small towns dotting the North Shore Highway all the way to the Canadian border often sell unique and memorable items and are worth a browsing stop. In particular, the beautiful town of Grand Marais, about 110 miles northeast of Duluth on US 61, is a haven for many artists, and the downtown region is alive with galleries and studios.

Restaurants

If you're more comfortable dining at familiar restaurant chains, then Two Harbors is the place to stop before heading on up the Lake Superior coast. Pretty much every fast-food chain in America is represented here, including Dairy Queen, Pizza Hut, and Culvers. If you're more interested in sticking to family owned-and-run establishments, there are plenty of those to choose from, too, either in Two Harbors or along the North Shore Drive. For burgers and sandwiches, and breakfast all day long, try **Judy's Café** at 623 Seventh Avenue, Two Harbors (218–834–4802), or for traditional North Shore smoked fish as well as pickled herring, salmon spread, and cheese, head to **Lou's Fish House,** 1319 US 61, Two Harbors (218–834–5254). For a north woods dining experience, try the **Northern Lights Restaurant** on US 61 in Beaver Bay (218–226–3012), with wild game and Scandinavian dishes, and for informal, family-style meals, there's **Our Place** on Minnesota Highway 1, Finland (218–353–7343). **Vanilla Bean Bakery and Café,** 812 Seventh Avenue, Two Harbors (218–834–3714), is a cozy bistro for designer coffees or meals.

RED WING

Perhaps best known as the home of the Red Wing Shoe Company, Red Wing is a charming little town with a beautiful, regal downtown composed of refurbished old warehouse buildings and absolutely amazing churches that date from 1855. Set deep in a valley surrounded by beautiful fishing lakes, scenic hilltop views, rivers, picturesque farms, and apple orchards, Red Wing has the added advantage of being populated by some of the most genuinely friendly and helpful people you'll ever meet.

Getting There

You have two choices: You can either take the scenic drive to Red Wing via US 61 from St. Paul, or you can get on a train at the Amtrak station in St. Paul (730 Transfer Road; 800–872–7245) and take it all the way to the historic **Old Milwaukee Depot** at 420 Levee Street in Red Wing. You may want to stop by the depot while in Red Wing anyway, since it doubles as the visitor center and there are lots of maps, brochures, and free local newspapers with restaurant coupons and information on events and happenings around

No tickets are sold at the Red Wing Amtrak station, so make sure you buy a round-trip ticket at the Twin Cities station.

town. The depot, established in 1904, is located next to downtown Red Wing and all its sights, too, so there's no need to worry about transportation unless you have plans outside of town.

If you opt to drive, a nice alternative to US 61 is to cross the river just before Hastings and jump on Wisconsin Highway 35 south at Prescott. Follow WI 35 to Bay City, and then turn on to U.S. Highway 63 west to cross the Mississippi to Red Wing between Hager City and Bay City. WI 35 is a two-lane highway that passes through beautiful old hardwood forests and gently sloping farmlands dotted with old farmhouses, stone silos, and shallow creeks. It also roughly follows the Mississippi River here, providing spectacular views of the waterway and the bluffs across the river on the Minnesota side.

If you want to get to Red Wing quickly, US 61 out of St. Paul can save you about 15 minutes off your total driving time. There's not much to look at until you get to Hastings, Minnesota. Once you pass through Hastings, though, it's all trees and farmland again.

For more information about the area, contact the **Red Wing Visitors and Convention Bureau,** 420 Levee Street; (651) 385–5934 or (800) 498–3444; www.red wing.org.

Attractions

A good place to start exploring Red Wing is **Bay Point Park** on Levee Street. Located right on the Mississippi River, this is also the home of **Boathouse Village,** one of the only remaining "gin pole" boathouse installations in the country. The village looks just like a bunch of little houses floating in the water, with floating walkways connecting the "neighborhood" together. Close by is **Levee Park,** located just behind the historic 1904 Milwaukee Depot. Both parks have picnic tables and play areas for kids.

At the corner of Third Street and East Avenue at 443 West Third Street is the historic **Sheldon Theatre** (651–385–3667 or 800–899–5759; www.sheldontheatre .org), the country's first municipal theater. First opened in 1904, the theater was such an unabashed collection of sculpture, arches, marble columns, and gilded plaster detail, it was once described as a jewel box. Nowadays the 466-seat theater is used for everything, including children's plays, concerts, acrobats, and films. If you just want to walk in and look at the inside of this beautiful building, the helpful men and women at the ticket counter will gladly let you in to take a peek. Guided tours are offered Saturday at 1:00 P.M. for $2.50 per person.

Red Wing has its share of museums, including the somewhat unconventional **Red Wing Shoe Museum,** 314 Main Street (651–388–8211; www.RedWingshoe.com). Owned and operated by Red Wing Shoes, the museum treats visitors to exhibits imparting the history of the company as well as an interactive display that helps you learn the process of making a pair of shoes. There are other displays, too, including a kiosk in which you can match occupation to shoe. About 9 blocks away at 1166 Oak Street is the **Goodhue County Historical Museum** (651–388–6024; www.goodhuehistory.mus.mn.us), which contains more than 150,000 paintings, photographs, geological and natural history displays, and artifacts concerning Goodhue County from prehistory to the present.

At the end of East Fifth Street is majestic **Barn Bluff,** immortalized by Henry David Thoreau in 1861 after he hiked to the top. The bluff is listed on the National Register of Historic Places, and a marked stairwell is available to hikers. An even easier climb (or drive) to the top of the bluffs is in **Memorial Park,** located at the end of East Seventh Street. On your way to the top of **Sorin's Bluff,** you'll find hiking trails, bike paths, and caves that may or may not be wise to explore. From either bluff, you get a great view of Red Wing and the Mississippi River, as well as the beautiful valley and tree-covered

---

Bald eagles on their annual migration congregate in Red Wing's Colvill Park from November through the end of March. Often multiple eagles can be spotted in a single tree, looking for abundant shad in the Mississippi River.

---

bluffs that stretch around the town. For another view of the valley, **River Boat Rides,** located at the Levy Wall (651–592–3494), offers relaxing, one-hour-plus boat rides along the rugged bluffs of the Mississippi River. Be sure to bring your binoculars, as everything from deer, beavers, bald eagles, and wild turkeys have been seen on these rides. Passengers are encouraged to pack a picnic lunch to take with them for the trip. Rides are $15 a head.

In wintertime Red Wing and its neighbor, Welch, become ski country. Twelve miles northwest of town, just off US 61, is the **Welch Village Resort** (651–222–7079; www.welchvillage.com), which features some of the best downhill skiing in the state. Right next door, **Welch Mill,** at 14818 264th Street Path (800–657–6760; www.welchmillcanoeandtube.com), offers canoe and inner tube rentals and to-and-from shuttle service to the Cannon River in spring, summer, and fall. For cross-country skiers, there's the **Cannon Valley Trail** (507–263–0508; www.cannonvalley trail.com) in Cannon Falls, nearly 20 miles of countryside that follows the original Chicago Great Western Railroad line that once connected Cannon Falls and Red Wing. Call (888) 665–4236 for information and to purchase required ski passes.

Ten miles north of Red Wing and just off US 61 is the glamorous **Treasure Island Resort and Casino** (651–388–6300 or 800–222–7077; www.treasureislandcasino .com), a tropical-themed casino and hotel that features 44 games tables, 2,500 slot machines, a 10-table poker room, and a 40-foot waterfall, and smoking and non-smoking gambling areas. The casino is decorated with palm trees, and the slot machines and gambling tables are spread far enough apart that the casino never feels too crowded. The attached hotel has an indoor pool with another waterfall, a fitness room, and a child care facility, while outside is a campground with 95 pull-through sites and a 137-slip marina.

Accommodations and Camping

If you plan to spend the night in Red Wing, you have many options. The most elegant of the hotels in the area is downtown Red Wing's historic **St. James Hotel** at 406 Main Street (651-388-2846 or 800-252-1875; www.st-james-hotel.com), established in 1875 and a member of the National Trust's Historic Hotels of America. The elegant hotel has only 61 guest rooms, so you'll want to call ahead of time to make reservations.

Many beautiful old houses in Red Wing have been converted to bed-and-breakfasts and inns. Most of them are on the National Register of Historic Places, and many were former residences of Red Wing Shoe Company tycoons. The **Golden Lantern Inn** at 721 East Avenue (651-388-3315 or 888-288-3315; www.goldlantern .com), wasn't just home to one Red Wing Shoe president—three former presidents of the company once lived here. The Golden Lantern has since added whirlpools and fireplaces to some of the rooms and offers a full breakfast each morning to visitors. At 1105 West Fourth Street is the **Moondance Inn** (651-388-8145; www .moondanceinn.com), which offers a five-course gourmet brunch to weekend guests and rooms with private bathrooms and double whirlpools.

For more conventional lodging, there's an **AmericInn Motel** at 1819 Old West Main (651-385-9060), which offers guests a free continental breakfast and has a pool and sauna on the premises; a **Best Western Quiet House & Suites** across the high-way from Pottery Place Mall off US 61 (651-388-1577; www.quiethouse.com), offers both indoor and outdoor pools as well as complimentary coffee in every room; a **Super 8 Motel** at US 61 and Withers Harbor (651-388-0491), has an indoor pool and allows pets to stay with guests for a small additional fee; and the **Parkway Motel** at 3425 US 61 west (651-388-8231 or 800-762-0934), has snowmobile trails, hiking trails, fishing lakes, and a golf course within walking distance.

If you're more happy "roughing it" while on vacation, there's the **Hay Creek Valley Campground** (651-388-3998 or 888-388-3998), located 6 miles south of Red Wing on Minnesota Highway 58. The campground has a heated swimming pool and a restaurant, the Old Western Saloon, on the premises and borders a stocked trout stream. Right next to the campground is the Hardwood State Forest with trails laid out for horseback riding, hiking, snowmobiling, and areas set aside for in-season hunting.

Shopping

Antiques addicts beware—Red Wing has some amazingly good deals on antique furniture, toys, jewelry, and collectibles in general. The two main shopping areas in town are situated near each other, too. There's the Downtown District, which is composed of beautiful old warehouse buildings and storefronts that have been refurbished and turned into antiques stores, thrift stores, and restaurants, while about 12 blocks away, down Old West Main Street, is the Historic Pottery District, where you can buy antiques from **Al's Antique Mall** at 1314 Old West Main Street (651-388-0572), or shop at antiques and outlet stores in what was once a pottery factory at the **Historic Pottery Place Mall** at 2000 Old West Main Street (651-388-1428).

The Downtown District has the widest variety of shops to choose from. At **Mem-**

ory Maker Antiques in the Boxrud Building at 415 Main Street (651–385–5914), you can find everything from 50-cent postcards to vintage dishes to antique wardrobes. Twigges of Galena at 415 Main Street in the St. James Hotel's shopping court (651–388–3033) has lots of twig furniture as well as home items such as Yankee Candles and quilts. At Main and Bush Streets is the Uffda Shop (800–488–3332) selling all things Scandinavian, such as gnomes, Norwegian sweaters, *lefse* grills, porcelain, *solje* jewelry, and, of course, Ole and Lena joke books.

Restaurants

While the majority of Red Wing's restaurants can be categorized as traditional American fare, quite a few add a unique twist to those traditional dishes. The Staghead Restaurant at 219 Bush Street (651–388–6581) offers a changing and eclectic menu of steak, Italian dinners, and specialty sandwiches; the restaurant has a huge wine list and more than 30 imported and domestic beers on tap. Former Staghead chef and Hüsker Dü bassist Greg Norton now owns and cooks at the Norton's (715–792–2464; www.thenortons restaurant.com) with his wife. The upscale menu has a little something for everyone. The incredible food and the quaint wooded location make this place worth the trip across the river into Wisconsin. Fiesta Mexicana, 2918 Service Drive North (651–385–8939), serves authentic Mexican food for the lunch and dinner crowd and is quite possibly the only nonchain Mexican restaurant you'll find within a 50-mile radius. Bev's Café at 221 Bush Street (651–388–5227) offers classic home-style meals from hash to roast beef dinners and a fish fry on Friday. For a very elegant evening, the historic St. James Hotel's restaurant, the Port (651–388–2846; 800–252–1875; www.port-restaurant.com) serves a limited but tantalizing dinner menu. Call ahead for reservations.

If you just want a cup of coffee and something to munch on while you read the paper, you're in luck. Red Wing has several cozy little nooks to grab a cup of java, including Lily's Coffee House & Flowers at 419 West Third Street (651–388–8797; www.lilyscoffeehouse.com), which serves soups, sandwiches, pastries, coffee, and espresso drinks; Braschler's Bakery and Coffeeshop at 410 West Third Street (651–388–1589) makes its own pastries and muffins to accompany its large menu of caffeinated beverages; Tale of Two Sisters Tea Room and Gift Shoppe at 204 West Seventh Street (651–388–2250) offers a full English tea or just a cup of coffee to patrons.

For the sports bar fan, Andy's Bar at 529 Plum Street (651–388–4471), has 10 TVs with satellite hookups to accompany its menu of beer, appetizers, burgers, and chicken dinners, while in downtown proper, the Barrel House, at 223 Main Street (651–388–9967), serves light food, pizza, and beer, with daily happy hour specials.

In the Area

Twenty-three miles south of Red Wing across the Mississippi River on Wisconsin Highway 35 is the historic town of Pepin, Wisconsin. Named after the Pepin brothers, who were two of the first French trappers in the area, the village was settled in 1846 and was known for years as a steamboat boomtown and a vacation spot for wealthy Chicago socialites who summered on Lake Pepin. This is the place to visit if you're interested in fishing, boating, or bird-watching—the 13,000-acre Tiffany Wildlife Area, right next to Lake Pepin, is a regular roosting spot for bald eagles and hawks, while Lake Pepin itself has several beautiful marinas with public docking ramps.

Perhaps the most famous of Pepin's residents was Laura Ingalls Wilder, immortalized in *Little House on the Prairie*. Every

September, Pepin celebrates Laura Ingalls Wilder Days with events including a Laura knowledge contest, a parade, demonstrations of traditional crafts and industries, and bus tours of Wilder's birth site. For more information about Laura Ingalls Wilder Days, contact the Laura Ingalls Wilder Days Committee, Pepin Visitor Information Center, P.O. Box 264, Pepin, WI 54759, or call (800) 442-3011.

STILLWATER

Stillwater is technically considered a Twin Cities outer-ring suburb, but it's a good half hour's drive from the Cities themselves, especially in wintertime. Long in competition with the Twin Cities for everything from being the state's logging and industry capital to making a bid for the state capital itself, Stillwater is a beautiful riverside city with much to offer antiques shoppers, architecture connoisseurs, book collectors, and nature lovers. There's more than enough to do in the Stillwater area to make it at least a day trip, if not a relaxing weekend getaway.

That the economy is on an uphill climb in Stillwater has never been more apparent—everywhere you go, brick-and-wood storefronts have been restored and repainted, and specialty stores, wineries, and espresso bars have set up shop where there were once just thrift shops and diners. With all of its parks and bicycle trails, Stillwater is sure to offer something that appeals to you and your family.

For more information about Stillwater, check out www.ilovestillwater.com, or call the **Stillwater Chamber of Commerce** at (651) 439-4001.

Getting There

Take Minnesota Highway 36 east until you reach Stillwater.

Attractions

In springtime (approximately late March), you can catch sight of **bald eagles** sunning themselves on breaking ice floes in the river. In summer the town comes to life with the **Rivertown Art Fair** (third weekend in May, Lowell Park; 651–430–2306) and the Saturday morning farmers' markets.

Stillwater has many festivals, such as the popular **Lumberjack Days,** a citywide street festival complete with parades, live music, and logrolling competitions held each July. Contact the chamber (651–439–4001) to learn about more festivals.

From Stillwater you can ride the beautiful "floating wedding cake" **steamboats** that travel up and down the St. Croix River on a daily basis through spring and summer. Six paddlewheel boats take passengers for long and relaxing rides along the limestone cliffs overhung with oaks and firs that make up most of the river valley (contact St. Croix Boat and Packet Company, 651–430–1234). If solo boating is more your style, you can rent fishing boats and equipment from either **Beanies** at Maui's Landing (651–436–8874; www.boatingatbeanies.com) or kayaks from **P. J. Asch Otterfitter**s at 413 East Nelson Street (651–430–2286; www.pjaschotterfitters.com).

Another great way to see Stillwater and the St. Croix is from the air—in a hot air balloon. **Aamodt's Hot Air Balloons** have been taking satisfied passengers up into the air for years (call 651–351–0101 or 866–5–HOT–AIR for launch sites and to make reservations, or check the Web site at www.aamodtsballoons.com for more info). There's also the **Minnesota Zephyr** at 601 North Main Street (651–430–3000 or 800–992–6100; www.minnesotazephyr.com), an elegant, refurbished dining train that takes passengers on a three-and-a-half-hour trip through Stillwater and along the bluffs of the St. Croix River Valley. The trip includes a five-course white linen dinner and the musical stylings of the Zephyr Cabaret, which performs hits

Stillwater's famous lift bridge spans the St. Croix River, connecting Minnesota and Wisconson. TODD R. BERGER

of the '40s and '50s. Another option is the **Stillwater Trolley** at 400 East Nelson Street (651-430-0352; www.stillwater trolley.com), for a narrated trip through the older neighborhoods and downtown of Stillwater.

In winter many of the sports stores in town rent cross-country skis and snow gear. **St. Croix Outfitters** at 223 South Main Street (651-439-4891) is a good place to start.

Accommodations and Camping

Stillwater boasts bed-and-breakfasts housed in quaint old hotels and Victorian mansions listed on the National Register of Historic Places as well as modern hotels

with the expected amenities. Formerly the Lumber Baron Hotel, the **Water Street Inn** at 101 South Water Street (651-439-6000; www.waterstreetinn.us) is a beautiful red-brick building that's located right by the St. Croix and is furnished with turn-of-the-20th-century period pieces. The **1849 Brunswick Inn** at 114 Chestnut (651-430-8111; www.brunswickinnstillwater.com) features gas fireplaces and double Jacuzzis in the rooms. Another fine choice is the **Elephant Walk** at 801 West Pine Street (651-430-0359 or 888-430-0359; www .elephantwalkbb .com), where each room is decorated with exotic finds from around the world. You're welcomed with a complimentary bottle of wine, cheese, fruit, and homemade crackers in your room.

If you're looking for a comfortable hotel room, **Holiday Inn Express** at 2000 Washington Avenue (651-275-1401) fills the bill nicely. **Days Inn Stillwater,** 1750 West Frontage Road (651-430-1300; www.stillwaterinnmotel.com), is located along MN 36 southwest of downtown. The comfortable hotel offers everything from basic rooms to suites with cozy Jacuzzis. The nearby **Super 8 Motel** (651-430-3990), lets kids younger than age 12 stay for free and includes free HBO.

For RV campers, there's the **Golden Acres RV Park & Picnic Area** at 15150 North Square Lake Trail (651-430-1374), which has 54 campsites with water, electrical, and sewer hookups available (no tent camping allowed). The campsite, located right on the banks of Square Lake, has a nice swimming beach and a reputation for being a good place to go fishing.

Shopping

Stillwater is antiques central, with shops that sell everything from collector's dolls and teddy bears to handmade Amish quilts and furniture. In Main Street Square at 124 South Main Street, you can buy pottery, jewelry, and vintage clothing at **Country Charm Antiques** (651-439-8202) or consignment clothing at Nearly New (651-430-1188). **Seasons Tique** at 229 South Main Street (651-430-1240) carries beautiful Christmas tree ornaments and decorations from around the world all year long. For the larger budget, **Enigma** at 213 South Main Street (651-439-2206) carries new and antique furnishings from Europe and Asia, and the **J. P. Laskin**

In 1994 Stillwater was declared America's first "Book Town," an international designation sponsored by Welshman Richard Booth to honor notable book-friendly towns worldwide. Stillwater's multiple antiquarian and new booksellers line Main Street downtown. For more information about Stillwater's bookstores, visit www.booktown.com.

Company at 306 East Chestnut Street (651-439-5712) carries handmade American goods made by Amish people and Native Americans, as well as handblown glass artifacts.

Stillwater has several independent bookstores to choose from. **St. Croix Antiquarian Booksellers** at 232 South Main Street (651-430-0732), carries more than 50,000 books on history, art, philosophy, Americana, and everything in between, while **Loome Theological Booksellers** in the Old Swedish Covenant Church at 320 North Fourth Street (651-430-1092) specializes in secondhand and out-of-print books on theology, religion, and philosophy. The **Valley Bookseller,** 217 North Main Street (651-430-3385; www.valley bookseller.com), is an independent bookstore selling new titles. The beautiful store is bright and sunny and features a strong children's section, a large selection of fiction and local history titles, and an exotic bird aviary in the middle of the store.

Restaurants

Stillwater has no shortage of coffeehouses and espresso bars. At the **Dreamcoat Café,** 215 South Main Street (651-430-0615), you can order sandwiches or ice cream to go with your coffee—on weekend nights, local acoustic acts perform at this neighborhood cafe. At the other end of Main, **Supreme Bean Espresso Café** at 402 North Main Street (651-439-4314) serves delicious sandwiches and pastries that you can take outside to eat on the patio.

There are just as many places to go for dinner in Stillwater, too. Featuring a beautiful view of the St. Croix as well as traditional American fare is the **Dock Café** at 425 East Nelson Street (651-430-3770; www.dockcafe.com). **Brine's** at 219 South Main Street (651-439-7556; www.brines-stillwater.com) serves hot deli sandwiches, soups and salads, and the famous "Brine Burger," which is a heck of a lot better than it sounds. For German food, try the **Gasthaus Bavarian Hunter** at 8390 Lofton Avenue North (651–439–7128; www .gasthausbavarianhunter.com), which features live accordion music Friday and Sunday evenings.

For more refined dining, the historic **Lowell Inn** at 102 North Second Street (651–439–1100; www.lowellinn.com) serves elegant dinners in a variety of themed rooms.

Stillwater is also the home to several wineries with on-site tasting rooms, including **Saint Croix Vineyards** at 6428 Manning Avenue (651–430–3310; www .scvwines.com) and **Northern Vineyards Winery** at 223 North Main Street (651–430–1032; www.northernvineyards.com). Call ahead for an appointment at either place, just in case they're already booked.

In the Area

Just south of Stillwater and across the St. Croix River is the city of **Hudson, Wisconsin,** which is basically a little Stillwater. There are plenty of antiques stores, jewelry stores, and coffee shops, as well as beautiful storefronts and turn-of-the-20th-century architecture throughout the downtown area. On the west end of Coulee Road is the turnoff to Birkmose Park, which, if you take the drive to the top, gives you a great view of the harbor as well as a few imposing-looking Native American burial mounds. Hudson is also the home of the **San Pedro Café** at 426 Second Street (715–386–4003; www .sanpedrocafe.com), which features excellent dishes with a Caribbean flair, such as jerk chicken and rubbed, slow-roasted BBQ pork.

North of Stillwater on Minnesota Highway 95 is the **Boomsite,** a large body of water where fresh-cut trees once poured in through the river mouth and were then collected by the hardworking men of Stillwater's logging past. Now the Boomsite is a wonderful park surrounded by forest

with an easily accessible path down to the beach. This is a beautiful, well-maintained park, a fun place to stop and relax and let the kids run around before getting back on the road.

TAYLORS FALLS

In order to properly appreciate autumn in Minnesota, a drive to Taylors Falls in the last two weeks of September or the first two weeks of October is absolutely necessary. During autumn, the leaves of the trees growing in the mineral-rich soil turn fluorescent shades of scarlet, gold, and yellow, looking more like bright springtime flower petals than dying tree leaves.

But don't just visit in the fall. Taylors Falls is just as beautiful in springtime, with millions of tiny purple, white, and blue wildflowers springing up between even the smallest of sidewalk cracks. In the warm months, bird-watching is a popular pastime all along the St. Croix River, and canoes can be rented at Interstate State Park for those who want to get a closer look at the cliffs that line the river. For more information, you can call the Taylors Falls Chamber of Commerce at (651) 465–6315 or visit its Web page at www.taylorsfallschamber.org.

Getting There

We, of course, recommend taking the scenic route up to Taylors Falls from the Twin Cities. If you take U.S. Highway 94 east to MN 95 north to Taylors Falls, you'll be treated to scenes of beautiful old hardwood forests and the St. Croix River all the way. If you just want to get to Taylors Falls, the quickest route is to take either I–35E north or I–35W north (depending on where in the Twin Cities you are) to I–35, then take I–35 north to U.S. Highway 8 east and follow US 8 all the way to Taylors Falls. It's a little less scenic, being a major highway and all, but you'll travel through the cute towns of Chisago City, Lindstrom, and Center City, and you can still get a glimpse of the beautiful St. Croix Valley along the last few miles.

Attractions

Taylors Falls attractions run the gamut of breathtaking, cliffside views of a landscape carved out by Ice Age glaciers to wild water park rides to self-guided tours through a historic neighborhood with houses dating from the 1850s. You can take a trip down the St. Croix on your own in a rented canoe or get on a steamboat for a relaxing luncheon tour.

The centerpiece of the Taylors Falls, Minnesota, and the St. Croix Falls, Wisconsin, border is **Interstate State Park,** (651–465–5711) just off US 8 in Taylors Falls, known for its rare flora and fauna. Perhaps the most distinguishing features of the park, however, are the dark gray basalt formations scattered throughout the region. Believed to once be full-size mountains, the dense stone was slowly eroded by glaciers into solitary pillars, winding towers, and the deepest glacial potholes in the world. The potholes are really something to see. It's nearly impossible to glimpse the bottom of the deepest ones. So much groundwater seeps into the holes that the park has to regularly pump the water out. It's amazing how thousands of years of erosion can shape even the densest rock into these near-perfect, soft-edged circles that curve their way nearly 100 feet down through solid basalt.

Aside from the unique geological formations, Interstate State Park is crisscrossed with nature trails that lead visitors through thick forests (breathtaking in the height of autumn), up into the greenstone cliffs and Precambrian basalt flows that encircle the Minnesota side of the park, and then into open fields of tiny purple trilliums and other native wildflowers. Bird-watching is another popular pastime

in the park. Eagles and their hatchlings can be seen almost every summer. For another view of the park and its wildlife, catch a ride on the riverboat *Taylors Falls Princess.* The boat dock is located right next to the entrance to Interstate State Park, and you can buy tickets at the dock. For more information, call (651) 465–6315 or visit www.taylorsfallsboat.com.

For man-made entertainment, head over to **Wild Mountain** (651–465–6315 or 800–447–4958; www.wildmountain.com). To get there, go north US 8 in Taylors Falls, follow MN 95 to County Road 16, go right onto CR 16 to Wild Mountain. Park visitors can play on one of the giant waterslides, float down an 800-foot lazy river in an inner tube, splash around Wild Adventure Island (an interactive water playground), slide down one of the two 1,700-foot-high alpine slides, or race around on the park's go-kart track. In winter Wild Mountain becomes a ski and snowboard park, with more than 100 acres of beginner, intermediate, and advanced skiing terrain as well as Wild Shoots snow tubing.

While most of the historic houses in Taylors Falls are private residences and not open to tourists, you can stop by the **Folsom House Museum** at 272 West Government Street (651–465–3125). Listed on the National Register of Historic Places, along with the rest of the Angel Hill neighborhood, the Folsom House is a five-bedroom Greek revival home furnished with the original furniture, books, family pictures, and memorabilia belonging to Minnesota state senator W. H. C. Folsom and his family in the 1800s. The home is open to tour groups Wednesday through Monday from Memorial Day weekend to mid-October each year.

Accommodations and Camping

A few of the historic houses in Taylors Falls have been converted to bed-and-breakfasts. The **Cottage Bed & Breakfast,** 950 Fox Glen Drive (651–465–3595; www.The-Cottage.com), was originally designed as an 18th-century English country house and offers guests a spectacular view of the St. Croix River. The house is furnished with English and French country period pieces and is minutes away from several state parks and Wild Mountain. Even more interesting—especially from a historical perspective—is the **Old Jail Bed & Breakfast** at 349 Government Street (651–465–3112; www.oldjail.com). Exactly what it sounds like, the Old Jail has three furnished suites available to rent, each with its own private bathroom, kitchen, sitting room, and entrance. The Old Jail is located a short walk from the St. Croix River, Interstate State Park, and downtown Taylors Falls. Having just as good a view as any other place in town but offering much more conventional accommodations is the **Pines Motel** at 531 River Street (651–465–3422; www.pinesmoteltaylors falls.com).

For campers, **Wildwood RV Park & Campground,** 1 mile west of Taylors Falls off US 8 (800–447–4958; www.wildwood camping.com), offers sunny or shaded campsites for both tents and RVs, with immediate access to hiking and bicycle trails, a swimming pool, and a miniature golf course. The campsite also has well-maintained showers and flush toilets, as well as water, electrical, and sewer hookups.

Restaurants

The **Drive In Restaurant** at 572 Bench Street (651–465–7831) is a quaint, '50s-style drive-in with wonderful burgers, shakes, and homemade root beer served by waitresses in hoop skirts wearing roller skates. Patrons of the Drive In also get to enjoy a great view of the St. Croix and the steamboats passing by while they eat either in their cars or at one of the picnic tables set up outside the restaurant.

For indoor dining, stop by **Romayne's on Main,** a sports bar and grill at 391 Bench Street (651–465–4405).

If you're just looking for a cup of coffee, you're in luck—Taylors Falls has one of the nicest coffeehouses in Minnesota. Located next door to the oldest independent public library in the state, **Coffee Talk,** 479 Bench Street (651–465–6700), is a beautifully renovated Victorian house with a small front porch and a gigantic, beautiful flower garden with lots of comfortable, quaint wicker furniture and chairs spread around in the back. Inside there are paintings by local artists and plenty of seating for customers upstairs and down. The menu includes espresso and coffee drinks and fresh pastries, but the main sell of this place is the beautiful, morning glory–covered trellis that leads the way to the closest thing to a 19th-century English garden you may ever walk into.

In the Area

While driving up to Taylors Falls on MN 95, a stop at the little village of **Marine on St. Croix** is a must. The community, composed of stately old houses surrounded by fantastic flower gardens and ancient hardwood and conifer forests, is so still and quiet and beautiful it feels completely apart from the rest of the world. Established in 1838 as a lumber town, Marine has kept the look of a 19th-century settlement while becoming less an industrial town and more an out-of-the-way retreat for artists and writers. Inspired by the forests, ancient stone silos, and farmhouses that pepper the landscape and, of course, by the St. Croix River, they create their art. Writer Garrison Keillor once compared Marine to his mythical hometown of Lake Wobegon, while the directors of such films as *Grumpier Old Men, Beautiful Girls* (which was also shot in nearby Stillwater), and *The Cure* all chose to film on location here.

Marine on St. Croix is mostly made up of residences, but there are several places worth stopping by. The 2-block downtown district on Judd Street, now on the National Register of Historic Places, has a gas station and general store, perfect for making pit stops, and the Village Scoop ice-cream parlor. The **Brookside Bar and Grill,** 140 Judd (651-433-5132), has a real spring-fed stream running through its basement to keep the beer cool. There are also plenty of cross-country skiing and hiking trails that start in town and head out into the forests.

If you take US 8 across the river to Wisconsin from Taylors Falls, you'll come to **St. Croix Falls, Wisconsin** (715-483-3580; www.stcroixfallschamber.com). Located on the east side of the St. Croix River, the historic downtown area has many antiques shops and farm stores that sell knickknacks and produce. The countryside around the town is dotted with llama and ginseng farms, ancient farmhouses, and about a dozen abandoned one-room schoolhouses that date from the time when wealthy landowners built schools on their land for their own as well as their employees' children.

If you take US 8 all the way to US 63, you'll reach the town of **Turtle Lake, Wisconsin,** home to the St. Croix Casino & Hotel, 777 US 8 and US 63 (800-U-GO-U-WIN; www.stcroixcasino.com). An easy-paced, almost neighborly feeling casino decorated like a north woods lodge, the St. Croix has live entertainment every weekend.

RELOCATION 🏠

Minneapolis–St. Paul has always been an attractive place for relocation, given the region's consistently strong economy, the high quality of life, access to world-class educational resources, the numerous corporations based in the Metro, the lower crime rates than comparable metropolitan areas, and its vibrant cultural scene. Not surprisingly, many persons relocating to Minneapolis and St. Paul come from neighboring states, new Twin Citians accustomed to the cold. In recent years, however, thousands of Hispanic, Hmong, Somali, and Russian immigrants have chosen to come to Minnesota, adding new faces and languages to the Twin Cities community.

Although some of the quirks inherent to the Twin Cities may be hard for newcomers to understand (ice fishing, annual New Year's Day swims in area lakes, Twin Citians' inability to merge smoothly into freeway traffic, onramp meters on freeways, "snow emergencies," and the rivalry between Minneapolis and St. Paul), the friendly nature of Minnesotans and the conveniences of the 15th largest metropolitan area in the country will quickly make just about anyone feel at home.

This chapter is designed to aid newcomers to the Twin Cities, with details about looking for work, buying real estate, renting, and choosing neighborhoods. We then give you listings for useful resources such as libraries, motor vehicle departments, and tourism bureaus (which can send you relocation packets in addition to comprehensive area info). If you don't find what you are looking for here, ask a native; 9 times out of 10, the famous quality of "Minnesota Nice" will come through and he or she will steer you in the right direction.

FINDING A JOB

The Twin Cities is a mecca for jobs in manufacturing, banking, retail, airlines, information technology, medicine, law, publishing, state government, insurance, and many other fields. The following are a few sources to consult as you look for your perfect job.

Temp Agencies

Temp agencies can often provide short- or long-term employment in a variety of fields. They can be very useful for newcomers to an area who have not yet secured a full-time job. All the national temp agency chains have offices in the Twin Cities, as do many local agencies and specialized businesses that hire temp workers only in certain industries. The following are a few places to get you started.

Adecco: The Employment People
900 Second Avenue South,
Minneapolis
(612) 339-1153

101 East Fifth Street, St. Paul
(651) 224-4040
www.adecco.com
Multiple additional locations
in the Twin Cities
Adecco specializes in clerical, financial, technical, engineering, administrative, and light industrial jobs.

Allied Professionals
3209 West 76th Street, Edina
(952) 832-5101
www.alliedprofessionals.com
Allied focuses on medical and dental temporary positions, including jobs for nurses, X-ray technicians, dentists, medical secretaries, and home care assistance.

 *Some of the largest employers in Minnesota are in Maplewood, with several thousand employed by 3M alone.*

Celarity: Staffing Creative Professionals
7835 Telegraph Road, Bloomington
(952) 941-0022
www.freelancecreative.com
Celarity matches workers with jobs in creative fields, including graphic design, marketing, technical writing, editing and proofreading, and Web design.

Pro Staff
40 South Seventh Street, Suite 104, Minneapolis
(612) 339-2220

Norwest Center, Skyway Level,
55 East Fifth Street, St. Paul
(651) 291-7811
www.prostaff.com
Multiple additional locations in the Twin Cities
Pro Staff is a national company specializing in hiring temps for companies looking for workers in the fields of accounting, creative services, office support, finance, and light industrial.

Strom Engineering
10505 Wayzata Boulevard, Minnetonka
(952) 544-8644
www.stromengineering.com
Strom Engineering finds temporary and permanent positions in engineering, technical, industrial, personnel, consulting, support services, and more.

Teachers on Call
3001 Metro Drive, Suite 485, Bloomington
(952) 703-3719
www.teachersoncall.com
Educational professionals can get their foot in the door with the help of Teachers on Call.

Employment Agencies

Of the many employment agencies in the Twin Cities, some specialize in certain fields, while others place candidates in every kind of job. Some employment agencies charge a substantial fee to help you find a job; others charge their fee to the employer that hires you. Ask questions before you sign anything.

The Affiliates
800 Nicollet Mall, Minneapolis
(612) 349-2810
www.affiliates.com
The Affiliates specialize in helping workers in the legal field find jobs, including lawyers, legal secretaries, and support staff.

Career Professionals
4930 West 77th Street, Suite 260, Edina
(952) 835-9922
www.gocpi.com
Career Professionals focuses on recent college graduates, finding entry-level positions in customer service, marketing, financial industries, sales, retail, and administrative settings.

Creative Group
800 Nicollet Mall, Minneapolis
(612) 333-7990
www.creativegroup.com
Creative Group serves clients looking for work in marketing or advertising, including art directors, copywriters, graphic designers, Web site developers, marketing managers, and similar positions.

Thomas Moore, Inc.
1221 Nicollet Mall, Suite 710, Minneapolis
(612) 338-4884
www.thomasmooreinc.com
Thomas Moore matches accountants, financial professionals, and information technology specialists with jobs at Twin Cities companies.

State Agencies

Minnesota WorkForce Center
777 East Lake Street, Minneapolis
(612) 821-4000

2455 University Avenue West, St. Paul
(651) 642-0363
www.MNWorkForceCenter.org
Multiple additional locations in the
Twin Cities
The Minnesota WorkForce Center is operated by the state. It offers free or inexpensive services, including access to its huge
database of available jobs, help with
résumés and interviewing skills, free local
faxing, and free computer usage. After
registering with the agency, you can have
descriptions of available jobs of interest
e-mailed directly to you. Positions run the
full spectrum of the Twin Cities economy,
including education, human services, state
government, and executive management.

Classified Ads

The two major dailies in the Twin Cities,
the *St. Paul Pioneer Press* and the *StarTribune,* have exhaustive classified job listings, particularly in their Sunday editions.
The listings in the *StarTribune* are generally more extensive, although the *St. Paul
Pioneer Press* is stronger in listings for
jobs in the East Metro. Both newspapers
allow you to search the classifieds on their
Web sites for free (visit www.startribune
.com or www.twincities.com).

Several national Web sites allow you
to search for jobs in the Twin Cities based
on specific criteria. Some allow you to
post your résumé to the site for free, and
some will e-mail job openings that match
your criteria to you.

BUYING A NEW HOME

The Twin Cities have recently seen an
explosion in the value of homes and sky-
rocketing rents. The median price of a
home has risen to over $220,000 in the
metropolitan area, nearly double what it
was in the mid-nineties. With continuing
low mortgage rates, home values are likely
to continue to rise for the foreseeable
future. The following are a few places to
get you started on your search for a new
home in the Cities.

Real Estate Agencies

Here are some of the major, national
agencies that work through franchised
operations in the Twin Cities metro area,
as well as the larger independent agencies
that are based here. Many allow you to
search for houses through their Web sites.

Century 21–Luger Realty
4536 France Avenue South, Edina
(952) 925-3901
www.century21luger.com
Century 21 is one of the largest residential
real estate franchisers in the world, with
more than 100,000 independently owned
and operated franchised broker offices in
more than 30 countries and territories
worldwide. Its local, independently owned
branch, Century 21–Luger Realty, was
founded by Jim and Judy Luger in 1976. It
has achieved the highest honor conferred
by Century 21, the Centurion Award, rank-
ing it among the top 3 percent of all Century 21 offices worldwide. The company
has also earned the coveted Quality Service Award, resulting from a client satisfaction rating of over 95 percent. Luger
Century 21 represents the entire Twin
Cities metro area, including the outlying
suburbs.

Coldwell Banker
Burnet-Minneapolis Lakes, 3033
Excelsior Boulevard, #100, Minneapolis
(612) 920-5605

Burnet-Highland Park, 1991 Ford
Parkway, St. Paul
(651) 698-2481
www.cbburnet.com
The Minnesota division of Coldwell Banker

St. Paul skyline. SAINT PAUL RCVA

national, Coldwell Banker Burnet makes a genuine effort to make buying and selling homes as convenient as possible for clients, connecting potential buyers with local, accredited mortgage companies and payment plans specifically suited to each individual. More than 25 Coldwell Banker Burnet offices serve the Twin Cities metro area, both the Cities and the surrounding suburbs.

The Minneapolis Lakes office is Coldwell Banker's No. 1 office nationally and is equipped to handle relocation needs, set up mortgages, and refinance existing properties in the entire Twin Cities metro area, with an emphasis on properties in Minneapolis and St. Paul proper. More than 300 sales associates report to the Chain of Lakes office, and their strong intraoffice networking and communication with other offices and brokers ensures that your needs are broadcast to the largest possible audience of buyers and sellers.

In St. Paul the Highland Park office deals with properties in St. Paul, Mendota Heights, Highland Park, Lilydale, Inver Grove Heights, and Eagan. Eighty-five sales associates report to the office. All Coldwell Banker Burnet offices are equipped with up-to-date real estate software and technology.

Counselor Realty
7250 France Avenue South, Suite 300
Edina
(952) 921-0911
www.counselorrealty.com
Established in 1964, Counselor Realty is a local Minnesota company with strong ties to the community and 9 branches throughout the metro area in Brooklyn Park, Coon Rapids, Edina, Maple Grove, Spring Lake Park, Wayzata, White Bear Lake, and Fridley. Counselor Realty prides itself on providing superior service tailored to each client's individual needs, as well as total integrity and honesty with

clients. The agency has built its reputation through word-of-mouth referrals from satisfied customers and has firmly established itself with the local community by involvement through local charities and causes.

Edina Realty
3270 West Lake Street, Minneapolis
(612) 926-4606

700 Grand Avenue, St. Paul
(651) 224-4321
www.edinarealty.com
Founded in 1955 by Emma Rovick, a Minnesotan housewife with three kids and a $2,000 loan, Edina Realty Home Services was built on a strict standard of quality and service that lives on today. Now part of a company that is one of the largest real estate companies in the nation with a mortgage division (Edina Realty Mortgage), a title division (Edina Realty Title), and a relocation division (Edina Realty Relocation), Edina has more than 90 independently run offices throughout the Midwest. As the first Minnesotan real estate company to own a mortgage and title company, to have computer services for sales associates, and to have a 24-hour interactive real estate hotline number, Edina Realty has experienced unprecedented growth in the past decade. Edina realtors pride themselves in being able to match customers with their first-choice, affordable dream house as quickly and efficiently as possible without pressuring customers to settle for anything. The company Web site has many tools available for home buyers to use, including a mortgage calculator and full listings of all of the homes Edina represents. There are five Edina offices in the Twin Cities proper, and 30-plus throughout the metro area suburbs.

Prudential Plus
4901 West 77th Street, Suite 125, Edina
(952) 835-4400
www.prudential.com
With six offices in the Twin Cities metro area, Prudential Realty is part of the Metrowide Group of Prudential Realty, which provides its independently run offices with a regional support group and national relocation information and services, making it a favorite relocation service among businesses nationwide. All offices have in-house closers and information on mortgages and home insurance on-site, making it an especially complete real estate agency to deal with.

RE/MAX Results
11200 West 78th Street, Eden Prairie
(952) 829-2900

1071 Grand Avenue, St. Paul
(651) 251-4800
www.remax.com
RE/MAX Results is not only the Twin Cities' oldest and largest RE/MAX brokerage, but it is also one of the nation's top-ranked firms in sales per associate. RE/MAX Results specializes in corporate relocations, and, as such, has many Corporate Relocation Specialists (CRPs) on staff. The CRP designation represents the highest level of achievement earned through the Employee Relocation Council. All RE/MAX Results associates either hold the designation or have been thoroughly trained in the relocation process. RE/MAX Results has nine strategically located offices to service the metro area's strongest and fastest-growing markets, including Eden Prairie, Plymouth, and Woodbury.

Roger Fazendin Realtors
15550 East Wayzata Boulevard, Wayzata
(952) 473-7000
www.rogerfazendin.com
Founded in 1965 by Roger Fazendin, Roger Fazendin Realtors is the largest family-owned and operated residential real estate company in Minnesota. The company has expanded from its humble beginnings of Fazendin and a couple of realtors to include his son, Dan Fazendin, who now owns the company, and Dan's wife, Lynn, and their son, Dan Fazendin Jr., as well as more than 30 other professional

real estate agents and a dozen other employees. Dan Sr. has served as president of the Minneapolis Association of Realtors, chairman of the Regional MLS committee, and president of All Points Relocation Service, and the agents that work under him are supremely qualified, practicing broker reciprocity and having good connections within the local financial community. All of their listings are available for viewing through their Web site, including color photos and basic floor plans.

OTHER SOURCES FOR FINDING HOMES

Both Twin Cities newspapers carry extensive listings of homes for sale in the Metro, particularly in their Sunday editions. Pick up a paper, or check out their Web sites: *StarTribune* at www.startribune.com or *St. Paul Pioneer Press* at www.twincities.com.

There are general sites on the Internet for searching for homes in the Cities. The following sites allow you to search by city and other specifics, with additional information about finding movers, financing, contacts, and more.

www.realestate.com
www.realtor.com

RENTING

The Twin Cities offer rental properties from historic apartments with hardwood floors, beautiful woodwork, and lots of character to modern apartments in complexes with many amenities. Rental units are going for an average $775 per month, actually down from what it was in recent years due to prolific home-buying.

There are several ways to find an apartment in the Cities. One easy option is to consult with an agency. Two agencies in the Twin Cities with excellent reputations are **Relocation Central** (2756 Hennepin Avenue South, Minneapolis and other Twin Cities locations, 612–870–0525;

www.relocationcentral.com) and **Apartment Mart** (612–927–4591; www.apartmentmartmn.com). Neither business charges a fee to the renter to locate an apartment.

Both Twin Cities newspapers carry extensive listings of apartments and houses for rent in the Metro, particularly in their Sunday editions. Pick up a paper, or check out their Web sites: *StarTribune* at www.startribune.com or *St. Paul Pioneer Press* at www.twincities.com.

Several national Web sites allow you to search for apartments in the Twin Cities. The following sites should provide some good leads.

www.rent.com
www.rentnet.com
www.apartments.com

If you are looking for a roommate, one option is to contact **Roommate Referrals,** 1600 West Lake Street, Suite 105, Minneapolis; (612) 827-5565; www.roommates.com. For a fee this company can match you up with persons looking to share their apartments or, if you've already found a place, with persons looking to move in with someone else. You get a list of matches, allowing you to screen potential roommates by telephone.

NEIGHBORHOODS

Few places have such defined neighborhoods as the Twin Cities. Each neighborhood has a distinct personality, its own churches, and often its own religious, ethnic, or social groups, as well as city parks and schools specific to the neighborhood, independently owned markets and delis, and active planning committees that do everything from petition city government for roadwork and cleanup crews after storms to organize big neighborhood events like live music in the parks and evening and weekend educational seminars. Moving from one neighborhood to another is almost like moving to another town at times, with benefits and drawbacks to each location. With more than 80 specific neighborhoods in

Minneapolis and another 20-plus in St. Paul, new residents have the opportunity to choose exactly what kind of place they'd like to live in, whether it's in swanky, funky Uptown Minneapolis; the vibrant, artistic, mixed-ethnic community of Frogtown in St. Paul; or one of the pleasant suburbs north, south, east, or west of the Cities.

Minneapolis

COMO

The Como community of Minneapolis is named after Como Avenue. The thoroughfare continues to Como Park in St. Paul, where another residential community is located. The Minneapolis Como neighborhood is filled with middle-income homes. Van Cleve Park is a matter of pride for the community and includes baseball fields, a pool, and a community center.

DOWNTOWN

Downtown is one of the Twin Cities' quickest growing neighborhoods. The area is expanding rapidly as high-rises and renovations replace once vacant or dilapidated properties. Living options in downtown Minneapolis include apartments, condominiums, and lofts. In the past few years all three types of properties have been developed next to the old milling district and beside the Warehouse District along the Mississippi riverfront. So you're in luck if you're looking to live downtown; however, remember most properties garner a premium price.

The benefits of living downtown are almost endless. There are numerous employment opportunities without the headache of commuting. The cultural and shopping opportunities abound—where else are so many four-star restaurants, performing arts venues, varied stores accessible by foot? And when the weather becomes inclement, most buildings downtown are connected by skyways, so a

Residents of the Marcy Holmes neighborhood in Minneapolis have the advantage of living in a quiet residential neighborhood but the convenience of living across the Mississippi River from downtown Minneapolis—located just on the other side of the Hennepin Avenue Bridge.

downtown resident doesn't have to experience the unpleasant elements.

LINDEN HILLS

One of the Twin Cities' most expansive neighborhoods, Linden Hills offers several compelling reasons to move to this charming neighborhood. Linden Hills is nestled between Lake Calhoun and Lake Harriet, two of The City of Lakes' most breathtaking bodies of water. Its location isolates the area from the bustle of Uptown and downtown but allows easy access to the lakes, which offer almost infinite recreation opportunities, from bicycling and walking to riding a sailboat on a sunny summer day.

Linden Hills' appearance is reminiscent of a small town. Specialty shops and restaurants are located on Linden Avenue. The restaurants offer choices ranging from barbecue to Hmong cuisine. The idyllic shopping district is one of the many selling points of one of Minneapolis's hippest neighborhoods.

MARCY HOLMES

Marcy Holmes is named after the two neighborhood parks located within the community. The neighborhood is a healthy mix of students, senior citizens, college professors, and young families. Beautiful Victorian houses sit side by side with apartments in this community next to the University of Minnesota.

Another great part about living in Marcy Holmes is its proximity to Minneapolis attractions. The historic St. Anthony neighborhood borders Marcy Holmes, and the James J. Hill Stone Arch

ℹ️ *You'll notice a lot of* Peanuts *characters around St. Paul. They're a homage to Charles Schulz, who grew up in the city, and each is unique. People drive around and take photos of the different characters. It's a fun way to get to know the city.*

Bridge, now a pedestrian bridge, offers one of the best views and shortcuts to downtown. Home prices are low compared with the rest of the city.

PROSPECT PARK

The Prospect Park neighborhood is recognizable because of its water tower, which overlooks the Minneapolis community. The water tower, no longer in use, sits atop the highest point in Minneapolis and is one of the most scenic vistas in the area. The neighborhood is composed mainly of classic, expensive homes that sit on the many winding roads surrounding the water tower. The homes in Prospect Park are some of the most attractive in the Twin Cities. Prospect Park has easy access to all of the Twin Cities major thoroughfares.

SEWARD

Seward is the Twin Cities' idealistic, former hippie neighborhood. The area is lined with beautiful old homes, and many have lovely gardens. The neighborhood has many schools and diverse shopping options. Ethiopian restaurants and diners coexist in this neighborhood, where community is emphasized. Churches of various faiths as well as New Age and wellness businesses exist in this charming community.

UPTOWN

The Twin Cities' hippest neighborhood, Uptown is the community that locals visit for fun. Others choose to live in this wonderful cosmopolitan hub because of the numerous cultural amenities. An example

of comfortable high-density living, the area is packed with restaurants and retail shops. Calhoun Square, an urban shopping center, is at the center of the area's shopping scene.

A favorite spot for summer recreation and relaxation, Uptown is walking distance from Lake of the Isles and Lake Calhoun. The community effervesces with excitement each summer when it hosts the Uptown Art Fair. As a result of the excellent living in the Uptown neighborhood, rents and home prices are generally expensive.

St. Paul

COMO PARK

Not to be confused with the Como neighborhood in Minneapolis, St. Paul's Como neighborhood is centered around Como Park, Como Zoo, and Como Lake. Residents here have the pleasure of being located near many pleasant neighborhood coffeeshops and restaurants, and many of the bungalows and smaller two-story homes are reasonably priced.

FROGTOWN

Arguably St. Paul's most ethnically diverse community, the Frogtown District has been a magnet for poets, artists, and immigrants for many years. With some of the lowest property values in the city, who could blame them? In the 1990s urban revitalization programs sold houses here for under $40,000, allowing home buyers to take possession with no money down and delayed mortgage payments. Property values for these same houses are on the rise (with the rest of St. Paul), as are the small storefronts and restaurants owned by the Thai, African-American, Vietnamese, Cambodian, and Hmong residents who populate this area.

HIGHLAND PARK

Highland Park, in the southwestern corner of the city and bordered by the Mississippi

River, is a delightful area of the city, with many bungalows, larger two-story homes, and a smattering of upper-tier properties. The area surrounds the shops and restaurants centered at the intersection of Ford Parkway and Cleveland Avenue South, with numerous specialty retailers, bookstores, ethnic restaurants (as well as fast-food fare), and a major grocery store within a short drive from home. Almost surprisingly, given the pleasant nature of the neighborhood, Highland Park is also home to the Twin Cities Ford Plant, producing Ford Ranger pickups and other vehicles in the expansive factory on the banks of the Mississippi. The tree-lined streets, quiet boulevards, and bike paths of the neighborhood show no hint of industrial sprawl.

MACALESTER-GROVELAND

Macalester-Groveland is one of the Twin Cities' premier urban neighborhoods. The neighborhood has several excellent schools and is filled with numerous businesses. The name of the neighborhood is in part derived from Macalester College, a highly respected liberal arts institution of higher learning, which has a significant presence in the area. The area includes diverse restaurants and shops.

MERRIAM PARK

This attractive St. Paul neighborhood was named after the Merriams, a prominent Twin Cities family. The community is ideally located almost halfway between downtown St. Paul and Minneapolis. An important part of the neighborhood is the University of St. Thomas.

North

FOREST LAKE

Founded in 1855 by Louis Scheil, a German immigrant, this area has long been a summer haven for tourists from Chicago and beyond and is now known as one of the most popular resort towns in the area. The city has managed to keep its small-town charm even with the introduction of many big-city conveniences, especially the outstanding medical care and the many businesses that have moved into the area. Activities in Forest Lake are centered around Lakeside Memorial Park, where outdoor concerts and other cultural events take place at the gazebo in summer. Ice-skating and ice fishing are popular in winter.

NEW BRIGHTON

The land around New Brighton was originally inhabited by the Dakota and Ojibwe tribes. They were drawn to the area for its rich farmland and abundant wetlands, which were perfect for growing wild rice. French and English settlers first came to the area in the mid-1800s, looking for land to homestead and farm. By 1858 the settlement was named Mounds View Township, which was later broken up into the communities of New Brighton and Mounds View. Today New Brighton has a population just over 22,000, and many of the residents work within the city limits at the industries that have been established here.

ROSEVILLE

Rose Township was originally named for Isaac Rose, one of the first white settlers in the area. Rose and his family settled on a claim near what is now St. Anthony Road and Fairview Avenue—look for the historical marker if you happen to pass by. When the federal government ordered a survey of the area, Rose went to work on the surveying team, and, as a result, the township was named for him. In 1948 the area was organized and incorporated as the towns of Roseville, Falcon Heights, Lauderdale, and part of St. Paul.

Residents of the Como Park neighborhood often remark about how beautiful it is to hear the wolves at Como Zoo howling at night, especially in winter.

Today Roseville is a mostly residential community of pleasant houses with expansive gardens, specialty shops, and restaurants. The city of Roseville owns 23 park sites, ranging in size from 2 to 220 acres, including a large concert amphitheater in Central Park. The John Rose Minnesota Oval & Roseville Ice Arena has huge indoor and outdoor rinks available for hockey, figure skating, open skating, and speed skating. High school hockey games are held here on a regular basis, and the public is allowed to attend for a nominal charge.

Roseville's biggest housing boom took place in the early '70s; as a result, most of the residential areas are filled with split-level ramblers and bungalows.

SHOREVIEW

Socrates A. Thompson, the first white settler on the land that makes up present-day Shoreview, came to the area from St. Paul looking for a good place to farm. He decided on the east shores of Turtle Lake and was soon joined by other settlers from as far away as Germany and Switzerland.

In 1941 the U.S. government opened the Army Arsenal plant on the west side of Shoreview, bringing many new workers into the area. This expanse of residential property turned Shoreview from a small, lakeside, rural community into a Twin Cities suburb, and the township was officially made a city on January 1, 1974.

Today Shoreview is approximately 95 percent developed, surrounded by expanses of farmland, lakes, and woods. The land and houses formerly belonging to struggling immigrant farmers are now sold at a premium. Residents enjoy proximity to the Twin Cities as well as a strong sense of community.

VADNAIS HEIGHTS

Since its humble roots as a small rural farming community, Vadnais Heights has grown into the successful, thriving residential suburb and business community it is today. Within the city limits can be found many open, protected wetlands, lakes, and ponds, around which have sprung idyllic neighborhoods with relatively expensive houses. A solid industrial core and many service manufacturing jobs employ more than 5,000 residents, while many others make the easy commute into the Twin Cities.

South

APPLE VALLEY

Originally a small farming community named Lebanon, Apple Valley and its low-cost farmland first started drawing city developers as early as 1960. When the city was incorporated in 1968, the area was renamed Apple Valley for developer Orrin Thompson Homes's habit of putting an apple tree on every single family lot. Located 12 miles south of Minneapolis off Minnesota Highway 38, Apple Valley today is a small business and residential community that is approximately 75 percent developed and 25 percent parks, marshes, woodlands, and wilderness conservatories. Apple Valley is also home to the Minnesota Zoo, one of the state's best-known attractions.

BLOOMINGTON

With its proximity to the Minneapolis–St. Paul International Airport and more than 30 hotels, Bloomington is often the first and last stop of visitors to the Twin Cities. Home of the Mall of America and several prestigious golf courses and country clubs, as well as more than 85,000 residents, Bloomington is a city in the middle of an economic boom. Because of Bloomington's proximity to Minneapolis and St. Paul, this is a choice community for those who don't want to live in the Cities but have to commute there for work. Surrounded by open country and maintained parklands, Bloomington is the home of the world's first virtual high school: Mindquest, which enrolls students from as far away as India through the Internet.

EAGAN

In Eagan's early days, a tree now known as the Lone Oak Tree served as a communication center for the city. Public notices and announcements were posted here long before the town of Eagan grew into a modern city around it.

Aside from its rich agricultural history, Eagan has a thriving business community. Major employers in the area include Cray Research, Blue Cross–Blue Shield, Northwest Airlines, West Publishing, and Coca-Cola. Eagan borders several beautiful, large parks, including Lebanon Hills Regional Park and the Caponi Art Park, which features an outdoor sculpture garden.

EDEN PRAIRIE

Eden Prairie's history can be traced back to the mid-1800s, when an 1851 treaty opened the land west of the Mississippi River to settlement. According to legend, the town Eden Prairie was named by American author Elizabeth Fry Ellet, who visited the area at the request of the *New York Times*. She described the area in her resulting article as the garden spot of the territory, and the name Eden Prairie was coined.

Today Eden Prairie is a refuge for commuters who want a quiet, beautiful town to escape to after a busy day at work. It's surrounded by parklands, including Bryant Lake Regional Park and its boating and fishing lake.

PRIOR LAKE

Located in the southwestern Twin Cities suburbs, Prior Lake is centered around the 16-square-mile lake that shares its name. Named for landowner and railroad employee Charles H. Prior, who brought the Chicago, Milwaukee, and St. Paul Railroad lines through the town, Prior Lake has been a summer spot for tourists and a busy port of business since 1872.

Of Prior Lake's attractions, perhaps the best known is Mystic Lake Casino, Minnesota's largest gaming and entertainment establishment. Prior Lake is also home to the world-class Wilds golf course, designed by Tom Weiskopf and Jay Morrish. *Golf Digest* magazine regularly names it one of the best courses in the state.

It's the proximity of residents to the eponymous lake that makes water recreation the No. 1 activity in the area. With its many swimming beaches and boating marinas, Prior Lake is a favorite resort spot for watersport enthusiasts. Lakeside living, however, is linked with expensive homes; the farther you get away from the waterfront, the more reasonably priced the houses get.

SAVAGE

A steamboat landing, located at the point where the Credit River meets the Minnesota, marks the birthplace of the town of Hamilton. The early history of this community, renamed Savage in 1902 for Minneapolis businessman Marion Willis Savage, was largely shaped by its transportation connection to these two major waterways. In 1941 Cargill, Inc. moved to Savage and set up massive shipbuilding yards to construct oceangoing oil tankers for the U.S. Navy.

The present-day city of Savage is a dynamic community offering many housing options, all with easy access to the surrounding urban areas. An interesting mix of older homes and new construction, Savage is the fastest-growing and most populated community in Scott County.

East

AFTON

Nestled between wooded river bluffs and the St. Croix River, the historic town of Afton is a rural community of approximately 3,000. Located on the eastern edge of Washington County, the quiet residential community has a small business district comprised of restaurants, marinas, unique shops, and services. The village is surrounded by parks, farms, and nature preserves, and the residential area is made up of mostly upper-bracket houses.

One of Afton's best-known landmarks is the Afton Alps Recreation Area. Open year-round, Afton Alps offers skiing, snowboarding, snow tubing, golfing, and mountain biking in a beautiful scenic setting.

BAYPORT

Settled more than 150 years ago, Bayport, known as South Stillwater until 1922, was known as a bootlegger's paradise during Prohibition. Today the small community boasts a charming downtown area, including a park, several marinas, and quaint little shops and restaurants in a downtown made up of turn-of-the-20th-century brick-and-wood buildings. Formerly a center of the lumber industry, today Bayport's main employer is Andersen Windows, one of the country's largest producer of windows and patio doors.

LAKE ELMO

With the growth of the Twin Cities metro area, city dwellers seeking the quiet life have found Lake Elmo. Located on the old mail trail between Stillwater and St. Paul, the city boasts a big blue lake of the same name and eight other smaller lakes as well.

Settled in 1880 and incorporated in 1920, Lake Elmo is another historic town that has kept its quaint, turn-of-the-20th-century feel. Because it has resisted growth as its neighbors have expanded, it has retained its small-town feel. Downtown Lake Elmo is made up of old brick-and-wood buildings and an old grain elevator, all of which have been turned into first-class restaurants, antiques shops, and other businesses. Lake Elmo is also home to the Washington County Fairgrounds and an annual August county fair. The town's population is around 7,000 residents.

MAHTOMEDI/GRANT

Founded in the mid-1800s as a Methodist summer colony, Mahtomedi soon became a desirable location for summer homes and resorts due to its proximity to beautiful White Bear Lake. Both Mahtomedi and the nearby former township of Grant, one of Minnesota's newest cities, are dotted with hobby farms and working farms as well as natural areas set aside for parkland. White Bear Lake is deep enough for waterskiing and boating in the summertime, and is a popular ice fishing spot in the winter.

Many of the homes in Grant are located on the rolling acres of hobby, horse, or agricultural farms, while Mahtomedi offers more variety, including town houses, condominiums, and newer residential developments centered around small parks.

MAPLEWOOD

The city of Maplewood was originally not much but farmland lying on the outskirts of St. Paul near the town of North St. Paul. In the past 30 years, however, Maplewood has earned an identity separate from St. Paul as an attractive community in which to work, live, and raise a family.

Maplewood's three most distinct features are the Maplewood Community Center—containing a fully appointed fitness center with a pool, a senior lounge, and a craft center—the Maplewood Mall, and the worldwide corporate headquarters of the 3M company, a major employer in the area.

Like many other Twin Cities suburbs, Maplewood is rich in parks and recreation areas. The city-funded Maplewood Nature Center offers environmental programs for children and adults, with interactive displays and marked trails for seasonal use.

MARINE ON ST. CROIX

Established in 1839 as a lumber town, Marine on St. Croix is now one of the prettiest, greenest little towns you'll ever come across. Located next to the St. Croix River and about 45 minutes from St. Paul and Minneapolis, the town is made up of old, New England–style houses with elaborate flower gardens lining the roads and sidewalks, old-growth hardwood trees, and little creeks running through the town that terminate in waterfalls in the city's parks. Marine on St. Croix was used as the location site for several big-budget Hollywood films, including *Grumpier Old Men, The Cure,* and *Beautiful Girls.*

NORTH ST. PAUL

Founded in 1870 by developer Henry Castle as Castle Site, this lakeside community was primarily farmland until 1880, when it became a major manufacturing hub in the area. Today the area manages to combine the benefits of a bustling commercial and industrial district with the feel of a quiet residential area, with tree-lined neighborhoods, a historic downtown area, and many community events along the shores of Silver Lake.

STILLWATER

Founded in 1839 by trader Joseph Renshaw Brown, Stillwater is a town that's worn many nicknames in its past and present. The best-known one, of course, is the Birthplace of Minnesota. Stillwater's also been called The Queen of the St. Croix because of its booming lumber industry, North America's First Booktown because of its many specialty and antiquarian bookstores, and Prison City because of the huge territorial prison built here in the mid-1800s. Modern Stillwater offers a wide selection of restaurants and antiques shops, as well as beautiful parks and picturesque marinas.

Stillwater is home to some of the finest examples of 19th-century residential architecture in the state. A short drive from the downtown area are homes built in the Queen Anne, second empire, and stick styles of the 1800s as well as the prairie style of the 1900s. Many of the older homes have been restored and reopened as bed-and-breakfasts.

Given the beautiful setting and vibrant community, Stillwater properties are some of the most expensive in the region, particularly if you have your heart set on a Victorian masterpiece with a turret and big front porch.

WHITE BEAR LAKE

Created as a health resort town in the 1880s, White Bear Lake is a bustling business and residential community set on the clear waters of White Bear Lake. Located just 20 minutes from St. Paul, White Bear Lake has a beautiful, turn-of-the-20th-century downtown area with modern residential areas situated around parks and wetlands. Golf courses, beaches, lakes, and nature trails can be found within the city limits, and White Bear Lake itself is the largest lake within the metropolitan area, making it a great place for boating and fishing in the summer and cross-country skiing and ice fishing during the winter.

WOODBURY

With both beautiful residential neighborhoods and a thriving business community, Woodbury has enjoyed a population explosion over the past 10 years. Originally named Red Rock Township by the first settlers who came to the area in the 1840s, the area was later named after Judge Levi Woodbury of New Hampshire, who never actually set foot in the city. Many of the original settlers came from the eastern United States and from Germany, Sweden, Denmark, Ireland, and Switzerland.

Today commercial development has helped create a strong community with a high quality of life, making Woodbury a great place to live and do business. Although most of Woodbury is strictly residential, the city is also home to businesses from large corporations to small businesses and retail outlets. Some of Woodbury's industries and employers are 3M, State Farm Insurance, and the Woodbury Health Care Center.

Citizens of Woodbury enjoy four community parks: the Bielenberg Sports Center, Carver Lake, Ojibway, and Tamarack Nature Preserve, the latter three offering more than 120 acres of parkland connected by paved and turf trails. Woodbury has many neighborhood parks, too, with amenities such as basketball courts and ballfields.

West

DEEPHAVEN

A small city surrounded by protected bays and woodlands, Deephaven is located on the south shore of Lake Minnetonka. The city is so close to the water, in fact, that few of its residents live more than 1 mile from the beaches of this beautiful lake. Deephaven has more than 76 acres of parkland, with Thorpe Park being the largest, offering picnic areas, a lighted hockey rink, basketball courts, and many flower gardens.

EXCELSIOR

The historic town of Excelsior is a perfect blend of the old and the new, combining a villagelike atmosphere of antiques shops and inns with modern hotels and restaurants. First settled in 1853, downtown Excelsior is full of old buildings and houses that date from the turn of the 20th century and have been made into part of the Lake Minnetonka Historical Society's guided tour route. Excelsior borders Carver Park Reserve and its 3,500 acres of parkland, campgrounds, and horseback and snowmobile trails, as well as Minnewashta Regional Park and its public swimming beach.

MINNETONKA

Residents of this Twin Cities metro suburb may just have the best of both worlds—a thriving, competitive business community set in a beautiful residential area. Minnetonka has more than 40 city parks and is set close to the shores of Lake Minnetonka. Careful city planning over the years has allowed its beautiful woodlands, wetlands, and creeks to survive intact inside the city itself.

ORONO

Once known as Starvation Point, the village was renamed and organized as Orono in 1899. The population of Orono grew over the years at a purposefully slow pace to preserve much of the wildlife, wetlands, and farmlands in the area. This picturesque residential community is surrounded by many neighborhood and city parks, including Noerenberg Memorial Park, and five public marinas. City ordinances require minimum sizes for residential lots, so each home owner has at least two acres of land, and many home owners own five acres of land.

WAYZATA

Pronounced "why-ZEH-tah," Wayzata is a small city located on the north shore of Lake Minnetonka. The name comes from the Dakota's god of the north, a giant who blew cold winds from his mouth. Today this area is a beautiful spot for a weekend retreat as well as a luxurious residential area with access to many downtown specialty shops, restaurants, and boutiques. The town has the only free trolley service in the Twin Cities, which takes visitors and residents around town spring through fall.

LIBRARIES

Hennepin County Library
17524 Excelsior Boulevard, Minnetonka
(952) 847-5725
www.hclib.org
Twenty-five additional locations in
Hennepin County suburbs
The suburban Hennepin County Library system has locations throughout the Minneapolis suburbs. Borrowing privileges are available to suburban Hennepin County residents. In addition to the general library collections, the Hennepin County Library

offers an eLibrary through its Web site and at branch libraries, with many databases available in languages commonly spoken in the seven-county metro area, including Hmong, Somali, Russian, and Spanish. The library also has KidLinks and TeenLinks collections of electronic resources for children, including children's search engines and word processing, as well as easy electronic information about the library's holdings of materials for children and teens.

The Hennepin County Library's hours vary widely by location; call for more information.

Minneapolis Public Library
250 South Marquette Avenue, Minneapolis
(612) 630-6000
www.mplib.org
Fourteen additional locations in Minneapolis

The central Minneapolis Public Library moved to a temporary location on the skyway level in the former Federal Reserve Bank building at 250 South Marquette Avenue in 2002. The library will remain in the bank building during the construction of the new central library on the site of the old library building at 300 Nicollet Mall, which is scheduled for completion in 2006.

The former site of the library dated from 1961, and although the library has some 3.2 million items in its collection, the largest of any public library in the state and the third largest per capita of any public library in the country, the previous building (razed in 2003) allowed direct access in browsable stacks to only about 15 percent of the library's holdings. Items from the remainder of the collection, generally books and other items more than 10 years old, had to be requested from a librarian and pulled from subterranean stacks by a library employee and sent to the library floor for a patron's review—not the most efficient system for researchers, students, and the general public looking for a variety of books on a given subject.

The temporary library allows access to part of the library's holdings on open shelves and the rest by request through a librarian. Similarly, the new library now taking shape in downtown Minneapolis will allow direct access to 35 percent of the library's holdings, a huge improvement over the old 15 percent. Architect Cesar Pelli designed the new library, which will also offer a much larger children's book area, a public commons, a cafe, a retail bookstore, a center for teens, a computer training room, meeting rooms, and an auditorium. The new library will be connected to the downtown skyway system. The Minneapolis Planetarium, which was housed in the old library building, will be built atop the new library, pending funding, but it's looking positive—as of press time, fund-raising was well on its way.

The new library will be a landmark in downtown Minneapolis. The five-story building will have an exterior of clear, patterned, and opaque glass, allowing patrons to browse and read using largely natural lighting throughout the building. The specially designed glass will also protect the library's collections from ultraviolet damage. Bands of Minnesota stone will form layers between the glass panels. The see-through building will provide a more integrated feel for the library with the surrounding downtown community, not to mention spectacular views of the Minneapolis skyline and Warehouse District.

The temporary library is open 10:00 A.M. to 5:00 P.M. Monday, Wednesday, and Friday; 11:00 A.M. to 6:00 P.M. Tuesday and Thursday; and noon to 5:00 P.M. Saturday. Patrons can enter from the plaza on the Nicollet Mall side of the building, from Marquette Avenue, and from the skyway

---

Twin Citians are notorious for the speeds at which they enter city highways. They definitely try to merge onto the freeway already traveling at freeway speed—and they expect that you will accelerate rapidly, too.

The recently remodeled St. Paul Public Library on Rice Park downtown. TODD R. BERGER

Lake convenient access to general books and other materials. Although suburban libraries in Ramsey County date from the 1920s, the Ramsey County Library system was established in 1951. Today the seven libraries house more than one million items, and patrons can also access the Internet from library terminals, use Microsoft Word at all branch libraries except North St. Paul, and enjoy such amenities as a Dunn Bros. cafe in the Roseville branch library. Any resident of the seven-country metropolitan area can get a library card. Hours vary widely, depending on the individual library's policies; call for more information.

St. Paul Public Library
90 West Fourth Street, St. Paul
(651) 266-7000
www.stpaul.lib.mn.us
Twelve additional locations in St. Paul
The elegant St. Paul Public Library building in downtown St. Paul dates from 1917. Having reopened in 2002 after a $15.9 million renovation, the beautiful Italian Renaissance revival building brashly shows off its historical and artistic interior. The renovation included restoration of the building's detailed hand-painted ceilings, Mankato stone and plaster details, and compressed cork floors, as well as updating the library's telecommunications connections to allow high-speed Internet access. The library building is connected to downtown Saint Paul's skyway system via a tunnel between the Saint Paul Hotel and RiverCentre. Other features include an enlarged children's room, larger public browsing areas, a cafe on the first floor, and a new entrance from Kellogg Boulevard.

The central library's collection includes some 350,000 items. Patrons can browse the collection on Monday 11:30 A.M. to 8:00 P.M.; Tuesday, Wednesday, and Friday 9:00 A.M. to 5:30 P.M.; Thursday from 9:00 A.M. to 8:00 P.M., and Saturday from 11:00 A.M. to 4:00 P.M. Although the central library is closed on Sunday, several of the St. Paul Public Library's branch locations are open

across Marquette Avenue (the skyway is closed on weekends). Minneapolis residents can obtain a library card at the central library and all branch locations or online; residents of other Twin Cities communities can use library cards from their local library to check out materials from the Minneapolis system after registering at the library.

Ramsey County Library
Administrative Offices, 4570 North
Victoria Street, Shoreview
(651) 486-2300
www.ramsey.lib.mn.us
Six additional locations in Ramsey County suburbs
The Ramsey County Library allows residents of the St. Paul suburbs of Arden Hills, Maplewood, Mounds View, North St. Paul, Roseville, Shoreview, and White Bear

that day. Cards are available to residents of St. Paul. Borrowing privileges are free to those with a valid Minnesota library card.

University of Minnesota Libraries
Wilson Library, 309 19th Avenue South,
West Bank Campus, Minneapolis
(612) 626-2227
www.lib.umn.edu

The University of Minnesota–Twin Cities Libraries contain the largest collection of materials in the state, including some 6 million books, 37,000 periodical subscriptions, 2.6 million government documents, and 400,000 maps. The library system's extensive holdings are housed in five major libraries and 14 branch locations on the U of M's campuses in Minneapolis and St. Paul. In addition to the main Wilson Library general collection, the system includes such specialized collections as the Veterinary Medical Library on the St. Paul campus, the Science and Engineering Library within Walter Library on the East Bank of the Minneapolis campus, and the Eric Sevareid Journalism Library in Murphy Hall on the East Bank. The U of M Library is also the regional depository for Minnesota and South Dakota of all publications produced by the U.S. Government Printing Office, and the library boasts more than one million full-text journal articles stored in electronic databases.

University students, faculty, staff, and research assistants enjoy free borrowing privileges to the library's collections. The general public can borrow books and other materials from the library by joining the Friends of the Library, with a minimum donation of $80 annually, or by requesting an interlibrary loan at a public library. The hours of Wilson Library and the other libraries and collections on campus vary widely, depending on the individual library's policies and the academic schedule of the university. Call Wilson Library for more information.

MOTOR VEHICLE REGISTRATION AND DRIVER'S LICENSES

As a new resident of Minnesota, you have 60 days after moving to the Twin Cities to register your vehicle and obtain a driver's license if your vehicle is registered in another state and/or you have a driver's license from another state. Commercial vehicle drivers have 30 days to obtain a commercial driver's license.

To obtain Minnesota plates and register your vehicle, you will need the current vehicle registration card or certificate of title, your insurance information, the odometer reading from your vehicle, a driver's license (or other valid form of identification) and, if you are leasing your vehicle, a copy of the leasing agreement. The cost to register your vehicle is based on set fees for plates, filing, public safety tax, and title, as well as on the value of your vehicle for the registration tax. For passenger cars the title fee is $5.50, the filing fee is $8.50, the public safety vehicle fee is $3.50, and the plate fee is $4.25 for standard plates. Personalized and specialized plates (such as Critical Resources plates) are an additional charge. The registration tax for first-time registration of a vehicle in Minnesota is based on the value of the vehicle. The tax for cars older than 10 years is set at $35 for new registration and renewals.

If you have a valid driver's license from another state, you will need to pass a

---

You don't need to be a resident of the town or county in which the Motor Vehicle Registrar Office is located to obtain a driver's license or vehicle plates there, and it is often a much shorter waiting time at suburban offices than at the main offices in Minneapolis and St. Paul. For a full list of Twin Cities registrar offices, contact the Minnesota Department of Public Safety at (651) 296-6911 or www.dps.state.mn.us.

---

knowledge test and vision check to obtain a Minnesota driver's license. If your license from another state has been expired for more than a year or you move to Minnesota from another country, you will also need to pass a skill (road) test. You will need to present your current driver's license when applying for a Minnesota license. A regular driver's license for adults over 21 costs $37.50; for those under 21, it's $17.50.

Motor Vehicle Registrar Offices are located throughout the seven-county metropolitan region. The following offices serve Minneapolis and St. Paul.

**Driver and Vehicle Services
Government Center, 300 South Sixth Street, Minneapolis
(612) 348-8240**

**Driver and Vehicle Services
Sears, 425 Rice Street, St. Paul
(651) 291-4267**

TOURISM BUREAUS

Both Minneapolis and St. Paul have convention and visitor bureaus with a wealth of information about the Cities, on such topics as relocation, current arts and sporting events, restaurants, real estate agents, neighborhoods, and many other resources.

The **Greater Minneapolis Convention and Visitors Association,** 250 Marquette Avenue South, Minneapolis (612-767-8000 or 888-676-6757; www.minneapolis.org), offers a visitor guide, a very complete listing of visitor and resident resources, travel/hotel reservations, events calendars, and discounted tickets to certain events.

The **Saint Paul RiverCentre Convention and Visitors Authority,** 175 West Kellogg Boulevard, Suite 502, St. Paul (651-265-4900 or 800-627-6101; www.stpaulcvb.org), offers detailed information about the city's attractions, restaurants, hotels, neighborhoods, and more. A free visitor kit, with much information useful to new Twin Citians, is available through the bureau.

SENIOR SCENE

The Twin Cities and its suburbs are home to more than 100 retirement communities and nursing homes, many of which are located on scenic lakefronts or surrounded by parklike grounds. This chapter covers just a few of the residences senior citizens have to choose from in the greater Twin Cities metro area and is in no way meant to be all-inclusive. For more information about nursing homes, call the Minnesota Department of Health at (651) 201–5000, Care Providers of Minnesota at (952) 854–2844, the Minnesota Health and Housing Alliance at (651) 645–4545, or the AARP at (952) 858–9040.

Today, more and more emphasis is placed on senior citizens receiving assisted care in their own homes instead of relocating to a group nursing home. With more than 60,000 senior citizens in Minnesota in need of day-to-day care, many nursing homes are filled to capacity, and most opt to stay relatively small and intimate in order to provide quality care to residents. To accommodate the growing senior population in the state, many hospitals and managed care facilities offer assisted living options to seniors that are covered by either Medicare or their own insurance plans. These services range from having a nurse stop by on a regular basis to having a home care worker live full-time with seniors, helping out with everything, including grooming, medication, shopping, and housekeeping.

Senior citizens are a vital force in the Twin Cities, as evidenced in many successful political campaigns that have run primarily on senior concerns and issues. This is in no small part because of the Twin Cities' being home to some of the most dynamic senior rights advocacy groups, including the Gray Panthers, the AARP, the Minnesota Senior Federation, and many of the other lesser-known organiza-

tions that are listed in this chapter. These groups have effected positive change in the way government, employers, and businesses view senior citizens. They have also changed for the better the way all adults are treated in nursing homes and medical facilities across the country.

RETIREMENT COMMUNITIES

Alterra Sterling House
1005 Paul Parkway, Blaine
(763) 755–2800

5891 Carmen Avenue East,
Inver Grove Heights
(651) 306–0919

305 East Thompson Avenue,
West St. Paul
(651) 453–1803
Alterra Sterling House, known nationally as a pioneer in senior care, offers assisted living to older adults who want to retain their independence while receiving the personal services they need—the company is a national leader in freestanding residences specifically designed for individuals with memory impairments such as Alzheimer's disease. Residents live in their own private apartments, complete with kitchens and private bathrooms, receiving individual care and personal assistance in a cheerful, homelike atmosphere. This allows residents to enjoy privacy yet still have access to a full-time professional staff that caters to their personal needs.

For up-to-date information about retirement communities in the Twin Cities, New Lifestyle *magazine has a great Web site at www.NewLifeStyles.com listing regularly updated community overviews.*

Bethany Village Home
2309 Hayes Street NE, Minneapolis
(612) 781-2691

Located in northeastern Minneapolis, Bethany Village Home is a 16-room Christian facility that provides care to senior citizens who need assistance in their day-to-day living. Their supportive and sensitive staff provides assistance with such activities as dressing, bathing, medication management, and anything else that may be needed to help residents retain their independence. A licensed nurse supervises medical management; rehabilitation services include physical, occupational, speech, and intravenous therapy.

Studios and one-bedroom apartments are furnished and decorated by the residents. Each unit has a private bathroom, carpeting, drapes, individual climate control, master TV antenna, telephone outlets, and an emergency call system.

Colonial Acres Health Care Center
5825 St. Croix Avenue North,
Golden Valley
(763) 544-1555

Located in the metro suburb of Golden Valley, Colonial Acres' professional health care team excels in meeting individualized needs, from subacute care to rehabilitation to continuing care. The on-site Special Care Unit offers individuals with Alzheimer's or progressive memory loss quality nursing care in a Christian environment. The facility provides personalized dining areas, comfortable lounges, specially designed activity programs, and an enclosed outdoor yard—a safe, secure environment for residents. A specially trained staff is on-site to offer support to families and residents to cope with Alzheimer's progression through monthly support groups and individual counseling.

The Commons on Marice
1380 Marice Drive, Eagan
(651) 688-9999
www.commonsonmarice.com

The Commons on Marice is an elegant senior living community offering independent and assisted living, a progressive memory center and intergenerational learning opportunities. The luxurious apartments include a full kitchen and a private bathroom with a walk-in shower equipped with grab bars. The residents' common grounds include a two-story atrium where residents can tend a garden, enjoy entertainment, or simply gather for conversation with neighbors. The library, fireplace, lounge, and billiards room provide residents with additional opportunities to gather.

The Commons' main claim to fame is fine dining—meals are prepared from scratch by an executive chef using only the finest ingredients. All meals are chosen by residents from a changing and extensive menu, and meals are taken when the resident chooses to do so and not on any predetermined schedule. There's also an ice-cream parlor, an Intergenerational Learning Center, a chapel, and a Wellness Center offering everything from massage to aromatherapy. The Commons offers around-the-clock staffing, a 24-hour emergency call system, and programs aimed at three levels of living, from independent residences to assisted living to a Memory Center for residents with Alzheimer's.

Covenant Manor Retirement Community
5800 St. Croix Avenue North,
Golden Valley
(763) 546-6125 or (800) 296-4114
www.covenantretirement.com

Covenant Manor is the first accredited continuing-care retirement community in Minnesota—one of only 260 in the nation to achieve this honor. Loving care is the essence of Covenant Retirement Communities, from assistance with daily activities to rehabilitative care following injury or illness to long-term skilled nursing care. Established in 1886, Covenant Manor provides homes to more than 5,000 senior adults in 15 retirement communities found throughout the country.

Apartments of various sizes include a full kitchen and balcony, and some are equipped with dens and fireplaces. House-keeping, maintenance, dining services, and amenities such as recreational facilities all contribute to residents' comfort, and regular group activities are scheduled. Residents enjoy the comforts of a community that cares for them physically, socially, emotionally, and spiritually. Wellness programs, exercise facilities and programs, dietary services, and residential and nursing services are all a part of the Covenant facilities, and everything from assisted living to rehabilitative care is available from a licensed skilled nursing facility located right on the grounds.

Lake Ridge Manor
310 Lake Boulevard, Buffalo
(763) 682-1434

Located just 30 minutes west of Minneapolis in a quiet rural community, Lake Ridge Manor combines exceptional professional health care with personal attention to help residents achieve their highest level of ability and independence. Providing a family-like, Christian community, the home's gracious common grounds overlook beautiful Lake Buffalo. A licensed nurse supervises medical management; rehabilitation services include physical, occupational, and speech.

Residents are in charge of personally furnishing their single or double (private or semiprivate) residences. Each apartment has a private bathroom, carpeting, draperies, individual climate control, a master TV antenna, telephone outlets, and an emergency call system. Both short- and long-term care are available.

RidgePointe
12600 and 12800 Marion Lane West, Minnetonka
(952) 540-6200
www.ridgepointeseniorliving.com

RidgePointe offers one- and two-bedroom apartments surrounded by gardens to active, independent seniors and adults. The complex is located conveniently near shopping centers, restaurants, medical facilities, theaters, and cultural centers. The complex itself has a group dining room, a fitness center, a hair salon, a convenience store, and hobby rooms on-site. There's also daily scheduled transportation to shopping, medical appointments, and church services for residents; and amenities figured into the apartment rent include weekly housekeeping, a complimentary continental breakfast, all utilities except telephone and electric, basic cable television, individual climate control, and centrally located elevators in each apartment building. For recreational purposes, there's a card room, a complete library, a billiards room, and a tropical atrium and art gallery connecting the resident buildings.

Twin Lake North
4539 58th Avenue North, Brooklyn Center
(763) 533-1168

Twin Lake North's independent living six-apartment townhouses are surrounded by beautiful grounds that allow residents countrylike comfort with city convenience. One- and two-bedroom apartments are available, and rent includes utilities plus an attached garage. Many apartments include private balconies. Additional amenities include daily activities, a clubhouse, a heated pool, and transportation.

SERVICES AND PROGRAMS IN THE METRO AREA

Many organizations in the Twin Cities are concerned with protecting the welfare of our senior community. These organizations deal with everything from helping senior citizens and their families choose a suitable retirement community to matching grandparentless children with volunteer senior citizens. For more information about senior advocacy groups in the Twin Cities, contact the AARP at (952) 858-9040 or (866) 554-5381.

> For informed referrals to medical
> programs, specially trained personnel,
> or special housing arrangements, call
> the Minnesota Home Care Association
> at (651) 635-0607.

Alzheimer's Association, Minneapolis/North Dakota Chapter
4550 West 77th Street, Edina
(952) 830-0512
The Alzheimer's Association is available to answer questions about Alzheimer's disease and to direct you to services, educational workshops, support groups, and information.

CARELINK
www.carelinkusa.com
CARELINK is an interactive resource to link families with long-term care facilities throughout Minnesota. Up-to-the-minute information gives caregivers current resources to better define individual plans of care for senior citizens.

DARTS
1645 Marthaler Lane, West St. Paul
(651) 455-1560
www.darts1.org
DARTS provides professionally coordinated transportation and in-home services for Dakota County seniors and their families. As a volunteer-based, nonprofit organization, DARTS pioneers services that support the full participation of seniors in community life, seeking out group activities and volunteer opportunities for seniors in the metro area and providing transportation to those functions.

Elderhostel
(877) 426-8056
www.elderhostel.org
Elderhostel is dedicated to providing extraordinary learning adventures for people age 55 and older. About 3,000 programs are offered in sites around the world, including some in Minnesota. Elderhostel's learning vacations provide opportunities for older adults to take noncredit courses in many subjects—history, culture, food and wine, the outdoors, and more—while enjoying extracurricular activities with others who share similar interests. This is learning just for the pleasure of learning. Visit Elderhostel's Web site or call the above phone number to be put on Elderhostel's mailing lists.

Estates in Transition, Inc.
5427 Pompano Drive, Minnetonka
(952) 938-5253
Estates in Transition, Inc. has been helping individuals with household organization, financial management, and personal and care management since 1982. It is particularly concerned with senior advocacy in all the aforementioned cases.

Evercare Minnesota
9900 Bren Road East, Minneapolis
(800) 393-0993
www.evercareonline.com
Evercare provides health care services to both Medicare and Medicaid recipients and offers programs to keep frail individuals living independently as long as possible. Started in 1987 by two nurse-practitioners in Minnesota, Evercare has grown from a small Medicare pilot program to an international, award-winning health care organization that's the largest organization of its kind in the country.

Gentle Transitions
7001 Cahill Road, Edina
(952) 944-1028
www.gentletransitions.com
Gentle Transitions is a fully insured moving company that provides moving services for relocating senior citizens, offering pre-move planning, sorting, and packing, through to unpacking and settling into a new home.

Gray Panthers of the Twin Cities
3249 Hennepin Avenue South, #220, Minneapolis
(612) 822-1011
The long-established Gray Panthers have

worked on local, state, and national levels to fight ageism and press for legislation that promotes age equality. Call to find out about what's going on in your local network.

HandyWorks
Greater Minneapolis Council of Churches, 1001 East Lake Street, Minneapolis
(612) 721-8687, ext. 329
www.gmcc.org/handyworks
HandyWorks' chore and home maintenance services provide assistance to older adults and people with disabilities with household chores and minor home repairs to help them continue to live independently in their own homes. For some people, HandyWorks is a solution to a temporary situation—an illness or recovery from an injury. For others, HandyWorks becomes an essential service to help them remain living in their homes by providing routine cleaning, yard work, and snow removal.

Home Instead Senior Care
1444 Cliff Road East, Burnsville
(952) 882-9300

8960 Spring Brook Drive NW, Suite 200, Coon Rapids (763) 792-0041

4445 West 77th Street, Suite 224, Edina (952) 929-5695

5730 Duluth Street, Suite 203, Golden Valley
(763) 544-5988

2580 White Bear Avenue, #104, St. Paul (651) 747-8722

1349 South Robert Street, West St. Paul (651) 747-8720
www.homeinstead.com
Home Instead Senior Care is the world's largest provider of comprehensive companionship and home care services for seniors. From a few hours a day, up to 24 hours' care, seven days a week, Home Instead helps with everyday tasks to enable older adults to live independently.

Jewish Family and Children's Services of Minneapolis
13100 Wayzata Boulevard, Suite 400, Minnetonka
(952) 546-0616
www.jfcsmpls.org
Jewish Family and Children's Services of Minneapolis is dedicated to helping older adults maintain their autonomy, independence, and safety. The Older Adult Services staff includes social service and nurse case managers who are specialists in the field of aging and are knowledgeable about community resources—the staff also includes professionals who speak Yiddish and Russian. One phone call to JFS puts you in touch with a case manager who will answer your questions and schedule a time for an in-home visit. Some of the services offered include housecleaning, personal grooming, Kosher Meals on Wheels, in-home health services, transportation to medical and dental appointments, grocery shopping, consultation with family and caregivers, household financial management, volunteer visitors, and individual and family counseling. Fees are based on income and ability to pay.

Keystone Community Services
2000 St. Anthony Avenue, St. Paul
(651) 645-0349
www.keystonecommunityservices.org
In 2004 Merriam Park Community Services and Neighbor to Neighbor merged to create Keystone Community Services, which provides senior services including activities for mind and body, Meals on Wheels, jobs and training, and supportive services that help seniors overcome obstacles to independence.

Lutheran Social Service of Minnesota
2485 Como Avenue, St. Paul
(651) 642-5990
www.lssmn.org
Senior programs through Lutheran Social Service, one of Minnesota's largest statewide nonprofit charitable organizations, include assisted living, nonmedical

in-home respite, counseling, debt counseling, foster grandparenting, grandparents raising grandchildren support, conservatorship, senior companions, Meals on Wheels, and healthy living workshops.

Metropolitan Area Agency on Aging, Inc.
1600 University Avenue West, Suite
300, St. Paul
(651) 641-8612
www.tcaging.org
This state-designated agency advocates and educates on issues of aging and plans, coordinates, and offers services that help older adults remain in their homes. This is a great resource that offers a range of help or links to help for everything from teaching seniors how to use the Internet, home-delivered meals, senior employment, and in-home assistance and care to counseling, prescription, and community service hotlines.

Children of Aging Parents (CAPS)
offers advice on all aspects of senior
care, as well as support for those facing
difficult decisions regarding such. Call
(800) 227-7294.

The Minnesota Board on Aging
540 Cedar Street, St. Paul
(651) 431-2500
www.mnaging.org
The Minnesota Board on Aging is committed to providing leadership to ensure that the needs of the state's older citizens are met. The board provides many opportunities and programs to enhance quality of life. Programs include Senior Linkage Care (800-333-2433), Eldercare projects, legal advocacy, coordinated health insurance, counseling, congregate housing services, nutrition programs, and services as an ombudsman for older Minnesotans.

Minnesota Department
of Veterans Affairs
20 West 12th Street, Room 206C, St. Paul
(651) 296-2562
www.mdva.state.mn.us
The Minnesota Department of Veterans Affairs provides information to seniors on benefits for former armed forces personnel in Minnesota.

The Minnesota Relay Service
(651) 602-9005 (TDD or Voice)
The Minnesota Relay Service connects those who are deaf, hard of hearing, and speech impaired to hearing people via the telephone, 24 hours a day, 365 days a year. There are no restrictions on the length or the number of calls placed by users. One service is CapTel, where specially trained operators type the telephone users' verbal responses, relaying conversations to the CapTel user almost simultaneously with the spoken word. All calls are confidential.

Minnesota Senior Federation
1885 University Avenue, Suite 171,
St. Paul
(651) 645-0261 or (877) 645-0261
www.mnseniors.org
The Minnesota Senior Federation is dedicated to maintaining a democratic, grassroots organization that trusts in the common sense of its members. Uniting seniors and their own organizations, the MnSF acts as a body of peers, leaders, and decision makers, influencing state policies regarding seniors and providing community information and services to benefit people of all ages with an emphasis on health, housing, retirement planning, and legal issues. The MnSF publishes a monthly newspaper for members—call for current membership information and dues.

Osher Lifelong Learning Institute
250 McNamara Alumni Center
200 Oak Street SE, Minneapolis
(612) 624-7847
www.cce.umn.edu/olli

OLLI is a voluntary, noncredit education and service program for older adults. It is an affiliated program of University College at the University of Minnesota College of Continuing Education. The organization offers courses, luncheon programs, informal summer programs, educational tours, service opportunities, and special events. Courses are offered for an eight-week session each fall and spring and a six-week session each winter that meet weekly for one-and-a-half- to two-hour sessions. Courses focus on a wide range of interests—literature, psychology, world cultures, history, politics, economics, science, wellness, and the arts.

Outfront Minnesota
Sabathani Center, Suite 204,
310 East 38th Street, Minneapolis
(612) 822-0127
www.outfront.com
Call the Outfront Minnesota to receive a confidential copy of Resources for Older Gays and Lesbians for yourself, family, or friends. This resource includes several social groups, family and individual support, medical and mental health, housing, employment (volunteer, stipended, and paid), job search help, and many other services to make lives more comfortable.

Recovery, Inc.
(612) 824-5773
Recovery, Inc. organizes and sponsors free self-help groups throughout the Twin Cities to help people regain and maintain mental health when dealing with mood and personality disorders such as depression, anger, frustration, fear, and anxiety.

RSVP
2021 East Hennepin Avenue, Suite 200, Minneapolis
(612) 331-4063
The Retired and Senior Volunteer Program invites persons 55 and older to make volunteering a part of their lives. RSVP provides free assistance in locating volunteer opportunities, along with supplemental insurance and limited reimbursement

of travel expenses. Volunteer opportunities are available throughout the eleven counties.

Saint Paul Parks and Recreation
300 City Hall Annex, 25 West Fourth Street, St. Paul
(651) 266-6378
The Saint Paul Parks and Recreation Special Programs section invites adults at least 50 years of age to spring into new activities. Bimonthly the Special Programs staff publishes a newsletter called *The Pioneer Spirit,* listing upcoming activities and registration materials—call the above phone number to get a copy mailed to you. There are special events and weekly groups with activities such as craft making, bowling, cards, movies, senior choir, and senior exercise.

Satin Dolls & Company
(952) 546-8865
Satin Dolls is a volunteer group of senior dancers and entertainers associated with the Lenox Community Center of St. Louis Park. The accomplished troupe travels throughout the Minneapolis area presenting 45-minute shows of dance routines interspersed with specialty acts at senior centers, organization meetings, nursing homes, fairs, churches, and synagogues. Donations presented to the volunteers are given to the Lenox Senior Center in support of their programs, which have been featured on local television and have received favorable write-ups in several publications.

Senior Community Services
10709 Wayzata Boulevard, Suite 111, Minnetonka
(952) 541-1019
www.seniorcommunity.org
Senior Community Services provides in-home counseling and case management to frail elderly and their families throughout suburban Hennepin County to help older adults remain independent as long as possible. Its services include transportation, homemaking, medical care, and

Many travel agencies offer substantial discounts to senior citizens, as well as tour packages tailored specifically for seniors.

assistance with health insurance. The staff meets with seniors in their own homes to identify and connect with the combination of services that will fit their specific needs.

Senior Nutrition (Volunteers of America)
5905 Golden Valley Road, Minneapolis
(763) 225–4023
Volunteers of America has several programs under the Senior Nutrition category. Senior Dining provides healthy, diverse noon meals for people age 60 and over on weekdays at 40-plus locations in Hennepin and Anoka Counties for a suggested contribution of $3.00. Home Delivered Meals has more than 34 locations that bring food to seniors' doorsteps. The Wellness Initiative provides strength and flexibility classes, grocery shopping assistance, and one-on-one nutritional counseling by a registered dietitian. And the new Nutrition Education Web site helps seniors access nutrition education through current articles, links, and activities.

TeleFriends
2021 East Hennepin Avenue, Suite 200, Minneapolis
(612) 331–4063
Senior volunteers provide reading support, encouragement, and assistance to grade-school children via the telephone. TeleFriends provides age-appropriate books to volunteers and students.

SUPPORT PROGRAMS

Adult Day Programs
2021 East Hennepin Avenue, Suite 200, Minneapolis
(612) 331–4063
Adult Day Programs offers long-term, daily support for seniors, including transportation and day care for adults with social activities, lunch, field trips, and more.

Elder Ride
(612) 332–9544
Elder Ride provides van rides for seniors to medical and nonmedical appointments.

Hennepin County Coordinated Transportation
(952) 541–1019
HCCT plans, develops, promotes, and coordinates transportation resources for older adults in Hennepin County.

CHILD CARE 🧸

There are more than 290 child care providers and preschools in the Twin Cities metro area, ranging from small, home-based day care centers that cater to infants and toddlers to public schools that have specialized programs for children as young as two years old. Minnesota law has specific guidelines for child care providers. Minnesota's licensing procedure for potential child care providers is a strict one, too, requiring thorough background checks, drug testing, proof of completion of a child development course and a family day care training program, and unannounced site inspections that continue long after the license is granted. Providers must have at least $100,000 in liability insurance for each child enrolled, as well as a $25,000 policy on the facility itself. Minnesota law dictates that each day care must adhere to specific adult-to-child/infant ratios, usually of no more than six preschool-aged children per adult or two infants per adult.

The upside of this is that parents are able to rest much easier knowing their children are placed in such rigidly monitored day care facilities. Most day care centers in the Twin Cities have large, fenced-in play areas attached; serve one or two hot, homemade meals that meet USDA guidelines; and are run by people willing to go through rigorous screening procedures to become day care providers. The downside is that child care expenses in the Twin Cities are easily above the national standard, costing parents between $4,000 and $22,000 per year per child, with an average monthly bill of about $700. The following listings are by no means exhaustive but should give you a good foundation for your search for child care.

AFTER-SCHOOL CARE

Almost every school in Minneapolis and St. Paul offers some sort of after-school program for children, continuing education classes for adults, or weekend activities open to both children and adults as part of their continuing effort to both get parents involved in school and to keep public schools an important focus of their community. For information regarding after-school activities in your neighborhood, contact Minneapolis Public Schools at (612) 668-0000 or www.mpls.k12.mn.us, or the St. Paul Public Schools at (651) 767-8100 or www.stpaul.k12.mn.us.

MONTESSORI SCHOOLS

Founded by Dr. Maria Montessori in 1907, Montessori education has gained favor with the public over the past decade. In Minnesota many Montessori schools have been incorporated into the public school system, bringing their tradition of encouraging independent thinking and cultural literacy to inner-city children who might otherwise not have the financial option of attending the formerly private schools. As all Montessori schools generally allow children as young as three to attend classes, a Montessori education is a viable alternative to traditional day care.

When choosing a Montessori school for your child to attend, it's important to remember that no two Montessori schools are exactly alike. One might put an emphasis on arts and crafts, while another might concentrate on math and science. Curriculums are subject to change, too, so the only way to know for sure what type of Montessori school is in your neighborhood is to personally check it out—which the schools strongly encourage anyway, as parent involvement is just as vital a part of the system as the students and teachers themselves. *Note:* Montessori preschool classes fill up quickly, and parents are encouraged to apply to their school of choice at least six months in advance.

In Minneapolis, Montessori schools that have specifically pre-K (from one year old on up) and kindergarten classes are Bernie's Montessori School (612-333-5460) at 115 Second Avenue South and Children's Village Montessori (612-378-7730) at 2812 University Avenue SE. In St. Paul there is Children's House Montessori (651-690-3403) at 1194 Randolph Avenue and Oak Hill Montessori School (651-484-8242), at 4665 Hodgson Road.

GROUP DAY CARE CENTERS

New Horizon Child Care
2733 Park Avenue, Minneapolis
(612) 871-0233

111 Marquette Avenue, Minneapolis
(612) 332-7866

2204 Lower Afton Road, St. Paul
(651) 735-7311

401 Robert Street North, St. Paul
(651) 224-4256
www.newhorizonchildcare.com
One of the largest child care providers in the Twin Cities with more than 50 branches in the metro area alone, New Horizon Child Care aims to give children under their care a safe place to play as well as a head start on their future academic careers. New Horizon has a curricu-

lum for children, based on their age and developmental levels, which includes art, drama, computer, music, reading classes, field trips, lots of storytelling, and indoor and outdoor exercise (depending on weather). Infants as young as six weeks old are accepted into the program, as well as children as old as 12.

Children's World Learning Center
3708 West 44th Street, Minneapolis
(612) 922-6727

807 Second Street SE, Minneapolis
(612) 379-0857

525 Huron Street SE, Minneapolis
(612) 623-4642

2070 Burns Avenue, St. Paul
(651) 731-1815
With some 40 locations in the Twin Cities metro, this all-purpose day care is extended to children as young as six weeks old to kids as old as 12, with the exception of the Minneapolis facility on Second Street SE, which only takes infants age six weeks to five months. The facilities offer transportation to and from home, and meals are provided three times a day.

NANNIES

Although there aren't a lot of nanny resources in the Twin Cities, the resources available have exemplary reputations. The state-required screening process of the nannies and the potential hiring parents, as well as the extra screening completed by the individual agencies themselves, ensures a roster of child care professionals. Nanny care is not just for infants—the agencies listed below have nannies qualified to take care of infants and children up to age 14.

Nannies from the Heartland, 5490 Balsam Lane North, Minneapolis; (763) 550-0219; www.nanniesheartland.com

Nanny Professionals, 2456 Arkwright Street, Suite 703, St. Paul; (651) 221-0587; www.nannyprofessionals.com

The Greater Minneapolis Day Care Association (612-341-1177; www.gmdca.org) connects parents to day care centers and child care providers in the Twin Cities metro area.

CHURCH-BASED CARE

Many of the hundreds of churches in the Twin Cities metro area offer weekday and/or weekend day care for young children. It would be difficult to list every church that offers day care, just because these programs are sometimes offered only in the summer or are even canceled due to lack of community support. Your best bet is to call the churches directly to find out if they are offering day care—church-based care generally costs about $150 per week for full-time care.

Lexington Kids Christian Childcare (651-646-6484), located at 701 North Lexington Parkway in St. Paul, is a Christian-oriented day care that offers children six months to school age a playground, computer labs, and various monthly activities. **Calvary Lutheran Pre-Kindergarten** (763-545-5933), located at 7520 Golden Valley Road in Golden Valley, is another Christian-oriented preschool for children ages two to five, with an academic curriculum that encourages children to start reading and writing prior to entering the public school system. Calvary has a full-time kindergarten as well. **Holy Trinity Latch Key** (612-729-8358; www.htlcmpls.org), located at 2730 East 31st Street in Minneapolis, is Lutheran based but open to any child grade K–4. Holy Trinity offers a curriculum with art, science, music, and field trips. The one stipulation for acceptance is that children be toilet trained.

SPECIAL NEEDS

Ronald McDonald House
621 Oak Street SE, Minneapolis
(612) 331-5752
The Ronald McDonald House of the Twin Cities is a home away from home for 48 families living farther than 45 miles from the Twin Cities who have children with cancer or another life-threatening illness and are accessing a local medical treatment facility. The purpose of Ronald McDonald House of the Twin Cities is to

The University of Minnesota's Center for Early Education & Development (612-624-5780) keeps a database of early childhood programs throughout the Twin Cities.

support and strengthen families during this critical time.

Crisis Nursery of Anoka
County–Childrens Home
1400 131st Avenue NE, Blaine
(763) 785-9222
Crisis Nursery offers emergency care family services, including help for battered women, teen parents, and abused or neglected children. Families are encouraged to call ahead to set up a meeting, in either home or at Crisis Nursery's office, to see what action would be most beneficial. Referrals are available, so call with any problem and the staff will do their best to direct you to the most appropriate organization.

SUPPORT GROUPS

Chrysalis—A Center for Women
4432 Chicago Avenue South,
Minneapolis
(612) 871-0118
www.chrysaliswomen.org
Chrysalis holds classes and workshops for women, with a special emphasis on helping couples with children deal with divorce or separation—these meet the county requirements that divorcing families must attend. Child care is available during counseling and classes (Chrysalis has a thorough child care program as well), and counseling is extended to children ages 6 to 17 whose parents are separating or divorcing.

Prevent Child Abuse Minnesota
1821 University Avenue West,
Suite 202 South, St. Paul
(651) 523-0099 or (800) CHILDREN
www.preventchildabusemn.org

CHILD CARE

A good way to determine whether a church has a day care program is to simply drive by. If a church has a playground attached to the facilities, there's a good chance that it has children's programs.

Prevent Child Abuse Minnesota provides support groups for children and parents—adults talk about challenges and ideas while, in a different room, children learn new coping skills. Weekly meetings are offered around the metro. The organization also provides materials on preventing and coping with abuse, advocates strength-based family services and policies, and gives guidance to families in crisis.

Resource Center for Fathers and Families
1201 89th Avenue, Blaine
(612) 521-3409

With locations in Minneapolis, St. Paul, Blaine, and New Hope, the Resource Center for Fathers and Families has programs aimed at single, married, or divorced fathers who want to improve their relationship with their children, including anger management groups, parent education classes, and support groups. The center also has information for fathers on legal issues, including referrals and up-to-date information on public policy and child support issues.

Southside Family Nurturing Center
2448 18th Avenue South, Minneapolis
(612) 721-2762
Southside Family Nurturing Center offers parenting classes to men, women, and couples alike. The program features classes on the prevention of abuse and neglect, parent and child activity nights, anger management, and therapeutic group discussions and individual counseling.

EDUCATION ⬤

Education is a matter of consider-
able civic pride in the Twin Cities
and is viewed as essential to the
area's continued success. The area's
school districts strive to incorporate the
entire community in improving the quality
of learning, and the influence of K–12 education is felt beyond the confines of the
students in the classroom in important
areas such as parent involvement, athletics, and local school boards. The State of
Minnesota places a premium on education, and therefore an astounding number
of local residents are directly or indirectly
involved in the school system. Education
has always been highly valued in the Twin
Cities, and Minnesota as a whole, thus
parents, politicians, and educators usually
work together. The end result is one of the
best states for education in the nation.

This section's focus is on metro area
public education, particularly Minneapolis
and St. Paul. In addition, there are profiles
of a few of the area's private preparatory
schools, both nonsectarian and parochial,
and profiles of institutions of higher education.

PUBLIC SCHOOLS

Organization

The organization of Minnesota public
education (K–12) is based on a stable and
efficient school board government. A significant issue with state school districts is
consolidation, especially in rural areas.

As Minnesota's population has swelled,
the number of school districts has shrunk.
Many suburban school districts have rapidly expanded to immense megadistricts,
but they have shrewdly avoided the political difficulty of dividing districts. Today
the state of Minnesota has 339 school districts, from traditional K–12 districts to sig-

nificantly less numerous but growing charter districts. Also counted are one experimental district, Pine Point, within the Park
Rapids District, as well as cooperative,
intermediate, education, and enhanced
paired districts; all the different types of
school districts have missions and objectives specified by the State of Minnesota.

All districts are subject to review and
are granted powers by the state legislature and government. When school districts are negligent, their powers may be
rescinded and inspected by the Minnesota
School Board Association (MSBA). The
MSBA frequently serves as a surrogate for
direct state intervention in the school districts.

Minnesota school boards' size and
lengths of elected terms differ, and they
are frequently authorized to make personnel, curriculum, and budget decisions. The
Minneapolis school district is the largest in
the state, with 43,429 students enrolled
for the 2003–04 school year, and is governed by seven "at large" elected school
board members, who serve four-year
terms. School District 623, the Roseville
Area School District, in contrast, elects six
members every odd year.

Both state and local government make
enormous financial appropriations to Minnesota public education. The state serves
approximately 850,000 K–12 students
annually. The state is fervently committed
to providing a quality education for all
students. The Twin Cities have an important organization dedicated to improving
Twin Cities K–12 public education, the
Association of Metropolitan School Districts, which represents 260,000 students
from Minneapolis, St. Paul, Edina, North St.
Paul–Maplewood–Oakdale, and Bloomington, to name a few of the 26 member districts. Organization is an essential
component of Minnesota and Twin Cities
K–12 public education, and efforts are con-

tinually made to better serve the area's children.

Grade Level

Most area school districts are divided into elementary (K–6 or K–5), junior high (7–8 or 7–9) or middle school (6–8), and high school (9–12). The state's two largest school districts, Minneapolis and St. Paul, differ in matters of grade level. Minneapolis has a standardized districtwide system of elementary (K–5 or K–8), middle school (6–8), and high school (9–12). St. Paul's demarcation of grades includes elementary (K–8 or 1–8), middle school (6–8), junior high (7–8), high school (9–12), as well as innovative 4–6, K–12, and 4-year-old programs. Twin Cities suburban public schools frequently use a system similar to Minneapolis for grade levels, and although junior highs continue to persist, middle schools have become much more prevalent over the past couple of decades.

Standards

Minnesota, unlike many other states, did not develop statewide standards until 1993. Because Minnesota consistently has had a 90 percent graduation rate (18- to 24-year-olds), many argued against the trend toward state graduation standards. At the beginning of the '90s, the legislature and what is now the Minnesota Department of Education jointly initiated a statewide graduation standards program. The resulting Minnesota State Graduation Standards, approved in 1993, had two distinct components: basic skills tests and the profile of learning.

Under these standards students had to pass the basic skills tests and successfully complete the minimum profile of learning requirements in order to graduate. But developing and implementing the profile of learning generated much debate. Concerns with the standards' content and with how they were taught led to a compromise, which gave local schools boards the authority to decide which content standards students had to complete and how many standards were necessary for graduation. In 1999 the legislature launched an unsuccessful attempt to abolish the profile of learning.

The attempt proved successful in 2003. The profile of learning was repealed and replaced with the Minnesota Academic Standards. The new law defined five core academic content standard areas: language arts, math, science, social studies, and arts. Standards for math, language arts, and arts were adopted in this law, and science and social studies standards were adopted the following year. These standards are supplemented by specific grade-level benchmarks. The standards and benchmarks will be reviewed on a four-year cycle beginning in the 2006–07 school year. In addition to providing the core academic standards areas, school districts must offer elective courses in health and physical education, vocational and technical education, and world languages, and must create their standards as well. School districts may switch to the new graduation system at any time but must continue to offer the old graduation standards to students who started grade 9 under the old profile of learning standards.

In addition, the Minnesota Comprehensive Assessments (MCA-IIs) were developed to help schools and districts measure student progress in mastering the state's new reading, writing, and mathematics standards. They are gradually replacing the basic skills tests, starting with the students who entered grade 8 during the 2005–06 school year. Students begin taking the MCA-IIs in grade 3 and their performance on these statewide assessments can be used as one of multiple criteria to determine grade promotion or retention. To graduate students will have to pass the MCA-II writing test given in grade 9 (beginning in spring 2007), the MCA-II reading test given in grade 10 (beginning in spring 2008), and the MCA-II math test given in grade 11 (beginning in spring 2009). All public schools and charter schools must administer the tests. Students must pass these required state exams, must successfully complete a required number of course credits, and must meet any local graduation requirements in order to graduate from a Minnesota public school.

Teachers

Minnesota has one of the nation's premier public education systems. Central to the state and the Twin Cities success are the 55,862 teachers statewide. Funding and class size are important, but nothing can overshadow passionate, well-educated, committed, student-centered teachers. Minnesota has relatively strict requirements for teaching. Education Minnesota, the state's teachers' union, espouses and promotes only the highest caliber of members in its ranks. The strength of teaching in Minnesota can be attributed to a number of factors, from the Department of Children, Families, and Learning to individual school districts, but quality education begins with each individual teacher's commitment to the children of Minnesota.

Requirements for teaching in Minnesota are more rigorous than in many other states. First, in order to receive a license, prospective teachers must attend an institution accredited by the state. Then they must successfully complete classes in a specific area of study; e.g., English, social studies, mathematics, or science. In addition, the state has designated requirements for teachers, which vary depending on the grade levels in which the license can be used. All licensed teachers in the state must pass a course in human relations. Since 1973 each teacher's education institution has been required to provide a course addressing race, culture, socioeconomic status, and general interpersonal communication.

The Minneapolis public school district features the only urban family involvement program in the nation. If you are interested in participating call "Team Up for Learning" at (612) 668-3959.

Specific licenses have additional requirements. For example, in social studies, and most prospective grade 6–12 disciplines, teachers must take a number of state-specified courses in teaching technology, assessment, kinesiology, special education, and drug and alcohol abuse. Beyond academic requirements, passing a relatively simple test of general knowledge, the Praxis I, is required. Finding employment as a teacher in the Twin Cities is highly competitive, especially in liberal arts subject areas such as social studies and English. Math, science, and special education teachers, in contrast, are in high demand.

Education Minnesota represents the teachers of the state. Education Minnesota developed after the first merger at the state level of the nation's two largest unions of the Minnesota Federation of Teachers (affiliate of the American Federation of Teachers) and the Minnesota Education Association (affiliate of the National Education Association). The 1998 merger was completed to improve the bargaining position of Minnesota's teachers.

Minnesota's teachers are esteemed throughout the nation. Almost 37 percent of Minnesota teachers have received advanced degrees. The average salary among Minnesota teachers is $43,330 annually, and statewide the student/teacher ratio is 16:1.

Special and Gifted/Talented

Over the past couple decades local educators have moved toward integrating special education students in the classroom to reflect society at large. The largest school district in the state, Minneapolis, has developed an approach to special education that is followed by most school districts statewide. Of the 128 schools in the Minneapolis school district, only 6 are special education–only facilities.

Both St. Paul and Minneapolis emphasize diagnosing and beginning special education students as early as possible. Both schools have early-childhood special education programs, which follow the proscriptions of state law: Students who are assessed to require additional educational enrichment prior to K–12 education receive it. St. Paul addresses these students with the Early Childhood Special Education program (ECSE). Minneapolis has a similar pre-K–12 program and promotes job seeking and job retention skills for high school special education students. Twin Cities special education integrates these students in the classroom so that they can fully participate in the community as adults.

Minnesota special education is among the best in the nation because of the stringent requirements of its teachers. Statewide, master's degrees or greater are required for all special education teachers. The Twin Cities has nationally recognized special education programs; in particular, the University of Minnesota was ranked fifth by U. S. News & World Report. The University of Minnesota sponsors special education outreach programs, such as the Institute on Community Education, which provides social support to individuals with developmental problems.

Gifted and talented students are targeted with programs to meet their educational needs. St. Paul addresses gifted education at the elementary level with DISCOVER, where students are assessed and identified for enriched education. Most elementary districts have School-wide Enrichment Models (SEMs), with programs for gifted students and teachers to meet their needs. At the senior high level, the International Baccalaureate program provides a challenging liberal arts curriculum. For Minneapolis talented students there is the Gifted Catalyst Program, which develops the strengths and talents of this important student group. Another essential part of gifted education statewide is a postsecondary option, where Minnesota high school students enroll in college and university classes and earn coursework toward graduation.

Alternative Education

The seven-county metropolitan area of the Twin Cities features several programs to meet the individual needs of students. Alternative education programs lead to degrees for nontraditional students who have dropped out of school or require a more flexible learning experience. The state features 145 area learning centers (ALCs), with many other options available within the Twin Cities. From night school GED programs to charter schools, the state has always been an innovator in education for every student.

School Choice

The Twin Cities have without great commotion implemented school choice programs. Integration in the Twin Cities has been relatively civil over the past few decades; compliance has occurred largely through districtwide magnet programs in both St. Paul and Minneapolis, which provide all area students with extensive choices in public education.

Minnesota state statute allows students to attend the public school of their choice, regardless of the community they live in and where their parents pay taxes. If the student is of low socioeconomic status, in some cases transportation may be provided free of charge. As long as there is space in the school, and the student completes registration before individual district's deadlines, then he or she is ensured admittance. Because of the success of open enrollment, the idea of vouchers has only been bandied about but not considered a serious public education option. The success of Minnesota school choice can in part be attributed to the relative parity in funding between Twin Cities school districts. If this condition did not exist, local public education expert Joe Nathan of the nationally recognized Center for School Change argues that school choice would surely fail. Minnesota is proud of the equitable school choice system developed by the state, which offers educational opportunity to every child.

Magnet schools are a major component of Twin Cities school choice. Minneapolis has a combination of magnet and community schools, where specific magnet programs and comprehensive options are available. Comprehensive takes a general, wide-breadth approach to curriculum, whereas the magnets feature a wide array of options. Some of the programs included at the high school level are travel and tourism, aviation and aerospace, communication and technology, education, international baccalaureate, automotive and liberal arts, and several more specific areas of study. There are also magnets available beginning in kindergarten, as well as community schools, which make it easier for families to participate in their particular elementary school's education policies. Minneapolis school choice provides almost infinite options for Minneapolis's children.

The St. Paul district's magnet system is similar to Minneapolis's, with some minor differences. In the jargon of St. Paul public education, there are magnet/city-wide and neighborhood schools. Again, the system is developed as a voluntary form of desegregation and offers numerous educational opportunities in specific and broad areas of study.

In both districts magnet programs admission is competitive; however, the majority of students get into the program they desire during their first application. Magnet programs are an important part of the Twin Cities' school choice program, which offers specialized education for every area student.

Charter Schools

Minnesota passed the nation's first charter school law in 1991, and since then, both locally and nationally, there has been an exponential growth of charter schools.

Minnesota sparked the movement, and has numerous charter schools to meet students' needs. As a laboratory for innovation in education, Twin Cities charter schools have distinguished themselves. Charter schools are independent educational entities, where experiments are permitted in the classroom. Minneapolis alone sponsors seven charter schools. The charter schools vary widely in curriculum and environment. The Cyber Village Academy is a school dedicated to serving students with "a serious challenge to learning." Annually, approximately 150 homebound students participate in this program for students who may otherwise fall behind or drop out of school. The Heart of the Earth serves Twin Cities American Indians in a K–12 school, while Minneapolis's five other charter schools provide educational opportunity for students who may have otherwise given up on education. St. Paul also has several charter schools to meet the needs of specific student groups, including the Acorn Dual Language School, which is a school for students whose first language is Hmong or Spanish, and City Academy, where "hard to teach learners" receive an education.

Homeschooling

Homeschooling is another sector of Minnesota education to experience significant growth in the past couple decades. Numerous organizations have developed to meet the requirements of homeschoolers and the complex labyrinth of local,

EDUCATION

Extensive homeschooling information is available from the Minnesota Home-schoolers Alliance, P.O. Box 23072, Richfield, MN 55423; (612) 288-9662 or (888) 346-7622.

state, and federal laws with which they must comply.

Minnesota has several laws that protect students from being denied a compulsory education (MS 120 A 22, sub. 9), which also set minimum curriculum requirements for schools across the state, including homeschools. Other statutes ensure that homeschool teachers are competent, and address other issues relevant to quality of education. Homeschool students are required annually to successfully complete a state exam to prove that they are being provided with a sufficient education. For the most part, homeschool students have scored well academically compared with their peers. Homeschooling is yet another option for Twin Cities students, requiring substantial planning and hard work by parents and teachers.

Athletics

Athletics play a significant role in Twin Cities education. The number of sports available for both boys and girls varies greatly across school district boundaries. Most schools have boys' baseball, soccer, football, basketball, and hockey. For young women sports include soccer, softball, basketball, gymnastics, and hockey. Girls' hockey is by far the fastest-growing sport in the state, the result of the sport becoming available at most large Minnesota high schools. Over the years, the Twin Cities have produced a number of outstanding athletes of both genders.

Local residents support their area athletic teams with an outpouring of enthusiasm. March in Minnesota is tournament

time, when high school sports fans become captivated with state championships over three successive weeks. Minnesotans love high school hockey. The Minnesota High School Hockey Tournament draws sellout crowds, and enormous television ratings, as the Twin Cities and greater Minnesota schools engage in annual rivalries. The men's and women's basketball tournaments are also well received throughout the state, as is the annual state football championship the day after Thanksgiving, the Prep Bowl.

The Minnesota State High School League (MSHSL) is the organization that oversees the state's interscholastic athletics and fine arts programs. As a nonprofit, the MSHSL promotes fairness and good sportsmanship by standardizing rules and acts as a bureaucratic force protecting the integrity of statewide athletics. Since 1916 the MSHSL has overseen athletic and fine arts programs, where students have "gone to state." Each year more than 200,000 students participate in MSHSL-sanctioned events.

Parent Involvement

Parents are encouraged to actively participate in their child's education, whether it's in the classroom or in local school board elections. In fact, Minneapolis has one of the nation's most proactive programs for parent involvement.

The first place parents can involve themselves is at the local polling place. There they can support school board members who espouse an agenda most closely resembling their own. In addition, school districts periodically have levies or referenda regarding funding. Twin Citians are usually willing to support more taxes if they believe it will markedly improve K–12 public education.

The Twin Cities school districts have specific initiatives for parent involvement. In 1996 the Minneapolis school district adopted family involvement standards, the only program of its kind in an urban school district. The program bridges the gap between students, parents, and the community to promote learning. Training and access to resources help families enrich their student's educational experience. Parent involvement creates an important link between Twin Cities children and the community.

English Language Learners (ELL)

In the past decade the Twin Cities have undergone a transformation in student composition, particularly in the two largest urban districts, Minneapolis and St. Paul. English Language Learners have always been a significant part of student demographics. In the late 19th and early 20th centuries, large groups of Czech, German, Swedish, Norwegian, Polish, Jewish, and other immigrant children entered Twin Cities public schools. Today ELL programs have been established to make the transition easier for Hmong, Somali, Tibetan, Bosnian, Hispanic, Amharic (Ethiopian), Russian, and other students whose first language is not English. The Minneapolis K–12 school guide is an excellent example of the school's commitment to ELL education; on the very first page, seven languages ask, "Do you speak a language other than English?"

Minneapolis is the most diverse school district in the state, with school attendance figures for 2001–02 at 45 percent African American, 14 percent Asian American, 11 percent Hispanic American, 4 percent Native American, and 26 percent Caucasian. Minneapolis schools have 24 percent ELL students or approximately 12,000 in the district. An ELL student must meet two requirements: The student's first language is not English, and he/she scores poorly on an English reading or language proficiency test. Throughout the district specific ELL programs are available at most schools. For example,

the Ericcson Community School has Hmong and Spanish ELL programs. ELL programs are also significant parts of many area school districts, St. Paul. With 51,275 ELL students statewide, serving this population will continue to be a major objective of public education.

PRIVATE SCHOOLS

The Twin Cities are home to nationally respected private schools. Many of the schools are denominational parochial institutions, but in most cases they include children of diverse faiths in their student body.

The area also features schools with innovative academic programs, which mirror charter schools with one exception—tuition. Many of these schools are quite expensive; however, many do offer scholarships for children with low socioeconomic status. Admission is another difficult matter, since some of the schools have fairly rigid admission requirements for K–12 education.

Minneapolis

Minnehaha Academy
3100 West River Parkway, Minneapolis
(612) 721-3359
www.minnehahaacademy.net
Minnehaha Academy offers a pre-K–12 education with a distinctly Christian orientation. The school's approach to teaching and curriculum does not endorse a particular Christian denominational outlook but does emphasize "challenging minds and nurturing souls."

Minnehaha Academy has three campuses: one in suburban Bloomington and two Minneapolis campuses, idyllically located on West River Parkway overlooking the Mississippi River. Founded in 1913, Minnehaha Academy was established to educate children in Christian faith. Since then the school has expanded but continues its mission of providing an excellent education rooted in faith.

EDUCATION

St. Paul

Cretin-Derham Hall
550 South Albert Street, St. Paul
(651) 690-2443
www.cretin-derhamhall.org
Cretin-Derham Hall (CDH) is one of the premier private high schools in the Twin Cities area. The school is recognized throughout the area for providing a disciplined Catholic education. CDH is also respected statewide as an athletic powerhouse, especially in football and baseball, where students almost annually compete in state championships.

Cretin-Derham Hall's roots date from 1871. The Christian Brothers founded Cretin High School exclusively for young men, and in 1905 the Sisters of St. Joseph Carondelet founded Derham Hall. The schools did not merge until 1987, creating a much larger coeducational Catholic high school. After all these years Catholic values remain central to the school's academic experience. CDH inculcates in its students such values as leadership, service, diversity, and equity.

Cretin-Derham Hall has been a name synonymous with athletic success in the Twin Cities. Many CDH athletes have gone on to national success after graduating. In baseball the school boasts major-league great Paul Molitor. The school is also renowned for developing football players who went on to successful college and even NFL careers. Former Florida State quarterback and Heisman Trophy winner Chris Weinke is one of the most recent CDH stars to achieve enormous success after graduation.

Friends School of Minnesota
1365 Englewood Avenue, St. Paul
(651) 917-0636
www.fsmn.org
A school developed by parents, educators, and members of the Quaker community, the Friends School of Minnesota is in the fine tradition of Quaker education nationally. The Friends School prepares children with a specific Quaker curriculum in grades K–8.

The curriculum at the Friends School is characterized by several teaching techniques. One important aspect of the school's academic experience is a weekly silent meeting, where students and staff reflect on the events of the day. As a part of the Quaker tradition, students also have daily moments of reflection. The curriculum emphasizes hands-on education, especially with young children. The school has a community focus in the classroom, and group gatherings are a regular component of the curriculum, where students discuss group dynamic problems. Essential to the educational experience at the Friends School is the inquiry process, which encourages students to be thirsty for answers when learning.

St. Paul Academy and Summit School
1150 Goodrich Avenue, Goodrich Campus, St. Paul

1712 Randolph Avenue, Randolph Campus, St. Paul
(651) 698-2451
www.spa.edu
St. Paul Academy and Summit School provides a private education on two beautiful campuses in St. Paul. The school's mission is to prepare students for life by providing academically challenging programs.

Another area private school that developed as the result of a merger, St. Paul Academy and Summit School are the result of consolidation to create a coeducational school. St. Paul Academy was founded in 1900 to educate young men, and Summit School first opened its doors in 1917. The two schools have been one since 1969 and have provided an excellent college preparatory education in beautiful, historic facilities.

North

Totino-Grace
1350 Gardena Avenue NE, Fridley
(763) 571-9116
www.totinograce.org
Totino-Grace, a private Catholic high school, serves the northern Twin Cities suburbs. The school's mission centers on learning, faith, service, and community. As the second largest of the 13 Catholic high schools in the Archdiocese of St. Paul and Minneapolis, the school has an annual enrollment of more than 1,000. Totino-Grace was founded in 1965 to meet the needs of the rapidly expanding Twin Cities north suburban area. Since then the Twin Cities suburbs have expanded much farther, but Totino Grace remains an important area Catholic high school.

South

Academy of Holy Angels
6600 Nicollet Avenue South, Richfield
(612) 798-2600
www.ahastars.org
The Academy of Holy Angels, one of the Twin Cities' most picturesque campuses, is equipped with excellent education facilities. The campus is on 26 acres in suburban Richfield, where the school actively pursues a diverse student population.

Beyond the beautiful campus, the academy has several important selling points. The 850 students in grades 9–12 have ample academic resources available. Amenities include a theater, computer labs, and a library with more than 12,000 books. The school has excellent athletic facilities, which include a domed football stadium, two gyms, and a weight room with modern exercise equipment. The Academy of Holy Angels specializes in a Catholic education with state-of-the-art education facilities.

Totino-Grace High School is named in part for Jim and Rose Totino, owners of Totino's frozen pizzas, who made a large donation to the private Catholic school.

The International School of Minnesota
6385 Beach Road, Eden Prairie
(952) 918-1800
www.ism-sabis.net
The International School of Minnesota (ISM) is a private preparatory school for pre-K–12. The school is a member of the SABIS School Network that includes 31 schools worldwide and traces its history back to 1886 in Lebanon.

Located in Eden Prairie, a southern suburb of Minneapolis, ISM has an impressive 55-acre campus beside Bryant Lake. The school was founded in 1986 with an enrollment of only 24 students; since then the school has rapidly expanded to over 500 students. High school students at ISM have advanced placement programs in many academic fields, such as art, biology, history, French, English, and several more college-level courses.

East

Hill-Murray School
2625 Larpenteur Avenue East,
Maplewood
(651) 777-1376
www.hill-murray.org
Hill-Murray is a respected Catholic private high school for the east metropolitan Twin Cities. The school enrollment is 940 students for grades 7–12, and it has an impressive 14:1 student/teacher ratio. Academics with a moral perspective are emphasized at Hill-Murray, and the results show in student standardized test performance. On average, 94 percent of the school's graduates attend college.

Athletics are another important aspect of a Hill-Murray education. There are 23 varsity sports teams, and the Pioneers excel in many, especially hockey, where they have regularly competed in state high school tournaments. Hill-Murray has provided an excellent Catholic education for more than 40 years.

West

Blake School
Blake Campus, 110 Blake Road, Hopkins

Highcroft Campus, 310 Peavey Lane, Wayzata

Northrop Campus, 511 Kenwood Parkway, Minneapolis
(952) 988-3520
www.blakeschool.org
Blake School is one of the area's elite private preparatory schools and provides a nonsectarian, coeducational experience. The school features three campuses in the western Twin Cities metropolitan area and one next to the Walker Art Center in Minneapolis.

The Blake School's academic programs are challenging and intensive. Though the school is nonsectarian, it does promote a specific set of values, which include respect, love of learning, integrity, and courage. All students participate in artistic, academic, and athletic activities designed to prepare Blake students for higher education.

Breck School
123 Ottawa Avenue North, Golden Valley
(763) 381-8100
www.breckschool.org
The Breck School is recognized as one of the Twin Cities' finest private schools. The school offers Episcopalian values in the curriculum and is coeducational. Breck has a beautiful campus just outside Minneapolis and features 37 acres for school activities.

HIGHER EDUCATION

It's hard to imagine a metropolitan area with more diverse higher education options than the Twin Cities, from nationally recognized colleges and universities to esteemed community colleges and technical institutes that transcend the traditional notion of trade schools to prepare students to participate in the area's dynamic economy.

The area's higher education institutions have long, storied histories. The University of Minnesota celebrated its sesquicentennial in 2001. Throughout its history the school has shaped the quality of public education in the state and has provided a relatively inexpensive undergraduate education through significant state subsidies. The area's community colleges are evenly distributed throughout the Twin Cities to serve as a feeder system for the University of Minnesota and the Minnesota state colleges and universities. Another feature of Twin Cities' higher education is the many nationally recognized private colleges located in the area.

Continuing education has become an increasingly essential component of most school's missions. Area colleges and universities have extensive, flexible continuing education programs to satisfy the needs of nontraditional students and adult learners. "Distance learning" is an innovative means for busy adults to complete undergraduate and professional degrees.

Numerous Twin Cities graduate programs and schools are nationally recognized for educational excellence and professional training. For more information on specific educational programs, most area higher education institutions have Web sites. *Peterson's 4-Year Colleges* is also a good source of information on Minnesotan institutions. Several area institutions are mentioned in *The 331 Best Colleges* by Princeton Review.

Minneapolis

Augsburg College
2211 Riverside Avenue, Minneapolis
(612) 330-1000
www.augsburg.edu

Located approximately 1 mile from downtown Minneapolis, Augsburg College is the Twin Cities' Evangelical Lutheran institution of higher learning. The college provides a distinctly secular education, though it retains its affiliation. The college, founded in Marshall, Wisconsin, in 1869, relocated to Minneapolis in 1872. Since then Augsburg has grown in scope and enrollment, with annual enrollments of slightly more than 3,000 students.

Teaching students is at the core of an Augsburg education, and it is reflected in many programs and activities. Professors concentrate on teaching rather than research and publication. Average class size is only 15. Another asset is the plentiful multicultural support programs, ranging from Pan-Afrikan and Pan-Asian to Hispanic/Latino student services.

Augsburg offers programs in most disciplines. For many majors the college has an area of emphasis, such as "Sociology-Crime and Community" or "Social Psychology." Augsburg also offers majors not found at some other institutions of higher learning, e.g., Nordic Area Studies, which reflects the heritage of the region and the continuing influence of Scandinavian Lutheran culture.

Activities abound at Augsburg and enrich students' educational experience. With nine male and eight female intercollegiate sports, the "Auggies" are members of Division III of the NCAA in the MIAC (Minnesota Intercollegiate Athletic Association). More than 50 clubs and organizations are on campus, including forensics, cheerleading, and the student newspaper.

Capella University
225 South Sixth Street, 9th Floor, Minneapolis
(888) 227-2736
www.capella.edu

Capella University is the Twin Cities' first and only "distance learning" undergraduate and graduate school, primarily offering courses online but also offering directed studies programs. About 1,300 students are enrolled at the school in more than 20 nations worldwide.

Since receiving accreditation in 1997, the school has received significant media attention for its high-tech version of higher education. The school offers 650 accredited online classes, which are accessible anywhere and anytime a computer is available. Capella offers the online "cybrary," the school's Internet version of a library. The university has five primary schools: Undergraduate Studies, Technology, Psychology, Human Services, and Education, plus nearly 70 specialized areas of study. Conferred degrees at Capella University include B.S. and M.S. Adult students are the most common group in the student body.

Dunwoody College of Technology
818 Dunwoody Boulevard, Minneapolis
(612) 374-5800
www.dunwoody.edu

Dunwoody College of Technology is an excellent Twin Cities unified trade school. The institute is a nonprofit that offers 16 technical programs. Founded in 1914, Dunwoody has trained more than 250,000 students for technical careers. Located next to the breathtaking Walker Art Center Sculpture Garden, the school sits on the edge of downtown Minneapolis and has one of the most panoramic views of the city, where many of its students move on to successful careers in various trades.

Dunwoody is recognized as one of the premier trade schools in the nation. Just a

E-learning is a rapidly expanding service area of the economy; Minneapolis-based Capella reflects this trend, and was named one of the 500 fastest growing companies by Inc. *magazine.*

few of the programs offered at Dunwoody are construction accounting, electronics, technology, auto collision repair, heating and cooling systems, and welding. There are continuing education and Web-based tech classes, such as night classes offered for construction industry trades. Dunwoody recognizes the importance that trades continue to play in the Twin Cities' dynamic economy by providing a high quality education, and their high placement results demonstrate the institution's success.

Minneapolis College of Art and Design
2501 Stevens Avenue South, Minneapolis
(612) 874-3700 or (800) 874-MCAD
www.mcad.edu
Minneapolis College of Art and Design (MCAD) is the leading art educator in the Twin Cities. Since 1886 MCAD has served area art students. Today the art college shares a large portion of the state-of-the-art Minneapolis Institute of Arts (MIA) building. MIA is one of three excellent art museums in Minneapolis, all within a few miles of MCAD.

MCAD programs are available in more than 20 fields, which include comic art, advertising, and photography, plus business-friendly areas of art, such as furniture design and advertising design. Besides the rigorous studio art portion of most majors, important foundation and liberal arts courses are required.

MCAD confers many specialized graduate degrees. Offered are masters of fine arts programs as well as one-year post-baccalaureate and certificate programs in design, fine arts, and media arts. MCAD's continuing education courses are open to the general public, and include distance learning and design programs.

Minneapolis Community and Technical College
1501 Hennepin Avenue, Minneapolis
(612) 659-6000 or (800) 247-0911
www.mctc.mnscu.edu
Minneapolis Community and Technical College (MCTC) is dedicated to serving the increasingly diverse Twin Cities student population with liberal arts and career/technical programs. The focus at MCTC is on creating an environment where recent high school graduates, working adults, and continuing education students are comfortable and excel together in various educational fields.

Diversity is a major commitment at MCTC. As the state's most ethnically diverse school of higher education, MCTC has an important mission: providing a quality education to students who speak more than 80 languages and dialects. In part this is accomplished by the English as a Second Language program, which serves these frequently skilled students, who may need to improve their English language proficiency. Additionally, the average age of the student body, 29.6 years, is decidedly nontraditional. MCTC offers programs that lead students into successful careers. A few of the most popular programs are liberal arts disciplines, law enforcement, nursing, and computer support. Associate in arts (AA) and Associate in science (AS) degrees are popular at MCTC, as are technical certificate programs.

MCTC has dedicated and continues to allocate substantial funds and resources for technology, such as its online courses and its New Technology Center/Library.

MCTC abuts Loring Park, one of the Twin Cities' most beautiful parks, and is within walking distance from all downtown Minneapolis's attractions and employers.

The University of Minnesota–Twin Cities
231 Pillsbury Drive SE,
240 Williamson Hall, Minneapolis
(612) 625-2008
www1.umn.edu/twincities
The University of Minnesota–Twin Cities pervades all aspects of the area's culture from sports, education, research and development to medicine, law, politics, and business. Known in the Twin Cities as the U of M, or simply the U, the institution is the flagship of Minnesota public higher

education and a matter of tremendous civic pride. With an annual undergraduate and graduate student enrollment of more than 60,000, the U of M dominates southeast Minneapolis and is omnipresent throughout the Cities.

The University of Minnesota public education system includes five campuses. Outstate campuses are located in Crookston, Duluth, Morris, and Rochester. The University of Minnesota–Twin Cities has two campuses. The vast majority of programs are on the Minneapolis campus, where the administration is housed. The St. Paul campus is much less urban, with 155 acres of beautiful property devoted to agriculture and natural resources programs.

The academic options at the U of M are seemingly endless. The two largest colleges are the College of Liberal Arts (CLA) and the Institute of Technology (IT). Eleven U of M programs are ranked in the top 10 in the nation, including Chemical Engineering, Psychology, Geography, Economics, and Forestry. Besides the 20 distinct colleges of the U of M, there is University College, the continuing education program, which is important in serving Twin Cities nontraditional students.

In 1999 the University of Minnesota opened the new McNamara Alumni Center and Gateway Center, the culmination of decades of work and fund-raising. University of Minnesota alumni appear in almost every imaginable field. Two vice presidents and Democratic Party nominees for president of the United States, Hubert H. Humphrey and Walter Mondale, attended the U of M. The school counts five alumni in the Pro Football Hall of Fame: Bud Grant, Leo Nomellini, Alan Page, Bobby Bell, and Bronko Nagurski. The list of alumni includes Seymour Cray, the founder of Cray Research and an important figure in the development of the supercomputer; Earl Bakken, who created the first battery-operated pacemaker and founded Medtronic; and 1998 Nobel Prize winner Dr. Louis Ignarro, who was instrumental in the development of Viagra.

Bob Dylan attended the University of Minnesota and lived and performed in the adjoining Dinkytown neighborhood from 1959 to 1960. Many of Dylan's former stomping grounds still stand in the area, and longtime residents are more than happy to tell stories of the native.

Another U of M Nobel Prize winner is Norman Borlaug, who received the award in 1970 for engineering the "green revolution," which resulted in unprecedented food yields for feeding the third world. University of Minnesota alumni have had enormous impact on the Twin Cities by creating 1,500 technological companies, which contribute $30 billion annually to the state economy.

The U of M newspaper, the *Minnesota Daily,* has operated for more than a century and is regarded as one of the nation's best college newspapers. The University's radio station, KUOM, better known as Radio K, provides student radio programming from dawn to dusk daily. Many *Minnesota Daily* and KUOM alumni have moved on to success in the Twin Cities and national media. As a link to the University of Minnesota, the alumni association publishes a bimonthly magazine, *Minnesota,* a glossy publication filled with facts about the school and its history.

St. Paul

The College of St. Catherine
2004 Randolph Avenue, St. Paul
(651) 690-6000 or (800) 945-4599
www.stkate.edu
Located on an idyllic 110-acre wooded campus 5 miles from downtown St. Paul, the College of St. Catherine champions the cause of women's higher education.

As the largest Roman Catholic liberal arts school for women in the state, the College of St. Catherine, or St. Kate's, has a notable history. Founded in 1905 by the

The College of St. Catherine in St. Paul. TODD R. BERGER

Sisters of St. Joseph Carondelet, their mission is improving women's educational opportunities. That said, St. Kate's does offer limited programs for men at its much smaller campus in Minneapolis as well as the graduate school.

St. Kate's emphasizes a distinctly Roman Catholic spiritual and ethical approach to education. St. Kate's curriculum emphasizes depth and breadth and is reflected in critical inquiry, multicultural studies, and interdisciplinary teaching in the classroom. Offered at the college are more than 45 different majors, from art and biology to theater and theology. Liberal arts is the most popular area of study, while health care is an important option. The College of St. Catherine is the Twin Cities' oldest and largest health care educator and includes highly regarded programs in nursing, occupational therapy, and pre-med.

One of St. Kate's greatest educational innovations was the creation of "Weekend College" in 1979. Weekend College is designed to meet working women's needs for a college education. Classes meet every other weekend on Friday evening, Saturday, and Sunday. Twelve practical, career-oriented majors are offered in the Weekend College program, including elementary education, accounting, communication, and nursing. Programs like Weekend College extend educational opportunities to students who might not otherwise receive a college education.

Concordia University–St. Paul
275 Syndicate Street North, St. Paul
(651) 641-8278 or (800) 333-4705
www.csp.edu
Concordia University provides higher education in a Christian environment. The origins of Concordia date from 1893, when

the Lutheran Church–Missouri Synod created a high school to prepare students for its ministry. The school became coeducational in 1950 and began granting bachelor's degrees in elementary education in 1962 for the first time as a college.

Today educational opportunities are available in numerous fields. Liberal arts, business and health care are popular areas of study. The college continues to offer many specialized career majors in the ministry, such as directors of church, parish music, Christian outreach and Christian education, as well as preseminary studies.

Hamline University
1536 Hewitt Avenue, St. Paul
(651) 523-2800
www.hamline.edu
Hamline University is Minnesota's oldest university. The United Methodist Church organized the school in 1854 in Red Wing. Shortly thereafter, it relocated 50 miles north to its present site in St. Paul. Hamline was a progressive area leader in higher education and was the third coeducational college in the United States. The cornerstone of Hamline's curriculum is liberal arts.

Hamline offers degrees and majors in numerous areas of study. Undergraduate bachelor's degrees in liberal arts disciplines are the most popular certificates granted. Also conferred are master's, doctorate, and law degrees. The campus is composed of approximately 2,000 undergrad students in areas of study ranging from the familiar such as history, art, and anthropology, to urban studies, Latin American studies and musical studies. Besides the Hamline Law School, there are several additional graduate programs: the Graduate School of Education and the Graduate Liberal Studies Programs.

The Hamline Plan is a specific curriculum program instituted universitywide that outlines and targets the institution's specific educational goals. Throughout their studies student are exposed to an interdisciplinary focus—students are educated in particular majors but taught to think

beyond the confines of their specific fields. Hence, students in all areas of study are expected to improve their abilities in several key areas (writing, speaking, computing, and reasoning) regardless of their major. Another essential component of the curriculum is "culture and issues." Students are encouraged to consider how culture interacts with such issues as gender, race, and age. Finally, the curriculum promotes "work and leadership" through seminars, internships, and career development courses. The overall goal of Hamline's curriculum is creating good citizens through a liberal arts education.

Luther Seminary
2481 Como Avenue, St. Paul
(651) 641-3456
www.luthersem.edu
Luther Seminary educates ministers for the Evangelical Lutheran Church in America (ELCA). It is the largest of eight ELCA seminaries in the United States. The seminary expanded over 50 years to its present size after the consolidation of six area institutions serving a similar function. The campus is located on a pastoral bluff in St. Paul, where they provide degree programs in Old Testament, New Testament, history of Christianity, Christian lay ministry, and family ministry; also offered are graduate studies and doctor of ministry programs.

Macalester College
1600 Grand Avenue, St. Paul
(651) 696-6000
www.macalester.edu
Macalester College is a preeminent private liberal arts college. The college is respected locally and nationally for maintaining high academic standards and championing internationalism and multiculturalism. Macalester is the recipient of enormous endowment monies, particularly from the DeWitt-Wallace fund, which helps underwrite the costs of tuition, through scholarships and other awards, for students of low socioeconomic status.

Macalester was founded in 1874 by the Reverend Dr. Edward Duffield Neill. A superintendent for Minnesota Territory Schools, Neill did not move the college to its present site until 1885. In its early years the college received significant financial support from philanthropist Charles Macalester, for whom the college was named.

Macalester College's diversity is reflected in the exceptional students it attracts from the nation and abroad. Nestled in the exquisite Macalester-Groveland neighborhood, the college creates an excellent learning environment. Macalester's demographics consistently have represented one of the most diverse schools of higher education in the nation. The roughly 1,800 full-time come from 49 states, D.C., and around the world—10 percent are from more than 78 countries. There are 35 majors and minors are offered at Macalester, including geography, Russian, and glassics, as well as African-American studies, women's and gender studies, urban studies, and several interdepartmental fields. A major area of focus at Macalester is the arts, particularly music and theater. Macalester hosts four or five theater productions a year. In addition, the college features extensive organized music groups, which include: Symphony Orchestra, Mac Jazz, New Music Ensemble, Festival Chorale, Flying Fingers (a traditional bluegrass group), the Electric Guitar, and several other diverse music organizations.

McNally Smith College of Music
19 East Exchange Street, St. Paul
(651) 291-0177 or (800) 594-9500
www.mcnallysmith.edu
Formerly Musictech, McNally Smith began in 1985 as "the Guitar Center of the Twin Cities" but since its inception has rapidly expanded into other music-related fields (hence the name change). The school is now known as a "college of contemporary music and recording arts." Professional musicians, music technicians, and educators formed the school to serve the needs of the burgeoning local music scene. Classical and traditional music schools of

higher learning were already established in the Twin Cities, but a formal school for studying popular and rock forms was strikingly absent—McNally Smith filled this gap. Students have many options for study such as guitar, bass, percussion, vocals, engineering, theory, production, brass and woodwind, and music business. The programs confer associate of applied science in music degrees and diplomas. McNally Smith has a school in Germany as well.

Metropolitan State University
700 East Seventh Street, St. Paul

1501 Hennepin Avenue, Minneapolis
(651) 793-1212
www.metrostate.edu
Metropolitan State University provides flexible and affordable education to non-traditional students in the Twin Cities. Convenience is emphasized in order to provide educational opportunities toward earning bachelor's and graduate degrees.

Metro State has served the Twin Cities since 1971. The university's original objective was to offer a program for working adults. This has remained Metro State's focus, though the university has broadened its objectives. In 1983 the first graduate program, master of management and administration, was launched. Today Metro State's enrollment is approximately 9,000 annually and continues to support education of diverse and underserved student populations.

Metro State offers more than 30 majors. Most majors are training toward occupations, such as accounting, social work, law enforcement, and nursing. Metro State Accounting students frequently distinguish themselves by annually placing in the top 10 percent on the CPA exam.

Metro State campuses are conveniently located to facilitate greater academic success. The Dayton's Bluff neighborhood, just outside downtown St. Paul, is the largest campus. Another campus is in the heart of downtown Minneapolis. In addition, Metro State has three smaller campuses strategically placed throughout the Twin Cities,

Metropolitan State University in St. Paul. TODD R. BERGER

which minimize the time students must spend getting to school and brings classes closer to their homes.

Northwestern College
3003 Snelling Avenue North, St. Paul
(651) 631-5100
www.nwc.edu
Northwestern College is a nondenominational, conservative, private Christian college. In recent years Northwestern has undergone significant growth; for the 2002–03 academic year enrollment was 2,480 students. Part of the growing enrollment is linked to the expansion of the adult degree completion program, Focus, and the Center for Distance Learning.

Northwestern College began as the Northwestern Bible and Missionary School in Minneapolis in 1902. Over time educational and vocational opportunities have been greatly expanded, with the creation of the Northwest Theological Seminary in 1935 and the College of Liberal Arts founded in 1944. Then the college

acquired a former Roman Catholic seminary in 1970; the large, wooded, gated campus was renovated and reopened as Northwestern College in 1972.

Christian doctrine is central to the educational mission at Northwestern College. Despite firm established Christian doctrines, students follow remarkably diverse faiths. For the 2000–2001 academic year, Northwestern had students representing 44 religious denominations. Unlike with many of the Twin Cities commuter campuses, 63 percent of students live on campus, and, reflecting current higher education trends, the college student body is composed of 61 percent women. Northwestern College offers a distinctly conservative Christian education option for Twin Citians.

St. Paul College
235 Marshall Avenue, St. Paul
(651) 846-1500
www.saintpaul.edu
Formerly St. Paul Technical College, St.

Paul College is a remarkable educational institution. Foremost among its accomplishments is its astounding job placement statistics; consistently 90 to 100 percent of its students find positions in their field of study. Technically trained employees are highly sought by Twin Cities employers. St. Paul College provides more than 50 occupational fields, which include formal trades such as cabinetmaking, carpentry, and auto body repair, as well as numerous medical and computer service occupations, e.g., medical laboratory technician and computer programmer. Deaf education is another prominent field of study. St. Paul College offers an affordable education in numerous fields and places graduates in frequently high-paying and rewarding trades.

University of St. Thomas
2115 Summit Avenue, St. Paul
(651) 962-5000
www.stthomas.edu

In 1885 Archbishop John Ireland founded St. Thomas Aquinas Seminary. This higher education institution quickly grew beyond the bounds of its original purpose, as a high school, college, and seminary, with only two departments, Theology and Classics. However, the Twin Cities largest Catholic university was prepared to gradually expand into numerous other areas of study.

The first four-year baccalaureate degrees were conferred by then St. Thomas College in 1910. The college increased its liberal arts emphasis and broadened its demographic in 1977 when it became coeducational and accepted women for the first time. Today the school is composed of 54 percent undergraduate women, with more than 75 major fields available.

St. Thomas has evolved into a private Catholic university with a liberal arts emphasis. Traditional majors such as theology, Latin, and classical languages have been retained, as well as more popular majors such as history, English, or geography, plus recent majors like justice and peace studies. The annual enrollment at St. Thomas is approximately 11,000 students. St. Thomas began offering graduate education and social work programs in 1996, plus its business and psychology graduate programs, as well as a law school.

Continuing education is another paramount focus at St. Thomas. Since New College opened in 1975, the needs of part-time, adult, and nontraditional students have been readily met with innovative methods, such as off-campus classes to make convening easier. The program changed its name to the School of Continuing Studies in 1998 to reflect its commitment to students following a non-traditional educational path.

St. Thomas boasts several campuses. The main campus is 78 acres approximately halfway between downtown Minneapolis and St. Paul, on the western edge of historic Summit Avenue, where St. Paul's old money resides. In addition, since 1992 the Graduate Department of Psychology, the School of Education, and the Graduate School of Business have called downtown Minneapolis home, in a beautiful state-of-the-art facility. St. Thomas also owns smaller campuses in out-state Owatonna and the Mall of America.

Student activities abound at St. Thomas. Both men and women have a large slate of intercollegiate sports, such as basketball, swimming, cross-country running, and men's and women's hockey. St. Thomas publishes a newspaper to serve the university community, the *Aquin*. The seminary also publishes *Catholic Digest,* a world-renowned Catholic magazine.

William Mitchell College of Law
875 Summit Avenue, St. Paul
(651) 227-9171 or (888) WMCL-LAW
www.wmitchell.edu

In 2000 William Mitchell College of Law celebrated its centennial as a legal educator. During this time the institution has had many different names, but the goal has remained the same: providing a quality legal education for recent college graduates or, more frequently, students returning to school after a long absence. William Mitchell began as a night school, and it was prescient in creating a flexible schedule where nontraditional students could succeed.

William Mitchell is the only Twin Cities higher education institution solely dedicated to legal education. It began as the St. Paul College of Law in 1900, then in 1956 merged with the Minneapolis-Minnesota College of Law to form the William Mitchell College of Law (named after a 19th-century Minnesota Supreme Court Justice).

Alumni of William Mitchell are an important group in Twin Cities government and law. The school's most famous graduate was Supreme Court Chief Justice Warren E. Burger of St. Paul, who attended one of the four predecessor law schools of William Mitchell. The Warren E. Burger Library was built in 1990 in his honor and is one of the finest law-school libraries in the nation.

William Mitchell College of Law is one of three law schools in the Twin Cities.

TODD R. BERGER

North

Anoka-Ramsey Community College
11200 Mississippi Boulevard NW,
Coon Rapids
(763) 433-1240

Cambridge Campus
300 Polk Street South, Cambridge
(763) 433-1840
www.an.cc.mn.us

Anoka-Ramsey Community College (ARCC) has served the north metropolitan Twin Cities since 1965. As the suburbs of Minneapolis and St. Paul have expanded, Anoka-Ramsey has grown to meet the area's needs. The college is part of the Minnesota State Colleges and Universities (MnSCU), which was established to guarantee a quality education.

After opening the first campus in Coon Rapids, presently one of the Twin Cities' fastest growing suburbs, the college added the Cambridge Campus in 1978 and shrewdly anticipated an area that would undergo significant urbanization. The community college provides a postsecondary education for students of all ages.

Anoka-Ramsey's student demographics mirror many other area community colleges. Developed by the state colleges as a feeder system for four-year degrees, 54 percent of the student body intends to transfer to a four-year program, the average student is approximately 22 years old, and more than 90 percent work while attending ARCC. The student body is predominantly female, composed of 65 percent women and 35 percent men.

Numerous programs can be started, and in some cases completed, at Anoka–Ramsey. They range from accounting, art, astronomy, music, and law enforcement, to Spanish, sociology, mathematics, and zoology. The community college offers associate in arts (A.A.) and associate in science (A.S.) degrees.

EDUCATION

Bethel College and Seminary
3900 Bethel Drive, Arden Hills
(651) 638-6400
www.bethel.edu
Bethel College offers a four-year liberal arts education with an evangelical Christian perspective. Approximately 5,000 students attend the college, nestled on 214 wooded acres on the shore of Lake Valentine.

The Baptist General Conference created Bethel Seminary in 1871. Preceding Bethel College was a secondary academy and a junior college, before the liberal arts college was formed in 1948. In recent years, Bethel has undergone significant expansion and even added master's programs in nursing, education, communication, counseling psychology, and organizational leadership.

North Hennepin Community College
7411 85th Avenue North, Brooklyn Park
(763) 488-0391 or (800) 818-0395
www.nh.cc.mn.us
North Hennepin Community College (NHCC) serves the northern Twin Cities. The 80-acre campus has an annual enrollment of 9,000 students, with 4,000 full-time students. NHCC has many liberal arts programs, which earn credit toward bachelor degrees. Associate in arts (A.A.) and associate in science (A.S.) are transferable to all Minnesota State Colleges and Universities (MnSCU) schools as well as the University of Minnesota. Also offered at NHCC are career-oriented programs, such as nursing and accounting, and professional development and enhancement classes. Continuing education is another important part of NHCC's mission; it is reflected in the 5,000 part-time students enrolled at the community college. Numerous classes are offered to enrich people's lives in the community.

NHCC has a vast array of clubs for student participation. Among the options available for student involvement is the student newspaper, as well as career-oriented clubs such as the Student Nurse Association and Business Leaders of America.

United Theological Seminary
3000 Fifth Street NW, New Brighton
(651) 633-4311
www.unitedseminary-mn.org
United Theological Seminary (UTS) is the Twin Cities' ecumenical theological school. More than 20 denominations are represented at UTS, where the mission is "To prepare women and men for effective ordained and lay leadership in church and society." Building bridges and creating worldwide Christian unity is the focus at UTS, where tolerance, empathy, and diversity are central to the seminary's educational program.

UTS's history is fairly brief in the Twin Cities, but its antecedents are rooted in the Evangelical and Reformed Church Seminary of Plymouth, Wisconsin (founded in 1862), and the Yankton School of Theology, which began serving the German Congregational churches in South Dakota in 1869. Not until 1960 did the seminaries merge and form UTS.

A progressive theological education is provided at UTS. Instruction reflects recent developments in curriculum, and the educational experience at UTS emphasizes field learning as well as classroom study. Interdisciplinary perspectives are included within the curriculum of all fields at the seminary. Also of paramount importance to UTS is supporting students of diverse racial, ethnic, sexual orientation, and denominational traditions.

UTS offers programs in ordained ministry, lay ministry, academic vocations, professional, and individual enrichment. Degrees include conferred master's degrees in divinity, arts in religion and theology, religious leadership, and women's studies. Doctor in ministry is also offered. There are specialized programs, which are available at few other seminaries, including Indian ministries, rural ministries, and religion and arts.

East

Century College
3300 Century Avenue North,
White Bear Lake
(651) 779-3300 or (800) 228-1978
www.century.mnscu.edu
Century College is dedicated to creating educational opportunity for its community in the east metropolitan Twin Cities. Students of all ages may attend the college based on their needs, whether to build a foundation for a four-year degree or solely for the joy of learning as a continuing-education student. There are classes to satisfy almost everyone's interest.

Century College was created when Lakewood Community College and Northeast Technical College merged in 1996. Both institutions had long histories serving the area. Since 1967 Lakewood provided an inexpensive education for many students who otherwise wouldn't have been able to afford it. Northeast Technical College performed a similar function since its inception in 1968.

More than 60 technical and occupational programs are offered at Century College, as well as more than 100 degrees, certificates, and diplomas. Students with limited financial means may begin a four-year degree program in numerous subject areas, such as English, geography, and Biology by earning associate of arts (A.A.) and associate of science (A.S.) degrees. When students complete their A.A. or A.S. and transfer to the University of Minnesota system or the Minnesota State Colleges and Universities (MnSCU), all credits are accepted toward a B.A. or B.S.

Another important function of Century College is continuing education. Century College serves more continuing-education students than any other college in Minnesota, making up 55 percent of the student body.

Minnesota School of Business
and Globe College
7166 10th Street North, Oakdale
(651) 730-5100

5910 Shingle Creek Parkway,
Brooklyn Center
(763) 566-7777

1401 West 76th Street, Richfield
(612) 861-2000

1455 County Road 101 North, Plymouth
(763) 476-2000
www.globecollege.com
Minnesota School of Business has four Twin Cities campuses. There are also campuses in northern Minnesota in St. Cloud and in southern Minnesota in Shakopee and Rochester. At all locations Globe College offers a quick track to many careers in business as well as technical fields. Also included are accounting, dental assistant, paralegal, medical assistant, software developer, and e-commerce design. There are many other career paths available at Globe College. Besides regular classroom instruction, Globe College offers distance education, which allows students to take classes online.

South

Argosy University
1515 Central Parkway, Eagan
(651) 846-2882
www.argosyu.edu
Medicine is an important part of the Twin Cities economy, and Argosy University has the most comprehensive allied health care associate programs in the area. Students can pick from numerous health care programs. Here are a few of the associate degree programs available: histotechnology, radiologic technology, dental hygiene, medical laboratory technician, veterinary technology, and radiation therapy.

Brown College
1440 Northland Drive, Mendota Heights
(651) 905-3400
www.browncollege.edu
Brown College is an important local technical and trade school. The school boasts many graduates from its programs in local television and radio positions. Brown pro-

vides an education that employs its students in their fields of study. Since it opened in 1954, the range of programs at Brown has rapidly expanded. The school has a second campus in Brooklyn Center.

Today Brown College has 16 programs in fields as varied as culinary arts and criminal justice. The culinary arts program was added in 1998 and is a member of Le Cordon Bleu French cooking school. Le Cordon Bleu began in Paris in 1895; since then, exclusive, limited culinary arts programs have been licensed by the institution. Another important program is the Department of Visual Communications, where students first develop traditional computer skills, which build from basics to advanced skills, such as computer animation and multimedia production. Also of note at Brown is the radio and television broadcasting program, where many local media technicians and producers have received their education. In addition, Brown has digital electronics and computer technology, telecommunications, PC/LAN, and e-commerce programs.

Inver Hills Community College
2500 East 80th Street, Inver Grove Heights
(651) 450–8500
www.inverhills.edu
Inver Hills Community College fulfills the needs of students working toward a four-year degree, to improve job skills, or simply to explore subjects of personal interest. The community college serves the south and east suburbs of St. Paul.

It offers numerous programs for degrees and certification. The associate in arts, or A.A. degree, is a popular stepping-stone toward four-year degrees in more than 50 academic areas, which include sociology, economics and nursing, as well as more uncommon major fields, such as fish, game, and wildlife, and public health education. Another important two-year degree is the associate in science, or A.S., which is more career oriented (e.g., accounting, criminal justice, aviation, and construction management). The associate

in applied science is a two-year degree aimed at immediate employment upon completion, and includes medical secretary, building inspection, and management/marketing. Finally, Inver Hills offers several vocational certificates. The certificates qualify students for various vocations, or can be used to improve jobs already held. Many high demand technical degrees are available, especially computer-oriented programs, including desktop publishing, medical-office systems, computer applications and many more.

Normandale Community College
9700 France Avenue South, Bloomington
(952) 487–8200
www.normandale.edu
Normandale Community College serves the needs of the southern Twin Cities by offering associate degrees, certification programs, and classes for personal enrichment. The community college is easily accessible from Interstate 494 and is located on a 90-acre site, complete with the beautiful Normandale Japanese Garden. Founded in 1968, the school has an enrollment of 8,000 students. Normandale offers programs in occupational fields, including law enforcement, radiologic technology, hospitality management, dental hygiene, and computers/information management. Other popular programs include two-year liberal arts degrees.

Northwestern Health Sciences University
2501 West 84th Street, Bloomington
(952) 888–4777
www.nwhealth.edu
Northwestern Health Sciences University offers classes in a frequently overlooked portion of medicine: natural approaches to health and health care. There are programs in acupuncture and herbal studies, professional massage, integrative health and wellness, and the College of Chiropractic. The university's origins are as a chiropractic school, but it has grown to include the aforementioned programs as well as graduate programs.

The university recently received

accreditation for master's programs in Oriental medicine and professional acupuncture. The Oriental medicine program requires more than 3,000 hours of instruction over four years, with 200 hours of observation and greater than 600 hours of clinical practice. Not nearly as rigorous are undergraduate programs, which are approximately two years in duration. Programs are also offered for nontraditional and/or adult learners. All students must complete foundation, core, and clinical courses before completing their program. Another important activity before graduation is a "summary paper" about their field of study, written with the help of a faculty member. The summary paper develops students' analytical skills and requires reflection in their chosen field of study. As medical technology increases, Northwestern Health Sciences University's programs have experienced growing importance as ancillary adjuncts for medicine.

West

Rasmussen College
12450 Wayzata Boulevard, Minnetonka
(952) 545-2000 or (800) 852-0929

3500 Federal Drive, Eagan
(651) 687-9000 or (800) 852-6367

8301 93rd Avenue North, Brooklyn Park
(763) 493-4500 or (877) 495-4500
www.rasmussen.edu
Rasmussen College has been a two-year college for business and professional careers since 1900. During the past century, the college has expanded its programs. Presently, there are nine majors. Students may chose from information technology, accounting, child care specialist, medical records, restaurant management, and other fields of study. The programs are flexible and allow students to expeditiously embark on new careers.

Students can determine the pace at which they want to complete their program—in as little as nine months or over the standard period of two years. Institutions like Rasmussen are essential to the Twin Cities economy, quickly creating qualified employees for high-demand careers. The college has three convenient Twin Cities locations, Minnetonka in the western suburbs, Brooklyn Park in the northwestern suburbs, and Eagan, in the southern suburbs. In addition, Rasmussen College has campuses both north and south of the Twin Cities metropolitan area.

HEALTH CARE
AND WELLNESS

Minnesota has been a medical industry hub and site of health care innovation for decades, even before the founding of the world-famous Mayo Clinic and Medtronic. Ironically, a good deal of this reputation came from rumors started by PR agents in territorial times, who were horrified to find that the rest of the country likened Minnesota to an American Siberia. With the hordes of health-challenged immigrants who moved to the state in the 1850s to 1870s to follow these claims of rejuvenation came doctors and scientists who were just as willing to test the healing powers of Minnesota's climate, including Dr. William W. Mayo, whose sons founded the Mayo Clinic in Rochester, and Dr. Brewer Mattocks, who wrote the highly partisan book *Minnesota as a Home for Invalids.*

Even today Minnesota, especially the Twin Cities region, is a major force in the medical community, and the medical industry is strong in the Twin Cities as well.

Minnesota's health care system has been at the top of the field for many, many years. The strong emphasis on research that the Mayo Clinic started at the turn of the 20th century has been carried out all over the state, ensuring that hospitals in the Twin Cities and throughout Minnesota will continue to keep far ahead of the times.

HOSPITALS AND HOSPITAL COOPERATIVES

Abbott Northwestern Hospital
800 East 28th Street, Minneapolis
(612) 863-4000
www.abbottnorthwestern.com

Abbott Northwestern Hospital has grown to become the Twin Cities' largest health care provider, with a tradition of compassionate care, outstanding service, and leadership in education and clinical research. The huge facility treats a wide range of health-related issues, from family practice to cosmetic medicine and surgery, cancer treatment, neuroscience, and behavioral studies.

Children's Hospitals and Clinics Children's-Minneapolis, 2525 Chicago Avenue South, Minneapolis
(612) 813-6100

Children's-St. Paul, 345 North Smith Avenue, St. Paul
(651) 220-6000

Children's-West, 6050 Clearwater Drive, Minnetonka
(952) 930-8600

Children's-Ridges, Fairview Ridges Hospital, 201 East Nicollet Boulevard, Burnsville
(952) 892-2202

Children's-Roseville, Twin Lakes Health, 1835 West County Road C, Roseville
(651) 638-1670

Children's Clinics-Woodwinds, 1875 Woodwinds Drive, Woodbury
(651) 232-6800

Children's-St. Francis, St. Francis Regional Medical Center, 1455 St. Francis Avenue, Shakopee
(952) 403-3360
www.childrenshc.org

Children's Hospitals and Clinics was created by the merger of the children's hospitals in St. Paul and Minneapolis. With

268 staffed hospital beds at their main Minneapolis and St. Paul campuses, they are the largest children's health care organization in the upper Midwest, with services available in all major pediatric specialties.

Comfort is an important facet of each Children's Hospitals facility. Each child's room has a VCR, television, and radio. Videos are available for checkout, and a computer on a rolling cart, stocked with CD-ROM games, can also be brought into the child's room. Many rooms feature built-in beds for a parent to sleep in. A wheelchair-accessible garden of sculptures, flowers, and wild plants soothes visitors and provides a place to eat, relax, and play. Several floors of the hospital have decks with lawn furniture and grills. Playrooms full of toys, colorful play structures, art supplies, and games are on each floor of the hospitals. Playrooms are the center of activities, including cooking, movie days, visits from zoo animals, and bingo. Special efforts are made to accommodate children who need to stay in their rooms.

Children who are away from school 15 consecutive school days or longer can continue their studies with a teacher from the St. Paul public school system. Sessions are limited to one 50-minute session per day. You will be asked to sign an authorization form to permit your child to participate in the school program. The child life specialist will communicate your child's needs to the hospital-based schoolteacher.

Fairview Health Services
University of Minnesota Medical Center, Fairview, Riverside Campus,
2540 Riverside Avenue, Minneapolis

University of Minnesota
Children's Hospital, Fairview, University Campus, 520 Delaware Street SE, Minneapolis
(612) 273-3000

Fairview Southdale Hospital
6402 France Avenue South, Edina
(952) 924-5000

Fairview Ridges Hospital
201 Nicollet Boulevard, Burnsville
(952) 892-2000
www.fairview.org
University of Minnesota Medical Center, Fairview, is among the most respected teaching institutions in the nation. It ranks among the best hospitals in the country, according to the *U.S. News and World Report*. The medical center balances responsiveness to patients' needs and wishes with access to innovative treatments and technology to deliver superior health outcomes. Located on two campuses on the east and west banks of the Mississippi River in Minneapolis, the medical center provides comprehensive services from primary care, emergency care, and the delivery of thousands of babies each year to care of patients with the most complex conditions, including organ and blood and marrow transplantation, heart disease, cancer, neurosciences, and behavioral illnesses.

University of Minnesota Children's Hospital, Fairview, is a renowned pediatric teaching and research hospital that provides superior health care for children from around the world. The hospital is located on the east and west banks of the Mississippi River in Minneapolis and is the primary teaching hospital for the University of Minnesota Medical School. University of Minnesota Children's Hospital provides a broad range of pediatric programs, and services—including pediatric mental health, general surgery, imaging, neonatal, and pediatric intensive care; plus cardiac, cancer, and cystic fibrosis services; as well as blood and marrow and organ transplantation.

Fairview Southdale Hospital's 290-bed facility offers health services and

MinnesotaCare (651-297-3862; www .dhs.state.mn.us) provides health care insurance to residents who have trouble affording it. Premiums are based on family income and size.

advanced medical technology. Rated in 2005 as a top 100 hospital for cardiovascular services by Solucient, a national health care benchmarking company, the hospital specializes in cardiac care, stroke and vascular care, oncology, mental health treatment, eye care, and maternal and newborn care, plus spine, neurology, neurosurgery, urology, orthopedic surgery and joint replacement. It offers a 24-hour emergency department along with urgent care for evenings and weekends. A full-service hospital providing the latest in same-day surgery and rehabilitation services, Fairview Southdale believes that offering the finest health care includes addressing the physical, emotional, and spiritual needs of patients and their families.

Fairview Ridges Hospital, opened in 1984, is located on the Ridges Campus in Burnsville. This medical facility holds 150 beds and has a staff of more than 1,000 employees, 700 physicians, and 600 volunteers. Fairview Ridges specializes in obstetrics, pediatrics, emergency medicine, and both inpatient and outpatient surgical services. The hospital offers counseling, chemotherapy services, intensive care, orthopedics, imaging, and rehabilitation. Staff provide expert personal attention, from diagnosis through treatment, because of its direct connection to the entire network of Fairview Health Services. Fairview Ridges Hospital also has ongoing programs and community partnerships to help individuals and families stay well.

Hennepin County Medical Center
701 Park Avenue, Minneapolis
(612) 873-3000
www.hcmc.org
Hennepin County Medical Center (HCMC) is a public teaching hospital in downtown Minneapolis owned and operated by Hennepin County, governed by the seven-member Hennepin County Board of Commissioners, and affiliated with the University of Minnesota Medical School. HCMC is the centerpiece of Hennepin

County's health services system. HCMC provides specialized and general medical care, often through hospital referrals.

The Minneapolis Medical Research Foundation is the third-largest nonprofit medical research organization in Minnesota. The MMRF was founded by a group of concerned physicians and citizens 45 years ago at Minneapolis General Hospital (now HCMC). The MMRF has a long history of innovative research resulting in clinical breakthroughs, such as the world's first dual lung transplant, the Midwest's first kidney transplant, and Minnesota's first blood dialysis. It continues to serve the citizens of Hennepin County through its programs: alternative medicine, brain and immune disorders, cancer center, children's hunger and growth, diabetes and obesity, heart disease, HIV/AIDS, kidney research, Berman Center for Clinical Outcomes, sleep disorders, smoking prevention, trauma/shock/sepsis, traumatic brain injury, and women's health.

Because HCMC serves many patients from the Native American community, an Indian Health Advocate is available to ensure that the special needs or cultural preferences of Native American patients are treated with sensitivity and respect, and that both American Indian health practices and Western medicine can be brought to the care of the patient.

Mayo Clinic Rochester
200 First Street SW, Rochester
(507) 284-2511
www.mayoclinic.org/rochester
The world-famous Mayo Clinic has been a pioneer in medical research and disease treatment for more than a century. While it is located almost 90 miles south of the Twin Cities, the very existence of the hospital is one of the reasons there is such a strong medical community in Minnesota. Mayo Clinic Rochester, the original Mayo Clinic, began its research program in 1901, when Dr. Henry Plummer joined the Mayo Clinic as the fourth partner and urged the two Drs. Mayo to

invest as much time in research as they did in treatment. This course of action led to some incredibly revolutionary discoveries that changed the face of medicine, including developing a method for staining fresh-frozen tissue from surgical specimens so that they could be studied under a microscope for diagnostic purposes; the isolation of thyroxin, a system for grading cancer (created in 1920) that is still used all over the world today; and the creation of the Sheard-Sanford photelometer photoelectric eye, the BLB mask for high-altitude pilots, the leprosy and tuberculosis suppressant Promin, the first human centrifuge, cortisone, and the Gibbon pump. The Mayo Clinic Rochester was also the site for some of the earliest successful heart transplants and open-heart surgeries.

Today more than 2,000 physicians and 35,000 allied health staff work in the Mayo system, treating nearly half a million patients annually. Their specialties include (but are far from being limited to) cancer treatment, dermatology, diagnostic radiology, Native American studies and medicine, internal medicine, cardiovascular disease treatment, allergy studies and treatment, plastic surgery, HIV study, and general practice/family medicine.

Mercy Hospital
4050 Coon Rapids Boulevard,
Coon Rapids
(763) 236-6000

Unity Hospital
550 Osborne Road, Fridley
(763) 236-5000
www.mercy-unity.com
Mercy and Unity Hospitals are nonprofit hospitals that have been serving the northern Minneapolis–St. Paul metropolitan area for more than 40 years. Together, Mercy and Unity are dedicated to providing cost-effective, quality health care to the more than 250,000 households in the neighboring 26 communities and nearby out-of-state towns. Mercy and Unity Hospitals are affiliated with Allina Health Sys-

Guided tours of the historic Plummer Building at the Mayo Clinic can be arranged through the hospital, or self-guided tours may be taken on your own during public hours.

tem, the largest integrated health care system in Minnesota.

Mercy Hospital is located in Coon Rapids, and Unity Hospital is located in Fridley. The hospitals function as virtually one entity, with shared resources to help ensure quality, cost-effective care. Mercy and Unity respond to a wide range of health care needs with specialty services including behavioral health, cardiac, emergency, family centered care, oncology, and bariatrics. The hospitals offer medical transportation, health education, and support groups. In addition, Mercy Hospital provides specialized services for senior citizens, such as Meals on Wheels, Hot Meals for Shut-ins, and the Senior Identification Program.

North Memorial Medical Center
3300 Oakdale Avenue North,
Robbinsdale
(763) 520-5200
www.northmemorial.com
Located in the northwestern Twin Cities suburb of Robbinsdale, the independently owned North Memorial is a familiar face in an always-changing health care community. North Memorial's history of responding to the health care needs of its communities has lasted for more than four decades and continues to be the main ingredient to its success.

North Memorial's early leadership in emergency care was one of the factors that led to its being the successful emergency and trauma services center it is today. The first totally integrated hospital-based medical transportation system in the state of Minnesota began at North Memorial, which now includes two helicopters, 100 ambulances, and 575

St. Joseph's Hospital in downtown St. Paul is the oldest hospital in Minnesota. TODD R. BERGER

employees. North Memorial also founded the I Can Cope cancer education program that is now used in hospitals throughout the country and by the American Cancer Society.

St. Francis Regional Medical Center
1455 St. Francis Avenue, Shakopee
(952) 403-3000
www.stfrancis-shakopee.com
Named a top-100 hospital in the nation, St. Francis Regional Medical Center completes its expansion project in late 2006. Doubling in size, St. Francis continues to attract new physicians—specialists including orthopedists, spine surgeons, cardiologists, and oncologists—and offers the best technology to advance the care. Hospital services include the St. Francis Cancer Center, emergency department, St. Francis Sleep Diagnostics Center, St. Francis Family Birth Place, St. Francis Breast Center, St. Francis Children's Pediatric Unit, St. Francis Rehabilitation and Sports Medicine, St. Francis Health Services, and sev-

eral primary and specialty clinics. St. Francis is jointly owned and sponsored by the Benedictine Health System, Allina Hospitals & Clinics, and Park Nicollet Health Services.

St. Joseph's Hospital
69 West Exchange Street, St. Paul
(651) 232-3000
www.stjosephs-stpaul.org
The first hospital in Minnesota, St. Joseph's was founded by the Sisters of St. Joseph of Carondelet in 1853. Today the downtown St. Paul Catholic hospital serves patients in the eastern Metro, with specialties in heart care, cancer care, mental health and chemical dependency treatment, and maternity care. St. Joseph's operates a 24-hour emergency room and comprehensive services for inpatient care. The hospital has been a member of the HealthEast Care System since 1987, which operates several hospitals, clinics, and rehabilitation centers throughout the eastern Metro. The respect and compassion

routinely shown by staff members at the hospital reflects the vision of the founders of this historic hospital.

United Hospital
333 North Smith Avenue, St. Paul
(651) 241-8000
www.unitedhospital.com
United Hospital is a premier acute care medical facility in St. Paul. A part of the Allina Health System, United has 572 beds, offers staffing privileges to more than 1,000 physicians, and employs more than 3,000 professionals. The hospital facilities include a birth center, a pain center, the John Nasseff Heart Hospital, and a center for breast care; the hospital specializes in behavioral health studies and treatment, emergency care, heart/lung medicine, oncology, rehabilitation services, and surgery.

United Hospital is St. Paul's largest private not-for-profit hospital.

REHABILITATION CENTERS

Hazelden Foundation
and Renewal Center
15245 Pleasant Valley Road, Center City
(651) 213-4000 or (800) 257-7800
www.hazelden.org
Hazelden has a history spanning more than 50 years of pioneering leadership in the care of chemically dependent people and their families. It is internationally recognized for its broad spectrum of interrelated services and continuum of care, which includes assessment and rehabilitation for adolescents and adults, aftercare and family services, renewal services, extended care and continuing care, professional development, counselor training, and clergy training and counseling. A nonprofit organization dedicated to helping people recover from alcoholism and other drug addiction by providing residential and outpatient treatment for adults and young people, Hazelden offers programs for families affected by chemical dependency as well as training for a variety of professionals. Hazelden is also known as

the world's premier publisher of information on chemical addiction and related areas.

New Beginnings
190 North Shore Drive, Waverly
(763) 658-5800 or (800) 487-8758
www.newbeginningsatwaverly.com
New Beginnings is nationally recognized for its treatment of alcohol, cocaine, methamphetamine, and other drug dependencies, providing intensive and individualized treatment programs for adults and adolescents. New Beginnings offers a unique treatment environment. Located on several acres of private wooded lakeshore property in the converted summer home of former vice president Hubert H. Humphrey, away from the noise and tension of urban life, the program components are designed to help men and women overcome the physical, emotional, spiritual, behavioral, and social aspects of addiction. New Beginnings programs were founded on the belief that people who are suffering from addiction deserve treatment that is specifically designed for them.

New Beginnings at Waverly offers intensive individualized treatment programs that include residential and outpatient levels of care. All dimensions of addiction are addressed under the principle that successful treatment demands the efforts of an interdisciplinary team that includes the patient, family, clinicians, and other professionals.

HMOS

HealthPartners
8100 34th Avenue South, Bloomington
(952) 883-6000
www.healthpartners.com
HealthPartners is a nonprofit, consumer-governed family of health care organizations focused on improving the health of its members, its patients, and the community. HealthPartners provides health care coverage to nearly 630,000 members

Earl E. Bakken invented the first wearable cardiac pacemaker in Minneapolis. The company he cofounded, Medtronic, continues to be a world leader in medical technology, based in Minneapolis.

through a broad range of medical, dental, individual, and Medicare plan products and through direct patient care to more than 350,000 patients at more than 50 HealthPartners Clinic sites across the Twin Cities and at Regions Hospital in St. Paul. HealthPartners has a contracted network of nearly 15,000 community providers and a national network of more than 400,000 providers.

More than 9,600 employees staff the various HealthPartners organizations. The HealthPartners family includes the HealthPartners Medical Group, Health-Partners Central Minnesota Clinics, HealthPartners Dental Group and Clinics, Regions Hospital, Regions Hospital Foundation, Health-Partners Research Foundation, Health-Partners Institute for Medical Education, and Group Health, Inc.

HealthPartners and its related organizations offer products, both fully insured and self-insured, to meet the needs of large employers, small employers, individuals, and seniors.

The HealthPartners Medical Group is one of Minnesota's largest medical groups with more than 580 physicians practicing in primary care and 35 medical and surgical specialties. HealthPartners Dental Group includes 58 dentists with expertise in preventive dentistry, oral surgery, periodontics, endodontics, prosthodontics, and pediatric dentistry.

SPECIAL CLINICS

Phillips Eye Institute
2215 Park Avenue, Minneapolis
(612) 336-6000
Phillips Eye Institute is a premier specialty center devoted exclusively to the diagnosis, treatment, and care of eye disorders and diseases. Located in Minneapolis, the institute integrates the latest technologies in eye care with unprecedented staff expertise. Phillips Eye was originally designed to function as a freestanding eye specialty center associated with Mount Sinai Medical Center and was named for Mount Sinai's largest benefactor, Jay Phillips.

Nearly 8,000 patients a year visit the institute for refractive surgery (LASIK), vision rehabilitation, and other inpatient services. The institute also has an established pediatric ophthalmology department for its younger patients.

HEALTH ASSOCIATIONS

Alzheimer's Association
(952) 830-0512 or (800) 232-0851

American Cancer Society
Minneapolis (952) 925-2772
St. Paul (651) 644-1224

American Diabetes Association
(763) 593-5333

American Heart Association
(952) 835-3300 or (800) 331-6889

American Lung Association
of Minnesota
(651) 227-8014

American Parkinson's Disease
Association
(800) 223-2732

American Red Cross
(651) 435-7669

Arthritis Foundation of St. Paul
(651) 644-4108

United Way
(612) 340-7400

COUNSELING

Catholic Charities, Archdiocese of St. Paul and Minneapolis
(612) 664-8500

Jewish Family and Children's Service
(952) 546-0616

Lutheran Social Services of Minneapolis
(651) 642-5990 or (800) 582-5260

MEDIA 📺

Much of what a newspaper says about a city goes beyond the printed word. Insight is gleaned by analyzing what's front-page newsworthy, how much (or little) heft the arts section has, and what the classifieds reveal about the cost of homes. In the Twin Cities we have two dailies to analyze as well as plenty of free publications dispensed in business entryways across the Metro. Add two slick city magazines, sold by subscriptions and on newsstands, and the local print media is surprisingly vast and diverse. The radio stations, too, run the gamut, but again, the Twin Cities lean toward the local—Clear Channel has a firm presence, but we've always found our many home-grown personalities more interesting than the for-the-faceless-masses national shows, and we love, love, love our local public radio stations. For TV we have all the standards, plus a professional independent station that puts out some of its own programming. Analyze away.

DAILY NEWSPAPERS

St. Paul Pioneer Press
345 Cedar Street, St. Paul
(651) 222-1111 or (800) 950-9080
www.twincities.com

The *St. Paul Pioneer Press* is Minnesota's oldest newspaper, founded as the *Minnesota Pioneer* in 1849.

Today the paper is known as being on the cutting edge of news journalism. Winning three Pulitzer Prizes, including one for breaking the Gophers basketball scandal, the paper was named one of the nation's top-10 daily and Sunday sports sections in 2003. The newspaper retains bureaus in Washington, D.C., and at the State Capitol in St. Paul. It also has a Metro West bureau in Minneapolis. While it has a smaller readership and distribution than Minneapolis's *StarTribune*, it has arguably just as good coverage of the area and is only 25 cents on weekdays and $1.00 on Sunday as opposed to the

The St. Paul Pioneer Press *is one of two major dailies in the Twin Cities.* TODD R. BERGER

StarTribune's 50 cent daily price tag and $1.75 on Sunday.

StarTribune
425 Portland Avenue, Minneapolis
(612) 673-4000
www.startribune.com
Since 1867 the *StarTribune* has been a part of the Twin Cities community with an outstanding newspaper that's read by 1.5 million people each week and an online network of services that has become the region's preferred source for online information.

Bigger than the *Pioneer Press,* especially in the employment/job search and business sections, the *StarTribune* is considered the leading area paper in sports coverage as well. Their main sportswriter, Sid Hartman, is considered the ultimate "homer"—that is, a Twin Cities–biased booster sportswriter—and has been with the paper for so long that staffers joke he was there when the first issue hit the streets.

MAGAZINES

Minnesota Monthly
600 U.S. Trust Building, 730 Second Avenue South, Minneapolis
(612) 371-5800 or (800) 933-4398
www.minnesotamonthly.com
Full of interviews with local political figures and celebrities, restaurant reviews, and features ranging from controversial reports on small-town sexual harassment suits to staying healthy longer, *Minnesota Monthly* is a vibrant publication that showcases all the facets of Minnesota and its people. A monthly publication, it can be bought at most magazine racks and bookstores in the Twin Cities. *Midwest Home* is also published by Minnesota Monthly Publications. It's full of recipes, garden secrets, and interior designing tips.

Pick up a copy of City Pages *or* Pulse . . . of the Twin Cities *to get an idea of what's happening in town. Both weeklies have a good calendar of entertainment events in the Cities.*

Mpls/St. Paul Magazine
MSP Communications
220 South Sixth Street, Suite 500, Minneapolis
(612) 339-7571
www.mplsstpaul.com
For 30 years, *Mpls/St. Paul Magazine* has been providing readers with up-to-date information on Twin Cities events and dining, as well as features on local celebrities and important members of the community. The magazine runs travel articles, lodging information outside the metro area, and universally pertinent features concerning health, beauty, child-rearing tips, and everything in between.

Utne Magazine
1624 Harmon Place, Minneapolis
(612) 338-5040
www.utne.com
Utne is a nationally distributed monthly magazine that reprints articles from thousands of alternative media sources, providing interesting perspectives on current events, environmental issues, lifestyles, politics, books, and the arts. The magazine hosts a popular online discussion room, Cafe Utne (accessible through the magazine's Web site), with postings about many of the topics the magazine covers.

OTHER PUBLICATIONS
Business

Twin Cities Business Monthly
MSP Communications
220 South Sixth Street, Suite 500, Minneapolis
(612) 339-7571
www.tcbm.com

> *The satirical weekly* **The Onion** *(612-370-1372; www.theonion.com) now has a Twin Cities edition.*

Twin Cities Business Monthly, published by the same company that publishes *Mpls/St. Paul Magazine,* includes profiles of successful businesspeople and companies in the metropolitan area and information about business education, technology, and other topics of interest to business-oriented readers.

Ethnic Community

Asian American Press
417 University Avenue, St. Paul
(651) 224-6570
www.aapress.com
Not only does *Asian American Press* cover news of interest to Asian Americans in the Twin Cities region but it also provides excellent coverage of international news geared to the Asian population, from local business profiles to politics to festival information (local and other) to the struggles new immigrants have adjusting to life in a new country.

The Circle Newspaper
3355 36th Avenue South, Minneapolis
(612) 722-3686
www.thecirclenews.org
Approximately 25,000 Native Americans from various tribes live in the Twin Cities, and *The Circle* monthly newspaper is dedicated to publishing news, arts information, community calendars, and resource information for Native Americans in the region.

Gente de Minnesota
Latino Communications Network
2019 East Lake Street, Suite 7,
Minneapolis
(612) 729-5900
www.gentedeminnesota.com
Published in Spanish, *Gente de Minnesota*

is a weekly newspaper that serves the Hispanic population of the Twin Cities with local, national, and international news, as well as sports, entertainment, and Spanish-language TV program listings.

Hmong Times
962 University Avenue West, St. Paul
(651) 224-9395 or (888) 229-9577
www.hmongtimes.com
With some 70,000 Hmong residents, the Twin Cities have the largest population of Hmong of any urban area in the world. The community is served by the English-language *Hmong Times,* with news, community information, religion, sports, and agriculture coverage. Published twice a month, the newspaper reaches a wide audience among the community, which began settling in Minnesota after the Vietnam War.

Family Papers

Downtown Journal
1115 Hennepin Avenue South,
Minneapolis
(612) 825-9205
www.skywaynews.net
Another free weekly newspaper distributed throughout the Twin Cities, *Downtown Journal,* formerly *Skyway News,* provides information on local politics and events, interviews with local celebrities, a calendar of art and music events, and a decent map of the skyway system of downtown Minneapolis.

Family Times
P.O. Box 16422, St. Louis Park 55416
(952) 922-6186
www.familytimesinc.com
Family Times truly is geared to the entire family. News about children and senior events alike is listed here, as well as wellness information for everyone in the family. There's an extensive theater section in the back and a decent calendar of events for all members of the family.

Good Age
**1115 Hennepin Avenue South,
Minneapolis
(612) 825-9205
www.mngoodage.com**
This senior-oriented monthly publication contains pages of information on health care issues and developments dealing with medical expenses, support groups, and nursing homes, as well as lots of advice and tips on how to stay at your peak physical and mental shape for as long as possible. There's also information on less age-specific things like filing taxes and shopping for a new house.

Minnesota Parent
**1115 Hennepin Avenue South,
Minneapolis
(612) 825-9205
www.mnparent.com**
Presenting itself both as a support group and a how-to guide to parenting, *Minnesota Parent* contains information on essentials like enrolling your children in school or helping them survive a divorce. The greatest part of this magazine, however, is the exhaustive calendar of events in the back, containing times, prices, and contact info for just about every museum and park in town.

Minnesota Women's Press
**771 Raymond Avenue, St. Paul
(651) 646-3968
www.womenspress.com**
The biweekly print flagship of Minnesota's Feminist Voices, the *Minnesota Women's Press* provides a fair and open-minded view of women in politics and feminist issues that affect women and men alike, as well as profiles and interviews with political personalities and prominent women in the Twin Cities. The publication is well written by members and volunteers of MFV as well as outside contributors, many of them prominent businesswomen and writers from the area.

Senior Times
**P.O. Box 16422, St. Louis Park 55416
(763) 541-9363
www.familytimesinc.com**
The sister publication of *Family Times,* the award-winning *Senior Times* is geared to the senior community. The paper is full of news about living on your own and adjusting to retirement, as well as about senior events and activities around the Twin Cities and surrounding communities.

Food and Entertainment

Buon Gusto
**126 North Third Street, #506,
Minneapolis
(612) 746-4766
www.buon-gusto.com**
This is a fun little food-related publication that's released bimonthly and carried at most gourmet grocery stores and some restaurants. Covering everything from haute cuisine to Minnesota hot dishes and carrying many interviews with local chefs and restaurant owners as well as reviews of local cooking supply stores, this newsletter has information for the weekend cook and professional alike. It also has great recipes, usually about six in every issue.

City Pages
**401 North Third Street, Suite 550,
Minneapolis
(612) 372-3788
www.citypages.com**
Since the 1970s, when it was called *Sweet Potato, City Pages* has been consistently providing great coverage of local politics, music events, and Twin Cities culture in general. The weekly calendar and A-List deliver the best information on what to do with your spare time, whether it be catching a lecture at the university or seeing a show at your neighborhood coffeehouse, while the interviews with notable Min-

nesotan artists and musicians are both entertaining and informative. The restaurant reviews are also worth noting, serving up the good and not-so-good news about area eateries.

Lavender
3715 Chicago Avenue South, Minneapolis
(612) 436-4660
www.lavendermagazine.com
The best known of the local gay and lesbian publications, *Lavender* contains interviews, features, events calendars, and book and music reviews of interest to the gay, lesbian, and transgendered population. Published biweekly, it's carried in record stores, coffee shops, and bars throughout the Twin Cities.

Pulse . . . of the Twin Cities
3200 Chicago Avenue South, Minneapolis
(612) 824-0000
www.pulsetc.com
Founded in 1996, *Pulse* provides decent coverage of music, art, and film community activity happening throughout the Twin Cities, as well as covers many controversial political feature stories. Available at most convenience stores and alternative media venues in the area, *Pulse* officially hits the streets every Wednesday, although slow press dates sometimes keep it from being available until later in the week.

Rain Taxi Review of Books
P.O. Box 3840, Minneapolis 55403
www.raintaxi.com
Distributed nationally, this quarterly publication contains tons of book reviews (all genres) as well as interviews with established and up-and-coming authors from around the world.

Twin Cities Blues News
P.O. Box 65671, St. Paul 55165
(612) 642-5170
www.mnblues.com
Full of information about new blues

recordings, blues acts coming to town, and reviews of regional blues festivals, this publication contains some of the more interesting music interviews in town with both old and new bluesmen (and women). Released monthly and carried in record stores and coffee shops throughout the area, this is full of essential blues info to even the most casual of enthusiasts.

Health, Religion, and Support Publications

Edge Life
Leap Productions
14590 Bowers Drive NW, Ramsey
(763) 427-7979
www.edgelife.net
Falling somewhere between a New Age and Christian publication, *Edge Life* contains articles about miracles and biblical prophesies and articles about how they've been fulfilled—reincarnation, faith healing, and archeological excavations that may or may not prove the existence of God. The paper is distributed throughout most of the Midwest during the first week of every month and is carried at most bookstores in the Twin Cities.

Essential Wellness
4270 Honey Tree Pass, Danbury, WI
(888) 667-7866
This monthly paper is an excellent source of information about alternative healing techniques, breakthroughs in homeopathic and alternative medicines, and features written by practitioners of alternative medicine. There's information on where to find alternative and homeopathic doctors and treatment centers in the Twin Cities area, from massage therapy to herbal vendors.

Fate Magazine
P.O. Box 460, Lakeville 55044
(800) 728-2730
www.fatemag.com
Fate is a full-color, 130-page monthly

that's been published continuously since 1948, making it the longest-running publication of its kind. It features accounts of the strange and unknown, from psychics, spiritualists, archaeological hot spots, and fringe science to authoritative UFO and paranormal investigations and readers' personal mystic experiences.

Neighborhood Free Publications

Almost every neighborhood in the Twin Cities has a free paper that can be found in neighborhood convenience stores or appears on your doorstep. These papers cover local news, school district announcements, flea market schedules, city council efforts on the part of the district in question, and sometimes, like in the *Villager,* news that affects the entire city. Here are just a few listings of neighborhood papers and the areas they cover:

> *Northeaster*—northeast Minneapolis
> *Southwest Journal*—southwest Minneapolis
> *Southeast Angle*—southeast Minneapolis
> *The Villager*—St. Paul, Highland Park area
> *The Riverview Times*—Harriet Island St. Paul riverside community
> *Midway/Como Monitor*—St. Paul Como Park area
> *Grand Gazette*—St. Paul Summit Hill/ Grand Avenue area
> *Seward Profile*—Minneapolis, Seward/ Cedar-Riverside/Cooper/North Longfellow neighborhoods

Sports

Minnesota Motorcycle Monthly
7265 Balsam Lane North, Maple Grove
(763) 315-5396
www.motorbyte.com/mmm
This publication contains everything from reviews of new motorcycle gear to motorcycle vacation tips to full-length travel logs contributed by readers and staff writers. Check out the anti–Harley Davidson "Geezer with a Grudge" column for some really scintillating insight into the mind of a longtime motorcycle owner.

Twin Cities Sports
701 Fourth Avenue South, Suite 500, Minneapolis
(612) 337-9007
www.twincitiessports.com
This monthly free magazine covers all aspects of personal sports in the Metro, with features on such things as in-line skating at the Metrodome, profiles of athletes, and a very detailed calendar of events. The magazine can be found at many restaurants, bars, grocery stores, and bookstores in the Twin Cities.

RADIO STATIONS
AM Stations

KFAN-1130 AM
1600 Utica Avenue South, #400, St. Louis Park
(651) 989-1130
www.kfan.com
KFAN is the Twin Cities sports radio leader. The Fan features interesting sports talk and occasional discussions about current affairs. The talk personalities on KFAN are the station's strength. Morning drive host Dan Cole, "the Common Man," is a seasoned veteran of local talk, who offers an offbeat look at various topics. The Fan is also the radio home of the Minnesota Timberwolves basketball games.

A couple stations showcase the thriving local music scene: the University of Minnesota's Radio K (770 AM and 106.5/ 100.7 FM) and the Current (89.3 FM).

KKMS-980 AM
2110 Cliff Road, Eagan
(651) 405-8800
www.kkms.com
KKMS is a Christian talk radio station owned by Salem Communications. It features the Salem Radio Network and Family News in Focus.

KSTP-1500 AM
3415 University Avenue, St. Paul
(651) 646-TALK
www.am1500.com
KSTP is one of many Hubbard Broadcasting Inc. media stations in the Twin Cities. In recent decades KSTP has specialized in conservative talk radio. The station airs nationally syndicated personalities, including Rush Limbaugh, Dr. Laura Schlesinger, and Paul Harvey, and local programs such as *Garage Logic* with Joe Soucheray, and a political talk show that features "Minnesota's Mr. Right" Jason Lewis. Another interesting on-air personality is Barbara Carlson, a former Minneapolis city council member and mayoral candidate, who offers her brash opinions for weekday morning drive time.

KTIS-900 AM/98.5 FM
3003 Snelling Avenue North, Roseville
(651) 631-5000
KTIS is a religious music and talk station, with frequencies on the AM (900) and FM (98.5) dials.

KUOM-770 AM/106.5 and 100.7 FM
University of Minnesota, 610 Rarig Center, 330 21st Avenue South, Minneapolis
(612) 625-3500
www.radiok.org
The Twin Cities' largest and most popular college radio station is KUOM or, as it is known locally, Radio K. Radio K plays alternative, techno, ska, hip-hop, and much more. It features music from independent labels and local music as well as major label music. Radio K has the most diverse playlist in the Twin Cities. Plus

Radio K's schedule abounds with piquant specialty programs, such as *Radio K International* and *Rude Radio* (a ska, dub, and reggae show). Additionally, there is *Off the Record,* a program devoted to local and recently released music, which features weekly performances by local bands in Studio K. Radio broadcasts stop at sundown, except the FM stations, which broadcast 24 hours a day on weekends. Radio K is also available 24-7 online.

KYCR-1570 AM
2110 Cliff Road, Eagan
(651) 405-8800
KYCR, the Patriot, is a Twin Cities Christian radio station featuring Christian talk, music, and lectures and discussions about religious matters.

WCCO-830 AM
625 Second Avenue South, Minneapolis
(612) 370-0611
www.wccoradio.com
WCCO Radio was, until the '90s, the undisputed leader in news and talk. In the past decade, ratings have slid as demographics aged, yet WCCO remains a vital force on Twin Cities radio. The station continues as the broadcast home of Minnesota Twins baseball as well as University of Minnesota Golden Gophers football and basketball.

FM Stations

KBEM-88.5 FM
1555 James Avenue North, Minneapolis
(612) 668-1735
www.jazz88fm.com
Jazz 88 focuses on light jazz, fusion, classic jazz, and cool jazz but also programs that include exotica, Latin, and bluegrass music. KBEM features traffic information every 10 minutes during morning and afternoon drive time. Jazz 88 also features programs that focus on Twin Cities jazz.

KCMP-89.3 FM
45 East Seventh Street, St. Paul
(651) 290-1212
www.minnesota.publicradio.org
KCMP, more popularly known as the Current, debuted in 2005, thus driving the number of Twin Cities Minnesota Public Radio stations to three. The Current plays a broad spectrum of artists, with a strong showing of independent and local music—don't be surprised to hear Frank Sinatra sandwiched between classic country and local hip-hop. It sounds strange, but it works, as evidenced by the huge listenership the Current built in its first year on air.

KDWB-101.3 FM
1600 Utica Avenue South, St. Louis Park
(651) 989-KDWB
www.kdwb.com
KDWB plays contemporary hits, with an emphasis on dance, especially on weekend evenings. The station has been popular with local teens for decades because of its programming. If you want to hear hits, KDWB is where Twin Citians go.

KFAI-90.3/106.7 FM
1808 Riverside Avenue, Minneapolis
(612) 341-3144
www.kfai.org
Since 1978 KFAI has served the Twin Cities with an extremely wide array of programming. This community radio gem began in a church loft and has over the years grown to two frequencies: the original 90.3 and, in 1994, the 106.7 signal for St. Paul and eastern Twin Cities suburbs. KFAI programming is remarkably diverse. Prominent features of the program schedule are arts, public affairs, world music, community affairs, jazz, and rock. In addition, KFAI hosts several weekly bilingual programs to serve the local immigrant communities. KFAI features Khmer, Hmong, Somali, Eritrean, and Ethiopian programs.

KMOJ-89.9 FM
501 Bryant Avenue North, Minneapolis
(612) 377-0594

KMOJ is the Twin Cities home to soul, jazz, blues, and reggae. It is one of only two area community radio stations. KMOJ gives its community, North Minneapolis, a voice on the air with music and public discussions of issues important to the neighborhood. Beyond North Minneapolis, KMOJ is enjoyed by many throughout the Twin Cities.

KNOW-91.1 FM
45 East 7th Street, St. Paul
(651) 290-1212
www.mpr.org
KNOW is the Twin Cities Minnesota Public Radio news, information, and talk station. The programming consists of a mix of local, nationally syndicated, NPR, and BBC broadcasts. KNOW has an MPR sister station at KSJN, which emphasizes classical music.

KQQL-107.9 FM
1600 Utica Avenue South, St. Louis Park
(952) 417-3000
www.kool108.com
If you are looking for golden oldies, KOOL 108 is the Twin Cities frequency on the FM dial. The station is known for "good times, great oldies" and plays a surprisingly diverse chunk of rock music. If you love classic rock, check out the *Saturday Night Oldies Party.*

KQRS-92.5 FM
2000 Southeast Elm Street, Minneapolis
(612) 617-4000
www.kqrs.com
KQ 92 is the Twin Cities' most popular classic rock station. It began as an early FM maverick radio station in the late '60s but in the '70s began to take on its classic rock position. Since then KQ has been enormously popular—so popular, in fact, it caused the local affiliate with the *Howard Stern Radio Show* to leave the area and change formats. Morning talk show host Tom Barnard, a derivative midwestern version of Stern, is so popular that KQ's ratings now regularly eclipse local radio ratings leader WCCO. Beyond the "the KQ

MEDIA

Morning Crew" led by Barnard, the station plays a consistent rotation of Pink Floyd, Led Zeppelin, Foreigner, and Tom Petty.

KSJN–99.5 FM
45 East Seventh Street, St. Paul
(612) 290-1212
www.mpr.org
KSJN is Minnesota Public Radio's Twin Cities classical station.

KSTP–94.5 FM
3415 University Avenue, St. Paul
(651) 642-4141
www.ks95.com
KS 95 has held the honor of being the Twin Cities' favorite top-40 station for decades and continues to play "the best variety of the '80s, '90s, and today!"

KTCZ–97.1 FM
1600 Utica Avenue South, St. Louis Park
(612) 989-9797
www.cities97.com
Cities 97 is the Twin Cities adult contemporary station. KTCZ's motto is "music you thought was too good to hear on the radio." Cities 97 regularly showcases deeper, nonhit tracks by artists such as Sting, Los Lobos, and Steely Dan.

KXXR–93.7 FM
2000 Southeast Elm Street, Minneapolis
(612) 617-4000
www.93X.com
93X is the station for fans of acts like the Red Hot Chili Peppers, Korn, and Metallica. The station serves up nonstop new metal and industrial music.

WLKX–95.9 FM/KBGY–107.5 FM
15226 West Freeway Drive, Forest Lake
(651) 464-6796
www.spirit.fm
WLKX/KBGY is a Twin Cities adult contemporary Christian channel. WLKX reaches the Metro, northern suburbs, and western Wisconsin; KBGY reaches the Metro, southern suburbs, and a wide area of southeastern Minnesota.

WLTE–102.9 FM
625 Second Avenue South, Suite 300,
Minneapolis
(612) 339-WLTE
www.wlte.com
WLTE plays a large selection of light rock; some perennial favorites are the Eagles, Air Supply, Anita Baker, and Phil Collins. The station also features unusual specialty programs. One particularly interesting show is *On the Air with John Tesh*. It is a weekly program about music and musicians hosted by New Age guru and former *Entertainment Tonight* cohost John Tesh.

TELEVISION STATIONS

TPT2–Channel 2
172 East Fourth Street, St. Paul
(651) 222-1717
www.tpt.org
TPT2 is the Twin Cities public television station. It recently changed its call letters from KTCA to TPT2 to signify its commitment to the community. Of course, TPT is an acronym for Twin Cities Public Television. TPT2 has continually served the community with a healthy mix of national PBS and local public television programming.

TPT2 features more children's television programming than any other Twin Cities station. *Sesame Street* and *Teletubbies* are featured on the daily schedule, as well as *Newton's Apple,* a locally produced science program for nearly 20 years.

For adults TPT2 has national PBS hits such as *Frontline,* the *NewsHour with Jim Lehrer* and countless national public television specials. Additionally, TPT2 has created a wealth of locally produced programming. Local public affairs programs like *Almanac,* and *Newsnight Minnesota* distinguish the station and serve the community.

WCCO–Channel 4
90 South Eleventh Street, Minneapolis
(612) 339-4444
www.wcco.com

WCCO has a long history in television and radio in the Twin Cities. In fact, the acronym, WCCO, stands for Washburn and Crosby Company, the former name of the Twin Cities–based international corporation, General Mills. However, WCCO has lost some of its local focus as both the television and radio station have been owned by the CBS Corporation for well over a decade.

WCCO continues to link itself through "the Home Town Team," the WCCO news team, as well as several other programs and initiatives to the community. One is *Hometown Heroes,* where WCCO-TV encourages Twin Citians to nominate people who make significant contributions to the community; later some of the outstanding local citizens nominated are interviewed and honored on WCCO news. Another WCCO community-based program is *Community 4 Kids,* where adults in the community mentor troubled area youths.

Surveys are available on the WCCO Web site regarding matters of public interest to the Twin Cities. Information from surveys is frequently used on the air by the WCCO news team. It is yet another effort to connect the station to the community.

KSTP–Channel 5
3415 University Avenue, St. Paul
(651) 646-5555
www.kstp.com

KSTP is recognized locally and nationally as an innovator in the television industry. Hubbard Broadcasting, Inc. owns KSTP as well as additional stations in New Mexico and New York. KSTP was the first television station in the Twin Cities, signing on the air on April 27, 1948. It also was the first full-color television station and the first to broadcast daily newscasts in the nation.

News is important to KSTP and its "Eye Witness News Team." KSTP was a local pioneer in investigative journalism and weather reporting. "Weather Center 5" is always a step ahead of the competitors in weather technology and forecasting; whether you are going up north for the weekend or are concerned about an ominous storm, KSTP and its meteorologists have the answers. It is also the only affiliated station that remains under local ownership, which is reflected in the station's news and programming. KSTP is the Twin Cities ABC affiliate but has its own unique identity because of the strong local ownership.

KMSP–Channel 9
11358 Viking Drive, Eden Prairie
(952) 944-9999
www.kmsp.com

In 2002 the Twin Cities UPN affiliate, KMSP Channel 9, and the Fox affiliate, WFTC Channel 29, switched call letters and places on the TV dial—an effort by the Fox network, which owns both stations, to reach a larger audience with a Fox channel bunched together with the other major stations in the Cities.

Fox News Sunday is the network's competition against such Sunday news institutions as NBC's *Meet the Press* and CBS's *Face the Nation.* They carry plenty of Twin Cities sports. NFL football and Major League baseball are featured prominently on Fox. In addition, professional hockey is on Fox; the Twin Cities NHL team, the Wild, is broadcast locally on Fox and also UPN's WFTC.

KARE–Channel 11
8811 Olson Memorial Highway, Minneapolis
(763) 546-1111
www.kare11.com

KARE is the Twin Cities home of NBC. Besides NBC programming, it consistently has the highest-rated news broadcasts at 6:00 P.M. and 10:00 P.M. Paul Magers and Diana Pierce have coanchored the ever-popular six and ten o'clock broadcasts for well over a decade. KARE has created

The local television comedy Nate on Drums *airs on KSTC's Channel 45 Friday night at 12:30.*

local initiatives such as "11 Who KARE," which recognizes citizens who have made significant contributions for the betterment of the Twin Cities. In addition, KARE produces programs like *Whatever,* aimed at teens. *Whatever* features teen reporters examining subjects of interest to the group, which is frequently underserved by national and Twin Cities media.

KMWB–Channel 23
1640 Como Avenue, St. Paul
(651) 646-2300
www.kmwb23.com
KMWB is the Twin Cities WB network affiliate. KMWB airs WB programs, such as *Dawson's Creek,* plus syndicated programming, movies, and infomercials. *The Jerry Springer Show* calls KMWB its Twin Cities home. There are also plenty of reruns of recent sitcoms to sate the viewing appetite of Twin Citians.

WFTC–Channel 29
11358 Viking Drive, Eden Prairie
(952) 944-9999
www.wftc.com
WFTC is the Twin Cities Paramount, or UPN, affiliate. After many years as an independent, WFTC now airs UPN programming. However, the station retains its unique version of television news.

KPXM–Channel 41
10700 Old County Road 15, Suite 285, Plymouth
(763) 417-0041
www.paxtv.com

PAX TV recently bought this longtime independent station. One of the many goals at PAX is to buy low-performing stations and make them competitive. PAX TV is new to the Twin Cities. So far, it lacks a local presence and is still developing much of its programming schedule.

KSTC–Channel 45
3415 University Avenue, St. Paul
(651) 645-4500
www.kstc45.com
KSTC is an interesting newcomer to Twin Cities television. The channel specializes in expanded news coverage and creative programming. Hubbard Broadcasting, Inc. owns KSTC and is the parent company of KSTP. But KSTC, unlike KSTP, is not an ABC affiliate, which permits much greater leeway in programming. In organization, KSTC is a "duoply," the first allowed by the FCC (permitting more than one station in a designated market area).

KSTC aims at expanding its sister station, KSTP's, news programming. In addition to KSTP's 10:00 P.M. news, news coverage now begins at 9:00 P.M. on KSTC. This allows more in-depth stories and commentary.

KSTC also broadcasts creative and quirky programs. The weekly program schedule has included local programs such as *Horror Inc.,* a Saturday late-night program featuring, and a current example is *Nate on Drums,* a locally produced comedy. KSTP has a long history in the Twin Cities—its sister station, KSTC, is an independent newcomer without a network affiliate, which allows it to make atavistic, creative programming decisions.

WORSHIP

An amazing variety of religious groups are represented in the Twin Cities, with hundreds of churches—many are on the National Register of Historic Places—spread throughout the Twin Cities. Besides established religions such as Catholicism, Judaism, and Islam as well as Evangelist, Lutheran, Mennonite, and Methodist denominations, other traditions, celebrations, and orders have come to the Cities with new waves of immigrants. Among these new arrivals are the Hmong people from Asia. More Hmong live in Minnesota than any other state as of the 2000 census, and every December the Hubert H. Humphrey Metrodome is the site of the Hmong New Year celebration. The event is spectacular, with beautiful costumes, parades, traditional dancing, and singing. The event brings Hmong immigrants from all over the country to the Twin Cities, as well as curious non-Hmong residents of the area. The annual event was renamed the Hmong-American New Year in hopes that the entire Twin Cities community would feel welcome to participate and not just the immigrant population. As Minnesota's nonwhite, non-Christian population continues to grow, organizations like the Minnesota Cultural Diversity Center have been arranging more and more open festivals celebrating the metro area's cultural richness both in social customs and religious observances.

It is this openness and acceptance of new cultures and religions that makes the Twin Cities so special. Catholicism has long been one of the primary faiths in the area, as evidenced by the many beautiful old Catholic churches throughout the region. Still, during Ramadan, Muslims can be seen walking to mosque dressed in beautiful traditional robes. In December street celebrations of Hanukkah, complete with food and live music, are a regular tradition in both Twin Cities downtown areas. Many cultures and religious groups have found a home here in the Cities, and no sooner does a new group move in than organizations spring up to welcome and support them in their new home. And for those wishing to experience new cultures themselves, there's nothing that says "welcome to the neighborhood" quite like attending a Minnesota polka mass!

Churches and religious centers are an important aspect of Minnesota culture, and vice versa. Most neighborhoods in the Twin Cities were traditionally built around churches, and these churches are an integral component of their neighborhoods. Churches in the Twin Cities remain an active part of the community, setting up soup kitchens and sleeping quarters for homeless people, FoodShare and Food Shelf grocery giveaways, and shelters for battered women, orphans, and runaways. On the lighter side of things, many religious centers in the Twin Cities also double as reasonably priced day care centers during the workweek, and most have regular festivals and picnics open to the general community, sponsor neighborhood rummage sales for charity, and arrange summer camps for kids.

If you're looking for volunteer opportunities, any and all the religious centers in the Twin Cities would be more than happy to have your help. **Loaves and Fishes** (1917 Logan Avenue South, Minneapolis; 612-377-9810; www.loavesandfishesmn .org) is the primary local service for providing free dinners to disadvantaged families throughout the Twin Cities. Operating from seven strategically located facilities, Loaves and Fishes serves hot, nutritious meals to an average of over 2,300 persons each weeknight.

ISAIAH, located at 2720 East 22nd Street in Minneapolis (612-333-1254; www.gamaliel.org/isaiah) provides leader-

Basilica of Saint Mary. GREATER MINNEAPOLIS CONVENTION & VISITORS ASSOCIATION

ship training and a vehicle for congregations to take action in the public arena to achieve social, economic, and racial justice in our metropolitan and regional communities. ISAIAH is a membership-driven organization of 85 congregations located in the Twin Cities metropolitan and St. Cloud regions.

Lutheran Social Service of Minnesota, located at 2485 Como Avenue in St. Paul (651-642-5990; www.lssmn.org), started in 1865 when a Swedish pastor and his congregation began taking in children orphaned by poverty and tragedy. The congregation soon opened the Vasa Children's Home to serve orphans and from there grew into what it is today: the largest statewide nonprofit social service agency, offering crisis shelters, group homes, counseling, and adoption services for people of all income levels and religious affiliation. The Lutheran Social Service helps more than 100,000 Minnesota children, families, seniors, and people with disabilities each year.

The **Center for Ethical Business Cultures,** located at 1000 LaSalle Avenue, Suite 153 in Minneapolis (651-962-4120; www.cebcglobal.org) is not a religious organization, but it has many similarities to religious charities and groups. The purpose of the center is to help businesses create healthy, ethical, and profitable environments in-house as well as at community and global levels. CEBC's priorities include ethical leadership, work-life and employee-employer relationships, and corporate citizenship. With the ongoing nationwide spate of corporate scandal, this nonprofit provides a necessary service—and it's no coincidence it's based in Minnesota, where business leaders have long invested in the community.

No matter what your religious persuasion, two important stops in the Twin Cities are the Basilica of Saint Mary and the Cathedral of Saint Paul. The Basilica of Saint Mary, or just "the Basilica," as locals call it, is the first basilica built in the United States, taking seven years to build

before holding its first Mass on May 31, 1914. Located at the corner of 17th Street and Hennepin Avenue in Minneapolis (612-333-1381; www.mary.org), the Basilica has ingrained itself firmly into the community around it, organizing events ranging from amazing bell choirs open to the public to a full-scale annual summer rock concert—the Basilica Block Party—of which proceeds go to help maintain the historic building. Rose Ensemble chorale group has an artists residency here. Tours of the building are available—call or check the Web site.

The Cathedral of Saint Paul, located at 239 Selby Avenue in St. Paul (651-228-1766; www.cathedralsaintpaul.org) is impossible to miss once you're in St. Paul's capitol district. It took more than 50 years to complete and is absolutely stunning. The gigantic building, topped by a dome with an exterior height of 307 feet, is filled with carved marble statues of saints, gold accents, painted murals, and large stained-glass windows. The cathedral dome is an important landmark of the city, lending St. Paul a European feel that the rest of the Midwest can only envy. A $35 million renovation of the historic cathedral resulted in replacing the copper domes, cleaning and sealing the granite walls, repairing interior damage, and updating the lighting, heating, and cooling systems. The replacement of the main copper dome involved 60 roofers and more than 100 craftspeople (carpenters, electricians, ironworkers, and plumbers) to put the new 70-ton dome in place. The spectacular results have returned St. Paul's great landmark to its historic state. The cathedral is the working headquarters of the archdiocese and has a regular attending congregation of nearly 3,000. Many regularly scheduled choral and orchestral concerts are held here (the acoustics are spectacular).

Minnesota FoodShare

Minnesota FoodShare is just one example of how the diverse religious and neighborhood communities in the Twin Cities come together to help people in need. FoodShare, one of the region's largest and most successful charities, is the result of what happens when neighborhood religious centers with soup kitchens and grocery giveaways get together to form a community organization. Members of the FoodShare project include Catholic Charities, the Minnesota Rabbinical Association, and the Minnesota Council of Churches, as well as many members of the business community, including several popular nightclubs. Organized officially in 1982, Minnesota FoodShare now delivers literally millions of pounds of food each month to people in need through neighborhood churches, grocery stores, and home delivery programs.

One church that has been an active member of Minnesota FoodShare is Pastor Paul's Mission. For nearly 25 years, Pastor Paul Arnopoulos has been helping feed homeless and disadvantaged Minnesotans through Disciples Ministry Mission in north Minneapolis, an area that even now is still struggling with poverty. Every day staff members hand out bags of groceries and cook hot meals for families in need, distributing approximately 14 million pounds of food each year. More than 12,000 families from Minnesota and Wisconsin depend on the mission for help, and Pastor Paul has dedicated his entire life to making sure they get it.

Supporters of the mission and the FoodShare project come from some unlikely sources. The most well-known one is the Acoustic Garage Sale, a rock benefit put on each year by the First Avenue nightclub. Each January First Avenue brings in several dozen local and national acts to play the Main Room stage, and all door proceeds go directly to Pastor Paul's Mission. Concertgoers have the option of bringing in canned and boxed food in lieu of the door price, and that, too, is taken to the mission. After the show well-known local and national music personalities donate musical instruments, autographed photographs, albums and CDs, and other items to be auctioned off for additional money for the mission.

Minnesota charities all work together to feed those in need. The charities keep in touch with one another, and if one charity is having trouble meeting its neighborhood's needs, another pitches in to bring any surplus. This network of charities makes Minnesota's Food Share program among the most successful in the country.

Other Worship Resources and Organizations

Archdiocese of St. Paul and Minneapolis
266 Summit Avenue, St. Paul
(651) 291-4400
www.archspm.org

Bethesda Lutheran Homes & Services, Inc.
275 North Syndicate Street, St. Paul
(651) 603-6279
www.blhs.org

Catholic Aid Association
3499 Lexington Avenue North,
Arden Hills
(651) 490-0170
www.catholicaid.com

Good News For Israel
6408 Minnetonka Boulevard,
St. Louis Park
(952) 926-7369
www.gnfi.org

Greater Minneapolis Council of Churches
1001 East Lake Street, Minneapolis
(612) 721-8687
www.gmcc.org

Islamic Center of Minnesota
1401 Gardena Avenue NE, Fridley
(763) 571-5604
www.icmorg.org

Joint Religious Legislative Coalition
122 Franklin Avenue West, Minneapolis
(612) 870-3670
www.jrlc.org

Minnesota Zen Center
3343 East Calhoun Parkway, Minneapolis
(612) 822-5313
www.mnzencenter.org

St. Paul Area Council of Churches
1671 Summit Avenue, St. Paul
(651) 646-8805
www.spacc.org

Unitarian Universalist Association
122 Franklin Avenue West, Suite 303,
Minneapolis
(612) 870-4823
www.psduua.org

Wat Lao Minneapolis
1429 Northeast Second Street,
Minneapolis
(612) 789-9382

INDEX